ANANDA RANGA PILLAI

ANANDA RANGA PILLAI

THE 'PEPYS' OF FRENCH INDIA

C. S. SRINIVASACHARI

GYAN

Published by

Gyan Publishing House
5, Ansari Road
Daryaganj, New Delhi-110002
Phone: 011-47034999, 9811692060
E-mail: books@gyanbooks.com

Distribution Network
gyanbooks.com
India, USA, Canada, UK, Australia, France

ISBN : 978-81-212-3115-2 (PB)
First Published, 1940

2nd Impression 2020

Printed at: Gyan Press, Delhi.

Ananda Ranga Pillai
Author: C. S. Srinivasachari

ANANDA RANGA PILLAI

THE 'PEPYS' OF FRENCH INDIA

BY

RAO SAHEB C. S. SRINIVASACHARI M.A.
Professor of History and Politics
Annamalai University, Annamalainagar

WITH A FOREWORD
BY
DR. SIR SHAFAAT AHMAD KHAN, *Kt*,

PUBLISHED BY
P. VARADACHARY & CO., MADRAS

CONTENTS

FOREWORD

BY

SIR SHAFAAT AHMAD KHAN, *Kt.*, D.LITT.

RAO Saheb C. S. Srinivasachari, Professor and Head of the Department of History and Politics, Annamalai University, has established a sound reputation by his industry and initiative. A brilliant orator, with a flair for fluency and a devotion to scientific research, he has proved himself to be one of the most accurate historians of British India in the South. He, along with Dewan Bahadur Dr. S. Krishnaswami Aiyangar, never grudged himself to the object of his affection, 'The Journal of Indian History', and devoted years of patient toil until the Journal has taken deep root in the South. The Journal which I fondled as a baby, has now, thanks to his and Dr. Aiyangar's nourishing diet, reached a vigorous and virile manhood. His devotion to the Indian History Congress is marked; and he has not missed a single session of the supreme organ of Indian historical scholarship since it was inaugurated by me at Poona, in June 1935. His amazing industry and sound judgment have placed him in the front rank among scholars of British India. Last year he published an excellent 'History of Madras', in connection with the Madras Tercentenary Celebrations. He has now prepared a most useful symposium of Ananda Ranga Pillai's *Diary*.

In his introductory chapter, Professor Srinivasachari traces the steps by which the *Diary* was unearthed. Till 1846, its existence was unknown and it was discovered by M. Gallois Montbrun, whose son was Mayor of Pondicherry for a long time. A faithful transcription was made by Mr. K. Rangachariar, Assistant to Sir Frederick Price and Superintendent of Records in the Secretariat, Fort St. George. The person who deserves most credit for unearthing the

Diary and bringing it to the hands of the English authorities was the late Mon. A. Singaravelu Pillai, Curator of the Historical Records of French India. He first inspected the *Diary* in 1897 and perused it a second time in 1900.

The chapters in the *Diary* make a fascinating study; and Professor Srinivasachari has strung the various items together by notes of the highest value to the historian. The *Diary* is one of our chief authorities for the period and we can follow the march of momentous events in India with an almost photographic fidelity. The South was living a very active and self-conscious life, acknowledging no principle of stability in her constitution or politics and making India a mosaic of hundreds of fragments. The *Diary* gives us pen-portraits in which Dupleix and his associates live again and seem to breathe epics of Pondicherry's strange vicissitudes from its humble beginnings, of detailed tragedies and highly finished episodes, of studies of the plastic characters of French proconsuls and of idylls detached from the main currents of French Indian history. The whole period is instinct with energy and vital with experience. The tempestuous personality of Dupleix moves with epic majesty through the intrigues of Indian rulers, through rapine and disorder fomented by adventurers and free-lances and ends in his recall. Dupleix dominates the scene and we have a good picture of this remarkable man. The organising thoroughness of this person is keyed up to the English dynamics. Dupleix's strange and enigmatic personality flits through these pages with strange steps. The gravest defect in his character and administration consisted in the fact that he lacked stable sincerity and could not readjust his former passions to a new view of his interests.

Pillai's *Diary* shows that Dupleix's whole administration down to the smallest detail bears the attribute of personality. He watched the lights and shadows of sentiment and feeling among the neighbouring rulers with the consummate skill of a supreme artist in intrigue. He received a posthumous beatification, but never got terrestrial satisfaction. The reason for it is to be found in his attitude towards his employers. He suppressed material particulars from the Company, and the latter were not fully acquainted with the financial aspects of his grandiose projects. While our admiration for Dupleix's bold enterprise and astonishing resource is boundless, it is necessary to have a drop or two of Irish blood in one's veins to believe in the efficacy of some of his quixotic enterprises. He delved into the subsoil of thought and had his finger on thirty to forty intrigues, adventures and enterprises which were sometimes conducted concurrently.

India in the eighteenth century was broken up into a thousand pieces and it has taken nearly 150 years to complete the task of reintegration and consolidation which has been taken up in earnest with energy and resource during the last fifty years. Dupleix's tragedy lay in the fact that he was rarely in a position to execute one-fourth of his schemes; and as he had dispersed his forces over an immense area, he could not concentrate his energy or his resources on any one pivotal point. In times of anarchy and disorder, there is no limit to the play of personality in action, and it is not surprising that a handful of bold adventurers decided to carve out careers for themselves. Nor is it surprising that the arrangements into which Dupleix entered with a light heart were thrown into grievous disarray by the staggering abruptness of the strange decisions to which he resorted with his curious flair for mysterious negotiations. Dupleix had the ultimate vision; but he forgot to concentrate on proximate emergencies. For some time he had the cards in his hands; he held all the trumps and appeared to be the most astute player alive. Then, in the flush of assurance and adventure, he lost his acumen and fumbled all his cards. Is it surprising that what began as a crusade was inexorably converted into an intrigue? The contrast between La Bourdonnais and Dupleix is too vivid to be easily forgotten by the student.

Chapter III should be read by everyone with the liveliest interest. The whole forms a picture of which the lights might have been given by Rembrandt, but the outline would have required the force and vigour of Michael Angelo. Professor Srinivasachari's account of the capture of Madras and its sequel in Chapter IV will also arouse the attention of the student. His footnotes in the Chapter are invaluable; while his simple unvarnished style gives a correct perspective of the administration of the period. The attacks on Fort St. David are described with a breadth of detail and with fresh material which lift the narrative above the level of a mere compendium of Pillai's entries in his *Diary*. Professor Srinivasachari's notes on Chanda Sahib's release on pages 107 and 108, throw fresh light on the subject; and he has discussed the question with his characteristic industry and thoroughness. The operations round Cuddalore and Pondicherry are graphically described in Chapter VII and lose none of their effect by the solid and massive presentation of prosaic details. Chapter VIII transports us to a sphere of activity which electrifies that period; Chanda Sahib, the stormy petrel, who ascended the sky like a meteor and dropped down like a stick, now appears on the scene. Schooled in adversity and well versed in the intrigues and plots of nearly half a dozen courts, this bold and dashing *condottiere* was taken in hand and patronised by Dupleix. The latter wished to exploit his influence for his grand design, and Southern India was launched upon a career of mysterious negotiations and bizarre intrigues.

In Chapter XII there is a brilliant account of the way in which Dupleix faced odds; Muhammad Ali's dealings with the British are analysed; and Ghazi-ud-din Khan's advance is discussed with great lucidity and thoroughness. Dupleix's efforts to get allies are discussed in Chapter XIII; and the narrative closes with a pathetic account of his failure. While Dupleix preserved his hypnotic supremacy, nobody competed with its spell. Then disasters thickened fast, and from September 1753 Pondicherry received "only news of loss of armies, damage to ships, strength and success of enemies." The financial situation was hopeless; and Pillai remarks in his *Diary*:—"How can the Governor expect success when all his actions are unjust? Victory will attend him only when his heart is right. I am certain of this." (December 7, 1753). The French had failed to take Trichinopoly by assault and Godeheu now appeared on the scene. He offered a sharp contrast to Dupleix. A man of much insight, with considerable experience of administration, Godeheu applied himself to the task of settlement with great energy and thoroughness. Dupleix departed for Europe by the *Duc d' Orleans* on the morning of the 14th October, nearly 13 years after he landed from Bengal. He had hoped, according to the Diarist, to leave his bones in Pondicherry; yet now he had been "dismissed accused and arrested." Godeheu was succeeded by De Leyrit who had troubles of his own and grappled with them with a curious mixture of vacillation and strength. Chapter XVI records the bold adventures of Bussy in the Deccan, and transports us to a region where that courteous and shrewd adventurer had a painful intimacy with intrigue and want, but overcame them by the brilliance of his arms and the wisdom of his counsels. Of all the proconsuls whom France sent to India, he was the shrewdest.

The troubles of the French now thickened fast, and Lally's campaigns which were started in an atmosphere of expectation, ended in disaster. The temper of his mind and the fiery passion which gleamed luridly across the gulf of race, language and creed, ensured the victory of the steady, plodding and persevering English. Lally's scornful arrows, shot off at random, even when they did not hit the target, were picked up and carried to their victims. The failure of French campaigns was not his fault; it was his fate. Success henceforth took up her abode in Madras. The English now consolidated their position in the South; and since they were entrenched in Bengal, their dominance in the polity of India was now assured. Unlike the Dutch, whose gaze was pathetically fixed on dividends and who received the reward of their mercantile puritanism in political oblivion in India, the English emerged as a great power in the land, and their empire was now assured. If a person is at the summit of a volcano, the least he can do is to smoke. Dupleix's grand ideas and imperial designs lay extensively in ruins, and the empire of his dreams crumbled up into dust. The morning had been golden; the noontide was bronze and the evening lead. The last chapter comes into its own as a stately *finale*.

I have given sufficient indication of the wealth of material which is contained in this book, and I have no doubt whatsoever that it is indispensable to all the students of the period. By preparing this work, Professor Srinivasachari has placed students of history under a deep debt of gratitude.

31, Stanley Road,
Allahabad,
March 8, 1940.

SHAFAAT AHMAD KHAN.

INTRODUCTION BY THE AUTHOR

Ananda Ranga Pillai, the famous *Courtier* of Dupleix, has left documents of great value for the history of Pondicherry and of the French in India. Of them, the *Diary* (or *Journal*) which he maintained during a quarter of a century is the most important and forms the major item. The *Diary* extended from 1736 to 1760; and though it is not available to us in its entirety, there being several lacunae, we know that it is a good summary of the views and feelings of the most acute Indian observer of contemporary events, giving, wherever possible, what may be deemed to have been the Indian point of view. It is said that Ranga Pillai's *Diary,* when it was discovered by Mon. A. Gallois Montbrun in 1846, was not complete either, there being extant only 13 registers in folio of the entries he made from day to day, in the years 1736–60, of all those facts and details of gossip that he witnessed and heard during the time. There were also then extant three other registers of the same format, containing the original text of the Journal, which his nephew, Tiruvengadam Pillai, continued up to 1799 after the death of his uncle. From Mon. Edmond Gaudart, *Gouvernour en retraite,* Pondicherry, we learn that these sixteen registers disappeared without any member of the family of Ananda Ranga Pillai knowing how it happened. The extensive copy made by Mon. A. Gallois Montbrun in 1846 from these sixteen registers has not since been found either in entirety. In 1892, a second copy of the *Diary* of Ranga Pillai that was available at Pondicherry was placed at the disposal of the Record Office of the Madras Government. This copy which is now at Madras, has enabled the publication of the English Translation of the *Diary* in 12 volumes, under the auspices of the Madras Government,—the first three volumes (1904–1914) edited by Sir J. F. Price and the subsequent nine volumes (1916–1928) by Professor H. H. Dodwell. The second copy made directly from the original by M. Ariel in 1852, now forms part of the Tamil Collection of the National Library of Paris; and the translation by M. J. Vinson of a small portion of the *Diary* is from Ariel's copy.

Ananda Ranga Pillai, the 'Pepys' of French India

M. A. Gallois Montbrun published at Pondicherry in 1849 " Notice sur la Chronique en langue Tamoule et sur la vie d'Ananda-Rangappillei." Mon. Montbrun, in the enthusiasm that he felt over his discovery of the *Diary*, painted an over-coloured picture of Ranga Pillai in which he was made out to have been the intimate *confidante* of Dupleix and the inspirer of all his political moves and activity and the influence which he exercised on the great Governor was exaggerated by a good measure. He says that the first portion of the *Diary*, covering the years 1736—45, was one in which Ranga Pillai was largely merely an on-looker; but for the second portion lasting from 1746 to 1760, during which he was intimately associated with the political life of the French Company as its Agent, his entries show a more direct and active association with the French Government and its doings. But according to Mon. Montbrun, even the first portion has the same historical value as the second; he thus writes of it: " Just as it is, however, and although much inferior to the rest of the work, this part (the first part) of the chronicle of Ananda Ranga Pillai which is on the whole a curious and interesting document, leaves most of its qualities to guess work. The manners of the times, the Hindu character, the indigenous administration, the personalities of the epoch,—everything comes to be placed in turn, not as in the outline of the writer who usually dreams to depict from what happens before his eyes, but like the mechanical action of the daguerrotype process which adds to the permanency and controls only the reproduction, renders the objects much more exact without being artificial, without previous planning and without afterthought. This observation, nevertheless,—one is not disappointed at it,—applies purely to the descriptive part of the work, which is, one could say, full of colour; for our author, as I have said already, excels in probing to the depth or in tracing back to the origin of an event. Endowed with great delicacy of observation, especially concerning men, he sets himself to arrive at his conclusion, leaving room clearly to have a glimpse of the personage that he draws in, but rarely stops to paint a picture ".

The second part of the *Diary* discloses a developed picture of the fine experience and maturity of the author. The Diarist not only gives descriptive sketches about the personaliites with whom he came in contact, but also furnishes rich and precise information about the government of Pondicherry, about Dupleix and his successors. Mon. Montbrun would say that if we gathered together all the scattered pieces of information embodied in the work, we would be enabled to get a complete full length picture, " full of life and exactitude ", about the great Governor and his influential wife, of Labourdonnais, of De Leyrit and of the great Indian princes and potentates of the time. With regard to the Diarist's picture of De Leyrit's rule, we are told that Ranga Pillai's *Journal* gives " an impression of the depression and unhappiness of the epoch, but at the same time presents the characters in greater exactitude." Prof. Dodwell is not less emphatic on the importance of the *Diary* for the historian. He wrote, in his Introduction to the last volume of the English Translation, that though no one would ever take the trouble of reading the *Diary* for its own sake, still it should be valuable as dealing with a particularly critical period during which not only Ranga Pillai rose and fell, but the struggle was decided whether India was to be dominated from Paris or London. " During the greater part of these twenty-five years, the momentous struggle was being fought out in South India and upon those sullen waters which roll unceasingly on the pale, palm-fringed sands of the Coromandel Coast. Of the men and circumstances of the time Ranga Pillai was a close and interested observer; and he was the only Indian observer whose views are directly positively known to us. No doubt there were many whose memoirs would have been more precious. Chandā Sāhib's thoughts upon Dupleix, Yusuf Khān's opinions on the campaigns of Lally, would have revealed important aspects of the conflict. But they could hardly have displayed more fully and closely the Indian attitude towards events which were so deeply to influence the course of modern Indian history. For a considerable time, the Diarist was the foremost Indian merchant in an essentially mercantile community and the main intermediary between the Governor and the Indians whom he governed. His business it was to know all that was going forward in the Indian quarter, to learn the news that the bankers' agents received from their correspondents, to watch the course of trade and feel the pulse of sentiment. For a considerable time too he played the part of Foreign Secretary to the Governor, translating letters or getting them translated, suggesting appropriate answers, settling the minutiaē of Oriental etiquette and himself corresponding with distant ministers." [Pp. xviii—xix—Introduction to *The Private Diary of Ananda Ranga Pillai,* Vol. XII (1928)].

Ranga Pillai is precise in his formation and does not fill his *Journal* either with empty rumours or with mere bazaar news; and the political information that he gives is of great value. He did not intend his *Diary* for the use of the historian, but wrote primarily for his successors "in order to perpetuate in his family the Souvenir of the events of his time." Mon. Montbrun has stressed on the capacity and depth of Ranga Pillai in tracing back the origin of an event and on his fine powers of observation, especially concerning persons. We are thus enabled to judge from his *Journal* very accurately of personalities from the instances of their qualities and defects and the events created by them because these are given in such an abundant measure, though mixed up with a multitude of insignificant facts and figures.

Let us now turn to a short biography of the Diarist. He was born at Ayanavaram near Perambore, a suburb of Madras, on the 30th of March 1709. His father, Tiruvengadam Pillai, was a prosperous trader at Madras from which he was induced by the persuasions of his brother-in-law, Nainiyappa Pillai, to go and settle at Pondicherry. Nainiyappa had acquired considerable prosperity and reputation at Pondicherry, where he had easily asserted himself as the most prominent of the Hindu citizens. It was always the practice of the French Company to have a Chief Agent from among the non-European citizens of the settlement, who was to serve as the intermediary between the Company and the Indian merchants in all the commercial transactions of the former. This Agent enjoyed a commission paid on all their transactions by the buyers of goods imported by the Company and by the suppliers of goods to the latter for export, as well as a very small percentage of profits in terms of rupees. He was entitled

'Mudaliar' in the sense of the word which signified the 'first' [derived from the root 'Mudal']. As such, he enjoyed the honours due to persons of high rank, like the privilege of going into the fort in a palanquin and having a white umbrella, the *roundel,* carried before him. He was also a judge of the Tribunal of the *Chauderie* and helped to decide cases arising among Indians. The first of the Mudaliars or *Courtiers* of Pondicherry was Lazare de Motta, Thanappa Mudaliar, who had helped the French even during the siege operations round San Thomé in 1673-4 and was a prosperous merchant of that region and had entered the service of the French Company in 1676 as their *Dubash.* Motta was an Indian Christian and enjoyed particular influence only with the members of his own community. François Martin, the founder of Pondicherry, who did much for the promotion of its prosperity, made the Agent the head of the Malabars (Hindus) and assured all the Indians who settled at Pondicherry of their free exercise of their caste usages and religious rites. This promise was renewed by his successor, the Chevalier Hébert, by a declaration issued in the name of the King, in July 1708.

The family of Ananda Ranga Pillai was "one of the first to yield to the call of France." His uncle, Nainiyappa, had been settled for some years at Pondicherry where he secured the lease of tobacco and betel for two years. He soon made himself indispensable to the Company by his services to them, which enabled them to overcome some of the fraudulent practices of the suppliers of the cloth for export, who demanded an increase of 12% on the price originally fixed. On a subsequent occasion, when Lazare de Motta could not dispose of the coral imported by the Company, Nainiyappa enabled them to sell all the stock at a good price. In consideration of these services, Hébert made him Agent in the place of Lazare de Motta in 1708. But the Jesuits who were very influential at Pondicherry and controlled the congregation of the Indian Christians, were jealous at the appointment of a Hindu to the post of Agent; and Hébert himself soon turned out to be hostile to Nainiyappa. The Jesuits had addressed to the royal court at Versailles a petition in which they demanded and urged the closure of all Hindu temples in Pondicherry except two and the appointment of a Christian to the post of Agent. King Louis XIV admitted their demands, but counselled the Governor and the missionaries to exercise care and caution in the matter of closure of the temples; and Nainiyappa was given six months' time to become a good Christian, failing which he was to be dismissed. These orders were communicated to Pondicherry only in 1714, three years after they were actually issued; and the delay was due to the apprehensions of the Directors as to their repercussions. The Governor and Council found themselves in a very difficult situation. They could not well afford to dispense with the services of Nainiyappa who enjoyed great influence at the court of the Nawab of the Carnatic and who, they were convinced, would be very helpful to them in the execution of the royal order for the closure of the 'heathen' shrines, without giving rise to any convulsion within the Hindu community. They therefore adroitly associated with him a Christian, Savari by name, who was a relation of the family of Thanappa Mudaliar,—since his son, Muthiappa, was dead and his grandson, Kanakaraya, was still a youth,—as Co-Mudaliar (or co-ordinate Agent). Of course, Nainiyappa's influence made that of Savari pale into insignificance. But even he could not quell the excitement that was roused among the Hindus who were indignant at the royal order for the closure of their temples. The Jesuits took advantage of this and charged the Hindu Agent with having deliberately caused all the troubles himself. When Governor Dulivier who had succeeded Hébert, interdicted Hindu ceremonies and processions with music on Sundays and Catholic holidays and when he particularly refused permission for the performance of the *Amāvāsya* ceremonies (New Moon Day rites) which happened to fall on Sunday, February 3, 1715, there was a wholesale exodus of all the Hindu population and the Black Town of Pondicherry remained empty for four days. The Governor and the Council had to guarantee solemnly to the deserters the free exercise of their religion in order to persuade them to return to their homes.

Meanwhile, the Chevalier Hébert, having made amends to the Jesuits and secured the favour of the Ministry and of the Directors, returned to Pondicherry with enlarged powers and with the titles

'Envoy of the King and General of the Nation.' He deprived Dulivier of all influence and compelled him to retire completely from the service of the Company. He also now resolved to dismiss Nainiyappa; but the latter was strongly supported by the resident agents of the Company of Saint Malo, who fully appreciated the value of the Mudaliar for the proper maintenance of their trade prosperity. Also, Hébert's candidate for the office of Agent was only a Christian youth, about 20 years of age, Pedro Kanakaraya Mudaliar, "without experience and fortune." Hébert, however, did not give up his purpose of dismissing Nainiyappa. Soon after the ships of the Malouins had departed from Pondicherry, Hébert had Nainiyappa and several other Hindu leaders arrested on a charge of complicity in the events leading to the exodus of the Hindu population in February 1715; and he contrived to sentence him to flogging at the hands of the executioner at a public place, to a very heavy fine, to imprisonment for three years and to subsequent banishment. This unjust decision roused the indignation of some Frenchmen and, particularly that of Jacques Vincent, the Accountant of the Company of Saint Malo and the first husband of Madame Dupleix. At their prompting, Nainiyappa submitted a petition to the King of France for a revision of the trial and got, in answer thereto, an order for his restoration. But, unfortunately, he died in prison some days previous to the receipt of the order. His property had been, meanwhile, seized by Hébert who contrived to misappropriate a good portion of the jewels and valuables. Hébert had also persecuted Tiruvengadam Pillai, the father of the Diarist, and contrived to have him condemned to corporal punishment. Tiruvengadam Pillai only escaped this humiliation by the fact of his having a month previously retired to Madras. Jacques Vincent made himself the champion of Tiruvengadam Pillai as well and got from the Superior Council the cancellation of his punishment which had been decreed without their authority. It is a matter of gratification for the reader to know that Pedro Kanakaraya Mudaliar, the rival of Nainiyappa for the post of Agent, "prayed, the moment the Governor gave the sentence, on behalf of Tiruvengadam Pillai, to oblige him by commuting the punishment to a fine of 1,000 pagodas to the profit of the Company."

A royal decree arrived, cancelling the sentence against Nainiyappa and constituting a special commission to inquire into all the charges against Hébert. The latter was recalled and Le Prévostiére, First Councillor, became the *ad interim* Governor on account of the death of D'Hardancourt, who had been nominated to the place. The new Governor soon proved that the Company had been extensively ruined by the embezzlements of Hébert. A retrial of Nainiyappa's case was ordered and resulted in the cancellation of the sentence against him; but though his honour was vindicated, his fortunes had been totally ruined, the compensation that his family was enabled to secure from the Company being very little.

Now, once again on the advice of Jacques Vincent and of other friends of the family, Guruvappa, the eldest son of Nainiyappa, resolved to go to France and implore from the King himself for justice and the vindication of his father's memory. With the consent of Tiruvengadam Pillai and other members of the family, he embarked at Madras for France in February 1719. He was very sympathetically received at the court of Versailles and got a decree from the King's Council for the restoration of the property sequestrated from his father, which had been in charge of the Company, and for his nomination as Agent and Mudaliar of the reconstituted Company. He was also baptised as a Christian in the Royal Chapel at Versailles with King Louis XV himself acting as his god-father, and ennobled, receiving the ribbon of Chevalier of Saint Michael. Immediately after he returned to Pondicherry in August 1722, he took up the functions of the Agent, Mudaliar and the Head of the Malabars; and his uncle, Tiruvengadam Pillai, was nominated to be the Deputy Agent. Thus the Christian, Chevalier Guruvappa, was harmoniously associated with the Hindu, Tiruvengadam Pillai, in the enjoyment of this high office and their combined influence was naturally very great. Unfortunately, Guruvappa Pillai died within two years after his assumption of office, in August 1724; and in another two years, Tiruvengadam Pillai followed him to the grave. Ananda Ranga Pillai was only a little over 16 at the time of his father's death; and he had now to manage the affairs of a large family. He was too young and inexperienced to receive either the post of his father or that of his cousin and had therefore to shift for himself for the time. He started a small trade on his own account. It is known that he sold areca-nuts in the shop near the great bazaar, to which he so often refers in his *Journal*. He maintained this small retail trade all his life; and it is in this modest shop that he later on liked to take a little rest daily and to meet his old friends and collect all news and reports. Ranga Pillai had, like others in a similar walk of life, some knowledge of Tamil literature and of the indigenous methods of reckoning and accounting. Later, he learnt French and spoke it correctly, though he knew "less to write than to read". In all papers preserved in the archives of Pondicherry, he invariably put down his name as Rangappa and signed it in Tamil characters. He also spoke the common Portuguese *patois* of the Malabar Coast, which had been for a long time prevalent in South India; he had also some tolerable acquaintance with Persian, the official language of the country powers.

Governor Lenoir (1726–35) had a high opinion of Ranga Pillai and his business talents. His successor, Dumas (1735–42), put him in charge of the Company's trade at Porto Novo which was then a prosperous weaving centre. Ranga Pillai had already established a small agency for himself at that place and got from its Mussalman governor the personal privilege of exemption from 50% of the duty on goods that he might ship from that port. The Company also profited from that privilege. The business of both the Company and our young friend prospered till the Maratha invaders of 1740 created anarchy in the Carnatic and pillaged Porto Novo among other places.

Ranga Pillai was then associated by Dumas with his own business and that of his brother, Gabriel Dumas, and employed in providing goods for exportation to Mocha and the Isles of France. For the purpose of supplying calico and linen that formed the principal articles of commerce, Ranga Pillai started, under his own auspices, a large establishment of weavers, etc., at Lalapet near Arcot. In March 1737, when Kanakaraya Mudali, the Agent, became seriously ill, Dumas appointed, with the unanimous consent of the Council, Ranga Pillai to the temporary vacancy in the office. But he could not be permanently made Agent, as Kanakaraya was enabled to rejoin duty, being speedily restored to health. Ranga Pillai continued to enjoy the kindness of Dumas to a marked extent till his retirement; and when Dupleix succeeded him in the Governorship in January 1742, he found no reason to regret the departure of his late patron. Dupleix was fully aware of all the interest that his friend, Jacques Vincent, had shown in the family of Nainiyappa; also in the course of his first sojourn at Pondicherry, he had come to know well Tiruvengadam Pillai and utilised his services and those of his son. During his administration at Chandranagore, he arranged to have business relations with Ranga Pillai. He fully appreciated his intelligence, his probity and his activity in business; and he made him his personal trade agent.

Even during the tenure of the Company's Agency by Kanakaraya Mudaliar which lasted down to 1746, Dupleix kept Ranga Pillai in personal favour and made him acquainted with some of the most delicate affairs of the government. But Madame Dupleix had no sympathy for him; and Ranga Pillai in his *Diary* makes her solely responsible for poisoning the mind of the Governor against himself, for making him delay in appointing himself to be the regular Agent and for even letting out that office to auction. But there was also fault on the side of Ranga Pillai himself; and the blame was not to be shifted wholly to Dupleix's shoulders. He had sustained heavy losses and was in considerable arrears in the settlement of his accounts with the Company; and besides, he owed a heavy sum to Dupleix himself. Naturally enough, on account of these circumstances, the Governor was not very enthusiastic on his behalf. But Pillai had shown great abilities and considerable discretion in his dealings with the native potentates; and above all, when the sons of the Nawab Anvar-ud-dīn Khān marched into the neighbourhood of Pondicherry with intentions of hostility in January 1747 and set fire to some villages, he succeeded in gaining them over to the French interest and in bringing about an understanding between them and Dupleix. During the siege of Pondicherry by Admiral Boscawen (September–October, 1748), Ranga Pillai gave additional proofs of his activity and fidelity and remained steadfastly at his post, contriving to efficiently revictual the town in those dark days. The subsequent events of the years 1749-50, which resulted in the short-lived triumph of Chandā Sāhib and Muzaffar Jang, while elevating Dupleix's prestige to a great height, reflected a corresponding glory on the Diarist. He obtained the jaghir and command of the fort of Chingleput and of all the villages that belonged to it, and of which his father-in-law, Seshadri Pillai, had been the poligar for a number of years; a little later, he got from the Mughal authorities the high-sounding title of *mansabdar* of 3,000 horse. But the maintenance of the *mansab* rank meant more expense than before; and the jaghir which was estimated to yield annually normally one lakh of rupees, was more often in possession of the enemy powers than of himself. The reputation to which Ranga Pillai had now raised himself entailed on him the necessity of keeping up a sumptuous magnificence in his household; and " everybody from Salabat Jang himself downwards who wanted a favour knew that they had to turn to the good offices of Mahārājarājasrī Ranga Pillai Avargal ". His house came to be the resort of all sorts and ranks of men, of Indian potentates, fallen nobles, impecunious princes and all kinds of adventurers, who invariably returned from him with words of good advice and some small pocket money besides. Ranga Pillai thus spent all his income and more. Soon his trade prosperity declined on account of the war, while the closing of the route to Karikal put him to grievous loss and increased his debt to the Company; nor was his renting of the revenues of the newly acquired or claimed districts in the Carnatic happy at all. The antipathy of Madame Dupleix "whose ear was receptive of the sound of only one word, money, remained implacable in her dislike of the man "; and she persuaded her husband to make one of her own creatures, Papayya Pillai, the Receiver-General of the Revenues of the Carnatic.

At the beginning of 1751, Ranga Pillai found himself in a very depressed condition. Dupleix was not at all communicative with him on important political matters as he was before; and his daily interviews with the Governor were only limited to some commercial matters relating to the Company. The closing years of the Governorship of Dupleix saw the continuance of this financial depression both for the Diarist and for the Company. During 1751 Ranga Pillai had no contract at all with the Company and did not get any advance. In the succeeding years his business dealings with the Company were comparatively negligible; and only some of his old friends, Des Frenes, Barthelemy, Dubausset and Moracin continued to confide in him and to encourage him with contracts for the supply of cloth for their own export trade.

From the landing of Godeheu at Pondicherry, in 1754 September, Dupleix began to insist on a strict presentation by the Diarist of the accounts of his own personal dealings with him and also of those he had with the Company. Ranga Pillai, on his side showed no alacrity in producing them and maintained that large amounts of reduction were due to him and that the Governor had already promised him these reductions in the contracts of rents that he had entered into. Mon. E. Gaudart says that Ranga Pillai produced the accounts desired by Dupleix only on the evening (14th October 1754) preceding his departure, just like any ordinary creditor of the Company. Naturally he received none of the usual welcome. He records in his *Journal* that Dupleix was very agitated, and did not keep to his seat. After having submitted the accounts, he said:—" You have during the last 13 years showed evidence of great kindness to me. You will remember me and my continued goodness to you." Dupleix replied: " I shall do so." It is all that we know of the last interview of these two men who have contributed, " the one to produce and the other to preserve the most beautiful pages of the history of our colony."

The next day, October 15, at three in the morning, Dupleix embarked on board the ' Duc d'Orleans ', saluted by 21 gun-shots. At day-break Ananda Ranga Pillai returned to the sea shore to have a farewell look at his patron. The ' Duc d'Orleans ' had already weighed anchor; and our Diarist verified that he did not see the coloured flag at the main masthead of the ship, as was usual when Governors departed. He became sad: the recollections of the past began to fill his memory. He pictured in his mind the occasion of Dupleix previously landing on the same shore 12 years and 9 months before as Governor and being received with great pomp and with all the honours due to his high office, and escorted into the Fort by a considerable number of friends and courtiers. "He whose great desire was to end his days in India, is now seen deprived of his office, abandoned by his friends, arrested and sent to France accused. Fortune is capricious. Who is assured of all its favours? Nāsir Jang, master of the Deccan and lord of six and a half subahs thereof, yet trembled, for his courtiers etc., conspired to kill him. He disappeared as victim of a conspiracy hatched by his Nabobs. His (Dupleix's) arms carried French glory up to the Narmada; he had made the throne of the Padshah tremble. What had become of the man formerly so powerful? Madame is the sole cause of his all troubles. Is it not written in the *Saptha Sastras*: 'Unhappy is the man who is guided by his wife.' He will reap evil who takes a woman's advice."

The Diarist received some degree of consideration from Godeheu who was aware of the esteem that he had enjoyed at the hands of several of the Council and especially of Duvelaer. Soon after his arrival at Pondicherry, Godeheu told Ananda Ranga Pillai that he held him and his children to be the members of the family of the Company. He restored to him all his previous privileges, renewed in his favour the farming of some of the districts of the Carnatic and recommended to the new Governor, Duval de Leyrit, that he might well utilise his services in the administration and in the conduct of negotiations with the Indian princes. De Leyrit would not, however, consciously befriend and protect those persons who were the chief collaborators of his predecessors; and Ranga Pillai was always kept at a distance from him in the transaction of all public affairs. After the arrival of Lally and when De Leyrit was practically reduced to the rank of a mere pay-master of military expenses, the experience of Ranga Pillai and his profound knowledge of the resources of the Indian inhabitants of Pondicherry were very useful to the General, particularly in the matter of the reckoning and the realisation of the contributions and forced loans to which he had to resort in order to meet the military charges. The Diarist dreamt, indeed, for some time of the possibility of all the Carnatic being brought back once again under French domination through Lally's powerful lead and of the white flag of France once more floating on the ramparts of Fort St. George itself as in the glorious days of 1746. The French triumph over Fort St. David was but very ephemeral; and the retreat of Lally from the siege of Madras was followed by a series of bad reverses for the French. Ranga Pillai lost both heart and hope, while Pondicherry became quickly encircled and narrowly besieged by the enemy forces. The disunion that prevailed among the Europeans themselves, the violent passions into which Lally so frequently flew, the disgraceful quarrels between the officers of the King and the servants of the Company that occurred so often, and above all, the incompatibility and want of harmony between the irascible Lally and the phlegmatic De Leyrit, leading to mistake after mistake, both in the military and diplomatic fields, as well as to gross indiscipline among the troops and a quasi-anarchy that manifested itself even in the very streets of Pondicherry—these are all well pictured in the vigorous language of the Diarist, whose descriptive power had not at all suffered from either his growing bodily ailments or from the visible setting of the sun of French dominion.

Foreseeing the disaster that was to befall Pondicherry, Ranga Pillai had, on the 24th September 1760, sent off all the members of his family, with some papers and jewels packed in bundles in haste. Only his nephew, Tiruvengadam Pillai, remained with him along with a few servants. Ranga Pillai wrote under this date: "Till now I was under the influence of the sign of *Apasavya,* according to the predictions, so that the town and myself have been in affliction .... The influence of the sign of *Savya* begins on 21st Panguni (30 March 1761) and my fortune thereafter is to be seen by experience." This is the last inscription made in the *Diary* by Ranga Pillai himself. A gap followed till January 10, 1761, on which date, his condition became serious; and his nephew Tiruvengadam Pillai noted all the phases of the short illness of his uncle down to January 12, 1761 the date of his demise. It was, says Tiruvengadam Pillai, a great illness that beset his uncle, and his voice was scarcely audible. Yet, he removed on the last day of his life, to the big drawing room of his house and dictated to his nephew a letter to be sent to his son-in-law, Chidambaranatham Pillai. He reproached him for not responding to his pressing calls, and signed his name, adding in his own hand these words: "This should be considered my last letter." He was then carried to his chamber and stretched himself on the bed. Tiruvengadam Pillai left him for a moment to despatch the letter, and found that on his return "the body of his uncle had become cold."

At last, four days after Ranga Pillai had been carried to the burning ghat, Coote's English Grenadiers replaced the French guard at the Vaḷudāvur gate and the English flag was hoisted over the ramparts of Fort Louis. Ranga Pillai did not entertain any idea of abandoning Pondicherry till it became too late for him to do so; and Providence ordained, with true historic justice, that his bones should be reduced to ashes only in the town in which he had spent the best part of his life and to which he devoted so much of his affection. "Within a twelve-month the proud and dazzling *Gouvernement* which Dupleix had built, had undergone the same fate, dismembered and sold piece-meal to adorn the palace which Muhammad Alī was about to build (at Madras) under the protection of the English guns." The victorious and revengeful English not only ordered the dismantling of the Fort and walls of Pondicherry but also the demolition of all public buildings. It was a piece of luck that Ranga Pillai died in time and was spared the pain and humiliation of witnessing this wilful destruction.

By his marriage with Mangathayi Ammal, daughter of Seshadri Pillai, the Poligar of Chingleput, Ranga Pillai had three daughters: Pappal, Kalathi and Lakshmi, and two sons, Annaswami and

Ayyaswami. Both the boys were very young at the time of their father's death; and the elder, Annaswami, was only 13, having been born in 1748. Their mother had died on the 18th April 1756. She was, Ananda Ranga Pillai says, "beautiful like the Goddess Lakshmi." He performed her obsequies on a grand scale and had her body cremated on a pyre made of sandal wood.

Tiruvengadam Pillai, a younger brother of Ranga Pillai, had died on September 8, 1754 at the age of 40, leaving two children: a daughter, Kolandai Ammal and a son, Appavu. The latter being more aged than his own sons, Ranga Pillai treated him with great affection, had him educated well and used to bring him along with him to all ceremonial functions and solemn occasions. Another of his nephews, Tiruvengadam, helped him much in his commercial affairs. He assisted him in his last days and became, after his death, the head of the family. He secured, not without trouble, his succession to the office of Agent; and he received good consideration at the hands of the Governors who ruled at Pondicherry from 1765 to 1793. He died in the last year of the 18th century and left a journal which yet awaits careful editing and translation.*

* Mon. Gnanou Diagou, the translator into French of the 'History of the Carnatic' by Narayana Pillai (*Histoire Détaillée des Rois du Carnatic par Narayanampoulle*, traduite du tamoul et annotée par Gnanou Diagou) has written to me, under date 8th May 1940, on the *Diary* volume maintained by Tiruvengadam Pillai that has been in possession of Mon. Gallois A. Montbrun, thus; "I was engaged in the study of it for over a year. The volume is in a bad condition. One must read the entries thrice at least before they would become legible. But there is not much fruit. Unlike Ranga Pillai, Tiruvengadam Pillai did not perform important tasks. He devoted his time mainly to endeavouring to recover the amounts due to his uncle. For that purpose he saw many Europeans but they did not communicate to him interesting or important news."

Mon. Gnanou Diagou is a member of the family of the old *courtier*, Pedro Kanakaraya Mudali. Another book preserved in Ananda Ranga Pillai's house and recovered from it by Mon Jouveau Dubreuil, was translated some years ago by Mon. R. P. Oubagarasamy Bernadotte, with an introduction by M. E. Gaudart. It is entitled "Un Livre de

Of the daughters of Ranga Pillai, the eldest, Pappal, died at Madras in 1747, some days before her intended marriage. Another married Kandappa Pillai at Karikal, and the last was married to Chidambaranatham Pillai of Venkatammalpettai. These two marriages, along with that of his niece, Kulandai, were celebrated on a magnificent scale in June 1755.

In the first chapter entitled 'Introductory' the author has given a detailed account of the vicissitudes through which the *Diary* of Ranga Pillai passed to the stage of its translation into English under the auspices of the Government of Madras; here stress is laid on the part played by the late A. Singaravelu Pillai, Curator of the Historical Records of French India, in unearthing it and bringing it to the notice of the English authorities. Since this book went to the press, the author had had information from Professor G. Jouveau-Dubreuil of Pondicherry, of his acquisition of portions missing from the transcription of the *Diary* from which the English translation was made; he was also permitted to give a very short summary of the entry for December 16, 1750 in which some interesting information regarding the actual assassination of Nāsir Jang is given. Thus several lacunae may be filled up in the matter of the information supplied by the Diarist from this new discovery of Professor Dubreuil.

The core of this book is the series of articles entitled 'The Historical Material in the Private Diary of Ananda Ranga Pillai

Compte de Ananda Ranga Poulle, Courtier de la Compagnie des Indes Traduit du Tamoul par le R. P. Oubagarasamy Berdanotte, Professeur au College Seminaire de Pondicherry: Introduction et Notices Biographiques par Edmond Gaudart, Gouverneur en Retraite." In the original which I was given by courtesy of Mon. Gaudart the privilege to go through, the Agent of the India Company entered the details of the operations on loans given on the security of jewels and the more important of his borrowings and advances received from the Company and from the Agents on account of delivery of goods. It is held to be an authentic document and in a few of the operations recorded therein it is in perfect agreement with the *Journal*, which Ranga Pillai maintained during quarter of a century. Tiruvengadam Pillai utilised the last pages of this register to an account of the record of the operations of his uncle to regulate his debts.

Ananda Ranga Pillai, the 'Pepys' of French India (1736–1761)' that appeared in 19 parts spread over several years in the issues of the Journal of Indian History, (Volume VI, 1927 to Volume 17, 1938) Madras. The matter has been modified and supplemented in places so as to form a continuous narrative of the events, most historical, chronicled by the Diarist in his peculiar revealing manner. The narrative of the Diarist, in the English translation published by the Government of Madras, has been kept up as the central core of the book; while notices of the Diarist and his other records made by several generations of scholars at Pondicherry and elsewhere have also been useful. The grateful thanks of the author are due among others to the late A. Singaravelu Pillai, Curator of the Pondicherry Records and M. Edmond Gaudart, *Gouverneur en retraite,* for supplying him with valuable details as to the resuscitation of the *Diary* and supplementary records left by the Dubash.

To Dr. Sir Shafaat Ahmad Khan, M.A., D.Litt., M.L.A., of the University of Allahabad, the author feels most grateful for his generous and scholarly foreword to the book. He is also very much indebted to Professor G. Jouveau-Dubreuil of Pondicherry for supplying him with the pictures of the Diarist and of Pondicherry in 1760 and with information regarding the missing entries in the Diary and to Mon. Gnanou Diagou, Avocat and a descendant of the family of Lazare de Motta, for valuable details supplied.

The author is very grateful to Diwan Bahadur Dr. S. Krishnaswami Aiyangar for having encouraged him to work on this subject and helped him in the serial publication of his articles in his valuable *Journal of Indian History.* To Mr. V. R. Ramachandra Dikshitar, Lecturer in Indian History, University of Madras, he is likewise greatly indebted for suggestions regarding the narrative as well as for help in the reading of proofs. Mr. R. Bhaskaran, M.A., Lecturer in History and Politics, Annamalai University and Mr. R. Ayyaswami of the Annamalai University Library, likewise generously helped him in the matter of translation of French passages and extracts. Mr. V. Vriddhagirisan, M.A., M.Litt., Senior Research Scholar in the Annamalai

University, has been most assiduous in helping him in various ways, particularly in the compilation of the elaborate index.

Mr. S. S. Srinivasaraghavan, Managing Director of Messrs. Thompson and Company, Limited, who has ungrudgingly and patiently helped in the printing and get-up of the book and Mr. D. K. Govindachariar, Proprietor of Messrs. P. Varadachary & Co., who are the Publishers have both laid the author under great obligation to them. It is a pleasure for him to testify to the kindness he has experienced from all these gentlemen.

ANNAMALAINAGAR,
June, 1940.

C. S. SRINIVASACHARI.

Ananda Ranga Pillai, the 'Pepys' of French India

CHAPTER I

INTRODUCTORY

ANANDA Ranga Pillai[1] belonged to a family of prominent merchants who had made themselves conspicuous both at Madras and at Pondicherry. His father, Tiruvengadam Pillai, who was previously trading at Madras, emigrated early in 1716 to Pondicherry at the instance of his brother-in-law Nainiya Pillai who was *courtier* or chief native agent for the French at Pondicherry. Chevalier Hēbert who was the Governor of Pondicherry in the years 1708–13 and 1715–18 saw that the depression in French trade caused by the death-like coma that seized the French Company in the first two decades of the eighteenth century had resulted in the ruin of their credit as well as commerce, and strove to the small extent that was in his power to raise funds and improve trade. The invitation extended to Tiruvengadam Pillai to settle at Pondicherry was among such measures. After a period of eclipse in the favour of the French Governors, due to the disgrace of Nainiya Pillai and the ill-treatment of his son Guruva Pillai by M. Hēbert, Tiruvengadam

1 In a Telugu work, entitled *Ananda Rangarātchandamu*, a work on prosody dedicated to Ananda Ranga Pillai and written by one Kasturi Rangayya Kavi (published by Messrs. V. Ramaswami Sastrulu and Sons, Madras, 1922), we have an account of the genealogy and family of Ranga Pillai. He was born at Yayapuram (Ainavaram?) near Perambur. His father Tiruvengadam Pillai was a clever and prosperous merchant and skilled in dealing with European merchants. His mother was Lakshmiammal; and he married Mangathayi, daughter of a merchant, Seshadri by name; he had four daughters, Lakshmi, Swarnambal, Janaki and Tripurasundari, and two sons, Muthu Vijayananda Ranga (born on a Thursday, *Prabhava, Dhanur Masa, Suddhashtami* and *Revati Nakshatra*) and another, Kumara Vijaya Tiruvengadam Pillai.

Pillai who had meanwhile returned to Madras, was reinvited to Pondicherry and brought with him five other influential merchants. About the same time the French Company was reorganized under the name of *Perpetual Company of the Indies* (1723) after John Law, the Scotsman, made his famous and ill-fated attempt to pull France out of her financial difficulties.[2] The reorganized Company fitted out to Pondicherry three vessels laden with a large amount of bullion which enabled the latter place to retrieve its lost credit and pay off the debts of the Old Company (1721). It was now that Tiruvengadam Pillai and Guruva Pillai, the disgraced *courtier*, who had meanwhile gone to France and personally laid his grievances before the Regent, the Duke of Orleans, were restored to their previous positions by M. de la Prēvostiēre who became the *ad interim* successor to M. Hēbert in 1718 and continued in office till his death in October 1721. Governor Lenoir who was Governor for the first time in the years 1721-23, built with great effort French credit with the native merchants, in spite of the lack of a steady and continuous supply of goods and bullion

The introduction which gives us these details also narrates how Ranga Pillai's father Tiruvengadam Pillai grew to be powerful at Pondicherry and helped in securing justice and honour for his relative, Guruva Pillai, from the French King himself as against the Governor of Pondicherry. Ranga Pillai's knowledge of the various European races settled in India and their languages is set forth in exaggerated terms. The latter portion of the account maintains the same flattering vein and gives him a prominent share in all the achievements of Dupleix and the French—the release of Chandā Sāhib, his successes, the fall of Nasir Jang, the establishment of French influence at the Nizam's court, etc. The description is too exaggerated and flattering to be taken at its face value and is in the ordinary mode of the praise of literary patrons. There is also to be noticed the *Ananda Ranga Vijaya*, a *Champu Kāvya*, composed by the poet, Srinivasa, about A.D. 1752 and celebrating the lives and achievements of Tiruvengadam Pillai and Ananda Ranga Pillai. It tells us how Tiruvengadam Pillai grew to be powerful at Pondicherry and helped in securing justice and honour for his relation, Guruva Pillai, from the French king himself.

2 G. B. Malleson, *History of the French in India* (1893 ed.), pp. 43–58.

from home.[3] M. Beauvallier de Courchant who succeeded Lenoir, took care not to undo the work of his predecessor. What with these efforts and with the loyal co-operation of Guruva Pillai who died however prematurely in 1724 and of Tiruvengadam Pillai who lived for two years longer, the nearly extinct commerce of Pondicherry began to revive rapidly; and in the years following it made still greater progress.[4]

M. Lenoir who succeeded again as Governor had always a high regard for Tiruvengadam Pillai and allowed his young son Ananda Ranga Pillai 'whom he considered a promising young man', to continue the work on which his father had been engaged. The latter was appointed to be the chief native merchant of the French trading-house at Porto Novo.[5] Ranga Pillai established, according

3 J. Burgess, *The Chronology of Modern India, 1494–1894* (1913), pp. 164–165.

4 M. Lenoir who replaced M. Beauvallier as Governor for the second time in September 1726, was able to transmit to Europe in the course of 3 years merchandise valued at nearly 31 lakhs of rupees; and this is a testimony to 'the great commercial progress made by the settlement and to its entire recovery from the state of nullity and depression into which it had fallen in 1722 and 1723...... With its prosperity Governor Beauvallier had begun, and after him to a far greater extent, Lenoir had carried on, those improvements in the town which had been in contemplation ever since the time of Martin.'—Malleson, *History of the French in India*, pp. 59–60.

5 The station was at first occupied by the Portuguese towards the close of the 16th century. Later the Dutch obtained a *cowle* for it from the Indian governor of Gingee in 1643, and with a short break of 1678–80, remained in continuous occupation of the place till 1825. In 1745 they transferred to this place their factories at Cuddalore and Fort St. David. In 1781 the English seized Porto Novo; but they returned it back to the Dutch after the conclusion of peace. Again, it was taken by the English in 1795 and restored to the Dutch in 1818. By the treaty of March 1824, it was finally handed over to the English in the next year along with the other Dutch possessions in India. The Danes had also a small trading-factory at the place, near the river-bank. The English made a settlement (i.e., a factory) there in 1683; but their attention was centred on Kunimedu; and their factory fell into neglect; and they never acquired any sovereign rights there. In 1749 Chandā Sāhib gave the town to Madame Dupleix. Sir Eyre Coote drove the French out of the

to Sir Frederick Price, large trading-houses at Lalapettai and Arcot 'which were soon carrying on a brisk business in the exchange of European goods for the merchandise of the country'. Governor Dumas who succeeded Lenoir in 1735 had a very high opinion of Ranga Pillai and placed confidence in him to such an extent that almost before he completed his first year of office, he came to raise Ranga Pillai to that position in which the latter felt a desire to maintain a diary to the regular writing of which he attached great importance.[6]

Till 1846, *i.e.*, till after more than a century after the *Diary* began to be regularly written, its existence was unknown, when it was unearthed by M. Gallois Montbrun,[7] whose son was Mayor of Pondicherry for a long time. The efforts of French scholars did not seem to have made any progress further than transcriptions

place after his victory of Wandewash in 1760; and it was raided by Haidar Ali who fought the famous battle of Porto Novo in its vicinity (1780-81)—See Francis, *South Arcot Manual*, pp. 279–281; Hodgson's *Report on the Dutch Settlements* (1818). The first mention of the place is according to *Hobson-Jobson* (new ed., p. 727) in Bocarro's *Decada* (*c.* A.D. 1613); and the name was perhaps intended to mean New Oporto rather than New Haven. The Tamil name is Parangi (Feringhi) Pettai (European Town); and the Muhammadans call it Muhammad Bandar. A settlement at the place had been made by Krishnappa Nayak of Gingee and given the name of Krishnapuram.

6 Thus when he sent his younger brother, on the occasion of his first mission on behalf of the French Government to Madras, he gave strict instructions to the latter to keep a regular diary and note in it everything of importance that occurred. (Vol. i, Introduction, p. 12). And we see that after the death of Ranga Pillai, his nephew, Tiruvengadam Pillai, continued to maintain a record which ran to the beginning of 1770 and is still in the possession of his family. The full titles and honours to which Diarist attained were as follows:—

Courtier de la Compagnie Francais des Indes; Chef des Malabars' a Pondicherry; Mansubdar de Trois Mille Chevaux; Commandant du Fortret Jaguirdal, du District de Chingleput.'—taken from A. Gallois Montbrun's *Notice sur la Chronique en Langue Tamile et sur la vu D' Ananda Rangapillai* (1849).

7 The copy which M. Montbrun made was imperfect; he apparently made only selections from the *Diary*. He later supplied a portion of the

and translations of selections and extracts from the *Diary;* nor did M. Vinson, the most prominent of them, proceed beyond the close of the first Anglo-French War in his book *Les Français dans l' Inde* (1894).

The Government of Madras adopted the suggestion of Lieut.-General H. Macleod, the Consular Agent at Pondicherry at the time, and Professor (afterwards Sir) G. W. Forrest[8] who was the Director-General of the Imperial Records at Calcutta (1894–1900), and ordered a transcription of the *Diary.* The first transcription was made from the incomplete copy of M. Montbrun and not from the original. A later and more faithful transcription was made by Mr. K. Rangachariar, Assistant to Sir Frederick Price and Superintendent of Records in the Secretariat, Fort St. George, who discovered that some of the original volumes of the *Diary* were missing and not traceable and also that 'portions of M. Montbrun's copy, of which no originals could be found, had disappeared since

blanks by a supplemental volume which was not available to Sir Frederick Price when he began editing and translating the *Diary.* M. Ariel made another copy of the *Diary* which he presented to the Bibliotheque Nationale of Paris. A translation was made in 1870 by M. Laude of that portion of the *Diary* which gives an account of the siege of Pondicherry in 1748 by Admiral Boscawen. M. Julien Vinson, the well-known Tamil scholar and Professor of the Special School of Living Oriental Languages at Paris, translated portions of the *Diary* in 1889; and he followed up this first production by publishing in 1894 another volume amplifying these under the title of '*Les Français dans l' Inde.*' This does not go beyond 1748 and refers only to a few selected topics. Refer also to Montbrun's *Life of Anandaranga Pillai* quoted above.

8 Forrest, in the course of examining the documents of Fort St. George which threw light on Clive's part in the Carnatic struggles, incidentally examined the relevant records in the Pondicherry Archives. It was on one of these visits to Pondicherry that the *Diary* was brought to his notice; and it was mainly his suggestion that induced the Madras Government to obtain a copy of the *Diary* and arrange for its translation and publication. [Page viii of Preface to Forrest's *Life of Lord Clive,* vol. i (1918).] Forrest often quoted in this work from Ranga Pillai's *Diary,* five volumes of which had been published then. Forrest attached great historical value to the *Diary* and regarded Ranga Pillai as a shrewd observer.

General Macleod's transcription was made.' A statement was given by Sir Frederick Price[9] of (1) the originals of the *Diary* then extant showing the periods for which they were available; (2) copies in the possession of M. Montbrun for which no originals could be found; and (3) portions of the *Diary* for which neither originals nor copies were forthcoming. The principal *lacunæ* occur from November 1738 to June 1740; from October 1750 to April 1751; from December 1753 to September 1754; and from September 1758 to January 1759. It is very doubtful if the copy made by M. Ariel for the Paris National Library would contain the missing portions[10] and possibly, without much doubt, these breaks represent lost volumes.

The late Mon. A. Singaravelu Pillai, Curator of the Historical Records of French India, was largely instrumental in unearthing the *Diary* and bringing it to the hands of the English authorities. He supplied to the writer the information regarding the manner in which the *Diary* came to be translated which is given below, in English translation, of a note supplied by him to the author dated 23rd December, 1927. It contains, among other things, the following sequence of events connected with the unearthing and publication of the *Diary*.

"When in 1870 the statue of Dupleix was set up in Pondichēry, M. Laude, Advocate-General, brought out *Le Siēge de Pondicherry in 1746* consisting of extracts from the *Diary of* Ananda Ranga Pillai.

"Next, M. J. Vinson, the noted Tamil Scholar and a son of Hyacin de Vinson, Judge at Pondichēry, and Curator of the Government Public Library, brought out (in 1894) the well-known *Les Français dans l' Inde.*"

"After him this important *Diary* was neglected by scholars; and the English have the credit of resuscitating interest in it.

9 pp. xvi and xvii of the Introduction to vol. i of the *Diary*.

10 M. A. Singaravelu, Curator of the Old Historical Records at Pondicherry, has thrown information on this point by examining the records of the Societie de Histoire de l' Inde Française.

"Hearing that the original volumes of the *Diary* were in a disorganized and confused condition in the house of Ananda Ranga Pillai, I requested permission from M. Tiruvengadam Pillai, the head of the family, to set about personally arranging and classifying, mainly chronologically, the *Diary* and a large number of historical documents lying in a big box in the house, on which insects were making great ravages. M. Tiruvengadam Pillai had two sons, of whom the elder was an invalid without any interest in this matter. The younger was a clever and learned man, and evinced great interest in the documents and the *Diary;* and he was eager to have these not only edited in Tamil, but also translated. He proposed first to publish the verses sung by poets in Tamil describing the life and achievements of the Dubash and then to take up the matter of the publication of the *Diary*. Some pages of the *Life* were indeed printed; but the work could not be continued owing to difficulties. Unfortunately both the sons of Tiruvengadam Pillai died soon after this time.

"It was in 1897 that I first inspected the *Diary;* in 1900 I perused the volumes a second time, but found that many of the precious documents had disappeared, like others before them. In 1902 the Madras Government deputed Mr. K. Rangachariar to go to Pondicherry and compare the two volumes of proofs with him with the original volumes of the *Diary*. By the will of God, or by a piece of luck coming in my way, Mr. Rangachariar consulted me; and I went through some portions and found that the translation of the *Diary* from 1736 to 1746 was not made from the original volumes of the *Diary*, but from a copy of extracts. He was surprised and declared that the material with his Government was only this copy from which Sir Frederick Price and himself had been translating. I assured him that I would secure for his use the original volumes of the *Diary* from which a complete transcription might be made afresh. He readily agreed to this plan and the Madras Government accorded their generous sanction to this arrangement. I went over to the house of M. Montbrun and handed over to Mr. Rangachariar two volumes of the manuscript original of the *Diary* which, even to-day, continue to be in the possession of the Madras Government. Mr. Rangachariar used to go over to Pondicherry, stay with me for three or four months at a stretch, examine the proofs of his translation along with me and clear all his difficulties. He did this on three or four occasions and corrected his translation in the matter of the correct spelling of the names of ships and men in particular, verifying them and other points from our archives and Government records. It was I that have been uniformly helping in these and other ways in the work of the English translation of the *Diary* from its beginning down to the present year, with the twelfth volume of the work in the press. The letters addressed to me on this subject are so numerous as to occupy two drawers fully. I have just written, clearing certain doubtful points raised in the course of their translation of the twelfth volume, by the Record Office, Madras; and I am ready to help in a similar manner, in the answering of subsequent queries that may be made. The General Introduction given as a preface to the first volume of the Translation by Sir Frederick Price was prepared with the help of the French manuscript note supplied by me. Both Sir Frederick Price and Mr. Dodwell, his successor in the task, consulted me, as well by correspondence as by meeting me personally, in respect of their doubts and difficulties. Even now I am corresponding with Mr. Dodwell at London. When I asked him why my name and services were not noted in the General Introduction, he replied that it was a mistake of omission on the part of his predecessors and that the omission would be rectified soon. In the first page of the Introduction to the eighth volume (1922), he wrote as follows: 'The present instalment of the *Diary* covers the period from May 3, 1751 to December 8, 1753. As will be seen from the list of entries they are very irregular. No reason can be assigned for this, as it has not been possible to check the Madras transcript with the original *Diary* which was formerly preserved at Pondicherry or even with the transcript made by M. Gallois Montbrun. Mr. Singaravelu Pillai to whom the discovery of the *Ms.* was originally due and to whose courteous and learned aid, I have often had recourse, informs me that the Gallois Montbrun papers were irreparably damaged in the cyclone which raged at Pondicherry in 1916 and that the original *Diary* for this period had long since disappeared. More than one passage in the Madras transcript is evidently corrupt; the most important cases of this are indicated in my foot-notes.'

"The primary evidence as to my resuscitation of the original *Diary* from oblivion is to be found in the journal, *Bālabhārati;* first volume. pp. 169-173, published by Mr. V. V. Subrahmanya Iyer of Bharadwaj Ashram, Shermadevi. It thus says: ' . . . . . When the late Mr. K. Rangachariar came over to Pondicherry and sought for a competent hand to help him in arranging the matter of the *Diary,* it was my precious friend and Assistant Curator of the Government Record Office, M. Singaravelu Pillai, that came to his help and rendered assistance in all possible ways. Had it not been for his aid that translation would have remained valueless. The trouble that he took in searching out the volumes of the original *Diary* and its transcript lying in the houses of Ananda Ranga Pillai and Montbrun was great. The most important parts of the Montbrun transcript were destroyed in the storm that raged at Pondicherry eight years back. His (Singaravelu Pillai's) grief at this loss is greater than the grief of one who has lost an immense fortune. So great is his love of learning. Mr. Dodwell who is at present editing the English translation has also written warmly in praise of the help rendered by him.'

" The portion of the original *Diary* extending from April 9, 1760 to January 12, 1761, was discovered by me in 1900 in the course of an examination of the papers and books in Ananda Ranga Pillai's house. There was no copy of this either with M. Montbrun or in the *Bibliotheque Nationalē* of Paris. I had two copies made of the *Ms.*, reserving one for my own use and sending the other through M. Julien Vinson to the *Bibliotheque Nationalē.* This copying was done in January 1901. The late Mr. Bharati took my copy for perusal and handed it after use to Mr. Srinivasachariar, son of Mandayam Krishnamachariar of Triplicane, ... who wanted to publish it in his journal, *India Vidjaya,* in Tamil. But he could not get the necessary permission for such publication from the members of Ananda Ranga Pillai's family . . . . . Finally Mr. V. V. Subrahmanya Iyer published in his *Bālabhārati, in extenso* that portion of the volume discovered by me till April 22, 1760. . . . . His untimely death and that of his son are well known to us. My copy of this portion of the *Diary* has disappeared along with his death, as my numerous queries relating to it addressed to his successors in work and his relatives have proved fruitless.

"A copy of this portion, prepared by the late Mr. K. Rangachariar, is now in the Madras Record Office; its original also is now there. A translation of it is now in press. This is the last volume of the *Diary* of Ananda Ranga Pillai.

"Mr. V. V. S. Iyer has further written in p. 170 of his *Bālabhārati* thus: 'The copy of this portion of the *Diary* was copied by M. Singaravelu Pillai and the then Curator of the Pondicherry Record Office. It was placed at my disposal by my friend Mr. Srinivasachariar. For this I am very grateful to my friend and M. Singaravelu Pillai.'

"Another testimony to my discovery of this portion of the *Diary* is this: Both in M. Vinson's *Les Français dans l' Inde* and in the collection of M. Montbrun there is no mention of this *Diary* portion. This has been omitted necessarily from the first English translation; but in the final translation of vol. i it is mentioned in the list of volumes, as drawn up by Mr. Rangachariar, in the General Introduction.

"Yet a point to be noted as testimony is this. In 1902 when I made an investigation into the condition and number of the original *Diary* manuscripts in the possession of the descendants of Dubash Ananda Ranga Pillai, a letter was written by Vijaya Durai Ranga Pillai (the then head of the family) giving a list of the manuscript volumes in his possession, the original of which I am enclosing herewith. From this list you will see that the first volume of the manuscript original extends from April 28, 1750 to October 29, 1750, which shows that the two previous volumes of the manuscript were not in his possession. If he had them with him he would have included them in his list. This letter will be clear evidence that I discovered the first two volumes from the house of

M. Montbrun and was instrumental in sending them on to the Madras Government through Mr. Rangachariar . . . . . These will clearly prove that I discovered the original *Ms. Diary*, vol. i and ii.

"In 1910 when M. Charles Gallois Montbrun, brother of M. A. Gallois Montbrun, the Mayor of Pondicherry, was the chief of our Library here, an inventory was made of the important documents and books in the possession of his family; and it was found that there were only ten volumes of Ananda Ranga Pillai's *Diary* (1736-60)."

Below is given the translation of the letter to M. A. Singaravelu, regarding the volumes of the original *Diary* in possession of the Dubash's family in 1902.

Letter of Vijaya Durai Ranga Pillai, dated Pondicherry, January 10, 1902, *and addressed to M. Singaravelu Pillai.*

My Dear Friend,

I am in receipt of your letter. I was prevented from replying to it even the day before yesterday (as I intended) because some of the books required were then with my father. As a result of my examination to-day I find the following manuscript books of the *Diary* here.

April 28, 1750	..	October 29, 1750.
April 24, 1752	..	April 5, 1753.
September 4, 1754	..	March 29, 1755.
April 10, 1757	..	September 21, 1758.
April 12, 1759	..	April 8, 1760.
April 9, 1760	..	April 12, 1761.
May 26, 1766	..	April 30, 1767.
May 1, 1767	..	February 8, 1770.
April 10, 1795	..	January 15, 1796.

There is no other volume besides these . . . . . One gentleman from Madras came to me yesterday and told me that he had copies of those volumes not here and that the originals are not here. Is this true? Who has got the originals now? . . . . . .

Yours faithfully,

VIJAYA DURAI RANGA PILLAI,
'ANANDA RANGA PILLAI'S HOUSE'

Pondicherry.

The English Translation as it has appeared has been provided with a table of contents prefixed to each chapter and with amplified marginal notes on each page.

CHAPTER II

THE FIRST YEARS OF THE DIARY

THE DIARIST BEGINS HIS NARRATIVE

The first volume of the English Translation published by the Madras Government in 1904 carries on the quick moving narrative of the *Diary* to April 22, 1746, from its beginning in September 1736. It starts with an account of the grant made to the French at Pondicherry by the Nawab of Arcot, Dōst Alī Khān,[1] of permission to coin money of their own. The *farman* was received with much ceremony and many salvoes of cannon, but not without a large *nazar* to the Nawab and various presents to his *durbar* amounting in all to about 40,000 pagodas. The Diarist who had not developed a high appreciation of Dumas about his time says: 'If M. Lenoir had been Governor now he would not have spent so much money'; (September 10, 1736). Nor was he satisfied with the arrangements

1. The Nawab secured the *farman* from the Emperor Muhammad Shāh which empowered the French to mint the current coin of the realm. The letter addressed on this occasion by Dōst Alī to Dumas runs thus: 'The reputation you have acquired of being a true and faithful friend is known everywhere. In the view therefore to gain your friendship, I grant you permission to coin rupees at Pondicherry, of the coinage of Arkat, conformably to the Parwana which I send you.'—quoted from M. l'Abbe Guyon's *Histoire des Indes Orientalis* by Malleson (p. 73). The moneys coined by the Arcot Nawabs were the *pagoda* and the *rupee*. From the time of Sa'ādat-ullah Khān, *huns* with Persian letters on the reverse were struck at Arcot; and the Nawab Wālājāh (Muhammad Alī) struck coins, known as the Wālājāhi, Kuruki, Star and Feringhipet pagodas (*huns*). There were silver rupees struck besides (Sir Walter Elliot, *Coins of Southern India* (1886), p. 144).

The French rupee was coined at the rate of 2,335 per 100 seers; the expenses of coining amounted to Rs. 16 per 1,000. The gold pagoda was equal in value to about 9 shillings sterling. 320 rupees were considered equal to about 100 pagodas. The reputation of the Indo-French money became very great; and the annual amount struck off did not fall short of five or six millions of rupees. (See Ranga Pillai's *Diary* for December 1736 about the mint accounts and Malleson, p. 73). About the time of the starting of the mint the market price for a seer of silver varied from seven pagodas five fanams to seven pagodas six fanams.

made for the working of the mint through a merchant, Sungu Seshachala Chetty, under the influence of Kanakaraya Mudali, Ranga Pillai's predecessor in the office of the Company's Chief Dubash and *Courtier*. He speaks grievously of the fact that while Governor Lenoir negotiated hard for the acquisition of the right of coinage, Governor Dumas was the recipient of the honours and the glory, which included a decoration with the Order of St. Michael and the title of Chevalier.

The *Diary* from July to November 1738 has its interest for us centered in the occupation of Karikal, the original object of Dumas being to purchase it from the Rajah of Tanjore. A daily post was established between Pondicherry, Tanjore and Karikal. The failure of the peaceful mission that went to the Rajah of Tanjore to secure possession of the place is attributed to Governor Dumas 'who mismanaged the whole affair from beginning to end.' The French were, however, enabled to seize the port with the help of Chandā Sāhib who made over the place to them in February, 1739, there prevailing entire confusion at the Tanjore court at that time in the shape of rapidly succeeding revolutions.[2]

News of the invasion of Nādir Shāh and the sack of Delhi reached Ranga Pillai who wrote an account of what he heard of the revolution in his *Diary* for May 23, 1739, with the exclamation: 'If such indeed be the fate that befell the Emperor of Delhi, need we wonder at the calamities that overtake ordinary men!'[3]

The Invasion of the Marathas (1740)

The interest of the Diary is greatly enhanced with the first approach of the Maratha invaders. On May 15, 1740, it reports

2 Burgess, *Chronology of Modern India*, pp. 177–8. There was intense confusion in the Tanjore kingdom marked by domestic revolutions and the rise of a pretender, Kāṭṭu Raja, in the years 1736–40 (see below).

3 Page 94 of vol. i. The *Diary* says that between 100,000 and 150,000 men perished in the course of the invasion according to the estimate which reached the Armenian merchants and that the Nizam was secretly in league with the invader. The number is, of course, greatly exaggerated.

that a body of Maratha cavalry, 40,000 or 50,000 strong, marched against Cuddapah and worsted a body of cavalry led by Abdun-Nabī Khān; and that the enemy were moving in the direction of the (Dāmalcheruvu) Pass,[4] while Nawab Dōst Alī Khān was marching with all his foot and horse to attack the enemy. News to the same effect was despatched by Imām Ṣāhib to Governor Dumas and the Diarist also received letters to the same effect and describing the depredations of the Marathas.[5] Ananda Ranga Pillai took care to send his agent with an escort of the Company's sepoys to bring away his broadcloths and other goods from Arcot, as many from that place and from Wandiwash, Gingee, Vālikandapuram and Vellore were evacuating their houses and entreating accommodation in Pondicherry. Letters received from Madras stated that many had already similarly fled there with much treasure. The wife of Nawab Dōst Alī came to Pondicherry for refuge from Wandiwash; and a few weeks later came the wife of Safdar Alī, his sisters and his young son who were all very hospitably received by the Governor. Safdar Alī[6] who had been recognized as Nawab by the Marathas in August, secretly concluded a treaty with

4 Dōst Alī was hemmed in and slain in the Dāmalcheruvu Pass, along with his younger son (May, 1740); his Diwan, Mīr Asad, was taken prisoner.

5 Col. Mark Wilks [*Historical Sketches of the South of India* 2nd ed.), vol. i, p. 156] says that Safdar Alī, the elder son of the Nawab, and Mīr Asad, the Diwan, becoming jealous of Chandā Sāhib's power, secretly negotiated with the Marathas inviting their invasion, without the knowledge of the Nawab. Chandā Sāhib was the son-in-law of the Nawab and along with Safdar Alī really managed the affairs of the government. He acquired Trichinopoly in 1736 and was confirmed as the governor of that region. This invasion is stated by Orme to have been instigated by the Nizam; but this is not likely as the Nizam was then absent at Delhi and too deeply engrossed in the affairs there and he had subsequently to proceed to the Carnatic with a large punitive expedition to restore order

6 The object of Safdar Alī and Mīr Asad was frustrated. Dōst Alī's defeat and death at the hands of the Marathas dislocated their plans which presumed that the aged Nawab would shut himself up in Arcot or Vellore and that the invaders would pass, according to previous

them by which they consented to evacuate the province on the secret understanding that they should receive a large portion of the districts in possession of Chandā Sāhib as the price of his effectual removal. The Maratha army quitted the Carnatic; and Chandā Sāhib, deceived by appearances, sold off the provisions which he had accumulated in Trichinopoly on the first alarm of invasion.[7]

The Marathas, according to Ranga Pillai, remained quiet during October and November and pretended to be busy making terms with the Nawab for the payment of tribute. They then gave out that they were preparing for a battle with Chandā Sāhib at Trichinopoly. They actually swooped down on Tiruvannamalai and raided the surrounding country from which many inhabitants escaped to Cuddalore and captured a convoy of treasure which was being sent to Arcot. The *Diary* gives detailed news as to the

compact, to the pretended attack of Safdar Alī and Chandā Sāhib and leave the former free. Dōst Alī took the field with a small force and perished before either Chandā Sāhib or his son could join him. Safdar Alī had advanced as far as Arcot when he heard this news; and with fear for his safety he shut himself up in Vellore, trying to negotiate with the enemy through the medium of Mīr Asad who had fallen into their hands in the battle. The Marathas quickly saw that any price might now be exacted from Safdar Alī by the simple threat of selling themselves to Chandā Sāhib.

Safdar Alī sent gifts to the Governor of Pondicherry and a letter of grateful thanks for French services to his family. The contents of the letter are given by the Diarist in his entry for July 7, 1740. This letter gives the details of the battle between Dōst Alī and the enemy and an account of the fall of the Nawab.

7 He had also sent his wife for safety to Pondicherry; and he himself accompanied Safdar Alī on a state-visit to Pondicherry in September. Ranga Pillai, commenting on Chandā Sāhib's declining to join Safdar Alī in paying a return visit to the Governor, says that it arose from a desire not to go under the wing of another and to be dealt with independently and with due honours. (*vide* p. 131 of vol. I). Afterwards Chandā Sāhib visited the Governor separately and received a return visit. But unfortunately there is a blank in the original *Diary* which barely mentions these visits and adds that Chandā Sāhib accompanied Nawab Safdar Alī to Arcot and then, with the latter's permission, conducted his forces to Trichinopoly. (Note for September 17, 1740).

capture of Porto Novo by the Marathas in the last week of December and an account of the depredations of the Maratha soldiery, their raid into the Dutch factory of the place and their plunder of it and of the town, the total estimate of the value of the plunder being about 150,000 pagodas.[8] This account is based on the contents of a letter received by the Diarist from Porto Novo and mentions the imprisonment by the Marathas of the Dutch Deputy-Governor Astruc and several other Dutchmen who were released later.

The siege of Trichinopoly begun by the Marathas about the middle of December, was in fair progress when detachments of the Maratha soldiery marched into the Cuddalore territory, pillaged the town of Tirupapuliyur and moved towards Sadras, raiding places on the way. At Sadras they were repulsed from the Fort by a volley of cannon shot. They then turned back pillaging as usual the villages on their route. (29th January—2nd February, 1741). All obstructions in the suburbs outside the walls of Pondicherry were cleared for purposes of defence. Couriers arrived at intervals bearing letters from Raghuji Bhonslé; but their contents were not known to the Diarist. In March, he details news of the probable fall of Trichinopoly where Chandā Sāhib could not hold out any longer, of the efforts made by Safdar Alī and others to subscribe a large sum with which to buy off the Marathas from the siege and of the refusal of the latter to cease operations in the absence of orders from their chief. (Entry for the 15th March—which tells us that Nawab Safdar Alī, his mother, Chandā Sāhib's wife and others subscribed among themselves 22 lakhs of rupees; and that the wives of Chandā Sāhib and Badē Sāhib[9] wrote to the Marathas offering to pay this amount, but without effect.)

The *Diary* for the 27th March, 1741, relates how Badē Sāhib advanced to the relief of Trichinopoly with a large convoy of

8 A reverse is said to have been sustained by the Marathas at Porto Novo. (Burgess, *Chronology of Modern India*, p. 180).

9 One of the brothers of Chandā Sāhib who was in charge of Madura and who had also sent his wife for safety to Pondicherry.

provisions and horsemen and foot, and how the Marathas intercepted him with a body of 2,000 cavalry near Dindigul from which he sallied out and routed them; later how Raghuji Bhonsle marched with 10,000 horse and invested the camp of Badē Sāhib at Maṇalpārai and how in the battle which ensued both Badē Sāhib and Sādiq Sāhib, the son-in-law of his elder sister, fell. The *Diary* further tells us that the Marathas sent the corpse of Badē Sāhib in a palanquin to Chandā Sāhib.[10] In a subsequent letter recorded by Ranga Pillai, he tells us that Badē Sāhib was alive and did not die from his wounds.

We also note how the Pindaris who had attached themselves as irregulars to the Maratha armies of a later date in large numbers[11]

10 Orme narrates this event as if there was only one encounter between Badē Sāhib and the Marathas, and how the latter cut off his head and sent it as confirmation to his brother. 'Another detachment attacked Sādiq Sāhib approaching from Dindigul with 1,500 horse and 3,000 foot, who were likewise defeated after a sharp fight which ended with the death of Sādiq Sāhib.' (*History of the Military Transactions of the British Nation in Indostan*, 4th edition of 1803—Madras, Reprint of 1861—vol. i, p. 44.)

11 Yule and Burnell in *Hobson-Jobson* (p. 712)—say that the Pindaris seem to have grown up in the wars of the later Muhammadan dynasties of the Deccan and in the latter part of the 17th century attached themselves to the Marathas in their revolt against Aurangzib. The supposed earliest reference to them is their helping Dunnaji Jadu as against Zulfiqār Khān in the campaign of 1706–7 in South India. Mr. A. F. M. Abdul Ali, in his edition of Colonel James Tod's Manuscripts relating to the Origin, Progress and Present State of the Pindaris (Gwalior, 1815) (see pp. 212–242 of Indian Historical Records Commission, Proceedings of Meetings, Vol. XIV—Fourteenth Meeting held at Lahore, December 1937) says that the earliest mention of the name Pindari is to be found in the *Tārikh-i-Muhammad-Qutb-Shāhi* and that the Sultans of Golconda and Bijapur employed in their expeditions into South India after the battle of Rakhas Tagdi a very large number of irregular cavalry composed entirely of free-lancers, many of whom came from outside the Deccan or even India. The next mention of the term Pindari is to be found in the accounts of Aurangzib's expeditions into the Deccan, and Jonathan Scott's *Aurungzebe's Operations in Dekkan* (Part III of Ferishta's History of Dekkan from the First Muhammedan Conquests etc—Vol. II. (1794)) mentions them as the auxiliaries of the Maratha plunderers.

accompanied Raghuji Bhonsle in this expedition and how the and the Poligars and the Kallars of Tondaiman scaled th walls of Trichinopoly from all sides on the 25th March;[12] an Chandā Sāhib submitted to the Marathas at midnight of the sam day and was disarmed and kept a prisoner. The Fort was place by the Marathas in charge of Murari Rao, assisted by 14,000 o their best troops. Chandā Sāhib and his son were sent clos prisoners to Satara in the neighbourhood of which they wer confined in a strong fort.

Nothing of much importance is noted in the *Diary* except tha Dumas retired from the Governorship and embarked for Franc on the 20th October accompanied by La Bourdonnais and hi squadron which had come from Mascareigne (Isle de France) o which he was Governor from 1735 to 1746. Dupleix, the nev Governor, landed at Pondicherry on the 14th January, 1742; an a few months later a flag and a kettle-drum were received by th Governor from the Emperor of Delhi at an imposing reception.

Domestic Revolution in the Carnatic

On the night of Saturday, the 13th October, 1742, Nawal Safdar Alī was murdered in bed by order of his cousin Murtaz Alī Khān, the Governor of Vellore; and the Diwan, Mīr Asad, wa heavily chained and imprisoned. These tidings reached Pondi cherry on the 16th October. The Diarist reports the movement of Murtazā Alī Khān who was installed as Nawab by his partisan and also chronicles the news from Madras where Nawab Safda Alī's widow and mother were staying as well as his young son Muhammad Sa-īd[13] who, as soon as he was proclaimed Nawab recompensed the English for the hospitality shown to him b

12 Orme distinctly says that Chandā Sāhib delivered up the cit and himself on the 26th March, 1741.

13 Orme (vol. i, p. 45) says that Safdar Alī had sent the wome and children of his family, together with his treasures to Madras preferring the English by the advice of Mīr Asad who suspected Dupleix He also made several visits to Madras (*vide* H. D. Love, *Vestiges of Ol Madras* (1913), vol. ii, pp. 282–4).

granting them as a gift[14] five villages in the neighbourhood of Fort St. George and the liberty of coining Arcot rupees and pagodas.

The revolution at Arcot did not long favour Murtazā Alī. Murari Rao of Trichinopoly declared against him; and the army broke into open mutiny. Terrified at the demands of the soldiers, Murtazā Alī escaped from Arcot to Vellore in women's cloths; and the son of Safdar Alī was duly proclaimed Nawab by the Diwan Mīr Asad. Ranga Pillai records the camping of Mīr Asad with his men at Valudāvūr in the neighbourhood of Pondicherry and the mis-doings of the ill-disciplined soldiery of the Nawab. He says: 'The havoc previously committed by the Marathas was nothing compared with this. It is true they plundered and pillaged, but the people managed to save at least something from their hands, and so continued to eke out a living. But now the country has been utterly laid waste.'[15]

The Invasion of Nizam-ul-Mulk

The next noteworthy event chronicled was the advance of the aged Nizām-ul-Mulk to Arcot in the last week of February. He came with an enormous number of horse and foot—'as though the sea was rising and flooding the land'—'the camp extending from the banks of the Pennar,—taking in Vellore—to the dam of the Kaverippakkam tank.' According to the reports which reached him, the object of the Nizam's expedition was to transfer the possession of Trichinopoly to the Mysoreans. But nobody knew what would happen; and Dupleix put Pondicherry in a state of defence, mounting cannon on the walls, storing powder and shot in convenient places and forming a volunteer corps of Europeans.

After intimidating into submission the petty chiefs of the country and appointing one of his chief officers, Khājā Abdullā

14 This grant was possibly ordered by Nawab Safdar Alī, but it was not actually made until a month after his death. Ananda Ranga Pillai refers to this grant as a rumour in his entry for 26th October 1742.

15 Entry for the 2nd February, 1743.

Khān[16] to administer the Carnatic and take charge of the young son of Safdar Alī, the Nizam moved down on Trichinopoly. The mere weight of his name and numbers compelled Murari Rao to evacuate the Fort (29th August, 1743). The Diarist tells us that Murari Rao who was promised the possession of the hill fort of Penukonda, gathered renown from this exploit; and the Nizam carried on operations with only a semblance of reality, but without ever actually offering battle. 'By these means, Āsaf Jāh who is an astute man, gained his object, but at the same time Murari Rao gathered renown.'[17] The *Diary* notes that both the French at Pondicherry and the English at Madras sent presents to the Nizam and at the same time strengthened their own fortifications. In December 1743, Dupleix issued an order to the effect that all the officials should build houses at Mortāndi Chāvadi on the outskirts of Pondicherry and that the new town should be styled *Dupleix-pēttai* and that any one who called it by its old name should be liable to a fine—an early illustration of his love of self-glorification.

The Maratha danger reappeared quickly even before the Nizam returned from the Carnatic. A letter to Dupleix from the son of the French agent at Arcot in February, communicated the news that the Marathas[18] were besetting the army of the Nizam and had got through the passes and the country round Arcot had been deserted by the people. The troublous times were attributed by the Diarist to the appearance of a great comet (no doubt that known as the Cheseaux's).

16 Orme distinctly states that Khājā Abdullā was appointed Nawab of Arcot and all its dependencies. This person left with the Nizam on the latter's return to the Deccan, leaving one of his dependents in charge of Arcot—probably his son—Wilks says that the Khājā was only to be deputy.

17 This piece of news was later confirmed by a letter addressed to Dupleix by Imām Sāhib, an officer of the Carnatic since the time of Dōst Alī, who had extensive money dealings with Pondicherry. The Governor was greatly rejoiced at this. Imām Sāhib had made himself a favourite at the Nizam's court and had advised the Nizam to march into the Carnatic.

18 The news, according to the Diarist, states that the Marathas had even killed Nāzir Jang (of course false).

The Nizam returned to Golconda in March 1744 and publicly confirmed in the Nawabship Khājā Abdullā who had accompanied him. But this was followed by the latter's sudden death.[19]

The Accession of the House of Anvar-ud-din

Anvar-ud-dīn Khān,[20] the founder of the second Carnatic Dynasty, was then appointed Nawab by the Nizam and he took charge of his duties at Arcot in April; he made Mahfuz Khān his elder son Deputy-Nawab, and appointed Muhammad Alī, his younger son to the governorship of Trichinopoly, having got the Nizam's permission beforehand to make these appointments. He came to the Carnatic with the suspicion of having poisoned his predecessor. He was accompanied by Safdar Alī's son Muhammad Sa-īd who was specially commended to his protection by the Nizam, who expressed a desire to raise the boy to the Nawabship when he should come of age.[21] The impropriety of this charge of the boy to the care of Anvar-ud-dīn is severely commented on by Orme,[22]

19 The Khājā was found dead in his bed the morning after he was confirmed. The hand from which death came could never be discovered. (Orme, *History of Indostan*, vol. i, p. 52—no doubt based on contemporary sources including Paupia Brahman's *History of the Carnatic up to 1749*)—Orme Manuscripts, quoted in H. D. Love, *Vestiges of Old Madras*, vol. ii, p. 286, n. 5. His sudden death happened on the very next morning after he took leave of his master to return to his *subah*, when he was about to get ready for the early morning prayer (p. 51. *Tuzak-i-Wālājāhi* of Burhān Ibn Hasan. tr. by S. M. H. Nainar: Part I. (1934)).

20 He was the son of an erudite lawyer Anvār Khān, had served with distinction at Surat and elsewhere under Ghāzi-ud-dīn, the father of Nizām-ul-Mulk and was latterly governor of the districts of Ellore and Rajahmundry from 1725 to 1741. He was in charge of the city of Golconda during the Nizam's absence in the Carnatic.

21 Fort St. George to the Directors; September 5, 1744. The letter quotes this piece of information.

22 Orme suspected the Nizam of having dissembled throughout this transaction, and wrote thus: 'The general joy with which the youth was received eclipsed all the homage that was paid to the sovereign power of his guardian; and it is supposed that the provisional Nabob did not behold without jealousy these demonstrations of the public attachment to the son of Subder-ally, (vol. i, p. 55).

and the family and relations of Dōst Alī were very much chagrined at the nomination of Anvar-ud-dīn by the Nizam to be Nawab, in spite of his repeated promises that the boy should have his father's post.

The story of the assassination of the boy, Muhammad Sa-īd, commonly known as Sāhibzada (June, 1744) by a body of Pathan soldiers, which produced another revolution in the ruling family of the Carnatic, is told in detail by Ranga Pillai (entry for 4th July) who gives the details of the outrage and says that the Pathans were incited by Murtazā Alī Khān who had for a long time waited for an opportunity of the kind. Some suspected Anvar-ud-dīn himself of having practised on Murtazā Alī to bring about this murder. He strongly denied all connection with the murder;[23] but he was not able to exculpate himself in the opinion of his subjects who 'complained loudly of the avarice and parsimony of his gove ment, and contrasted it, much to his disadvantage, with that of

23 The Fort St. George Despatch to England said that Murtazā Alī hired the Pathans to assassinate the Nawab (Anvar-ud-dīn), Sāhibzada and some others, intending to seize upon the government; and that in the *turban* of one of the assassins was found an obligatory note signed and sealed by Murtazā Alī Khān for 200,000 rupees to be paid to them on their executing the deed; and that the Nawab escaped, though there was a second attempt on his life which miscarried also. The same despatch tells us that the Nizam was greatly displeased with Anvar-ud-dīn whom he first suspected, but was convinced of his innocence when the note of Murtazā Alī Khān was produced in which the Nawab's name was also mentioned as one of the victims (P. to England, vol. xiv, September 5, 1744) quoted in Love, *Vestiges of Old Madras*, vol. ii, pp. 287–8. Burhān Ibn Hasan, in his *Tuzak-i-Wālājāhi* is explicit that an Afghan, Yadu'l Khān got the signal from Ahmad Tāhir Khān, father of Muhammad Husain Khān Tahir, on the occasion of the marriage of the latter's daughter and struck the boy-prince with a dagger under the pretext of a dispute on account of delay in getting the arrears of pay due to him. There had been bitter enmity between the Tahirans and Nawab Safdar Alī. Husain Khān Tahir was the jaghirdar of Amburgadh and diwan to Nawab Dōst Alī. He was dismissed from office by Safdar Alī and superseded by Mīr Asad. The Tāhirans and Murtazā Alī conspired together and had brought about the assassination of Safdar Alī and the imprisonment of Mīr Asad.

their former Nabobs.' Among the people suspicion was mutually divided between Anvar-ud-dīn and Murtazā Alī.[24] Finally the Nizam conferred upon Anvar-ud-dīn the Nawabship which he continued to hold till his death in 1749 at the battle of Ambur. He was however held in no great estimation by the people; and an Indian of note, Papaiya Brahman, the Younger, wrote of his government as being 'the most spiritless, covetous, severe and unjust' among all the late rulers of the Carnatic and says that 'the whole body of superior, inferior and meaner ranks of subjects in the province, continually lamented for having so bad a Government over them.'[25]

Shortly after these events, rumours of an approaching English squadron reached Pondicherry; and in September a ship which was approaching was suspected to be English; preparations for defence in case of a sudden alarm were made.[26] In September 1745 the Nawab Anvar-ud-dīn visited Pondicherry, accompanied by his Diwan, Sampati Rao and several other officers. He was received with great honours and pomp (September 10 and 11, 1745); and the result of this was to renew the friendship existing for long between Arcot and Pondicherry; this was to stand Dupleix in much good stead in the coming war.

24 Elphinstone, *The Rise of the British Power in the East* (ed. by E. Colebrooke, 1887, p. 81). He bases his information on Orme and Wilks.

25 H. D. Love, vol. ii, p. 288.

26 *Diary* entries for September 29, 1744 and October 31

CHAPTER III

LA BOURDONNAIS ON THE SCENE

THE DECLARATION OF WAR WITH ENGLAND

IT was in the last week of August 1745 that despatches[1] were received by Dupleix communicating the intelligence of war with England. A few days after this Nawab Anvar-ud-dīn arrived in Pondicherry where he was received with great pomp and shown over the fortifications. Ranga Pillai estimates the Nawab's age at eighty or eighty-five years. The visit was a political one;[2] and the Nawab was accompanied by his Diwan, Sampāti Rao, Bangāru Yāchama Nāyak, Dāmalcheruvu Venkatapathi Nāyak and other chiefs. The significance of this visit was known a few months later.

News of war reached Madras in the middle of September; and the English[3] began to strengthen their fortifications, watching, mounting artillery on the Fort walls and equipping the batteries

1 The frigate which conveyed these despatches was wrecked on a rock when approaching Mascareigne (see note 2, p. 268); a few survivors collected these, got into a boat and delivered them to M. de la Bourdonnais who forwarded them by another ship to Mahe whence they were sent on by land to Pondicherry through some Brahmans. Ranga Pillai's record of the contents of these despatches has unfortunately perished in the original.

2 Thence the Nawab went on to Fort St. David and Uḍaiyār-pālaiyam. His tour was in some measure calculated to raise contributions from the European settlements [H. Dodwell, *The Madras Despatches* (1744–1755); (1920), p. 19.]

3 From about the September of the previous year, the Madras Council had been observing Pondicherry and arranging for rapid communication overland with Bengal. They ordered the building of two swift despatch-boats at Bombay; and Governor Morse, in reply to M. Dupleix's letter of November 23, proposing that peace should be preserved eastward of the Cape of Good Hope by mutual agreement, replied by a P. Consultation of November 26 that he was not authorized to enter into any such compact. A squadron under Commodore Curtis Barnett left England for the East secretly a month after the war was

on the sea-shore with guns. Dupleix was anxious to receive accurate information as to the doings at Madras, particularly during the time that Barnett's squadrons cruised near the coast.

It was in November 1745, that Pondicherry was swept by three severe cyclones,[4] the first of which caused great damage (night of November 3) inundating the town and destroying three newly-formed suburbs. Two lesser cyclones followed on November 23 and 27, the former date being a New Moon day and Tuesday, under the influence of the star Kēṭṭai.

In February 1746, news came from Mahe that a squadron five to ten French ships was on its way hither and was in likelihood heading for the roadstead of Pondicherry. The Eng were also apprised of this fact from Anjengo and Telliche The Diarist calculated (entry for February 5, 1746)[5] that

declared and other ships followed in the months of October and the next February. Barnett arrived off Fort St. David in July 1745 and reached Madras towards the close of August. Soon after Commodore Barnett reached the Coromandel Coast, the Nawab, who had previously written to Madras to forbid hostilities with the French (received on July 14, 1745) now repeated his injunction (August) and got the same reply—that Morse 'will not be the first to disobey your Commands in this Respect, provided there is the same deference paid to them by the French. Otherwise I (Morse) may presume it is not your Excellency's design to put any restraint upon me to my Disservice and to the Advantage of the Enemy. . . the Commanders of his Majesty's ship are not under my direction, I cannot oblige myself to answer for their conduct.' (Madras letter to the Nawab, dated July 16, 1745). Anvar-ud-dīn, after the second reply, came to San Thomé, accompanied by one of his sons and Diwan Sampāti Rao and received two of the Council. The subject of their conversation is not on record. Barnett, perhaps influenced by these circumstances, refrained from attacking Pondicherry, though he might have easily done so. On the approach of the north-east monsoon, he sailed for the Archipelago.

4 Alfred Martinean's *Les Cyclones a la Cōte Coromandel* (Pondicherry, 1917), pp. 4–8, extracting from the original of the *Diary* (T. iii, pp. 289, 280 *et* 292).

5 The French had adopted the New Style of dates long before it was used by the English who followed to Old Style down to 1753. Hence the discrepancies between the dates of the Diarist and those of Orme, etc.

English had in all twenty-two sail including the prizes taken from the French, 'so that when their fleet encounters ours, the enemy would be two and a half times stronger. Taking this into consideration, should a force advance on Cuddalore, the English would be obliged to keep about five or six of their fleet for the protection of that place, and two or three might be required to remain at Madras. This would reduce the enemy's ships by half their number, and when they then met ours, the latter should be able to deal with them effectively and reach the roads here.'[6] This is the explanation for the detailing of a force of 500 men towards Cuddalore whose inhabitants were thrown into a panic. Four English ships[7] neared Pondicherry, sailing in pursuit of a fugitive Portuguese ship coming from Chandranagar; precautions were taken against a possible assault on Pondicherry; while the English at Fort St. David requested the English captain to retaliate by an attack on the batteries of the French town (February 8). The attack did not take place; and the Diarist shrewdly remarks: 'The object of the English in acting as they have done is to imitate the course followed by the French near Fort St. David, who made but a show of warlike operations; and in this respect they have outdone them.' Nevertheless he eulogizes Dupleix's skill and writes of the Madras Governor as being 'a worthless fellow and a man devoid of wisdom'; and he continues: 'Although Pondicherry receives no ships, her Government lacks funds, the enemy has seized her vessels, she is feeble and wanting in strength, and her inhabitants are in misery; although she has all these disadvantages, no sooner is mention made of her than the Nawabs, and other magnates in the interior become alarmed . . . . . All this is owing to the ability, readiness and luck of the present Governor, M. Dupleix.'[8]

6 *The Diary*, vol. i, p. 297.

7 Dupleix's demonstration against Fort St. David was withdrawn as a consequence and this fact is noted in a Madras *P.C.* dated January 31, 174⅚.

8 *Diary*, vol. i, pp. 299–300. Dupleix's 'method of doing things is not known to any one, because none else is possessed of the quick mind with which he is gifted. In patience he has no equal. He has peculiar

Pondicherry was not perturbed by the threatenings of the English ships and her inhabitants went about fearlessly, even crowding on the beach at nights when the English ships in the roadstead were brilliantly lit. Dupleix wrote a letter to Nawab Anvar-ud-dīn, complaining of English troops encamping in his territory close to Pondicherry and planning to attack it and promising not to do violence or retaliate unless the English should give occasion; and he added: 'If at any time the English should give us occasion to fight, we cannot then remain passive. Should therefore an encounter take place within your territories, you must not blame us. We write to you beforehand in order that you may not blame us afterwards. Be it known to you that it is the English who have compelled us to write this letter to you.'[9] (Diarist's entry for March 18, 1746). Shaikh Rahīm-ullā, the Nawab's representative of the country round Fort St. David, wrote to Dupleix a letter asking for French help in seizing the fourteen villages forming the suburbs of Fort St. David, according to the order that he had

skill in carrying out his plans and designs; in the management of affairs and in governing; in fitting his advice to times and persons; in maintaining at all times an even countenance; in doing things through proper agents; in addressing them in appropriate terms; and in assuming a bearing at once dignified and courteous towards all.' The Diarist goes to the extent of comparing him with Aurangzib and Louis XIV.

9 Compare this with Governor Morse's letter to the Nawab, dated March 17, explaining how he had held to his engagement notwithstanding French provocation to which the Nawab replied on April 1, as follows:— 'I received your agreeable Letter acquainting me that you and the Gouvernour of Tēvanāmpatam (Fort St. David) pay a great regard to my Orders, and have made use of no Hostilities to his Majesty's Sea Port Towns, and desiring that the Gouvernour of Pondicherry may be enjoined to behave in like manner. This pleases me highly, and I assure you that your Behaviour in every respect is very satisfactory to me. You may depend upon it that the Gouvernour of Pondicherry shall not be suffered to behave in a different manner. I have sent him my *Taukeed* in such a way as is necessary upon this occasion. Pray believe me to be your Friend and let me have the pleasure of hearing frequently of your Welfare.' (*Madras Records, P.C.*, vol. lxxvi, April 3, 1746). For some nights in March, the town-gates of Pondicherry were closed

received from the Nawab. This letter was answered on the next day (April 2) after it was received to the effect that French assistance would be given if the Nawab himself should write to Dupleix direct.[10]

Dupleix was also at pains to keep on good terms with the Danes just then. A French ship which was attacked by English ships in the roadstead of Tranquebar was attempted to be protected by the Danes who had, in the words of Ananda Ranga Pillai 'obliged the French in everything that they asked.' He showed great honour to the Deputy Governor of Tranquebar who halted at Pondicherry on his way from Madras.

The Appearance of La Bourdonnais

Commodore Barnett, the commander of the English fleet, died at Fort St. David (May 10), after a few days of illness; and the command of the English squadron devolved on Captain Edward Peyton who was far less capable than his predecessor. But for this change of command, the fortunes of Madras might have been different; and the Diarist gleefully recorded that 'public opinion now says that the tide of the victory will henceforward turn in favour of the French as it has hitherto flowed on the side of the English.' He said that the Goddess of Fortune had departed from Madras to take up her residence at Pondicherry where Dupleix was making vigorous preparations in defence and collecting stores for a large army. He was expecting the fleet that La Bourdonnais had fitted out, carrying three thousand and three hundred men

earlier than usual for fear of a possible English attack. The Nawab's assurances to Dupleix sent through his Deputy, Shaikh Rahīm-ullā, described below, seems to produce an impression of inconsistency and a desire to please both parties without being sincere to either. Mahfuz Khān, a son of the Nawab, came to Vaḷudāvūr near Pondicherry and received a French deputation; he was welcomed into Pondicherry with the same honours as his father got and he later sent to the French two brass cannon from Trichinopoly (February–March).

10 *Res.* of the Pondicherry Council of April 2, as reported by the Diarist.

which left Bourbon and Mauritius at the end of May.[11] On June 12, Ranga Pillai heard the news that five Europe ships reached Mascareigne[12] in February, bringing orders to M. de la Bourdonnais that he should attack the English and the latter had fitted out the recent arrivals and other ships for hostilities and sent advance intimation to Dupleix that he would reach Pondicherry by the end of May. It was also known that the coming ships would touch at Karikal where some boxes of silver would be disembarked. Dupleix had therefore sent some soldiers and Mahe sepoys to Karikal in order to strengthen it against attack. From the beginning of June, his eyes were continually straining to look out for the coming fleet; and Ranga Pillai was sure that by June 30, the squadron would certainly be in the roads of Pondicherry.[13] At last news was received from the Dutch Council of Negapatam on June 21 that the French squadron was well on its way up the Coromandel Coast and would reach Pondicherry in a day or two. At last the precious squadron reached the Pondi-

11 *Memoir pour le Sieur de la Bourdonnais* (1755); and Julien Vinson's *Les Français dans le Inde, Dupleix et Labourdonnais* (1894). p. 25, footnotes.

12 Bourbon, now called Reunion, was sometimes known as Mascareigne, after its reputed discoverer Mascarenhas; and the name of Mascarene Islands is still applied to the whole Archipelago. Ranga Pillai, more often than not, meant by Māsukkarai (the Tamil equivalent of Mascareigne) only Mauritius (Isle de France) occupied by the Dutch and called after Prince Maurice of Nassau and later seized by the French about 1725. Bourbon was the less important of the islands. M. Vinson was the first to see that in the *Diary Māśukkarai* meant very often the *Isle de France, vide* (1) Vinson, *Les Français dans L'Inde*, p. 14 note and (2) Price's Appendix I to the English Tr. of the *Diary*, vol. i.

13 See entry for the 12th June, 1746, p. 61 in vol. ii of the *Diary* (English Trans. by Price and Rangachari, 1707); *ibid.*, p. 68 where the Diarist records (June 13); 'The eyes of all here are fixed upon the sea looking for the appearance of the tradeships. The non-arrival of these is a divine punishment for the manifold vices of the townsfolk. But He knoweth that they can endure the strain no longer, and I trust that He will look upon them with compassion and restore them to happiness.' (pp. 112-3.)

cherry roadstead in the night of July 8 after having given battle with some apparent success to the English men-of-war under Captain Peyton, a little to the south of Negapatam.[14]

A few days after the arrival of the fleet under M. de la Bourdonnais, Ranga Pillai heard among the latest news items received from France that Dupleix had proposed that he should be transferred to Chandernagar which should be the head-quarters of the French settlements instead of Pondicherry, or should be constituted an independent government like Mascareigne and that he had offered, in the event of the acceptance of his proposals, to serve as Governor for the full term of his life. The orders of the Company were expected to be favourable to Dupleix's wishes and

14 According to the Diarist the combat lasted from four in the afternoon to seven in the evening; and La Bourdonnais fired some five thousand rounds repulsing the six English ships which escaped, owing to their having the advantage of the wind. The French suffered severe losses and their boxes of ammunition in two ships exploded. 'It is said that two English ships were either sunk or damaged beyond repair and that their crews perished.' (*Diary*, vol. ii, p. 113.). Orme (*Military Transactions*, vol. i, fourth edition, Madras Reprint, 1816, p. 62) says that the English had greatly the advantage in the weight of their cannon, (they had twenty-four pounders as against the eight and twelve pounders of the French) though the number of their men did not amount to one-half of that of the French squadron. Peyton had his squadron nearer to the wind than that of the enemy; and the fire of the smaller French cannon did very little execution. One of the French ships was dismasted and shattered and had to be sent away to Bengal for repair. Peyton did not venture on a second engagement and made the next evening for the harbour of Trincomali—See Mill's *History of India* (1858), vol. iii, p. 45 and Beveridge's *A Comprehensive History of India* (1865), vol. i, p. 413; and Vinson, pp. 25–26; and Malleson, *The French in India* (1893), p. 196; and Dodwell, *Dupleix and Clive* (1920), p. 11.

The arrival of La Bourdonnais' fleet created great joy in the minds of the citizens of Pondicherry. In the previous year no ship arrived from France, and none was despatched likewise from Pondicherry; while those bound for China, Manilla and Achin were all captured by the English. There was complete depression in trade; and the arrival of this fleet was like the 'discovery of a hidden hoard or lost treasure to them.'

to be sent by the seven ships which were shortly expected from Europe; and he would be most probably succeeded by M. de Leyrit from Mahe. He had seen in La Bourdonnais a rival to himself for the Governorship of Pondicherry.

Misunderstandings between Dupleix and La Bourdonnais

Misunderstandings began between Dupleix and La Bourdonnais even within a few days after the latter's arrival; and the Diarist notes, in his entry for July 13, that the two were at heart jealous of one another's rights and privileges, though they preserved an outward appearance of amity.[15] La Bourdonnais held that the control of the military operations rested wholly with

15 M. de la Bourdonnais resented the beating of the *tambour* accorded only to officers of inferior degree; and not the *tambour-aux-champs* which was accorded only to officials of high degree. That Dupleix was not given a similar honour when he first landed at Pondicherry was made the ground of a precedent. He preferred a complaint against this to Dupleix who would not comply with his request, saying that he himself was an independent Governor and was vested by the King with command of the fleet. Dupleix maintained that La Bourdannais ceased to be independent when he set foot on shore and became his own subordinate.

Dupleix, in the course of a private conversation with the Diarist (July 16, 1746) expressed that La Bourdonnais had an ungovernable temper and was a babbler and that according to the version of his own officers it was his neglect that permitted the escape of the English ships after the engagement off Negapatam and that all of them could have been easily captured. (*Diary*, vol. ii, pp. 128–130 and pp. 166–7.) La Bourdonnais states in his own *Memoirs* that being without provisions and having on board a great number of sick and wounded men, he could not pursue the enemy. In his letter to Dupleix, he wrote thus: 'The fear of missing Pondicherry, the large amount of money for you on board, and, more than that, the scarcity of food, of which many ships had only four and twenty hours' supply, made me contemplate the frightful situation in which I should be, if I were to fall to the leeward of the place; this determined me to bear up for Pondicherry.' (Quoted by Malleson; foot-note on pp. 127–8). This explanation, Dupleix said, 'I suppose, must be accepted'; but he added that under similar conditions in the future the English should not be let off thus and that the French should fight to the last. 'One side must be destroyed by the

him and that he was not bound to consult the Governor in matters connected therewith. ' Thus business is transacted between them with but little cordiality. The future development of this remains to be seen.' [16]

The news that reached the Diarist in the days following consisted first of the arrival of envoys from Tanjore and the Raja of Sivaganga for negotiating an alliance between these chiefs and the French, and of the Dutch at Negapatam having received some of the wounded English and giving sail-cloth, cables and other necessary materials for repair of the English ships which were being refitted at Trincomali. The arrival of the French fleet frightened many merchants and inhabitants of Fort St. David and Cuddalore[17] (including Orkandi Rangappa Nayakan, the *dubash* of Mr. Hinde, the Deputy Governor of Fort St. David) to send their valuables to Porto Novo to which now removed the

other; there should be no alternative.' When Dupleix became the Governor of Pondicherry, La Bourdonnais was there and even so early explained his project to capture Madras when war should be declared. Dupleix approved of the plan and sent Paradis, an able Swiss soldier and engineer, on a secret visit to Madras. The latter drew up a memorandum and prepared a plan of attack. At that time La Bourdonnais returned to Mauritius after re-establishing the French factory at Mahē. He however studied the memorandum and plan of Paradis and wrote to Dupleix that the capture of Madras was feasible. Dupleix himself had Madras once more thoroughly explored and procured a plan of the place from his wife's daughter who had married an Englishman (G. W. Forrest—*The Siege of Madras in* 1746 *and the Action of La Bourdonnais* (1908)).

16 Diarist's entry for July 14. 'Almost at once (*i.e.*, after La Bourdonnais landed at Pondicherry) the ancient dislike which he and Dupleix had cherished for each other flamed up into activity ...... within the week Dupleix too was abusing La Bourdonnais to all who would listen to him'—Dodwell, *Dupleix and Clive*, p. 11.

17 To obviate the risk of a possible appearance of the English fleet on his rear and draw it within fighting distance, La Bourdonnais proposed to attack Fort St. David; and if an English fleet should bear up to assist the Fort he would then attack it, to which Dupleix said that the place was not worth the attack (Malleson, *The French in India*, pp. 134–5).

Dutch traders and artisans of that place who had betaken themselves to Cuddalore during the late Maratha inroad. The people of Madras also were greatly concerned; many of the wealthy merchants were removing their families and goods to Arcot; and the Governor, Mr. Morse, was 'much broken in spirit'; but 'vigorous arrangements are being made for the defence of the fort and the ships are being brought nearer the shore and are being supplied with arms and ammunition.'[18] The Diarist also heard that the properties of the late Commodore Barnett were being transferred from Fort St. David to Madras and that three ships laden with treasure had sailed from Madras for Bengal. He also noted the chief points of talk going on of the plans of war and other topics of political interest, such as 'the friendly relation subsisting between the authorities at Negapatam and the English, the construction of ships by the latter at Trincomali, a cruise of the squadron commanded by M. de la Bourdonnais to seek the English; the prospect of the destruction of all the English ships

18 *Diary*, vol. ii, p. 127. In Madras Major Knipe's design for strengthening the west front of the Fort was taken up on hand by Mr. Joseph Smith, an engineer; but owing to the rains of the wet season of 1745 and the expensiveness of the designs, the work was not vigorously pushed on; and at the time of the French attack in September 1746, only the wet ditch with its escarp and counter-scarp walls on the west had been finished. The original design was eventually completed after the restoration of Madras to the English in 1749 and before Lally's siege of it in 1758–9. The garrison of Madras consisted only of about two hundred Europeans 'good and effective', besides the gun-room crew of about one hundred men and the militia and the peons of Pedda Naick. 'When full allowance, however, for these omissions, has been made, it is evident that Madras, abandoned by the British squadron and deprived of a military commander of energy and experience, was not in a condition to cope successfully with the force of some three thousand and four hundred men, which M. de la Bourdonnais was able to bring against it.' (Love, *Vestiges*, vol. ii, pp. 351–2). In it is given the muster-roll of the Madras garrison, September 1, 1746, taken from *The East Indian Chronologist*, an anonymous work published at Calcutta in 1802.

of war, the desirability of capturing Madras and of hoisting the French flag there—were it only for four days—in order to retrieve the name of the French.......'[19]

The plans of both Dupleix and La Bourdonnais were two-fold, including the destruction of Peyton's squadron and the capture of Madras—the latter being 'an old ambition of La Bourdonnais.' The defeat of Peyton was the necessary preliminary to be achieved; a large quantity of munitions of war including several 18 pounders were shipped;[20] and La Bourdonnais embarked on August 3, declaring before his officers that he would either destroy Peyton's squadron and bring him prisoner or meet a like fate. On hearing this, Governor Morse wrote to Nawab Anvāru'd-dīn and to his Diwan saying that he suspected that the French had designs on Madras, that war at sea alone had been proclaimed between the English and the French, that the latter should not attack the former on land and that as towns possessed by either party lay in the territories of the Nawab, neither the English nor the French could attack these without his permission. Also the Nawab despatched two messengers to Madras and two others to Pondicherry with instructions to send him news of all that might happen.[21] Dupleix, we learn, was prepared to grant passes of safety for native vessels provided they did not carry goods belonging to the English; but he returned an evasive answer to the Nawab's letter which reached him on August 13 and required him not to endanger the security of Madras.[22] Meanwhile La Bourdonnais anchored off Negapatam, where after making apologies for having purchased from the English the French ships that they had captured, the Dutch Governor and Councillors entertained him with great hospitality (August 17). Even when the guest was still at table news was brought to him that five

19 *Diary*, vol. ii, p. 158.

20 Dupleix to La Bourdonnais, July 20, 1746, quoted by Malleson, p. 134 (foot-note).

21 Letter of Subbayyan, the French agent at Arcot, which reached Pondicherry on August 18.

22 The reply was to this effect—'No harm to the inhabitants of Madras is contemplated by the ships of war. On the contrary they have come there to punish the enemies of its people' (*Diary*, vol. ii, p. 201.)

English men-of-war were in sight, on which the French Admiral immediately returned to his ship. The French waited for the morning to engage the enemy; but no English ships could then be seen or for some time. The French squadron cruised about till it fell in with the enemy.[23] The two squadrons were three days in sight of each other, after which the English ships, availing themselves of the advantage of sailing better than the French, disappeared; and La Bourdonnais returned to Pondicherry with his squadron (August 23) thinking that the English fleet would remain on the coast 'at least with the hope of deterring him from attempting any operations against the English settlements.'[24] La Bourdonnais spoke with Dupleix regarding his plans for an attack on Madras; he was ill with fever and diarrhœa and had to be bled in the arm. Rumours of the differences that had arisen between the two got abroad; and our Diarist[25] heard from M. Desmarets on the 29th that La Bourdonnais demurred to fighting the English on land and required the written order of

23 Even as Peyton approached he saw the French ships now showing a new tier of guns. He refused action and not falling in with any reinforcements, sailed for Pulicat (August 22). 'He there received news that Madras was threatened by the French, but fortified himself for further flight by another council of war and sailed for Bengal. He had not even taken the trouble to write to Madras when he touched at Pulicat' (*Dupleix and Clive*, p. 12).

24 La Bourdonnais thought Peyton more courageous than he was in fact. He supposed that Peyton had withdrawn 'only in order to fall upon the French when, with half their people ashore, they were besieging Madras. Indeed his presence on the coast would have made the siege of Madras an exceedingly rash undertaking....... He longed to attack Madras, but shrank from accepting the responsibility of possible failure.' (Dodwell, p. 12.) News of Peyton's arrival off Pulicat reached Madras after two days; and the Madras Council sent a sloop to him with an urgent appeal for assistance. 'But Peyton escaped this appeal by the haste of his departure.'

25 The prospects of his becoming the *Courtier* (Chief Dubash) in succession to the late Pedro Kanakaraya Mudali and in preference to the latter's brother, Lazar Tanappa Mudali, who was backed up by the priests and to Annapurnaiyan who wanted to work through Madame Dupleix by means of bribes, had by this time become almost certain; but he did not openly profess his sense of elation at this.

the Pondicherry Council to that effect; that high words ensued between the two and that the Councillors were summoned, but declined all responsibility stating that the Governor and La Bourdonnais had not consulted them when they first planned the undertaking.

The Council held on 26th discussed the plans for laying siege to Madras; the next day a deputation waited on La Bourdonnais,[26] and the Council sat for three hours after its return. The Diarist at this stage could only say that there would be certainly war, but could not be sure of any details. But things were so uncertain between the two leaders that on August 28 the Diarist wrote, 'We know that the enterprise against Madras, has for the time being, been abandoned. The object of this expedition is to scour the sea between Madras and Negapatam until the setting in of the monsoon and attack any English ships that may be sighted. The fleet will then, it appears, sail for Mascareigne. I have written what rumour says.'[27]

Thus was the situation uncertain in Pondicherry, on the eve of the starting of La Bourdonnais' expedition, with both Dupleix and La Bourdonnais not willing to shoulder the entire responsibility.

It was on August 25, which was the French King's Birth-day, that the metrical ode in Telugu composed in the Diarist's honour by Kasturi Rangayya (*Anandarangarāṭchandamu* referred to already) a noted scholar of Trichinopoly, was set to music by Trichinopoly Mangapati Aiyan. 'Dancing-women were taught to sing it, and they gave a performance of it this night at the garden-house of Muthaiya Pillai in Sēḍai Street before a public assembly, consisting of my friends and others.' (Diarist's entry for August 25, 1746), vol. ii, p. 238.

26 Dupleix wanted to have d'Auteuil, his own man, lead the land-forces against Madras; but La Bourdonnais understood his motive well enough and 'pleaded illness as an excuse for not setting out on the expedition on which the Governor has so strongly set his heart, but would not consent to any other person being appointed in his stead.' At the same time the Governor sent a letter to Nawab Anvaru'd-dīn asking politely for help with 3,000 men in attacking Madras, thus attempting to pre-justify his own action. (See letter of La Bourdonnais to Dupleix, August 26, in his *Memoires*, No. 27.)

27 *Diary*, vol. ii, p. 252. It was even said that the project of Dupleix to seize Madras and become its Governor would end in failure.

CHAPTER IV

THE CAPTURE OF MADRAS AND ITS SEQUEL

THE PRELIMINARY DEMONSTRATION BEFORE MADRAS

LA BOURDONNAIS, to test the situation at Madras, sent eight ships of war to make a demonstration before its Fort. The ships arrived in the Madras roads on August 29, and according to a letter written by the Pastor of the Church of St. Paul at Mylapore,[1] fired a broadside on a country sloop and an English ship lying in the roadstead. After two hours of firing,[2] the squadron moved off to Mylapore, then put to sea and disappeared. The English ships were damaged and about twenty-five of their crew killed in the action. On the whole, the cruise was deemed unsuccessful; and according to a letter from Madras conveying the message of Madame Barneval, the third daughter of Madame Dupleix, all people talked disparagingly of the French, that

1 This was interpreted to Dupleix—entry of the Diarist for September 1, 1746 (vol. ii, p. 260).

2 Malleson states that the squadron captured the two ships in the roads (*History of the French in India*, p. 140). But the *Diary* of Ranga Pillai says that the squadron, on its return from Madras, captured an English ship and a sloop returning from Bencoolen (vol. ii, p. 264.)

La Bourdonnais' letter to the French Controller-General, dated September 2, 1746, also says that the squadron captured, only on its way back, a couple of small prizes, though the object was to capture the ships which were anchored off Madras. The capture of the prizes took place off Covelong, twenty miles south of Madras, and not in the Madras roads. (Appendix by J. F. Price, vol. ii, p. 408.) This is further supported by an extract from the Tellicherry Factory Diary (Malabar Records, No. 6) dated September 23, 1746, recording the information of a *pattamar* (small vessel) that on August 19, there were eight French ships at Madras under the command of a cousin of La Bourdonnais, which after some fire, left the place and on their way took the two English ships coming from Bencoolen. The evidence is in other respects somewhat exaggerated (*Diary*, vol. ii, pp. 408–10)—See also Orme's *History*, vol. i, p. 66—where it is said the French squadron appeared and cannonaded the town, but without doing any damage and did not venture to attack the English ship with armed boats.

hereafter they could not even alarm the English and that, if they had continued in the Madras roads, their whole fleet would have been captured.[3]

Dupleix, in the course of an intimate talk with the Diarist, albeit the latter suited his answers to the Governor's views, detailed the difficulties that he was experiencing from La Bourdonnais in attempting to make him act in concert with himself. He blamed the Ministers at Paris as being responsible for having made La Bourdonnais truculent, particularly the Controller-General, M. Orry, and M. de Fulvy to whose venality no doubt he owed both the condonement of his acts of injustice in Mascareigne and his appointment as Admiral. Further, Dupleix urged the Diarist to disabuse the minds of the Muhammadan nobles outside Pondicherry of any impression that the delay in the expedition to Madras was due to himself. 'When La Bourdonnais was told that an order of the Council would be given to him, he pleaded illness and said he would set out on the expedition as soon as he felt better. I therefore suggested to him, that during his absence on account of ill-health, he might depute some other suitable officer

3 M. Barneval was a merchant under the English East India Company living in Fort St. George. Madame Barneval was ashamed that the French could not stand their ground and she wanted this poor impression of the French to be conveyed to Governor Dupleix immediately. (*Diary*, vol. ii, pp. 271–2). The letter added that after the appearance of the French fleet, some English merchants and ladies fled to Pulicat; but the Dutch would not allow them to remain there. There was much apprehension among the Indian population who ran away from the town in various directions. But all had a poor impression of the French; and their talk was unbearable to the priests of Mylapore who wanted the news to be conveyed in their name to Dupleix. The latter was greatly annoyed at this impression and exclaimed to the Diarist, 'Although Madras was at one time in such a great state of alarm, it was M. de La Bourdonnais who relieved it from this by sending his squadron to attack it.' His misunderstandings with La Bourdonnais were so intense that he even asked Ranga Pillai not to order manufacture of any goods indented for by him (entry for September 7, 1746).

The *Journal of John Hallyburton* (*vide infra*) says that the Dutch Chief, Woutuen de Jongh, of Pulicat, refused protection to the English women and children who had consequently to return to Madras.

for the command. His answer to this was that it was a business the execution of which rendered his presence indispensable. Nevertheless I have not abandoned the undertaking. I will—come what may—see to the capture of Madras.'[4]

The Diarist further heard from some Muhammadans who had recently arrived from Madras that its Governor, Mr. Morse, had sent his wife with all his treasure to Pulicat, that the citizens were greatly paralyzed with fear and that, if at that juncture five hundred European soldiers had landed from the French ships, Fort St. George would have fallen easily; but the English had, since the retreat of the French ships, recovered their courage and grown wary and hence they could not now be easily dispossessed of the place.

The next day Dupleix received a letter from Nawab Anvar-ud-dīn that he had previously prohibited English operations against Pondicherry and he was surprised to learn of the French designs and attack on Madras[5] and they should abstain from

4 Dupleix's reply to the Diarist on September 4 on the subject of the projected expedition—He was particularly anxious that the people should know how he was enthusiastic over the affair and how basely La Bourdonnais threw impediments in the way of his plans. The Diarist naively added in his entry, 'He (Dupleix) dwelt upon this subject for about four Indian hours. I all along continued to express views in consonance with his inclinations praising him unreservedly wherever I could.'—This is an instance of the Diarist frankly confessing his practice of humouring the great.

5. In this letter of the Nawab, the word used for Madras is Pādshāh-Bandar (*i.e.* The Emperor's Landing-Place). From the context there is no doubt that the name refers to Madras. The same name is applied to Madras in two other letters of the Nawab. 'How this name came to be applied to Madras has not been discovered'—foot-note on p. 284 of the *Diary*, vol. ii.

The next letter of the Nawab was received by Dupleix on September 8. It was very curt and declared that the Nawab would advance on Pondicherry in case of disobedience of his orders (*vide infra*). Orme observes wrongly that the Nawab took no action on Governor Morse's representation; because it was not accompanied by a present. This view is held by many writers. The Diarist corrects this view.

further hostile measures. To this a reply was sent that no harm would be done to the people, but that the French war-ships would be guided solely by the instructions given to them by their King. The Nawab followed this up with another letter in which he threatened to advance against Pondicherry and accusing the French of transgressing all bounds. Dupleix's reply to this second letter was couched in the same terms as his first one and declared that the captains of the French ships would not listen to the orders of any but their own King. A curious explanation was made the following day to the Nawab, in the form of a copy of a letter which was addressed to Nizām-ul-mulk which pretended to justify in detail the grounds[6] for the contemplated attack on Madras.

On the morning of September 11, La Bourdonnais embarked for the expedition against Madras; and the Diarist was asked to send his younger brother, Tiruvengadam Pillai, as *dubash* at Madras during the time that the operations should be in progress. The administrative arrangements contemplated were that, as soon as Madras should be captured, M. d' Esprēmēnil was to assume the office of Governor, and M. Paradis that of Deputy-Governor and all the Europeans and the rest should be under their control.[7]

6 This letter, in the words of the Diarist, said that the French King was angry with the English at Madras for having unjustly seized French ships and also another bound for Manilla, which bore the name and flag of the Emperor of Delhi. It was thus that the French King resolved to seize the city of Madras, to avenge the insult offered to his faithful friend, the Emperor of Delhi. The French at Pondicherry were only carrying out their King's mandate and the Nizam was requested to help them in whatever way he could. Copies of this letter were sent to Imām Sāhib and other Muhammadan nobles, including the amaldars of Mylapore and Poonamalle who were likewise requested to help, being warned at the same time that they would be punished in case of failure to comply. These latter communications were handed over to M. de Esprēmēnil for delivery to the addressees in person.—(*Diary*, vol. ii. pp. 291–3 and Vinson's *Les Françes dans L'Inde*, pp. 73–74).

7 'La Bourdonnais dit que, sur sa demande, Dupleix lui donna un second commissaire, qui ētait son gendre d'Esprēmēnil, 'pour veiller, conjointement avec le premier, avec interēts de la Compagnie.' (Note on p. 75 of Vinson's *Les Frances dans L'Inde*, foot-note).

The expedition actually began to sail in the night of September 12.[8] The Diarist advised his brother who set out by land to keep M. de Esprēmēnil and others informed of everything done by La Bourdonnais and to keep a concise diary of the occurrences of every day, besides reporting all things of importance that took place daily.

La Bourdonnais' Attack

Dupleix's letter to the Amaldar of Mylapore delivered to him by M. de Esprēmēnil reiterated the assertion that the expedition had been undertaken because a ship bearing the flag of Muhammad Shāh, the Emperor of Delhi, had been captured by the English

8 The Fort St. George Consultations break off after the middle of June 1746; and we have to rely on the Fort St. David Consultations and letters to England and the papers relating to an inquiry held by the Company into the conduct of their President and Council, for the English version of the operations; there are also short reports from the other English settlements of Calcutta and Tellicherry—preserved in the *Coast and Bay Extracts*. vol. v, October 15, 1746 and *The Tellicherry Factory Diary*, vol. vi, September 28, 1746, respectively.

On the French side, besides the Pondicherry archives and the *Diary* of Ranga Pillai there is the *Memoir* of La Bourdonnais which is 'replete with details which are supported by copies of original documents'. Unofficial accounts are those of Orme which appear to be derived mainly from the *Journal of John Hallyburton*, now preserved among the Orme MSS. in the India Office. There is also the narrative of Humffries Cole, an eye-witness, which was published anonymously in the *London Magazine*, supplemented by two accounts of Thomas Salmon in his *Universal Traveller* (Love, *Vestiges*, vol. ii, p. 352).

Hallyburton was Secretary to Governor Morse, and was one of those who escaped to Fort St. David from Madras after its capture. He took part in its defence and in subsequent military operations. His *Journal of the Fleets and the taking of Madras from the 29th of April to the 9th of December, 1746*, has been made use of by Orme (vide *Catalogue of MSS. in the European Languages of the India Office*, vol. ii, part i; *The Orme Collection* by S. C. Hill, 1916, p. 19).

and that the Muhammadans and the French were friends and that the latter proposed capturing Madras on the account of the former and would not molest their town.[9]

On September 18, news was received from Mylapore that La Bourdonnais who reached Madras[10] on the 5th and landed his men a short distance to the north of the present Ice House, had since moved to the suburb of Chintadripet, that the English Governor Morse had become insane and his place was taken up by Mr. Stratton, Chief of Vizagapatam (this was obviously incorrect), that the guns on the Fort had been spiked or cast away and the English had thrown open the gates of the city (*i.e.* Old Black Town). This was supplemented by the news that seven ships which left France, had touched at Mahe and were on their way to Pondicherry. This piece of news greatly elated the Governor and raised in him hopes of prosecuting the expedition of the French very successfully.

On the night of September 18, a letter from La Bourdonnais was received at Pondicherry that his forces had occupied the

9 Both Dupleix and the Diarist commented on this that the Muhammadans were not conscious of their own might, that they managed to preserve their forts and territories because the whole of India was supposed to be under the sway of one sovereign and for no other reason. 'If as in Europe and other continents each province in India formed a distinct realm and had its own independent king, they could easily be conquered and would soon vanish.' Also, so poor was the strength of their fortresses and the nature of their defences and the courage of their soldiers that '1,000 (French) soldiers, two mortars and 100 bombs' or even less would be 'sufficient to reduce Arcot, Cuddapah, Sīrppai (Sīrappa) and all the other Muhammadan strongholds and countries on this side of the Krishna.'

10 The French landed 600 men at Trivembore, a few miles south of San Thomé, on the morning of the 3rd (old style). They marched along the shore and the fleet kept pace with them. At noon the rest of the troops disembarked on the east side of the Triplicane Temple, opposite the Mile-End House, Chepauk, entrenched themselves for the protection of their ammunition and stores and threw up a battery for five mortars on the beach at the south-end of the Cooum river-bar. The English shots fell short of this camp. The French expeditionary force consisted of 1,100 Europeans, 400 *coffres* and 400 Indian troops—and

Governor's garden-house[11] while the English could only answer them with ineffective shots from the Fort. At last news was received that the Fort surrendered on the 21st (Wednesday, 9th Purattāśi). As soon as the news was received, a public announcement was made of the victory and a thanksgiving service was held amidst great rejoicings (entry for September 22.)

The Sequel of the Capture

On the 24th Dupleix nominated M. Dulaurens to manage all matters pertaining to finance at Madras; on the next day, the Governor heard from M. de Esprēmēnil that the Diarist's younger brother at Madras never communicated any intelligence to him, but was always intimate with La Bourdonnais and asked the

there were besides 1,800 European mariners on board. Slightly smaller numbers are given by Col. Love. On the 5th the force moved to Chintadripetta; and on the 6th they occupied the Governor's garden-house, situated to the north-west of the Fort. The guns on the walls and bastions of Black Town which lay immediately to the north of the White Town (or the Fort) were spiked and the guards withdrawn by the English who thought their numbers too weak to attempt at anything more than the defence of the Fort. Only one officer, Lieut. P. Eckman, was against this measure.

11 This was situated to the south-west of the Island Ground in the grounds of the present General Hospital (*vide* Talboys Wheeler's *Map of Madras in 1733*); and also the maps on p. 84 of *Vinson*, and on p. 356 of *Love*, vol. ii. (Plan de Madras et du Fort St. George *pris par les Francois le September 21, 1746*) where a battery of ten mortars was erected under cover of the building. This battery opened on the next day (September 7, old style), shell-fire on the Fort. At dusk of the same day three French ships took their post opposite the Fort and cannonaded it from the sea. The firing continued the next day; and the French shells were dropped with precision on the citadel (Fort Square) within the Fort. And on the evening of this day a letter written by Madame Barneval on behalf of Governor Morse, asking for terms, was brought to the French camp. (See *Plan de Madras et du Fort St. George* in 1746, after Paradis, given in *Love*, vol. ii, and the narratives of Orme, vol. i, pp. 67–68; of Cole (quoted by Salmon in his *Universal Traveller*, vol. i) and of the Secretary of La Bourdonnais quoted also by Salmon (quoted in *Love*). La Bourdonnais insisted that his possession of the place must be the basis of negotiations; he feared that the English

Diarist to recall him. Subsequently the Governor gave instructions that the latter was to continue at Madras, but report all that took place between him and La Bourdonnais to M. de Esprēmēnil promptly. Other officials were of course sent to Madras to assist in its management.

A letter written by Mahfuz Khān, the son of the Nawab, and addressed to La Bourdonnais at Madras was forwarded to Dupleix who received it on September 26. It enjoined on the French to evacuate Madras and depart in their ships under threat of an invasion. Dupleix's reply to it was so worded that it was

squadron under Peyton might at any time reappear and would not allow any delay in the negotiations. He had received information which turned out to be incorrect that some ships, probably English, were sighted off Pondicherry. In the afternoon of the 9th (old style) after bombardment was resumed, Francisco Pereira came with a further message from the Governor asking for a renewal of the armistice till the next morning. This request was declined; La Bourdonnais bombarded the Fort furiously in the night; and on the morning of the 10th conditions of the capitulation were drafted and signed by the Governor with the approval of his Council, in which a proviso was inserted for the English right to ransom the place (the terms being given by the Secretary to La Bourdonnais) that was further assured on the 28th (old style, being October 9, new style) September, by an act authentically given by La Bourdonnais declaring that the Governor and Council should cease to be prisoners of war. Malleson says that La Bourdonnais had undoubtedly some discussion regarding a ransom, but the question was referred for further deliberation; and that it was a doubtful one is shown by the words employed in the 4th article (of the capitulation) in which it is stated that 'if the town is restored by ransom....' La Bourdonnais' own *Memoirs* should be taken with the greatest caution, as they were written with the view of exculpating himself from the specific charges, including the question of ransom, brought against him; and his official correspondence with Dupleix was a far surer guide. And the question as to whether any absolute engagement for the ransom was entered into at the time of the surrender, formed one of the specific charges against La Bourdonnais. In the letters that he wrote to Dupleix both on the night of the day of the surrender (*i.e.* the 21st) and two days later, he did not mention his promises to ransom the place and declared that the surrender was at his discretion (*vide* his *History of the French in India*, 1893, foot-note on pp. 149–150).

to appear as though La Bourdonnais himself wrote it and took shelter under the usual plea that the French had first to obey the orders of their King.[12] Even as early as this Dupleix was feeling the possibility of the restoration of the exiled Chandā Sāhib and instructed his *dubash*, the Diarist, to sound the agent of the widow in the matter of his recall which, when realised, was to work such a wonderful, though brief, change in French fortunes.

The Governor's differences with La Bourdonnais became marked with the passing of the days. According to a letter which reached him on September 29, the latter disregarded his orders and left his letters unanswered, browbeat D'Esprēmēnil and others, took away a quantity of merchandise, specie and ordnance on board his ships from both the Fort and the town, ransomed

In his first letter, written soon after the surrender of the place, La Bourdonnais stated that he had just entered Madras. In his second letter written on the night of the same day, he wrote, 'I have them (the English) at my discretion and the capitulation which they signed has been left with me without their having dreamt of demanding a duplicate.' In the report that he made on the 23rd, he said: 'The conditions on which it (Fort St. George) surrendered, place it, so to say, at my discretion. There is, nevertheless, a sort of capitulation signed by the Governor, of which I subjoin a copy; but it does no more, as you will see, than authorise me to dispose of the place.' Malleson is fully convinced that the talk between La Bourdonnais and the English deputies regarding the ransom was inconclusive and that it was finally resolved by them to leave this question to future adjustment. When he was pressed by the deputies for a more explicit explanation as to the ransom being regulated in a definite manner, La Bourdonnais replied:—"Gentlemen, I do not sell honour...... In regard to the ransom of the town and in everything that is interesting, you shall be satisfied with me; (and taking the hat of one of the deputies, he said) here is nearly the manner of how we will regulate matters: this hat is worth six rupees; you shall give me three for it; and so of the rest."

12 The tone of the reply was rather defiant and it ended with the ambiguous words: 'You have intimated to us that you will make a progress through the country. When you do so you will come to know us and our affairs better.' In the same spirit Dupleix received the widow of Dōst Alī on her arrival at Pondicherry with inferior honours and remarked, 'Those times have gone.' (*Diary*, vol. ii, pp. 334 and 339).

the Fort to the English for eleven lakhs of pagodas[13] and also resolved to sail for Mascareigne, while de Esprēmēnil and other Pondicherry officials, becoming greatly irritated with his conduct, had betaken themselves to Mylapore. La Bourdonnais' letter which arrived almost simultaneously with the previous one, explained how he had decided to seize all the English Company's goods, a portion of the ammunition and arms, leave the rest to them and restore the fort to them on their undertaking to pay eleven lakhs of pagodas in two years and engaging never more to fight against the French. The next morning after this letter was received, all the European residents of Pondicherry except the Governor met at the house of the Deputy Governor, re-capitulated the services of Dupleix, how he retrieved the situation of the French, established French power at Karikal, and aided La Bourdonnais in many ways and how the latter was indifferent to the Madras expedition and how Dupleix undertook the whole responsibility for the expedition and how the victory was solely

13 Above this stipulated amount, according to one version La Bourdonnais was promised by bond as a separate bribe, one lakh of pagodas. The Directors of the English Company of the time were convinced of the truth of this on the testimony of the members of the Madras Council. The same charge was brought against La Bourdonnais by two Frenchmen, de Esprēmēnil and Kerjean, nephew and son-in-law to Dupleix, respectively. La Bourdonnais repudiated these charges on several grounds. On his return to France La Bourdonnais was thrown into the Bastille on charge of collusion with the English, but was acquitted and set free after a protracted trial lasting for three years from 1748 to 1751. 'His acquittal by his own government which was inspired by the deepest resentment against him, is a strong fact in his favour...... (he) acted with the gravest indiscretion and that sufficiently accounts for his strange and, in a political sense, sufficiently culpable conduct.' [*Vide* Birdwood's *Report on the Old Records of the India Office* (2nd reprint) footnote on pp. 242–9]. The documents in Law Case, No. 31, dated March 3, 1752, preserved in the India Office, and relied on by Malleson in the first edition of his work, were examined by Birdwood in the above note which concluded with the statement that all it could furnish was an extract implying that any money ever paid to La Bourdonnais was by way of *dasturi* or *douceur*. Malleson refutes this conclusion in very vigorous language and says, 'A high official,

due to his foresight. Lastly, the meeting questioned any right of La Bourdonnais to ransom Madras on his own authority and the propriety of his seizing English property and claiming the right to answer for his action directly to the French Company. On the lines suggested by the representation of this meeting[14] Dupleix wrote a letter to La Bourdonnais forbidding him to proceed further.

Thus the memorable month of September came to a close—La Bourdonnais writing to Dupleix on the 26th that he had almost agreed to a ransom and on the same day receiving a letter from the latter and the Pondicherry Council informing him of the constitution of a Council for Madras over which he was to preside. Already Dupleix had written on the 23rd that he had promised to deliver Madras to the Nawab immediately on its fall; and this probably made La Bourdonnais hurry on the conferences with

negotiating, against the orders of his superior, for the ransom of a town, to accept *dusturi*, that is, percentage on the amount of ransom, for disobeying his own superior officer at Pondicherry......is incredible,' p. 597. Malleson also quotes La Bourdonnais' own account in his *Memoirs* of the ransom engagement (p. 149). Actually the English Company accepted the evidence of Morse confirmed by other witnesses as proof of the actual payment by Mr. Morse of 88,000 pagodas of secret service money to La Bourdonnais, the funds being raised by bonds on the Company and before the treaty was signed. (*Love*, vol. ii, pp. 369–70). A letter from Madras, dated October 17, 1747, quoted by Forrest says:—"The French have come to a treaty with the Governor and Council for the ransom of the place at eleven lakhs of pagodas, payable in 3 years, half in India, half in Europe; they to carry off half the company's goods and half the cannon and warlike stores; but here's to be a garrison of 400 French till January." The value of the company's goods was about 4 lakhs of pagodas in silver, broad-cloth etc.; La Bourdonnais was believed to have screwed, in diamonds, jewels, etc., a purse of about 150,000 pagodas. Hostages were delivered for the whole amount.

14 It said, 'Now we hear that M. de La Bourdonnais is treating with the English for the return of Fort St. George to them. If he has restored it, we dare not show our faces in this Mussalman kingdom.' (*Diary*, vol. ii, p. 353.)

Morse relating to the definitive treaty of ransom[15] which was drawn up on September 26, but was not signed till the 21st of the next month.

On October 2, the Council of Pondicherry sent an order[16] investing de Esprēmēnil with supreme power at Madras and directing the imprisonment of La Bourdonnais if he should refuse to obey the former. There was much ingenious speculation as to the possible reaction of La Bourdonnais to this step. According to the Diarist's information, La Bourdonnais defended himself on the ground that he had been authorised in writing by the Pondicherry Council to exercise his discretion, not only in the siege, but also in the further administration of the Fort and the town; and again because the capture of Madras had been planned and effected by them all without any authority from the French King to wage war on land; and finally he had seized all the treasure he had found in the Fort and *had settled* with the English for the payment of eleven lakhs of pagodas as a condition of restoring the Fort to them. It was maintained, on the other side, that the Council of Pondicherry had cancelled the powers of La Bourdonnais and ordered him to take an oath of allegiance to M. d' Esprēmēnil on pain of arrest. The letter containing all this information reached Pondicherry in the afternoon of October 4; the Council sat that evening as well as the next morning and the whole of the next day (6th). On the 7th news reached Pondicherry that La Bourdonnais had, on the 4th, under the pretence that the English fleet had been seen off Pulicat, sent the troops of the Pondicherry contingent on board the vessels, and with the help of his trusted officers deprived de Esprēmēnil of his authority and placed Paradis and three deputies under arrest—threatening

15 *Vide* La Bourdonnais' letter to Dupleix quoted in his *Memoirs* and translated by Salmon. The treaty when first drawn up consisted of seventeen articles to which some articles were added later.

16 The declarations sent by Dupleix announced that the simple act of ransoming by La Bourdonnais was null and void and was to be regarded as never having been executed, and created a Provincial Council to administer justice, beside appointing de Esprēmēnil the Commandant and Director of the Town.

them that he would leave them prisoners to the English at Madras on October 15, the day on which he had covenanted to restore it. To this Dupleix could only reply by a letter that the Pondicherry contingent should not evacuate Madras and should not be compelled to embark on La Bourdonnais' ships (letter of Dupleix, dated October 6).[17] From his brother Thiruvengadam Pillai who had been sent as *dubash* to Madras along with the expedition, the Diarist heard that La Bourdonnais had proclaimed the rendition of the Fort to the English, telling the merchants that they were to obey the orders of the English Governor henceforth and was embarking merchandise with all possible speed on his own ships.[18] After this Dupleix could no longer indulge the hope of annulling the treaty of ransom; La Bourdonnais now rigorously kept out of Fort St. George all who were favourably disposed to the French Governor and garrisoned it with his own soldiers and *coffres* who had followed him from Mascareigne and Mauritius and would not reply to the points of Dupleix's letters. The Diarist considered that he had taken steps to secure the spoils of Madras for himself and that 'we shall not be far wrong if we put the value (of the plunder obtained by him) at a crore of pagodas, for we must remember that Madras, as a town, has not its equal in all India; is called throughout the land the golden city and as such has been compared to the city of Kubēra.' The Diarist was ignorant of the exact terms of the treaty of ransom; while he heard that M. d' Esprēmēnil and others were returning to Pondicherry and La Bourdonnais was preparing to set sail, he also heard on October 12 that La Bourdonnais had come to know that the English had buried two lakhs of pagodas under the flag-staff and consequently he was angry with Morse, destroyed the agreement he had made in their favour and put Morse and his

17 Quoted by Malleson, (foot-note on p. 168). The Diarist says that Dupleix's grief was boundless and that his reputation had declined much in the estimate of the outside public (vol. ii, p. 367). He also writes that the proposed visit of Dupleix to Madras would serve no useful purpose and that he would not go.

18 Gist of the letters of Thiruvengadam Pillai from October 4 to 8 and entered by the Diarist on the 9th.

companions in confinement, had re-landed the troops from Pondicherry and re-occupied the Fort. He also wrote to Dupleix stating that as the English had deceived him, he had now destroyed the treaty and remanded them all to custody and asked that D' Esprēmēnil and others who had departed might be sent back to resume possession of the Fort. In accordance with this the Pondicherry Council ordered that D' Esprēmēnil should return to Madras, wherever on his way the order might reach him; and the Governor felt relieved and was happy.[19] A section of the party of D' Esprēmēnil returned to Pondicherry, including Tiruvengadam Pillai, from whom Dupleix tried to know of the amount that La Bourdonnais should have made. The latter turned round on his first letter[20] and followed it up with another on the

19 Entry for October 12.

20 The vacillation of La Bourdonnais noted by the Diarist becomes clearer from a perusal of the progress of events from day to day. On October 2, as already stated, a commission arrived from Pondicherry appointed D' Esprēmēnil to supersede La Bourdonnais as Commandant at Madras. La Bourdonnais retorted that he recognised no authority as superior to his own. On the 4th he effected the embarkation of the Pondicherry troops on board ships, became the master of the situation and arrested the three Councillors. He then instructed Paradis, the captain of the Pondicherry contingent with him, to sound Dupleix as to whether he would agree to the treaty of ransom, provided the rendition of Madras was deferred from October to January or February. Dupleix wrote to La Bourdonnais on October 7, stating that he would entertain the project. On the 8th three ships of war from France with a number of soldiers on board arrived at the Pondicherry roadstead. They conveyed a message that the new French Minister, M. Machault, who had superseded M. Orry in December 1745 and had been even some months before this recognized as Minister-Designate, had ordered that the Commander of the Squadron should carry out without opposition all orders of the Superior Council. Dupleix sent the same day a copy of these instructions to La Bourdonnais with an intimation that they had been approved of by the new Minister. (La Bourdonnais later questioned the validity of the letter which was dated October 1745 and declared that a letter sent by M. Orry to him about that date confirmed his exercise of independent authority.) On the 10th La Bourdonnais replied to Dupleix that he would obey the orders of the Minister after he himself should receive them. A few

succeeding day in which he said that he had restored Madras to the English. The Pondicherry Council sent him a reprimand for this; but before the letter could reach him, he (La Bourdonnais) had forwarded another letter to the Governor which reached Pondicherry on October 13 and in which he said, 'I have neither restored Madras to the English, nor have I placed it under the control of the Council at Pondicherry. I do not know what I shall finally do. I am as yet undecided.' The Diarist was much perplexed at the conflicting news he heard of La Bourdonnais' change of views and remarks that his procedure was quite inconsistent with what he had seen and heard up to now of

hours after this he received letters which probably contained the orders. From that moment his attitude to Dupleix changed. When he received the reply of Dupleix to the overtures he had made through Paradis, he wrote back the conditions on which he would make over Madras to the Pondicherry authorities and depart; *viz.*, one of his own officers was to be appointed the governor of the place and it ought to be evacuated by January 1, 1747. (A precis of the five new articles is given in Love, *Vestiges*, vol. ii, p. 368, taken from Salmon). The Pondicherry Council replied to these letters on the 13th and 14th in which they insisted that D' Esprēmēnil should be the Commandant of Madras assisted by a Council of four of whom two might be nominated by La Bourdonnais; and the place could not be evacuated by January 1, nor till a complete division of the prize property should have taken place. But before the Council's letter of October 14 reached La Bourdonnais, a violent storm burst on the Madras coast on the night of the 13th and made havoc among the French ships in the roadstead. It was only on the 16th that the weather moderated; and on the 17th, La Bourdonnais became fully acquainted with the whole extent of his losses—four ships being lost, four others blown out to sea and dismasted while the loss in men alone amounted to more than 1,200 men (three ships were lost according to the Tellicherry Factory). Even before he knew the full extent of his losses, La Bourdonnais resolved to give up Madras to the Pondicherry Council, leaving them a copy of the capitulation. On the 21st he wrote to them that he had signed the capitulation with the English, to which the Pondicherry Council had raised objections on the 13th and 14th and sent the same to Pondicherry with a letter declaring that he would hold the French Council responsible, individually and collectively, for all contraventions of its conditions. After partially refitting his shattered squadron, La Bourdonnais, on October 23, ordered a grand parade of the

Europeans in India who used always to act in union.[21] Meanwhile only vague rumours of the storm on the Madras coast reached the Diarist who however remarked that the tempest was brought about by God to humble La Bourdonnais' pride and that 'He has deliberately caused this disaster to his ships, in view to an accusation being brought against him both here, and in France, and thus effecting his ruin.'[22]

La Bourdonnais withdraws from Madras

Another point of contention between La Bourdonnais and the Pondicherry Council was as to the authority whom the three ships from Europe which had arrived at Pondicherry on October 8 should obey. La Bourdonnais made an attempt to bring under his command the captains of these ships ordering them not to remain in the Pondicherry roadstead after October 25; but they only filed the letters of La Bourdonnais with the Pondicherry Government and signed an agreement that they would obey the orders of the Council of the place at which they were and that as they were now at Pondicherry they would act in accordance with the orders of the Council there. La Bourdonnais' climb-down was partially due to this circumstance.[23]

troops, made over the command to D' Esprĕmĕnil and at once set out to open sea and left Madras in a gathering storm—the place to which he 'would have given an arm never to have set foot in it.' The addition of the five new articles was grudgingly assented to by the English whose Governor Morse and four Councillors signed the treaty on October 21. Mr. Morse cleared out of Madras the wares of the merchants before La Bourdonnais' departure, as he was uncertain of the turn that affairs would take under Dupleix's direction (p. 28, vol. iii of the *Diary*).

21 Knowing as we do, there is generally concord and good understanding amongst Europeans, and that they never disagree, we cannot see what he (La Bourdonnais) means by saying at one time that he has restored Madras, and at another that he has not, and thereby disgracing others. The ways of Europeans who used always to act in union, have apparently now become like those of natives and Muhammadans.' (Entry for October 16, p. 395 of vol. ii of the *Diary*).

22 See also p. 39 of vol. iii in which he says, 'God caused a storm to arise, and through it, pronounced judgment on that evil man.'

23 Malleson, *History of the French in India* (1893), p. 178, foot-note.

The Pondicherry Council decided that the ships then lying in the Pondicherry roads, including the three from France, should proceed to Achin (in Sumatra) and return towards the close of the year. La Bourdonnais at the same time wrote to the captains of the ships directing them to proceed along the coast to join him. While they were hesitating as to their course of action, they fell in with the squadron of La Bourdonnais who assumed the command of the whole fleet and anchored in the Pondicherry roadstead on October 27 with a view to take round the ships to the Malabar Coast and then have the damaged ships refitted at Goa. He then proposed to return with a force sufficient to counterbalance the English fleet and wanted to borrow from Pondicherry all her available soldiers and heavy guns. Dupleix and the Council of Pondicherry definitely declined to adopt La Bourdonnais' plan, on the ground that Pondicherry might be attacked at any time by Peyton's squadron and the bulk of the fleet should proceed to Achin whence it might be recalled in any emergency. He refused to land at Pondicherry; and the Council refused to go on board his ship; and neither party would trust the other. La Bourdonnais then proposed to form two squadrons and not to interfere with the Council's command over the Company's ships. The uninjured ships soon reached Achin; and the Admiral, despairing of making for that place with his damaged vessels, bore up for Port Louis which he reached on December 10, after staying in the Pondicherry roads but for two days.

Of these events the Diarist records but little information. He heard on the 27th that the five ships which sailed from Pondicherry for Achin had joined La Bourdonnais on his return from Madras; and on the next day the Council deliberated on the action of the latter in ordering the ships to keep company with him. On the 28th he announced his arrival in the Pondicherry roads; on the following day the Superior Council considered the interference of La Bourdonnais in persuading the captains of these ships to obey his orders under the argument that his 'instructions from the King's Minister gave him the complete command of everything sailing under the Company's flag'. There is no other information from the Diarist forthcoming. La Bourdonnais' after-career was miserable. At Port Louis he was directed to return with his squadron to France; a storm shattered his ships off the Cape of Good Hope; he however reached Martinique; and impatient to reach France, he sailed in a Dutch ship which was captured by the English and was made a prisoner of war. Subsequently he was allowed to go on parole, was thrown into the Bastille and after three years of imprisonment, was declared innocent of the charges brought against him and released, only to die[24] (September 9, 1753).

Troubles with the Nawab

Even before La Bourdonnais' departure there arose troubles from the Nawab's side. Mahfuz Khān, the eldest son of Anvar-ud-dīn, sent a detachment of cavalry to occupy Mylapore and the surrounding country and to prevent all ingress into Madras, while permitting any egress from the town. Dupleix received news of this on October 26 and proposed that the Diarist should go to him on a mission of explanation. The latter argued that it would be best to appear indifferent towards Mahfuz Khān's

24 'By means, nevertheless of handkerchiefs steeped in rice-water, of coffee dregs and of a pen made of a piece of copper money, he had succeeded in writing his biography—and this, published at a time when the fate of Dupleix was trembling in the balance, contributed not a little to turn the popular feeling against that statesman.' It was only the English East India Company and the members of the Madras Council, that could prove the charge of bribery 'both preferred on every account to be silent'. (Malleson, p. 187.) According to Birdwood (*Report on the Old Records of the India Office*, 2nd reprint, p. 245 [note]) the Law Case, No. 31, of March 3, 1752 (already referred to) rose from the objection of the Court of Directors of the East India Company to meet the bonds on which the sum required for the ransom of Madras was raised, on the ground that, in part at least, the bonds had been given not to save the Company's property, but the private property of the Governor and his Council. Morse and others, including the bond-creditors, examined by the Court, were really on their own defence; and the exculpating opinion of Birdwood says that 'the only impartial evidence incriminating La Bourdonnais to the extent of his having received a

blusterings and at present impolitic to treat with him.[25] Letters to this effect were written and despatched to the Nawab and to Mahfuz Khān; and copies of these were sent to Diwān Sampāti Rao and to Hussain Sāhib; and it was pointed out by Dupleix in the letter to the Nawab that the French King sent the warships on the latter's behalf against the English and both the Nawab and his son had urged the previous year a war against the English and the action of Mahfuz Khān was very surprising. It ended with a warning that the French would resist the Nawab's forces and 'bring to bear against him the courage which overthrew the English.'[26]

Petty raiding parties were sent out by the Muhammadans on Madras and plundered stray persons, with the connivance of the

complimentary gratification (*dusturi*) is that of Fowke.' Birdwood's opinion is that Morse and his Council agreed to make La Bourdonnais a private present for exempting Madras from pillage. They raised 88,000 pagodas for the purpose. 'This sum was mostly otherwise expended; and the difficulty having arisen with the Court of Directors about refunding this and other sums embraced in the ransom, it was plausibly pleaded that this particular sum was paid to La Bourdonnais to secure the execution of a treaty of ransom, which was never executed but disavowed by Dupleix.' We saw in Note (13) Malleson's opposite conclusion as to La Bourdonnais' guilt.

25 The Diarist said (p. 36 of vol. iii), 'If you (Dupleix) send representatives to treat with the Muhammadans, they will think that the slightest display of hostility on their part causes you alarm, and it will encourage them to bluster more and more, in the hope of extracting from you as much money as they can.'

26 It further said, 'If you, however, should act without due caution, we are determined to give you a proof of the power of our valour. We will then raze the fort and town of Madras to the ground, and will work out our own policy, as circumstances may dictate. You will behold all these things with your own eyes.' And the Nawab soon realized that the threat was indeed a real one. Mahfuz Khān was told that he had started only to plunder a wrecked ship (Madras) and would find only shattered planks. The Amaldar of Mylapore was also warned not to annoy the French when passing in and out of Madras. (Entry for October 26.)

Pedda Naick[27] who escaped the moment it was decided to seize and imprison him. But M. de Esprēmēnil strictly forbade all hostilities on the score that he had no orders from the Governor of Pondicherry permitting them, though several Frenchmen had been taken prisoners by the enemy. Rumours also reached the Diarist that the Muhammadans were bent on attacking even Pondicherry and were doing so only at the instigation of the English who were to be carefully watched and subjected to severe restraints.

Madame Dupleix suggested to her husband and got his consent that she should write to Mahfuz Khān asking him to change his mind; and on this—however much to be condoned by European judgment—the Diarist remarks: 'What shall I say as to the good sense of the husband who allowed his wife to write to Mahfuz Khān without a thought of the fact that the rules of Muhammadan etiquette regard with but scant favour a woman as a correspondent......?' The Diarist even tried to persuade her to delay sending the letter till the effect of the Governor's despatch should be known, but without avail.

Dupleix appears to have assured Nawab Anvar-ud-dīn, in reply to the latter's curt letter of September 8, that Madras, when taken, should be delivered over to him. He certainly informed La Bourdonnais that he had given such an assurance, though the latter seems to have doubted its sincerity. Immediately after the fall of Madras, Mahfuz Khān wrote to La Bourdonnais[28] demanding the fulfilment of the promise as well as the immediate cessation of hostilities. He began to carry out his threat as soon as La Bourdonnais left the coast; his forces assembled at San Thomé

27 The Pedda Naick of Madras was the hereditary police officer of the Black Town. He had to maintain a fixed number of peons to keep order in Black Town and in the adjoining *pettas;* he could arrest offenders and bring them before the Choultry Court; he held land in remuneration in the *petta* named after him. His duties were defined in successive *cowles* given him by Governors like Chambers, Langhorne and Thomas Pitt. He was also known as the *Paliagar* of Madras. The office was hereditary in the family of Kodungur Pedda Naick, for a long time.

28 Forwarded to Dupleix on September 26, and mentioned above.

and at the Mount; and on October 26, a reconnoitring party of horsemen arrived at the bridge which connected the Island Ground with the high road that ran to San Thomé and which had been broken down by the English on La Bourdonnais' landing. Two men who were sent to remonstrate, Mm. Gosse and De Kerjean were seized; D' Esprēmēnil went to Pondicherry by boat to consult Dupleix on the new situation; the walls of Black Town were rearmed, while the Nawab's troops occupied Triplicane and the Egmore Redoubt (near the present South Indian Railway Station) and erected a battery in the Company's garden as La Bourdonnais did; they then spread to the northward and completely encircled Black Town. A mixed force of Frenchmen, East Indian soldiers and Mahe sepoys, 500 in all, marched from Pondicherry for Madras on the last day of October and the Nawab's officers in the neighbourhood of Pondicherry made threatening demonstrations. Thus events were rapidly tending to the glorious victory of the French at the battle of the Adyar which broke up the delusion of Muhammadan strength.[29]

---

29 Orme: vol. i, p. 76.

CHAPTER V

FURTHER DOINGS OF THE FRENCH

MAHFUZ KHAN'S ADVANCE ON MADRAS AND DEFEAT

DUPLEIX received frequent communications regarding the distribution of Mahfuz Khān's forces. According to a letter which reached Pondicherry on November 4, 1746, Mahfuz Khān was encamped on the foreshore of the Nungambakkam Tank; and his army lay at the Governor's Garden[1] (the present General Hospital and Medical College grounds, to the north-west of the Fort). Some of the Muhammadans in order to facilitate their approach to the walls of the Fort and of the Black Town in a general assault, made an effort to cut away the bar of surf-driven sand at the mouth of the Cooum and the North River, in order to drain their waters, particularly of the latter stream which formed a wet ditch to the west side of the Fort by which it passed. At the same time they took possession of a spring (The Seven Wells in the north of Peddanaickenpetta) lying to the north of the Black Town which was then the only source of supply of good water to the inhabitants. M. Barthēlemy who was in charge of Madras in the absence M. d' Esprēmēnil, rearmed the walls of Black Town; but he had orders from Pondicherry to remain strictly on the defensive. However when his water-supply was cut off, he was forced to sally out on an attack.[2] On November 2, M. de La

1 M. Barthēlemy's *Letter* to Dupleix (p. 75 of vol. iii of the *Diary*).

2 Orme says that the operations of the Nawab's troops showed 'a degree of intelligence very uncommon in the military operations of the Moors.' On finding their communication with the spring interrupted, the French opened fire from the bastions of the Black and White Towns on the enemy troops who had spread round to the northward, thus completely investing Madras. The fire produced their quick retreat from the river-bar and other places which were exposed to it; but they still kept possession of the ground near the spring which was out of the reach of cannon-shot from the bastions. The Muhammadans were also joined by the Pedda Naick with his peons and a body of Poligars (Orme; *History of Indostan*, 4th ed., vol. i, p. 74).

Tour with a body of 400 men and two field-pieces marched out of the town, attacked the troops in the Governor's Garden and to the west of it and put them to a total rout.[3] "Before a shot could reach his camp, Mahfuz Khān had mounted his elephant and escaped. After pursuing the fugitives for upwards of five Indian hours, the French troops returned to the camp from which the Muhammadans had fled, and plundered the valuables found there." Dupleix was overjoyed at this news and imagined that after this repulse Mahfuz Khān would come to his senses, and sue for peace, giving out that he would be going back to Arcot on account of the Nawab's illness. He even expressed a desire to proceed to Madras in order to settle matters personally.

Mahfuz Khān collected all his troops into one camp about two miles to the west of the town, but hearing that Dupleix had despatched a fresh detachment from Pondicherry, he quitted his post the next day (November 3) and took possession of San Thomé, which the French reinforcement under M. Paradis expected to reach on the morning of the 6th and where it would be joined by a body of equal strength issuing out from Madras under the command of M. de La Tour, the hero of the previous encounter. Mahfuz Khān took up a position on the northern bank of the Adyar River and planted his artillery on the bank, thus preparing to prevent the crossing of Paradis. The detachment under de la Tour which was to issue from Madras failed to arrive in time to attack the enemy from the northern side. On the morning of

3 The work of the two French field-pieces was so much superior to the awkward management of the enemy's clumsy artillery which could fire only once in a quarter of an hour. The first discharge of the field-pieces threw the whole body of the enemy into confusion; 'however they kept their ground some time, as if waiting for an intermission of the fire; but finding that it continued with vivacity, they took to flight with great precipitation.' The French did not lose a man in the attack. (See Orme, vol. i, p. 75: Malleson's *History of the French in India* (1893), p. 193; and the letter of Barthēlemy to Dupleix quoted above). Ranga Pillai got a similar account of the battle from Guruvappa Chetty and caused a copy of it to be made in his correspondence-register for the purpose of reference (Entry in the *Diary* for November 4.)

November 4, Paradis's detachment forded the river in the face of the enemy's fire which 'as usual was very ill served'. As soon as they gained the northern bank, they fell on the enemy with their bayonets; the Nawab's line broke and retreated into the town of San Thomé, 'where they again made a show of resistance from behind some pallisades which they had planted in different parts of the south side.' After a brief resistance the whole army of Mahfuz Khān fled to the westward and soon afterwards retired to Arcot.[4]

Paradis had no guns during the action; but he was a most capable officer and resolved to face the enemy though the promised co-operation from the Madras garrison did not come. To retreat would have but too surely invited the cavalry charge of the enemy eager to avenge their defeat of two days previously. Thus he plunged without hesitation into the river, and led his infantry and his raw Indian troops, to attack the three arms of the enemy, ten times their superior in numbers. Paradis had made himself

4 The French fire was so hot and quick for the Muhammadans that their horse and foot fell back promiscuously on each other in the narrow streets of San Thomé. confusion of the throng was so great that they remained for some time exposed to the fire of the French, without being able to make resistance, or to retreat. Many were killed before the whole army could get out of the town and gain the plain to the westward.' Mahfuz Khān was one of the first to escape. Scarcely had the Muhammadans fled out of the town when the detachment of de La Tour arrived and assisted in the pillaging of the enemy's baggage. The French troops were reported to have murdered some of the Moors whom they found concealed in the houses they were plundering. Dupleix informed the Diarist that de La Tour joined Paradis at Triplicane only after San Thomé had been pillaged. Orme, Love and Malleson say otherwise. According to the Diarist, Dupleix was very angry that de La Tour should not have effected his junction with Paradis a little earlier, in which case the Muhammadans would have been completely crushed. 'Want of promptitude on his part spoiled the undertaking.' (Diarist's entry for November 7). Only two Mahē sepoys were wounded on the French side, while 200 to 300 men fell on the enemy's side.

very acceptable to Dupleix by his violent opposition to La Bourdonnais and was now raised to be the Governor of Madras after the victory. Of course Dupleix would not think of giving Madras into the Nawab's hands[5] and declared thus: 'We cannot give Madras up without orders from our King. The restoration of the fort does not rest with us. So long as we have life left we will not surrender it.' Mahfuz Khān asked that his younger brother, Muhammad Alī, should join him with reinforcements at Conjeevaram where he was staying. Muhammad Alī had but lately returned from a campaign against the Marathas under the order of the Nizam; and conflicting rumours were received from Arcot, some of them condemning the action of Mahfuz Khān and others threatening an attack on Madras to be undertaken by Nawab Anvar-ud-dīn himself, if the French should not hand the place over to him immediately.

This battle is regarded by Malleson as one of the most memorable of Indian battles, 'being the first of its kind, that it proved to the surprise of both parties, the absolute and overwhelming superiority of the disciplined European soldier to his Asiatic rival.' It reversed the positions of the Nawab and the French Governor and was 'the first decided step to the conquest of Hindustan by an European power.' (*History of the French in India*, pp. 195–196; and *Decisive Battles of India*, 4th ed., pp. 14–17). The prestige and the *morale* were transferred henceforth from the Muhammadans to the European settlers. In consequence of this transfer, every subsequent battle of the European with the Indian was half-won, before it had been fought. The contemporary Orme says that the French by this battle broke through the charm of the timorous opinion about the courage and bravery of the Muhammadan troops, 'by defeating a whole army with a single battalion'. The same opinion of the significance of the battle is expressed by Dupleix himself in his own *Memoires;* (see Mill's *History of British India* (1858), vol. iii, p. 52).

5 Dupleix wrote letters to the Nizam informing him of the doings of Mahfuz Khān in (supposed) defiance of his father's orders, the defeats sustained by him in the two battles of Madras, the taking of Madras by the French under the (pretended) authority of Anvar-ud-dīn, the capture of French vessels by the English and their tricks, and the seizure of a ship bearing the Emperor's flag. A like letter was written to Imām

THE FRENCH OCCUPATION OF MADRAS

Dupleix now resolved to annul openly the treaty of ransom which had been made by M. de La Bourdonnais of the exact terms of which our Diarist was ignorant. Paradis who had been notoriously hostile to La Bourdonnais and all his works was now in sole charge of Madras; and was, according to the Diarist, 'living on plunder and taking his ease.'[6] The English at Madras were paroled, according to the custom obtaining in Europe; and it was further intimated that they were preparing to leave the place. Not a vestige of the Muhammadans was to be seen in Mylapore from which even the Gujaratis, Tamils and Telugus had fled to the Chingleput Pāḷaiyam. Inducements were offered to the merchants of Madras to settle at Pondicherry; and the goods

Sāhib requesting him to explain the situation to the Nizam (substance of letters written from Pondicherry as entered by the Diarist for November 12).

To a conciliatory letter written by the rather friendly Hussain Sāhib from Arcot requesting the delivering of Madras into the hands of Mahfuz Khān, with a veiled threat that a refusal would bring about a united attack on Madras both by land and sea—on land by the combined forces of the Subhadars of Cuddapah and other places, Yāchama Nayak and other poligars; and on sea by the English with thirty ships—the Governor sent a reply of adamant refusal (pp. 104–5 of vol. iii of the *Diary*). The Diarist also sent, by direction of Dupleix, a circular letter to the Poligars of Karunguzhi, Kaverippak, Arni, Gingee and other places complaining of the unjustifiable conduct of Mahfuz Khān in having provoked the French to war and having imprisoned their envoys and put them in chains. The elder brother of Chandā Sāhib was glad at the turn of events, characterized the defeat of Mahfuz Khān as a judgment inflicted on him by Providence, and entreated Dupleix to take steps for the liberation of Chandā Sāhib and to inflict other measures of punishment on Anvar-ud-dīn Khān's sons. Dupleix had always clearly perceived the necessity of winning over the goodwill of the Poligar chiefs who formed the feudal backbone of the Carnatic administration.

6 Paradis plundered Mylapore both on the day of his victory and later in a methodical manner and completely gutted it. Many of the Madras merchants were ruined by the sack of Mylapore. 'That (the plunder) of Madras when it was seized by the French was nothing compared with it.' (Diarist's entry for November 25, p. 134 of vol. iii.)

of the English Company which had been seized were now transferred to Pondicherry. On November 11, Paradis formally proclaimed that the treaty was annulled[7] and that Madras was the property of the French East India Company for the King of France. Morse, the ex-Governor of Madras, Monson, the Deputy-Governor and several other Englishmen were sent over to Pondicherry. Paradis put his manifesto into execution with great rigour. Dupleix, under pretence of doing honour to Morse caused him to enter the town in an ostentatious procession which exposed him to the view of the crowd; and Ranga Pillai well remarks: 'It may be imagined, then, how much Mr. Morse must have felt his position, when the eyes of all the people in the town were thus concentrated on him. To picture the grief which he must have experienced and the measure of it is not in my power.'[8] The fortunes of many of the English inhabitants of Madras were ruined; and several of its military officers refused to give their parole alleging that the breach of the treaty of ransom released them from their obligation; they escaped from the settlement by night and reached Fort St. David which had recovered from its alarm and to which merchants were now slowly returning. The young Clive was one of those who escaped

The Diarist puts down five lakhs of pagodas as a modest estimate of the value of the spoil taken by the French at Mylapore. The plunder of Mylapore was a sore grievance in the eyes of the Nawab and his officials and was obviously a target of attack on the French for long.

7 The proclamation allowed those who took an oath of fidelity to the French King, the liberty of continuing in Madras and carrying on their trade as formerly. Those who refused to take the oath, but were inclined to go to Pondicherry, were permitted to do so; others could have passports to go where they pleased upon their parole, within two days; they should not however reside at St. Thomas' Mount or Kattiwak by Ennore. (Letter of Mr. Godwin, Senior Merchant of Madras, to Mr. Hinde at Fort St. David, detailing the conditions forced on the English at Madras—*Factory Records*, Fort St. David, vol. v, November 5, 1746—quoted by H. D. Love—vol. ii, pp. 375–76).

8 Entry for November 24 (p. 131 of vol. iii of the *Diary*), Malleson's view is different, but not authoritative.

from Madras to Fort St. David.[9] It was only in August 1747 that Governor Morse who had been exchanged for M. Le Ris, Governor of Mahē, was allowed to go to Fort St. David, where he remained till he was summoned to go to England to give an account of his conduct at Madras from the time that the French took possession of the place.

About the middle of November, 1746, Paradis took measures to safeguard the White Town, and blew up the Governor's Garden House lying to its west. He made a survey[10] of the Fort (White Town) which served as the basis of a map published in La Bourdonnais' *Memoire*. Later in the course of 1747, the Black Town was repopulated; its fortifications were completely levelled to the ground; and all its houses lying within one hundred and twenty yards of the north wall of the Fort were razed to the ground; while certain additions on the west were made to the fortifications of the White Town. Paradis was succeeded by D' Esprēmēnil as the Governor of Madras early in 1747; and the latter tried to induce many of the Tamil merchants who had abandoned the town to come back to it. The English Company when they heard of the loss of Madras raised Fort St. David to be their chief settlement on the coast and appointed John Hinde, its chief, to be the President and Governor, with Major Stringer Lawrence as the commandant of the garrison. The Company forbade the Council of Fort St. David to enter into any treaty with the country government or any other power regarding the

9 Sir John Malcolm says in his *Life of Clive* (vol. i, p. 46) that he escaped disguised as 'a native'. He took part in all the fighting at Fort St. David and got his commission there in 1747 and was present at the siege of Pondicherry in 1748 and became the Deputy-Governor of Fort St. David (1756).

10 In this plan, a copy of which has been prepared for Love's work, the environs of the town are incorporated, which are admittedly drawn from memory and therefore not correctly depicted. 'The map was afterwards reproduced with all its errors by many publishers both French and English.' (See *Love*, vol. ii, note 1, p. 377; and map opposite to p. 356.)

payment of any ransom[11] for the redelivery of Madras; and even in case the Nawab should restore the settlement to them, it should only be kept very bare, and all effects in it ought to be removed to Fort St. David,[12] which heneeforward came to be the target for Dupleix's attacks.

Dupleix and the Nawab—First French Attacks on Fort St. David

The *killēdārs* of the neighbourhood, so far as the ideas expressed by them in their replies to Dupleix's messages are reflected by the Diarist, were not annoyed at the defeat of Mahfuz Khān or at the sentiments expressed by the French Governor. The *killēdār* of Timiri condemned the action of the Muhammadans in having imprisoned the three French envoys and declared that their proper course was to be friendly with the French as far as possible. Muhammad Miyān of Chidambaram expressed similar sentiments; the chief of Karunguzhi wrote of his condemnation of the attitude of Mahfuz Khān. Dupleix wrote to Anvar-ud-dīn, on the one hand, saying that he was willing to restore Madras if the latter would grant territory including Villianallur and the surrounding taluk yielding an annual revenue of 20,000 pagodas; and on the other, he ordered that letters should be sent to Raghuji Bhonsle, the Peishwa and Raja Shahu complaining of the misgovernment of the country by Anvar-ud-dīn, bewailing the disappearance of the Navāyat family (of Sādatullah Khān) from rule and indirectly urging the release of Chandā Sāhib from

11 According to Forrest the final treaty of La Bourdonnais with Governor Morse and five of his Council, signed on October 21, stipulated that the French should evacuate the town before the end of the ensuing January, after which the English were to remain in possession of it without being attacked by them during the war; and a sum of £440,000 was to be paid by the Governor and Council, £240,000 in six equal monthly instalments before October 1746 and the balance by bills on the company in London.

12 Proceedings from England, dated July 24, 1747—quoted in full by Love. (*Public Despatches from England*, vol. 51, pp. 47–49); *Vide* pp. 53–54 of H. Dodwell's *Calendar of the Madras Despatches (1744–1755)*.

captivity,[13] so that trouble might be fomented for the old Nawab. He secretly planned the capture of Fort St. David and the surrounding villages from the English and in his own tortuous way attempted through his agent at Arcot to get the sanction of the Nawab for his intended expedition.[14]

Muhammad Alī, the younger son of Anvar-ud-dīn, who had written a letter of expostulation to Dupleix, expressing a desire therein to preserve the French alliance on condition of Dupleix showing his loyalty to the old Nawab, received nothing but a complimentary reply to the effect that the sole desire of the French was to retain his friendship. When it was known at Pondicherry that the old Nawab was suffering from acute diarrhœa and that written instructions had been despatched both to Mahfuz Khān and Muhammad Alī not to move from their stations, Dupleix became more open. Mahfuz Khān's advance from Sriperumbudur further east and Husain Sāhib's continued

13 In the first draft of the letter to be sent to the Marathas, it was written: 'If you send Chandā Sāhib, I (Dupleix) will be responsible for the money payable by him.' The Diarist suggested that his master should not commit himself to the obligation of ransom in that explicit way; and consequently the following words were substituted: 'As regards the amount for which Chandā Sāhib holds himself liable, I (Dupleix) will endeavour to collect it, as your agent.' 'I will use all my influence to ensure that this money reaches you. Without my help he would not be able to collect a cash.' It appears from Ranga Pillai's *Diary* that Nawab Safdar Alī, shortly before his assassination, had promised his mother to ransom Abid Sāhib, the son of Chandā Sāhib, by paying five lakhs of rupees, and that his agent, Kasi Das Bukkanji, had been actually given that amount. These letters of Dupleix were sent on December 5, along with a letter to Muhammad Alī Khān, the elder brother of Chandā Sāhib at Satara and another to the latter from the wife of Chandā Sāhib, imploring him that this was the proper time for him to advance against Arcot and imprison Anvar-ud-dīn with the help of French guns and sepoys and the support of Murtazā Alī Khān of Vellore. (See pp. 141–3 and pp. 149–50 of the *Diary*, vol. iii.)

14 The French *vakil* at Arcot reported that the Nawab could not be approached on this matter and the idea of capturing Fort St. David should be entirely abandoned. Both Sampāti Rao, the Diwan, and Husain Sāhib, a powerful chief at the Nawab's court, were against such

detention of the French prisoners at Arcot gave him further justification. He schemed boldly for the release of Chandā Sāhib from Maratha captivity and for the deposition of Anvar-ud-dīn and his two sons from rule. Paradis has been recalled from Madras in order to lead the projected attack on Fort St. David; he was harrassed on his way near Tirupporur by Mahfuz Khān's troops and had to fight his way through to Sadras where a reinforcement of 200 soldiers and 150 sepoys was ordered to join him from Pondicherry.[15]

Dupleix took measures to make it appear that he had a large number of soldiers and sepoys in Pondicherry. His men marched frequently to and fro in the neighbourhood which was consequently deserted by the people and left uncultivated. Muhammad Alī marched from Gingee towards Fort St. David, but made a detour of three leagues to the westward, skirting Tiruvati and Panruti, avoiding any conflict with the French troops. He was accompanied by 1,500 horse and a number of rocket and match-lock men and

a matter being even broached to the Nawab. Husain Sāhib even tried to persuade the wife of Chandā Sāhib who was living at Pondicherry to leave the place and take her abode in some strong fort in the Nawab's territory; and he would not release the three French prisoners, even though his master had definitely ordered their freedom.

15 The fight was much more serious than what Dupleix made it appear to the Diarist (pp. 163–65 of vol. iii). Orme says that Paradis set out from Madras with a detachment of 300 Europeans to guard the booty which he had collected and was now carrying off, one portion of the detachment marching before the baggage and the other behind it. Mahfuz Khān's cavalry, about 3,000 horse, continually harrassed the rear, retreating as soon as the French prepared to fire, while his infantry fired from the shelter of thickets. Paradis, apprehensive of being overtaken by the night in the plain and anxious to reach Sadras, marched away with the first portion of the detachment and the baggage, leaving the rear to continue the skirmish as best they could. Twelve French soldiers were taken prisoners by the enemy; and Paradis would not venture to proceed from Sadras till he should be reinforced by a large detachment from Pondicherry—probably for the greater security of his own booty. Mahfuz Khān was satisfied with the advantage he had gained and proceeded to join his brother. (vol. i, pp. 79 and 80).

elephants. He marched to Fort St. David and encamped in its suburbs,[16] afraid of pitching his camp elsewhere lest he should be set upon by the French in a sudden attack. Small reconnoitring parties were sent out from Pondicherry; an expedition followed

16 The early history of the Fort and its acquisition are best told in Garstin's *South Arcot Manual*, (1878) (pp. 18–60) and in Francis' *South Arcot Gazetteer* (1906), vol. i (pp. 33–50). The Fort was garrisoned by about 300 to 400 English soldiers and 200 East Indians and equipped with about one hundred guns. The Indian troops posted round the Fort numbered about one thousand; and all the houses situated on the north-western side of the Fort were being demolished and levelled. 'The Fort was small, but better fortified than any of its size in India and served as a citadel to the Company's territory.' The town of Cuddalore (the Old Town) was about a mile to the south of the Fort, separated by a river from it. It was 1,200 yards from north to south and 900 from east to west; three sides of it were defended by walls flanked with bastions. The sea-side was open, but was partially skirted by the river just before it reaches the sea. To the westward of the Fort and situated in the Company's territory were two or three populous villages.

Mr. Hinde, when he was Deputy-Governor of Fort St. David, had, prior to October 1746, made extensive improvements to the Fort; and in announcing the capture of Madras to the Directors, he was able to tell them that the Fort had been rendered 'infinitely more secure than it was'. It was however only after the French had threatened the place two or three times, that the western ditch was widened to a breadth of 100 feet, by the diversion of the river. 'Bomb-proof barracks were erected; a horn-work on the north and two lunettes on the east and west,' besides some other works were commenced in 1747; and all houses including the hospital and the whole village of Tēvanāmpatṇam (Tegnapatam) within 800 yards of the Fort were pulled down and cleared away, except the Dutch Factory to the north. (Garstin, *Manual of the South Arcot District*, pp. 63 and 64). The town of Cuddalore was, as already noted, surrounded on three sides by a wall and with a small redoubt at the north-east corner, which was further protected by a spit of sand which the surf has thrown upon the shore to the north-east and was divided by a backwater from the town. (Refer to map showing plan of the Fort and Town at the time of the French attack in May, 1758, given in Orme, vol. iii (1862). Also refer to the copy of the map reproduced in pp. 62–63 of Francis' *South Arcot District Gazetteer*.)

on December 19, which[17] fought an action with the Nawab's horse and had to retreat with some loss of supplies and with a few killed and wounded (December 20, 1746). M. de Bury who commanded in this action which took place near the English Company's Garden House at Manjakuppam (the present Collector's Bungalow) attributed the failure to the indiscipline of the officers each of whom 'persisted in having his own way', and to the lack of sufficient powder and ball and provisions. Dupleix himself told the Diarist that he was anxious to appoint Paradis to the

17 This is the so-called first French expedition against Fort St. David which consisted of 900 Europeans, 600 sepoys, 100 Africans and a few field-pieces and mortars. The English garrison was very small. The French appeared to be masters of the coast and had the inspiration of recent victory. But de Bury who superseded Paradis as the commander, in spite of the best efforts of Dupleix, did not take proper precautions to station guards and to picket his camp at the English Garden House; his officers were taking rest, and his men were dispersed with their arms grounded, when they were set upon by the united forces of Mahfuz Khān and Muhammad Alī, consisting of 6,000 horse and 3,000 foot, Muhammad Alī having on the previous day been joined by his brother. A panic seized the French and they hastened to recross the Peṇṇār against a constant, but irregular fire. The English garrison at Fort St. David sallied out as soon as they saw the French retreating, but did not come up in time to assist in preventing the French crossing of the river. The retreating French recovered from their panic as soon as they had crossed the river and were drawn up in such good order that the enemy forces considered it prudent not to attack them. They lost about 120 Europeans killed and 12 wounded besides a quantity of military stores and much of their baggage; but their field-pieces were saved. (Orme, vol. i, pp. 81–83; Malleson, pp. 201–4). A slightly different account of the battle from that given by Orme is given in the *Memoire* of La Bourdonnais, on the authority of a French officer of artillery who was present. 'This makes no mention of the piling of arms in the Garden described by Orme, but says that the fight began as soon as the French approached that spot. It also states that there was a battery of six guns in the Garden which the French tried unsuccessfully to capture.' It admits that the whole affair was totally mismanaged (see p. 55 of Francis—*South Arcot Gazetteer*). The date of the battle is the 5th Dhul-Hajj, 1159 A.H. according to the *Tuzak-i-Wālājāhi*.

chief command, but the other officers refused to serve under his orders and that the latter were but served as they deserved.[18]

Muhammad Alī asked Mahfuz Khān to join him which the latter did about December 29, when their united forces amounted to 4,000 or 5,000 infantry, ten to fifteen guns and 400 to 500 rockets, besides the cavalry. Dupleix now planned the capture of Cuddalore Town by sea and from thence the launching of an attack on Fort St. David, but feared that the English ships which were expected from Bengal and from Tellicherry might render his position critical. Even Paradis feared such a contingency and thought that Fort St. David could be captured only if the Muhammadans retired or if the English fleet should refrain from attacking. On the other side there was an equal amount of indecision. Mahfuz Khān was vacillating in his attitude; and Muhammad Alī was half inclined to make peace with the French; while the old Nawab was reported to have written to both of his sons to come to some terms with the French, break up the camp and return to Arcot, as the country was already ruined owing to failure of rain. It was rumoured that the Governor of Fort St. David had given presents to both Mahfuz Khān and Muhammad Alī and was holding out hopes of the arrival of English ships when he promised to give them larger presents; and that so reinforced he would attack Pondicherry.

While the English and the French were thus both marking time, the French army continued in its camp at Ariyānkuppam; and on the night of January 10, a party of 500 men advanced in

18 'It was then my hope that they might return discomfited. This is what has actually come to pass, and I am pleased, although I am somewhat cast down at the thought that our men have sustained a defeat...... If Paradis does not go, neither the Muhammadans nor the English will have the least fear. Your (Diarist's) prediction has proved correct.' (Gist of Dupleix's talk with the Diarist on the occasion of the receipt of the news of the defeat.) (p. 189 of vol. iii of the *Diary*.)

It was after this defeat that Dupleix was convinced that any open attempt on Fort St. David would be futile, so long as the Muhammadans were there and began a serious correspondence with the Nawab and his sons, persuading them to withdraw.

boats to attack Cuddalore, but had to retreat owing to the high surf of the sea and the consequent impossibility of entering the river which runs along the eastern side of the place and thus attacking its exposed quarter. Dupleix was thus disappointed a second time in his views against Cuddalore.[19] He now attempted to cause a diversion of the enemy troops by carrying the war into the country round Madras. He directed the commandant of Madras to send a detachment into the neighbouring country where there were no troops of the Nawab. The French found large quantities of grain in several places which they set fire to, having no means to carry them off. These measures did not have the intended effect of diverting Mahfuz Khān and Muhammad Alī from Fort St. David and they continued to stay on in their encampment.

Treaty with the Nawab

Dupleix heard early in January of the arrival of the three ships under M. Dordelin (which had arrived from Europe in the previous October and had proceeded to Achin when La Bourdonnais returned to Port Louis) and of another belonging to La Bourdonnais' squadron at the Madras roads; he was elated at the news, since it might persuade the Nawab to withdraw his troops immediately.[20] Surely enough news quickly followed that

19 This attempt was decided upon in Council on December 30; and it was preceded by a smaller expedition of 100 soldiers and Mahē sepoys who set out in three boats, but had to return owing to the powder and muskets being wetted. (December 31st; see Diarist's entry for January 1, 1747). A party of 400 *peons* (undisciplined Indian troops who had with them their own arms and continued their own manner of using them) advanced on the 10th in two divisions by two different routes to attack the Muhammadan camp; but they returned without making any attack as the two did not join in proper time at the appointed place.

20 'Rangappa, we have good news; our four ships with a Dutch sloop which they have captured, have reached Madras. When the English, Mahfuz Khān, Muhammad Alī Khān and their troops hear of this, how will they like it?' Thus Dupleix asked the Diarist who replied

the Nawab had released the French prisoners he had with him and had sent them to Pondicherry with a letter from himself and Muhammad Tavakkal, the resident agent of the Nawab at Pondicherry, who seemed willing to arrange for a satisfactory

that this would produce a serious misunderstanding between the Moors and the English; and Dupleix said he was also of the same opinion, adding, 'when the English ships which were in the roads at Pulicat, saw ours arriving at Madras, they made off, but there was a Dutch sloop which our squadron seized.' (Entry for January 13 and 14, 1747, pp. 254 and 256 of vol. iii of the *Diary*.)

Dupleix informed the Nawab duly of the arrival of these ships at Pondicherry on January 20, exaggerated the augmentation of his own forces thereby and represented that the English at Fort St. David had been abandoned by the rest of their countrymen. It now seemed to lie easily within the power of Dupleix to launch an attack on Fort St. David both by sea and land. He did not make the attempt; he daily expected the arrival of the hostile English squadron; he was too far advanced in negotiating with the Nawab's government for a withdrawal of his troops; and above all, as Malleson says, 'he was hampered by the character of his naval and military commanders. Dordelin was feeble and unenterprizing; de Bury as we have seen, worn out and incapable' (*History of the French in India*, p. 205). And two of the ships had been dismasted and all of them had to be fitted out with the necessary munitions and stores. The ships were later sent to the Malabar Coast to engage the English ships which were said to be cruising off Anjengo and Tellicherry and to capture these places if possible. The Angria chief was reported to have offered the services of 6,000 men; and the Rajah of Travancore was also written to negotiate for the assistance of the Angrias; and the squadron sailed from Pondicherry on February 8, 1747, with the letter addressed to the Travancore ruler.

Tulāji Angria who had succeeded Sambhaji in the headship of his family's piratical power (the famous Kanhōji's) took advantage of the capture of Madras by La Bourdonnais and began stopping and plundering small native craft belonging to Bombay. 'Considerable anxiety was caused in Bombay, at this time, by the appearance of three French men-of-war cruising on the coast, with the evident intention of waylaying the Company's ships from Europe.' Tulāji's energies were mainly directed at this time against Canara where he sacked Mangalore and Honore carrying off on each occasion a large booty. J. Biddulph, *The Pirates of Malabar* (1907), pp. 220–222).

settlement provided he was given a large *douceur*.[21] A letter was written to Muhammad Alī to the effect that the French were prepared to give him the villages attached to Cuddalore and Fort St. David, reserving the latter place alone for a while longer and then to make it over also to the Muhammadans if required, provided he withdrew with his troops and did not give up these places to the English. Dupleix was inclined to ignore Mahfuz Khān altogether in these transactions, evidently because he was too irreconcilably alienated from the French and to have the negotiations settled through his younger brother alone, if possible.

When news reached Fort St. David that some English ships

21 According to information gained from Muhammad Tavakkal, the Nawab was overwhelmed with debts and thoroughly wearied; he wished to make peace with the French and withdraw his troops; and apparently the Nizam had ordered the Nawab to withdraw from the struggle. The Nawab had appointed a new person to collect the tribute of the Carnatic, 'Sadasiva Rao, a Mahratta, who is the son of Simanaji Rao, the younger brother of Baji Rao'—the same, apparently as Sadhashiv Bhao, son of Chimnaji Appa (The accuracy of this statement is open to doubt; or the Diarist apparently made a mistake regarding the person so appointed). Muhammad Tavakkal wrote letters to Husain Tahir and to Sampati Rao that the French Governor was not willing to pay anything to the Nawab, unless the latter asked for it, and that he was aware of the latter's difficulties with the Marathas and with the Nizam. To add to the complications of the situation, a letter arrived from Chandā Sāhib, in which he said that the Nizam was angry with Anvar-ud-dīn for having suffered a shameful defeat at French hands and intended appointing his (Chandā Sāhib's) son as Nawab; and in case 'Nawab Asaf Jah (the Nizam) objects to this, Sau Bhaji Rao is determined to take command of an army of 30,000 horsemen, with the view of expelling Anvar-ud-dīn Khān and installing Chandā Sāhib in his place' (Diarist's entry for January 24). Another letter from Arcot stated that the Nizam had issued a circular letter to all the chiefs of the southern country, directing them to proceed to the banks of the Krishna, that the troops at Arcot were preparing to do so, and that Anvar-ud-dīn had communicated the Nizam's command to his sons. A series of factors had thus contributed to weaken the resolution of the Nawab and his sons, if there was any, to continue firm against the French and to incline him more and more towards accommodation with the French.

had reached Anjengo and Tellicherry, Dupleix tried to counteract its effect by the report that about 6,000 of Tulaji Angria's men had offered to help M. de Leyrit, the Chief of Mahē, if he would take possession of Tellicherry, Anjengo and other English factories on that coast and that the ships under M. Dordelin which had recently arrived, together with two others, were being sent to Mahē for that purpose.

Negotiations with the Nawab's representatives continued, till Muhammad Tavakkal definitely declared that he received a communication from Arcot that the Nawab would definitely recall Mahfuz Khān and Muhammad Alī and would expect that the French in return would put a stop to the depredations of their soldiers in the country round Madras and would but fly the Mughal Emperor's flag over Fort St. George for a period of eight days. The Muhammadan troops would retire from the vicinity of Fort St. David as soon as Dupleix would withdraw the French soldiers encamped at Ariyānkuppam.[22]

In the meantime when negotiations were going on, messengers came to Pondicherry from Nāsir Jang with a letter and presents

22 Diarist's entry for January 27 and 26 (pp. 276, 278 of vol. iii). Dupleix gave immediate orders for the withdrawal of the soldiers from the Ariyānkuppam camp and even agreed to keep the flag flying over Madras; he denied any liability to give presents to the Nawab, but consented to make large gifts. After flying the Mughal flag, he would write to the Nawab asking him for the cession of Madras; and after getting a written order from the Nawab to that effect, he would then hoist the French flag over the citadel. Anvar-ud-dīn seemed to demand a present of several lakhs, to which Dupleix sent a reply message as it were, to the following effect: 'you have taken the part of the English, and dishonour, in addition to expenditure of money for the support of your soldiers, has hitherto been your only portion. You have never obtained any credit or gained any advantage. Now side with us, and we will save you all trouble. We will , at our own expense, maintain your troops. Keep your proper place and we will bring you renown and show you the road to fortune. Give us but a trial.' Except for this message Dupleix was not inclined to give more presents than to the value of 30,000 or 40,000 rupees. (Diarist's entry for January 31, pp. 287-8 of vol. iii).

who were received with great ceremony. Unfortunately the Diary of Ranga Pillai who describes in great detail the splendid procession of reception, is blank in the portion where the contents of the letter should be. The rumour was that Nasir Jang was actually on the march against the Marathas and the Nizam had given strict orders that the Nawab and his son should hasten to join him with their forces on the Krishna. Mahfuz Khān was unwilling to depart; and it was even rumoured that he was inclined to advance against Pondicherry itself. Dupleix and the Diarist attributed this delay to a desire to cover the disgrace of their previous defeats and to get a larger *douceur* if possible. A party of Muhammadan troopers actually tried to advance on Ariyānkuppam but were beaten off (February 13). It was followed by the further reinforcement of the enemy whose camp was moved to the immediate neighbourhood at Bahur and who plundered a few adjoining villages.[23] Muhammad Tavakkal now conveyed the orders of his master, Husain Sāhib, that Dupleix should give a guarantee that he would not attack Fort St. David and should pay five lakhs of rupees and then alone would the negotiation for the withdrawal of troops be considered; he repaired to Muhammad Alī's camp, remonstrated with him for having raided French villages when negotiations were in progress; and the latter attempted to transfer the blame on to his brother. Thereupon Tavakkal transferred himself to Mahfuz Khān's camp,

23 Mention is made by the Diarist of the depredations of *Pindarees* and *Kābās* in this connection. They set fire to the houses in the villages; and several of them were captured and very severely punished by the French. The *Kābās* (according to H. H. Wilson, *A Glossary of Judicial and Revenue Terms, etc.* (1855), p. 243) were a 'people to the north of the Maratha provinces, said to be a piratical tribe in the Gulf of Kach.' The Kābādis who might have been a connected tribe were conveyers of articles in wooden panniers. The Pindaris are mentioned in the south, for the first time as having participated in the last wars of Aurangzib against the Marathas. (Yule and Burnell, *Hobson-Jobson* (new ed.), p 712). The words *Pindarecs and Kābhas* are definitely mentioned in the letter written from Mahfuz Khān's camp to Muhammad Tavakkal throwing the blame of incendiarism on them. (P. 317 of the *Diary*, vol. iii.)

explained away the circumstances under which the French captured Madras and fought the battle of the Adyar and finally induced him to promise to withdraw his troops, and make friends with the French.

As a result of all this Dupleix decided to invite Mahfụz Khān to Pondicherry in order to settle the differences finally. Both the brothers agreed to come to Pondicherry. Mạhfuz Khān was invited by Muhammad Tavakkal, M. Delarche and the Diarist on February 18; he came to Pondicherry on the next day in great state and settled with the Governor the terms of the proposed convention. Muhammad Alī excused himself from a personal visit to Pondicherry on ground of illness, but agreed to abide by the conditions agreed to by his brother.[24] There was the usual haggling over the presents to be given to the various parties;[25]

24 Muhammad Tavakkal who was the main instrument of these negotiations was granted a title of honour, 'Salik Daud Khan', gold bangles to wear on the wrists, and a medal having the same inscription as that on a like decoration worn by the late *courtier*, Kanakaraya Mudali. The Diarist felt that he had also shared prominently in these negotiations; but Madame Dupleix, from whom everything had been kept back and who imagined that he was reaping a rich harvest and she had been kept from her own share, would have easily blackened him had the negotiations failed (pp. 349—354 of vol. iii of the *Diary*—entry for February 23). The entry for February 26 contains a long record of reflections with regard to his own skill in diplomacy, with the reputation that he thought he enjoyed in the opinions of other men and with similar extravagant fancies of his own services. A peculiar account is given of the struggle between the English and the French, of the subsequent events and of how he was mainly responsible for the thwarting of the enemy's designs and the triumph of Dupleix's plans. While writing these extravagant self-laudations, the Diarist is sober enough to add; 'all this (high reputation) came to me by the grace of God alone, and not through any talent on my part; ' but he is also foolish enough to supplement it with the following:—'I could record, at still greater length, all the credit that I acquired in this business, but as self-laudation is a most unwise thing, I have written as above, giving only hints with regard to it.' (P. 381 of vol. iii).

25 Orme says that Mahfuz Khān was paid 50,000 rupees and also given a present of European trinkets to the value of 100,000 rupees more.

but finally the Muhammadan camp struck its tents and both Muhammad Alī and Mahfuz Khān marched away in the direction of Arcot, and the occasion was publicly celebrated both at Pondicherry and at Madras. At the latter place an English ship which anchored in the roads in ignorance of recent events was captured, and a portion of her cargo containing silver confiscated, to the tune of £600,000 at which more rejoicings were displayed than if their own ships had arrived from Europe. Attempts were also made, though not very successfully, to induce again the Madras merchants to come and settle at Pondicherry; and brisk preparations went on for a fresh attack on Fort St. David;[26] and Paradis was chosen to head the expedition in spite of the disapproval of the other officers; and the resolution to launch the expedition immediately was taken as the approach of the English squadron was almost daily expected. This was the third projected attack on the English settlement.

These amounts should be regarded, from what the Diarist says in great detail of presents, as inclusive of the value of all the presents given to the various personages on the Nawab's side.

26 Besides the capture of the English ship at Madras, another English ship which touched at Fort St. David set sail for Bengal without landing the soldiers or any part of the cargo, though these were consigned to the Governor and Council of Madras. It was only on the last day of February that the ship which had escaped from the Madras roads in the previous November and escaped to Ceylon, returned to the coast and landed at Fort St. David £ 60,000 in silver and twenty recruits from the garrison (Orme, vol. i, p. 86).

CHAPTER VI

CONTINUED OPERATIONS ROUND FORT ST. DAVID

The Third Attack on Fort St. David and After

The Diarist describes in great detail the forces that proceeded from Pondicherry on March 11, 1747, under the command of MM. de La Tour and Paradis and their repulse of an English force near the boundary hedge of Fort St. David. The shots of the French cannon were more effective and their *Caffre* troops escaladed the Uppalavādi battery with ladders and drove back the enemy sepoys from the post. The French force subsequently attacked the English Garden-House at Manjakuppam whither the English had retired after their defeat and occupied it. Just when all the French troops, soldiers, *Caffres*[1] and Mahē sepoys, made ready to proceed to assault the Fort, a sentinel descried seven ships making for the anchorage and carrying the English flag. Thereupon the French officers held a council of war and decided that they should immediately retreat, since Pondicherry would be in a helpless condition, should the English ships proceed thither. In their hasty retreat, chests of powder were thrown into water; cannon were spiked or otherwise similarly disposed of; bags of rice were ripped open and their contents flung into wells; and casks of brandy were staved in and their liquor was allowed to flow off. The troops however repulsed a body of pursuers and reached Pondicherry safely on the evening of the 13th. According to the Fort St. David *Consultations,* dated March 1 and 2 (old style), the English defended the line of the Pennar for a whole day; and the French had to retire in haste. According to the Diarist, ' if the English fleet had arrived but two days later, the

1 A term applied first by the Arabs and then by the Portuguese to the black Negro troops who were then largely employed (Yule and Burnell: *Hobson-Jobson* (1921), p. 141).

French who had advanced well-equipped and with great energy, would undoubtedly have captured Fort St. David and have hoisted their white flag on it.'[2]

After the English fleet arrived with the British squadron and saved Fort St. David from threatened capture, the seas were practically closed to French trade and remained so till the end of the war.[3] The squadron which was under the command of Commodore Griffin ought to have reached the Coromandel Coast in the previous year, but had wintered at Achīn and reached Bengal only in December, where it was again delayed for some needed repairs. But the English ships were not sufficiently manned and any attack by them on Pondicherry was out of the question; and 'the utmost he could do was to blockade the French settlement and keep Dupleix inactive.'

Meanwhile Dupleix continued to ingratiate himself with the Muhammadan *killedars* of the neighbourhood, like Mudāmiah, the deputy of Nawab Abdul Nabī Khān of Cuddapah who had a *jaghir* in Chidambaram, Shaikh Ahmad of Porto Novo which was a large weaving centre for blue cloth that was exported largely to Bourbon, Achīn and other places, and Muhammad Alī Khān, the brother of Chandā Sāhib and the *faujdar* of Polur. He had also a new seal in Persian prepared for his use, the titles

2 He declared to Dupleix that Fort St. David should have been seized as soon as Madras was captured, as 'it was a snake at the head of our bed which must not be allowed to remain;' and that it would have been easier to have succeeded in the attempt while the French ships were still on the coast. He was confident that, with the coming of good times to Dupleix after April, the Fort would certainly fall.

3 'From time to time news came which made Dupleix hope to be able to renew the languishing commerce of the settlement; but the English squadrons were too tenacious and too pervasive for these hopes to be realized.'—*Dodwell.* The truth was that Pondicherry was depleted of its defence by the necessity of detaching a considerable force to garrison the captured city of Madras, while English ships hindered the importation of food-grains from the fertile northern coast and 'formed a perpetual menace to both Madras and Pondicherry, should they find either stripped of its garrison' (*vide* Introduction to vol. iv of the *Diary*, p. vi, and *Dupleix and Clive*, p. 23).

in which ran as follows: 'Acknowledging the supremacy of the Emperor Muhammad Shāh, the Victorious in Battle, He who is called Monsieur Dupleix, the Governor-General of Pondicherry, whose sway extends over Hindustan (*i.e.* the Governor of all the *French* in India), renowned for his valour and success in arms.'[4] The Nawab was displeased with the French attack on Fort St. David made without his special sanction and after, as he alleged, Dupleix had promised in the course of the previous negotiations not to attack it; and a letter had to be written to Husain Sāhib at Arcot that it was the English that first molested some Frenchmen coming from Arcot and made prisoners of some of them and also attacked a French detachment coming from Karikal and plundered some of the French villages. It concluded:—'Can they (English) do as they please, while we must remain quiet without doing anything?...... Will you give them the necessary orders, or shall we do as we think best?'[5] Muhammad Tavakkal wrote a letter asking that the French troops should be at once recalled from Fort St. David, if they had not already been; and that this was the reason why the *parwana* for the four villages already granted was being withheld by the Nawab. Muhammad Alī Khān, the son of the Nawab, was suspected of unfriendly feelings and designs, and an attempt was made to propitiate him by the gift of a gold-laced hat.

4 The Diarist adds that the inscription was the same as the old one, with the addition, 'Muzaffar Jang Bahadur' meaning, 'the valorous and successful in arms' (vol. iv, p. ii).

5 In this connection the Diarist was charged with having told Muhammad Tavakkal in the course of the preceding negotiations that Fort St. David would not be attacked. Dupleix did not believe it; and Ranga Pillai maintained that all that he expressed was that Dupleix would not listen to anything, and that he and the English must settle their disputes in their own way, and that the French could do nothing except under orders from Europe. He finally convinced Dupleix that such a promise on the part of the French should have been invented by Ṭavakkal himself in order to get out of difficulty (pp. 14-16 of vol. iv of the *Diary*).

Affairs in Fort St. David and in Madras

Turning to the position of the English at Fort St. David, the Diarist recorded, under date March 27, 1747, that huge ramparts were being built round the Fort, and the Gadilam was to be turned in its course so as to flow south of the Fort straight into the sea, instead of bending away as it did to the south-east. A mint was opened at the Fort 'which was crowded with merchants and *dubashes* from Madras'; fresh earthworks were built at the bound-hedge and near the Fort.[6] There were more than 1,500 men on board the English ships who were employed in the works. Guns were mounted and soldiers posted at Cuddalore where the English women and children from Madras were being sheltered. Contrasting this with the sorry spectacle of Madras under French rule, the Diarist lamented that the town (Madras) was going to ruin under an incapable governor (Duval d' Espréménil) and under the evil influence of Madame Dupleix who had been poking her nose into the affairs of the Madras merchants.[7] The English ships effectively blockaded Pondicherry, captured several

6 Mr. Dodwell says that this entry as regards the fortifications is highly anticipative; as it was not resolved according to the Fort St. David Consultations of 1747 to make alterations in the defences until March 30 = April 10, and to turn the Tēvanāmpatṇam (Gadilam) river until April 25 to May 6. (The *Diary*, vol. iv, p. 41, foot-note 2.)

7 'It surprises me that though such a town as Madras has newly fallen into our hands, yet no intelligent and suitable man has been appointed to guard and keep it in order. As the master of Pondicherry does not know how to govern properly and will hear no advice, the town is going to ruin. And not only are the town and its inhabitants being ruined, but the Governor, M. Dupleix, has brought disgrace on himself in more ways than one. Firstly whatever he does of himself, he does wrongly, for he always acts without taking advice. Secondly his wife wants to share in the government....... Thirdly the master of Madras is deaf. He can understand nothing unless it is given to him in writing....... He has never lived in the realm of intelligence...... there is no proper *dubash* to manage affairs...... What wonder that the town is ruined when these people are gathered together? Any one of these evil men would ruin the country; but when three or four are joined together what may not happen? Any wise man can see; I cannot

French merchantmen coming from the northward and sold their goods at Fort St. David. The English blockade prevented grain-vessels from reaching Pondicherry where there was much scarcity while plenty reigned at Cuddalore. The merchants of Madras steadily refused French solicitations to settle at Pondicherry, saying that the English would never give up their city. They feared that the French might forcibly convert them to the Christian faith and would not allow them any civil liberty; and they would not listen either to the overtures of the Diarist or to the solicitations of Madame Dupleix; and they would give no answer so long as they should be solicited on both sides; and Dupleix believed that while the Dubash had failed to get the merchants to live at Pondicherry, his wife would be more successful in the task.

The Situation with the Country Powers

The death of Mr. John Hinde, the Governor of Fort St. David, which occurred on April 25 and his burial the next day

write at full length, so I have written briefly.' Again, 'He (Dupleix) makes no proper enquiries; nothing is done properly. Such conduct brings no profit either to the Company or to the Governor. The merchants lose their hard-earned money and the Governor his reputation. Seeing that he cannot govern properly the town in which he lives, how can he be expected to govern a distant and important town like Madras?'...... Personal pique at being denied a hand in the Madras affairs may have had some share in the vitriolic nature of these remarks, which, however, disclose the true defects of Dupleix's character and action. The property of a number of Madras merchants was taken away by the French officials who divided the goods among themselves. In reply to the protestations of Ranga Pillai, Dupleix would often repeat to him to write to the merchants promising to give them back their property, if they should come and live at Pondicherry. But the latter always wrote about their grievances and begged the Governor to do something for them. The Diarist suspected that Madame Dupleix was inducing the Madras merchants not to give true answers to him and his men.

Contrast this opinion of Dupleix with that expressed by the Diarist in vol. i, pp. 299–300.

at the Church at Tēvanāmpatṇam (probably in a tomb in the cemetery north-west of the Fort, of which no trace remains now) is recorded by the Diarist under date Wednesday, April 26. Two days later, he records an interesting account of the situation in the Carnatic, where Nāsir Jang who had been put in charge of the districts south of the Krishna by Nizām-ul-Mulk, wrote to Anvar-ud-dīn Khān to march to him with his troops or, if he could not go, to send Muhammad Alī instead. Anvar-ud-dīn was reported to contemplate the recall of Mahfuz Khān from Nāsir Jang, then marching against Tanjore in person to recover arrears

The policy of Dupleix was evidently to transfer all the trade from Madras to Pondicherry, 'by the simple expedient of removing thither all the native merchants and their property'. The Armenians indeed pretended to acquiesce in the plan; they even behaved as if they persuaded other merchants to do the same. But this was 'little more than a cover under which to remove their property elsewhere' (Dodwell, *Dupleix and Clive*, p. 18). The Indian merchants were more obstinate. They were threatened with a proclamation dated March 2, 1747, that they should register all property in their possession, and that in default of compliance within three days, search would be made in every house, and all goods and articles found therein would be confiscated to the Company. Another order issued by the Council of Pondicherry soon after ordered all merchants and other persons at Madras to quit it for Pondicherry within eight days; and to transfer their goods within this period to the Fort from which they were to be shipped off to Pondicherry, where they were to be delivered to the owners; and that any person not complying with this order would have his property confiscated (*vide* Diarist's entries for March 6 and 7, 1747; pp. 403 and 405-6 of vol. iii; also letter from Pondicherry to the Company, dated, February 6, 1747). But even at the close of 1747, the Pondicherry Council could not record even a little success in the matter; and they reported as follows:—'All the methods we have employed—promises, threats and confiscation—to induce the native merchants to come and dwell here, have been fruitless. Most favourable conditions were annexed to their removal—the possession of all their property, and the most formal assurances of never being molested either in their trade or religion...... But no one has come, save a few wretches, neither rich nor respectable. This obstinacy is in fact very humiliating to us". (quoted by Dodwell who says that this order was repeated a few days later with no more effect than that of the previous one, although in the interval half of the Black

of tribute on his own visit to the latter. Muhammad Alī was at this time in Conjeevaram and was in frequent communication with Fort St. David. This situation caused Dupleix to write a letter of conciliation to Nāsir Jang and also one to Imām Sāhib (who had previously been an officer under Dōst Alī and was now in the Nizam's service and acted 'more or less as the representative of French interests') in which an offer was made to exchange Madras for the regions of Villiyanallur and Vaḷudāvur,[8] with a request that letters should be written in Nāsir Jang's name to the English, the Dutch, the French and the Danes commanding them to cease fighting and keep peace in the Mughal country on pain of their trade being stopped and they themselves being expelled. Rumour reached Pondicherry in the beginning of May that the English had asked the Nawab for 500 horse and 2,000 foot and the latter had promised to send them; but neither the Diarist nor the Governor believed that it could be true. Also it was bruited about that the English had decided to collect their ships and cannonade Pondicherry for some five or six nights.[9] The movements of Nāsir Jang who made as if to march to Arcot, together with the news that Nizām-ul-Mulk had made peace with the Marathas and Mīr Ghulām Husain of Tinnevelly had made up

Town had been demolished.)—Letter to the French Company, November 30, 1747, from Pondicherry and Council Order, dated December 1, 1747. The latter decree of the Pondicherry Council said that all goods will be confiscated unless the owners should settle in Pondicherry within six months.

8 'In February 1747, the Council Superior wrote to the *Compagnie* proposing three ways of dealing with Madras: (1) to keep the place in order to exchange it for Louisburg, when peace should be made with England; (2) to sell it back to the English Company; (3) to exchange it for territory near Pondicherry as in the text, *Cons. Sup' a' la Compagnie*, Feb. 6, 1747, P.R.F. 18. This letter in the text is interesting, for it shows that Dupleix did not wait for the Company's orders.' (Prof. Dodwell's *Note* on p. 72 of vol. iv of the *Diary*.)

9 Commodore Griffin, even shortly after his first arrival, opened negotiations with the Nizam's government regarding Madras. A letter from Nāsir Jang to the Commodore received on June 6 (*i.e.*, June 17, new style) deplores the carelessness and want of diligence of the Madras

with Mahfuz Khān, increased the fear of a hostile demonstration by the English fleet. There was also continued activity on the part of the English at Fort St. David who were busy destroying the houses in the village to the north and clearing the ground round the fortifications of all impediments. The chiefs in the neighbourhood of Madras were also hostile; and the *poligars* of Durgarazpatnam and Nellore ill-treated M. d'Esprēmēnil who left Madras for Bengal, suddenly and much to the surprise of the Council of Pondicherry. It was, indeed, true that Nawab Anvar-ud-dīn, when he heard of the complaint from the French about this, wrote to his son, Abdul Wahāb Khān who was the faujdar of Nellore, that the French property taken by him should be immediately restored and to the English Governor at Fort St. David that Frenchmen should not be molested and their letters not interfered with. When two Frenchmen who were proceeding from Karikal to Pondicherry were seized by the English peons

Governor in surrendering the Fort when he could have stood a siege. It concludes with a vague undertaking which might mean anything or nothing. This ran as follows:—

'Now the victorious Ensigns of my most potent Army ...... are marching towards the Kingdom of Carnatica for settling affairs there. And as it is unalterably his Excellency's most just and lawful Sentiment to do justice to the whole Empire, by punishing the oppressors and protecting and aiding the oppressed, and is what I am also delighted in, I have now, and once before, wrote to my friend Anawardean Cawn Behauder ...... to cause that the lawful Proprietors are righted and dispossess the Usurpers; and by the Almighty's Grace the said Cawn Behauder will put the Orders into Execution, agreeable to his Duty which requires him to do so ....' (*Fort St. David Consultations*, vol. xv, August 31, 1747; quoted by Love.) The letter to Nāsir Jang was preceded by one from Mr. Hinde to the same personage, complaining of the conduct of the French and requesting that he should order the restoration of Madras. This is mentioned by the Diarist in his entry for June 11 (p. 93 of vol. iv). A deputation was to be sent to Nāsir Jang with presents from Fort St. David, the embassy was ready to start when news arrived that the Nizam had marched from Hyderabad to Aurangabad; and this embassy was put off for the time being.

at Tiruvati, the Nawab sent an order to the English Governor to release them and a copy thereof in Persian to Dupleix.[10]

The dreary negotiations and counter-negotiations with the Mughal officials continued, in the course of which the French tried to get the support of Mahfuz Khān and of Nawab Anvar-ud-dīn and to get their prisoners exchanged for those of the English. In the beginning of October, the English ships passed by from Fort St. David, cast anchor in the Pondicherry roads threateningly, then proceeded to Madras in whose roads they burnt a French ship, and later sailed to the north-east and went out of sight.[11] News came a few days later that this ships reached Bengal, though they actually reached Balasore only in December. News reached Fort St. David that two men-of-war and eight of the Company's ships which they had been escorting, had left England in the beginning of January and were then about fifteen days' sail distant. Griffin was anxious about the safety of the English shipping in the Bay and deferred his voyage to the Archipelago, determined to cruise about the Madras coast, to prevent more ships from falling into French hands.

10 The order the text of which is given in the *Diary* (vol. iv, p. 108) is deemed by the Diarist to have 'cringed, rather than commanded'.

11 'To-day the Governor sent for me and said, "The English have burnt the *Neptune* in the Madras Roads. This is the result of Flacourt's being captain. No one else would have behaved so badly, for as soon as the English ships came in sight, he went ashore in a masula-boat. Such conduct cannot be borne with. The English have gone and done this mischief at Madras, because two French ships were there. Now I will no longer spare Fort St. David" ....' (Entry for October 7). It was rumoured in Pondicherry that M. Dordelin's ships had sailed from Mahe about the beginning of October, and Dupleix expected it for some days with great anxiety. On their way from Goa to Mahe, they succeeded in capturing an English ship and a sloop with thirteen lakhs of dollars (the *Anson* bound from England for Bombay, and the *Fakharo Markab*, a country-ship probably belonging to Bengal; and the prize was estimated by the Pondicherry Council at two million livres (£100,000). The object of Griffin's squadron was to cruise off the coast in order to save English ships from falling into enemy hands.

The happenings at the courts of the Nawab and Nāsir Jang[12] frequently roused the anxiety of Dupleix and the Diarist. When Anvar-ud-dīn heard that owing to repeated English requests, Nāsir Jang had made a resolve to go down into the Carnatic, he (the Nawab) wrote to Mahfuz Khān to bring about a frustration of the march saying that 'what between French arrogance, English cowardice and the famine (prevailing), the country was ruined and could not bear the expenses of his (Nāsir Jang's) army'. The news of Nāsir Jang departing from the Balaghat after finishing his negotiations with Mysore was very welcome to the old Nawab who had so moulded several at the Nizam's court, as to be speaking always of the bravery of the French and the cowardice of the English. Moreover, the old Nizam who was engaged in operations round Daulatabad, had ordered Nasir Jang to return to the Deccan, in order to help him against a projected Maratha invasion, headed by Sadasiva Rao the Bhao, son of Chimanaji Appa.

Later, we learn from the Diarist that Mutyālu Nāyakan who went to Nāsir Jang's camp on behalf of the English spent a large amount of money in presents without getting anything in return and that both Nawab Anvar-ud-dīn and his Diwan Sampāti Rao declared jestingly that the English had lost their good fortune and their wits together. The only outcome of the situation was that Morari Rao Ghorpade and his Maratha horse began plundering the country round Venkatagiri Fort, Vellore, Ambur and

12 Nāsir Jang seems to have entered into, or at least begun negotiations for an agreement with the English that he would recover Madras for a sum (ten lakhs of pagodas according to the Diarist and three lakhs, according to the English records, *Country Correspondence* 1748, No. 5, p. 2 and 3,000 pagodas for each day the army marched and 2,000 pagodas for each day he halted; *vide* entry for October 25, 1747, and Mr. Dodwell's note on the subject of the amount, p. 189 of vol. iv of the *Diary*). Later when this failed, the Fort St. David *vakils* with Nāsir Jang made new proposals, by which the English were to have 1,000 horse under two jamadars, which Mahfuz Khān was persuaded by the French to frustrate. A letter to Pondicherry from Nāsir Kuli Khān, the *diwan* of Mahfuz Khān, dated December 1747, says that Mahfuz Khān had contrived to stop the projected expedition.

Vaniyambadi; and the people at Arcot and Lalapettai were alarmed for fear of the Maratha horse, 'having no place of refuge on the coast to fly to, owing to the troubles between the French and the English.'

On March 10, the Diarist made an entry that Mutyālu Nāyakan, the English *vakil,* had arrived at Arcot from Nāsir Jang's camp with presents from him. Anvar-ud-dīn was commanded by a *parwana* to order all the *poligars* to assist the English as against the French, while another order directed Dupleix to abstain from further hostilities against the English; and Mutyālu Nāyakan was accompanied by a band of Mughal and Maratha horsemen and three hundred peons. So after all the English had secured some measure of diplomatic success. All that Dupleix could do was only to fulminate against the enormous sloth of the Arcot darbar where it was difficult to get admission and it took fifteen days to have a letter answered. The French could only resort to the dirty expedient of intriguing for the seizure of Mutyālu Nāyakan on his way from Arcot to Cuddalore; but the latter appears to have learnt something of the plans against him. For this purpose an adventurer in the French service, Abd-ul-Rahmān was detailed off with a hundred horse and ammunition to waylay Mutyālu and to instigate the Poligar of Vettavalam to help in this task. It was even thought to be a desirable achievement to take captive Mr. Floyer, the Governor of Fort St. David, and Mr. Griffin along with him, if possible. Mutyālu Nāyakan was too clever to get caught and reached Fort St. David safely. The Diarist now began to say that Mr. Floyer was highly displeased with his *vakil* for not having got any substantial help from Nāsir Jang and for having spent a lakh of pagodas uselessly.

All that the French now cared about was that, if the Marathas invaded the Carnatic, as they threatened to do, the people at Arcot would be busy defending themselves, and then they could settle everything about Fort St. David in spite of Nāsir Jang's *parwana* to the Nawab to assist the English; and so both Governor and Dubash counted on the possibility of the

English not getting any help from Arcot when they should launch their intended gigantic attack against the English.

Another Barren Attack on Fort St. David

The English began in December to actively strengthen their batteries; and for fear of being unable to hold their outworks, they demolished the Deadman's Battery on the west of the Fort, since the latter was within easy range of the fire of its guns.[13] They collected stores and provisions in the Manjakuppam Garden-House and were on their guard; they summoned a council of war on January 5, 1748, to decide how Dupleix's projected attack which was well known, should be met. Nearly two thousand soldiers and Mahē sepoys were collected by the French and posted at Ariyānkuppam, ready to attack Fort St. David. The town of Cuddalore was deserted by most of the merchants and other inhabitants and was almost completely denuded of its womenfolk. Ranga Pillai notes a curious incident regarding the brother of the *dubash* of ex-Governor Morse; that he was caught in the act of carrying on secret correspondence with Madame Dupleix and even implicating Morse himself.[14] Dupleix himself did not believe that Morse was guilty of any such treasonable correspondence.

13 The chief bastions and outworks of the Fort St. David were as follows:—

Bastions—Porto Novo, Chellumbrum (Chidambaram), Vizapore (Bijapur), Trividee (Tiruvati), Chingie (Gingee) and Golconda. Round Redoubts near Cuddalore and Tevanampatnam. Outposts at Tirupapuliyur and Bandipalayam. (See pp. 13–14 of *Fort St. David Consultations*, 1711). For a plan of the Fort and its outworks—see Orme (ed. 1862), vol. II—p. 307.

14 The preliminary examination of Mr. Morse alluded to by the Diarist cannot be traced in the English records. It was likely that inquiries were made of him; but 'Ranga Pillai's version is incredible'. Lakshmanan, the person implicated, was finally brought to trial by court-martial in June; and his letters, so far as they were secured by the English, 'do not appear to have contained any very valuable secrets,

The French troops moved out of Ariyānkuppam on January 13, while a letter was written to Nawab Anvar-ud-dīn informing him of the starting of the French expedition and justifying their conduct in view of the alleged violence of the English. Dupleix himself accompanied the expedition, which, while within nine miles of its objective, descried the approach to the coast of six ships and a sloop showing English colours. These, which constituted Griffin's squadron arrived at Fort St. David on January 17.[15] Dupleix[16] at once ordered his troops and baggage to retreat. Ranga Pillai has entered in his *Diary* the camp news that Appu Mudali who accompanied the troops wrote to the Diarist from day to day during the march and retreat (January 14-17); and we are told that all the troops were full of zeal, and the former expeditions were not one-eighth as well managed as this, and this was 'entirely due to M. Dupleix who cared nothing

but there was no doubt of his correspondence and he was condemned to be hung.' Mr. Dodwell's *note* on the Diarist's entry (*vide* note 1 on p. 312 of vol. iv).

15 Pondicherry was left practically undefended, as all the garrison had gone into camp, and the Fort was guarded only by the Councillors' writers and old men who had been armed with muskets.

16 The Diarist, with his usual fickleness and animus against Madame Dupleix, condemns his master's rashness in having set out on the expedition without considering all the possibilities and only relying on Madame's reports as to what happened—'He marched against Fort St. David inconsiderately and inconsiderately returned. Every one is continuously making jests at his expense and indeed it is plain that none can earn respect who follows a woman's counsel' (*entry* for January 17). The Diarist adds that two days before Dupleix started he had received information that the English squadron had been asked to return to Fort St. David with about 500 soldiers on board; but Dupleix would not believe this news and held that the Fort would not be receiving reinforcements and would have to shift as best as it might. Besides Dupleix said that 'Mr. Morse had been consulted in secret and that he had advised the Fort to be surrendered as Madras had been, since there was no other means of safety, in consequence of which the English were already removing their goods.' The Diarist adds that Dupleix did not pause to consider whether Mr. Morse was likely to have said such a thing or not.

about what he ate or when he slept, ate the same food as his men and took no thought for his personal comfort'. Thus ended another attempt of Dupleix to capture Fort St. David which was protected not only by the ships of Griffin's squadron but also by three fresh ships from England and three Company's ships from England *via* Bengal.[17] News came that a large expedition was also preparing; and at the same time Stringer Lawrence, a retired Captain of the King's Service took command as Major of the garrison of Fort St. David. 'His arrival and the discipline which he at once proceeded to enforce, mark the time from which the Company's troops became an efficient military force.'

Its Sequel

From this time there were frequent skirmishes and collisions. In one encounter between French boats and an English one,

17 The garrison of Fort St. David was reinforced by the arrival of 100 Europeans, 200 Topasses (soldiers of Eurasian descent) and 100 sepoys from Bombay, besides 400 sepoys from Tellicherry; and in the course of the year 150 soldiers had been landed from the Company's ships from England. In January 1748, Major Stringer Lawrence arrived with a commission to command the whole of the Company's forces in India (Mill, *History of British India* (1858), vol. iii, p. 55). Dupleix had to acknowledge the superiority of English ships and sailors in his letter to Montaron, January 30, 1748. News reached Pondicherry and the ear of Diarist that fresh ships besides those that had already reached Fort St. David were coming from England with reinforcements—this is deemed to be more likely a confused rumour of the coming of Boscawen's squadron, the news of which had already reached Fort St. David, (February 2, 1748, entry). Nine ships of the Royal Navy (one of 74, one of 64, two of 60, two of 50, one of 20 guns, a sloop of 14, a bomb-ketch with her tender) commanded by Admiral Boscawen and eleven ships of the English Company carrying stores and troops to the number of 1,400 men, set sail from England towards the end of 1747 with instruction to capture the Island of Mauritius on their way. The expedition was deterred from this after an examination of this coast of the Island and on account of the loss of time that the enterprise would occasion. The expedition arrived off Fort St. David on August 20, when 'the squadron, joined to that under Griffin, formed the largest European force that any one power had yet possessed in India.'

eleven Englishmen were killed; another resulted in the English setting fire to some French ships. Of course the usual complaint reached Anvar-ud-dīn regarding the burning of the boats. As if troubles were not enough, there arose a new complication. Shahji Raja of Tanjore, the son of Sarabhōji Raja according to the Diarist, sent an envoy to Pondicherry, by name Kóyāji Kāttigai promising that he was prepared to make an alliance with the French. Dupleix was very doubtful if any substantial gain could come out of any engagement with this person and ordered the messenger to be sent away. This Shahji[18] was an obscure pretender to the Tanjore throne which, after the death of Tukoji (1728–35) who was the last son of Ekoji, suffered a

18 Tukoji Raja died about the year 1735. He had five sons: (1) Bava Sāhib; (2) Saiyaji; (3) Anna Sāhib; (4) Nana Sāhib; and (5) Pratap Singh. Of these the first two were legitimate and the last three illegitimate. Nos. 3 and 4 died before their father; and Bava Sāhib who succeeded, died about a year after. Bava Sāhib's widow; Sujana Bai, was now raised to the throne by the ministers. But soon a pretender under the name of Savai Shahji, generally known as *Kāttu Raja* (Forest King) came forward and, with the aid of the Muhammadan commander of the Tanjore Fort, succeeded in usurping the throne. He was soon deposed in favour of Saiyaji, the second son of Tukoji; and the latter had in his turn to give place to Pratap Singh. The pretender Savai Shahji was in reality the offspring of a slave woman named Rupi, to Sarabhōji, the second son of Ekoji, counterfeited as the son of one of his queens. A previous counterfeit prince had already been disposed of. This second counterfeit was set up by one Koyanji Ghangte (Kóyāji Kāttigai?) who alleged that he was the Savai Shahji and was the lawful heir to the throne. He was afterwards called *Kāttu Raja*, because when he was proclaimed as Raja, he came from the Udaiyārpālaiyam jungle whither he had been taken by Ghangte for the purpose of securing the aid of its *poligar* for him. This pretender later secured the aid of the English at Fort St. David and of the Dutch at Negapatam. This prince was deposed by Saiyaji, the legitimate son of Tukoji. The *Tanjore District Manual* alleges that there were two rulers between Bava Sāhib's wife and Pratap Singh *viz.*, Savai Shahji, the son of Sarabhōji, and the other Saiyaji, the son of Tukoji. The latter has been consistently ignored in the pedigrees kept up by Pratap Singh who was after all an illegitimate son. And hence there was a likelihood of the identification of the two as one.

number of rapid revolutions before the Government became settled on the accession of Pratap Singh in 1740. Dupleix's dismissal of Kāttigai was probably due to his fear of provoking the enmity of the Tanjore ruler at a time when the English fleet was expected on the coast. It was also consistent with the recommendation of Le Riche of Karikal made in the previous year that the times were not suitable for such an enterprise. He ordered the Diarist to write letters to Pratap Singh of Tanjore, and Mānōji Appa, his chief minister, saying, 'We thought Shahji was dead, and are astonished that you have written to M. Paradis, the chief of Karikal, to say that the old Raja Sarabhōji's son, Shahji, the

Mill distinctly speaks, on the authority of an authentic manuscript of Tanjore, of the pretended son of Sarabhōji and of Sahujee (evidently Saiyaji) the youngest of the sons of Tukoji and attributes all the revolutions to the Muhammadan commandant, Sayid, whose execution was the first act of Pratap Singh's reign. (Book iv, chap. ii, p. 62 of vol. iii). Wilson in his note on Mill who declared that Orme was misinformed—as he considered both Shahji and Pratap Singh to have been sons of Sarabhōji—says that Saiyaji, as Duff calls him, was a legitimate son of Tukoji. Mr. Dodwell in his note (on pp. 350–1 of vol. iv of the *Diary*) says that the attempt of the *Tanjore Manual* was to reconcile the versions of Orme and Duff; and that it was not supported by the *Memoir* which was written by Elias Guillot, the Dutch Governor of Negapatam, in 1739, which was strongly in favour of the identification of the two persons Shahji and Saiyaji; and the Dutch were exceedingly well informed on all Tanjore affairs. He says: 'I take it that the Shahji who reigned from 1737 to 1739 claimed to be a son of Sarabhōji; whether he was or not I cannot pretend to decide, nor yet whether the person whose uncle visited Pondicherry was the actual prince who reigned. .... I think it probable that the man who now was approaching Dupleix and who, at the close of the year 1748, was to visit Fort St. David with more success, was the Shahji, who had reigned over Tanjore.' The native tradition embodied in the *Tanjore District Manual* distinctly says that the first pretended son of Sarabhōji was got rid of by the order of the latter himself when he came to know of the deception. The second counterfeit was set up many years afterwards by one Koyanji Ghangte (Kóyāji Kāttigai of the Diarist) who was the brother of the pretender's alleged mother. This is corroborated by other information also. Moreover the Abbé Guyon—the historian of French India—says that Pratap Singh stifled his rival Saiyaji in a bath of

late tyrannous Raja, has been kept in Pondicherry; it surprises us as much as if a dead man had come to life again. We could get no advantage from helping him; and so why should we concern ourselves with so unlucky a man?......[19] Copies of these letters were sent to Paradis. All the while paddy and stores were being steadily accumulated, and the neighbouring *poligars* were cautiously sounded. Dupleix, whether truthfully or otherwise, told the Diarist that the Dutch had joined the French and declared war against the English and that was why the English with all their shipping were afraid to attack Pondicherry. In reality Louis XIV had declared war on Holland and 'in a few months Dutch troops were to appear beside the English before Pondicherry'.

Thus the events drifted on to the last episode of this first Anglo-French struggle.

milk; and if that should have been true, the pretender Savai Shahji should have been a different person and not the same as had been killed by Pratap Singh in 1740.

The name given to the pretender in the Fort St. David records is Sahajee Maharaja. The Marathi inscription in the Big Temple at Tanjore calls him Savai Shahji and *Kāttu Raja*. According to the Marathi inscription, he obtained help even in 1738 when he deposed Sujana Bai, from the English at Fort St. David and the Dutch at Negapatam under specious promises. Another writer, Mr. K. R. Subrahmanian (in his *The Maratha Rajas of Tanjore*, 1928, pp. 44–6) is inclined to support the view that there was no Saiyaji at all and that the same person, Shahji, superseded Sujana Bai for a while at first and aftewards permanently. The Dutch Memoir of 1739, Ananda Ranga Pillai's *Diary* for 1748 and the English account of the claims of Shahji in 1749—all say that he was the legal heir and not Pratap Singh. But the first of these sources only proves that the Dutch, having supported Shahji, pretended that he was the legal heir. The French *Dubash* only wrote what he was told of the claims of Shahji as the son of Sarabhōji; and the English records of 1749 could not prove the legitimacy of their candidate. None of these sources mentions Saiyaji; and a French record of 1749 accuses the English of having attempted to pull down the reigning prince Pratap Singh and place a phantom in his stead. So the writer concludes that there was only one person, Shahji, the *Kāttu Raja*; and there is no reason to suppose that Tukoji had a legitimate son, Saiyaji, who ruled for a year before Pratap's accession.

19 Diarist's entry for February 27.

CHAPTER VII

OPERATIONS ROUND CUDDALORE AND PONDICHERRY

EVENTS AT PONDICHERRY TILL THE ARRIVAL OF BOUVET'S SQUADRON

MUTYALU Nāyakan, the English *vakil* who had gone on a mission to Nāsir Jang's camp, returned, as already noted, with *parwanas*, from the Nizam to Nawab Anvar-ud-dīn and all the *poligars*, enjoining them to assist the English as against the French, together with one to Dupleix ordering him to abstain from further hostilities. The attempts planned to seize him on his way from Arcot to Fort St. David, came to nothing. Dupleix and the Diarist made much of the fact that Mutyālu Nāyakan had spent more than a lakh of pagodas for no substantial return and the English Governor, Mr. Floyer, was greatly displeased with him and would not receive for some days the presents which had at first been left outside the town. The Diarist who heard rumours about the arrival of some Maratha horse and about a panic having been produced consequently at Arcot and in its neighbourhood, thought that the people at Arcot would be busy defending themselves and thus the French could settle everything about Fort St. David in spite of the Nizam's *parwana* to Arcot. He made this suggestion to the Governor, adding his own belief that, astrologically, the English fortunes would go down to their lowest in the middle of April. But paddy continued to be scarce and dear at Pondicherry; and possibly there was 'also a scarcity of silver there, owing to the delayed arrival of Europe ships and the stoppage of French traffic to Manilla and the Red Sea', while the rate of exchange at Fort St. David was much higher. Even the pagodas current at Pondicherry had been for some years debased, being lower than the 8-touch normal standard.[1]

1 'About 1740, all the European settlements had been greatly troubled by the debasement of pagodas struck in the country mints. Pagodas of 8-touch (*i.e.* fine) had been the normal currency; but mints

A few horses with a camel and some bullocks and a standard were captured by a party of French horsemen and sepoys from the camp of the Rajput and Maratha horse who came with Mutyālu Nāyakan on April 8. Dupleix got greatly elated in spirit, declared that evil times had begun for Fort St. David and that he would surely take that place with the help of even two ships. Meanwhile news was received from Europe that France had declared war on Holland, that the French King was greatly elated at La Bourdonnais' capture of Madras—Dupleix's complaints against him not having reached Paris by that time—and that all believed that by this time the French flag would be floating triumphantly at Fort St. David, Anjengo, Tellicherry and Vizagapatam. Dupleix was eagerly expecting St. George's squadron which comprised three men-of-war and had left for the east in the beginning of 1747.[2] Shaik Ahmad Sāhib's letter to Pondicherry from Porto Novo, given by the Diarist under date May 22, tells us of a rumour that French ships had appeared off Batavia and that English and Austrian ships were coming to their help. Dupleix commented on this, saying that the Dutch were so alarmed at what had happened in Europe as to betray their own weakness; while extraordinary precautions were taken at

such as Alambarai, issued coins of 7 and 6-touch. As a consequence of this debasement, the English coined the *star pagoda*. The French also attempted measures of reform, such as prohibiting the introduction into Pondicherry of pagodas under 8-touch. Though this was not successful, bargains were still made in such coins and settled in other specie at the current ratio.' Dodwell. Note. 2—on p. 6 of the *Diary*, vol. v. Silver seems to have been the alloy usually mixed with gold.

2 This squadron was first dispersed by a storm, sailed again in May 1747 from the Isle d'Aix, and in the same month was destroyed by the English admiral, Lord Anson, off Cape Ortegal, along with the escort of La Jonquiere. 'Three ships however had disappeared in the storm; and these reached the French Islands in October 1747. Other vessels were lying there more or less ready for service. With these a squadron of seven sail was formed, under the command of Bouvet, to carry much-needed supplies of money to Pondicherry. His instructions expressly stated that this was the principal object of his mission.' (Dodwell—*Dupleix and Clive;* pp. 23-24.)

Negapatam where there were constant rumours of an imminent attack by French ships.[3] Dupleix was of the opinion that perhaps the French Government might have issued orders to capture the rich towns of Batavia, Colombo, *etc.*, that the French ships at Mascareigne should have been asked not to sail for Pondicherry before the arrival of the squadron from Europe, and the ships must have gone from that place to the Archipelago to intercept the four English ships that were being expected from China and to attack Batavia. Dupleix had not got any news either from Europe or from Mascareigne; and the frigate that came with Europe news was captured by the English and taken to Fort St. David; and the letters found in it must have mentioned the capture of Madras, what was to be done with it and the despatch of many ships;—' for it was only after this that the Governor of Negapatam began to pull down houses and so forth, and prepare for war.'

Meanwhile Dupleix received some presents that Nāsir Jang sent him along with a letter which assured him that the latter received Mutyālu Nāyakan, the English *vakil*, with but ill-favour and that he had always admired the greatness of Dupleix's valour. Moreover, news reached Pondicherry that Anvar-ud-dīn was not on good terms with his eldest son, Mahfuz Khān, that Fatteh Singh and Raghuji Bhonsle had assembled their troops at Ākulakotta for a march on the Carnatic and that Chandā Sāhib had taken leave of the Marathas. Above all information was received as to the death of the Emperor Muhammad Shāh

3 'Veḷipālayam, on the outskirts of Negapatam, has been pulled down and all the houses near the fort have been razed to the ground. All the cannon in the batteries at Veḷipālayam have been carried into the Fort. The merchants of the town and the rich men from Trichinopoly and Tanjore who went thither to make money are alarmed and have fled to Jaffna, Udaiyārpālaiyam and Ariyalur. They would fear to touch even a crow from Pondicherry or Karikal.'—Diarist's remarks to Dupleix; but he put down his own private reflection; 'I reflected that the confusion of our affairs was only concealed from the world by the glory we have been lucky enough to win; otherwise it would have been evident to all.'—pp. 29 and 30 of the *Diary*, vol. v.

at Delhi on April 28 and of Nizām-ul-Mulk some weeks later. When Nizām-ul-Mulk died, his younger son, Nāsir Jang, was with him; and the news of his death[4] caused great grief both to Nawab Anvar-ud-dīn and his son Mahfuz Khān.

The Last French Attack on Cuddalore

Dupleix was so anxious about the rumoured approach of the English fleet that he paid but scant attention to this serious news about the country powers. He believed that the English had heard from Negapatam of the arrival of French ships in its vicinity and that was the reason for Commodore Griffin taking on board his ships all available men and supplies and making himself ready for action; the Commodore sighted, on June 21, Bouvet's ships off Fort St. David and the same night prepared to engage them. The entry of the Diarist for June 22 states that the English ships were lying off Pondicherry in the hope of encountering the French fleet which was expected to arrive in a day or two. On the next day the ten ships of Griffin were not found in the

4 Varying dates are given for the death of the Nizam. Grant-Duff dates it as having occurred on June 19, 1748. The *Country Correspondence* of the English gives it as May 21, June 1, as quoted by Dodwell. Burgess states (p. 188 of his *Chronology of India*) thus; 'June, Jumada II, Asaf Jāh, Nizām-ul-Mulk dies.' The death of the Emperor Muhammad Shāh, the astrological details of which are given by the Diarist, can be dated on this basis for April 17—28, but there is a day's difference according to another reckoning which puts it down as April 27; Rabi II, 27, H. 1161. The date given in Beale's *Oriental Biographical Dictionary* (revised by Keene, 1894) for the Nizam's death, is 22nd May, 1748 (old style) 4th Jumada II. A. H. 1161, *i.e.*, 37 days after the death of Muhammad Shāh. This date is confirmed by a letter of Imam Sāhib to Pondicherry quoted by the Diarist in his entry for July 7, 1748. The news of the Nizam's death reached Arcot only sixteen days after its happening, which was fixed by the Diarist for June 2. A rumour was prevalent that the Nizam took poison and died as he heard that his eldest son Ghāzī-ud-dīn Khān was ordered to be executed by the Emperor. Anvar-ud-dīn was in fear of an attack by Murtazā Alī of Vellore and there was confusion in Arcot (p. 75 of vol. v of the *Diary*.)

roads, having sailed the previous midnight northward; while a sloop had sailed for Fort St. David and only a ship which used to lie in the Pondicherry roads was still there.

Dupleix sent some European horse and sepoys to Madras, being still uncertain as to the aim of the English move or the exact location of the French fleet. The Diarist however shrewdly suggested that it must have been the French ships that were sighted off Fort St. David on the 20th and caused great confusion in Cuddalore and made the people there remove their money and valuables to Porto Novo and other places; but the French ships which carried the much-needed supplies of money ' could not land their silver here and had therefore gone to Madras ' and would soon send news after unloading. This surmise proved correct, as news soon arrived on the noon of June 23, that eight ships and two sloops dropped anchor at Madras the previous day.[5]

5 The whole of the incident, if it may be called one, is as follows:— When the French squadron under Bouvet made for the coast, his first concern was to reconnoitre the English squadron. 'On June 21 he sent a fast-sailing boat ahead which reported that ten men-of-war and several merchantmen were lying in the St. David's roads. He himself approached within about a league to survey the enemy, but after consulting his senior captain, resolved to sail for Madras, and there land the treasure and men he was bringing instead of running the risk of an action. This he accomplished (at Madras) on the 22nd, and then hastily quitted the coast. Dupleix complained of this abrupt departure. Had Bouvet only put into Karikal, he declared, he would have learnt that Griffin had only four ships ready to sail; and, by attacking, could have made an end of the English squadron.' (Dodwell, *Dupleix and Clive*, p. 24). Dupleix repeatedly asked the Diarist why the French ships should go to Madras, when there was Karikal to the south, where they would have been safe (Diarist's entry for the 23rd) and would not be satisfied with Ranga Pillai's explanations.—' But whatever Dupleix thought about it, Bouvet would undoubtedly have been bringing his mission into the most serious peril had he ventured on attacking Griffin, who was not so unprepared as Dupleix stated (in his letter to the French Company, dated January 15, 1749) ....but apart from these (two rudderless ships) the English squadron comprised six line-of-battle ships with a frigate and two of the Company's ships. Nor were the English taken by surprise. About

Dupleix severely commented on the inaction of Commodore Griffin, who should have pursued the French ships till he had caught them up and given them battle. 'But he waited till they were out of sight and then sailed in shore, lay to the south of our roads and only sailed slowly off the next day. You will see him flying before our ships when they return....... I will send the troops that are now ready, or I will go myself, against Fort St. David in five or six days and cause great confusion there.'[6] Bussy told the Diarist that a new squadron under M. le Chevalier d' Albert was being sent out to India and that Bouvet had seized a Dutch vessel laden with powder and shot and carried it to Madras. Every one was encouraged by the news of the departure of the new squadron from Europe and of the landing of 500 soldiers by Bouvet at Madras, while Dupleix should have been particularly gratified by the news of the ordering of La Bourdonnais' imprisonment and of the seizure of all who helped him. The Governor even confiscated the papers of one or two Frenchmen and arrested another for alleged complicity in La Bourdonnais' misdeeds at Madras. He got all the sepoys and the

nine o'clock on the evening of the 20th, an English scout came in with the news that she had sighted a French squadron, and Bouvet did not appear until 2 p.m. on the following day.' (Dodwell, p. 24.)

6 His remarks to the Diarist—pp. 62–63 of vol. v.—Griffin's conduct was certainly blameworthy. Examining the Fort St. David Consultations, the Admiralty records concerning Griffin's court-martial, and Griffin's own Journals and Letters, Mr. Dodwell would convict him of hesitation and delay, but would approve of the essential justice of the finding of the court-martial that he was only guilty of an error of judgment in not sailing early...... He admits that, if Griffin had sailed immediately after he boarded (*i.e.* in the early morning of the 21st), he could probably have brought the French to action that day; but he quietly remained at anchor until the enemy was in sight from the masthead, and the sea breeze had set in from the south. The council of war that he held decided nothing; later, when the French drew near, he contemplated putting out to sea and again consulted his captains; finally he resolved to wait till the wind moderated and only got out to sea at 1 a.m. on June 22. 'The result of all this hesitation and delay was that Bouvet got safely off to Madras, while Griffin was cruising vainly off Pondicherry and was clear of the coast when at last the English sailed

European and Muhammadan horsemen in Pondicherry ready for an attack on Fort St. David,[7] as the French ships from Madras had arrived, and, more than that Griffin's squadron had sailed north leaving the English settlement uncovered.

A detachment was sent to attack Cuddalore on June 27 which did not assault the place either that night or even the next day. The French troops numbered 2,000 men according to the Fort St. David Consultations; and of them 900 were Europeans. Major Lawrence who commanded the English forces gave out a report that he was withdrawing his men from the town of Cuddalore into the Fort and intended to confine himself only to the defence of the latter. But with nightfall he threw a strong garrison into the town and mounted all the guns he could spare, upon its ramparts. The result was that when the French, unconscious of this ruse, carelessly advanced upon the place at night on the 28th, believing that they would not meet with any resistance, they were thrown back with great loss and in utter confusion and had to fly away in all directions. According to the report recorded by the Diarist, about 500 sepoys, fifty Europeans and ten horses were missing :

north in search of him. Griffin himself felt that his conduct was liable to strictures.......'. The court-martial found that he should have sailed with the land-wind before the enemy came in sight; and the Admiralty exonerated him from the charge of lack of zeal or courage.

Bouvet also was attacked for not falling upon the English ships riding at anchor in Cuddalore when their crews were ashore and two of their men-of-war were rudderless. 'His principal business was to carry supplies to Dupleix who was so short of money that he was on the point of sending his plate to the mint. The relief he brought materially assisted Dupleix in maintaining his position till the arrival of the news of peace....... Bouvet was to all appearances justified in his decision to avoid action.' He had less guns than Griffin who had six men-of-war and two Company's ships, besides the two rudderless ones. Dodwell points out that Bouvet emerges with more credit than his rival.

7 The Diarist held (entry for the 27th June) that the two objects of the advance on Fort St. David were (1) to secure the arrival of the men landed at Madras by Bouvet, if conveniently managed; and (2) to bring M. Paradis in safety to Pondicherry, by surrounding the English settlement.

while 'if only the English had known the panic that arose when they fired on us, and if they had sent out but fifty men with swords, every man would have been cut off ...... the soldiers were taken with panic threw away their arms and fled in tens and twenties. For two hours they did not know friend from foe or what way they went......'[8]

Dupleix was greatly discomfited by this repulse and, according to the Diarist, attributed the fault to M. de Mainville who was

8 Diarist's entry for Saturday, June 29, 1748. According to him the first report brought to Pondicherry gave false news of French success and of their having scaled the walls of Cuddalore and cut to pieces the Carnatic sepoys there. This news which Madame Dupleix seems to have got, greatly elated the Governor's spirits; and he was highly pleased that Cuddalore should have fallen without a blow owing to his wife's counsel. Soon, however, contradictory news was brought that the spy who led the French troops pretended to reveal all the secrets of Cuddalore and had really told the English when he would bring the French and cunningly slipped away on arriving at Cuddalore. The French troops threw away their arms and fled to Tiruvati, Panruti, Mēttupālaiyam, Bhuvanagiri and other places, while a friendly poligar of the English, Akkal Nāyakkan, waylaid them, seized their clothes and other weapons and left them with hardly a rag to cover them. 'If those within had known there would be such a panic, and if they had only opened the gates and surrounded the French, all would have been cut to pieces...... The English refrained from marching out for fear of an ambush and only mounted the ramparts and fired from there. The French, losing their way, wandered hither and thither for nearly two hours and fled not knowing whither they went.' There was again brought, or pretended to have been brought, news that the French, in revenge for having been beaten off the previous night, scaled the walls of Cuddalore the next morning (*i.e.* the 29th) got inside and cut to pieces all they could find and the white flag was flying on the upper storey of a Chetti's house. The Governor was inclined to believe even this bluff which was finally given the lie only by the report of two soldiers returned from the camp. The Diarist's remark is instructive as illustrating the pernicious influence exercised by Madame Dupleix.—'If anyone but Madame had been managing matters, some one would have been punished for this. Our army's defeat by the spy's treachery, and its headlong flight have tarnished the glory that was formerly won; and if this had happened under any one else's management, surely he would have been hanged—no less punishment would have served.' This

mis-informed as to the directions given by the spy regarding the movements of the French; otherwise he was afraid he would be blamed for having entrusted the management of this affair to his wife. Thus was Dupleix's last chance of capturing Fort St. David foiled. Since the last attack on that settlement had been foiled by the arrival of an English fleet, the aspect of affairs had changed with Griffin's squadron in the Bay, and Bouvet not being able to help him actively. He had heard of the despatch of a strong fleet by the English which was expected to reach the Bay

set-back to her ambition did not make the Diarist hope that she would give up interfering in public matters again. He thought she cared little for her husband's anger, but was much alarmed lest he should give the management of affairs to some one else.

Malleson is of the opinion that the French should have advanced against Cuddalore as soon as they observed its walls dismantled and that the fault was not Dupleix's, but that of the men in charge. This attack on Cuddalore was defensive in its nature, as he knew that a large English fleet was coming out with the express object of laying siege to Pondicherry and as he wanted to secure Fort St. David during the absence of Admiral Griffin and thus deprive the English fleet of any base of operations on the coast.

Mr. Dodwell remarks that Orme has a story (p. 91 of his *History of Indostan*—vol. i, (1861)) that Major Lawrence wanted to make the French believe that he did not think Cuddalore tenable and so removed the cannon to Fort St. David in the day, but restored them and the garrison to Cuddalore, with the necessary secrecy, as soon as night came on. Orme got this from a letter of Clive, dated July 19, 1762, and included in Orme MSS.—India I, pp. 137–141, summarised in Hill's *Catalogue of Manuscripts in European Languages* in the Library of the India Office—vol. ii, Part i. The Orme Collection (1916, p. 268)—In this letter Orme gives, among other details, as to how Mr. Floyer and Major Lawrence tricked the French into a useless attack upon Cuddalore. But Mr. Dodwell says that not a gun or man was withdrawn from Cuddalore and the Fort St. David Council had given out that they intended to abandon the town, and that it was likely that, had the Fort itself been attacked in strength, the Cuddalore garrison would have been withdrawn.

The French troops did not march directly south from Pondicherry, but kept inland, and on the evening of the day of the attack were close to the southern part of the English bounds; that was why Lawrence reinforced the garrison of Cuddalore by a party of sepoys and went

at any time. He had lost the final chance of capturing the English settlement and had henceforth to stand purely on the defensive and began to strengthen as much as possible the fortifications of Pondicherry before the expected enemy should appear. Paradis was got from Karikal to Pondicherry to carry out the additional fortifications with energy and expedition. He was appointed Commissary of the troops and held in high honour and granted the cross of a *Chevalier de l' ordre militaire de St. Louis.*

thither in person. The French attempted, shortly after night had fallen, an escalade on the southern side of the town where the wall was low and easily climbed. The English garrison was on the alert and beat back the attackers with great loss. 'The precipitation of their flight prevented the English fire from doing much execution among them.'

According to a letter written by an English officer, Hyde Parker, to the Secretary at the India House and quoted by Mr. Dodwell from the India Office Miscellaneous Letters Received (1749–50, No. 7), the French began firing near the Porto Novo Gate of Cuddalore, where the English had only two companies of soldiers with about eighty or ninety peons and sepoys. They had not even much of ammunition with them as it had been sent to Fort St. David a few days before....... 'But what struck terror into the French was, when the firing was hot at the Porto Novo Gate, our people by some mistake (though a lucky one) began firing all round Cuddalore, which put the French into great confusion, imagining we had all our force at Cuddalore.'

Abdul Rahmān, the Jamadar of the French sepoys, reported to Dupleix that the French troops followed the spy blindly, some of the Europeans were exhausted and others blinded and that the heavy fire of the enemy scattered them on all sides, and that no one would have escaped from such a trap if but fifty men had opened the gates and attacked them. He added to the Diarist:—'Many fights have I seen and heard of; many battles have I fought; but never before have I seen men losing their senses at the sight of the enemy and throwing their arms in such a panic. As for the enemy, never have I seen men lose such a chance, or fear to open their gates for nearly two hours. But they feared us and kept inside. Never have I seen such a thing before!'

M. de Mainville and the other officers who took the field told the Diarist that they disliked Dupleix entrusting state affairs to his wife and accused her of trying to make an end of them by treachery. (Entry for July 1, pp. 91-94 of *Diary*, vol. v.)

Events Preceding the Arrival of Boscawen's Fleet

Meanwhile the restlessness of the Indian powers increased. There arose a rumour reported by the Indian powers that Nāsir Jang was alarmed at his father's place having been given to Qamar-ud-dīn Khān's son;[9] and that Murtazā Alī Khān was preparing to take advantage of the new Nizam's alarm by preparing to seize Arcot; while Chandā Sāhib was reported to have reached

9 (See Irvine's *Later Mughals*, vol. i, p. 263; vol. ii, pp. 104–5, 138 *et seq.*; The *Siyar-ul-Mutakharin* (tr. ed.) vol. iii, pp. 276 *et seq.*; *The Muslim Review*, vol. ii; R. D. Banerjea's *Article on Mir Shihabuddin—Beale—Burgess, etc.*) Qamar-ud-dīn Khān was the son of Muhammad Amīn Khān Chin, the son of Mīr Baha-ud-dīn, the younger son of Ālam Shaikh, who came to India in 1687 and rose to be the Chief Wazir of the Mughal Empire after the defeat and death of the Sayyad Brothers in the Mughal revolution of 1720. Muhammad Amīn Khān died soon after in the early part of 1721; and his son, Qamar-ud-dīn Khān became chief minister in 1724. He continued in the service for the entire reign of Muhammad Shāh, served in the campaign on the first invasion of Ahmad Shāh Abdali and was killed by a cannon ball during the battle of Sirhind (March 1748). Qamar-ud-dīn's eldest son, Intizām-ud-Daula, here referred to (described as the second son by Beale) was appointed to the rank of Second Bakshi on the accession of the Emperor Ahmad Shāh in 1748 and was made Wazir in 1753, after the dismissal of Nawab Safdar Jang. Ghāzī-ud-dīn Khān, Firōz Jang, the father of Nizām-ul-Mulk, was the son of Khwāja Abid, the elder son of Alam Shaik and the elder brother of Mīr Baha-ud-dīn, the father of Muhammad Amīn Khān Chin. Muhammad Amīn Khān Chin was thus first cousin of the father of Nizām-ul-Mulk; and both he and Nizām-ul-Mulk were the leaders of the Turani revolution against the Sayyad Brothers. Under Muhammad Shāh the great Wazirs were for the most part members of the Turani party; and after his death, the Hindustani party gained the upper hand only for a short time when Abul Mansur Khān Safdar Jang of Oudh was appointed Wazir in 1748.

Qamar-ud-dīn Khān's son, Intizām-ud-Daula, was one of the leaders of the court party against Safdar Jang, the Wazir, along with Ghāzī-ud-dīn II, Firoz Jang, the eldest son of Nizām-ul-Mulk who was confirmed in his father's office of Amīr-ul-Umara in 1748. Ghāzī-ud-dīn II was caught in the snares of Maratha intrigue and lured to the Deccan in 1751–52 with the hope of wresting its viceroyship from his younger brother, Salabat Jang; but he was poisoned by one of his step-mothers at Aurangabad. Ghāzī-ud-dīn II's son, Mīr Shihab-ud-dīn, afterwards

the northern bank of the Krishna with a large body of Maratha horse. The news that reached Pondicherry was that Chandā Sāhib had obtained his release, by means of Raja Sahu's wife, from the great Raghuji Bhonsle by promising to pay 2,10,000 rupees and that he had also definitely settled the question of Trichinopoly.[10] It was rumoured that Chandā Sāhib would

to become so notorious, was confirmed as Amīr-ul-Umara after his father's death and created Ghāzī-ud-dīn III, Imad-ul-Mulk. The latter turned against his cousin Intizām-ud-Daula and with Maratha help, superseded him in the Wazirship and blinded and subsequently murdered the Emperor Ahmad Shāh (June, 1754).

Muin-ul-Mulk, *alias* Mīr Mannu, the second son of Qamar-ud-dīn Khān the Wazir, was appointed governor of Lahore and Multan by Muhammad Shāh. He was defeated by Ahmad Shāh Abdali in 1751, forced to cede the Punjab and Sind to him and was confirmed in these two subahs by the Afghan conqueror and ruled over them till his death in 1754. There was no truth in either of the sons of Qamar-ud-dīn Khān being appointed to supersede Nāsir Jang in the Deccan.

10 Chandā Sāhib is said to have been released by the Marathas much earlier, in 1745, according to Cultru. Wilks, probably with the authority of Orme, says that Chandā Sāhib departed from Satara early in 1748 and proceeded slowly to the south, awaiting the communications of his friends. On the banks of the Krishna his help was solicited both by the Poligar of Chitaldrug and the Rani of Bednore; but owing to the jealousy of a Navayat captain of the Bednore forces, Chandā Sāhib took the side of the ruler of Chitaldrug. In the battle that ensued, at Myconda, south of the Tungabhadra, Chandā Sāhib's eldest son, Abid Sāhib, was slain, and he himself was taken prisoner to Bednore. The Rani of that place was desirous of keeping him a prisoner; but her troops and jamadars marched off under the command of their prisoner. Orme seems to continue the story as he says that he received an invitation from the ruler of Chitaldrug to take command against Bednore. In the ensuing battle he obtained a complete victory for his new ally. 3,000 of the enemy's horse after the defeat offered their service to him, as well as 2,500 troops of his own ally. He was thus the head of nearly 6,000 men when he interfered in the Deccan and Carnatic politics. Dodwell thinks that it is presumably his release from his second captivity that is referred to by the Diarist.—Orme, vol. i, p. 121; Wilks, vol. i. (1869), pp. 159–60, (see note 11 below). Both Orme and Wilks are held by Dodwell to have been inaccurate.

reach the Carnatic in August, and Dupleix declared in joy :—' would even sacrifice French blood to procure Chandā Sāhib return, so great is my goodwill.' The Diarist also offered h congratulations to Chandā Sāhib's family, on his release an departure.[11]

Another rumour that the Diarist heard from the vakil oı Alī Naqi Sāhib at Arcot, was that the people belonging to the Emperor had stabbed Nāsir Jang in an interview with him (which was of course wholly unfounded). Dupleix surmised, as soon as he heard the news, that the people of Arcot would take refuge in Pondicherry and so he would get great sums of money, probably by selling the privilege of admission. Imām Sāhib wrote from

11 Chandā Sāhib is held by Cultru to have been released in 1745 without any sort of French intervention. There were some negotiations going on between the Marathas and the Navāyat relations of Chandā Sāhib in the Carnatic even in 1744. He wrote to Dupleix, according to Cultru, that Balaji's Rao's nephew had paid several lakhs on his behalf to Raghuji Bhonsle and also promised to give suitable presents to the Nizam for securing his countenance for his release and departure, and that Raghuji Bhonsle had given him leave of departure. But Chandā Sāhib seems to have continued to remain in Maratha captivity as both the Pondicherry Council and Ranga Pillai bear testimony to the fact of his captivity in 1746 and 47. 'Perhaps the previous release was only conditional and Chandā Sāhib was so sanguine as to write of promises as accomplished facts. Perhaps he only exchanged Raghuji Bhonsle for Balaji Rao as his jailor. In 1745 the Pondicherry Council agreed to lend Chandā Sāhib a lakh of rupees; but it had no funds as its disposal then. After the French victory of 1746. Dupleix and Chandā Sāhib's relatives began to concert measures for his liberation. Even then "Dupleix refused to guarantee the payment of his ransom, but offered to act as the Marathas' agent in its collection; and a few days later he advised Raza Sāhib to assemble all the forces of his family and fall upon Anvar-ud-dīn who was then lying sick at Arcot. He promised to pay the lakh offered in the previous year, as soon as Chandā Sāhib reached the Carnatic."

Chandā Sāhib wanted to send his eldest son. ·Abid Sāhib, to the Nizam, to treat with him for the Carnatic (Diarist's entry for the 24th January, 1747); and if the Nizam was unwilling, Balaji Rao would consent to help Chandā Sāhib with 30,000 horse and the latter should re-establish Hindu rule in the territories seized in recent years by the

Nāsir Jang's camp at Aurangabad that the dead Nizam had left an enormous quantity of treasure and that a lĕtter of congratulation should be written to the new Nizam; and in a few days a *parwana* would be sent by Nāsir Jang for the grant of the jaghirs of Vaḻudāvur and Villiyanallur, together with an order to Nawab Anvar-ud-dīn for the surrender of the jaghir villages. Letters were written to Imām Sāhib and Nāsir Jang requesting a speedy grant of the favour asked for in respect of the proposed jaghir villages. Nawab Anvar-ud-dīn sent a letter of compliment in which he wrote of his confirmation in the subah of Arcot by Nāsir Jang; a similar letter was sent to the English also. But news

Mughals. Thus "the restoration of Trichinopoly to Hindu rule was one of the conditions of Chandā Sāhib's release at the time. If so, it would completely explain Nizām-ul-Mulk supposition." Subsequently, according to the Diarist (entry for July 18, 1747) Dupleix had promised to pay three lakhs of rupees, in the place of the one lakh promised by the Pondicherry Council, one lakh as soon as he should leave Satara, the second lakh when he should reach Cuddappah, and the third when he should reach Arcot.—Presumably, according to Dodwell, Dupleix promised thrice as much as his Council had authorised; and the loan when made was not to pay Chandā Sāhib's ransom, but to pay his troops on the march (Note on p. 125 of the *Diary*, vol. iv.) Chandā Sāhib could not march as the Nizam and Nāsir Jang were then encamped in his way. The failure of Chandā Sāhib to march then was caused partly by the interposition of the Nizam and partly by the failure of Dupleix to furnish the necessary sums—"which was beyond his power at any moment between June 1747 and June 1748." According to Dodwell, Chandā Sāhib did not escape from Maratha custody till the middle of 1748; and the conditions of his release are described in the Diarist's entry for July 14, 1748 (vol. v, p. 97).

'There is much here that is obscure. Whence came the funds for the payment of the ransom? Apparently not from the French who were actually quarrelling with the Nawabs over a loan for their own use. Ranga Pillai mentions diamonds being sent to Chandā Sāhib from Trichinopoly, presumably by his wife; but they are spoken of as though not completing the full sum. Again, how was the Trichinopoly question settled?...... A letter from Chandā Sāhib received some two months later, but which seems to refer to this period, says that his affairs had been settled, thanks to Dupleix's message by Jayaram Pandit, Raghoji's Vakil......" News received at the same time as this letter reported

continued to report that Murtazā Alī Khān was still collecting troops with a view to attack Arcot from which people were sending property and goods to places of safety (entries for July 10 and 11). Three days later news arrived that Chandā Sāhib had crossed the Krishna with 70,000 horse, and Murtazā Alī Khān had made proposals to him, that the latter should receive Trichinopoly and his son Abid Sāhib[12] should get the fort of Gingee and 'the country as it was before it was attached to the Carnatic' and the former should be in possession of Vellore. It was also reported that Chandā Sāhib's elder brother, Muhammad Alī Khān, wished to seize the fort of Arni and the Conjeevaram territory, to demolish the Vishnu and Siva temples at the latter place and build mosques in their sites. The Diarist remarked that these plans were like 'a pot made of parched flour.' Dupleix was angry that he should be denied a share in the spoils and was 'as excited and angry as though everything had been settled.' These were only Murtazā Alī Khān's proposals and the Diarist assured the Governor that Chandā Sāhib would conquer

Chandā Sāhib south of the Krishna with 12,000 horse. Dupleix perhaps hoped that he would move south and drive Boscawen from Pondicherry, and he even asked Raza Sāhib to write to his father about it.......'

Chandā Sāhib did not enter the Carnatic till about a year after this time; and his movements are uncertain during the period. It was now that he should have engaged in wars with Bednore, etc., reported by Orme and Wilks, who however differ from one another. Mr. Dodwell surmises that Chandā Sāhib joined Muzaffar Jang, Governor of Adoni and Bijapur, very shortly after his release in June 1748 and was employed in raising money for his new master in the Subah of Bijapur, out of which arose the Bednore and other affairs—(*Dupleix and Clive*—*pp.* 32–7). It was now that he should have been persuading Muzaffar Jang to embark on the plan of first seizing the Carnatic and afterwards the Deccan.

Dupleix's close attachment to Chandā Sāhib through all vicissitudes is an idea that must be in the light of these taken in a greatly modified form.

12 Wilks says that Abid Sāhib accompanied his father from Satara and fell in the battle of Myconda between the Raja of Chitaldrug and the Rani of Bednore. (Vol. i, pp. 159–60) see note 1 on p. 154.

the whole country of Arcot and Trichinopoly and would win the Nawabship for himself and not be content with the title of a mere faujdar.[13]

Rumours quickly followed that Nāsir Jang intended to march to Golconda, leaving his own troops as well as his father's at Aurangabad and that he had raised 10,000 more horse; while an Arcot letter informed the Diarist of the possibility of the Emperor Ahmad Shāh himself advancing against Golconda and worshipping at the tomb of Aurangzeb, with the object, among others, of securing the immense riches said to have been amassed by the dead Nizam. Murtazā Alī Khān actually began to proceed against Arcot, while Muhammad Alī, Anvar-ud-dīn Khān's son, was ordered to return from Tinnevelly, where he was encamped, to Trichinopoly and to lay up provisions and strengthen the garrisons in Trichinopoly and Madura.

After a few days had passed during which the situation of the English remained unchanged,—except for a reported dispute between the English Governor Floyer and Commodore Griffin, described at length by the Diarist, but regarded by Mr. Dodwell as purely imaginary,—Dupleix made a suggestion, very characteristic of his own diplomatic tortuousness, that the Diarist should write to Imām Sāhib that the latter should send the French Governor presents as if they came from Nāsir Jang and accompany them with a letter of encomium and warm congratulations.[14]

13 The Diarist said: 'Murtazā Alī Khān may have made proposals, but when Chandā Sāhib arrives, he will show what he thinks and tell him to content himself with his fort. He will first give you your share and only then attend to his own business.' When I spoke thus in these soothing terms, he (the Governor) said: 'That is true; it does not matter whether he helps Chandā Sāhib or not. We shall help him. Besides, does he need anyone's help?...... but remind Chandā Sāhib's son that he must remember my share, and arrange for me to receive it.'—*Diary*, vol. v, pp. 127–8.

14 "The Governor said, 'Safdar Alī Khān sent to M. Dumas two cross-hilted daggers......and in consequence he was held in high esteem in Europe. Write now to Imām Sāhib desiring him to send me similar presents as if they came from Nāsir Jang'. I was also ordered

Dupleix even helped the Diarist to take from a book (probably Abbe Guyon's *Histoire des Indes Orientales*, published in 1744) the list of the jewels sent by Safdar Alī Khān to Governor Dumas through Mīr Ghulām Hussain and further required that Imām Sāhib should be urged to obtain and send Nāsir Jang, as *parwana* for the grant of Villiyanallur and Vaḻudāvur.

Again when the English squadron under Boscawen reached Fort St. David with eight ships of the line, and thirteen Company's ships on August 6–7 and when there was some rumour of negotiation between Mahfuz Khān and the English, Dupleix asked the Diarist to write a polite letter to the latter urging him not to help the English.[15]

to desire Imām Sāhib to write a letter as follows: 'As you have overcome your enemies and captured Madras and other towns, meeting everywhere with success, so that you have no rival, as your glory, power and valour shine like the sun, we request you to help the Nawab Anvar-ud-dīn Khān Bahadur and the other Nawabs, should they be troubled by the Marathas or other enemies. Moreover, I have written to Nawab Anvar-ud-dīn Khān of Arcot and the other Nawabs, ordering them to consult with you and act accordingly in all state matters. They will do this. Even the Padshah of these dominions is not so valorous as you...... In token of this we send you a dress of honour, jewels and weapons (as written above) such as the Emperor is wont to send his nobles.' I was also to say that, if he wrote such a letter and did the business, all the expenses involved should be repaid him; and I was to add, 'All Europe has read the letters regarding the help which you have rendered and the respect which you showed to me and to the French nation. If you will do me this favour, your name will shine like the sun throughout Europe, Turkey, Ispahan and other places......" (Diarist's entry for August 1, 1748, pp. 170–2 of vol. v). Comment on the morality of such a course is superfluous, even taking the standards of contemporary diplomatic ethics.—See Abbe Guyon's *History*—(London, 1757), vol. ii, pp. 128–29.

15 The letter was to this effect. 'If you (Mahfuz Khān) join them and they march against Pondicherry, the troops at Madras will advance and waste that part of the country with fire; or if you attack Madras, we will lay waste the country from here to Arcot....... If you refrain from helping them, we will send you rich presents and make you rejoice' (p. 185 of *Diary*, vol. v). The Diarist naively wrote as a sort of comment that Dupleix proposed this letter because he was

Mahfuz Khān was to be impressed with the critical state of Nāsir Jang's affairs and with the great difficulties that would arise if the French should oppose him. Subsequently a letter was written to the French *vakil* at Arcot, of an imaginary victory that the French had gained over the newly arrived English squadron which the latter was to report to the Durbar.

It was to be reported that the English admiral escaped with seven or eight sails to Fort St. David with torn sails and shattered hulls and that, as the English were liars and cowards, they lost half their strength at the outset and the remaining half was nought.[16]

Meanwhile the trouble that Pandari of Vettavalam was giving the Nawab grew acute. He captured Old Gingee and hoisted his flag there, which act enraged Mahfuz Khān very much; he freed the temple of Tirukoilur when it was occupied by one of the Nawab's Amaldars and seized the latter; and the Nawab himself with Mahfuz Khān and other captains had to encamp in the Vettavalam jungles with 2,000 men, in order to cut a way through to his stronghold. The Diarist reported on the 15th of August that the Muhammadans were finding their task very difficult in the jungles and the sound of hot firing was being heard.

There were likewise disturbances in the Trichinopoly country where an attempt was being planned to recover the fort from the hands of the Muhammadans and establish the rule of the son of Kāṭṭu Raja (probably the Poligar of Udaiyārpalaiyam who is still locally called the *Kāṭṭu Raja*). The Maratha invaders were to be helped by the people of Tanjore and Mysore, the Toṇḍaiman

exceedingly alarmed and troubled; he said, 'I have seen what hitherto has happened. So long as the enemy is at a distance, a man may easily boast himself a soldier, but when danger is near, he may turn tail.'

16 Six Dutch ships joined Boscawen at the Cape and accompanied him to Mauritius; then they sailed for Batavia; and thus Boscawen reached India with six ships less. 'On this foundation Dupleix built up a legend, which he sought to spread far and wide, of a severe British defeat at the French Islands.'—Dodwell, p. 28.

and the Maravan;[17] and thus Trichinopoly was to be recovered; it was to be put under the rule of Kāṭṭu Raja's son; while Vriddhāchalam, Srimushnam and other places were to be added to Tanjore, and the territories which were lately conquered from the Muhammadans were to be restored to their former owners.

THE FIRST ACT OF BOSCAWEN

Admiral Boscawen's powerful squadron[18] reached Fort St. David on $\frac{\text{July 26–27}}{\text{August 6–7}}$, 1748; and the news recorded by the Diarist as to its arrival at Fort St. David on August 4, was probably

17 In September 1743, Trichinopoly was captured by the Nizam's forces; and Murari Rao immediately after this quitted the Carnatic with all his Marathas. Pratap Singh of Tanjore maintained a friendly correspondence with the Peishwas, according to the authority of Grant-Duff. In two letters, one dated June 23, 1744 and the other October 21, 1745, written by Anvar-ud-dīn Khān to the English Governor, the Nawab speaks of victories gained by his troops over the Raja of Tanjore, the first won by Mahfuz Khān, and the second won by the Nawab himself assisted by his two sons, Mahfuz Khān and Muhammad Alī and by several petty chiefs including the Zamindar of Kālahasti; but these victories did not lead to anything further than the exaction of a bond from the Tanjore Raja for seven lakhs and of arrears of tribute. (Venkasami Row: *The Tanjore District Manual* (1883), pp. 779–80).

Even in the course of the Nizam's siege of Trichinopoly, the Kallars of the Tanjore District made nightly irruptions into the Mughal camp; and according to the Annual Letter of the Madura Mission to Rome for 1743, the Mughals sent in all directions through the Kallar country strong bodies of cavalry that laid everything waste. The Toṇḍaiman of Pudukkottai, Vijaya Raghunātha Rāya (1730–69), had according to the *Toṇḍaiman Vamśāvali*, the honour of a personal interview with the Nizam and got from him a jaghir. In 1745 the Marathas under Murari Rao again invaded the south, but were driven away after some time from the country round Trichinopoly by its Muhammadan garrison. On these occasions the Kallars gave the invaders great trouble and cut off a large number of Maratha cavalry stragglers who strayed into the kingdoms of Tanjore and Madura.

From 1744 down to 1748 the Madura country was held by officers appointed by Anvar-ud-dīn and Muhammad Ali; the latter was personally in charge of the country, apparently subordinate to his father; and the Records of Madura contain two Persian orders actually issued by him. When Muhammad Alī and Mahfuz Khān went north to assist their

only the report of its having been sighted farther south and of the news of it sent up express from Karikal. Dupleix was told by his wife that the Nawab had written a letter to the English Governor that he could not interfere in the Anglo-French quarrels, and that he might do with the French as he pleased. This was disbelieved by the Diarist because the Nawab, even if he was in great difficulties, would not, on account of his pride, have written

father in the crisis brought on by the liberation of Chandā Sāhib, Madura was left in charge of one Mayana (1748)—Nelson, *The Madura Country, a Manual* (1868), Part III, p. 268.

As regards the Marāvan mentioned by the Diarist, it must mean the ancient Ramnad country, which about 1730 was divided into five parts, besides which the northern was taken by Tanjore. The Sētupati of Ramnad who took the major portion was known by the name of *Periya* Maravan (the Elder Marava) and the Raja of Sivaganga was known as the *Chinna* Maravan; and English writers of the eighteenth century always spoke of the Greater or Lesser Marava Poligar countries. The Sētupati's *Dalavay*, Velliyan Sērvaikkāran, was a man of great energy and ability and got all real power into his own hands; he was very aggressive and made wars on Tanjore and the southern Poligars, interfered in the Carnatic wars and died about 1760. He is probably the Maravan referred to.

18 'When the news of the capture of Madras and the flight of Peyton's squadron reached England, the Company hastened to request more effective succour from the Government. As a result six ships of the line, with store ships, etc., were ordered to fit; at the same time it was resolved to raise twelve independent companies; half by draughts from the regiments stationed in Ireland, half by recruitment in Scotland, by gentlemen commissioned as captains, on condition of raising companies. The recruitment in Scotland did not prove very successful, and the companies had to be completed with rebels, deserters and highwaymen pardoned on condition of enlistment.'—Dodwell, *Dupleix and Clive*, pp. 26-27.

Boscawen, though junior to Griffin in service, was entrusted with the supreme command of this expedition; and the latter was ordered to leave four men-of-war with him, and with the remainder to escort the East India shipping home. The Company proposed a plan of operations for the expedition, that it should reduce Mauritius, Pondicherry and Chandernagore or any other French settlement and dismantle and demolish whatever it could capture. Boscawen set sail in November 1747, reached Mauritius in July, having been joined at the Cape by six Dutch ships. There, not finding a suitable landing place, and being ignorant of such a letter,[19] and also because a piece of secret news like this could not leak out so early. But he did not care to reveal his real thoughts and only answered suitably to Dupleix's wishes and sang to his tune. The Diarist wrote that many of the towns-people went away by stealth; and the appearance of the European quarter made him think that 'the Tamils are the more courageous—the alarm of the former at least makes me think so.' He had however a hope that the English fleet would only pretend to attack Pondicherry, but in reality besiege Madras, and that if the French ships should arrive soon, his town would be safe; while Dupleix would only hug to himself fondly the idea that the

the strength of the enemy, Boscawen, with the advice of a council of war, resolved to sail straight for the Coromandel Coast, as 'although their force was sufficient to reduce the island, yet the attack and the maintenance of it when taken, would not only retard, but might probably disable the armament from undertaking the siege of Pondicherry, which Mr. Boscawen was instructed to consider as the principal object of his destination.' Consequently the fleet left the Island on June 27, and arrived at Fort St. David where Griffin's squadron was. Griffin resigned the command to Boscawen and retired with one ship and two frigates to Trincomali, from whence in January he set sail for England—Orme: vol. i. *pp.* 91–98. The Dutch ships parted company at Mauritius and sailed for Batavia.

The date of Boscawen's arrival at Fort St. David is given as August 8, by Boscawen, and as August 6–7 by the Fort St. David Consultations; and as July 29–August ? by Orme.

Boscawen had exaggerated the French strength in Mauritius. The Dutch ships that accompanied Boscawen, left his squadron; this as already been remarked, gave rise to the report that the French ships which were in the Mauritius harbour had captured five of the English ships and that the English ships had fled at the mere sighting of them. (See *Diary, infra*, pp. 207 and 214). He was further confirmed in this matter by the arrival of a letter from Mahe which informed him of a ship that came there.

19 The Nawab's letter to Fort St. David was not actually received till August 21; and the Diarist's entry was on August 13. He wrote: 'He (Dupleix) can only believe this news if he believes that the towns-people here know what is in our letters.' And then he added 'As I always used to write, he is the man who, if he heard that a bullock had calved, would merely order the calf to be put in the stall.' The blame he attributes wholly to the influence of Madame Dupleix.

English had given up all hopes of assistance from the Nawab. When three English ships sailed close in-shore to Pondicherry, Dupleix got alarmed, assembled all the Europeans on the sea-face and had the cannon ready. When he ordered the toll-gate people not to allow anyone to leave the town, it caused great inconvenience and not a little alarm to the Indian inhabitants. On August 20, European and Muhammadan troops and 300 sepoys under Abdul Rahmān marched to Ariyānkuppam and Aḻiṣapākkam. The next day an English force consisting of the Carnatic people and 200 European troopers came up and attacked the French troops which retreated north of the Chunnāmbāru, while the English advanced in great force on the fort of Ariyānkuppam; while news also came that a ship and a sloop were sailing to Pondicherry from Fort St. David. On the same day a letter arrived from the French *vakil* Subbayyan who was staying in Mahfuz Khān's camp at Gingee to the effect that Nawab Anvar-ud-dīn was informed by the English *vakil* at Arcot that the English proposed to march against Pondicherry on August 19, and to capture Madras as well; and it was also requested that the Nawab should render them all assistance according to the *parwana* of Nāsir Jang, to which the Nawab was said to have replied that he was unable to help them at present. These things were done without the knowledge of Mahfuz Khān who was inclined towards the French; while Muhammad Alī Khān who was inclined towards the English was still at Trichinopoly.

The next day, August 22, thirteen or fourteen English ships anchored off Vīrāmpattanam; and thus the number of English ships, great and small, which had arrived near Pondicherry was twenty-two. Both in the morning and in the afternoon the English attacked the French camp, which on three occasions threw back the assaulters. The Diarist was of the opinion that if only the Europeans and the sepoys at Ariyānkuppam had gone to their assistance, they would have driven the English attackers back into Fort St. David. But no assistance or provision was sent to them; and they retired from Muttirusa Pillai's Choultry across the river to Ariyānkuppam Fort, being pursued by the English who then occupied the choultry.[20] And the French were at Ariyānkuppam. Eleven valuable days were spent by the English in the operations at Ariyānkuppam, 'in spite of the fact that there was no particular need to capture it at all.' And five more days were wasted in putting the fort into some sort of defence.

Meanwhile the situation in Pondicherry tended to grow worse. An attack from the ships on the night of the 22nd was feared. The Governor sent his wife and family to the Mission Church near the Diarist's house and covered its roof with a large quantity

20 Vīrāmpattanam is a small village about four miles south of Pondicherry to the east of Ariyānkuppam where there was a small fort. The river of Ariyānkuppam ran close to the fort. M. Paradis, who had come from Karikal, had completed the defences of Ariyānkuppam and made it the real outwork of Pondicherry against the English who were entirely unacquainted with the additions that he had made to its strength.

M. Julian Vinson gives (in his *Les Frances dans L'Inde;* p. 169 note) from *La Relation du Siege de Pondicherry* (Brussels, 1766) information regarding this fort.

'Le Fort d'Ariancoupam est une espēce de pātē ā cinq faces non flanquées constuit autrefois pour garantir des incursions des Mores une Aldēe ou village qui porte son nom. Il est entourē d'un fossé avec une bermé á laquelle on avoit joint depuis peu un chemin couvert, avec son glacis; il a au Nord une rivierē qui porte son nom ā une portēe de carabine, ā l'est le village touchant au glacis, au sud la riviére de Chounambard á mille toises de distance, et a l'ouest une campagne assez de-couverte. M. le Prévót de la Touche, capitaine, commandoit dans ce Fortin, et avoit sous lui Mm. Law et la Borderie, avec 40 soldats europēens et quelques sipays Il y avoit onze piéces de canon de fer de 8 et 6 livres de balles et quelques mortiers ā grenades.'

The English army as it marched out of Fort St. David on August 19, comprised 1,200 soldiers, 800 marines, 750 of the Company's foot, 1,000 seamen who had been taught the manual exercise and 120 Dutch allies from Negapatam, besides some artillery men, thus making in all 4,000 Europeans with about 2,000 native foot. The Pondicherry garrison, all told, consisted of but 1,800 Europeans and Topasses, and 3,000 sepoys. The English enjoyed a certain superiority in numbers; but their engineers were very deficient in practical knowledge and besides wanting in resolution. (*Orme MSS., India*—vol. i, pp. 111-120—Paper written by Clive in 1762 at Orme's request, in which he remarks on the ignorance of the English officers and soldiers in regard to the art of war, an opinion

of wet cotton. Each house was ordered to have a ready supply of at least 30 pots of water; and a large guard was set to watch the town. A suggestion was made by Dupleix that Chandā Sāhib's son should be asked to write to the English Governor at Fort St. David that the English should desist from attacking Pondicherry where himself and Nawab Dōst Alī Khān's family were living.[21] Dupleix wanted the Diarist to send the poor people to the Muhammadan villages and set fire to the huts. The Indian merchants wanted permission to send away their children; and there was great panic among the Tamils and uneducated Europeans. 'God knows what fear reigns in the town; man can neither measure, nor describe it.' This was on the eve of the English launching the attack on the Ariyānkuppam Fort, after bringing up their men and provisions to Muttirusa Pillai's Choultry, while the French occupied the whole bank of the northern side of the Ariyānkuppam River, and mounted cannon on the mud batteries near it.

endorsed by Orme.—p. 268. *Catalogue of the Orme Collection of Manuscripts*, vol. ii, part i, by S. C. Hill). Malleson says (p. 217) that his account of the fortifications of Pondicherry and of the siege operations was taken from the journal of an English officer present at the siege, reprinted in the *Asiatic Annual Register* for 1802.

The work from which Vinson quoted says that in the actions of August 22, the French sepoys were wavering under the English attack and would have been cut to pieces but for a body of horse and foot sent forward by La Tour to cover their retreat; and it sets the English losses at 100 sepoys. According to Dupleix writing to the Company, on the English side none but sepoys were engaged in this fight. According to Boscawen the French merely made a show of resistance at an entrenchment they had thrown up and immediately abandoned it on the English advance). (Dodwell, p. 234 of *Diary*, vol. ii, note). Abdul Rahmān however is said by the Diarist to have told Dupleix that, if he were given 500 sepoys, he would drive the English back into Fort St. David.

21 This letter was apparently written, though Chandā Sāhib's writer who penned it, declared that the English might reply thus:—'They may reply that we did nothing to the French for capturing Madras when Nawab Dōst Alī Khān's son was there, and it is the same now; or else they may tell us to do what we like......or again they may say that if we fear, we should leave the town...... They well believe we have written out of fear.' (p. 232 of the *Diary*, vol. v.)

CHAPTER VIII

THE CLOSE OF THE FIRST WAR AND THE DESCENT OF CHANDA SAHIB ON THE SCENE

The English Attack on Ariyankuppam

While the situation at Pondicherry was growing worse, news arrived that Chandā Sāhib had reached Sāvanūr and Bankāpūr with a large body of Maratha horse; and immediately Dupleix wanted that the Diarist should write to him urging him to march to the relief of Pondicherry. This made the Diarist think that the French horse and foot on the Pondicherry side of Ariyānkuppam River should have been in great danger, as otherwise the Governor 'should never have spoken as if already in the enemy's clutches' (24th August, 1748). As to the English attack on Ariyānkuppam Fort, its works, according to Orme, were sufficient to protect the place from a sudden onset,—being 'a triangle regularly fortified with three cavalier, a deep dry ditch full of pitfalls, and a covered way,'—the officer commanding their troops fell, on which the latter fled, being pursued for some distance by Shaikh Hasan Alī Khān.[1] Major Goodere, the commanding officer who was killed, was the most experienced officer among the King's troops, 'whose loss left Boscawen with no one

1 'Ranga Pillai's account of the attack on Ariyānkuppam is exceedingly disjointed. However it makes it clear that the attack did not only consist of the attempt to storm the Fort, which is all that Orme mentions. That attack was made at day-break by 700 men and failed. Here the greater part of the English loss was incurred. Then followed an attempt 'to gain a lodgment in the village almost adjoining it and there raise a bomb-battery.' This failed because the coolies with the entrenching tools ran away and left the English exposed to the fire of the French batteries on the other side of the river. It was then resolved to retire towards the ships and land cannon and material for a regular siege.' Dodwell's *note* on the Diarist's account—See foot-note on p. 252 of the English Translation of the *Diary*, vol. v. See map of Pondicherry showing the environing redoubts and forts—in the pocket of Garstin's *Manual of the South Arcot District* (1878).

competent to conduct the siege.' This repulse greatly affected the spirits of the English; Boscawen, however, persisted in reducing the fort, landed disciplined soldiers and eight pieces of battering cannon from his ships, while the French erected a battery of heavy cannon on the opposite side of the river, 'to obstruct and enfilade the approaches to the fort.' The English erected a battery in the plain on the south side of the river; but 'such was their neglect in reconnoitring, or their want of skill in their art that, when at day-break they opened the battery, most of the guns were found to be intercepted from the sight of the enemy's by a thick wood.'[2] Not that the French fire was effective at all. Ranga Pillai complained that the French had only small cannon and their fire could not reach the enemy, while their European horse under M. D'Auteuil were afraid of the English fire and had retired within the English bounds. Thus when the English erected another battery and, for greater security, threw up before it an entrenchment, even then the fire on either side did little execution on the other. On the twenty-eighth, the fire of the French from their batteries at the river and at Ariyānkuppam made the enemy retreat from their batteries and breast-works. Two days later (*i.e.*, on the thirtieth) a body of troops including a number of the volunteer company and horse captured the English battery near the church of Ariyānkuppam and took several of the enemy prisoners including Major Stringer Lawrence, the Major of Fort St. David.[3] But they had to retreat to the north side of the river, being pursued by a large body of the enemy.[4] One of the English shots struck a barrel of powder

2 Orme, vol. i, p. 100; and also Boscawen's Letter to Corbet, quoted by Dodwell in p. 268—note—of *Diary*, vol. v.

3 'Major Lawrence commanded this day in the entrenchment and rather than participate of the ignominy of taking flight with the troops, remained there with two or three officers; he was disarmed and obliged to surrender himself prisoner to a French trooper, who knowing, it is probable, the value of his prize, immediately hurried him away by the side of his horse to Ariancopang.'—Orme.

4 After the Engineers with Boscawen had failed to construct an effective battery, the Artillery officers were allowed to attempt it and

and blew up the French battery, in the course of the same day and nearly a hundred men were killed by the explosion.[5] This created a panic; and 'as the enemy's fire reached our people this side of the river and the Ariyānkuppam batteries, the people this side signalled those at the Ariyānkuppam batteries to retreat.' Then the French set fire to the powder, shot, shell and planks and rejoined the main army on the north side of the river, and thereupon the English surrounded Ariyānkuppam, took possession of it and planted two flags there. All the French withdrew to the bound-hedge of Pondicherry; Chandā Sāhib's wife and others prepared to depart from Pondicherry; the Diarist wrote: "Hitherto I did not think there was any danger; but now it seems otherwise." Razā Sāhib persuaded the Governor to let him go out of the town.

The English Siege of Pondicherry

Boscawen tried to repair the fort of Ariyānkuppam from 31st August to 5th September, while the French troops remained at the bound-hedge without advancing or doing anything. On the 6th, the English troops marched to the bound-hedge and the French, unable to endure their fire, fled to the gates of Pondicherry and set fire in their flight to the bound-hedge, near which the English had encamped. The town[6] was placed in a condition of

succeeded in opening so galling a fire that this attack was made by the French. Bruce and Lawrence were taken when the English advance-guard gave way on the first assault. Among the Orme Manuscripts catalogued by Hill (*The Orme Collection*) is an account of the Siege of Pondicherry by Lord Clive written in 1762 at Orme's request. (See p. 268). Clive herein remarks on the ignorance of English officers and soldiers at this time in regard to the art of war, an opinion endorsed by Orme. In this account Clive attributed the capture of Lawrence to a panic among the sea-men who formed part of the guard.

5 The destruction of the battery was immediately followed by a bombardment of the fort with shell; and it blew up in the afternoon.

6 The town within its walls extended about a mile from north to south and about 1,100 yards from east to west. It was fortified on the three land-sides with a wall and a rampart, flanked by eleven bastions;

siege, and there being a large quantity of gunpowder, guns and cannon, all were alarmed. Ranga Pillai wailed that the Governor had dishonoured himself by listening to his wife's advice in everything. As if to increase the demoralization, the Governor ordered the pulling down of the Vedapuri Iswaran Temple which lay close beside the Jesuit Church, at the instigation of the Jesuits and ostensibly for military reasons; but when he sent men to pull down a mosque that stood to the west of the Capuchin Church, Abdur Rahmān, the leader of the Jamadars, protested and the order had to be revoked. The impression among the

and there were two half-bastions at the north and south extremities nearest the sea. These were supplemented by a ditch and an imperfect glacis. The eastern side was defended by several low batteries, cannon mounted on which could command the roads. The citadel or fort was too small to make a prolonged defence. 'The greatest part of the ground lying round the town was inclosed, at a distance of a mile from the walls, by a hedge of large aloes and other thorny plants peculiar to the country, intermixed with great numbers of cocoanut and palm trees, which altogether formed a defence impenetrable to cavalry, and of very difficult passage to infantry; this inclosure began at the north close by the sea-shore and continued five miles and a half, describing a large segment of a semi-circle, until it joined the river of Ariāncopang to the south, at about a mile and a half from the seashore, and in this part the course of the river served to complete the line of defence. There were five roads leading from the town into the adjacent country and at each of the openings in the hedge was built a redoubt mounted with cannon. It is probable that the hedge, at the same time that it was intended to be a defence against sudden incursions, marked the limits of the territory conceded by the prince of the country to the French, when they first established themselves at Pondicherry; and hence obtained the name of Bound-hedge' (Orme, vol. i, p. 101). There was a similar bound-hedge round old Black Town in Madras. The redoubts were named respectively Ariyānkuppam, Villianore, Vaḻudāvur and Madras and North. The English forces first took possession of Oḻukkarai, which was about two miles to the south-west of the town and other places and from thence marched to the bound-hedge, the north-western redoubt of which they attacked; and the French, unable to endure the fire, fled to the gates and set fire to the bound-hedge. They might have defended this and other redoubts easily; but they withdrew the garrisons in all the other redoubts.

people was that justice could not be had, Christians were being unduly favoured and wanton insults were offered to the Hindu idols. It was certainly extremely impolitic on the part of the Governor to have alienated the Hindus by these acts, merely to please his wife and the Capuchins.[7]

The English opened a preliminary fire on the 9th, which was done from the sea with a view to divert the attention of the French from the English working parties ashore. The shells, however, did little injury to life and soon the Tamils came to be accustomed to them. On the 11th of September, Paradis marched with all the European and Muhammadan horse, about eight to nine hundred in all, and two cannon, to destroy the batteries that the English were erecting; but the latter lay hid in a trench and opened a sudden and devastating fire when the enemy drew near them. M. Paradis was mortally wounded in the head, while about a hundred were killed and wounded on the French side. The Diarist says that his account of this engagement was based on the information given to him by a European officer who was in the fight.[8] For some days more the English approaches were

The English determined to attack the town on the north-western side and to facilitate communication between the fleet and the camp, their ships were stationed to the north of the town. On the 10th of September, the English troops opened ground. After Paradis' engagement, the English approaches were continued very slowly, 'from a want of experience in such operations.'

7 The demolition of the temple was attended by wanton breaking and insulting of images ordered by the priests of St. Paul's Church and effected by the *Caffres* and other soldiers. The Diarist thus writes: I think the Governor believes that by destroying the temple he has done what no Governor has been able to do for the last fifty years; for even when the King of France wrote thrice to M. Lenoir, himself as powerful as a king, the latter declared it impossible, because all the Tamil inhabitants would have left Pondicherry in a body.' P. 311 of the *Diary*, vol. v. Paradis had converted a temple at Karikal into a fort, which the Raja of Tanjore had made a complaint of.

8 It was in this engagement that Clive distinguished himself with much gallantry in defence of the advanced trench. Clive gave a lively account of this affair in a letter to Orme, regarding the siege of

continued, but 'very slowly, from a want of experience in such operations.' The havoc effected by the spies and peons of Madame Dupleix is related by the Diarist as contributing to the prevailing demoralization and depression in his usual sentimental strain.[9]

The English approaches were gradually advanced to within 800 yards of the walls, marked by skirmishes and small engagements; while news filtered that Boscawen had written to Fort St. David that, as the rains were approaching, he would take the ships to winter at Trincomali or at the Nicobars and that he would renew his attack next January, and meanwhile Ariyānkuppam could be garrisoned with about a thousand men. It was also falsely rumoured that Mr. Floyer, the Governor of Fort St. David, was demanding the return of his men and said to have reproached Rear-Admiral Boscawen with having lost many men before the Ariyānkuppam Fort and with having been able to capture it only when the French had abandoned it.

On the 26th of September, there was a sharp fight near the bound-hedge on the north side between a body of English troops outside and about half the number of French sepoys inside. The English lost a large number of men and were forced to withdraw to their camp in spite of reinforcements having come to them.[10] Firing continued through the next few days, and they surmised

Pondicherry, previously quoted; in this account Clive says that, when Paradis was wounded, the main body withdrew without attacking; but the smaller party did not see this and came right up to the advanced trench when the captain on the English side was killed and two out of their three platoons fled; but Clive's platoon stood fast and drove the enemy back.

9 'But the people fear these English shells less than Madame Dupleix, who accuses them falsely and gets them punished and vexes them more than can be written'. pp. 347-8 of vol. v. of the *Diary*.

10 The Diarist estimates that about 1,500 Europeans should have been sent back to Fort St. David by the English from the day of the fight at Ariyānkuppam till now, besides 400 or 500 Carnatic and Muhammadan sepoys. The English shells did very little damage and the French were bound, according to the stars, to win from the beginning of the month *Arpisi* (October-November).

that Boscawen should have resolved to expend all his ammunition 'like a man breaking his pot.' He had come with 22 ships, 7,000 Europeans and cannon, muskets, mortar and other equipment, had been fighting for 40 days (on September 29, 1748) and had been entangled within the bound-hedge for 24 days, 'building his battery and unable to find a means of escape, although hopeless of victory.'[11] The approach of the monsoon was feared by the English, who had not chosen a good camping ground near the beach to the east where they could easily have landed their men and munitions, but one to the west where it was difficult to get their stores and where the rains would make the swamps and water-courses impassable.[12] On the night of the 2nd of October, the French were fortunate enough to capture two heavy English guns (24-pounders) which were being landed from the ships. Boscawen, finding the season far advanced, endeavoured to annoy the French as much as possible by his fire and thereby reduce them to the

11 The heavy batteries of the English did not open fire till September 20, and even then the French fire was and remained superior. The attack culminated in a fierce cannonade from both sea and land on October 8; but as this failed to produce any perceptible effect, as the monsoon rains were at hand and sickness was prevalent in the English camp, Boscawen embarked his stores on October 13, and withdrew two days later. At the beginning of the siege he had more than 3,600 Europeans, of whom close on a third had either died or been disabled.... On the whole, the English shells, though they produced at first much fear, did not do much damage or produce a panic owing to their slow movement which enabled people to steer clear of them. Their round shot was much more destructive. 'On the whole the principal feature of Boscawen's bombardment would appear to be its insufficiency; he needed many more and much larger guns to accomplish what he aimed at.' The area of the town and the surrounding tract was too great for the shells to do much damage. Frequently the Diarist complained that the sepoys under Madame Dupleix wasted their grenades and shot in aimless firing.

12 'After much hard labour the trenches were advanced within 800 yards of the walls, when it was found impossible to carry them on any nearer; for a large morass extended itself before this part of the

necessity of surrendering. On October 7th, the English ships arranged themselves in two lines in five fathoms of water and began a heavy fire upon the fort and town, which ranged as far as the Vaḻudāvur gate in the west and even further, while from the landside the firing was equally heavy. The next day the English ships remained anchored abreast of the town and fort; the Admiral's ship hoisted the red flag of action and poured an incessant fire from sunrise to sunset, nearly 32,000 shot and 300 shells, while from the western battery additional shot and shell poured on. 'The fire of the ships reached even the bound-hedge on the west and the fire of the western battery reached the shore on the east.' After a time the French ceased their counter-fire, and in the evening the fleet ceased its hail of shot. On the 9th the French opened fire from their new earth-works and one English battery was destroyed. The French fire was regarded by the Diarist to have been superior to that of the English which was certainly quite insufficient for the purpose it had in view. On the 13th, all the ships except that of the Admiral and a bomb-ketch set sail from before the town and anchored off Kottakuppam (a little to the north) taking all the stores and guns of the camp west of Pondicherry. Dupleix ordered Abdul Rahmān to attack the English battery and destroy and seize all that could be found there but without effect. On the morning of the fifteenth, the enemy fired parting shots against the bastions and walls. At midnight on that day they set fire to their entrenchments, and having carried their heavy stores to the ships, withdrew to the tents pitched on the high ground to the west of the bound-hedge, abandoning even this on the night of the sixteenth. A party tried to pursue the troops that retreated to Fort St. David, but had to retreat owing to the English in the fort at Ariyānkuppam opening fire. 'From Friday, September 6, when the French forced the

town, and the French had preserved a back-water, with which they overflowed not only the morass, but likewise all the ground lying between the trenches and the foot of the glacis.' (Orme—vol. i, p. 103).

bound-hedge, down to October 15, the English fired some days 1,000, 800, 700, 600, 500, 300, 200 rounds, but never less than 100. Never a day passed without the sound of shot and shell.'[13]

The effect of the retreat of the English was beneficial to the French position in the Carnatic and added not a little to the general belief in Dupleix's 'good fortune.' The Diarist generally attributed Dupleix's success more to his good fortune than 'to the prudence and foresight of his measures'.

Dupleix and Chanda Sahib's Family

Dupleix's attitude to Chandā Sāhib at the beginning of Boscawen's siege was friendly enough, as his arrival in the Carnatic was expected very soon. Anvar-ud-dīn's troops encamped near Vettavalam were not strong enough to suppress its rebellious *killedar.* The English having got over Nāsir Jang to their side and got from him *sanads* to Nawab Anvar-ud-dīn, the *killedars* and others that they should help them, found that no one replied favourably; the Nawab himself, as stated in the previous part, was said to have replied, in response to the English request for help, that he was unable to help them just at present. Dupleix treated Chandā Sāhib's wife with scant respect when she left Pondicherry and would not allow Razā Sāhib to go away. Mahfuz Khān who was inclined towards the French, experienced great trouble at the hands of Periya Ayya, the Pandari of Vettavalam, who confessed before his execution that he resisted the Nawab's authority because Mīr Asad had given him money to kill the Nawab. Moreover the poligars of the Trichinopoly country were creating havoc; hence Mahfuz Khān, though he was approached

13 *The Relation du siege* gives the figures as follows:—English shot 40,000 from both batteries and ships; 1,100 shells from the bomb. Ketch; 4,000 shells from the land-mortar. French shot 24,000, shells 2,000. (*Collection Historique*, p. 342, quoted by Dodwell.) Dupleix wanted the Diarist to arrange a drama about the victories of the French and for the singing of all events that had happened from the beginning of the war up to now,—an illustration of his weakness for show and flattery.

by the English for help, would not help them, but stayed on at Gingee. News came from Anvar-ud-dīn's court that the French would be well advised to make peace with the English by the mediation of the Nawab. It said, 'Mahfuz Khān and the other Muhammadans fear the French, but see that the English are strong, and we are uncertain of the issue, though they know it cannot be long deferred.'[14] In these circumstances it will be wise to write promptly to Husain Sāhib (Tahir) 'as the Nawab always does as he advises.'[15] There was also the talk of Murtazā Alī Khān of Vellore, who was then afraid of an attack from his brother Razā Alī Khān, sending help to the French, but the matter was never seriously thought of. All this made Dupleix very impatient of the Nawab and his indecisive policy, as well as of the delay in the expected arrival of Chandā Sāhib. 'The effects of this delay are evident in the treatment which Dupleix accorded to the Navait families resident in Pondicherry.' Annoyed at their inability to give him financial aid, he almost resolved to break with them altogether, and when he found them suffering from fear and apprehension during the siege, 'he let them go elsewhere, detaining only Chandā Sāhib's son as a hostage.' Thus, as Prof. Dodwell points out, 'the traditional view of the close and constant friendship between Dupleix and the Navaits left much out of account.'[16]

14 From the letter of the French *vakil* at Arcot, quoted by the Diarist in his entry for October 6, 1748.

15 A letter quoted by the Diarist said that the English had promised Mahfuz Khān twelve lakhs of rupees if he would join them, raise a battery and encamp at the Villiyanallur gate with his army and that he replied that he would neither help the English nor befriend the French lest he should make both his enemies and so he would not trust their promises. Finally he agreed to help them with 1,500 horse and 3,000 sepoys, while common powder and shots would be supplied to him by the English (pp. 397–9 of the *Diary*, vol. v.)

16 'Dupleix's policy was not nearly so consistent or far-reaching as has been alleged. He was indeed prepared so early as 1745 to lend money in order to assist Chandā Sāhib to become the Nawab. It was a policy in which not only he and his Council, but the Company also saw

The raising of the siege of Pondicherry by Boscawen left Dupleix still apprehensive of the safety of the road to Madras on which he carefully posted peons to guard the various stages. Dupleix now became anxious to regain the confidence of Chandā Sāhib which might have been lost by his harsh attitude towards his family during the siege and asked the Diarist to write to him that 'your wife, Alī Dōst Khān's wife and others went away against my will, by reason of the troubles; so in order to get them back I stopped your son, using my loan to you as a pretext, merely in order to prevent his departure.' Care was to be taken to produce a good impression on Chandā Sāhib and to make him come to Pondicherry in joy. Complimentary letters were also written to Murtazā Alī Khān of Vellore, to Nāsir Jang and Imām Sāhib.

Anvar-ud-dīn Khān who had meanwhile gone to Trichinopoly to join his son Muhammad Alī, resolved to attack Tanjore as its

considerable advantages. But those advantages were nothing more than might reasonably be asked by a trading company from a favourable Nawab. They did not include the predominant share in the power of the government, which fell to the French in the Carnatic and the English in Bengal, not in consequence of any deep-laid plan, but simply because the Nawabs were unable, of their own power, to maintain themselves in their respective provinces. In the Carnatic the Moghul organization seems never to have recovered from the effects of the great Maratha raid in 1740-41. The years intervening between that event and 1748 had brought with them murders and anarchy. The death of the Nizām at once released the disruptive forces which had still been held in check by the terror of his name. Murtazā Alī........began at once to collect troops, to form designs against Anvar-ud-dīn at Arcot and possibly to enter into negotiations with Chandā Sāhib (as pointed out in the previous section). Another movement indicative of the growing unrest was that of the Hindu principalities of the South—Tanjore and Mysore—who are reported to have planned the restoration of Hindu rule at Trichinopoly. And all this, daily reported to Dupleix, bred in him contempt for the statecraft of these princes and nobles, distrust of their good faith and a dim consciousness of the results that might be expected from active and vigorous intervention.' See pp. xvii-xviii of Dodwell's *Introduction*, vol. v.

tribute had been withheld and proceeded two stages on his way with a force of over 7,000 men. The Toṇḍaiman of Pudukottah resolved to join the Nawab, while Muhammad Alī was to march against the Tamil *poligars* of the south. Anvar-ud-dīn was greatly suffering from want of money, while the *killedars* and *jamadars* were giving much trouble. Dupleix thought that it was now time for Murtazā Alī Khān to seize the country of Arcot. He was anxious to learn the terms on which Abdul Jalīl, one of the Nawab's officers, helped the English. There was an exchange of prisoners with the English; and a letter of Boscawen connected with this matter was exaggerated and twisted into an acrimonious retort upon Dupleix.[17]

News was received at Pondicherry on November 20, that peace had been made in Europe between the English and the French and letters to this effect had been received by the English at Tellicherry where the sepoys were disbanded and that ambassadors from both sides had met to treat. A letter was received from Rear-Admiral Boscawen that there was to be a suspension of arms for six months from the date of publishing the ambassadors' order in any place; but Dupleix himself had received no confirmation of this news.

The Descent of Chanda Sahib and Muzaffar Jang

From November 24, 1748, to June 26, 1749, there is a gap in the *Diary,* and hence we do not have the interesting details of the concluding negotiations between Dupleix and Chandā Sāhib. The information given in the French Company's *Memoir* which was prepared later against Dupleix, was that, towards the end of February 1749, an embassy from Chandā Sāhib was received at Pondicherry and the arrangement that was arrived at was that Dupleix promised the assistance of a body of Europeans to place Chandā Sāhib on the *masnad* of Arcot and the latter should at once take into his pay 2,000 French sepoys and grant them the

17 Pp. 49–50 of vol. vi of the *Diary*.

area of Villiyanallur as *jaghir* which they had long been asking from Nāsir Jang in exchange for Madras.[18] We saw that our authorities like Cultru, Orme and Wilks are not definite as to the exact date of Chandā Sāhib's release from the hands of the Marathas; and Orme and Wilks give us an account of his participation in the wars between the Poligar of Chitaldrug and the Rani of Bednore, in which he lost his eldest son Abid Sāhib. Cultru's theory that he was released from captivity in 1745 without any sort of French intervention is not borne out by the evidence of the Pondicherry Council and Ranga Pillai as to the fact of his captivity in 1746 and 1747. Chandā Sāhib did not enter the Carnatic till about a year after this time (*i.e.* when he was released from Maratha captivity in June 1748); and during this period, he should have engaged in his wars with Bednore, Chitaldrug, etc. reported by Orme and Wilks who however differ from each other. Mr. Dodwell thinks that, shortly after his release, Chandā Sāhib joined Muzaffar Jang, the governor of Adoni and Bijapur, and was employed in raising money for his new master in the *subah* of Bijapur out of which arose the Bednore and other affairs.[19] Chandā Sāhib's attempts to bring the Raja of Bednore into subjection to Muzaffar Jang was perhaps animated by 'the vague hope of doing there what he had almost accomplished at Trichinopoly (in 1736–40), and establishing himself in an independent position.'

Hearing of the rumours of Chandā Sāhib's approaching descent into the Carnatic, Nawab Anvar-ud-dīn Khān sent for the French *vakil* at Arcot and told him to write to Pondicherry that his rival's son who was preparing to join his father should not be allowed to remain at Pondicherry and said that he himself would be writing to Dupleix about it.[20] And as a usual consequence, the merchants at Arcot were removing their goods and

18 Dodwell's *Introduction* to vol. vi of the *Diary*, p. v.

19 For the different versions as to these matters, see my note on pp. 154–7, of the *Journal of Indian History*, vol. viii, part ii, wherein all the available authorities are cited.

20 Diarist's entry for June 28, 1749.

valuables for the sake of safety to Vellore, Arni and elsewhere. Anvar-ud-dīn's letter also informed the French that Nāsir Jang was marching with Sayyad Lashkar Khān, 10,000 horse, cannon and a powerful army and that Chandā Sāhib, having lost his able son, Abid Sāhib, had become, as it were, a lame man.[21]

Anvar-ud-dīn returned to Arcot through Gingee; he sent his family for safety to Trichinopoly fort, settled all arrears of pay due to his sepoys and horsemen and set out in a few days with Mahfuz Khān, the Diwan, Sampāti Rao and Husain Sāhib Tahir, *killedar* of Amburgadh and encamped at Ranipet. While making these preparations, he endeavoured at the same time to keep the favour of Muzaffar Jang by writing to him a conciliatory letter.[22] News reached Pondicherry on July 3, 1749, that Muzaffar Jang, having settled the Bednore affair, himself and Chandā Sāhib were descending through Anantapur District. It was planned by Chandā Sāhib that he would settle with Hirāsat Khān, the *killedar* of Arcot and his own son-in-law for five lakhs of rupees, with Murtazā Alī Khān of Vellore for 10 lakhs and with Mīr Asad Khān Sāhib and other *killedars* for 25 lakhs;[23] and these settlements would be effected as soon as he should reach Satgadh,

21 'I hear that his second son, who lives at Pondicherry, is collecting forces to join his father. No one will hinder him, so permit him to go. You will be blamed if you keep him with you. Therefore on sight of this letter send him out. I write thus by reason of our friendship. On no account permit him to remain with you.'—Quoted by the Diarist, in p. 102 of vol. vi.

22 The letter according to the Diarist ran thus:—'I make no difference between you and Nāsir Jang; when Nāsir Jang was master, I folded my arms, obeyed his orders and paid him tribute; but as you have succeeded Nāsir Jang, the accounts and money shall be rendered to you instead of him, and I will obey your orders, and be responsible for the revenues. For the present I have resolved to send you five lakhs of rupees.' A different version of the letter, in which the aged Nawab declared that he did not have the heart to fight with the grandson of his old friend, Nawab Asaf Jah, is given in Burhan-ud-dīn's *Tuzuk-i-Wālājāhi* (Book I translated by Md. Husain Nainar, p. 112).

23 *Vide* the letter of Chandā Sāhib to his son Razā Sāhib, quoted by the Diarist in his entry for July 3, 1749. The great power to which

Vellore and Arcot. Panic increased at Arcot from which the *subah's* money-lenders like Kasi Das Bukkansi departed. It was declared by Razā Sāhib that Muzaffar Jang had been invested by Ahmad Shāh Pādshāh with a *parwana* for the six *subahs* of the Deccan and that he had actually received the *sanad* and dress of honour about the middle of June, and that in turn, Chandā Sāhib, who joined Muzaffar Jang a few days later with about six to seven thousand horse, had been granted a *sanad* as Nawab of Arcot, Gingee, Tanjore, Trichinopoly and Madura with all their dependent territories and forts, supplemented by a new title and a new *jaghir* of three taluks. Both had already set out for Arcot with fourteen thousand horsemen and fourteen or fifteen thousand foot; and Chandā Sāhib desired Razā Sāhib to join him at the foot of the passes (in the Eastern Ghats) with the Mussalman *jamadars*, Abdur Rahmān and others, and with a body of 2,000 sepoys and 2,000 soldiers, and a large quantity of cannon, mortars, shell, shot, etc.[24] Muzaffar Jang sent Dupleix a dress of honour and a letter, which the latter prepared to receive with all the pomp and grandeur with which he used to receive the Nizam's presents. The Diarist makes mention in another place of 4,000 sepoys besides 2,000 soldiers marching along with Razā Sāhib. Only 300 European volunteers under d'Auteuil accompanied Razā Sāhib. The impression that prevailed was

the Navaits had attained in the Carnatic under the dynasty of Sādat-ullah, persisted even under Anvar-ud-dīn and in spite of his attempts to suppress them. Burhan-ud-dīn, quoted above, protagonist of Anvar-ud-dīn's family, portrays in vigorous language in various places, the turbulence, insincerity and secret hostility of the Navait leaders, which formed one of the chief contributing factors to the political anarchy of the period.

24 The sepoys, etc., were transferred to Razā Sāhib and were to be paid for by him from March 1st. A bond was to be got from him for the total amount due, as well as a *parwana* for Villiyanallur from him as well; this was supplemented by a declaration and an assurance that Chandā Sāhib's *parwana* for the same place was to be issued as soon as he should reach Arcot.

that the old Nawab Anvar-ud-dīn longed to go to battle and that it would be a good thing if he, with all his years, had another fight and died therein.

The French *vakil*, Subbayyan, was to go to Arcot with letters and *nazars* for Muzaffar Jang and Chandā Sāhib and also with copies of the *parwana* granted by the Emperor to the Governor of Pondicherry in Dumas' time for a *mansab* of 4,500 horse and a *naubat* and of Razā Sāhib's *parwana* for Villiyanallur. On July 26th, news reached Pondicherry that, while Anvar-ud-dīn was about 18 hours' journey to the southward of Arcot, Chandā Sāhib and Muzaffar Jang were about the same distance to the northward of it. Three days later it was said that Chandā Sāhib had certainly reached Pallikonda, which is half way between Ambur and Vellore, but it was not known whether Anvar-ud-dīn had departed from Singari Pass to the west of Chengama.[25] This was the situation when the Diary abruptly breaks off without giving the details of the preliminaries to the battle of Ambur, the battle itself and the events following it. The thread of the narrative is resumed from September 4.

25 Chandā Sāhib is said to have advanced through the Damalcheruvu Pass to the north-west of Chittore; the French and their allies affected a junction with him, routed Anvar-ud-dīn at Ambur and then occupied Arcot. Ambur did not lie on the road which would lead an invading army from Damalcheruvu to Arcot. Mr. Dodwell queries why Anvar-ud-dīn should have taken his post at Ambur or why Chandā Sāhib should have turned aside from Arcot to meet him. Burhan-ud-dīn, in his *Tuzuk-i-Wālājāhi*, says that Husain Khān Tahir, the *jaghirdar* of Amburgadh, persuaded the Nawab to encamp before his fort, in the plain, with a treacherous motive; and he details the treachery of the Tahiran, as well as the way in which Muzaffar Jang was dissuaded out of his inclination to make peace with the old Nawab.

CHAPTER IX

THE TRIUMPH OF CHANDA SAHIB

EVENTS AFTER THE BATTLE OF AMBUR

WHEN Ranga Pillai resumed his Diary in the beginning of September, 1749, Chandā Sāhib and Muzaffar Jang, the victors of Ambur, were still at Arcot. Many of the *killedars* had submitted; but Mīr Asad, the *killedar* of Chetpattu (in the North Arcot District), who had been *diwan* to Nawabs Dōst Alī and Safdar Alī, stood out; and he was successful in his resistance, in spite of the fact that a body of 300 Europeans with two mortars and several guns was despatched from Pondicherry to coerce him.[1] Chandā Sāhib proposed to leave Arcot for Pondicherry by way of Gingee, accompanied by Muzaffar Jang. The Chetpattu affair seemed to have been settled for three lakhs of rupees and the soldiers and French officers who were despatched to that place returned on September 8. An important event that took place, at the time was the rendition of Madras to the English on Monday, September 1. The Diarist thus writes about that event:—'The Brahmans did *puja*, cocoanuts were broken, sheep sacrificed and other Tamil ceremonies performed, before the flag was hoisted; then an extraordinary salute was fired from the Fort and from the (Boscawen's) ships. We do not know where the Tamils were who left Madras and would not return in our time; but when their (English) flag was hoisted, ten lakhs of Tamils, Muhammadans, Lubbays, Pattanawars, coolies, etc., crowded into the town as joyfully as though the Fort and town belonged to each

1 Mīr Asad wrote to the English in November, complaining that they had not congratulated him on his successful resistance—(Country Correspondence, 1749, p. 54: of Madras Records)—note by Dodwell on p. 154 of vol. vi, of the *Diary*. Dupleix desired that Mīr Asad might come to a settlement with Chandā Sāhib and asked the Diarist to write to this effect to Shaik Muhammad Sharīf who was arranging terms (entry for September 4, 1749).

one of them'.[2] Of course the trade of the times was not prosperous. The country trade was dull; but while Madras was ruined, Pondicherry was not correspondingly benefited. Dupleix arranged about this time to invite various classes of weavers, *Kaikōḷars, Sēdars* and *Sēṇiyars* to settle at Villiyanallur in the vicinity of Pondicherry and to advance them ten pagodas a loom, in order to enable them to build houses and construct looms. This was as if an answer were to be made for the English planting of weaving villages at *Kālādipēttah* (*originally,* Collettpettah) near Tiruvottiyur and at Chintadripettah to the west of the Island Ground in Madras by Governors Joseph Collett and Morton Pitt in 1719 and 1734 respectively. These two suburban villages of Madras were peopled by weavers, painters, dyers and washers of the Company's cloth intended for export to Europe and were the necessary adjuncts of a trading settlement whose principal occupation was the manufacture and export of calico and other cloth. As early as 1742 the Madras Council wrote that 'the French had expended much money in settling weavers at Pondicherry, just as the English had done at Chintadripet, and with similar ill-success;' and therefore they argued that it would be useless to attempt such a settlement at Cuddalore.[3]

2 This is confirmed, as Mr. Dodwell notes, by the Fort St. David despatch to the Company, dated August 30, 1749 (old style):—The rendition has occasioned 'universal joy among the late inhabitants who thronged there in great numbers, immediately on hoisting the English flag.' 'All French efforts failed to induce them to return; and the French are mortified at the present token of attachment to the English. Its condition is indifferent; all the fortifications are undermined and all useful stores have been carried off.' (Despatch from Charles Floyer and Council to the Company, from Fort St. David)—p. 79 of Dodwell's *The Madras Despatches* (*1744–55*)—1920. Ranga Pillai himself grieved that the French were destined by God to rule over Madras only for two years, eleven months and ten days and that Madras had become 'the Little City instead of the Golden City as it was once called'—the wealthy inhabitants of the Black Town being very few when compared with those of the past.

3 One main reason of the ill-success of these attempts, according to Dodwell, was the relative dearness of grain in the coast towns. Dupleix's attempt to settle weavers at Villiyanallur seems to have succeeded much

Meanwhile, news was received that when Nāsir Jang heard that Anvar-ud-dīn Khān had been killed, he cast his turban on the ground in vexation and despatched his younger brother (?) with a small army, recalling in disgrace Sayyad Lashkar Khān who was sent first. Chandā Sāhib was planning to raise a large body of horse and foot in order to march with Muzaffar Jang to conquer Trichinopoly, Tanjore and Mysore. Both the leaders had appointed Taqī Sāhib who was *killedar* of Wandewash and sometime *diwan* to Dōst Alī to be the *naib* and *diwan* of Arcot—a step that Dupleix did not like. Dupleix also desired that Mylapore (including, of course, San Thomé) should not be delivered to one Muhiud-dīn Sāhib who came with a *parwana* for that place from Chandā Sāhib, but should be left in the hands of Father Antony, Padre of Mylapore, for whom a *parwana* was subsequently got from the Nawab.

The Victors at Pondicherry

On September 27, the Diarist went to Vaḷudāvur in order to welcome Chandā Sāhib and offer him Dupleix's compliments; and the next morning he made a state entry into Pondicherry, the Governor meeting him at the Villiyanallur gate.[4] The next day

better, as 1,200 families of weavers were said to have been settled there, till they were scattered by the war in 1752. Dupleix arranged that the weavers should repay the advances given to them at the rate of one pagoda per year; and they should be free from any tax on their yarn and cotton for the first two years after their settlement. By this, the Diarist tells that Dupleix hoped that ten times as many weavers as went to Chintadripet and Madras would settle at Villiyanallur. For the terms of the *cowl* that was given to the settlers at Chintadripet, refer to the Madras Council Consultation of October 21, 1734, quoted almost in full by Talboys Wheeler in his *Madras in the Olden Time* pp. 522–5 of the 1882 edition.

4 Chandā Sāhib is reported by the Diarist to have related to Dupleix all his vicissitudes since his release from prison from Satara. He detailed, particularly, the part that he took in the fighting at Chittirakkal Baman where his eldest son, Abid Sāhib, perished. Compare this with the conflicting accounts of his doings at Bednore as given by Orme and Wilks and with Dodwell's account, as given in a note on part vi. (J.I.H. vol. viii, Notes on pp. 154–6).

Chandā Sāhib went out to Vaḻudāvur to meet Muzaffar Jang who was encamped there and to escort him to Pondicherry. His state entry into Pondicherry is described with an apparent relish by the Diarist in his entry for September 30. A number of days were spent in festivities, in the course of which, the Diarist contrived to plead both with Chandā Sāhib and with Muzaffar Jang, for the assignation of a *jaghir* to himself, 'as a mark of remembrance, besides those stipulated for the French.'[5] The scarcity of money was very keenly felt by the Nawab and by Muzaffar Jang. The latter pressed Chandā Sāhib who in turn importuned Dupleix for an accommodation of two lakhs of pagodas. Even thus Chandā Sāhib's hopes of supremacy were high; he said to the Diarist:—'If you will send troops to settle my business with Tanjore and Trichinopoly, I will give many villages as an *inam* (besides those you now enjoy) and pay the Governor one or two lakhs and reward you also suitably... French troops will march to Aurangabad; and Masulipatam and other sea-ports shall be given to the French. I will also give a *jaghir* there. Moreover I will conquer all the countries from Mysore up to the Narbada and rule as the Nizam did formerly. The Marathas are coming

5 The French had stipulated that as a condition of their help that they should be given the *jaghirs* of Villiyanallur and Bāhur. And Muzaffar Jang had, in his abundant gratitude, given in addition the sea-port of Masulipatam and the district of Bāhur which last included the villages immediately surrounding the limits of Fort St. David. Dupleix was particularly anxious to hoist flags and tie *toranams* in the thirty-six villages of the Bāhur jaghir on the day of Chandā Sāhib's departure (see p. 220 of vol. vi of *Diary*). The tying of *toranams* was a formal announcement of possession. He was also anxious that if English soldiers or peons came from Fort St. David or Madras and seized the inhabitants by stealth, they should be stopped and expelled. The Bāhur villages were taken possession of on November 2, 1749. 'To Dupleix this may have seemed no more than a convenient rounding off of French territory; but to the English it bore the menacing aspect of a scheme to cut off all trade and communication with the interior of the country. Their fear was confirmed by certain sinister occurrences in the neighbourhood of Madras; (the action of Padre Antonio in taking possession of San Thomé); and thus the English Council were compelled to embark on a policy of opposition.'—Dodwell, *Dupleix and Clive*, p. 39.

to assist me with a lakh of horsemen under the Peishwa Sau Baji Rao, Fatteh Singh Bhonsle and others...'[6] But in spite of the brave show and high hopes indulged in by Chandā Sāhib, he was nervous lest he should not have enough money and French auxiliaries for the expedition. Muzaffar Jang himself was not to be greatly relied upon; he was, in the words of the Diarist, 'like a child that will lie in any one's arm'; also he was very close-fisted about money and constantly dunned his ally for a fresh supply. Moreover he was anxious to go north, since he heard that Murari Rāo was marching down on the Carnatic with several thousands of horsemen and Pindaris, turning everything upside down and planning to march on Arcot, while Nāsir Jang himself had begun to march southward from Aurangabad with 30,000 horse. Dupleix's chief concern now was to have the grant of the proposed *jaghir* completed before his allies should depart from Pondicherry; and there now arose a new difficulty regarding Mylapore, about which mention has been made already.

The English Occupation of San Thome

After Madras came back into the possession of the English, one of the first questions dealt with by them was the attitude that they should take towards the Catholic priests and others who were believed to have played a treacherous part at the time of the French capture of the place. Admiral Boscawen declared that the four priests of the Great Church in White Town (the Capuchin Church of St. Andrew in the Fort built in 1675) were greater enemies to the Company than any others and no man doubted of their affection and goodwill to the French and that he had 'certain proof of Mr. Dupleix has wrote to Goa desiring the Portuguese Viceroy to send the padre Antonio a Commission as Governour of St. Thomé and its Dependancies and a supply of men and money . . .'[7] Admiral Boscawen advised in September that Father Antony de la Purification of San Thomé should be

6 Diarist's report of a conversation that took place between him and Chandā Sāhib on October 6, 1749, p. 215 of vol. vi of the *Diary*.

7 Fort St. David Consultation, dated September 2 (old style) 1749. Father Antonio had been appointed Procurator of the Portuguese at

deported as treasonable papers had been found in his house. The despatch of Governor Floyer of Fort St. David to the Company, dated October 18, 1749, tells us that Father Antonio forbade,

San Thomé by the Viceroy of Goa and *havildar* of Mylapore by Chandā Sāhib. San Thomé's history is briefly as follows:—

San Thomé and Mylapore formed one town as it were. Mylapore was a place of ancient importance, identified by some scholars with the Maliarpha of Ptolemy, the Geographer (*cir.* A.D. 150). It was rendered illustrious in Tamil literary and religious tradition by its close association with the Saint Tiruvaḷḷuvar, author of the *Sacred Kuṛaḷ*, which treats of the Trivarga; and also with the activities of the great Śaiva Nāyanar, Tirugṇanasambanda, as well as of an early Vaishnava Āḻvar. it is sacred on account of its Śaiva temple, dedicated to Sri Kapālīsvarar, and was mentioned as an important place along the coast by the European travellers of the sixteenth century. San Thomé's fame rests upon its close association with the Indian Apostolate of St. Thomas. It is not certain whether the Church of San Thomé was first founded by the Apostle himself or by a later personage of the name Thomas. The tradition that the Apostle suffered martyrdom at St. Thomas' Mount, a little to the west, has been current from the time of Marco Polo, the Venetian traveller, who touched the Coromandel coast towards the close of the thirteenth century. When the Portuguese became powerful on the west coast, they visited the Betumah (house or chapel of the Apostle) which, according to tradition, had been existing on the Madras coast. Gaspar Correa, the historian, visited the spot and made repairs to the chapel in 1521. The Portuguese are said to have founded the Church of St. Thomas in, or soon after, 1522; and the Church was consequently the most ancient European building on the coast. A monastic settlement was probably formed at St. Thomas' Mount about 1522; in 1547 the famous Bleeding Cross was discovered at the Mount by the Portuguese and built into the church wall behind the altar; and gradually a town grew up at the base of the Mount.

The rise of San Thomé was rapid after 1550. It shot into great importance in the last quarter of the sixteenth century and came to be equipped with a fort. It was the seat of a bishop; and besides the principal church, it contained several others both within and outside the walls. The settlement included Mylapore and was known as San-Thomé de Meliapour and was under the control of the Captain of the City who was usually a Portuguese nobleman. San Thomé began to decline in trade, particularly after Madras was founded, and it fell into the hands of the Mussalmans of Golconda in 1662. It remained under Golconda rule till 1672 when it was attacked and taken possession of by the

under the severest penalties, any provisions to be carried through or out of his dependencies, with other insults until the English Council requested Boscawen's assistance; and the latter at once

French. The Mussalmans seem to have strengthened the fortifications whose area seems to have been nearly three times that of Fort St. George.

The French occupation of San Thomé was neither long nor peaceful. It lasted a little more than two years and was one long period of beleaguerment, first by the forces of Golconda and then by the combined forces of Golconda and the Dutch, till the place was starved into capitulation. The first siege was slow and ineffective; it was raised in March, 1673; and de La Haye, the French Commander, occupied the Triplicane village and temple, though the place had been given over to the English by the Golconda representative in the previous year. The English Governor, Langhorne, protested against this action of the French, but without any effect. Meanwhile, Martin, the future founder of Pondicherry, proceeded to Masulipatam and negotiated for a *farman* from the Sultan for San Thomé.

War had meanwhile been declared by Holland against England and France. Van Goens, the Dutch Governor of Ceylon, was soon before San Thomé with a powerful armament and began a blockade on the seaside, while the Golconda troops invested the place on land (August 1673). The English at Madras were too jealous of the French at San Thomé to co-operate actively with them. At last, after more than a year of resistance, de La Haye capitulated and surrendered himself into the hands of the Dutch who, according to agreement, delivered the Fort to the Sultan of Golconda (September, 1674). The English Governor of Madras urged the demolition of the San Thomé fortifications, as he was afraid that the French might recover the Fort, either by force or by negotiation. But the Dutch gained over to their side Madanna Pant, the minister of Golconda: and the French hope of recovering the place was frustrated.

One important consequence of the French evacuation of San Thomé was the withdrawal of François Martin, with a few followers to Pondicherry, where he founded a settlement on a small site for a factory which had been granted in the previous year by the governor of Gingee on behalf of his master, the Sultan of Bijapur. Thus originated the city of Pondicherry.

Urged on by the Dutch, who were apprehensive of French designs, the Sultan of Golconda ordered in 1675 the destruction of the fortifications of San Thomé; and only the chief buildings and the churches were spared from demolition. The English cast covetous eyes from

made the *padre* a prisoner and wanted to carry him to England and he also took possession of his papers.[8] Boscawen and the English Council had definite information that Dupleix was determined to get possession of San Thomé as a counterpoise to the loss of Madras. The Fort St. David Council wrote to Boscawen that

time to time on the place. Their chief merchant, Casa Verona (Kāsi Vīranna), farmed the place from the Muslims, tried hard to repopulate it and spent large sums in building houses there. When Golconda's authority was superseded by the Mughals in 1687, the Madras factors began negotiations with the imperial officers for the grant of the town to them. In 1697 the Mughal representative in the Carnatic demolished such fortifications as still remained in San Thomé. Nawab Dāūd Khān, who was generally ill-disposed towards the English, often threatened to develop San Thomé at the expense of Madras; and it was from San Thomé that he frequently threatened the safety of Fort St. George in the time of Governor Thomas Pitt (1698-1709). Thus the place continued under the authority of the Nawabs of the Carnatic with very little trade and a decaying population. In 1710 the Armenian merchants of Madras were suspected of having designs on San Thomé and intending to use it as their port. Successive Nawabs visited the place; and in the course of Mahfuz Khān's defeat at the hands of Paradis, the town was plundered by French troops in a ruthless manner.

8 The letters found in the *Padre's* house showed that Dupleix advised him to carry matters with a fair face till Chandā Sāhib's affairs were more settled—see p. 82 of Dodwell's *The Madras Despatches, 1744–55* From the entries of Ranga Pillai, it can be seen that, on the *Padre's* representation, Dupleix had the *parwana* that Chandā Sāhib gave to one Muhi-ud-dīn Sāhib for San Thomé cancelled; and that Razā Sāhib gave the required *parwana* for the place to the *Padre* in the presence of Madame Dupleix who was a relation of his and used her own influence in the matter. Moreover, Dupleix asked the Diarist, when he had news of the deportation of the *Padre* by Boscawen, to tell Chandā Sāhib that the Viceroy of Goa would be very angry about this affair and that he would write to him for a squadron of warships if Chandā Sāhib would promise to bear the expense (pp. 178, 199 and 219 of the *Diary*, vol. vi). Chandā Sāhib was later asked by Dupleix to write a Persian letter to the Viceroy of Goa to this effect.—'In order to make their (the Portuguese) name shine here, we (Chandā Sāhib) appointed Padre Antonio, a Portuguese, amaldar of Mylapore and conferred on him a name by which to give orders. But the English were jealous of Portuguese prosperity near their city. So Mr. Boscawen sent soldiers and peons to seize the *Padre;* they wounded four or five persons with

the *Padre* was to come with a detachment of French troops to build the fort that he had already begun; and they wrote to Muhammad Alī Khān at Trichinopoly[9] that the French intended to keep possession of San Thomé and had actually begun to build a fort there and that Boscawen was determined to take possession of the place in his name. They requested the immediate despatch of a *farman* for that place which 'will engage the English strictly to adhere to your interest'. Accordingly Muhammad Alī despatched a *farman* dated October 2 (old style), delivering Mylapore (*alias* San Thomé) to the English; and Boscawen hoisted English colours at the place on the October 11 (old style). Writing to the Company on November 2, 1749, the Fort St. David Council justified their action, as the French occupation of San Thomé would have ruined the trade of Madras and enabled them 'constantly to observe all our transactions.'[10] Chandā Sāhib had

him, plundered Mylapore, destroyed its beauty, captured the *Padre* and sent him on board ship. I cannot endure that the English should thus dishonour the Portuguese, and so I write to you. If you send ships of war, soldiers and ammunition to attack Madras, Cuddalore and Fort St. David, I will march with my forces, fight with them and punish them. Please regard the letters which M. Dupleix, the General of Pondicherry, writes to you about this at my request, as my own and act as the letters require.' Meanwhile Dupleix thought that he could, with the help of the Portuguese soldiers who should be asked to come overland, overthrow Nāsir Jang with ease. For the outcome of this letter to Goa see the sequel.

9 P. Country correspondence; vol. iii. September 21, 1749, quoted by Col. H. D. Love in his *Vestiges of Old Madras*, vol. ii, p. 399. The occupation of San Thomé was certainly proposed by Boscawen; but the Fort St. David Council did not seem to have tried to evade responsibility, as was represented to the Diarist by Dupleix who said that they had written to Europe that it was done without their knowledge and attempted to shirk their responsibility (p. 255 of vol. vi of the *Diary*). Dodwell points out that there was no particular reason why the English Council should have done so.

10 English occupation of San Thomé.—Note on the Padre de la Purification.

'*Extract from Despatch from Fort St. David*,' *October* 18, 1749.

'The first act that he (Chandā Sāhib) did, after arriving at this (Nabob's) Dignity was the recompensing his good allies, by granting

not, till that date, entered on any hostilities on this account against the English, as he was just then busy with his expedition to the south against Tanjore and Trichinopoly. Major Lawrence who was in command of the Madras garrison, was prepared to open fire on any body who should dispute the English possession of the place. The Portuguese, as if in answer to Dupleix's advice, sent a letter of remonstrance to the English at Fort St. David, claiming that the place was under the sway of their King. To this the English Council replied that there were no Portuguese colours flying when Boscawen took the place and that *Padre* Antonio declared that he was the representative of Chandā Sāhib and that they had a valid *farman* for the town from Muhammad Alī, the lawful Nawab of the province.[11] Dupleix told the Diarist, when Boscawen's fleet sailed to Cuddalore from Madras after San

them forty-two villages of the Villanour Country, which lay all round this Settlement (Fort St. David), and by way of reward to Mr. Dupleix in particular, the following towns and their revenues have been given to him and his relations, *viz*:—

Coibelong (Covelong) to Mr. Dupleix, Porto Novo to Madame Dupleix.

Alempara to Monsieur D'Autel, his brother-in-law.

St. Thomé to Padre D' (la Purification) a relation of Madame Dupleixes.

'So that we are surrounded in such a manner as for the French to have it entirely in their power to stop our trade or debar us from any supplies of provision from the Country, and we have great reason to believe, from what has already happened, they will not be wanting to make use of this advantage, for the Padre's zeal being either warmer than the other could not help discovering himself, by forbidding on the severest penalties, any sort of refreshments going to Madras through or out of his Dependances; and by insulting us in other respects, in so much that at last we were obliged to apply to General Boscawen for his assistance, who immediately sent and took the Padre prisoner, and is bringing him to England to be disposed of as His Majesty shall think proper.'

Forrest's *Bengal and Madras Papers*, vol. ii, 1688–1757.

11 See the Portuguese Viceroy's letter to Fort St. David, dated February 5, 1750, and the Council's letter to him in reply dated, May 14, 1750—both quoted by Love—vol. II, pp. 400–1.

Thomé had been taken by him, that he feared that Chandā Sāhib and Muzaffar Jang would attack Cuddalore as a measure of retaliation and therefore he had postponed his journey to Europe and was going to Cuddalore and Fort St. David,[12] Boscawen, however, had definite orders to proceed home.

Chanda Sahib's Expedition to Tanjore

To return to Chandā Sāhib:—He departed from Pondicherry on October 28, but the heavy rains prevented his rapid march; and for a few days he stayed on in the neighbourhood. He then camped in the vicinity of Fort St. David in the hope of being able to raise money on the mortgage of some villages; and it seemed as if he and Muzaffar Jang who accompanied him, set out 'to replenish their purses, rather than to complete their conquests.' Almost even before they had proceeded far, Muzaffar Jang quarrelled with Chandā Sāhib about money matters and threatened to return to his headquarters at Adoni. Chandā Sāhib had to mollify him by promising to pay him two lakhs of rupees in ready money and to put him in possession of Nellore, Sarvepalle and other countries worth about ten lakhs a year in the opinion of the Diarist. Muzaffar Jang promised to demand no more money for four months. There was also news of Nāsir Jang's rumoured advance to the bank of the Godavari from Aurangabad and of the advance of the Nawabs of Cuddapah and Kandanur to seize the fort and province of Adoni under instructions from the former. Muzaffar Jang got greatly frightened and ordered his troops to be ready to march back to Adoni; he said that as Chandā Sāhib got the subah of Arcot with European help, he could manage affairs by himself, but that he himself should go to Nāsir Jang and reconcile himself to the latter somehow or other. It was with great difficulty that Chandā Sāhib contrived to dissuade him from

12 Entry of the Diarist for October 24 (new style)—p. 223 of vol. VI of the *Diary*. Boscawen's fleet sailed from Fort St. David on October 21 (old style); the French did not believe that he intended to quit India, but imagined that he only wanted to avoid the stormy monsoon of the coast. They took advantage of this absence, short as they imagined it, to send their allies to Tanjore the very next day.—*Orme*, vol. I, p. 133.

departing and to reassure him and finally to make him swear on the *Quran* that both would stand or fall together.[13] The situation was complicated by the arrival at Pondicherry of letters written to the French chief of Masulipatam by the Nawab of Rajahmundry, Khajah Namat-ullah Khān, son of Khajah Abdullah Khān, who was for a short time *interim* Nawab of the Carnatic in 1743 under the orders of Nizām-ul-Mulk. Herein the French were advised to give up the alliance of Chandā Sāhib, join Nāsir Jang and obey his orders; and they were told they could live at peace in Masulipatam if they acted as he wished. Copies of these letters and of the Mughal Emperor's *farman* confirming Nāsir Jang as the *Subhadar* of the Deccan, which was sent along with them were despatched to Chandā Sāhib by the Diarist according to Dupleix's instruction.[14]

Meanwhile Chandā Sāhib, having failed to get any money in the country round Fort St. David, directed his attention to the *Poligar* of Udaiyarpalayam which was a considerable chiefship in the interior of the Trichinopoly District. The *Poligar* agreed to pay one lakh of rupees; but Chandā Sāhib insisted on a lakh of pagodas. The Udaiyarpalayam people delayed the payment of the amount they agreed to give, in the hope that news of the coming of Nāsir Jang might improve their position. Chandā Sāhib spent about a fortnight before Udaiyarpalayam and succeeded in getting therefrom only about 70,000 pagodas. Even this was got only when three or four guns had been fired and the Nawab's troops had entered the bounds of the *palayam*. He then joined Muzaffar Jang who was encamped about 12 *kos* from

13 Diarist's entry of a conversation he had with Jayaram Pandit on November 5, 1749, who desired that letters should be written to Raghuji Bhonsle, Fatteh Singh and other Maratha chiefs requesting them to maintain Chandā Sāhib in his position and hinder his enemies from attacking them.—p. 236 of *Diary*, vol. VI.

14 Khajah Namat-ullah Khān had shown his enmity to the French as early as 1747, when he attempted to waylay M. d'Espremenil who proceeded overland from Madras to Yanam and extracted money from him; and it was suspected at Pondicherry that Antannan, a French servant at the Yanam factory, was intriguing with the Nawab.

Tanjore. Dupleix was anxious to get a *parwana* for the villages round Karikal that he wanted for himself from the Raja of Tanjore. He expected that the affair of the Raja might be settled for about half a crore of rupees, which was also the modest estimate of Chandā Sāhib. Of course, in his accustomed vein of vainglory, Dupleix proudly exclaimed: 'Affairs have been settled with the Udaiyarpalayam and other *killedars*, because of their fear of me; else, at a time when Nāsir Jang had given orders to advance, no one would have joined Chandā Sāhib's army or paid him a cash.'[15]

Abdul Amīn Khān, the younger son (or brother) of Abdul Nabī Khān, Nawab of Cuddapah, wrote to Chandā Sāhib that it would be an easy task for him to capture Tanjore and Trichinopoly, but Gingee was very strong and should be kept in friendly hands; his elder brother was now the ruling Nawab of Cuddapah and he was the Nawab of Savanur and Bankapur;[16] he expressed a desire in the letter to open communications with Dupleix. He was to play later a prominent part in the intrigues that brought about the deaths of Nāsir Jang and Muzaffar Jang in quick succession. When Nāsir Jang marched south through Kalyan and Gulburga and his general, Sayyad Lashkar Khān, reached the banks of the Kṛishna, the Diarist heard that the Nawabs of Cuddapah and Savanur were moving against him; and the Nawab of Kurnool, Himāyat Khān, the other member of this infamous triumvirate, appears to have actually attacked and defeated a small force sent to him from Nāsir Jang.

Things did not advance well in Chandā Sāhib's camp. Though some money was got from Ariyalur, there was general unrest among the troops on account of growing arrears of pay; while Miyān Ma'sūd, the *diwan* of Muzaffar Jang, went to Chandā Sāhib's camp before Udaiyarpalayam and demanded a lakh of

15 See Diarist's entry for November 25, 1749—p. 272 of vol. iv.

16 There is some doubt about the identity of this person. The Diarist speaks of him in another place as Abdul Majid Khān. The families of the Nawabs of Cuddapah and Savanur were related. He probably confuses the Nawab of Savanur with Abdul Majid who succeeded Abdul Nabī of Cuddapah.

rupees for expenses; when the latter expressed his inability, he behaved disrespectfully and said, among other things, that he (Chandā Sāhib) should not continue to live. There was for some time great likelihood of a revolution breaking out in the camp, while Chandā Sāhib complained that the northern *poligars* did not join him effectively, as one Dabbili Rāyappa Raja, presumably an adventurer, who promised him a big sum of money for being allowed to seize Bommarājapālayam, was being detained in custody at Pondicherry.

Letters were received early in December at Pondicherry from Nāsir Jang and Muhammad Alī Khān. That of Nāsir Jang promised to forgive the French their past offences if they should separate from their allies and be faithful to the Nizam in the future; otherwise he would order that the French factories should be pulled down and would write to Bengal to the same effect. Muhammad Alī's letter solicited French friendship and asked Dupleix to make peace with Nāsir Jang and offered twice as much gains as the French might secure from his enemies. To this Dupleix replied, exhorting Muhammad Alī to obey Muzaffar Jang's orders and win his favour, and through it, French friendship.[17] He had news—at least so he told the Diarist—that Sau Baji Rao had surrounded Nāsir Jang and was harassing him and the latter had abandoned the idea of coming down to the Carnatic and so Chandā Sāhib need not fear him now. He was intent that Chandā Sāhib should settle the Tanjore affair for at least 50 lakhs of rupees, so that he might get back all the amounts he had advanced to Muzaffar Jang.[18]

17 Diarist's entries for December 7 and 9—pp. 289 and 290 of the *Diary*, vol. vi. The English records have another version of Nāsir Jang's letter received from Muhammad Alī by Dupleix—see Country Correspondence, 1749, p. 60.

18 The Diarist heard from Dupleix that these amounted to 40 lakhs; but Dodwell estimates that even if the advances made to Chandā Sāhib were included, the total would still fall far short of 40 lakhs. Muzaffar Jang's debts to Dupleix and the French Company fell short of 7 lakhs, according to M. Cultru, even at a much later date—(Dodwell's note on p. 292 of vol. vi of the *Diary*.)

Operations at Tanjore

The united forces of Muzaffar Jang and Chandā Sāhib crossed the Coleroon into the Tanjore country on December 13. The French contingent with them was composed of 800 Europeans, a train of filled artillery and 300 Coffres and Topasses. Chandā Sāhib was being pressed for money on all sides. He was anxious to settle the affair for a large sum with the help of the Frenchman Duquesne who was in camp; he applied to Dupleix for guns, flints and cartridges; he complained of the importunate demands of Muzaffar Jang for money and of the slights he received at his hands. He kept Dupleix in good humour by sending his own *inam parwanas* for Tirunallār, Kōttaichēri and another place on whose possession the French Governor was bent and promised to send the Tanjore ruler's *parwanas* for these three places as soon as a settlement should have been arrived at with him.[19] Dupleix agreed to send a supply of guns and ammunition to Karaikal whither Chandā Sāhib might send to fetch them. For six weeks Chandā Sāhib allowed himself to be duped by protestations of good faith and promises of speedy payment made by Pratāp Singh, the Raja of Tanjore. Chandā Sāhib first gave him a peremptory order to pay all arrears of tribute due from the death of Nawab Safdar Alī in 1742, and contended that whatever might have been paid in the interval to Anvar-ud-dīn was not a tribute to the legitimate suzerain, but only a forced contribution exacted by and paid to a rebel authority. Pratāp Singh shut himself up in his capital and offered to pay a ransom which was more agreeable to Chandā Sāhib than either the reduction of the capital or the conquest of the kingdom. He did not permit his

19 Chandā Sāhib's autograph letter received by Dupleix on December 14, said.—'Nawab Hidāyat Muhiud-dīn Khān has received great sums for one or two affairs he has settled, and slights me. If I quarrel with him, we shall fare ill; so I have entrusted this matter to M. Duquesne as then no one will question what is done.' Vol. vi, p. 305 of *Diary*.

troops to approach nearer than three miles of the capital and requested the French troops not to commit hostilities.[20]

News reached Pondicherry on December 19, that Nāsir Jang who had advanced as far as Gulburga had again gone back to Satara, but had ordered Sayyad Lashkar Khān to seize Adoni, Rāyachōti and other places (belonging to Muzaffar Jang) south of the Krishna and that the latter had already captured Rāyachōti and hoisted his flag there. Also the English were creating disturbances in the neighbourhood of Covelong which had been granted to Dupleix and over which French authority was being attempted to be enforced.[21]

Report reached the next day that Chandā Sāhib had asked the French commandant in his camp to write to Karikal that *toranams* might be tied in the villages of Tirunallār and Kōttaichēri *nadus*, as a token of the establishment of French authority,

20 'The wily Tanjorean knew that by protracting time, he should increase the distress of his enemies, and in his letters expressed himself with so much seeming humility that Chandā Sāhib suffered himself to be amused to the middle of December (O.S.) without having settled the terms of accommodation. In the meantime the king, corresponding with Muhammad Alī at Trichinopoly, joined with him in exhorting Nāsir Jang at Golcondah, to come and settle the affairs of the Carnatic in person...... He likewise solicited the assistance of the English, who exhorted him to defend himself to the last extremity; but sent to his assistance no more than twenty Europeans who were detached from Trichinopoly and entered the city of Tanjore in the night.' (*Orme*, vol. i, p. 134–5.) See the Diarist's details of the Raja's haggling in p. 399 of vol. vi.

21 Letter of M. Bruno, French representative at Covelong, near Chingleput, to the Diarist (pp. 309–10 of *Diary*, vol. vi).

Grant-Duff, the historian of the Marathas, thus details the circumstances of Nāsir Jang's troubles with the Marathas.—'Very shortly afterwards, intelligence was received of the defeat and death of Anvar-ud-dīn......on which Nāsir Jang applied to Rughoojee Bhonslay, for a body of his troops, promising to grant some cessions of territory as the reward of their service. He also summoned the whole of the Moghul dependents and tributaries in the Carnatic to be prepared to join his army, as he advanced to the southward. Moorar Rao Ghorepuray, as Jagheerdar of Ghooty, the Raja of Mysore, the Nabobs of Kurpa, Karnoul and Savanoor, and Muhammad Ally, second son of the late

though the Tanjore Raja's *parwana* had not been received Chandā Sāhib and Duquesne had surrounded the Tanjore fort as Manoji Appa, the general of the Raja, insisted on a fight, in spite of his master's dissuasion and encamped in front of them.[22] The fight, according to the version of the Diarist, is at variance with the generally accepted version. The Diarist heard that in the engagement on December 17, the Tanjore forces were scattered and begged for quarter which was granted and then the French advanced and seized a gate of the Fort. According to Malleson and Orme, the details are different. Malleson says that Duquesne, acting under positive instructions from Dupleix, captured three redoubts situated at a little distance from the walls on December 26; and three days later, after some fruitless negotiations, he assaulted and carried one of the gates of the town, after which the Raja gave in and concluded a treaty on the 31st, which included, among other provisions, that he should pay Chandā Sāhib and Muzaffar Jang 70 lakhs of rupees, remit the annual ground-rent due for the Karikal territory and add to the French possessions new territory comprising 71 villages.[23] According to Orme, Dupleix, finding that his exhortations to Chandā Sāhib had no effect, ordered the French captain to break off the negotiations by some signal act of hostility; and by this time

Anvar-ud-din, with his supporters, and the President of the Council at Madras (Fort St. David?) were the principal authorities who joined or sent their troops to accompany Nāsir Jang.' Before Shahu's death which occurred in December, 1749, Raghuji had sent his son Janoji to accompany Nāsir Jang into the Carnatic with 10,000 horse.—pp. 511, 512 and 520 of *History of the Mahrattas*, 4th ed., vol. i.

22 The Diarist wrote that he heard that Manoji Appa had raised a battery in the middle of the Mariamman Temple outside the Tanjore Fort and camped there with 4,000 horse, 30,000 foot and 500 or 600 English and Dutch (the figures are greatly exaggerated) and that he retired into the Fort after a fight on the 17th; M. Duquesne's letter received by Dupleix is alleged to make mention of an English flag in the Tanjore ranks which the French people took; the French then seized a gateway of the Fort of Tanjore (Diarist's entry for December 22, 1749).

23 *History of the French in India* (1893)—pp. 247-8.

Chandā Sāhib likewise thought it necessary to deliver an attack and made a hostile demonstration round the walls for four days continuously; and on the fifth day, the French troops attacked three redoubts about 600 yards from the walls and carried them. Early the next morning the Raja sent proposals for accommodation. Chandā Sāhib allowed him two days to consent to his proposals; and on the third, directed the French commandant to bombard the town with shells which act so frightened the Raja that he sent emissaries who, in their turn, wasted three days without concluding anything. The French commandant then renewed the bombardment and assaulted and carried one of the gates of the city.[24] Then the Raja became serious about the conclusion of peace and ratified the treaty on December 21 (o.s.).

Ananda Ranga Pillai writes of letters from Duquesne, Chandā Sāhib and Muzaffar Jang received at Pondicherry on December 22, and containing news of the fight with the Tanjoreans, their retreat, the French advance to the gate of the Fort and their capture of it, the grant of an armistice and the demand made for a crore of rupees by the allies. The seeming discrepancies between these versions are not very serious except, perhaps, the statement that a gateway of the Tanjore Fort was carried by the French attackers, much earlier according to our Diarist, than according to Orme and Malleson. Certain posts outside the town were certainly seized by the French on December 18, and envoys were sent out that day or the next day. But Duquesne seized, according to these historians, one of the gates of the city on December 28—a discrepancy of dates which can be accounted for only by a confusion of the new and old styles of reckoning. The Diarist wrote, on December 28, that the Raja of Tanjore, despairing because his counsellors (like Manoji Appa) had brought matters to such a pass, and preferring death to the loss of his fort and country, fell upon the enemy who had crossed the ditch and seized the entrance to the Fort, and drove them back to the Mariamman Temple where they were discussing terms yet. On January 5, Dupleix told the Diarist joyfully that Duquesne ha

24 *History of Indostan*, (fourth ed.),—Vol. i, pp. 135-6.

written to him that the Tanjore affair had been settled by him for seventy lakhs of rupees, and a *parwana* for the French occupation of Tirunallār and other villages, eighty in all, had been obtained from the Raja as an *inam* attached to Karikal and that he had secured the yearly *peshkash* of 2,000 pagodas for Karikal; lastly, the Raja having paid a part of the amount agreed upon, the army was encamped two *kos* this (northern) side of Tanjore. A supplementary letter received three days later said that Chandā Sāhib was to receive thirty lakhs in ready money and have some territories mortgaged for the balance and that he was to be requested to accept the amount in instalments. As usual, there was a lot of wrangling and procrastination over the payment of the stipulated sum. The French Commandant of Karikal complained that the Tirunallār *jaghir* of eighty-one villages were but worth 40,000 pagodas, instead of 70,000, as first reported.[25]

Throughout January and February the negotiations about the actual payment of money went on. It was the custom in those days that, in these military collections, the first payment rarely exceeded a fourth part of the whole assessment. The Raja was a past master in the art of procrastination and contrived to delay the payment in full of the first instalment for several weeks.[26] Dupleix saw clearly the danger of such procrastination, especially as Nāsir Jang was fast approaching the Carnatic. The death of

25 According to the Diarist, Dupleix is said to have told him—' He (Le Riche, the Commandant) wants to cheat the Company. As you are the Company's courtier, you must manage them to the Company's benefit. Appoint proper men to manage them.' So far from Dupleix realizing even the estimated sum from the newly added villages, they actually realized only about 30,000 pagodas between 1750 and 1754; (vol. vi, of the *Diary*, p. 358).

26 ' One day he sent gold and silver plate, and his officers wrangled like pedlars for the prices at which it should be valued; another day he sent old and obsolete coins, such as he knew would require strict and tedious examination; and then he sent jewels and precious stones, of which the value was still more difficult to be ascertained. Chandā Sāhib saw the drift of these artifices, and knowing them to be common practices,—submitted to wait, rather than lose the money of which he was so much in want.' (Orme, vol. i, p. 136).

the Maratha Raja Shahu at Satara in December 1749 had its repercussions even in remote Tanjore. Chandā Sāhib, as soon as he received the news, seriously thought of renewing hostilities and capturing the fort of Tanjore; he even raised some batteries with that object and wrote to Dupleix requesting him to write to the French captain and the *jamadars* of sepoys not to plunder the fort when it should be captured.

The Commandant of Karikal wrote to Dupleix that Chandā Sāhib entertained the design of capturing Tanjore and establishing his son as its ruler.[27] Dupleix who had a wider perspective of the political situation, was apprehensive that such an action on the part of Chandā Sāhib might anger the great Maratha chiefs like the Peishwa Balaji Baji Rao, Fatteh Singh, Raghuji Bhonsle, Sripat Rao and others and incline them to support Nāsir Jang;[28]

By February 10, articles of gold and silver and jewels worth about 7 lakhs only were paid to Chandā Sāhib (Diarist's entry for the date—p. 362 of the *Diary*, vol. vi).

27 Letter of Le Riche to Dupleix, dated February 10, 1750—quoted by Dodwell from the Pondicherry Records (*Diary*, vol. vi, p. 363).

28 The death of Raja Shahu produced a revolution in the Maratha state. The Peishwa acted with promptitude, made himself master of Satara fort, put down all pretensions of Shahu's widow and the aged Tāra Bai who set up a spurious grandson of hers as king, got over Raghuji Bhonsle to his side by confirming him in his eastern possessions and giving him full powers in Bengal, Berar and Gondwana and quieted the opposition of other ministers like the Sachiv. He made himself the ruler of the Maratha state, since the inveterate malice of Tāra Bai led to the imprisonment of the new king and the fall of the house of Sivāji. So far from Maratha leaders taking any offence at the action of Chandā Sāhib, they were very busy at home, in the domestic revolution that followed the death of Shahu. Bālaji himself was engaged in consolidating his own position of supremacy till the late monsoon of 1750.

Sripat Rao, the Pratinidhi, whom Dupleix mentions among the great Maratha leaders who might take offence at Chandā Sāhib's proposed capture of Tanjore, died in November 1746, three years before Shahu; and his younger brother, Jagjivan, was now the Pratinidhi, but was degraded and imprisoned by Bālaji Rao at this time for his adhesion to Sukwar Bai, the elder wife of Shahu (Kincaid and Parasnis, *A History of the Maratha People*, vol. ii, pp. 295 and 311). Fatteh Singh was like

and so he advised that Chandā Sāhib should consider the future and avoid evils that might happen. He gave orders to the French captain and the *jamadars* of sepoys not to plunder the fort of Tanjore, even if Chandā Sāhib should capture it[29] and obey the latter's orders.

Nasir Jang's entry into the Carnatic and Chanda Sahib's Retreat

Nāsir Jang had advanced by February 10 as far as Sīrpi; he sent two emissaries to Chandā Sāhib at Tanjore to treat for peace. Dupleix was anxious that Chandā Sāhib and Muzaffar Jang should not make any agreement without his knowledge and the emissaries of Nāsir Jang should be told that 'though we (Dupleix, Chandā Sāhib and Muzaffar Jang) have three bodies, our life is one; peace cannot be made without me (Dupleix); and if the matter is to be settled satisfactorily, they must come here (to Pondicherry).[30]

Moro Pant and Khāzi Dāyem—these were the two emissaries of Nāsir Jang—are said by the Diarist in one place to offer terms to Muzaffar Jang, while Chandā Sāhib was too busy with the Tanjore affair to care about the enemy's approach and that he was unwilling to do anything until the fort should be captured.[31]

an adopted son of Raja Shahu and was confirmed by the Peishwa in the possession of his *jaghirs* and in the title of the Raja of Akalkote. Raghuji Bhonsle was mollified as already told; his son Janoji Bhonsle who was with Nāsir Jang's army did not assert himself. Thus, as Grant-Duff says:—'The arrangements before and consequent to (Shahu) Raja's death had, as already adverted to, prevented the Mahrattas from seizing an opportunity of enlarging their conquests in the Deccan, afforded by the absence of so great an army in the Carnatic........' Vol. i (4th ed.), p. 524.

29 Chandā Sāhib actually forbade Goupil, the French captain, to deliver an attack on the fort on February 24.

30 Diarist's entry for February 10, 1759 (p. 367 of vol. vi).

31 On February 19, Chandā Sāhib forbade an attack on the city in spite of Goupil, the French Commandant, desiring and urging it. Regarding this Dodwell remarks that as yet Dupleix had not really

Dupleix suspected that Muzaffar Jang might be purposely spreading the rumour that Nāsir Jang was coming down rapidly into the Carnatic, because Chandā Sāhib was not letting him manage the Tanjore affair and he hoped, by spreading such news, to cause confusion and prevent him from taking the fort.

But in spite of rumours that Nāsir Jang had turned back, news arrived early in March that he had reached the Chengama pass. Chandā Sāhib had, meanwhile, retreated from Tanjore[32] and had encamped on the northern side of the Coleroon in the neighbourhood of Chidambaram which was surrounded and plundered by a body of Maratha horse under Murari Rao who retreated on the approach of the Muhammadans. Murari Rao was joined by Moro Pant; and the former fought a small action with the enemy near the old Coleroon, a little to the south of Chidambaram. Being continually harassed by the Maratha troops, and often repulsing them with the fire of the French field-pieces, Chandā Sāhib, Muzaffar Jang and the French troops reached Tiruvati (a temple-fort on the Gadilam, near Panruti Railway Station). Rumour came that the Marathas were actually joined by a body of English troops from Fort St. David, though it was not true. The Marathas had come up to the place, even before the French reached it; and the fear of Chandā Sāhib and Muzaffar Jang was very great. The former reached Pondicherry on March 11. Immediately afterwards he began his importunate

become the master of the situation. 'The French were as yet neither masters, nor even partners, but auxiliary troops serving for hire.' (*Dupleix and Clive*, p. 45).

32 Dupleix seems to have advised now the seizure of Tanjore where Chandā Sāhib and his ally might have 'maintained themselves until famine compelled the hosts of Nāsir Jang to withdraw.' He also suggested that, according to the advice preferred by the *killedar* of Gingee, a body of European troops should be sent there along with ammunition (Diarist's entry for February 10—p. 369 of vol. vi of the *Diary*). But even this did not seem to have been taken advantage of by Chandā Sāhib. Note Dupleix's words according to the Diarist—'I ordered them to march towards Jinji, but they have not gone there. I wrote...... that if they occupied the Vaḻudāvur Fort........they could even drive Nāsir Jang's army through the passes.'

demands for money. Dupleix refused to give him any amount, but promised to supply plenty of powder, shot and guns and also to pay the French soldiers and sepoys. But Chandā Sāhib was timid, declared that this was not the proper time to attack Nāsir Jang and desired to stay at Pondicherry till he should go away. Dupleix answered that he should advance and meet Nāsir Jang, as otherwise he would be dishonoured.[33] Muzaffar Jang entered Pondicherry on March 15, and likewise importuned Dupleix for money. The latter scraped up somehow or other three lakhs of rupees, one lakh of this sum being got from the Company's merchants; and Muzaffar Jang gave a bill of exchange for this sum as well as for four lakhs that Chandā Sāhib owed, on the treasury of the province of Adoni. The allies pitched their camp at Villiyanallur, almost under the very walls of Pondicherry, as if for protection from its guns. Large arrears were due to the troops and every day some tumult or mutiny among them was feared. Muzaffar Jang did not give to Chandā Sāhib anything out of the sum that Dupleix advanced. The sepoys, horsemen and bazaar people belonging to Muzaffar Jang's camp had to be sternly ordered by Dupleix, on pain of being shot, to quit the bounds of Pondicherry where they were loitering, and join the camp.

First Encounter with Nasir Jang

On the March 18, Nāsir Jang's troops occupied Gingee; but the *killedar* that was appointed to that fort allowed the French at that place to depart with their money in peace; while Chandā Sāhib's garrison at the fort quietly gave it up to the enemy. Chandā Sāhib's sepoys and horsemen greatly troubled him for the payment of the arrears due to him; and Dupleix had to order

33 'If you refuse to attack him you will dishonour me, your ally...... Put your trust in Him (God) and attack Nāsir Jang. If he falls in battle you shall march to Aurangabad; and I will give you the subahs of the Deccan; but if it falls out as you fear, it is the will of God.' (Entry of the Diarist for March 14, 1715)—p. 394 of the *Diary*, vol. vi.

M. d'Auteuil to encamp with French soldiers at Villiyanallur and see that the sepoys ceased to disturb Chandā Sāhib. But in spite of French reinforcements and protection, Maratha horsemen hovered on the outskirts of the camp, broke into a choultry at Villiyanallur and killed some Coffre troops. The sense of insecurity that prevailed in the camp was great; and a rumour got about that Nāsir Jang had reached Trichinopoly. On March 23, Chandā Sāhib sent his *gumastah*, Rajo Pandit, and Muhammad Razā Sāhib with letters from himself and Nāsir Jang's emissaries to the effect that they were willing to let Chandā Sāhib retain the subah of Arcot, as he had been connected with that province for a number of years from the time of Nawab Sadatullah Khān and as the French Governor would not be content unless he was confirmed as the Nawab of the Carnatic. This and another communication received from Chandā Sāhib the next day, made the Diarist suspect that 'he (Chandā Sāhib) was waiting to see which way the cat would jump' and hoped that Dupleix would advise the making of peace with Nāsir Jang, particularly as he himself was to be confirmed in the possession of Arcot.[34]

Uncertainty continued to prevail till the end of March when the sixth volume of the *Diary* terminates. An action took place on April 4, between Nāsir Jang's forces and the allies; but little injury was done to either side; on the evening of that day, thirteen French officers insisted on resigning their commissions and returning immediately to Pondicherry. This action, made in face of the enemy, is condemned as 'even more disgraceful than the mutiny of the English officers in Bengal in 1766.' The French troops had become unreliable and their officers demoralized. It is indeed true that the French contingent had borne the

34 Muzaffar Jang, whom Nāsir Jang was resolved to abase, seeing that Chandā Sāhib was wavering, sent a letter to Dupleix in which he urged that d'Auteuil and his army should attack the enemy and this was not the time to halt. Dupleix himself had, on the receipt of the offers made on behalf of Nāsir Jang, ordered the French troops to halt, expecting that peace would be made (Dodwell's note based on Dupleix's letter to the Company, dated October 3, 1750, quoted on p. 426 of the *Diary*, vol. vi.)

brunt of fighting at Ambur and before Tanjore. But the fighting before Tanjore was not serious; and many of the French officers, when the army had returned, insisted on being relieved from field-duty. Those who replaced them had been placated by the advance of a month's *batta*; but even so they hesitated. D'Auteuil wrote to Dupleix from camp on April 1, that fifteen officers refused to fight, because 'our army is too small to attack the enemy's 50,000 horse, besides 2,000 sepoys and ten or twelve guns belonging to the English . . . we can be safe only under the walls of a fortress; how can we conquer an enemy who has both men and walls, whereas we lack both?' Muzaffar Jang and Chandā Sāhib also wrote that all the officers and soldiers opposed d'Auteuil's fighting, as the enemy was strong with great stores of powder and shot, guns and good artillery men, and the Muhammadans could not shoot well before the English and could not fight without shelter nor bear the heat.[35]

After the cannonade of April 4, and the mutinous refusal of the French officers to continue in camp, d'Auteuil, finding that the soldiers refused to fight without their officers, retired on Villiyanallur, much to the chagrin and mortification of Dupleix, accompanied by Chandā Sāhib and 4,000 of his horse. Muzaffar Jang, however, refused to move, saying that Nāsir Jang's people had come to treat with him after the engagement of the previous day and that he preferred to remain where he was, even at the risk of his life. This meant that Muzaffar Jang had deserted his allies; Dupleix ordered a strict guard to be placed over the house where his family resided. Chandā Sāhib was inclined to throw the blame for this cowardly retreat on d'Auteuil; he declared that the Maratha officers were ready to abandon Nāsir Jang who, just before the engagement, was inclined to retreat; but Muhammad Alī, Mahfuz Khān and others tried to restrain him from such

35 Diarist's entry for April 1, 1750 (pp. 9 and 10 of vol. vii of the *Diary*). Later the *Diary* tells us that the Governor sent M. Bussy to advise the mutinous officers to obey and the latter went to the camp and persuaded them to agree to fight (Chandā Sāhib's explanation to the Diarist made on April 5.).

a dishonourable action. At such a moment he urged d'Auteuil to attack Nāsir Jang; but he obstinately refused as all his officers had departed; 'the Europeans scattered in all directions; d'Auteuil and a few soldiers went one way; Muzaffar Khān, the *jamadar,* went another way; and his sepoys, a third'. Muzaffar Jang declared that he could not incur the disgrace of running away out of fear; Chandā Sāhib was pursued by Maratha horsemen and could not reach Muzaffar Jang's camp; when in the early morning the retreating army was surrounded by the enemy, they fought so well that Mahfuz Khān fell and Muhammad Alī was wounded—quite false news told by Chandā Sāhib, who wanted to persuade others that he could have won in the engagement, if d'Auteuil had not retreated. Chandā Sāhib also wanted to persuade the Diarist that Muzaffar Jang was in no way at fault, that he had not any previous design of joining Nāsir Jang, in which case he would have secured the restoration of his family from Pondicherry and that affairs were spoiled by d'Auteuil and not by Muzaffar Jang. Of course Dupleix threw the entire blame on Muzaffar Jang; but he permitted Chandā Sāhib to negotiate with Murari Rao and his companion to abandon Nāsir Jang, in return for Tādpatri and the neighbouring country which were to be given to him.[36]

Nāsir Jang, on entering the Carnatic, first summoned Muhammad Alī to join him from Trichinopoly and wrote letters to Fort St. David requesting the English to send him a body of European troops. He ordered his own army to concentrate under the hills of Gingee and the protection of its walls. Nāsir Jang himself seems to have reached Gingee about the last week of March. Muhammad Alī joined him with about 6,000 horse at Valudāvur, about 10 miles from Pondicherry; the English detachment under Cope which had been sent previously to Trichinopoly to Muhammad Alī, accompanied him. On March 28, Nāsir Jang was encamped between Villupuram and Koliyanur; the English troops were said to be about 200 English soldiers, 100 *mestizos* and 200 *topasses* besides 400 sepoys.[37] Moreover additional troops from Fort St.

36 Diarist's entry for April 5,—pp. 17-22 of the *Diary*, vol. vii.
37 The figures are not accurate.

David were sent under the command of Lawrence. The camp stretched for about five miles from north to south and three miles from east to west. It was heard and recorded by the Diarist that the Marathas and Kallars in Nāsir Jang's camp made a sortie or two on the French camp on that afternoon, but there was nothing that could be called fighting. Even in this situation, an emissary from Nāsir Jang arrived to treat for peace, to whom, in the presence of Bussy, Muzaffar Jang replied that there could be no talk of peace without the approval of Dupleix. The emissary offered to grant *jaghirs* to both Muzaffar Jang and Chandā Sāhib and to repay the amounts they had borrowed from the French. Muzaffar Jang to whom the emissary came, sent for a French representative to be present during the conversations and his reply was given in the presence of Bussy.[38] Dupleix wrote to Chandā Sāhib that any negotiation should be conducted only through himself; otherwise, he was not for any compromise at all. Shortly afterwards Nāsir Jang's engagement took place, on account of which the English Captain Cope, and the French Commandant, d'Auteuil, exchanged 'mutual recriminations regarding the breach of peace between the two natio s.' Lawrence, with an English embassy, was also present in Nāsir Jang's camp; and he no doubt inspired Cope's recriminations with d'Auteuil.[39] Thus the beginning was made of the direct conflict between the two Companies on the eve of the great revolution that was to see the fall of Nāsir Jang and the triumph of the French.

38 Diarist's entry for March 31—pp. 435–48 of vol. vi. This is an effective support of Chandā Sāhib's opinion that Muzaffar Jang had no preconceived plan of making his own terms with and submitting to Nāsir Jang and that Dupleix's estimate of him was not fully justified.

39 Orme estimates the troops under d'Auteuil at 2,000 Europeans; and the English troops that came with Lawrence at 600. But Dodwell shows that, besides the detachment of 100 under Cope that came from Trichinopoly, only about 200 men were sent subsequently from Fort St. David (*Dupleix and Clive*, p. 46, foot-note 5.)

CHAPTER X

THE CLIMAX OF THE FRENCH EFFORT

DUPLEIX'S NEGOTIATIONS WITH NASIR JANG

NASIR Jang halted at Valudāvur after his triumph, where he received Murtazā Alī Khān of Vellore to whom he gave Arcot. Mīr Asad was made the diwan of the Nawab; and both agreed to pay the Nizam an annual tribute of 50 lakhs for the subah.[1] Wandewash was to be given over to Mīr Asad who suggested that, if Pondicherry were blockaded, Chandā Sāhib and Muzaffar Jang's mother who were there, would have to be given up and most of the sepoys would desert from the French side. Major Lawrence who was in Nāsir Jang's camp is said to have written letters to Dupleix and d'Auteuil that he would arrange to effect a peace between the French and Nāsir Jang. The Diarist's view was that the English could not remove from the mind of Nāsir Jang his fear of the French, and as they could not attack Pondicherry directly and Nāsir Jang insisted that he should not return without effecting something, 'they might have offered to make peace between us and him and have written to you.'[2] Nāsir Jang was advised by his nobles like Sayyad Lashkar Khān and Sayyad Sharīf Khān that the besieging of Pondicherry would prove a very arduous task and the English would not fight them as there was peace between them; they were of the opinion that the subah of Arcot should be given to Muzaffar Jang and peace should be made with the French; otherwise Chandā Sāhib would return with European aid and renew the struggle for the Nawabship of Arcot. This was all the more effective as Murari Rao, Janoji Nimbalakar, Chandra Sen and other Maratha sardars in

1 The Diarist tells us that Nawab Sadat-ullah Khān used to pay 12 lakhs a year; Anvar-ud-dīn agreed to pay 24 lakhs; and Mahfuz Khān 28 lakhs of rupees.

2 Entry for April 12, 1750, p. 36 of vol. vii of the *Diary*.
The letter of the English and the reply of Dupleix are given in Martineau's *Dupleix et l'Inde Française* (1749-54), p. 121.

the Nizām's camp were preparing to depart. In reply to communications received from Nāsir Jang and Shāh Nawāz Khān, Dupleix sent ambassadors, including two of his Council, Mm. du Basset and Delarche.[3] Shāh Nawāz Khān sympathized with the French; but apparently he was not able to persuade his master who demanded the surrender of Chandā Sāhib and declined to give him the subah of Arcot. The envoys returned to Pondicherry with a letter from Shāh Nawāz Khān explaining the situation, to which a veiled threat of war was sent as a reply. In fact, the envoys said that Shāh Nawāz Khān and his peshkar, Ramdas Pandit, told them secretly that, if they departed without hesitation, marched again with troops and fell upon Nāsir Jang's camp-

3 Orme states that the first letter of Dupleix to Nāsir Jang was not replied to by that prince; but Dupleix made use of this pretext to continue the correspondence. The Diarist wrote for April 15th, that Dupleix observed to him that although six letters had been sent to the Nizām with the usual compliments, no reply had been received, the cause being that the letters were not couched in proper form. The letters from Nāsir Jang and Shāh Nawāz Khān were only received two days later.

One of the two French envoys spoke Persian with tolerable fluency. Du Basset had gone on an embassy to Nizām-ul-Mulk at Trichinopoly in 1743; according to their original instructions, they were to demand the restoration of Adoni for Muzaffar Jang, while Arcot might be given to Chandā Sāhib or to the 'young prince', *i.e.*, the younger son of Ṣafdar Alī who was then residing at Wandewash. Dupleix himself subsequently wrote to the envoys that Arcot was to go to Muzaffar Jang, but later turned and agreed that Muzaffar Jang might be kept in prison, provided Adone was given to his family. Thus 'M. Cultru concludes with reason that Dupleix still had no policy except that of hiring his troops to the highest bidder'. 'With such ill-defined aims, the ambassadors could accomplish little beyond getting a general idea of the parties into which the court was divided. They also seem to have sought relations with the Pathan Nawabs of Cuddapah, Kurnool and Savanur, who were already discontented at their prolonged detention in the south.' (Dodwell's *Dupleix and Clive*, pp. 48-9).

Also Martineau's *Dupleix et l' Inde Française, (1749–54)*, p. 122.

guards by night, he would arrange to get Arcot for Chandā Sāhib and restore his territory to Muzaffar Jang.[4]

The French attacked Nāsir Jang's camp on the night of the 27th April, killed and wounded nearly 1,000 of the enemy as well as a large number of horse and cattle. A detachment under M. de La Touche as the captain of the attacking party, was sent out by d'Auteuil who had taken the command again; and he took by surprise one of the quarters of the camp and penetrated more than a mile.[5]

Intrigues and Factions in Nasir Jang's Camp

Ramdas Pandit is stated by the Diarist to have offered terms of peace by which Trichinopoly was to be given to Chandā Sāhib, as well as a *mansab* of 5,000 horse, a *jaghir* in the Arcot subah and permission to seize and plunder Tanjore.[6] It was also stated that Muhammad Alī had been promised Arcot and that the English had agreed to help him on receiving a *cowle* for Poonamallee and a part of the Devanampatnam country as *inam*. In the *darbar* of the Nizām, when the consent of the nobles was asked for the appointment of Muhammad Alī to the subah of

4 According to Orme (who, however, says that the French deputies remained in the Nizam's camp for 8 days) Dupleix obtained the real advantages intended from their visit, a knowledge of Nāsir Jang's strength and of the state of parties at his court. He continues:—'Suspicions were entertained of the clandestine conduct of the French deputies, and Major Lawrence was informed that some design was carrying on in the camp against the Soubah (Nāsir Jang) in which Shanawaze Khān, the prime minister, was the principal agent. The latter part of the report was not true; and the first could not be proved; however, the major, at an audience endeavoured to acquaint Nāsir Jang with what he had heard. . .', vol. i, (4th edition, p. 145).

5 It was the first of 'a score of such night-attacks made by both French and English, almost all of which were equally successful'.

6 Purport of a letter written by the Pandit and brought by Chandā Sāhib to the Governor (p. 89 of Vol. vii of the *Diary*). Ramdas Pandit was a partisan of Chandā Sāhib and strove hard in his interest.

Arcot, Shāh Nawāz Khān[7] said that the subah should be given to Chandā Sāhib who deserved favour. Sayyad Lashkar Khān said that he would very willingly consent to Muhammad Alī's appointment; but as the French were opposed to him, he thought it inadvisable. Muhammad Alī openly quarrelled with Sayyad Lashkar Khān for his remarks; and Nāsir Jang dissolved the assembly without giving the dress of honour to the former. Dupleix was also told that Murari Rao wanted to be friendly with him and believed that Nāsir Jang had a wholesome fear of the French. This quieted the apprehension entertained at Pondicherry that Murari Rao would be given the right of *chauth* over the Arcot subah on condition of his staying in the country, as was reported.

Muzaffar Jang's captivity did not seem to have been harsh, and he contrived easily to maintain correspondence with his mother, Dupleix and others at Pondicherry. He entreated Dupleix to send his mother to him; but the latter refused to depart saying it would be unseemly to go away without repaying the Governor what she owed him.[8] She was hoping that if her debt was paid before Nāsir Jang left the country, there would be a good chance of her son being released and treated well.

News meanwhile arrived that the English under Captain Cope took leave of Nāsir Jang and departed for Fort St. David owing to the expected arrival of Portuguese ships,[9] which was strongly

7 Shāh Nawāz Khān was always ill-disposed towards Anvar-ud-dīn and was opposed to his appointment to the subah of Arcot. MS. of Burhan-ud-dīn's *Tuzuk-i-Wālājāhi*, Book I, translated by M. H. Nainar (of the Madras University). The Khān continued his enmity towards the son.

8 Muzaffar Jang's mother was the half-sister of Nāsir Jang and his elder brother Ghāzī-ud-dīn Khān who were the sons of Nizām-ul-Mulk's second wife. The latter's first wife was the daughter of a Pathan noble; and Muzaffar Jang's mother was her daughter. Nizām-ul-Mulk had six sons. There was no truth in the scandal recorded by the Diarist that Nāsir Jang was the son of Nizām-ul-Mulk by a low woman.

9 'The despatch of ships from Goa for the recovery of San Thomé was expected as a result of Dupleix's intrigues with Goa. But there is

rumoured. Nāsir Jang is said to have given an interview to Muzaffar Jang and to have relaxed the severity of his confinement, possibly as a result of the letter that the latter's mother wrote to him. On May 3rd, the Nizām held a *darbar* before marching at which besides Sayyad Lashkar Khān, Shāh Nawāz Khān, Sayyad Sharīf Khān and his other diwans, were also present Nawab Abdul Nabī Khān of Cuddapah, Himāyat Bahadur Khān of Kurnool and other nobles. They all advised him to forgive Muzaffar Jang; while Jamīl Bēg Khān, the subhadar of Berar, advised the Nizam to conciliate the French and win them over to his side; and Sayyad Lashkar Khān and others offered the same advice as to Muzaffar Jang.[10] Nāsir Jang ordered his return march north; and the Diarist records that on May 5, he heard that Cope and Lawrence went to Nāsir Jang's camp when he was about to commence his march, with the request that the Poonamallee, Mylapore and Devanampatnam countries should be given as an *inam* to the English, in return for their services; but they had to return unsuccessfully;[11] and Nāsir Jang is said to have torn the letter of Lawrence, praised the services of the French to Muzaffar

no reason to suppose that the English feared at this time any Portuguese interference'. Dodwell in his note on p. 102 of *Diary*, vol. vii—*See* the writer's notes on the English Occupation of San Thomé by Boscawen, the letter of the Fort St. David Council to the Company justifying their action, the Portuguese Viceroy's letter of remonstrance to the English at Fort St. David and the latter's reply to him, May 4, 1750—the last two being quoted by Love in his *Vestiges of Old Madras*, vol. ii, pp. 400–1. The English possibly expected about this time a reply from the Portuguese Government at Goa (*Journal of Indian History*, vol. ix, pp. 341–45.)

10 Haji Fazil Khān, the steward of Muzaffar Jang's household, related these happenings as he had seen them, to Dupleix. (Diarist's entry for May 4, 1750).

11 Dodwell says that the English ambassadors to Nāsir Jang wrote on April 14, that a party was forming among the Nizam's ministers influencing him against them, at the instigation of the French; and they 'seem to intimate in their discourse that they hold the assistance we have given them in very little esteem.' On May 2, the ambassadors wrote:—'Yesterday we got Nāsir Jang's consent to our demands according to our former advices, and had our agreement reduced into writing in

Jang and dismissed the English envoys with scant ceremony; and M. de La Touche also said he heard that the English had departed in great displeasure.[12] The French hoisted their flag at Bāhur; and they heard that Nāsir Jang was perfectly willing that Tanjore and Trichinopoly be given to Chandā Sāhib along with a *mansab* jaghir, but the latter would not agree and wanted Arcot as well, though he was persuaded to yield for the present and to seize Arcot as soon as Nāsir Jang should have recrossed the Krishna. Chandā Sāhib knew that Dupleix would not consent to a settlement if Arcot were not given, and replied accordingly; he contrived that his demands should be made known to Nāsir Jang, knowing that the chances of a settlement would be indefinitely prolonged, unless Shāh Nawāz Khān and Ramdas Pandit were definitely won over to his side.

order for his signing it, that the *phirmaund* might be made out, but it is not yet perfected, and this day, his whole army has marched about six miles from us towards Arcot.' (Taken from the Orme *MSS.* India, volume ix, pp. 2175–7, containing the proceedings of the English embassy composed of Stringer Lawrence and Foss Westcott and accompanied by Captain Dalton, from March 24 to May 5, 1750). These contain letters from Dupleix to Lawrence and from the French Governor to Nāsir Jang, asking him to reconcile himself to Muzaffar Jang.

The Fort St. David despatch to the Company, dated October 24, 1750, abstracted by Dodwell in *The Madras Despatches, 1744–55*, (pp. 112-3), says that Nāsir Jang remained at Vaḻudāvur for about a month and then moved to Arcot; he desired the English to accompany him; but Lawrence etc., insisted on first receiving grants of the Poonamallee country, to which demand Nāsir Jang returned no answer; and the English troops were recalled and reached Fort St. David, (April 22, May 3).

12 The reception of the English by Nāsir Jang was warm at first; a week after their arrival, they complained they had good reason to suspect that the French were tampering with some of the countries. 'Indeed their services had not been such as to merit any considerable reward. They had proffered unwelcome military advice; they had refused to pursue the French in their flight; they had informed Nāsir Jang that they could not enter the French bounds. Moreover, they were accompanied by a native agent, who, though long employed by the English, made no scruple about betraying their plans and letters to the French.

Nāsir Jang's order that the French factory at Masulipatam should be captured, was carried out by the subhadar of that place. The soldiers in the factory at Yanam defended themselves, but had to yield. These factories were seized in order to compel Dupleix to better terms. But Dupleix was not daunted; he sent troops to capture the fort at Vaḷudāvur; but as it was too strong to be taken by Indian troops alone without European reinforcements, he resolved to wait till Nāsir Jang should have passed Arcot; there was also trouble with the sepoys (see below) who refused to act without their pay; and for the time the troops returned to Villiyanallur. He had ambitions that he could easily

On April 20, they refused to co-operate in an attack on Wandewash, unless their demands were granted. Again, they refused to join Nāsir Jang in an expedition to raise tribute in Tanjore. On May 1, although Nāsir Jang had agreed to their requests, 'this day the whole army had marched six miles from us towards Arcot.' So the ambassadors and their troops marched back to Fort St. David.' (Dodwell, p. 50).

Orme says of the English embassy as follows:—

'Meanwhile Major Lawrence . . .solicited Nāsir Jang to confirm the grant, which Mahommed Ally, now esteemed Nabob of Arcot, had made to the East India Company, of a territory near Madrass, in return for the assistance of their troops. He had often promised to comply with this request; but his minister, Shāh Nawaz Khān, regarded such accession as inconsistent with the majesty of the Mogul empire, and prevented the *phirmaund* or patent, from being issued from his office. Wearied with prevarication, Major Lawrence insisted on a peremptory answer, on which he was assured that he should be immediately satisfied, provided he would march with the battalion to Arcot . . . He did not think it prudent to comply with this proposal, lest the French and Chandā Sāhib should take advantage of his absence and invade the English territory. He therefore endeavoured to divert the Soubah from this purpose, by representing that it would give the enemy an opportunity of recruiting their forces and recommencing hostilities; whereas by remaining near Pondicherry he might, by cutting off their communications with the country, reduce them to such distresses as would oblige them to accept of peace on his own terms. This reasoning producing no effect, the major returned with his battalion to Fort St. David; . . ., (Vol. i, *Fourth Edition*, pp. 145-6).

send by sea munitions to Yanam and Masulipatam, from which they could be easily carried to Hyderabad and Aurangabad.[13]

Conflicting news reached Pondicherry from Nāsir Jang's camp. Shāh Nawāz Khān wrote on May 11th that he would be remaining at Arcot for four months, and, if in the meantime Chandā Sāhib gave satisfaction, the Arcot subah would be given to him, while Trichinopoly and a *mansab* jaghir for Tanjore would be granted immediately. Dupleix insisted that the places mortgaged to the French by Chandā Sāhib should be restored to their possession till the money was paid; and the French factories in the Northern Sarkars should not be interfered with. He even offered to guarantee that Muzaffar Jang did not draw the sword against his uncle, as the latter feared he might do, if he were released and joined the French as was very likely.[14] Nāsir Jang, it was reported, could not easily make up his mind; and it was also believed that Muhammad Alī Khān had been given Arcot and he had sent for 500 sepoys from the English as an escort and arranged to pay five lakhs of rupees to Nāsir Jang and had sent

13 Dupleix contrived to have the following conveyed to Nāsir Jang secretly:—'Tell him secretly, that, if Masulipatam and the country be given to me, I will help Nāsir Jang with all he needs to conquer the country as far as Delhi. I will send 4,000 soldiers to smite his enemies.'; also 'I will send munitions of war from here to Masulipatam and Yanam whence they can be easily carried to Hyderabad and Aurangabad; we of Pondicherry will conquer all who disobey him, and I will help him with all he needs to fulfil his desires.'—pp. 147 and 148—*Diary*, of the Vol. I. This offer was made in reply to the letter containing terms of settlement with Chandā Sāhib received by Shāh Nawāz Khān.

14 Abdul Nabī Khān of Cuddapah urged Nāsir Jang to release his nephew and give him his own country and Arcot, and then he would keep the French quiet and live at peace. Otherwise, he said, that if Muzaffar Jang should be carried away a prisoner, Nāsir Jang should, for the sake of effecting perfect security, conquer the French, capture their fort, imprison Chandā Sāhib and recover Muzaffar Jang's family who were at Pondicherry. The other nobles also advised Nāsir Jang to the same effect; but one or two poisoned his mind with the fear, that, if Muzaffar Jang were released, he would win over the nobles and the army and bring about great trouble to Nāsir Jang himself. (Entry for May 12, 1750).

for the amount from Trichinopoly.[15] A letter received by Jayaram Pandit at Pondicherry informed that Muhammad Alī was given the subah of Arcot and a dress of honour on the 11th May, *i.e.* on the night of the fifth of Jamādi-ul-Ākhir. Delay ensued in the matter of the proposal to release Muzaffar Jang and invest him with authority, as Nāsir Jang feared danger for himself through such a contingency.[16] Nāsir Jang continued to stay on for some days near Wandewash, negotiating for the payment of a big sum of money to himself from Taqī Sāhib who held the place and was a son-in-law of Dōst Alī. Once a storm of wind and rain beat down his tents; and in the confusion that ensued, a false rumour arose that Muzaffar Jang had escaped. The division of the Nizam's camp into the two parties respectively supporting the causes of Nāsir Jang and his nephew, is seen more and more clearly in the entries of the Diarist. The latter's partisans like Sayyad Lashkar Khān, Jamīl Bēg Khān and the Nawabs of Cuddapah, Kurnool and Savanur are said to have resolved to overthrow Nāsir Jang with their troops and to send Muzaffar Jang under a strong guard to Pondicherry for the sake of safety. Ramdas Pandit,[17] whom Grant-Duff calls

15 Dodwell points out that in a consultation held at Fort St. David on April 30, May 11, Floyer reported that Muhammad Alī had been appointed Nawab and desired that the sepoys in his service in the bounds of Fort St. David be sent over to him; and that, in consequence, it was resolved to advance their arrears amounting to 14,000 rupees and send them out. (Note on p. 154 of the *Diary*, vol. vii.)

16 'Shāh Nawaz Khān, Khāzi Dāyem and Moro Pandit are on Nāsir Jang's side . . . all tell him that if Muzaffar Jang were released, he would seize and imprison both him and themselves, that Saiyid Lashkar Khān, the mansabdars, jamadars and others would choose Muzaffar Jang as their leader, seize the country . . . That is why Nāsir Jang has abandoned the idea of releasing Muzaffar Jang, now fearing that he will become an enemy and seek his death'—pp. 177–8 of vol. vii of the *Diary*.

17 'The fall of Nāsir Jang was wrought by the intrigues of M. Dupleix. He gained a Brahmin, named Ramdas, a native of Sicacole, in the confidence of Nāsir Jang, and through him raised seditions in the

'the traitor Ramdass' was secretly in favour of Muzaffar Jang's elevation, pretended to seek Nāsir Jang's interest alone and at the same time did all in his power to encourage Sayyad Lashkar Khān and Muzaffar Jang's party, communicating to them all that passed with Nāsir Jang. It was only Shāh Nawāz Khān and his adherents that were opposed to Muzaffar Jang; all the others wished Nāsir Jang to be overthrown.[18] Dupleix even suggested that Muzaffar Jang might escape to Pondicherry by way of Alambarai where he would post some soldiers with boats and sloops, and from which he might go in a few hours to Kunimedu, Covelong or Pondicherry, whichever way the road should be clear, and arranged for some money being sent to him in pagodas as they would be easier to carry. The plot against Nāsir Jang was expected to bear fruit in 15 or 20 days.

Meanwhile information was received that Shāh Nawāz Khān had arranged that Trichinopoly and Tanjore should be leased out to Chandā Sāhib, after being made over to Dupleix who could occupy them and then lease them to his protégé. Arcot was to be under Shāh Nawāz Khān; and if Chandā Sāhib should act for four or five months as he desired, and should pay the tribute due for Trichinopoly according to agreement, then he would receive Arcot. The amount owing to Dupleix from Muzaffar Jang should be paid by Chandā Sāhib in return for the grant of Trichinopoly to him; and Muzaffar Jang's bond should be returned and his family sent away to him. Dupleix was assured by the envoy that the Mughals had made up their minds to seize Tanjore and grant it out; and though he expressed a fear that the Raja of Tanjore would apply to the English and the Dutch for help and promise them territory as against any French attack, still he was told that Shāh Nawāz Khān desired to become the captor of the Tanjore fort, though the French should actually conquer it. Finally, Dupleix agreed to be content with the grant

army, which Dupleix called into operation by an attack on the camp.' *History of the Mahrattas*—4th ed. Chap. xviii—Vol. I, pp. 525–6.

18 Diarist's entry for May 22nd, 1750—p. 183 of vol. vii.

of lands round Karikal equal to the cost of the expedition which would have to be sent to conquer Tanjore and to give an account of the total cost thereof.[19] Dupleix was further told that Muhammad Alī was hard pressed for money and unable to pay at once all the amount due for the Arcot subah; and his brother; Mahfuz Khān (who had been made prisoner at Ambur, subsequently released by promising to pay Muzaffar Jang 11 lakhs for the Trichinopoly country and had later joined Nāsir Jang's camp) was greatly depressed by the scant attention paid to him and threatened to turn *faqir* and go on a pilgrimage to Mecca.[20] Sayyad Lashkar Khān, Sayyad Sharīf Khān and others now departed with their contingents; while the Pathan Nawabs also sent their troops in advance; thus Nāsir Jang could not stay long and must soon depart. He agreed to appoint Taqī Sāhib of Wandiwash as the Diwan of Muhammad Alī, after which he proceeded to Arcot. Taqī Sāhib also agreed to make Muhammad Alī Khān of Polur (Chandā Sāhib's brother) swear to be friends with his namesake and gave plenty of trouble to Chandā Sāhib's wife who was at Wandiwash and whom he now turned out of the fort.

The Employment of Sepoys by the French

In the month of May when Dupleix presented medals to Abdul Rahmān and Shaikh Hasan with commissions for them as captains of the sepoys and the Diarist entered this fact in his account, he gave an account of the origin of the sepoys in the French service, which is deemed by Dodwell to be a generally accurate account. In 1740, when war was threatened between England and France sepoys were first entertained; but it was not Dupleix that entertained them, as the Diarist says of the enlistment of Shaikh Hasan and others. 'They were first employed

19 Conversation between Dupleix and Jayaram Pandit in the presence of Chandā Sāhib and the Diarist, according to the latter's entry for May 26th.

20 Shortly before Anvar-ud-dīn's death, Mahfuz Khān had been appointed as the deputy of his father at Arcot, by the diplomacy of his partisan Raja Sampat Rai. He had joined his father, before the struggle at Ambur (Burhan-ud-dīn's *Tuzuk-i-Wālājāhi*—Bk. I.)

at Mahē in the war with Boyanore, 1739–40, when Dupleix was still at Chandernagore. Early in 1742 Dumas ordered three companies of them over to the Coromandel coast to assist in defending Karikal against the Tanjoreans. Two companies were sent back in 1743 and broke; but others again were obtained in 1746 at the request of La Bourdonnais, who had seen them in action at Mahē in 1741. It is interesting to note that whereas the English soon appointed European drill-sergeants and a European adjutant to their Sepoy-Corps, Dupleix left the command and discipline entirely in Indian hands, except when sepoys were co-operating with European troops.'[21] Ranga Pillai gives Dupleix the entire credit of the enlisting of sepoys. He says: 'Dupleix entertained in his service, Shaikh Hasan, Abdul Rahmān and others who had formerly served in the troubles at Mahē on the coast of Malabar. After these troubles were over, Shaikh Hasan, Bikkan Khān, etc., came here with 200 sepoys. A year later Bikkan Khān and 100 sepoys were sent back; and Shaikh Hasan with his 100 sepoys was invited to stay. He did not receive enough even to buy *conjee* . . . . but news came of war being declared between England and France (September, 1744). Thereon Shaikh Hasan was summoned and directed to invite his elder brother (Abdul Rahmān) (who was out of service in Malabar) with 500 or 600 sepoys. Abdul Rahmān came accordingly. When . . . Dupleix seized Madras . . . Abdul Rahmān and his brother seized palanquins, elephants, horses, etc., . . . and the Governor permitted all to keep their booty . . . When the English were attacked at Fort St. David and they attacked the French at Pondicherry, he brought some men under the pretence of enlisting them as sepoys. . . He made more money on the expedition against Anvar-ud-dīn Khān by telling

21 Dodwell's note on the Diarist's account, in p. 168 of the *Diary*, vol. vii. 'The raising of actual native regiments was first undertaken by the French, and it was due to the coming struggle for mastery in Southern India, that we owe the first conception of a regular native army.' McMunn in *The Armies of India*, p. 4; also Dodwell: *Sepoy Recruitment in the Old Madras Army* (1922)—pp. 2–4.

Chandā Sāhib that he had raised 2,000 horsemen and sepoys. . .' Ranga Pillai is angry that he should have had a free hand in making so much money by plunder, and thinks that he cared very little for his commission as captain from Europe or his present or medals and looked to the getting of a high mansab for himself from the Mughals. Another detail that the Diarist supplied was that the sepoys still wore their traditional clothing of coats, trousers and turbans and their native commandants supplied them with it.[22]

Shaikh Hasan and Abdur Rahmān had frequently to suffer from the insubordination and mutinous spirit of the sepoys. The latter were usually in considerable arrears of pay. When Shaikh Hasan took Tiruvati fort from its *killedar* in June, the sepoys actually refused to march without their pay. After the fort was captured, it was with great difficulty that they could be restrained from plundering; Shaikh Hasan told Dupleix, according to the Diarist, that the sepoys abused him so violently that he feared for his life, and they declared that if they were not allowed to give back their muskets and be dismissed, they would become afraid for their lives and then kill their captain.[23]

French Capture of Masulipatam

On the first of June a sloop was despatched from Pondicherry to recover the Yanam factory which had been abandoned by its chief, Lenoir, on the approach of Khāja Namatullah Khān; but the Diarist thought that it was intended to procure the release of M. Coquet, chief of the factory at Masulipatam. Nāsir Jang gave orders that the two French factories of Yanam and Masulipatam should be seized; the factories were easily taken possession of by

22 Diarist's entry for June 1, 1750, p. 219—of vol. vii of the *Diary*.

23 Pages 265–66 of vol. vii of the *Diary*. Dodwell remarks that such mutinous episodes, due mainly to their pay being in arrears, were by no means uncommon among the French sepoys. 'The murder of Dewan Raghunath Das, a little later in the Deccan, shows that Shaikh Hasan's fears were not wholly imaginary. Bussy himself was at one time in apprehension for his life.'—*Ibid.*, footnote 1.

Khāja Namatullah Khān, the subhadar of Ellore and Rajahmundry about whom mention has been already made. He advanced on Yanam with 2,000 foot and 200 horse; and Lenoir, the chief of that factory had the trees surrounding it to be cut down and the ground levelled. Dupleix had tried in the course of his secret negotiations with Shāh Nawāz Khān that Nāsir Jang should direct that the French factories should not be interfered with and give a written order to that effect. Lenoir abandoned the Yanam factory, even before it was attacked by the enemy; he took shelter in one of the islands at the mouth of the river, situated to the north-east, where the French had taken refuge during the late Maratha invasion. At Masulipatam two French factors were taken prisoners and M. Coquet, the chief of the French factory, was asked to pay 15,000 pagodas. Lenoir retired to the island with all the goods, men and a few guns.[24] Presently the Yanam factory was recovered; and Masulipatam was captured later. Dupleix knew of the defenceless condition of Masulipatam[25] and resolved to take it by assault, regarding it as an acquisition essential for the realization of his future views.

On July 9, 1750, two large vessels with a boat were despatched with 200 soldiers, 150 sepoys and 10 *topasses* under the command of M. de La Tour with mortars, cannon and other equipment to

24 According to *Orme* (vol. i, p. 146), 'Nāsir Jang's officers proceeded without violence, plundered nothing and sealed up what they took possession of. The detriment sustained was not considerable.' 'The French repeatedly declared that the English from the neighbouring factory of Ingeram had helped the Moghuls to take Yanam. Even M. Cultru makes the same assertion. However the English correspondence cited above (Fort St. David Letters received 1750) shows that they had no hand in it.' (Dodwell—*Dupleix and Clive*—Note 1 on p. 51). Dodwell says that, despite Nāsir Jang's orders, only the four walls of the Yanam factory were left standing.

25 According to the Diarist, the amaldars of Masulipatam trembled and said they had behaved foolishly when they extracted money from the French factory and feared that the French would come and burn and destroy the whole country; while the merchants feared that the town would never regain its old prosperity (entry for 5th June, 1750—p. 231 of vol. vii of the *Diary*.)

attack and capture Masulipatam; and a lakh of rupees was also sent in order to provide the factories with goods. The vessels arrived before Masulipatam on July 11th, and took possession of the fort without 'the least opposition', while the Mughals attempted 'to blockade the place, but quickly desisted.' The French landed in the night and took the town with very little loss; they kept possession of it and immediately began to put it into a better position of defence. The Mussalman authorities declared that they lodged the French prisoners well and treated them respectfully; and so they were not to be blamed for obeying the orders of their master, Nāsir Jang. All the inhabitants were allowed to return; and the sepoys and Europeans were warned that they would be severely punished for any theft or plunder; and the Diarist notes with evident satisfaction that 'all those who fled from the town have returned, including even the Dutch and their families.[26] Nāsir Jang was sorely troubled by the loss of Masulipatam, where the French did not allow even the Dutch to fly their flag, though they did not in any manner interfere with the Dutch trade.[27] The Dutch Council at Negapatam protested that their factory site was given to them by the Mughal emperor, and they had his orders for flying their flag and hence the French ought not to have pulled it down. Dupleix replied that their contention held good so long as the port was in Mughal possession; but as the French had captured it, and 'as both flags cannct fly there, we have ordered theirs to be pulled down and that they can hoist their flag there only when they produce the orders of the King of France.' On October 22nd, the Diarist recorded that he heard that, owing to orders from Negapatam, the Dutch factory people at Masulipatam had sent all their goods by ship to Kothapatnam and Cocanada on the New Moon day; and as such a day

26 Diarist's entry for July 25th, 1750—p. 325 of the *Diary*, vol. vii.

27 Dupleix added, as Dodwell says, in his letter to Masulipatam; 'Nous persons que, si vous aviez, voulu joindre vos sollicitationsā celles des principaux marchands de Mazulipatam pour la delivrance des Srs. Coquet et Lasalle, nous ne nous fussions point trouvēs dans le cas de nous emparer de cette ville.'

was unlucky, a tempest arose and two Dutch ships sank with their cargoes of goods and money. The abandonment of the Dutch factory was intended as ' a protest against the action of the French in refusing to allow the Dutch flag to fly there.'[28]

Further Developments

Dupleix was frequently advised and persuaded himself into believing that for fear of him, Nāsir Jang hesitated to entrust the subah of Arcot to Muhammad Alī and nobody dared to accept the job. He resolved to tie *toranams,* as a mark of French occupation, in the regions of Tiruvati, Panruti and Villupuram and to get the mortgage amounts due to him from Mudāmiah, the faujdar of Chidambaram, who held the place from Abdul Nabī Khān of Cuddapah. Mudāmiah removed his goods and property to Devikottai, under the protection of the English; and Dupleix was advised by Ranga Pillai to send a few soldiers and sepoys with a couple of mortars in order to coerce him for the amount due. Mudāmiah complained that Muhammad Alī's men were demanding payment and protested that he would wait for instructions about the Chidambaram mortgage from Nawab Abdul Nabī Khān. Ranga Pillai and Dupleix distrusted Mudāmiah's professions and sent dragoons and sepoys against him; thereupon he fled to Devikottai with a number of people from Chidambaram. The French troops pursued him and his men agreed to remain in the fort and promised to pay a part of the amount in ready money and the balance in a few days. Evidently, he wished ' to be able to allege compulsion in case the other side called him to an account for the payments he made.' He negotiated with the Diarist for time in which to sell grain enough to pay 50,000 rupees and was told to give sowcars' bonds for the balance due.

28 The Dutch indeed landed a party of soldiers, a few weeks after the French captured the place, but were easily compelled to withdraw them. 'They seem to have displayed a political ineptitude similar to that which ruined their expedition to Bengal (1759).' After the English secured possession of the place they ceded their factory which was then in a very ruinous condition and all their rights along with it.

After reaching Arcot where he stayed for some days, he was told by Muhammad Alī that he could manage the *subah* if he were allowed to maintain 10,000 horse and receive all the collections, but not otherwise; he had not the help of the English to oppose the French and meet them in battle, as Nāsir Jang had refused to grant them the Poonamallee and Devanampatnam countries and Mylapore as *inam* and they had departed in consequence. The Diarist reported to Dupleix on June 11, 1750, that when Muzaffar Jang was imprisoned in the Arcot fort, he attempted to take his life by tying a cloth round his neck, but was prevented from doing so by Nāsir Jang's guards; thereupon he was comforted by Shāh Nawāz Khān, under instructions from Nāsir Jang, with a promise of 'the kingdom he desired and a dress of honour'. Nāsir Jang desired that the Pathan Nawabs who were anxious to depart should stay with him till he also started. Taqī Sāhib of Wandiwash was afraid of the French and now desired that the proposal regarding Chandā Sāhib should be carried out successfully although till lately, he was hostile to Chandā Sāhib. Dupleix was told that if French should capture the fort of Vaḷudāvur, matters would be hastened by Nāsir Jang towards a settlement; while Chandā Sāhib was desirous that French troops should occupy the countries of Villupuram and Tiruvati as well as Porto Novo in order that Nāsir Jang might be frightened into granting him terms.

Conflicting counsels prevailed at Arcot. It was reported that Muzaffar Jang promised to bring round Chandā Sāhib and fetch him to Arcot and that Mahfuz Khān advised Muhammad Alī that the French would kill whoever became the *subahdar* and would conquer the country.[29] Villupuram and Tiruvati were occupied by French sepoys. Chandā Sāhib was advised by his brother, Muhammad Alī Khān of Polur, to beware of going to Arcot for an interview, even though he should be promised safety by means of an oath on the *Quran*. It was also learnt that Shāh Nawāz Khān himself was preparing to set out for Pondicherry to pacify

29 Entry for June 13th—pp. 252-3 of the *Diary*, vol. vii.

Dupleix and Chandā Sāhib and to take Muzaffar Jang's mother, wife and children. The capture of Tiruvati frightened the Mussalmans at Chidambaram into compliance. Shāh Nawāz Khān himself is reported to have secretly written to Dupleix, that if he should seize the fort of Vaḷudāvur, he would obtain what he desired through the very efforts of his enemies. The Pathan Nawabs, Abdul Nabī Khān, Himāyat Bahadur Khān and Abdul Majīd Khān, refused to pay their *peshkash* to Nāsir Jang on the ground that they had not paid any even to his father and would pay him none now, their lands were plundered by the *poligars* and the Nizām was responsible for the cost of their maintaining troops to chastise them. Nāsir Jang became angry; and the Nawabs absented themselves from the *durbar*. A collision occurred between Nāsir Jang's people and their followers, and Shāh Nawāz Khān had to intervene to make peace.[30] There were also troubles between the Peshwa and Nāsir Jang; and the former had sent word to the latter urging him to return. As if these troubles were not enough, Muzaffar Jang made a second effort to escape from his prison-room; and Nāsir Jang had to put new and vigilant guards over him and took away from him the liberty of receiving visits and sending messages.

In the beginning of July it was rumoured at Pondicherry that a number of nobles of the Nizam had resolved to release Muzaffar Jang, establish him as the *subhadar* of the Deccan and seize or slay Nāsir Jang; and Muzaffar Jang's attempted escape, noted above, was in reality done with their connivance; and when it failed, the latter took all the blame on himself and pretended madness. Chandā Sāhib advised that agents should be employed to arrange matters secretly with the Pathan Nawabs for the deposition of Nāsir Jang. Letters were written cautiously by Dupleix, to Chandā Sāhib's men at the Nizam's camp couched in general

30 The Diarist, after recording these items of news, wrote:—'The Arcot people and other *killedars* who expected much are discontented. All Nāsir Jang's old friends have become his enemies. . . His commands are disregarded and he cannot prosper. . . '

terms;[31] and the messengers were given specific instructions to arrange an interview between the discontented nobles and the Pathan Nawabs.

THE ENGLISH JOIN MUHAMMAD ALI

While thus Dupleix was taking advantage of the situation in Nāsir Jang's camp, Muhammad Alī wrote to the English Governor Floyer, saying that the French were fortifying themselves in Tiruvati, and declaring that a *sanad* granting Poonamallee to the English had been drawn out and lodged with a substantial merchant at Arcot and would be delivered to them when Muhammad Alī should become the Nawab, in September, after Nāsir Jang should depart; he also sent a copy of the *sanad*, along with a bill of exchange for Rs. 20,000 to defray the expenses of the troops for two months in lieu of the Poonamallee revenues for that period.[32] As the French were preparing both openly and insiduously to make Chandā Sāhib Nawab, Captain Cope was sent out with a body of 600 men and a field-train on June 30th, and joined the Nawab who had marched down from Arcot with a body of horse, a little to the west of Tiruvati.[33]

Muhammad Alī Khān later advanced to Tirupapuliyur, near Fort St. David, with his brother, Abdul Wahāb Khān, his brother-in-law, Khair-ud-dīn Khān, Dewan Muhammad Abrar, Badē Sāhib son of Hussain Tāhir and other *jemadars*. He had

31 'So also you seek to remove evil from the country, and accomplish all that you undertake. I will therefore grant you all that you desire as soon as I hear that the matter has been settled.'—p. 304 of vol. vii of the *Diary*.

32 *The Madras Despatches* (1744-55), p. 114.

33 The Diarist wrote that Major Lawrence who was acting as Governor at Fort St. David, had recalled Cope; but Muhammad Alī told Cope who was about to start that he had only come down in reliance on English help; and that if they now departed under the pretext that a new Governor had been appointed, he would be unable to fulfil his promises to Nāsir Jang. Both he and Cope wrote to Lawrence for further orders. Entry for July 18, 1750, p. 31–4 of vol. vii of the *Diary*. Later, the Diarist entered for July 26th, that Mr. Lawrence had refused help before reinforcements arrived to guard Fort St. David and declared that he could do nothing of himself without orders. (p. 327).

about 4,600 horsemen, 4,000 peons and a body of 500 matchlock men of his own; while Cope had 700 Europeans, 13 field-pieces and about 2,200 sepoys and peons, besides a large number of horsemen etc. of the Nizām according to the information of the Diarist.[34] 500 horsemen were sent in the direction of Porto Novo and Chidambaram. It was feared that the English might go as far as Gingee. There was an engagement near Tiruvati on the bank of the river on August 1st, between Muhammad Alī's troops and the French, the English also taking part in the fight.[35] In the end, the English, after some cannonading, were compelled to withdraw. The situation thus dragged on, till Cope was recalled to Fort St. David, in the end of the month, 'as the French would not and we could not attack.' Muhammad Alī had written to Nāsir Jang that the countries promised to the English before, should now be offered to them, though, in June itself, he wrote that a *sanad* had been made out for them. Thus the situation about the middle of August was very unsatisfactory for the English; and Dupleix pushed on with his efforts, and brought things to the crisis at Nāsir Jang's camp ending in his assassination.

34 Muhammad Alī procured the assistance of 600 Englishmen under Cope; while the French troops consisted of 500 Europeans under La Touche, their best officer. According to Orme, the English ordered a body of 400 Europeans and 1,500 sepoys to take the field and the Nawab marched with an army of 20,000 men, of which more than one-half were the troops of Nāsir Jang.

35 According to Orme there was a skirmish which lasted till night (31st July) when the detachment was recalled. The next day Cope persuaded the Nawab to march against Tiruvati fort in order to draw the French from their strongly pitched camp. The Nawab asked his troops, under the advice of Cope, to scale the walls, but they refused to undertake so perilous an attempt. The army marched back the next morning (2nd Aug.) towards the French encampment and formed for battle within gunshot of their entrenchments. The French commander sent a messenger to ask the reason why the English came so near their posts; Cope replied that the English were acting as allies to the Nawab and would accompany him into all parts of his dominions and assist him against all his enemies. In the struggle which ensued, the French, being in their entrenchment, suffered less than the Nawab and the English (pp. 148-9 of vol. 1).

CHAPTER XI

THE EVENTS LEADING TO THE DIVERSION ON ARCOT

French Victory at Tiruvati and Bussy's Capture of Gingee

The Diarist was told on the second of September (1750) that, on the previous day, the French attacked Muhammad Alī Khān who was encamped at Kumaramangalam and forced him to abandon his camp and set fire to his tents and goods, while the English were abused for dishonestly abandoning him 'like a guide deserting a blind man in midstream.' The army of Muhammd Alī was computed by Orme at 5,000 foot and 15,000 horse; but his disposition and camp were absurdly arranged.[1] The French advanced with their field-pieces in front, baggage carts in the rear and cavalry on each wing; the enemy's cannon and musketry did no execution; and on the advance of the troops within 200 yards of their camp, their entrenchments were abandoned and cannon deserted. The camp was broken into and the cavalry was thrown into utter confusion. Some 20 cannon, 1,000 matchlocks and 2,000 muskets were taken from them; while the tents were set on fire and Muhammad Alī himself made his escape with great loss and hurried away in the direction of Arcot. On the French side only one officer and six or seven sepoys were killed. It was reported to the Diarist that Muhammad Alī was slightly wounded

1 'His camp extended between two villages which secured the flanks; the rear was defended by a river; while in the front there were several entrenchments occupied by the infantry; and in the other intervals where there were no entrenchments, cannon were planted; the cavalry, instead of being out on the plain, formed a second line within the camp.' (Orme, vol. i, p. 150). In the French attack, La Tour commanded the right wing, Bussy the left, and d'Auteuil the centre. The whole camp of Muhammad Alī and all his artillery, including 30 guns and 2 mortars, bearing the arms of Great Britain according to Dupleix's *Memoirs*, fell into French hands (Dodwell).

in the leg by a bullet. Dupleix planned that the troops at Tiruvati should march towards Arcot by way of Gingee or Wandiwash.[2]

Meanwhile Nāsir Jang continued to be indifferent to the state of affairs; and mutual recriminations were freely indulged in by his courtiers. Shāh Nawāz Khān charged Mīr Asad with treachery and with being in correspondence with the Pondicherry people, while Murtaza Alī Khān was told to attack Pondicherry with Mīr Asad who was rebuked for having originally advised that Muhammad Alī was to be helped at all. Shāh Nawāz himself is said to have boasted that, but for the Nizam's orders that he should return at once to Aurangabad, he himself would soon set out to attack the French.

Fearing that Muhammad Alī might take refuge in Trichinopoly, Chandā Sāhib was advised by Dupleix to write to the *killedar* of that place, persuading him not to admit the refugee prince into the fort and promising him a valuable *jaghir* as reward. It was also reported that Muhammad Alī was afraid to halt at Gingee whither Nāsir Jang had promised to send him reinforcements. Dupleix was also hopeful that, if French troops should advance in the direction of Arcot, the Pathan Nawabs of Cuddapah and Kurnool would, as they had formerly promised, have a good chance of seizing the person of Nāsir Jang; while Muhammad Alī would never approach the French troops that

2 It appears from the *Tuzuk-i-Wālājāhi* that Muhammad Alī had secured the friendship of the English by giving them the hope of the grant of the *jaghir* of Poonamallee, that Nāsir Jang was persuaded by the intriguing Pathan Nawabs and Ramdas Pandit to order Muhammad Alī to sever his relationship with the English, that he had ordered Abdul Nabī Khān of Cuddapah and Himmat Khān of Kurnool to subjugate Fort St. David and Madras respectively, that Muhammad Alī contrived to give a large bribe to Ramdas Pandit through Raja Sampath Rai and Raja Bashan Das and to persuade them and Shāh Nawāz Khān to see that the order for the expulsion of the English was withdrawn. When the battle was lost, Muhammad Alī fled to Gingee, but wished once again to proceed to Tiruvati to engage with the enemy; but he was suddenly recalled by the Nizām to his presence.

were advancing under M. Bussy and Shaikh Hasan, the *jemadar* of sepoys. The Diarist even heard that Nāsir Jang who had boastfully recalled all the troops he had sent away, declaring he would march in person against the enemy, had again ordered the artillery and troops to return without delay. Mr. Saunders, the new Governor of Fort St. David, which remained the seat of the Presidency till April 1752, was said to have received a letter from Muhammad Alī, demanding powder and shot for which he had advanced money and complaining of Cope's behaviour, while the latter justified his conduct, saying that the fault was not his, but that he had only obeyed Major Lawrence's orders to march back to Fort St. David.[3] The Diarist says that he heard that Floyer was at the bottom of the whole thing, while Morse was being kept under surveillance, and Lawrence was being frequently summoned to the Fort for consultation; and also the Major would be soon returning to Europe and be succeeded by Cope in command. Meanwhile events moved in quick succession. Nāsir Jang remained inactive at Arcot; and the English were sulky with Muhammad Alī and 'reduced to an almost compulsory inaction.' Dupleix sent orders to d'Auteuil to detach a sufficient force under M. de Bussy to attack Gingee, the possession of which great fortress would be decisive of the fate of the Carnatic.[4] Bussy carried the

3 Orme says that Major Lawrence was much offended by the prevarications of Muhammad Alī who first made excuses for payment and at last declared he had none, having exhausted his treasury by giving Nāsir Jang twenty lakhs of rupees. When there was no prospect of an action, as the French would not and the English could not attack, and as the English officers and men were daily falling sick, Lawrence, with the advice of Stark and Powney, recalled the troops. (Vide *Despatch to the Company from Fort St. David*, dated October 24, 1753.)

4 For details of the exploit of the capture of this famous fortress see Orme, vol. i, pp. 151–2; Malleson's *History of the French in India*, new edition, pp. 263–5; and Martineau's *Dupleix et l'Inde Française*, vol. iii (1749–54), pp. 134–8. The force at the disposal of Bussy consisted of 250 Europeans, 1,200 sepoys and four field-pieces. The capture of Gingee was hardly rivalled 'until 40 years later under Cornwallis, we (the English) stormed certain of the rock-forts in Mysore.'

fortress by escalade (11th September); and the feat was regarded as a wonderful achievement; while the loss of this fortress awakened Nāsir Jang to the true peril of his situation.

French Intrigues—Nasir Jang's Death

There followed an inaction of more than two months' duration till the beginning of December. On the side of the French, d'Auteuil seemed to be 'strangely resolved to rest on Bussy's laurels'. Dupleix indeed wrote to him urging him to advance at once against Nāsir Jang. Even before the capture of Gingee, he was anxious that the French troops should march towards Arcot, as then the Nawabs of Cuddapah and Kurnool would have a good chance of seizing Nāsir Jang, according to their promises.[5] One of the Maratha *mansabdars* in Nāsir Jang's camp, sent a message to Chanda Sāhib and Dupleix that, if the French had marched on Arcot immediately after taking Gingee,[6] the Nizam could easily have been seized, and urged that the time had now come for the French to move, in order to capture or slay Nāsir Jang and establish Muzaffar Jang on the throne. It was also added that as the Pathan Nawabs and other *sardars* were secretly working on the French side, French troops should have continued to advance beyond Chetpattu which they had reached, but from which d'Auteuil had hastily retired, on hearing that Nāsir Jang's forces had reached Dēsūr (twenty miles off) and justified his retreat by asserting that the Pathan Nawabs and others were only

5 Diarist's entry for September 5, reporting a conversation he had with the Governor (p. 376 of vol. vii).

6 *The Tuzuk-i-Wālājāhi* of Burhan-ud-dīn says that after the French had captured Gingee, Nāsir Jang ordered Muhammad Alī to lay siege to the captured place and to prevent any succour to the besieged from Pondicherry; and accordingly the latter sent his *Bakshi*, Md. Abrār Khān, with an army to Gingee. But the conspirators persuaded Nāsir Jang to transfer the forces of Muhammad Alī to protect Conjeevaram, which, they said, was threatened by the French troops at Chingleput; and thus Abrār Khān was recalled from Gingee and sent with augmented forces to Conjeeveram; thus, in the quaint words of Burhan-ud-dīn, 'the *maidan* of impudence became extensive for the French and for those corrupted by mischief.'

deceiving them with false promises.[7] Dupleix tried to console himself as best he could, by saying that the French troops had not retired for any lack of confidence in themselves, but only on account of the constant rains and flooded rivers, and they would advance as soon as the rains were over and the roads became passable. Things were much worse on Nāsir Jang's side. In the beginning of October, his army was encamped on the north side of the Cheyyar river which was flooded; for want of fodder and from the rains, horses and bullocks were dying in numbers; the artillery could scarcely cover four miles in a day; the horsemen were unwilling to march; and Nāsir Jang himself marched in the rear and not in the front of his army. The Diarist was told that many of the *sardars* had not marched with the troops, that Arcot was crowded with all sorts of people and rice was scarce and sold in camp at five *pucca* seers per rupee. In his opinion, d'Auteuil knew these facts well, but had retired ingloriously from Chetpattu and attempted nothing in spite of frequent encouraging letters from Dupleix. When Janoji Nimbalakar and Ramachandra Rao were ordered by Nāsir Jang to march as an advance guard, they refused, pleading it would be dangerous and they could do nothing and advised him that war should cease and peace be made. Shāh Nawāz Khān was of the same opinion and advised his master not to fight, as the army was small and a favourable time would offer itself later.[8] M. d'Auteuil demanded his recall from the field and pleaded sickness, the heavy rains and his men's reluctance to

7 *Vide* pp. 395 and 399 of the *Diary*, vol. vii. Dupleix had gained over to his side Ramdas Pandit who was high in the confidence of Nāsir Jang and through him had tried to raise sedition in the Nizām's army.

'Raja Ramdas was a low servant receiving the wage of one *hun* under the government of Nawab Shāheed (Anvar-ud-dīn) when the latter was the Nazim at Chicacole and gradually rose to importance in the durbar of Asaf Jāh. Later, by the kindness of Nawab Nāsir Jang he was given the title of Raja and was promoted to the position of the *Peshkar Bakshi* of the army'—*Eng. tr.* of the *Tuzuk-i-Wālājāhi* of Burhan-ud-dīn, done by Mr. Md. Husain Nainar of the Madras University.

8 Diarist's entries for October 10 and 12—pp. 401, 404, and 405 of vol. vii.

continue in camp in such weather; and 'Dupleix had much ado to prevent his marching his troops back to Pondicherry and forwarded to him every scrap of encouraging news that he received.' He then actually returned to Pondicherry on October 22; and Dupleix asked the Diarist to write to Muzaffar Khān, the *jemadar* of sepoys, to remain in the villages lying between Villupuram and Gingee and join the main body if he should be directed by de La Touche who had succeeded to the command, and not to send in the guns from Gingee.

Murtazā Alī Khān meanwhile contrived to send a message to Dupleix suggesting that he would secure Arcot from Nāsir Jang, that he might be made the Nawab and Chandā Sāhib might get Trichinopoly, or, as an alternative, that he should be confirmed in the possession of his *killa* and *jaghir* and be the *diwan* to Chandā Sāhib. Dupleix did not take this seriously at all. He deplored that d'Auteuil's indecision and weakness had spoiled the whole situation and that the rains should prevent the French from using their muskets and artillery which gave an advantage to the enemy.

Nāsir Jang had at last ordered his troops to march towards Gingee and himself joined the main body in the beginning of October. His army was considerably less numerous than when he entered the Carnatic; but he could still count, according to the authority of Orme, 60,000 foot, 45,000 horse, 700 elephants and 360 pieces of cannon.[9] On the evening of the 24th October, a body of Nāsir Jang's horse about 4,000 in number who were lying in ambush in several places round Gingee, were encountered by a few French dragoons and Muhammadan troopers. As it was heavily raining, the Muhammadan troopers could not fire and insisted on retreating to camp; the dragoons lost their way and many were killed. The French army marched the next day, but was obliged by the heavy rains, to retreat to Gingee where there were not sufficient provisions.[10]

9 According to letters received by Dupleix, the Mughal effective cavalry was not more than 15,000.

10 According to the letter of the *amaldar* of Gingee, quoted by the Diarist in his entry for the 27th of October, 1750.

Dupleix continued his active intrigues with Nāsir Jang's court where it was presently rumoured that Mīr Asad and Murtazā Alī Khān were in the immediate favour of Nāsir Jang and urged him to march against Pondicherry and Chandā Sāhib, and that the latter had a design to seize the suspected Pathan Nawabs who were consequently on their guard.[11] All the same, Nāsir Jang let Dupleix know, through Khāzi Dāyem, that he was not averse to negotiations, would let bygones be bygones and would even visit Pondicherry and become the friend of the French, adding that if he were to give way to Dupleix's demands, he would be regarded as weak, feeble and helpless. Dupleix replied in suitable terms to this secret offer, protesting that he had ever been Nāsir Jang's well-wisher and had not himself sought his enmity and had

11 According to the *Tuzuk-i-Wālājāhi* Mīr Dāyem Alī Khān, the sardar of the advance guard of Nāsir Jang's army, warned his master against the intended treachery of the Afghan Nawabs and the evil disposition of Raja Ramdas, on the very eve of his assassination. Nāsir Jang even gave an order for the killing of Muzaffar Jang; but Ramdas bribed the executors and sought to delay them. The Nizam mounted an elephant, unarmed and without being protected by any armour; he was surrounded only by a few torch-bearers and *bandars;* and he rode, as the day dawned, towards the elephants of Abdul Nabī Khān and Himmat Bahadur Khān and salaamed to them. But they pretended ignorance of his presence; and he saluted them a second time with a loud voice; and he followed up with the words that it was incumbent on them, brothers of the same faith, to fight the stranger. Then Himmat Bahadur aimed with his musket at the Nawab and shot him through the heart. In the confusion that ensued, Muhammad Alī departed for Trichinopoly with only Ghazanfar Alī Khān and a single guide. He was joined by a dozen servants of his at Tiruvannamalai. At Ranjangudi, its jaghirdar, Mutabir Khān Tāhir, pretended under cover of hospitality to receive him in the fort, with a view to get him secured. It was only by the presence of mind of Ghazanfar Alī Khān, who held the jaghirdar in firm grip that Muhammad Alī was enabled to escape; and the rescuer also quickly rejoined his master in safety.

See also Wilks: vol. i, note on p. 166 in which he gives the narrative of Nāsir Jang's end almost verbally from the *Serve-i-Azad* whose author was in the tent of the Nizam when the alarm was given and assisted him to dress.

always desired the country merchants and inhabitants to be at peace. He even offered to stop all fighting if the negotiations should begin. This was the situation on October 29, after which date there occurs a hiatus in the *Diary* which lasts on till the 16th of April, 1751. This is one of the principal lacunæ; and possibly this, like other breaks, represents lost volumes; and the *Diary* would probably have given us much interesting information about the negotiations with Nāsir Jang and about the circumstances under which the French attacked Nāsir Jang's camp on the fateful day of 16th December and the alleged mistake under which the attack was delivered just at the moment when Dupleix had made peace, whether genuinely or not.[12]

12 *Note on the site of the murder of Nāsir Jang and on Dupleix Fathabad*—

M. A. Lehuraux, writing to the author from Calcutta, under date 6-5-1939 about the place of Nāsir Jang's 'martyrdom' thus says:—

"From a manuscript which I read in the Bibliotheque Nationale, Paris, *viz.*, the Diary of Bussy's march from Pondicherry to Aurangabad with the new Nawab, Muzaffar Jang, the site of the murder of Nawab Nāsir Jang may be identified. The detachment under Bussy set out on January 15, 1751 from Perimby near Vilnur (Villiyanallur) and marched 7 *kos* = 19.30 miles, the official *kos* being 2.76 miles. They halted 2 days at an unnamed place and then, on the following day, proceeded on a second stage of 8 kos (= 22 miles) in course of which they *crossed the camp where Nāsir Jang had been slain.* In the third stage they reached a further 7 kos (= 19.30 miles) and passed near the fort of Wandiwash. It will, I think, be easy for anyone familiar with the topography of the country to locate Nāsir Jang's camp from these particulars; Mailam proximately represents the limit of the first day's march, 20 miles north of Perimby. Starting again from Mailam the detachment advanced 22 miles. Now Mailam is 28 miles south of Wandiwash. Therefore when the detachment had reached a spot some five miles south of Wandiwash, it had passed over the scene of the death of Nāsir Jang. I told you (in a previous conversation) I surmised there must be 4 identifying marks *viz.*:—

(1) a large ruined *mantapam* (noticed by Clive).
(2) Traces of a burnt-out village (Dupleix-Fathabad).
(3) Grave-stones indicating a vast battle-field,
(4) Local tradition of a great fight and the death of the Nizām.

A Hiatus in the Diary: October 1750 to April 1751—Summary of Events

Before the *Diary* begins again for us in April 1751, Muzaffar Jang who was raised to the throne after his uncle's assassination, had appointed Dupleix as his deputy in all the country south of the Krishna and made a grant to the French of Masulipatam and Divi Island; and it was deemed necessary that a French force should proceed to Golconda to secure Nāsir Jang's treasure and firmly establish Muzaffar Jang there before any party could be raised against him. Bussy was chosen to command the French

Now there is a ruined *mantapam* near Velimedoupet; and Ananda Ranga Pillai said that Nāsir Jang was encamped on the maidan of Velimedoupet;

(1) What is the origin of this *mantapam* of Velimedoupet?

(2) Is the *mantapam* of Velimedoupet the choultry Clive saw?

(3) Is the plain of Velimedoupet the scene of the battle?

(4) Is Velimedoupet none other than Dupleix Fathabad?

These are 4 questions that I venture to suggest to you for solution."

This suggestion may be very near the truth regarding the site of Nāsir Jang's murder wherein or near which, Dupleix might have built his monument of power.

Further Note on this Topic

"With regard to the site of Nāsir Jang's murder, Colonel Lawrence's 'Narrative of the war on the coast of Coromandel' states that Clive burnt the town (Dupleix Fathabad) and destroyed the monument on which the (commemorative) pillar was to have been erected." He did not plough the land. There is also no evidence that he destroyed the *chaudri* (*choultry* or *mantapam*) that had been erected, not to the glorification of the French, but to the memory of the murdered Nabob. Further, as the locality had been the scene of hard fighting, the neighbourhood should be found to contain Muhammadan grave-stones. Thus the locality is a spot "16 or 17 miles (eastward) from Gingee" (Orme) or 40 miles (20 *kos*) from Pulcheri (Sewī Azad). Within these limits, I must find—

(1) a fairly large *chaudri* (choultry) probably in ruins,

(2) Evidence of a burnt-out village (though this will be difficult to identify),

(3) Grave-stones, here and there,

(4) a local tradition of a great fight and the Nabob's assassination."

contingent and was rewarded with a present of 4 lakhs of rupees, while Dupleix received an immense sum in jewels and treasure, and all men of the French contingent received three months' pay in advance, besides valuable presents. Bussy had, as his second and third in command, Kerjean who was a nephew of Dupleix and Vincens who was his stepson. The contingent was composed of 300 Europeans and 1,800 sepoys with about 10 field-guns. Muzaffar Jang, on departing for the north, appointed Chanda

"The following localities are suggested as being the site:—

(a) Dupleix mentioned Sarasangupettai (on the route between Wandiwash and Villupuram) *vide* Anandaranga Pillai's conversation with Dupleix (*d.* 7th October 1752) (Vol. VIII of the *Diary*, pp. 239–241).

(b) Tanyal near Nemali, on the plain east of Dēsūr (the French attack was delivered at Dēsūr),

(c) Velimedoupet,

(d) Kattēri,

(e) Senāl,

(f) Sarodrium (Srotriem?) Kātteri."

Further, M. Lehuraux had discussed the question with Prof. Dubreuil and M. Fauchaux, "two distinguished explorers" of Pondicherry; and they were of the opinion that Nāsir Jang's camp could never have extended so far as Balachetti Chatram, near Conjeevaram. A map of 1770 shows this choultry as well as another in the neighbourhood of Dēsūr.

An old route-map of the period in the Pondicherry archives expressly states that Nāsir Jang's camp extended from Fattehpet and Balachetti Chatram "on the route to Chetpet". Further the French troops under La Touche turned the Nabob's camp and attacked him from the rear (Dēsūr). This movement could never have been accomplished successfully if the camp had extended so far as Balachetti Chatram near Conjeevaram. The French force would, in that case, have merely cut into the Nabob's army—a very perilous position exposing them to be caught between two forces. Prof. Dubreuil thinks that Nāsir Jang was killed at Sanal, between Nerkunam and Tellar. Mons. Fauchaux believes that the site is Tanyal. Dupleix himself seems to indicate the scene of the murder to be Sarasangupettai, between Wandiwash and Villupuram. (The note of the edition of the *Diary* of Anandaranga Pillai says of this:—"Not known, perhaps a corruption of Nāsirjangai konra pettai—the village where Nāsir Jang was killed.")"

Sāhib to the government of Arcot. While at Pondicherry, Muzaffar Jang and Chandā Sāhib wrote to the English, demanding the restoration of the sea-ports like Devikotta that they had occupied during the recent troubles. This revolution alarmed the ruler of Tanjore who now demanded English assistance in consequence of a treaty that he had concluded with Floyer. Muhammad Alī who escaped to Trichinopoly, put in his claims for English support; but he also opened negotiations with the French, as it was the harvest season and the longer he could remain at peace with them, the greater were the chances of his collecting any revenue. He therefore contrived to prolong negotiations with Dupleix and Chandā Sāhib for four months (December, 1750 to March 1751), and communicated regularly to the English all his discussions with them. Saunders, the English Governor, maintained that as Muhammad Alī had been appointed Nawab of Arcot by Nāsir Jang, he continued to be the legitimate and rightful Nawab till another appointment was made from Delhi; the English having received *farmans* for the districts granted by Muhammad Alī, a detachment was sent to Trichinopoly under Captain Cope to secure it from any attempts by Chandā Sāhib; and another detachment was sent to assist the ruler of Tanjore in consideration of a *farman* that he granted for Devikottai and its bounds. The English also intended to send men to Divi Island and Masulipatam to hoist English flags on the island and in the factory.[13]

(Chandā Sāhib and the French moved out from Pondicherry only in March, 1751, and after reducing one or two forts, proceeded to Arcot to receive the tribute of the *killedars* and other notables; and he prepared to advance against Trichinopoly only towards the end of May or later, by which time Saunders had sent a force under Captain de Gingens to oppose his march.

13 Despatch of the President and Council of Fort St. David to the Company, dated Fort St. David, January 24, 1751—summarised in Dodwell's *The Madras Despatches, 1744–55*—pp. 118–9.—*See* also Orme MSS. *O. V. 17;* 1; and *15;* 5; pp. 24 and 22 of Hill's *Catalogue of the Orme Collection of MSS.*

Meanwhile, events in Muzaffar Jang's camp had also moved fast. The Pathan Nawabs looked on with jealousy at the turn that affairs were taking. Pondicherry was now the pivot of the whole country; all matters were decided by the French, who were enriched by securing considerable accessions of territory.[14] Consequently there was great discontent which was bound to break out as soon as Muzaffar Jang should depart from the Carnatic. When he was encamped at Rayachoti, 5 days' march from Arcot and in the dominion of the Nawab of Cuddapah, the latter and the Nawab of Kurnool complained that Muzaffar Jang was allowing the Marathas to plunder their country contrary to his promise; and they seized some French horse and spoiled the French ammunition. The Pathan Nawabs had agreed, before Dupleix and under his pressure, that half the money found in Nāsir Jang's treasury should be divided amongst them, while their dominions should be increased by some districts, which were however much less than what they first demanded; and they also agreed that all the jewels should be reserved for Muzaffar Jang.[15]

In the skirmish that ensued, the Nawab of Cuddapah attacked the rear-guard of Muzaffar Jang's troops which escorted the

14 Muzaffar Jang, according to the *Tuzuk-i-Wālājāhi*, conferred on Dupleix the title of Zafar Jang, granted the French the *jaghirs* of Gingee, Tiruvati and other places, while Law, d'Auteuil and other French captains were given suitable titles, *mansabs* and presents. Himmat Bahadur Khān was given the title of Rustam Jang and the *jaghirs* of Raichur and Adoni. Abdul Nabī Khān got the *jaghirs* of Gandikotta, Gooty, and Gurramkonda; and Abdul Karīm Khān secured the *jaghir* of Sira; and Ramdas Pandit got the title of Raja Raghunath Das; while Abdul Rahmān got the title of Muzaffar Khān. Muzaffar Jang also wrote a friendly letter to Muhammad Alī Khān at Trichinopoly, according to the plan and counsel of Dupleix and Janoji, the Maratha, and sent it along with letters from the latter.

15 The Nawabs signed an agreement to this effect and swore on the *Quaran* an oath of allegiance to Muzaffar Jang; and they declared that Nizām-ul-Mulk himself had never been able to obtain from them this mark of submission—(Orme: vol. I, p. 160).

women,[16] whereupon the Nizām ordered his whole army to halt and prepared to march against the Cuddapah troops. Bussy who had received specific instructions to avoid all occasions of being drawn into committing hostilities, now intervened and persuaded Muzaffar Jang to first call upon the Nawab to explain the reason of his conduct. The Nawab, though defiant to Muzaffar Jang's message, sent word to Bussy that he was ready to submit to the Nizām through French mediation. This behaviour stung Muzaffar Jang to the quick and forced him to instant action. The troops of all the three Pathan Nawabs had already been drawn up in battle array and Muzaffar Jang marched to attack the rebels without French assistance, being impatient of the slow pace of their battalion. At first Muzaffar Jang's troops were repulsed; but the fire of the French artillery changed the fortunes of the day and forced the Nawabs to retreat. Muzaffar Jang, heedless of the advice of Bussy, pursued the fugitives, and left the French battalion behind once more, which however endeavoured to keep in sight of him. The Nawab of Savanur died on the field; while the Nawab of Cuddapah fled precipitately, being severely wounded. In his pursuit of the latter, Muzaffar Jang came up with the Nawab of Kurnool and proceeded to attack him personally, when, having lifted up his sword to strike, he was pierced in the head by the javelin of his opponent. Both the Nawab

16 *The Tuzuk-i-Wālājāhi* says that Muzaffar Jang was not feeling quite safe, because of the knavery of some of the amīrs of the army and the Afghans, especially of Himmat Bahadur Khān. Beyond Damalcheruvu, Mughal sepoys plundered the properties of the Afghans, in spite of their master's prohibition. In the course of the march, the Afghans, one day looted a cart belonging Muzaffar Khān (Abdul Rahmān), the *Ilaqadar* of the French forces. Abdul Nabī Khān offered to pay compensation, but Muzaffar Khān did not agree; and the struggle began. Abdul Karim Khān of Savanur perished; Himmat Bahadur Khān fled, heavily wounded; he was later killed by order of Nizam Alī and his head fixed on a spear. The Mughal army plundered Cuddapah on the way; but Abdul Majīd Khān, brother of Abdul Nabī Khān, sought peace by paying 3 lakhs of rupees. Kurnool was attacked and the wife and children of Himmat Bahadur were taken captive.

and his troops were overpowered and cut to pieces. The death of Muzaffar Jang left the French in great consternation, because they had now no pretension nor claim to interfere in the affairs. But Bussy did not lose his presence of mind, assembled the generals and ministers, and persuaded them to raise Salābat Jang, the eldest of the three brothers of Nāsir Jang, who had been kept in close confinement, to the throne. French arms had again been decisive; and Salābat Jang agreed to confirm all the cessions to the French made by his predecessor and granted additional villages round Masulipatam, as well as a large donation to the French contingent. As soon as Dupleix's approbation was received, the Mughal army left the country of Cuddapah and continued its march towards the Krishna.

Chanda Sahib's Movements: April-June 1751

The Diarist whose available narrative begins, after the hiatus, from April 16, 1751, mentions the capture of the fort of Chetpattu by Chandā Sāhib who had at last moved out of Pondicherry with a French contingent under La Tour and the imprisonment of Mīr Asad and his family. On April 18, news was received that Salābat Jang was encamped 12 *kos* on the other side of the Krishna, after taking Kurnool and making prisoners of its Nawab (Himāyat Bahadur Khān) and his family, and that when the army had advanced 16 *kos* beyond the river, where a large Maratha army was lying in wait for them, Salābat Jang made a settlement with them, through the mediation of his minister Ramdas Pandit, by consenting to give them a *sanad* for the *chauth* of the provinces of Golconda, the Carnatic and Trichinopoly and that the minister was rewarded by the Nizām with a *mansab* of 7,000 horse,[17] Salābat Jang left a son-in-law of Muzaffar Khān

17 The Peishwa, Balaji Baji Rao, had been jealous of Nāsir Jang's rise and had entered into negotiations with Sayyad Lashkar Khān, the governor of Aurangabad, through the mediation of Ramdas Pandit. Sayyad Lashkar Khān induced Ghāzī-ud-dīn, the eldest son of Nizām-ul-Mulk, to oppose the succession of Nāsir Jang and offer to cede to the Marathas, in return for their support, the two *subahs* of Aurangabad

(Abdul Rahmān) in charge of the *killa* of Kurnool.[18] The Diarist, recording affairs in the Carnatic, said that the Vellore affair was settled by Chandā Sāhib for 6 lakhs of rupees, which meant that there was a compounding with the evil-hearted Murtazā Alī. Shaikh Hasan, the sepoy leader who accompanied Chandā Sāhib along with de La Tour was to have the fort and *jaghir* of Arni, yielding two lakhs of rupees; and his uncle, Muhammad Kamāl, was also to receive a *jaghir*. Dupleix also arranged to give the

and Burhanpur. Thereupon the Peishwa left Poona towards the end of January, 1751, with a large army, accompanied by Fatteh Sing, Raghuji Bhonsle and other leaders. The Marathas demanded a contribution from Sayyad Lashkar Khān, which, on pretence of coercion, the latter levied to the tune of 15 or 17 lakhs of rupees; and then they spread over the country and occupied the two *subahs*, and finally proceeded to the banks of the Krishna. When Balaji Rao was at Pangal, seven marches from Hyderabad, he received alarming news from Poona that Tarabai was preparing, in league with Damaji Gaekwad, to undermine his supremacy; he resolved to return to Poona, and ordered Janoji Nimbalkar to make the best terms possible with the enemy. Salābat Jang who was ignorant of the Peishwa's situation, offered 17 lakhs of rupees, two in cash, and the rest in bills on bankers in Hyderabad, Aurangabad and Burhanpur. (*See* Kincaid and Parasnis—*History of the Maratha People*, vol. III, pp. 1–2; and Grant-Duff—*History of the Mahrattas* (4th ed.), vol. I, p. 527). Grant-Duff calls Ramdas Pandit, 'the traitor Ramdas, a fit instrument for the unprincipled ambition of Dupleix.' See also *Selections from the Peishwa's Daftar*, 6, *Ramaraja's Struggle for Power*—Letters *Nos. 167, 168, 180* and *201*.

The Diarist's entry, that news came from Satara that Shahu Raja's wife Tāra Bai Umma Bai had been imprisoned and that internal dissensions were likely, does not convey any clear meaning (p. 431 of Vol. VII). It was in reality a plot woven by two women, Tāra Bai and Uma Bai, the latter being the widow of Khanderao Dabhade who had been destroyed by the Peishwa. Tāra Bai saw in Uma Bai a ready ally for her plan. Uma Bai was to equip an army under Damaji Gaekwad and effect a junction with Tāra Bai who even sent emissaries to Ramdas Pandit who was in Salābat Jang's service and offered him the office of Peishwa if he would advance with the Nizam's army to her help. But the plan miscarried and the Peishwa was able to triumph.

18 Abdul Rahmān was the dewan of M. Bussy, and better known by his title of Hyder Jang. His father was a defaulter of revenue under the Nizam's government at Masulipatam and had been friendly to the

lease of the Tinnevelly country to Titarappa Mudali who afterwards became the renter of the district under Nawab Muhammad Alī and the English.[19] Titarappa was to pay 10 lakhs to Chandā Sāhib and a present of one lakh to Dupleix, besides presents to Madame Dupleix, Madananda Pandit and others, and was to give a lease deed for 5 years; and the Poligar of Sivaganga and other chiefs were written to, to give the renter all possible assistance in occupying the country. But rumour was rife that as Muhammad Alī was made strong at Trichinopoly by the English and as Chandā Sāhib was not in actual possession of the country, Titarappa's chance of occupying Tinnevelly was not great; while Kumarappa Mudali, the *dubash* of Governor Saunders at Fort St. David, sent word to Titarappa that he would arrange to get him the lease of the Tinnevelly country from Muhammad Alī and the English Council would write about it to Mr. Cope who was with the latter. But the cause of Muhammad Alī was not yet to gain the upper hand. The *Maravas* and others attacked

French. In his distress he fled to Pondicherry where he was kindly treated by Dupleix. 'His son, Abdool Rehmān, then a boy, soon acquired the French Language, was useful to Dupleix in carrying on his intrigues with Ramdass, and upon the success of them, accompanied Bussy when he went with the Mughal army'; and he was rewarded with the title of Muzaffar Khān, by Muzaffar Jang.

19 Anvar Khān was *faujdar* and *amil* of the Tinnevelly country in the time of Nawab Anvar-ud-dīn; he was succeeded by Mīr Ghulām Hussain Khān and Hussain Muhammad Khān who jointly managed affairs till 1749. After the battle of Ambur, Chandā Sāhib appointed, as *amil*, Ālam Khān who managed the district on his master's behalf in 1750 and 51. He was succeeded for a short time by Titarappa Mudali and Moodemiah, the agent of Chandā Sāhib. (Extracted by Caldwell from the letter of Mr. Lushington, Collector of Tinnevelly, dated May 28, 1802; *see* p. 125 of his *History of Tinnevelly.*)

Ālam Khān was, according to Orme, a soldier of fortune, who had formerly been in the service of Chandā Sāhib and afterwards in that of the king of Tanjore; he came to Madura, took the fort from one Abdul Hakimat Khān, and observing the course of events, proclaimed his adherence to the cause of Chandā Sāhib; he was in power in Madura in the beginning of 1751. (*See* Nelson's *Madura Manual*, Part III, p. 269; and *Orme*.)

the troops of Captain Cope and Muhammad Alī which advanced to take the Madura fort, broke them up and captured 3 cannon and a large number of muskets from them. Cope himself escaped with two wounds, while about 100 English soldiers were said to have fallen.[20]

Ranga Pillai notes, in his entry for April 30, 1751, that Dupleix sent the old *cowle* from Salābat Jang to Muhammad Alī and wrote desiring him to accept it[21] and deliver the fort of Trichinopoly to Chandā Sāhib's people; and to this the latter replied that he had already received from Ghāzī-ud-dīn Khān at Delhi, a copy of a *parwana* granting him the *subahs* of Payanghat and Balaghat (Carnatic) and directing him to take possession of them, along with a copy of the Mughal Emperor's letter to Ghāzī-ud-dīn Khān. Dupleix was greatly irritated at this reply and sent urgent letters to Chandā Sāhib urging him to settle

20 Orme says that Captain Cope offered to take Madura, though his detachment was ill-equipped for a siege, and proceeded with 3 field-pieces, 2 cohorns and 150 Europeans, accompanied by 600 of the Nawab's cavalry under Abdul Wahāb Khān, a younger brother of Muhammad Alī. Before Madura, these were joined by the detachment that Muhammad Alī had sent to the Tinnevelly country under another brother of his. The troops were repulsed from the walls and had to relinquish the attack. Captain Cope blew the cannon to pieces, but a very large body of cavalry deserted over to Ālam Khān both before and after the English broke up their camp. (pp. 169–170)—also *Orme MSS.; O. V.*

Ālam Khān is said to have subsequently proceeded and subdued the Tinnevelly country and appointed Nabir Khān at Tinnevelly and Mantimiya (Mundamiyah or Moodemiah) at Madura as his lieutenants and then joined Chandā Sāhib at Trichinopoly, where he died soon after his arrival, struck by a cannon shot (Saka, 1674)—*see* p. 48 of vol. II of W. Taylor's *Oriental Historical Manuscripts* (1835).

21 The *cowle* from Salābat Jang which was sent by Dupleix to Muhammad Alī, was not probably known to the Diarist, and is given as Appendix No. 1, in vol. III of the *Diary* by Mr. Dodwell. It is dated March 12, 1751, and granted the *sarkars* of Rajahmundry, Chicacole, Ellore, Masulipatam, Mustafanagar and Muzaffarnagar to Muhammad Alī along with two strong forts and a *jaghir* and also promising not to call him to account for the dues of his father and himself with respect to the Carnatic and Trichinopoly revenues.

the Arni matter without further delay and, without turning aside to Arcot, to proceed straight to Trichinopoly by way of Tiruvannamalai.

Having received the submission of the *killedars* of Vellore, Chetpattu, and Arni, Chandā Sāhib deemed the Carnatic to be secure enough for him under the circumstances and began his march for Trichinopoly, reaching Tiruvannamalai about the 20th of May. Dupleix asked the Diarist to write letters to the Rajas of Tanjore and Mysore and to 'the 72 *poligars* of Trichinopoly' whose names are enumerated, beginning with Maḻavarayan of Ariyalur, the Greater Marava (of Ramnad), the Lesser Marava (of Sivaganga) and enumerating *72 poligars* and the six divisions of the Kallars (the Colleries of Orme).[22] The list that Ranga

22 W. Taylor gives from the *Mackenzie MSS.* a list of the 72 *pāḷayams* appointed to guard the bastions of the Pandyan capital as they were in the time of Tirumala Nāyak, including Travancore, Ramnad, Sivaganga and Pudukotta, the three last being like the adopted children of the Madura Government, and Ayalur, Turaiyur, Iluppur, Marungapuri, Nattam, etc.

The following table, comparing Taylor's list with Ranga Pillai's enumeration may be useful. Where it has not been possible to equate names in the Diarist's list with those of Taylor, a blank space has been indicated.

	TAYLOR		RANGA PILLAI
1.	The Ramnad Setupati	..	Setupati
2.	Udaiya Tevar of Sivaganga	..	Udaiya Tevan
3.	The Reddi of Turaiyur	..	The Reddi of Turaiyur
4.	Puchi Nayakan of Marangapuri	..	Puchiya Nayakan
5.	Leckiya Nayakkan		Lakkayya Nayakan (of Kumaravadi)
6.	Viramalaipalayam; Kama Nayakan.		Kammaya Nayakan
7.	Iluppaiyur; Kamakshi Nayakan	..	Kamakshi Nayakan
8.	Nattam; Lingama Nayakan	..	Lingama Nayakan
9.	Pillai-Muzhungi; Muttaya Nayakan.		Muttayya Nayakan
10.	Ideiya-kottai, Ayalur; Valakondama Nayakan also Maduvur; Vallakondama Nayakan	..	Vallakondama Nayakan
11.	Ramagiri; Sami Nayakan	..	Samaya Nayakan
12.	Maruluttu; Amiya Nayakan	..	Ammayya Nayakan

Pillai gives has 34 *Poligars* as belonging to the Trichinopoly country and 38 as belonging to the south. The letter that was sent to these explained how Muzaffar Jang had given Dupleix the charge of all the country and the pāḷayams between the Krishna River and Cape Comorin and how the grant had been confirmed by Ṣalābat Jang: it then proceeded to state that Muhammad Alī was given a *cowle* from Muzaffar Jang and invited to act as Dupleix desired, and, instead of doing so, he had taken shelter in Trichinopoly and made frivolous excuses; and Chandā Sāhib and the French forces had, therefore, orders to capture Trichinopoly and punish Muhammad Alī and the poligars should not help him on pain of losing their fiefs and being punished, but should help Chandā Sāhib.

	TAYLOR		RANGA PILLAI
13.	Yemacalapuram; Kulappa Nayakan.		Kulappa Nayakan
14.	Kannivadi; Appayya Nayakan	..	Appaya Nayakan
15.	Palni; Chennama Nayakan	..	Sennava Nayakan (of Palni)
16.	Periakulam; Ramabhadra Nayakan.		Ramabhadra Nayakan (of Virupakshi)
17—25.		..	The nine Gounders and Poligars of Kangayam
26—32.		..	The seven Hill Poligars living in Kambam and Gudalur
33.	Malayalam; Nanjinattu Raja	..	Nanjanadu
34.	Ariyalur (Ayalur); Nayanār	..	Maḷavarayan (of Ariyalur)

THE POLIGARS OF THE SOUTH

	TAYLOR		RANGA PILLAI
1.		..	Sinnananja Tevan
2.	Sivagiri; Varagunarama Vanniyar.		Sivagiri Vanniyan
3.	Alakapuri Rettai-kudi (Rettai-kottai) Vanniyanar	..	Irattaikkudai Vanniyan
4.	Do.	..	Alagapuri Vanniyan
5.	Settur Tiruvannata Tevar	..	Settur Tiruvana Tevan
6.	Kolang-kondan	..	Kollangondan Vanda Tevan
7.	Ettaiyapuram; Ettappa Nayakar	..	Ettappa Nayakan
8.		..	Annichi Nayakan
9.	Dumbichi Nayakan	..	Tumbinji Nayakan
10.		..	Kama Nayakan
11.	Kollarpatti; Kalanka Nayakar	..	Kalanga Nayakan

Chandā Sāhib wrote shortly afterwards that he had to postpone his march to Trichinopoly, as the English under Gingens took Vriddachalam and hoisted their own flag there; Dupleix was so anxious that the place should be retaken and the English should be driven completely out of the neighbourhood that he arranged for Shaikh Hasan, the *jemadar* of sepoys, who had been sent to reduce the Chittore pāḷayams, should be required to come and help to beat the English. The horsemen on the French side gave some trouble as their pay was in arrears; and their demand had to be forthwith complied with; and a lakh of rupees was immediately despatched to Papayya Pillai, who was one of Madame

	TAYLOR		RANGA PILLAI
12.		..	Kandama Nayakan
13.	Eramadai	..	Elumadai Nayakan
14.	Chokkanpatti	..	Chokkathalavan
15.		..	Thadiyathalavan
16.	Panchalankurichi; Kattabomma Nayakan	..	Kattappa Nayakan
17.	Uttumalai Maruthappa Tevan	..	Marudappa Thevan
18.		..	Tāli Vēli
19.		..	Sūttala Tevan
20.		..	Saluva Tevan
21.	Urkad; Servakāran	..	Seturayan
22.		..	Nallakkutti
23.		..	Nambi Thalavan
24.		..	Ananja Thalavan
25.		..	Ramabhadra Reddi
26.		..	Ramaswami Reddi
27.		..	Kumaraswami Reddi
28.		..	Venkatachala Reddi
29.		..	Sankaranarayana Reddi
30.		..	Kechalappa Nayakan
31.		..	Pethana Nayakan
32.		..	Kadalakkudi Nayakan
33.	Nagalapuram; Iravappa Nayakan	..	Nagalapuram
34.	Melmandai Nayakan	..	Sirumalai Nayakan (of Melamandai)
35.		..	Indra Thalavan
36.		..	Kumara Thalavan
37.		..	Eravappa Nayakan

(only 37 poligars are enumerated by the Diarist)

Dupleix's agents and who was now appointed *receveur general des finances du Carnatic,* in which capacity he acted tyrannically and earned a very bad name for himself. In this connection, the Diarist described how large sums of money had been received by the French on Chandā Sāhib's account and arrangements had been made for a bill of exchange for 16½ lakhs of rupees on Kasi Das Bukkanji, payable at the Masulipatam factory, on account of the present which Muzaffar Jang had promised to make when he reached Golconda and which had been confirmed by Salābat Jang; he also wrote that Dupleix had ordered that all payments got, other than the sums due from Mīr Asad of Chetpattu and Murtazā Alī Khān of Vellore which were to be paid to Chandā Sāhib for the charge of his troops, were to be received for himself.

A number of pāḷayams mentioned by Taylor are not found in the list of the Diarist which includes several later creations. The chiefs of Perambur and Kattalur who were Tevans by caste were among the poligars of Tirumala Nayak's time; and Marungapuri of the Puchi Nayak family threw off an offshoot which formed a separate pāḷayam (of Karisalpattu-Varappur) of the Boma Nayaks.

A list of the names of the chiefs actually appointed by Visvanātha Nayak and by his co-adjutor and *dalavai,* Aryanatha Mudali, can be made out from the materials contained in Ward's *Survey* and in the two lists published in Taylor's *Oriental Historical Manuscripts* (vol. II, pp. 160–8) as well from an unpublished Mackenzie *MS.* Many of these chiefs are called Nayakars who were the descendants of the captains and soldiers who helped the Nayak rulers of Vijayanagar to conquer the Madura country. The traditional story of their migration is given in several of the Mackenzie *MSS.*; and they belong, for the greater part, to the castes of the Tottiyars and Kambalattars, corresponding to the Telugu Gollas and Yerragollas (Thurston and Rangachari—*Castes and Tribes of South India,* vol. vii, pp. 183–197). Among the other chiefs one is a Reddiar, another is a Tondaimanar (Kallar) and others are Gounders, Servaikarar, Tevans and Nayanars. Taylor's list divides the fiefs into 9 sections, the first comprising the bigger fiefs of Nanjinadu, Ramnad, Sivaganga and Pudukoṭṭai, the others being respectively those attached to the Manapar taluk, Dindigul taluk, Kambam and Gudalur, Madura and Trichinopoly, Tinnevelly, Coimbatore and Salem. The list should have been subject to perpetual fluctuations being 'increased or diminished with the absence or existence of any one preponderating power among them

THE ENGLISH AND CHANDA SAHIB ADVANCE ON TRICHINOPOLY

Captain de Gingens had with him about 500 Europeans and took the field in May in order to bar the way of Chandā Sāhib to Trichinopoly. He had also under him a force of *coffres* and sepoys and 8 pieces of cannon. His original instruction was that he was to wait in the vicinity of Fort St. David till he should be joined by Muhammad Alī's troops, from Trichinopoly. The English till then did not like to appear as principals in the struggle. After six weeks of waiting, Captain Gingens was joined about the middle of May, by 600 horse and about 1000 *peons* of

Ramnad was founded about 1605 by one Muthukrishnappa, rather restored to the ancient line of the *Setupathis*, according to the manuscript history of the *Carnataca Governors*, the account of the *Setupathis* translated by Taylor and the historical memorandum furnished to Nelson (in the *Madura Manual*, 1868) by Ponnuswami Tevan, the then manager of the *Zamindari*. Sella Tevar, *alias* Vijayaraghunatha Setupathi, was the ruler of Ramnad from 1748 to 1760. Sivaganga was an offshoot from Ramnad; and its existence as a separate fief dates only from about 1730; it was then ruled by Periya Udaya Tevar, the son of its founder Sasivarna Periya Udaya Tevar. The *Tondaimans* of Pudukottai, not mentioned separately by the Diarist, and evidently included by him in the divisions of the Kallars, came into prominence on account of their services to the Nayaks, about the close of the 17th century. They rose from one of the Kallar tribes settled near Anbil, in the land east of Trichinopoly, south of Tanjore and north of Ramnad, which were originally known as *Arasu*. Vijaya Raghunatha Tondaiman was the ruler at the time and took a very prominent part in the operations round Trichinopoly that followed.

See for the Poligar system, *Wilks*, vol. I, p. 34 note; Caldwell's *A History of Tinnevelly*, pp. 57–8; Wilson's *Historical Sketch of the Kingdom of Pandya*, p. 43; Nelson, Part III, Ch. IV *et seq*; *The Fifth Report of 1812* (1866 edn.)—vol. II, (Madras Presidency)—pp. 89–90; and C. S. Srinivasachari's paper, 'The Poligar system in the Tamil Country: Its Origin and Growth' contributed to the *Proceedings of the Indian Historical Records Commission, Nagpur Session, 1928.*

Mr. Dodwell's *notes* to the Diarist's List (pp. 6–9 notes) identify the then fief-holders of Ariyalur, Turaiyur, Kollankondan, and Kolarapettai; he fixes also the fiefs of several of the poligars mentioned by the Diarist; but the places mentioned by him are not in all cases the same as those of Taylor and can be explained by the assumption that the

Muhammad Alī. He then moved westwards and came in sight of Vriddachalam, whose fortified pagoda was garrisoned by 300 of Chandā Sāhib's troops. The place was on the high road to Trichinopoly; and its reduction was deemed to be necessary for the preservation of Fort St. David. The pagoda surrendered after a slight assault;[23] and after leaving a small garrison there, the English continued their further march and were joined by about 100 Europeans detached by Captain Cope from Trichinopoly and about 4,000 troops of Muhammad Alī, both cavalry and foot, commanded by Abdul Wahāb Khān, a younger brother of the latter. The exact place where the junction of the troops took place is not clear; according to Captain Dalton it was at Valikandapuram (the Volcondah of Orme and other historians). Gingens was encamped in a grove about a mile and a half from the latter place, while Chandā Sāhib's forces were posted about 4 miles to

original pālayams might have been shifted. Light's *Report* (Military Consultations) of 1781 has been thoroughly utilised by him in locating these.

The main sub-divisions of the Kallars which were returned in the greatest numbers at the Census of 1891 were Isanganadu (Visanganadu), Kungiliyan, Menadu, Nāttu, Piranmalainadu, and Sīrakudi. The Kallars of Madura are however divided into 10 endogamous sections which are territorial in origin. Mr. T. Turnbull, writing in 1817, says that the Kallars appropriated to themselves various *nads* (regions) in different parts of the southern districts; and in each of these territories they had a chief among them whose orders and directions they must all obey (Thurston and Rangachari—*Castes and Tribes of Southern India*—vol. III, p. 53). The Visinganattukallar, Piranmalai Kallar and Tannarasunattu Kallar seem to have been tribes living in the Pudukotta territory (vide *A Manual of the Pudukottai State*, (2nd ed. 1938); pp. 106–12; and Mr. S. Radhakrishna Iyer's *A General History of the Pudukottai State*, p. 67). The filiations of the Kallars are hard to fix; but they have got, according to tradition, some close connection with the Maravars and the Agambadiyans (See Sir Athelstane Baines: *Indian Ethnography (Encyclopædia of Indo-Aryan Research)*, pp. 81 and 47–48.

23 Chandā Sāhib's garrison surrendered as soon as they perceived the scaling ladders being put up by the attackers. The report that reached the Diarist tells that the defenders made a fairly prolonged resistance. Vriddhachalam was thus the only fort north of the Coleroon

the north. The rock-fort by whose side Volcondah village was situated, was that of Ranjangudi which was in the possession of a Mussalman *jaghirdar,* who, though a relative of Muhammad Alī's,[24] was afraid to throw in his lot definitely on the side of his kinsman and refused to open his gates to the English. Gingens first captured and burnt the village (or *pettai*) of Volcondah, but he could not take the rock-fort; while the *jaghirdar* permitted the French troops to go over to him. An action took place in the dry bed of the river which runs beneath the fort, into which the English troops fled for no apparent reason, though the officers including Clive who was then a lieutenant, did all they could to stop the disgraceful flight. This so-called battle of Volcondah [it was in reality the battle of Ranjangudi, *(June 30)*] was considered 'a disgraceful affair' by both Wilks and Malcolm. Orme says that Abdul Wahāb Khān's troops stood their ground; and it was only the English battalion that got so demoralised and broke up in panic.[25] The troops of Muhammad Alī 'behaved in this action better than ever they did afterwards, and even in the field of battle reproached the English for their want of spirit,' according

which remained loyal to Muhammad Alī, after the first English attempt to succour him failed. Clive and Pigot, one of the English Council, accompanied a small detachment sent by Saunders to Trichinopoly and convoyed stores to Vriddachalam which was then beleaguered by a hostile *poligar* (July, 1751). After having entered Vriddachalam and sent on the detachment further, Clive and Pigot set out to return to Fort St. David when they were immediately surrounded by the poligar's troops and escaped only after a close race. 'It was a close race and Clive's fighting nearly came to an end.'—See Forrest's *Life of Lord Clive;* vol. i; *p.* 135 and Francis; *Gazetteer of South Arcot District—pp.* 400–01.

24 The *Tuzuk-i-Wālājāhi* says that the jaghirdar of the place was Mutabir Khān Tāhir, son of Md. Husain Tāhir; he was therefore a Tāhirān and a hereditary enemy of Anvar-ud-dīn's family.

25 For details see Captain Dalton's *Memoir* (Memoir of Captain Dalton, H.E.I.C.S. (1886)) *pp.* 92 *et. seq.;* Orme, vol. i, *pp.* 172–4; Martineau's *Dupleix,* vol. iii, p. 194, and Forrest's *Life of Lord Clive,* vol. i, *pp.* 128–31, which says that some of Orme's statements are founded on a memorandum which Clive sent him in 1763. See *Catalogue of the Orme Collection of MSS.* by S. C. Hill—p. 272.

to Clive, in the memorandum that he gave to Orme in 1763. According to another version, the English were regarded as having lost all their courage in this engagement. The Diarist wrote that a letter which was received declared the English had a loss of 90 Europeans killed, including 2 officers besides the wounded, while in the detachment of Cope 110 persons had been either killed at Madura or died of sickness; but according to the English version they lost only one ensign and five or six men.[26]

The Diarist also makes mention of two envoys from the Raja of Mysore who came to Pondicherry with jewels and cloths as presents to the Governor who desired that the amount of the present might be given to him in ready money. It was possibly, as suggested by Mr. Dodwell, to frustrate this negotiation that Muhammad Alī sent an envoy named Seshagiri Rao to Mysore for assistance.[27] A Brahman who came to Pondicherry, alleged that he had been sent by Muhammad Alī, without the English knowing it, to desire Dupleix to send some one to Trichinopoly to hoist the French flag there. This was only one phase of the intrigue by which Dupleix urged Muhammad Alī to take up the offer of Salābat Jang of the Northern Sarkars and confirm it with a grant under the seal of Chandā Sāhib which latter was received by Muhammad Alī through M. Law. The person who was sent to Trichinopoly along with the Brahman, reported according to the Diarist, that the place was full of the English, and Muhammad Alī was only the nominal ruler.

26 According to a separate despatch from Governor Saunders to the Company dated August 15, 26, 'the Nawab's people and the *caffres* behaved well and our people ill. The unlucky action encouraged their (enemy's) people and depressed ours.'

27 The Dalavāi, Deva Raja, was not willing to embark on this enterprise; but his younger brother, Nañja Raja, was tempted by an extravagant promise of the cession of Trichinopoly and of all its possessions, down to Cape Comorin, to lend the required assistance and agreed to make provision for Muhammad Ali by giving him the *jaghir* of Hardanahalli, at the head of the pass to Trichinopoly (p. 2470 of Ch. XI of the *Mysore Gazetteer* (New edition); vol. II; Part IV), and also Wilks, vol. I, p. 172.

Chandā Sāhib had, after the action at Volcondah, followed Gingens to Utattur, situated about 25 miles from Trichinopoly and fifteen miles south of Perambalur. Two miles north of the place, the road from Trichinopoly passes between a hill and a ridge of rock which were described by Orme as the 'streights of Utattur' and by Dalton as 'the barrier to the Trichinopoly country'. Gingens was encamped in the streights, though they could have been avoided; and Dalton was posted as an advance-guard. The enemy forces were about 8 miles behind and thus the two forces watched each other for several days. On the 20th of July the English troops, consisting of a few dragoons, about 150 of the Nawab's horse and a company of sepoys were decoyed into an ambuscade of some 3,000 horse and foot. The cavalry escaped; but most of the sepoys were cut to pieces, and Lieutenant Maskelyne was taken prisoner. This disaster, though small by itself, followed so closely on the failure at Volcondah, that it had a most disheartening effect on the English. Chandā Sāhib thereupon advanced his camp three miles and offered a general engagement with a very large body of horse and sepoys. Dalton who occupied the outpost, retired with skill to the main camp of the English. Chandā Sāhib resolved upon a general action; but a heavy fire from the British artillery made him waver and soon compelled his troops to flight. This attack of Chandā Sāhib, though repulsed, made Gingens resolve to abandon the streights on account of the possibility of the enemy posting his cavalry between that place and Trichinopoly; he moved out the same night and after a quick march of eighteen hours, encamped close to the northern bank of the Coleroon and occupied a fortified pagoda (Bikshāṇḍār Kovil). They then crossed the river followed by the French and Chandā Sāhib, took possession of the Srirangam Island and the great pagoda. But even here they did not deem themselves secure from the enemy, crossed the Kāveri and took refuge on July 28th under the walls of Trichinopoly. The French also rapidly pushed on after the English; they and their allies took possession of Srirangam, conquered the mud-fort of Koiladi, near the eastern extremity of the island, crossed the Kāveri and encamped on the plain to the east of the town in the neighbourhood of what is known now as the French Rock which stood about a mile to the south-east of the fort.[28] The position of the English was certainly inferior at that time to that of the French. Gingens was not equal to meet the situation; there were cabals and quarrels among his officers; and according to Dalton, all the English officers were young soldiers, 'at that time little experienced in the country-method of making war'.

From the Diarist we learn that the French troops were not better off. Chandā Sāhib is said by him to have written that d'Auteuil and other French officers stubbornly refused to cross

28 The date of the French and Chandā Sāhib crossing the Coleroon is not certain. According to Orme, Chandā Sāhib and the French took possession of Srirangam soon after it was evacuated by the English; and about the middle of August they sent a strong detachment to attack Koiladi which was defended by a small body of English troops for several days and then given up. This success determined Chandā Sāhib to cross the Kāveri, and leaving a garrison in Srirangam, he encamped with the rest of his army to the east of Trichinopoly (Vol. I, pp. 180–1). As Dodwell points out, the French, according to Law, did not cross the Coleroon until September. The Diarist writes in his entry for September 14, that he heard from a letter of Chandā Sāhib that he intended to cross the Coleroon and occupy Srirangam. Apparently Chandā Sāhib first crossed the Coleroon alone, without the French and possibly 'withdrew when the French refused to follow him.' (Note on p. 29 of vol. viii of the *Diary*), as several letters from Chandā Sāhib are reported to have come from camp, on September 17, saying that he was about to cross the Coleroon into Srirangam.

According to the *Tuzuk-i-Wālājāhi*, (Part II) Husain Dōst Khān (Chandā Sāhib) broke the pot of his honour at the *maidan* of the Nawab's Tank, adjoining Utattur and hastened to Samiyavaram and encamped there. He stayed in that same place for a period of two months and twenty-days and engaged himself in taking possession of the kingdom and entrusting it to various agents. Ahsan-ud-dīn then marched with a French army according to the instructions of his master, Husain Dōst Khān and brought under his control the temple of Srirangam and Jhamgir (Jambukesvaram) which was like a fort; and "the vapour of his breath caused by the heat of his exertions to subdue the tract of land from the Kāveri up to the back of the hill of Dhobykonda (French Rock?) went as far as the sky."

the Coleroon after the engagements at Volcondah and Utattur and wished to return to Pondicherry with their soldiers and that Shaikh Hasan and his sepoys bore the brunt of the fighting both at Volcondah and in the taking of Srirangam and the neighbouring pagoda of Tiruvānaikōyil, while the French troops, instead of marching in advance as usual, lagged several miles behind the rest of the army. Presumably, the French refused to advance and allowed Chandā Sāhib to cross the Coleroon alone and occupy Srirangam as soon as the English quitted it. Chandā Sāhib was reported to be telling people that the Europeans had done nothing but talk big and write daily to Dupleix letters full of false complaints. The Diarist also heard news that Cope and his men got on so badly with Muhammad Alī Khān that they had resolved to depart. M. d'Auteuil was said to have resolved to leave Chandā Sāhib's camp; and the next day news was received from Chandā Sāhib that he had actually left the camp in anger and that M. Law who had already made a mark, might be made the commandant of the European troops. Dupleix was reported be very angry at d'Auteuil's departure, but unwilling to appoint Law as his successor.

Muhammad Alī himself sent a letter to Dupleix which was received on August 8, in which he pretended that he was ready to leave Trichinopoly under a safe conduct, according to the terms of Salābat Jang's *cowle* and willing to visit Pondicherry and discuss the whole situation. The Diarist also heard that he had sent emissaries to Ālam Khān at Madura and offered him terms in return for his assistance; he suspected greatly that Muhammad Alī was already suspicious of the English and could be easily persuaded into believing that they would be ready to abandon him. So when Governor Saunders wrote to Chandā Sāhib, taxing him with having unjustly seized the Trichinopoly country that had been mortgaged to the English by Muhammad Alī,[29] a reply

29 Saunders wrote to the Company that he had a mortgage bond for Trichinopoly and hoisted the English flag there and would protest against any French hostilities that might be committed there (letter dated August 15, 1751).

was sent, under Dupleix's instructions and according to his dictation and wording, that the country had been given by Salābat Jang to him and the English had no right at all to it. 'Advantage was taken of Mr. Saunders' sealed letter, to prepare an inner slip, as though addressed by Mr. Saunders to Chandā Sāhib, offering to deliver up the fort of Trichinopoly and the person of Muhammad Alī, provided such and such were done. This was to be folded up in the cover and given to the confidential people whom Muhammad Alī sends to M. d'Auteuil and Shaikh Hasan, to be carried to their master. As Muhammad Alī is already suspicious of the English and is secretly sending people to us for terms, it is hoped that this letter will cause quarrels between him and them and increase their ill-feeling. I hear that special letters to Chandā Sāhib and M. d'Auteuil were also written about this.' Comment is needless on this entry of the Diarist; and Dodwell remarks that this was 'a device characteristic of Dupleix, no matter whether proposed by him or not.'

The fort of Vriddachalam was to be taken by the French, as it was the only fort on this side of Trichinopoly, still in possession of the English and Muhammad Alī. Rango Pandit, Madame Dupleix's *amaldar,* was ordered to fortify his place in the neighbourhood and entertain topasses, sepoys and Portuguese artillery men for that purpose; but when he marched against the fort, the enemy sallied out and attacked him; and Rango Pandit had to run away, spiking his guns. The Diarist was glad that the attack miscarried, because, had it been successful, it would have redounded to the credit of that rascally Brahman (Rango Paṇḍit) and Madame Dupleix.[30] Not only was this set-back a source of depression to Dupleix; but the news that the Tanjore people were inclined to the side of Muhammad Alī and the English

30 The Diarist entry for August 18th, that the 200 men who marched from Cuddalore were encamped outside Vriddachalam when Rango Pandit's attack was repulsed, means probably the detachment that was sent out by Saunders with a large convoy of stores to the relief of Vriddachalam which was accompanied by Clive and Pigot and which dispersed, according to Orme, the troops of a neighbouring Poligar.—*Vide* note 23, above.

and hailed with joy the news of Ghāzī-ud-dīn Khān, the elder brother and a new rival of Salābat Jang, recognising the title of Muhammad Alī and even celebrated the hearing of the news as an occasion for thanksgiving and festivity, put him out greatly, though he affected to believe that the English should have spread the news which the Tanjoreans so readily took in. An agreement was made at Pondicherry with Gopal Rao, the *vakil* of Murari Rao Ghorepade[31] that the latter should take Chandā Sāhib's part either by openly attacking the enemy or by joining them and secretly working against them and that Chandā Sāhib should pay each trooper that the Maratha sent, Rs. 20 per month, besides an additional sum to him when matters should have been settled. Murari Rao was expected at Pondicherry and was to be welcomed with great honour and *eclat*.

On the last day of August, news was received that Governor Saunders had despatched to Trichinopoly from Devikottai a few soldiers with provisions, shot, powder and other munitions of war; that some of Chandā Sāhib's troopers and the Tanjore army attempted to attack them when they got near Trichinopoly, but that they broke through and reached the fort safely. Dupleix

31 Murari Rao (a grand-nephew of the famous Santaji) was the Maratha governor of Trichinopoly left by Raghuji Bhonsle; he took some part in the revolution that followed Sāfdar Alī's assassination and later evacuated Trichinopoly to Nizām-ul-Mulk and quitted the Carnatic (1743). He was hired by Nāsir Jang as the commandant of a body of 10,000 horse when the latter came down into the Carnatic and sent forward to the Coleroon where he met and harassed the army of Muzaffar Jang and Chandā Sāhib returning with the French battalion from the Tanjore expedition (February-March, 1750). When Muzaffar Jang had submitted to his uncle, and the French had retired hastily with Chandā Sāhib into Pondicherry (April), Murari Rao pushed on in pursuit of the French troops and greatly harassed them. He had established himself at Gooty in 1746 and got hold of Penukonda and became supreme among the *poligars* of the Ceded Districts. For his character, see Orme, vol. I, p. 363. He had a very interesting part to play in the operations round Trichinopoly and later against Haider Alī. (See the author's paper on Murari Rao Ghorepade in The Indian Historical Quarterly: Vol. XV: pp. 551-74).

was angry that the Tanjore people did not effectively obstruct their march and try to capture their munitions and provisions, to which the Tanjore *vakil* at Pondicherry gave an evasive reply.[32]

Clive's capture of Arcot—Events till the end of 1751

Dupleix resolved, according to the Diarist, to despatch 200 soldiers and officers, who had lately arrived, to Trichinopoly, on the 1st of September and asked Razā Sāhib to accompany them; the latter agreed to do so and begged for two lakhs of rupees at least with which he could pay off sepoys and horsemen who were heavily in arrears, but had to start only with half a lakh. Soon the news of Clive's diversion to Arcot came to be known. It was said by Madame Dupleix that it would not be advisable to recall Chandā Sāhib's or the French troops from before Trichinopoly, but that they would be sending troops from Pondicherry to help Polur Muhammad Alī Khān (brother of Chandā Sāhib) at Arcot. She asked that the two sons of Bangaru Yachama Nayaka of Venkatagiri[33] and other poligars of the

32 This refers to the second reinforcement sent by the English to Trichinopoly where great discontent prevailed among the officers and several had to be removed. A commission was given to Clive (Fort St. David Consultation of July 22|August 2, 1751); and he proceeded with a detachment into the country of Tanjore where he was joined by another from Devikottai under Captain Clarke who took the command of the whole which consisted only of 100 Europeans and 50 sepoys with one small field-piece. The French detached from Koiladi, 30 Europeans and 500 sepoys and had a skirmish with the English detachment, at a place 10 miles east of the latter. The English gained access to Trichinopoly by making a detour in order to avoid the enemy's camp. (Orme; vol. i, p. 182 and Forrest's *Clive*, vol. i, p. 137).

33 Bangaru Yachama Nayaka, surnamed Sarvagna Kumara, died in 1748, leaving two sons, Bangaru Yachama Nayak and Pedda Yachama Nayak. The latter quarrelled with his brother and attempted to get a *sanad* for the whole estate of Venkatagiri from the Nawab of Arcot who decided that the two brothers were to live in peace at different places. Their *vakils* were at Pondicherry, soliciting Dupleix's favour and being compelled to pay large sums both to Dupleix and to Chandā Sāhib. The younger brother died in A.D. 1754; and the elder received the *sanad* for the whole estate in the previous year from Nawab Muhammad Alī who had

neighbourhood should be written to immediately to send troops to Arcot, while Chandā Sāhib was asked to send as quickly as possible 2,000 horsemen to Arcot for the help of Polur Muhammad Alī Khān; and Sayyad Muhammad Khān of Tadpatri who had been ordered to go to the Musaravakkam *killa*, was now ordered to proceed to Arcot with his 200 matchlock men.

News was received on September 12, that the English had reached Conjeevaram and tied *toranams* there and were intending to occupy Kāveripākkam and Musaravakkam, while a small body of Polur Muhammad Alī Khān's men were encamped near Damarle (Damal) in order to attack the English. Dupleix tried to encourage the merchants who were alarmed by telling them that a very large army was being despatched from Pondicherry to Arcot, so that no fort or army could resist them, whereas in reality he could send only about 150 men of very inferior calibre. On the 15th of September, it was known in Pondicherry that on the previous day the English had hoisted their flag at the Nawab's palace and occupied the fort, while the day before (*i.e.* 13th September), Polur Muhammad Alī Khān and others had fled to Vellore.[34]

triumphed over his rival. It was reported by the Diarist that, after the death of Nāsir Jang, the two Nayak brothers were to pay Muzaffar Jang two lakhs of rupees and Chandā Sāhib one lakh. The former payment was made through Ramdas Pandit; and as a *jaghir* had been given for 4,000 horse, although the *mansab* was 5,000, the Nizām now gave the additional *jaghir* for 1,000 horse. Chandā Sāhib demanded three lakhs, but was paid one lakh through Dupleix who got bonds from their vakils.

34 Saunders wrote on August 15|26, that it had been resolved to leave 300 or 400 men to defend Trichinopoly fort, and according to the Nawab's desire, make a diversion in the Arcot country, with the rest, joining the Nawab's forces, with a view to raising contributions. Subsequently he wrote on the 30th September|11th October, to the Company that he had put in execution the design of making a diversion in the Arcot country, in order to draw off the enemy from Trichinopoly. 130 men under Clive embarked on August 22|September 2, from Fort St. David for Madras where they were joined by 80 more. The detachment that proceeded against Arcot, consisted of about 200 Europeans and 300 sepoys with 8 officers and 3 field-pieces. They marched from Madras on August 26|September 6, reached Conjeevaram three days later, got to

The English capture of Arcot did not greatly disturb the minds of the Pondicherry folk. Polur Muhammad Alī Khān wrote to say that when the English garrison at Arcot marched against Timiri fort, he sent his son with a small force of Murtazā Alī Khān of Vellore and repulsed them; and that, with reinforcements, the enemy could be quickly driven out of the Arcot *killa.* Murtazā Alī Khān sent word to the same effect and required reinforcements before the enemy could strengthen himself. Dupleix however realised the seriousness of the loss of Arcot and was so angry that the Diarist wrote, ' even I fear to stand before him '; how much more then will others fear? He urged that Chandā Sāhib who had already sent 1,000 horsemen, should write to his son, Razā Sāhib, to march at once to Arcot with another 1,000 horse; and also that he should immediately cross the Kāveri and attack Trichinopoly.

M. d'Auteuil and other officers had all along been written to by Dupleix that they were not to return to Pondicherry, but advance with Chandā Sāhib's troops. It was likely that when Chandā Sāhib crossed the Coleroon first, d'Auteuil obstinately refused to follow him and demanded to return. A letter from Chandā Sāhib received at Pondicherry on August 7, is reported by the Diarist in his entry for that date, to have contained the

the neighbourhood of Arcot on August 31|September 11, and took possession of the fort the next day, hoisting both the English colours and Muhammad Alī's flag and protecting the inhabitants.

It is to be stressed that, for sometime past, Muhammad Alī had been proposing a diversion in the direction of Arcot, and at first Saunders and the English Council thought that this might be effected by Gingens leaving a sufficient number of men in Trichinopoly and marching with a force into the Arcot country. But Gingens could not appreciate his capacity for the task and Clive persuaded Saunders that he could do it. News of the English march to Arcot did not reach Dupleix for a week.—*See* Mr. C. S. Srinivasachari's paper—Nawab Muhammad Alī and the Siege of Arcot—a paper in the Winternitz Memorial number of *The Indian Historical Quarterly*—Vol. XIV—pp. 545 *et seq;* and his paper—The Diversion on Arcot in 1751: Its Genesis—in the *Proceedings of the All India Modern History Congress, Poona,* 1935, (pp. 10–23 in Part II).

news that d'Auteuil had left the camp in anger and should have already arrived and reported the state of affairs and that Law might be made the commander of European troops. On September 17, another letter received from Chandā Sāhib said, according to the Diarist, that if d'Auteuil departed, Law might be appointed commander. To this Dupleix is said to have replied that he had recalled d'Auteuil and Bernier and appointed Law as commander with orders to cross the Coleroon and the Kāveri before the Nawab's troops. Law set out from Pondicherry for camp on September 8th and took over the command on 18th; and the real operations of Chandā Sāhib against Trichinopoly began only after this date.

In his letters, Chandā Sāhib said that Muhammad Alī had sent *vakils* to him, promising to accept the terms of the *cowle* formerly offered to him and to evacuate Trichinopoly twenty days later and asked that d'Auteuil who had the *cowle* with him, might be desired to hand it over to him. Dupleix had, by this time, become very suspicious of Muhammad Alī and was convinced that the latter was asking for a truce of twenty days in order merely to strengthen his position at Arcot and to collect provisions and stores for the defence of Trichinopoly, which he could not have the least intention to give up. He wrote thus to Chandā Sāhib and asked him not to allow even the least delay in crossing the Coleroon and the Kāveri.

On October 11, letters were received at Pondicherry that Chandā Sāhib's army was encamped round the fort of Trichinopoly and that Ālam Khān of Madura, to whom the English had written offering a place under Muhammad Alī, in return for his assistance, was marching to Chandā Sāhib's assistance, along with other poligars from the south, while the Raja of Mysore was inimical towards him openly. Ranga Pillai's *Diary* furnishes no details of the events happening before Trichinopoly in the fateful months October 1751 to February 1752; and there follows a hiatus during March and April. With regard to the Mysore negotiations with Pondicherry of which mention was made by the Diarist in his entry for July 8th, nothing seems to have happened. A letter of the captain of the English forces at Trichinopoly, written to Fort St. David was seized by the French on September 13th; therein, according to the Diarist's version, it was stated that the Mysore men had not yet arrived; but when they did, he would, in conjunction with them, attack the enemy. This meant that an agreement had already been made between the Raja of Mysore and Muhammad Alī. The Mysore *vakil* who had been sent to Pondicherry, still continued at that place; and when questioned by the Diarist, he declared that when he was accredited to Pondicherry, his master had no idea of assisting Muhammad Alī, but that troops had been marched only as a measure of precaution. He also added that Chandā Sāhib was ever talking ill of the Mysoreans to their *vakil* at his camp and threatening to seize their country. In October, as was seen above, the Diarist wrote that Chandā Sāhib and the Raja of Mysore were on bad terms. In the next entry of the Diarist, dated November 8, Chandā Sāhib is said to have written to Dupleix that he was again friendly with the Raja of Mysore whose *vakil* had proposed certain terms and that he had agreed to the demands which were as follows:—(1) That part of the Trichinopoly country which had long been in the possession of Mysore should not be interfered with; (2) the poligars who had joined Mysore should not be molested; (3) 2,000 horse and 5,000 foot of the Mysore army should constantly remain with Chandā Sāhib; and (4) the latter should assign for their maintenance lands adjoining Mysore and yielding 3 lakhs annually. Chandā Sāhib agreed to them and offered to cede Sondikuppam and certain countries seized by the Tondaiman for the maintenance of the troops, and not to molest any poligar except that of Turaiyur. Dupleix agreed to write to the Dalavāi of Mysore, promising to fulfil the terms of Chandā Sāhib's agreement, as desired by him.[35] It was likely that the agreement of

35 The Dalavāi, Deva Raja, was averse to engaging to help Muhammad Alī or interfere at all; but his younger brother, Nañja Raja, was tempted, by extravagant promises, to assist him. According to Mīr Husein Alī Khān Kirmāni (*History of Hyder Naik*: *tr* by Col. W. Miles, 1842—p. 35), Nañja Raja associated himself with Murari Rao and

Chandā Sāhib with the Mysore *vakil* was not intended to be a genuine one, but, as Mr. Dodwell suggests, 'only to delay matters until the Mysore preparations were complete' and to 'represent a stage in the bargaining between Mysore and Muhammad Alī which ended in his unfortunate promise to cede Trichinopoly.' As a matter of fact, though a letter was received at Fort St. David in October, 1751, from the Mysoreans promising to join Muhammad Alī, their contingent did not arrive at Trichinopoly till early in the following year.[36]

On the 13th of December, the Diarist heard that Nañja Raja (who was exercising all real authority and was usually called the young *Dalavāi* as well as surnamed *Karachuri* [hand and dagger], equivalent to the English phrase 'a word and a blow') had assembled at Dharmapuri, above the Changama Pass, 2,000 or 3,000 horse and 5,000 or 6,000 foot and that Murari Rao had visited him and was also there with 2,000 horse and that both intended to help Muhammad Alī. When Dupleix heard this news, his anger against Chandā Sāhib burst forth and he exclaimed that the latter had made enemies of the Rajas of Mysore and Tanjore, alienated the poligars, who hindered all cultivation and that he might be pensioned off with a *jaghir* or forced to retire to Mecca, as the country would be ruined if it remained in his possession longer. The Diarist was glad that the Governor was angry with Chandā Sāhib and wrote. 'God has dealt justly with Chandā Sāhib and punished him within the year for his having cheated me (of expected rewards)'.

As a measure of retaliation for Nañja Raja joining Muhammad Alī, Dupleix ordered that the Turaiyur people should tie *toranams* in the adjoining Mysore country. Nañja Raja and Murari Rao had time to plunder the Salem mint and fort.

other poligars and marched towards Trichinopoly with an army of 7,000 cavalry and 10 or 12,000 foot, the Raja however not consenting to this movement. The aged Dalavāi, Deva Raja, was averse to the proposals of Seshagiri Pandit, the ambassador of Muhammad Alī to Mysore (Wilks—vol. I., p. 172.)

36 See notes on pp. 58 and 69 of the *Diary*, vol. VIII.

To return to the doings at Arcot:—The alleged repulse of the English before Timiri fort reported by Polur Muhammad Alī and written by the Diarist in his entry for September 18, 1751, had probably a reference to Clive's first movement against Timiri on September 15th, when the English, according to Orme (vol. I, p. 184), marched out to meet the fugitive Arcot garrison of 600 horse and 500 foot drawn up near Timiri and forced them to retreat to the hills in their rear. Dupleix urged that Razā Sāhib should immediately proceed to Arcot; but the latter asked for 2 lakhs of rupees towards the charges of his 3,000 horsemen, as otherwise, they might retire from Volcondah to which they had advanced, to Gingee and refuse to accompany him (Diarist's entry for the 24th of September).

Meanwhile, Clive's troops had sallied out on Timiri (a fort situated about 7 miles south of Arcot, on the Arni road) on the 17th, but could not secure its surrender. On the night of the 25th September, when the reinforced enemy took up a stand within 3 miles of Arcot, Clive made a surprise attack and returned with some plunder. When the latter seized the Conjeevaram pagoda, Clive sent a small body to dislodge him and convoyed safely the 2 eighteen-pounders that were sent to him from Madras and beat back the enemy who advanced to attack the fort (27th September). When Razā Sāhib finally reached Arcot and took possession of the town and the palace, the famous siege began (4th October). Clive's sortie on the besiegers (5th October), the failure of a reinforcement under Lieutenant Innis to reach the besieged, the securing by Razā Sāhib of battering cannon from Pondicherry and of Murtazā Alī who came with 2,000 men, the latter's trick of pretending to quarrel with Razā Sāhib and inviting Clive to join in attacking him, the decision of Murari Rao to throw in his lot with the brave besieged, Razā Sāhib's offer of a proposal to Clive to surrender, the final attack of the besiegers on the 24th November, their failure and departure on the next day—most of these incidents are not noted by the Diarist; and he only records in a matter-of-fact manner how Razā Sāhib was driven from Arni to Chetpattu, by the English and the Marathas (entry for the

17th December) and how Clive marched on Conjeevaram which had meanwhile been taken by the French, reduced it and compelled the garrison to flee to Chingleput (entry for the 31st December).

Regarding the operations before Trichinopoly we have better information from the Diarist. In his entry for the 11th October, he wrote that letters were received on that day to the effect that Chandā Sāhib's army had been encamped round the fort of Trichinopoly. On the 8th November he reported that Chandā Sāhib had sent on Salābat Jang's *takid parwana* to Muhammad Alī and was expecting news of its receipt by the latter and of what might take place in consequence.[37] He is said to have also written that, if Muhammad Alī did not accept the *parwana,* the sepoys in the fort who had accepted a *cowle,* would make over the fort to him. Dupleix replied that Chandā Sāhib should not relax his efforts, but make every effort, day and night, to capture the fort without delay. Towards the close of November, news was received that Hasan-ud-dīn Khān and his troops attacked the battery built by Cope outside the fort gate and that Cope and Gingens were not pulling on well, the latter favouring Muhammad Alī Khān and the former opposing him. Towards the end of December there was a battle between the English and Hasan-ud-dīn Khān at Trichinopoly in which the latter was repulsed after a severe fight and rescued by Law and Ālam Khān moving to his assistance and rescuing Shaikh Hasan and those who remained

37 Chandā Sāhib mentions in his letter that a copy of the *parwana* was sent to the Governor of Fort St. David. It is interesting to note in this connection that Saunders, in writing to the Directors on 24th October (o. s.), mentions a letter alleged to have been sent by Salābat Jang, but suspected to be the production of Dupleix and Chandā Sāhib; and he remarks that it was curious that the letter should arrive on the same day as Chandā Sāhib's answer to his previous letter (see note above); and it was bruited about that Chandā Sāhib and others had counterfeit seals of the Mughal and his officers. Saunders offered that, Chandā Sāhib might hold Arcot, and leave Trichinopoly to Muhammad Alī, pending the Mughal's decision; but the offer was rejected—see Dodwell's *Madras Despatches,* 1744–55, pp. 145–6.

with him. The Diarist heard that Hasan-ud-dīn Khān was lured into an ambush and many of his men were cut off, though Chandā Sāhib, Ālam Khān and Law advanced to his help; and finally they were forced to abandon the battery which they had occupied.[38] Thus the year 1751 closed with the French fortunes beginning to sink in both the Arcot and Trichinopoly spheres. The triumphant march of Salābat Jang and Bussy to Aurangabad, their subjugation of the rebellious *killedar* of Nirmal, the great influence of the French at the Nizām's court—these are noticed by the Diarist in their places; but the details available of Bussy's doings are scanty.

38 M. d'Auteuil had been succeeded by Law, the nephew of the famous financier, who was obstinate, if anything, and resolved against Dupleix's advice that the city should be reduced not by storm, but by sap and mine. The English thought at first that Chandā Sāhib would merely blockade the place and not even besiege it (Saunders' letter to the Company of September 30|October 11). The French established themselves at Sarkarpalayam (Chuklepalayam of Orme) on the south bank of the Kāveri, about 1½ miles north-east of the city, and their principal battery was raised a little to the south of the north-east angle of the fort. They also mounted guns on the French Rock and in the Srirangam Island and on the rock of Erumbesvaram.

(For a plan of the dispositions and operations see Hemingway's *Trichinopoly District Gazetteer*—map between *pp.* 330 and 331; Forrest's *Life of Lord Clive*, vol. I. map facing *p.* 60 and Orme, vol. III. (ed. of 1862), maps and plans and Martineau's *Dupleix*, vol. III, map facing p. 206). The first fight took place when the French surprised the English entrenchments opposite the French Rock. Their guns were not effective and Law would not change their position. When a party of Mysore horsemen arrived about the middle of October, they accompanied a body of English troops under Dalton who put a large part of Chandā Sāhib's cavalry to flight. There were a few other engagements in December in which Chandā Sāhib's cavalry fared badly. The incident of the ambush is probably that narrated by Orme in *pp.* 204–5 of his first volume (1862 ed.).

CHAPTER XII

DUPLEIX FACES ODDS

French Negotiations with Mysore—Salabat Jang's Difficulties

Early in January 1752, Dupleix planned to convert the Villiyanallur temple into a fort, by raising batteries and constructing outer walls. Chandā Sāhib sent a letter informing that the Mysore Dalavāi was dead (the news was wholly false) and that the matter had been kept a secret for about three weeks and that Kāntayarāja, the former commander, had been appointed to his place.[1] Of course there was no truth in the news at all; but there was possibly some confusion in his mind between the two Nañja Rajas (written Nandi Raja in the *Diary*), the first, a cousin of Devaraja and the second, his younger brother who occupied the

1 In the reign of Chama Raja Wodeyar VII (1731–34), the three chief offices in the Mysore State were those of the *Dalavāi* (head of the army), *Sarvādhikāri* (head of finance and revenue) and *Pradhāna* (privy councillor); these were held respectively by Deva Raja who was the Dalavāi and Nañja Raja, his cousin, who combined in himself the other two offices. Chama Raja Wodeyar contrived to displace them; but they found means to recover their position quickly and to imprison the Raja and his wife. They raised to the throne Chikka Krishna Raja Wodeyar, a child of a distant branch of the ruling family. Nañja Raja died in 1747 and was succeeded by another person of the same name, who was the younger brother of Deva Raja and surnamed Karachuri. Nañja Raja was a truculent person and contributed, in great measure, to the eclipse of the dynasty and the rise of Haidar Alī. After a successful expedition into the Coimbatore country, he married his daughter to the nominal Raja, as a first step to his other ambitious projects. Haidar first came under his notice in 1749, during the siege of Devanahalli. He agreed, against the wishes of his elder brother, Deva Raja, the Dalavāi, to assist Muhammad Alī, and led an army of 5,000 horse and 10,000 infantry from Seringapatam to Trichinopoly, about the time of Clive's siege and subsequent defence of Arcot. His transactions and movements round Trichinopoly lasted till 1755 when he returned to Mysore at the summons of his brother, in order to meet and repel an invasion of Salābat Jang and Bussy. Deva Raja retired from government in 1757,

office of *Sarvādhikāri.*[2] Madame Dupleix persuaded her husband to write to the ruler of Mysore, asking him to help the French and not Muhammad Alī; and Dupleix himself was of the opinion that, but for the help of Mysore, Muhammad Alī could not have withstood the French so long.

Meanwhile, the troops of Razā Sāhib which had had to flee to Chettupattu, plundered, in February, the region of Poonamallee, Mylapore, the Great (St. Thomas') and Little Mounts, Saidapet and Kunnattur which were large and prosperous villages. The Indian merchants of Madras were reported to have run for shelter with their goods to Sadras and Pulicat; and the Diarist regretted that they did not go to Covelong which was in French occupation, and wrote that M. Le Blanc, the chief at that place, "troubles people, so that all fear him and prefer Pulicat or Sadras."[3]

disgusted with the cruelty practised by Nañja Raja towards the Raja and his partisans who had attempted to throw off the supremacy of the two brothers. Nañja Raja was responsible for the usurpation of Haidar Alī who got him imprisoned in 1767, "in so far as a single personage could be held responsible for it." (See the *Mysore Gazetteer* (New Edition) Vol. II, Modern, Part IV. *pp.* 2465 *et seq;* M. Wilks' *Historical Sketches of the South of India* (Ind. ed.) vol. i. *ch.* VII.).

2 *Vide Note* 1: Mr. Dodwell says in foot-note 2, on p. 90 of the *Diary*, vol. viii; "I am entirely at a loss to account for his (Chandā Sāhib's) statement that Nandi Raja was not the younger brother of the Dalavāi."

3 Razā Sāhib made a rally at Chettupattu after his defeat at Arni, and later at Covelong, with a design to attack San Thomé; but he was not in a condition to do it (Despatch of Fort St. David to the Company, dated January 25, 1752). From a subsequent despatch of Thomas Saunders, dated February 15, 1752, we learn that Razā Sāhib plundered and burnt some villages near Poonamallee and carried off to Pondicherry the furniture of the houses at St. Thomas Mount and Marmalong (Mambalam-Saidapet). The Pondicherry Council repudiated the English claim to these places; and the latter were unable to check these ravages for want of cavalry and their force at Madras was insufficient to defend even the Black Town (George Town) and the Pettahs; and Muhammad Alī had not sent the detachment of cavalry for which he had been so often pressed. (Madras Council's Consultation, dated February 3, 1752—pp. 1-2 of *Records of Fort St. George, Diary and Consultation Book of* 1752).

There is a hiatus in the *Diary* for three months (February 13th to May 12th). The entry for the latter date gives news from Salābat Jang's camp, according to which Nāmat-ullah Khān, who was a son of Khajah Abdulla Khān, Nawab-designate of the Carnatic, and who had been recently the Nawab of Rajahmundry, was to get the *subah* of Arcot and he was to come down with an army, subdue the refractory Pathans of Kurnool and suppress the disturbances caused by Muhammad Alī Khān, the English and the Raja of Mysore.[4] Khaja Nāmatullah Khān and Muzaffar Khān (Abdul Rahmān who had accompanied Bussy) advanced, by way of Gadwal, on Kurnool; but when batteries were about to be raised and the troops of Munawar Khān (younger brother of Himmat Khān who had successfully got possession of his brother's dominion) which were encamped near the fort were to be attacked, the French people, who were probably the troops attached to Muzaffar Khān, came away; and operations were consequently

4 Compare with a letter to the Madras Council alleged to have come from Salābat Jang, read at a Consultation of the 10th February, 1752 (O.S.), which exhorted the English "to quit Mahomed Ally's Interest, as He is a Rebel, and to espouse that of Chunda Saib" and "which by the confession of the Hircars coming from Pondicherry, we can't help entertaining some doubts with regard to its being really wrote by Salābat Jang . . ."—*Ibid.*—p. 3.

With regard to the refractory Pathans of Kurnool, it is to be noticed that in the *melee* that occurred at Luckireddipalli pass in the Rayachuti taluk, Muzaffar Jang fell, struck down by a javelin thrown by the Nawab of Kurnool (January 1751). Himmat (or Himāyat) Khān, the Nawab, had succeeded to power in 1733, had defied Nāsir Jang who had to conciliate him and accompanied his new master on the Carnatic expedition. Shortly after he left Kurnool, heavy floods passed down the Handri and the Tungabhadra and washed away portions of the fort walls. The Nawab requested permission to return to Kurnool; but Nāsir Jang declined permission. Later, a misunderstanding was created between the two by one Saif-ud-dīn and the ill-feeling was increased by the disappointment of the Nawab in his expectations of obtaining considerable immunities and an addition of territory from the Nizām. The Nawab was killed in the *melee* of Luckireddipalli; and Salābat Jang and Bussy carried the Kurnool fort by assault in March, 1751 and imprisoned the Nawab's wife and two sons. Kurnool was placed in charge of one Sayyad

affected. Hearing that Nāmatullah Khān had only a small army, the English and Muhammad Alī became emboldened and resolved "to drive away from Srirangam to Pondicherry or to destroy altogether Chandā Sāhib with his Muhammadan troops, M. Law and Shaikh Hasan with the French troops, before they can be joined by Nāmatullah's troops, Muzaffar Khān's troops and the troops that will arive by the Europe ships, as after that it would be impossible to dislodge the French."[5] The English, we are told by the Diarist, were resolved to fight to the end, and even spend the Company's money on continuing the war and fight harder than ever, even if Muhammad Alī could not find any more money.[6]

Ranga Pillai's note on the situation of Salābat Jang is interesting. Writing on May 12th, he says that the Nizām's treasury was empty; and his elder brother and rival, Ghāzī-ud-dīn Khān had been writing to many that Salābat Jang should not be recognised and the various killedars would not pay their *peshkush,* while the French troops were giving trouble on account of their arrears; and the jaghirdar of Pālaki (son of Raja Chandrasen) was giving trouble. Nor was the situation at Delhi any better, where the Mughal throne was about to be swallowed up by Ahmad

Ālam and of the Zamindar of Gadval; but in 1752, Ranmas Khān (*alias* Munawwar Khān) Bahadur, brother of Himmat Khān, returned from Arcot, whither he had gone, to seize the estate. He got a sum of money from the Nawab of Cuddapah, was joined by Khandoji Pandit with a body of 2,000 horse, and after six months of fighting and negotiation, got possession of the fort of Kurnool and made an amicable arrangement with the Nizām. Ananda Ranga Pillai wrote in his *Diary* (July 14, 1752) thus:—"I hear that Salābat Jang has ordered Coja Nāmat-ul-lah Khān and Muzaffar Khān at Kandanur to deliver up that fort and country to Munawwar Khān, Himmat Bahadur Khān's younger brother and join him at Hyderabad. As Muzaffar Khān has also written this to me, I think it must be true."—pp. 141–2 of the *Diary*, vol. viii.

5 Diarist's entry for May 12th, 1752. p. 95 of the *Diary*, Vol. VIII.

6 See the Madras Consultation of 13th April, 1752, resolving to press for money Muhammad Alī who said that the Mysore ruler would repay the advances made and ordered his officials to pay a part of the produce.

Shāh Abdālī's invasion. "Till now", the Diarist remarks, "the Mughals have exercised authority, but henceforth the Pathans will take their place, or the Rajas of Hindustan, the Rana of Udaipur etc., may become the masters."[7]

THE DEATH OF CHANDA SAHIB AND OF RAJA RAGHUNATH DAS

Very little is found in the *Diary* of the operations round Trichinopoly, of Clive's victory at Kāveripak, Lawrence's arrival from England and his assumption of command, Chandā Sāhib's retreat into Srirangam, the English blockade of the island, d'Auteuil's retreat to Uttatur and Clive's march on it—all of which took place before the end of April. He mentions that the English, Muhammad Alī Khān's troops and the Mysoreans intended to attack d'Auteuil at Uttatur, whereupon the latter retired to Valikandapuram. Also Law, Chandā Sāhib and the blockaded troops at Srirangam were suffering much from want of food and money; the sepoys and troopers had not received any pay at all for the last three months; and many had deserted to the enemy, who had occupied Koiladi, at the eastern end of the island, while others had resolved to obtain *cowles* and return with them to Pondicherry.

7 Ghāzī-ud-dīn Khān I (eldest son of Āsaf Jāh) was appointed to be the rightful Nizām by the Emperor in January 1751. Mahmud Khān Bangash invaded Oudh and invested Allahabad, but was routed by the Marathas and by Safdār Jang in April. Early (*i.e.* in March) in the next year, Ahmad Shāh Abdālī entered Lahore and annexed the subahs of Lahore and Multan. In April, Qalandar Khān, Abdālī's envoy, reached Delhi; and in May, Ghāzī-ud-dīn Khān left Delhi for the Deccan; he died at Aurangabad in the middle of October, being poisoned by his step-mother. In April 1752, Raja Raghunath Das, the Diwan of Salābat Jang, was murdered in a mutiny of his soldiery at Balki. Sayyad Lashkar Khān who succeeded him as Diwan, was ill-disposed towards Salābat Jang and secretly favoured Ghāzī-ud-dīn. (*see* Burgess, The Chronology of Modern India (1494–1894)—p. 193 and Sir J. N. Sarkār's article on A Correct Chronology of Delhi History in the J.B.O.R.S. Vol. XVIII, Part I. pp. 89–90).

In this distressing condition (about the middle of May), Dupleix received an entreating letter from Salābat Jang who begged him to order Bussy and Shaikh Ibrāhīm to guard his person night and day, saying:—" you protected me while he (Raghunath Das) lived, and must protect me now that he is dead."[8] Dupleix accordingly wrote letters urging Salābat Jang to do exactly as Bussy should advise,[9] and also to Abdul Baqar Khān,[10] who " is to be Diwan in the place of Raghunath Das ", advising him that according to Bussy's instructions, he (*i.e.*, Dupleix himself) was " induced to appoint him diwan ". He was advised to bear two things in mind: " one is to labour with a single heart in Salābat Jang's affairs; and the other is to be our (French) man and manage our (French) affairs with all fidelity." The death of Raghunath Das was a severe strain on Bussy's influence and dominance at the Nizām's court; and Dupleix had to write to Shaikh Ibrāhīm to do whatever Bussy should ask him to do and not disobey him even in the merest trifle.

The Diarist's entry for June 6, 1752, contains a bit of interesting news about Delhi affairs. The Afghans had captured the fort of Lahore and murdered Mīr Mannu and returned to their hills owing to the approach of the rains; and the Hindustan Rajas near Delhi had assembled together with a lakh of horse

8 Vide *supra*, note 21.

9 Saunders, the English Governor, wrote in a separate despatch, to the Company, dated July 5th, 1752, that he had tried various methods, in vain, to get letters conveyed to Salābat Jang, and had only received letters from him *via* Pondicherry. (Dodwell's *The Madras Despatches* (1744–55)—p. 171).

10 Professor Dodwell supposes that this person should be identified with Sayyad Lashkar Khān who was in fact appointed at once. Abdul Baqar Khān was, according to the Diarist, nominated Diwan of Salābat Jang by Dupleix. Sayyad Lashkar Khān was an officer of experience even in 1741, when he artfully secured the submission of Nāsir Jang who had risen in rebellion against his father, in the field of battle. He became the governor of Aurangabad later on. (See H. G. Briggs' *The Nizam*, Vol. I, p. 51 *et seq.*) Sayyad Lashkar Khān was succeeded as Diwan by Shāh Nawaz Khān, author of the *M'āsiru'l-Umrae Taimuria.*

and threatened the Emperor Ahmad Shāh with an ultimatum that he should abdicate and the throne would be given to a boy of Ālamgīr's family.[11]

Bad news from Srirangam reached the Diarist's ears on the 8th June in the shape of Chandā Sāhib having written to the Governor that M. Law had gone over to Muhammad Alī Khān and the English and ruined everything. M. d'Auteuil who had advanced to Valikandapuram, was attacked by Birki Venkat Rao with the Maratha troops, the Mysore faujdar and some English who were encamped at Samayavaram and forced to retreat to Ranjangudi, being unable to reach Srirangam; but Mutabar Khān, the faujdar of that place, would not admit them and, on the other hand, helped the enemy to get in their rear and attack them; and

11 Ahmad Shāh was the son of the Emperor Muhammad Shāh, whom he succeeded on the 15th April, 1748, Rabī II, A.H. 1161. After a reign of 6 years, 3 months and 8 days, he was deposed and imprisoned and afterwards blinded, together with his mother Udham Bai, by his prime minister, Imad-ul-Mulk, Ghāzī-ud-dīn Khān II, son of Ghāzī-ud-dīn Khān I, on Sunday, 2nd June, N.S. 1754. After this he lived more than 21 years and died on the 1st of January, A.D. 1775. After his imprisonment, Ālamgīr II, son of Jahandar Shāh, was raised to the throne. A *History of Ahmad Shāh*, has been abstracted by Professor Dowson in the 8th volume of Elliot and Dowson's *History of India* (pp. 104 *et seq*) which shows the condition of affairs. Muin-ul-Mulk, Rustam Hind, called commonly Mīr Mannu, was the son of Itimād-ud-daulā, Kamar-ud-dīn Khān. He was appointed governor of Lahore by the Emperor Ahmad Shāh after the battle of Sirhind, in which his father was killed. He died early in 1756, not now, as the Diarist wrote both on May 12th and on June 6th, 1752. Mīr Mannu governed the Punjab with vigour, chastised the turbulent Sikhs, withheld from Ahmad Shāh Abdālī the revenue of the four districts which he had stipulated to pay him after his second invasion of 1748, boldly resisted the third Abdālī invasion of 1751-52, and fought with the invaders in the country between the Chenab and the Ravi. He only submitted to the Abdālī after making a protracted defence of Lahore and got from the victor, the title of Farzand Khān Bahadur Rustam-i-Hind. He took part in the civil war at Delhi that followed the assassination of the eunuch, Jawid, and died only in 1756. Ahmad Shāh's reign was torn with internal strife and external invasion. (*see* Syed Mahomed Latif's The *History of the Punjab*. pp. 221-5)

d'Auteuil surrendered without striking a blow.[12] On June 15th, Ranga Pillai heard that Chandā Sāhib had tried to escape, as a faqir, from custody, but had been seized; and when the news reached Fort St. David, a salute was fired and sugar was distributed to the people. The next day he learnt that Chandā Sāhib, Shaikh Hasan, Law and others were surrounded in the Srirangam temple, and could get no provisions; and, in despair, Chandā Sāhib offered to pay a certain sum of money to Manoji Appa of Tanjore and Murari Rao, on condition that he was to be escorted beyond Tanjore and sent to Karikal. He was to be disguised as a faqir; and so he set out, escorted by Murari Rao. But Muhammad Alī's people found him out and declared that they would take him to the fort of Trichinopoly; then the people of Murari Rao and the Tanjore folk protested that they had given a *cowle* or safe conduct to Chandā Sāhib and carried him off in haste. Later, he was detained at the *Dalavāi Mantapam* and not taken to Tanjore, but sent on to Manoji Appa's tent. Two days later, *i.e.*, on June 18th, the Diarist received information that, when Chandā Sāhib was saying his prayers in Manoji Appa's camp, his head was cut off; and the head and the body were carried on a camel to Muhammad Alī at Trichinopoly. Dupleix found fault with Law for giving up Chandā Sāhib to Manoji Appa without insisting on getting a Maratha noble as hostage and being merely satisfied with asking the Tanjore general to take an oath, which he did by proxy and broke soon afterwards.[13]

12 The Madras Council Consultation of Monday, 3rd June (O.S.), abstracts two letters from Captain Clive, the first advising his having taken Volcondah (Valikandapuram) and, in it, d'Auteuil, 3 other French officers and 50 Europeans, besides 300 sepoys, 300 horse, 4 pieces of cannons, 2 mortars, and a large quantity of powder, ammunition and warlike stores; "the other (2nd letter) giving us the agreeable news that Chandā Sāhib, the night before, was taken prisoner." (Records of Fort St. George, *Diary and Consultation Book*, 1752, *Military Department*—p. 18).

13 Wilks wrote that Law was "justified by the fairest considerations of the natural interests committed to his charge, in recommending Chandā Sāhib to incur any risk, rather than surrender to the English;

It was widely believed at Pondicherry that Law misconducted himself at Srirangam; and the Diarist wrote that "it was by their own evil deeds that the army was swallowed up and they themselves (Law, Shaikh Hasan *etc.*,) fell into the enemy's hands." M. de La Tour who was senior to M. de Auteuil, refused to continue in service, as the latter who had married a sister of

and he unhappily trusted to the desperate faith of a Mahratta." According to Orme, Chandā Sāhib knew that the Tanjore general Manoji was at open variance with his prime minister and might be inclined to safeguard him, following only his personal interests, and he followed the overture with so much interest and seeming compliance, that both Law and Chandā Sāhib thought that they had gained him over to their interest. When Law demanded a hostage, the Tanjorean answered that a hostage would be no real check on intended treachery, and that, by giving one, the secret would be divulged and the escape rendered impracticable, and he promised, under an oath taken on his sabre and poniard, that he would send away Chandā Sāhib with an escort of horse to Karikal. As soon as the victim entered his quarters, Manoji had him imprisoned in a tent and put in irons. The next morning (1st June O.S.) there was a conference in Major Lawrence's tent between the Major, Muhammad Alī, Manoji and the Mysore general, when the proposal that the English should have the custody of the prisoner was violently opposed by the other three parties. To Manoji the Mysorean promised money, the Nawab threatened resentment and Murari Rao held out the fear of an attack; and he saw no method of saving the situation except by putting an end to the life of his prisoner. On the morning when Law surrendered at Srirangam, he had a conference with Lawrence that convinced him that the English were resolved not to interfere any farther in the dispute. The executioner was a Pathan, one of the Tanjore general's retinue. (Vol. I. pp. 236-42. 4th ed.).

Burhan-ud-dīn's *Tuzuk-i-Wālājāhi*, written in the interests of Muhammad Alī, naturally gloats over the fate of Chandā Sāhib, as being the visible manifestation of divine vengeance that he was treacherously murdered in the same choultry, the *Dalavāi Mantapam*, in which, 16 years before, he had profaned the holy *Quran* by a false and treacherous oath of protection that he gave to the distressed Rani Minakshi. Wilks says that his death was looked upon in this light by all Mussalman writers; but he had a manuscript which stated that Chandā Sāhib was murdered "at the instigation of Muhammad Alī." He however believes that the Maratha general, Manoji, would not have thus disposed of his prisoner and incurred the disgrace of open perfidy, had it not been for his fear of getting involved in further disputes. He thinks that, in the mock

Madame Dupleix, was appointed Major Commandant of Pondicherry. There were rumours, of course untrue, of Nawab Muhammad Alī having been killed by Murari Rao, which were not given credence to either by Dupleix or by the Diarist.

Stalemate in the Situation—Dupleix's Intrigues

In July, news came that the Raja of Mysore and Muhammad Alī had fallen out; and that the Mysore Dalavāi and Murari Rao who were not admitted into the fort of Trichinopoly, declared that they would certainly kill the Nawab and capture the place.[14]

conference held before Major Lawrence, the native chiefs were secretly agreed and that the Major was to be deterred from interfering by showing that he would thereby incur the resentment of all the confederates. (Vol. I—p. 177).

Malleson is of the opinion that "it is clear from Orme's version that Lawrence had it in his power to have saved Chandā Sāhib, and did connive at the death of the unfortunate man." (*History of the French in India*—p. 328. note).

H. H. Wilson only justifies the conduct of Lawrence by maintaining that the English were at that time not so well assured of their power as to pretend to dictate to the native princes. (Note on page 87 of Mill's *History of British India* (Vol. III)—1858).

Venkasami Rao says that Manoji, the famous general of Raja Pratap Singh, who undertook a successful expedition against the Maravas, shortly afterwards made himself "infamous by faithlessly and inhumanly disposing of Chandā Sāhib at Trichinopoly." Pratap Singh's chief minister, Sakhoji, was a great enemy of Manoji. (*The Tanjore Manual;* pp. 733 and 789).

The Madras Council Consultation of Monday, the 15th June, 1752, merely records a letter from Major Lawrence "advising that the Allies not agreeing who should have Chandā, to prevent disputes, his head was cut off and carried into Trichinopoly; that Shaik Hussan is a prisoner in Syringham to whom he had promised protection."

Dodwell points out (in note 3, p. 66 of his *Dupleix and Clive*) that, according to Saunders' letter to Dupleix of Aug. 22, 1752, Lawrence seems to deny that any conference was held; he adds that he does not attach much value to this, as he expressly says the opposite in his narrative (*Cambridge*, p. 28).

14 Major Lawrence and Clive both reported about the dispute that had arisen between Muhammad Alī and the Mysoreans as the former

Later news was received that Muhammad Alī offered to cede to the Mysoreans the fort and country of Trichinopoly as soon as he should be firmly established at Arcot; to which they replied that the agreement was to deliver up the fort and country as soon as Chandā Sāhib should have been defeated, on which event they were to have escorted him to Arcot, along with Murari Rao, and departed after installing him. The Diarist also notes that while the Dalavāi wanted to seize Trichinopoly and rule at the place himself, the nominal Raja of Mysore wished to check him, "lest he should seize him as his predecessors had seized the former Raja and take possession of the country,"[15] and that the Raja was trying to strengthen himself and then attack Nañja Raja.

would not give up Trichinopoly and its dependencies to the latter as the price of their help. The Mysoreans and the Marathas refused to march out from camp, and the Nawab could not join Lawrence in the proposed expedition to reduce Gingi, Chettupat, Chingleput and Vellore. The Madras Council resolved on the 29th June, O.S., that the English should not commit themselves to any precipitate action in the dispute which was "an affair of the utmost consequence," but should request the Dalavāi to send his *vakil* to Madras for negotiating for a settlement. Captain Dalton reported subsequently that Srirangam was, by agreement, delivered to the Mysoreans who were outwardly reconciled to the Nawab and that Murari Rao was not definitely on the English side, as he had a *vakil* at Pondicherry and frequently received letters from thence, and one of his captains had privately offered to desert to the English side, the moment his master joined the French. Dalton wrote later that Murari Rao was only designing to protract the war and to draw large sums from the Nawab as well as the Mysoreans who suspected that the Nawab and the Maratha were both endeavouring to ruin them; and Murari Rao even threatened to join the Mysore general to sign a letter to Dupleix, promising to abide by any agreement that he should make with him (Consultation Minutes of 13th July). Dalton later on discovered a plot of the Mysoreans to get possession of the Trichinopoly fort by arming the French prisoners and even murdering him. (Consultation Minutes of June 20th O.S.).

15 Dodda Krishnaraja Wodeyar I (1713–31) of Mysore was a weak ruler; and his ministers secured their own authority by affected humility. Chamaraja Wodeyar VII (1731–34) was at first successful in displacing Devaraja and Nañjaraja, his cousin, who occupied the offices of Dalavāi and *Sarvādhikāri*. But he was imprisoned along with his queen, by

The Diarist next records the news received from letters brought by the *Centaur* on July 13th, 1752 that no more war was to be waged on the Muhammadans and peace should be made and commerce continued without interruption; no man was to be sent beyond the bound-hedge, and the mansab jaghir villages possessed by the Company's servants were to be handed over to the Company itself. The Diarist was doubtful of the authenticity of this information and wrote he must ascertain its truth. Professor Dodwell notes how Dupleix's letters regarding his own and other jaghirs had excited considerable criticism in France and how the decrees of the Council of State, dated June 6, 1750, and December 30, 1751, forbade the receipt of presents or gifts from foreign princes.

On the 16th July, it was reported to the Diarist that Muhammad Alī had left Khair-ud-dīn Khān, his brother-in-law, and the English troops in the fort of Trichinopoly and that he had departed secretly, without the knowledge of the Mysoreans, with his brother, Abdul Wahāb Khān, for Valikandapuram on his way to join Lawrence and to Fort St. David. Of course, Dupleix still kept up his buoyant hopes; he spoke, more boastfully than was usual, that, if he had known of Lawrence's sailing for Madras, he would have ordered ships to seize his sloop; that he had frightened Governor Saunders at Madras by his letters and that

these and sent to Kabbāldurga, where he did not long survive. Chikka Krishnaraja Wodeyar II (1734–66) was the reigning prince at this time; he was only 5 years old at his accession and married in 1747 the daughter of Nañja Raja Karachuri, the new *Sarvādhikāri* and the younger brother of Deva Raja, the nominal Dalavāi. In 1756, the Raja, now 27 years of age, attempted by a *coup* to imprison Devaraja and Nañja Raja and take the power into his own hands; but the attempt failed; and Nañja Raja stormed the palace and cut off the noses and ears of the Raja's partisans before his very face. Later, Haidar compelled Nañja Raja to make atonement for his outrage to the ruler (*Mysore Gazetteer* (revised ed.)—Vol. II; Part IV, pp. 2472–5). Mīr Hussein Alī Khān Kirmani (in his *History Hydur Naik* (tr. by W. Miles) ch. V—VI) says that the Raja of Mysore was offended at the protracted operations of Nañja Raja before Trichinopoly and did not send any pay for the troops for 9 months; and he later reproached him in angry terms (pp. 39 and 61).

the English knew not how to answer him and stood abashed.[16] He was, nevertheless, anxious to know what happened in Madras after Lawrence's arrival, though the Diarist warned him that it was now a very difficult matter to obtain confidential news from the place, as it was strictly guarded. Dupleix planned to prevent Muhammad Alī's men from collecting any revenue in the country and from being enabled to pay his troops.

M. Kerjean, Dupleix's nephew who had accompanied Bussy along with Vincent, son of Madame Dupleix, to the Deccan, returned to Pondicherry by way of Masulipatam and Pulicat, in time to take part against Major Kinneer whom Saunders sent, against Lawrence's urgent protests, to besiege and attack Gingee, in deference to the desire of Muhammad Alī. The latter's situation was not very enviable; the sepoys were troubling him for their pay; the English would not advance him sufficient sums; and the Mysore agent, Birki Venkat Rao,[17] visited him in camp and importuned him for the cession of Trichinopoly to his master. Both Muhammad Alī and his brother, Abdul Wahāb Khān, who were encamped at Tiruvati, were afraid of a surprise night attack on their camp, from the Portuguese Volonté, whose real name was

16 Dupleix was fully alive to the critical situation that arose out of the surrender of Law and the death of Chandā Sāhib. Even before these calamities occurred, he had written to Saunders stating that he had been authorised by Salābat Jang to settle the affairs of the Carnatic by giving Trichinopoly to Muhammad Alī. Saunders waited for a day and wrote, after Chandā Sāhib was dead, that "Indeed, as Chandā Sāhib is dead, I can see no reason why it may not be easily accomplished." But now Dupleix demanded the release of all political prisoners, "as a preliminary to discussing terms," and Saunders declined; and hence the negotiations broke down. Dupleix was stiffened by the knowledge that he was to receive reinforcements from Europe. (Dodwell: p. 69; and Madras Consultation of Aug., 17, 1752.) The *Centaur* landed troops and chests of silver; and 300 soldiers were expected—Diarist's entry for July 13th and 14th, pp. 138 and 141 of the *Diary* Vol. VIII).

17 Birki Venkat Rao was a captain in the Mysore army and commanded the Mysore contingent, which included Haidar Alī and his brother, and joined Nāsir Jang's army at Madugiri in 1750.

Monis and who had a *nom-de-guerre, Kōṇapparangi* (the hump-backed European), and who was encamped nearby.

The entry of the Diarist for July 30, has a reference to the acquittal of La Bourdonnais who was actually released from the Bastille to which he was committed, early in 1751 and to his *Memoire* written during his incarceration.[18]

Minor Military Operations (August-October 1752)—Advance of Ghazi-ud-din

Rumours reached Pondicherry early in August, of a difference between Muhammad Alī and the English about his refusal to give Trichinopoly to the Mysoreans and his demands for money which the English were reluctant to advance further.[19] A few days later, news came that the troops of Muhammad Alī and the English had advanced against Gingee for the relief of which Kerjean was sent with a body of 300 Europeans and some topasses and sepoys. Major Kinneer, the English commander, found a main attack on the fort out of the question, without a much larger force and a long siege, though he had taken on his way the small fort of Villupuram. On their return from Gingee, the English troops encountered the advancing French and had to retreat after a brisk fire, back to Villupuram and Tiruvati. Dupleix told the Diarist that he had instructed the garrisons in the Tiruvati and Villupuram forts to surrender without fighting and when the English came on to Gingee, expecting that its garrison would do likewise, the latter should open a terrific fire on them; then the

18 Dodwell says that La Bourdonnais' *Memoire* which was instrumental in defeating Dupleix's attacks upon him was composed by the same advocate, M. de Gennes, who was later on to draw similar documents for Dupleix.

19 The Madras Consultation of 10th August, 1752, contains a resolution of the Council not to give the Mysoreans and Marathas any hopes of English assistance, but a previous consultation had resolved that "we shall rather persuade him to it than object . . . . to prevent the Mysore King's being disgusted, it be hinted to him that when the Nabob is once settled in the Province, if he can be prevailed upon . . . we shall have no objection."

English fled to Muhammad Alī's camp; and the Nawab, when he learnt of the advance of the army from Pondicherry and of La Volonte's encamping in his rear, fled with his own and the English armies to Tiruvannāmalai by way of Tumbūr.[20] After this victory of Vikravandi, for which Dupleix ordered a salute of 21 guns —and his wife hoped that God would bless the French with Muhammad Alī's head—his spirit was greatly elated with the news of a misunderstanding that took place between Muhammad Alī and his younger brother who reproached him for the march to Gingee, among other things, and departed to Tiruvannāmalai. Muhammad Alī was greatly troubled for want of money with which to pay his sepoys; and the Diarist heard that he was informed by Mr. Starke, the new Governor of Fort St. David, that strict orders had come from Europe not to interfere with the French and that he could do nothing for the Nawab who should write to Saunders at Madras. On August 19th, it was known that two nobles of Muhammad Alī were coming to Pondicherry to negotiate with Dupleix (which was done with English approval) and under his *cowle* of protection. After an amount of delay, in the course of which the two agents, Husain Muhammad Khān and Muhammad Masīh Khān, were shown the strength of the sea-face batteries of Pondicherry and a few English troopers who had been seized on the sea, Dupleix refused to talk of peace until the French sepoy-captain, Hasan-ud-dīn and other prisoners with Muhammad Alī should be released.[21] Towards the end of August, the *gumastahs* of Kasidas Bukkanji and other

20 All this is a great exaggeration. Major Kinneer only reconnoitred and did not make any attempt on Gingee; and after his defeat near Vikravandi at the hands of Kerjean, with one of his legs shot through with a musket ball, he gave orders for a retreat which was performed in very good order to Villupuram and thence to Tiruvati; and according to the Madras Council's Consultation Minutes, "the loss upon the whole is very inconsiderable and less than the enemy's, though they were superior in number," (Minutes of August 3, 1752 p. 29 of *The Military Consultations*, 1752.)

21 "The President acquaints the Board that the Nawab, by his vakil, had made overtures of peace to Dupleix who refused to hearken to

bankers received information that Ghāzī-ud-dīn Khān had crossed the Narmada and reached Burhanpur with 60,000 horse, and was accompanied by Mulhar Rao Holkar and other Maratha sardars. Sayyad Lashkar Khān and other Mughal nobles advised Salābat Jang not to quarrel with his elder brother; but on his not agreeing to this course, the Sayyad and a few mansabdars and jaghirdars had resolved to join Ghāzī-ud-dīn Khān and proceeded to Aurangabad; while Nizām Alī Khān, a younger son of Nizām-ul-Mulk might either join Ghāzī-ud-dīn or await his arrival at Hyderabad.[22] Ghāzī-ud-dīn occupied Aurangabad, with 150,000 men and was supported by Mulhar Rao Holkar and the main Maratha army and also by the bulk of the Mughal nobility of Aurangabad and Burhanpur.

any terms until the French prisoners are delivered up." Council Consultation of Madras, 17th Aug., 1752.

22 Ghāzī-ud-dīn Khān had opened negotiations with the Peishwa through the agency of Mulhar Rao Holkar and succeeded in inducing the Maratha chief to support his pretensions. From June 1751 to the autumn of that year, Salābat Jang was not threatened. During this interval Ghāzī-ud-dīn and Balaji Rao had time to cement their plans. Bussy stood behind Salābat Jang with his French soldiers and trained artillery and infantry. Balaji had stipulated from Ghāzī-ud-dīn the cession of the districts of Aurangabad and Burhanpur; and his first campaign against Salābat Jang had been interrupted. He received indeed from Salābat Jang a cash payment of two lakhs; but now his position had been strengthened and he resented an attack on a Maratha convoy ordered by Raja Ragunath Das. He ordered, in the autumn of 1751, the Holkar and the Scindia to join Ghāzī-ud-dīn and effect a junction with himself near Aurangabad, now occupied by Salābat Jang. Bussy advised the Nizām to leave Aurangabad to its fate and march on Poona itself. He also intrigued with old Tāra Bai who was the inveterate enemy of the Peishwa and, after defeating the latter near Poona, marched on that city. At Kukadi, he took the Marathas by surprise (22nd November) when they were engaged in religious devotions consequent on an eclipse of the moon; and he followed this up by sacking Ranjangaon and Talegaon and meeting a vigorous Maratha attack led by the Peishwa and by Dattaji and Mādhava Rao Sindia. Now the Peishwa changed his tactics, and directed his cousin Sadasiva Rao to open negotiations with Raja Raghunath Das, the Nizām's Diwan. He fomented discontent among the Mughal soldiery, asked Raghuji Bhonsle to harry the Nizām's eastern frontier between the

Meanwhile, a Mughal arrived at Pondicherry saying that he had brought with him the Padshah's *parwana* for Dupleix which had been requested to be granted by Raja Raghunath Das and had been issued by Mansūr Alī Khān[23] when the Peishwa had been overthrown and had been delayed as Raghunath Das died before he could send it on. He claimed to be a sardar of 1,000 horse, by name Yūsuf Bāshi Khān and to have brought also dresses of honour for Dupleix, his wife and her daughter, as well as a *parwana* of confirmation for the *subah* of Arcot, which was to be given to the French Governor to be sent on to Muhammad Alī, on condition that he would obey the former. He was persuaded to write a letter to Muhammad Alī Khān, asking him not to increase the trouble and go on warring against the French and promising him an *ināyat-nāma* from Sayyad Lashkar Khān that he had brought with him. To this letter which was

Godavari and the Penganga and contrived to get possession of the fort of Trimbak. Salābat Jang had to retreat to Ahmadnagar and on the advice of Bussy, and signed an armistice with the Peishwa (January, 1752).

It was on the return march from the armistice that Raja Raghunath Das was assassinated by a body of Mughal soldiers. Sayyad Lashkar Khān, the governor of Aurangabad, was now made the Diwan. (See Kincaid and Parasnis, *History of the Maratha People;* Vol. III. Ch. XLIX and Grant Duff's *History*, Ch. XVIII)—For the route of Bussy and Salābat on their march to Poona, *see* note on p. 359 of Malleson's *History of the French in India.*

According to the *Tarikh-i-Muzaffari* of Muhammad Alī Khān (Elliot and Dowson, Vol. VIII—pp. 316–318), Ghāzī-ud-dīn left his son, Shahab-ud-dīn Muhammad Khān, as his deputy in the office of Mīr Bhakshi (at the Imperial court) and proceeded towards the Deccan taking with him Malhar Rao and reaching Aurangabad in the month of Zi'l-Ka'da (July–August, 1752)—For the English attitude towards him see *Madras Military Consultations* (1752)—p. 41.

23 Safdar Jang, Nawab of Oudh and surnamed Mansūr Alī Khān, was the nephew and successor of Sādat Khān, the founder of the dynasty. He was appointed Wazir in 1748 on the accession of the Emperor Ahmad Shāh and conducted the entire administration for several years. He was dismissed from the Wizarat in 1752 A.D. (A.H. 1166).

Dodwell says that a large sum of money had been sent to Delhi to procure the *parwana*, and Bussy recommended Dupleix about this time to come to terms with Muhammad Alī.

despatched on the last day of August, a reply was received the very next day from Muhammad Alī, declaring that the Mughal envoy should have gone to him direct if he had really *parwana* confirming the grant of the Carnatic *subah* to him. He also wrote a letter to Dupleix saying that if he should be treated with justice, he would act according to the French Governor's desires and grant him all the jaghirs which Muzaffar Jang and Salābat Jang had given him, adding, " whatsoever may be further demanded ". This letter did not apparently please Dupleix, who, according to the Diarist, refused to send a reply and forbade Muhammad Tavakkal from going to him, as he desired, for beginning negotiations.

English Capture of Covelong and Chingleput and After

After the battle of Bāhur where Lawrence who had returned from Madras lured the French troops under Kerjean to fight him (September 6), Muhammad Alī, though elated by the victory, wrote another letter, in smooth words, to Dupleix, requesting his friendship and promising him additional jaghirs to the French people. To this Dupleix replied, urging Muhammad Alī to release the prisoners taken in the fight (Lawrence having allowed only Kerjean who was badly wounded, to return to Pondicherry) and promising that the released officers would not take up arms again. Muhammad Alī would not release the prisoners, nor even return the *palanquins* and *dhoolies* sent to fetch them, but continued to protest, through messengers, his readiness to be friends with Dupleix (Diarist's entries for September 7 and 9).

On the 12th of the month, Dupleix received, in a specially prepared *shamiana* amidst great pomp, the Pạdshah's *parwana* and presents; and in the entry for the next day, the Diarist gives a translation of the *parwana,* which addressed Dupleix as the Captain and Governor-General Bahadur Zafar Jang and exhorted him to continue " to regard Salābat Jang as a friend dear as your own life and afford him all the help of which you are capable." [24]

24 A Madras Council Consultation (Tuesday, 19th Septr. 1752) mentions a letter from Dupleix, enclosing a copy of the alleged 'Padshah's

All the while the French could do nothing from the military point of view, though Dupleix sent out Europeans and sepoys as well as cannon and munitions of war to those who escaped to Ariyānkuppam from the enemy, to show that " our army is ready for them ". Dupleix was eagerly looking out for reinforcements which he was expecting from Mascareigne in order that he might begin operations again. One small ray of hope shone for a moment for Dupleix when the French garrison at Covelong opened fire upon the troops of Clive and forced them to flee beyond the back-water where they stood in fear of an attack from the French garrison at Chingleput (Diarist's entry for September 18.)[25] After hard fighting from the 16th to the 19th, the garrison at Covelong had to deliver up the fort to the English; and St. Germain who advanced from Chingleput, not knowing that the fort had surrendered to the English, came close to it and being surrounded and fired upon, lost many men and was forced to flee. Ranga Pillai quotes, at length, a letter that he received from one Krishna Pillai of Covelong regarding its surrender, the first flight of the English troops and the final surrender of M. le Blanc and his bullying and extortion (entry for September 20). Clive's advance on Chingleput and his raising a battery and sending for mortars from Covelong to fire shells into the fort which, according to the Diarist, had sufficient provisions, powder and shot for a year, the subsequent surrender of M. Villeon, the commandant of

farman' approving of whatever he had done in favour of Salābat Jang and directing him to continue his assistance. Dupleix further offered to allow the English to compare the copy with the original. The Council resolved that they were of the opinion that the *farman* was spurious, "because the advices they lately received from Bombay and other parts are so contrary," and also because "it is extremely different from the form and stile in which papers of this kind are usually worded."

25 This refers to the repulse of the first attack of the English troops on Covelong (Sadat Bandar) when they fled precipitately from a garden near the fort. They had to be brought back by Clive who was advancing with the rest of his force and who "obliged them, not without difficulty, and even with violence, to rally and return with him to the garden." (Orme. Vol. I. p. 262).

the place—these are detailed by the Diarist.[26] Both according to the Diarist and the English, the Chingleput fort could have successfully stood a siege. According to the former, Dupleix's letters ordered the garrison to surrender the fort to the English; and it was supposed by him that as there were no Europeans, but only Carnatic sepoys in the fort, it was thought they could not continue to resist for long.

The military situation round Pondicherry had come to be so bad in the beginning of October, that Maratha horsemen advanced as far as the bound-hedge of the town, " driving off the cattle, plundering the country and wounding many "; and the people in the out-villages had to take shelter in the town. Since it was rumoured that Muhammad Alī was planning to march to Arcot, after making another attempt on Gingee and demanding from Taqī Sāhib of Wandewash arrears of tribute due, Dupleix revived his negotiations with the Mysore general and Murari Rao. The Diarist's entry for October 7th, says that Mīrza Abdul Nabī Beg was sent to treat with Murari Rao and Nañja Raja who were camping together. The conditions were that they should march together with their army and attack and slay Muhammad Alī; Murari Rao was to receive two lakhs of rupees and an equal sum when Muhammad Alī should have been disposed of. The Mysoreans were to receive Trichinopoly, in return for which they were to pay 30 lakhs of rupees. The French intrigues with these two had been going on for some time and were known to the English side.[27] The immediate consequence was that Murari Rao replied that he had given orders to the commander of the Maratha troops with Muhammad Alī Khān not to allow his horsemen to

26 See Clive's paper, sent among his many memoranda, to his friend, the historian Orme, and preserved in the India Office, among the *Orme MSS. India*, Vol. II. pp. 309–10. This is printed *in extenso* in Sir George Forrest's *Life of Lord Clive*—Vol. I. pp. 214–15—entitled "Siege of Cobelong and Chinglapet." See also Fort St. George letter to the Directors dated 3rd November, 1752, para 3, (in Forrest's *Bengal and Madras Papers*, Vol. II. (1688–1757).

27 The letter of Captain Dalton from Trichinopoly recorded in the Council Consultation of 17th August, shows that he had a suspicion that

plunder the villages of Pondicherry, but to help the French people. Muhammad Alī broke up his camp near Wandewash and marched back to Tiruvati, because, the Diarist wrote, the Mysoreans, Murari Rao and the Maravar were surrounding Trichinopoly in the hope of taking it. The Diarist gave the consoling encouragement to Dupleix that Muhammad Alī's 'play' was drawing to an end; and his petty successes in the last two months, his getting money from Taqī Sāhib, his luck in getting possession of Covelong and Chingleput—" all these are but the last flicker of the candle "; and that " he must suffer for his treachery even as Chandā Sāhib did." (entry for October 10, 1752). The English were angry with him at not getting the Wandewash money for them; the Marathas threatened to abandon him; and his army was breaking up. As the Maravar were troubling the Dindigul country, Nañja Raja and the followers of Murari Rao camped at Karur and wrote recalling Innis Khān, the paymaster, who was with Muhammad Alī. The Diarist recorded on the 20th of October that Dupleix and his wife had a definite understanding that, as Murari Rao's army was coming without him, 1¼ lakhs of rupees should be paid a month, that on the arrival of the army one lakh should be given, with another lakh and presents on Murari Rao's arrival and 2 lakhs more when he should depart. The agreement was written out; and Dupleix and his wife swore to keep it and, in token thereof, dipped their fingers in red and touched the paper. The last two entries of the Diarist for October describe the forced conversion of a dying man, the Governor and Madame, putting down by sheer force all opposition of his Hindu relations.

the ruler of Mysore was carrying on a secret negotiation with Dupleix. A later letter of Dalton's quoted in the Council Consultation minutes of 24th Aug., 1752, informs that the behaviour of the Mysore general and Murari Rao was so inconsistent and various, that it was evidently calculated to conceal their real intentions.

CHAPTER XIII

DUPLEIX ENDEAVOURS TO GET ALLIES

EVENTS IN THE DECCAN—THE NIZAM AND THE MARATHAS: 1752–53

THE first entry of the Diarist for November, 1752, gives the information that Ghāzī-ud-dīn Khān, the eldest son of Nizām-ul-Mulk, Āsaf Jāh, had reached Aurangabad, where the Peishwa, Balaji Baji Rao, to whom Salābat Jang had sent Sayyad Lashkar Khān for help, met him and that both offered Berar to Salābat Jang, but the latter refused to accept the offer and declared his resolve to fight. Also Salābat Jang had put under arrest the killedar of Hyderabad who threatened resistance, stationed M. Bussy[1] and the French troops there and after strengthening it, had marched forth, with a number of European soldiers, several thousand musketmen and about 10,000 horse towards Bidar. Ghāzī-ud-dīn Khān also marched from Aurangabad ten stages, with about 60,000 or 70,000 horse; and both sides were resolved

1 Bussy's anxiety was very great. "He wrote to Dupleix a letter which contemplated the possible necessity of retiring with Salābat Jang to Masulipatam or even to Pondicherry. In reply, Dupleix announced the despatch of reinforcements amounting to 300 Europeans, urged the possibility of negotiations which would leave Salābat Jang at least the position of Ghāzī-ud-dīn's deputy, and finally directed that if any thing should happen to Salābat Jang, Bussy should offer French support to his rival on condition of the renewal of all grants to the French." (Dodwell's *Dupleix and Clive*, pp. 87–88.)

Ranga Pillai had written on the 22nd September, that when Ghāzī-ud-dīn had advanced 35 *kos* on this side of the Narmada, Sayyad Lashkar Khān was sent to Poona to treat with the Peishwa, Bussy had been appointed to the charge of the *killa* at Hyderabad and urgent requisitions had been sent to Pondicherry for soldiers powder, shot, etc., (p. 227 of the *Diary*, Vol. VIII.)

On the eve of the poisoning of Ghāzī-ud-dīn, Bussy regarded his situation as all but desperate:—Dodwell quoting from Hamont's *Dupleix* and *Memoir pour Bussy expositif de ses créances sur la Compagnie de Indes* (1764).

on war. News was received at Pondicherry, on the 10th November, that Ghāzī-ud-dīn Khān was poisoned at the instigation of Salābat Jang, by his own cooks.[2] Dupleix was overjoyed at this, but wanted to make sure of it from letters from M. Bussy and others at Salābat Jang's camp.

When Salābat Jang heard of the death of his brother, he—so it was communicated to Kasidas Bukkanji's people at Fort St. David—wrote to Muhammad Alī Khān, confirming him in the Arcot subah, promising him the confirmatory *parwana* and other honours and giving him the title of Anvar-ud-dīn Khān Bahadur. When Salābat Jang sent Janoji Nimbalakar and Sayyad Lashkar Khān to the Peishwa to request his help, the latter wished to detain them; but Sayyad Lashkar Khān escaped, while the other was seized. Janoji was subsequently released and went to Aurangabad to settle affairs there in consequence of the death of Ghāzī-ud-dīn Khān. Two Maratha *sardars* who went along with Janoji to Aurangabad, had camped opposite to Salābat Jang. In December, news was received at Pondicherry of a battle fought by the Peishwa, Mulhar Rao Holkar and others against Salābat Jang who was surrounded and forced to offer terms, including the cession of Khandesh, Berar, Panhala and other districts dependent on Burhanpur, except the town of Burhanpur itself, as a *jaghir* to Baji Rao. The Nizam and the Peishwa exchanged visits; and both proposed to enter Mysore, as its ruler had not paid the tribute-money due for ten or twelve years. It was said that the Peishwa

2 According to Burhan-ud-dīn, Salābat Jang sent his own mother to Aurangabad where she was kindly received by her step-son, Ghāzī-ud-dīn Khān. One day, she offered to prepare, with her own hands, a salad of cucumber pickled in curds, for him and brought to him the salad mixed with poison, which he took in unhesitatingly. The date of his death was the 16th October, 1752. Kāsi Das Bukkanji's *gomastahs* sent word to Cuddalore that he fell sick on tasting the food and died on the third day. Kincaid and Parasnis say, in their *History of the Maratha People*, (Vol. III. p. 16), that it was the mother of Nizām Alī that poisoned Ghāzī-ud-dīn who died on the 16th October. He was "an extremely reserved and godly man who spent his days in the company of theologians and his nights in vigil." He was the father of the notorious Imad-ul-Mulk.

thought that he could not overthrow Salābat Jang who had French help and therefore proposed to accept the terms of peace if M. Bussy were sent to him. Bussy was escorted to the Peishwa's camp by Mulhar Rao Holkar and his son, Appaji Holkar, and treated with great respect. Finally it was agreed that Salābat Jang should fulfil Ghāzī-ud-dīn's promises to the Peishwa that he should retain the body of 25,000 Maratha horse in his service that Sayyad Lashkar Khān should be restored to favour and that Mysore should be attacked with the help of Mulhar Rao Holkar and the Maratha troops who should have half the tribute that might be collected. After peace was made, Salābat Jang bestowed on Bussy the title of Ghazanfar Jang, while Muzaffar Khān who made terms with Baji Rao and joined him after receiving a large bribe, was cast into chains and imprisoned.[3]

3 Though Ghāzī-ud-dīn was dead, the Marathas insisted on Salābat Jang carrying out his brother's promises to them; and they were supported by the Mughals of Burhanpur who, after their association with Ghāzī-ud-dīn, were afraid to become the subjects of Salābat Jang. The latter left the decision to Bussy who, according to Kincaid and Parasnis, preferred a solid peace to a doubtful war and advised the surrender of a considerable tract of land, provided Raghuji Bhonsle first withdrew from the eastern provinces. Raghuji was asked by the Peishwa to do so. "Raghuji and the Peishwa, though often mutually jealous and plunged into intrigue against one another, managed nevertheless, to avoid an open clash, and often actually joined hands in furthering the extension and prestige of the Maratha Raj." This statement of Mr. G. S. Sardesai [*vide Selections from the Peshwa Daftar*, 20, *The Bhonsles of Nagpur* (1717–1774)] is illustrated by Raghuji's compliance in the present instance, which led to the Nizām's cession of the whole country west of Berar from the Tapti to the Godavari to the Peishwa, by the Treaty of Bhalki concluded on the 25th November, 1752.

From *The Bhonsles of Nagpur* (1717–1774) we learn how Salābat Jang took into his service Muzaffar Khān, the trained artilleryman and how he was creating mischief for the Peishwa with the help of Ramchandra Jadhav (No. 134); and also of an agreement entered into between Raghuji Bhonsle and the Nizām through the influence of Sayyad Lashkar Khān and Janoji Nimbalkar (No. 135). Also we read of the Peishwa's disposition of the Maratha forces, after the death of Ghāzī-ud-dīn Khān, in the impending action against Salābat Jang (No. 148); of the attempt

It was also said that Balaji Rao, the Peishwa, insisted that Ghāzī-ud-dīn Khān had granted him the Carnatic and desired that Salābat Jang should confirm the grant, proposing that he himself should proceed to settle it and that his younger brother, Raghunath Rao and his cousin, Sadāsiva Rao, were at Bidar with 30,000 horse on their way to the Carnatic. The Peishwa was also said to have written a letter to Pratap Singh of Tanjore that he had acted wrongly in joining Muhammad Alī Khān and destroying Chandā Sāhib and he should now make peace with Dupleix and try to "take off the head of Muhammad Alī Khān, the causer of the disturbances." The months of January and February were full of rumours of the expected advance of the Peishwa to the Carnatic; it was feared by Dupleix that he might possibly intend to help the English and Muhammad Alī. In March, news was received at Pondicherry that Salābat Jang had seized Kondavīdu, Guntur, etc., given as a *jaghir* to Bussy and Kambampetta, etc., given as a

to attack the Nizām if he should be enticed away from Bhalki; and of Visvas Rao Ballal's letter conveying the news of the victory gained by the Peishwa's troops over the Nizām and the humble manner in which the latter sued for peace (letter dated 8-12-1752).

Ranga Pillai's news was to the effect that Mulhar Rao Holkar himself was wounded in the fight, that there were 2 battles and that 400 Europeans (about as many as Bussy had with him altogether) were killed and that Salābat Jang offered Baji Rao a great area of the country and about 35 per cent of the Arcot revenues provided he would do as Bussy should advise.

Balaji Rao, in his letter to Nawab Muhammad Alī, received January 5th, 1753, said that he besieged Salābat Jang's camp on all sides at Bhalki and distressed it to the degree of starvation and concluded peace through means of Bussy, upon the following terms:—

(1) The whole subah of Khandesh and half of the subah of Aurangabad were to be given to the Peishwa, according to the agreement made with Ghāzī-ud-dīn Khān.

(2) The Marathas were to collect *chouth* and *sirdeshmukhi* in all the subahs of the Deccan. M. W. Burway describes in his *Life of Maharaja Tukoji Rao Holkar II* [(1925)—p. 18] how strenuous attempts were made by unpatriotic Maratha *sardars* like Janoji Nimbalakar and Ramachandra Rao Jadhav to detach Mulhar Rao Holkar from the service of the Peishwa.

jaghir to Shaikh Ibrāhīm and that he had also dismissed 5,000 or 6,000 sepoys who were serving under them and ordered the remaining sepoys to be paid only 6 rupees a month or to be sent away if they did not agree; and that he had also dismissed M. Goupil who had been left in command at Hyderabad when Bussy was absent at Masulipatam, recuperating his health. Sayyad Lashkar Khān was dominant and he had joined with Janoji Nimbalakar and Raja Ramachandar Sen; and they would collect the money due to the discharged sepoys, in Masulipatam, for which a *sanad* had been given (Entry for March 26, 1753).[4]

(3) Both parties were to march jointly to take possession of the Carnatic and dispose of it as they should think fit. (*Records of Fort St. George—Country Correspondence of* 1753*—Military Department—No.* 2.)

"This conclusion, like the conclusion of Bussy's other struggles with the Marathas, hardly warrants the belief which historians have expressed in Bussy's victories; but Bussy's troops though strong enough to check the enemy, were not numerous enough ever to give them a decisive overthrow. Although these latter (the French), to judge by the resultant terms of the peace, had not won the decisive victories which were subsequently claimed for them, they had undoubtedly maintained Salābat Jang in his position as Subhadar of the Deccan at an incomparably smaller price than he would have had to pay without their assistance." (Dodwell's *Dupleix* and *Clive*—pp. 88-89.)

4 Bussy, after the peace with the Marathas, asked and obtained the district of Koṇḍavīdu, adjacent to Masulipatam. Raghuji Bhonsle had meanwhile renewed hostilities and appeared before Gulbarga, three weeks after he separated from the Peishwa and began his depradations. Bussy wished to relieve Salābat Jang from all military operations and advised him to give Raghuji several districts in the neighbourhood of Berar. This alienated several nobles from Bussy's side; and, unfortunately, a few days after the peace with Raghuji, Bussy fell dangerously ill near Gulbarga and departed for Masulipatam in January, 1753, leaving all the French troops and sepoys with Salābat Jang who proceeded without interruption to Hyderabad. Sayyád Lashkar Khān pretended that he could not furnish the pay of the French army at the usual periods; and he contrived to wean his master from French influence and carry him to Aurangabad, permitting no more than a small detachment of Europeans and sepoys to accompany him. He instructed the governor of Golconda to furnish no pay to those French men and sepoys who remained at

On the 8th of May, the Diarist received a letter from M. Goupil and another in Marathi, from Salābat Jang's camp on the Godavari, to the south of Aurangabad. The couriers were said to have brought a *parwana* to the French Governor for the Carnatic *subah*. The European soldiers and officers with the Nizām were four months in arrears of pay and the cavalry and the

Hyderabad and to distress them by every means except open hostilities. Goupil, the French commandant, divided his force into raiding detachments; and Sayyad Lashkar Khān was in constant correspondence with Balaji Rao and began to work in the Peishwa's interest; while Salābat Jang was in Aurangabad, nearer to Balaji and farther from Bussy.

The English vakil in Salābat Jang's camp wrote on May 6th, that Sayyad Lashkar Khān was very powerful and the French army doubted very much the sincerity of the Mussalmans. He subsequently wrote that Sayyad Lashkar Khān had prevailed on Salābat Jang to undertake his march to Aurangabad and that his resolution was "to disband the French army and to keep Salābat Jang separately which he has executed at present by acting as aforesaid." *Country Correspondence of* 1753 (Records of Fort St. George). *Nos.* 133 and 134.

Sayyad Lashkar Khān also entered into correspondence with the English Governor Saunders, offering to aid him with the whole power of the Deccan if they would assist him in his schemes for the expulsion of the French. Saunders entered into active correspondence and encouraged him to persevere in his undertaking. Towards the end of April, 1753, the plot seemed to be on the point of success; and Sayyad Lashkar wrote to Saunders:—"I have arranged the mode in which to rid myself of your enemies. The plan is in action and with the assistance of Providence the result will be what you wish. I expect to be with you by the end of the rains, and to arrange then everything in a satisfactory manner." (Malleson's *History of the French in India—pp.* 374–5.)

Sayyad Lashkar Khān's letter to Governor Saunders, read at a Council Consultation of July 10th, 1753, says that Salābat Jang was determined to settle the affairs of the Carnatic and "to extirpate the enemy" and that "a scheme is on foot whereby they will meet their deserts"; and that "in regard to the President's hint concerning assistance to be given to the lawful person (Muhammad Alī), Salābat Jang has the same thing in view, exhorting us to continue firm in his (Salābat Jang's) interest, as we have already given instances of our duty."

(p. 117 of *Diary and Consultation Book, Military Department,* 1753 (*Records of Fort St. George*)).

sepoys were eight months in arrears; and the troubles caused on this account by the horsemen and the sepoys might ruin the camp unless affairs could be improved by the transport of money from Pondicherry. They also told that peace had been made between Salābat Jang and his brother Nizām Alī through the kind offices of Sayyad Lashkar Khān and Raja Ramachandra Rao and that Salābat Jang attended but little to business and thought of nothing but drinking, eating and women.[5] In June Dupleix was writing to Bussy who had returned to Hyderabad and to Salābat Jang for a lease of the Carnatic at the rate at which it was given to Sādat-ullah.[6]

On the other side, Sayyad Lashkar Khān persuaded Ṣalābat Jang, according to the Diarist, to write to Pondicherry that the arrears due to the Europeans of the French contingent, should be met out of the 50 lakhs due from the Carnatic and that the balance should be paid to him without delay. He also proposed that the Europeans should remain either at Hyderabad or at Masulipatam, till after the rains, as large sums were due from the

5 Goupil objected to going to Aurangabad, urging that the place was unhealthy for Europeans. Salābat Jang had with him only a body-guard of 100 Frenchmen and a battalion of French sepoys, while the rest of the French troops were dispersed at Hyderabad and elsewhere. At Aurangabad it was given out that a French officer was contriving some mischief jointly with Nizām Alī who, along with another brother of his, was imprisoned in the fortress of Daulatabad. According to the letter of the English agent, Vasudeva Pandit, in Salābat Jang's camp, dated 8th August, 1753, the confidence which the Mughals placed in the French had now ceased; and Bussy who had arrived at Golconda from Masulipatam and intended to go to Aurangabad was informed by Salābat Jang "not to come to him saying that as the monsoon would continue four months longer he had better stay in Golconda and that after the monsoon he would send for him;" and also it was rumoured that a *sanad* would be granted, to Muhammad Alī Khān. See the Diarist's entry for June 21, 1753 (p. 385 Vol. VIII.)

6 Bussy arrived at Hyderabad in July owing to the pressure of Dupleix and his own officers who urged the necessity of his return. Dupleix wrote that "the French nation had fallen to a degree of contempt from which you (Bussy) alone can save it." Bussy's great difficulty was finance; he contrived to borrow a sum sufficient to pay off a portion of

Guntur and Masulipatam *sarkars.* In July the Diarist reported the receipt of a letter from Salābat Jang complaining that the French had not been paying any tribute at all for the Carnatic, although it had been delivered to them three years back; the letter added words to this effect:—" Though you know my straits for money, yet you have sent none, even after my writing about it." In August, news reached Pondicherry that Salābat Jang's younger brothers, Nizām Alī and another, had been imprisoned in the fort at Daulatabad and that Sayyad Lashkar Khān had ordered the French soldiers with the Nizām and their captain, M. Joinville, to depart and they had reached Golconda and written for orders about their future movements. Bussy was then at Hyderabad.

In September, 1753, Muzaffar Khān who was with Balaji Rao at Ahmadnagar wrote informing that the Peishwa had received a *parwana* from the Delhi Emperor to the effect that the Deccan *subah* should not be given to Salābat Jang, but to himself and that the Nizām should be seized and sent to Delhi, or, if possible, put to death; and the Peishwa had marched to Ahmadnagar with about 80,000 horse with the object of attacking and beating Salābat Jang. Muzaffar Khān himself had been ordered to enlist 10,000 musketeers and 4,000 cavalry with whom he was to march into the Carnatic. In November, the *sowcars* in Pondicherry brought about further complications in the situation. Balaji Rao and Tāra Bai had quarrelled again; and the latter had sent to Salābat Jang a

the arrears due to the sepoys. The paying of nearly 2½ lakhs of rupees to the French contingent was much disliked in the Nizām's court and was hotly resented by the Mughal nobles and all the troopers in the Nizām's army. The only method was to obtain a grant of the revenues which the French could collect for themselves. Bussy resolved to get the grant of the Sarkars of Chicacole, Rajahmundry, Ellore and Guntur, in addition to those of Masulipatam and Kondavīdu, already acquired.

Dupleix planned to get a lease of the Carnatic at the rate paid to the Nizām in Nawab Sādatullah's time, which, according to the Diarist, was said to amount to 12 lakhs, besides 2 lakhs for durbar expenses, 3 lakhs for the Marathas and separate *peshkash* for Trichinopoly and Tanjore; while Anvar-ud-dīn Khān had paid the Nizām 35 lakhs of rupees. Dupleix desired that he would pay Salābat Jang at Sādatullah's rate.

hundi for five lakhs of rupees for the getting ready of artillery and troops and promised to help him with twenty or twenty-five thousand horse, in order to destroy the Peishwa. Janoji Nimbalakar who was an old enemy of the Peishwa, told Salābat Jang that, if he obeyed Tāra Bai's wishes, he would join him with all the troops he could collect. Salābat Jang accepted the *hundi* and was preparing artillery and troops; while Baji Rao sent a conciliatory message to Tāra Bai advising her to think well before she acted and not assist her own enemies and ruin her own house.[7]

The last entry of the Diarist for 1753 concerning the Deccan affairs is dated November 30, and details a letter from Bussy to Dupleix that Salābat Jang had ordered him and the French troops at Hyderabad to proceed to Masulipatam promising to send for

7 After the death of Raja Shahu Chhatrapati, the Peishwa contrived to make Ramaraja king, but to keep all real power in his own hands January, 1750). The ambitious Tāra Baī, the grandmother of Ramaraja, was resolved to control the state and ranged the *Pratīnidhi*, Raghuji Bhonsle and Dabhade against the Peishwa. But the latter conciliated Raghuji and secured his good will by depriving the *Pratinidhi* of his *jaghir* in Berar and conferring it on him. Dabhade did not come to Satara and was indifferent to public affairs. He next humbled the *Pant Sachiv*, with whom Tāra Bai struck up an alliance and deprived the *Pratinidhi* of all power. According to the Sangola Agreement (1750) consented to by the king at the dictation of the Peishwa, the subah of the Carnatic which had been assigned to Babuji Naik, was transferred to the Peishwa who promised to pay a larger subsidy to the royal treasury. Tāra Bai was furious with Ramaraja for having consented to this agreement and conspired with Uma Bai Dabhade who resented the loss of his Gujarat fiefs forced on her son. She vented all her wrath on her powerless grandson and contrived to get him under her hold (Nov. 1750). She later intrigued, as we already saw, with Raja Raghunath Das and induced Uma Bai to send an army from Gujarat under Damaji Gaekwad. But the latter was defeated by the Peishwa and forced to come to an agreement with him (March 1752). Tāra Bai, foiled in every one of her attempts, grew desperate and declared that Ramaraja was not her real grandson, but only an impostor (September, 1752); she even suggested that Sambhaji of the rival house of Kolhapur might be brought to ascend the throne of Satara. (See *Selections from the Peshwa Daftar No. 6 Ramaraja's Struggle for Power*. Letter No. 190 dated 26-4-1751, revealing intrigues within intrigues for setting aside Ramaraja and placing

them, if necessary, when he visited Mysore and other parts and that he had actually advanced four stages this side of Hyderabad.[8]

Bussy reached Aurangabad where his enemies bent before him, Sayyad Lashkar Khān himself offering to surrender the seals of his office and requesting him to confer them on some other person. Bussy was clever enough to perceive the artifice of this seeming humility and soon came to terms with the Diwan. He had already set his mind on getting the four *sarkars* which were estimated to yield a revenue of 31 lakhs of rupees and to make, together with the yield of the territories already granted, a total of 42 lakhs. The *sarkars* were granted to Bussy personally for the maintenance of the French troops. According to Orme, after the preliminaries of the negotiations were finished, the grant was formally made in a grand durbar at Aurangabad, by Salābat Jang on the 23rd November, 1753 (O.S.) (3rd Dec. N.S.). The terms included the stipulation that the French troops should have the charge of the Nizām's person, that the latter should not

Sambhaji of Kolhapur on the throne, as well as another intrigue of Tāra Bai with Sambhaji to remove the Peishwa from power with the help of Damaji Gaekwad and the ex-*Pratinidhi*). Even in December 1752, the Peishwa was informed of the intrigues of Babuji Naik with Tāra Bai at Satara; and Jagjivan Pratinidhi reported to the Peshwa on 13-2-1753 that he had defeated Babuji Naik and taken his brother prisoner. A little later, Visvas Rao, the Peishwa's son, wrote to his agent with Tāra Bai, replying to the terms of agreement proposed by the lady who found herself completely discomfited.

8 This is hard to reconcile with Bussy having set out for Aurangabad in November, 1753 and his having arranged preliminaries on December 4, with Sayyad Lashkar Khān regarding the grant of the four *sarkars* of Chicacole, Rajahmundry, Ellore and Mustaphanagar and even interviewed Salābat Jang (Malleson, p. 379; Dodwell, p. 92).

According to Orme, Bussy left Golconda in the middle of October; and Salābat Jang, being then troubled by the prospect of another rupture with Raghuji, could not check the uncalled-for approach of Bussy; while Sayyad Lashkar Khān proposed the humblest obedience. The Madras Council wrote to Nawab Muhammad Alī, on November 6th (17th), 1753, that the French had sent several reinforcements to Golconda and Bussy was on his march to Aurangabad. (p. 136 of *The Country Correspondence, Military Department*, 1753).

interfere in any manner in the affairs of Arcot; and all other affairs in general should be conducted in concurrence with Bussy who should support and befriend Sayyad Lashkar Khān in his office. The patents for the four *sarkars* were sent to Moracin the French chief at Masulipatam with instructions to take possession.[9] Even before Bussy's acquisition of the *sarkars,* Dupleix was intriguing with the agent of Vijayaram Raja of Vizianagram who had previously helped the English when the latter's factories at Vizagapatam and other ports were attacked by Jāfar Alī Khān, under instruction from Salābat Jang. The Raja was promised more *mansab* jaghirs and honours and a supply of powder, shot and cannon, if only he should destroy the English settlements in the region.[10]

Operations round Tiruvati—French Alliance with Murari Rao.

In November 1752 the Diarist mentions a letter written by Dupleix to Murari Rao asking him to attack Mu'tabar Khān, the killedar of Ranjangudi who had betrayed the French and delivered

9 (*Orme—Book V,* p. 334 of Vol. I. 4th ed.) Sayyad Lashkar Khān was alive to the danger of allowing the French, possession of such a long tract of the coast; and he offered Bussy a much larger tract of country in the inland parts, provided he would desist from demanding these provinces.

10 See the Diarist's report of the secret message given by Dupleix to Jamāl Muhammad, Vijayarama Raja's messenger—pp. 362-3 of the *Diary, Vol. VIII.* Vijayarama Raja was the most powerful of the local renter-chieftains, and Jāfar Alī, the *faujdar* of Chicacole, who was disinclined to give up his charge to the French, persuaded him to join him in opposing Moracin's entry. The French however seduced Vijayarama Raja from observing this compact, by promising to lease him the Rajahmundry and Chicacole *sarkars* at a much lower rate. Jāfar Alī then called in the help of the Marathas of Nagpur who plundered the Dutch factory at Bimlipatam, but spared the English factory at Vizagapatam, as the *faujdar* had counted on their help and had been encouraged by them in his revolt, defeated Vijayarama Raja near Vizianagaram and fought with Moracin near Tumapala but suddenly recrossed the Godavari with enormous booty (p. 31. of W. Francis: *Vizagapatam District Gazetteer*).

over their goods and money (probably plunder taken from d'Auteuil's army after its surrender in May) to the English. Murari Rao was asked to take the town from him and promised half the plunder that might be got. About the close of that month, news was received of disagreement between the English and Muhammad Alī who was not able to continue his monthly payments; while Abdul Wahāb Khān, the Nawab's younger brother, had marched on Nellore and taken possession of it, but the English had sent people to intercept him and hinder him from proceeding until he had paid their dues.

On the 17th December, Muhammad Alī Khān and the English attacked the French camp at Bāhur and inflicted such heavy losses, that only 10 or 20 escaped to Pondicherry out of 200.[11]

Dupleix's intrigues with Murtazā Alī Khān of Vellore had begun as early as July; he was reputed to be very rich and might pay handsomely for French support. The Diarist's entries for December 20, 1752 and the next day mention the Khān as having fallen into the net of Dupleix. M. Le Gris was sent to Vellore to strengthen its fort where guns were being got ready to prepare for an attack on Arcot. Dupleix also intrigued to procure the escape of the French soldiers and officers who were imprisoned at Arcot; but the English learnt of it and sent away the prisoners under safe escort to Madras.[12] On December 22, Murari Rao's letter of negotiation was delivered to Dupleix with a list of his twenty-two demands, comprehending a *jaghir* besides certain forts, a lease of certain districts and the Sirpi, Yadiki and Tadpatri countries in *jaghir*. Dupleix agreed to them all, except that he insisted on Yadiki and Tadpatri being given only on lease and Sirpi not being given at all. Dupleix would also give Murari Rao

11 The English army returned to Tiruvati from the attack on Taqī Sāhib of Wandiwash by the 11th of November. On that day the monsoon burst on the country with a violent hurricane; and most of the troops and the men of the Nawab had to retire to Fort St. David and elsewhere for the season.

12 *Orme*, Vol. I. p. 275, describing the conspiracy of Murtazā Alī with the French prisoners at Arcot to rise and overpower the English garrison.

the right of the Carnatic *chauth,* in spite of his understanding with the Peishwa to whom Salābat Jang had agreed to grant it, but on condition that he assisted in driving away the latter's (Peishwa's) invading army. He also agreed to pay Murari Rao 1¼ lakhs every month, besides the present of 2 lakhs agreed upon. We are told that, in the course of the negotiations with the vakils of Murari Rao, the Governor and Madame Dupleix privately called three out of the four vakils and told them that, if they could by any means secure Murari Rao's assistance, they would be gratified.[13] Murari Rao's vakil, Subba Rao, continued to stay on in Pondicherry after the settlement was agreed on. By the middle of January Murari Rao had reached Pondicherry with a body of 4,000 men; and he marched, together with 500 Europeans and 2,000 sepoys to the vicinity of Tiruvati, upon which Major Lawrence and the Nawab returned from Fort St. David to their former encampment. The French attacked Muhammad Alī's army which, being unable to resist, fled towards Fort St. David and began to besiege the small party left in Tiruvati fort. When Muhammad Alī and the English had gone about 4 miles, the Maratha horse fell on the Nawab's

13 *Vide* Martineau's *Dupleix et l'Inde Française*, Vol. III, pp. 308-9. *Accords avec Morarao.* Murari Rao arrived at Vaḻudāvur where, after four days, the final terms of the agreement were agreed to. They were:—

(1) Papayya Pillai, receiver-general of the finances of the Carnatic, would pay him monthly 1¼ lakhs. (2) Dupleix should obtain for him the districts of Ascotte (Hoskote), Kolar, Gooty, Penukonda and the ordinary *jaghirs* of these four fortresses. (3) Both were to share equally in the booty whether got in the field or in fortresses. (4) Murari Rao should remain at the French side with his army, till the affairs of the country should be fully settled and till Dupleix should give him permission to return. (5) The payment of Murari Rao's army was to commence from the 20th December (4,000 cavaliers and 2,000 *fantassins i.e.,* foot-soldiers).

Ananda Ranga Pillai tells us that he was received at Pondicherry with the same honours as were paid to Muzaffar Jang. Martineau tells us that it was likely that it was planned to harass and attack the enemy as much on the side of Tiruvati and Cuddalore, as on the side of Bhuvanagiri, Porto Novo and Chidambaram as the control of this region should precede the march on Trichinopoly.

troops with great fury.[14] On the night of January 31, 1753, the Diarist heard that Muhammad Alī had reached Fort St. David with his army and the French were attacking Tiruvati fort. On February 16th it was recorded by the Diarist that a small body of the enemy, marching to Tiruvati from Fort St. David, were intercepted by the French and Murari Rao's troops and the officer in command and all his people, numbering 8 soldiers and 200 sepoys were killed and the cannon, muskets and provisions were carried to the French camp.[15]

14 Orme details the attack of the Marathas on Tiruvati, with three field-pieces, on January 20. Lawrence advanced two miles towards their camp, but when returning, was furiously surrounded and had to retreat with 100 slain. "Murari Rao, on his return to the camp, reproached the French for their cowardice, in not having supported him in the manner that had been concerted between them." Murari Rao continued to distress the enemy by sending out parties to prevent supplies reaching their camp; and Lawrence had to march with his whole force and escort his supplies from Fort St. David. These marches were excessively fatiguing and might have been dangerous, "had the French behaved with the same activity and spirit as the Marathas," who alone harassed and occasionally charged on their line of march. Dusaussaye the French captain, was very irresolute and talked ill of Murari Rao. Nawab Anvar-ud-dīn Khān (*i.e.* Muhammad Alī) wrote to Madras on the 28th January (N.S.) that Major Lawrence reached his camp on the 16th and engaged the enemy on the 19th when "the major behaved like a Rustam, an old hero, and punished them severely and took three of their guns"—referring probably to the first advance of Lawrence against the French camp (p. 7, *Country Correspondence, Military Department*, 1753). Martineau (Vol. III, p. 317) says that the affair was neither a victory, nor a defeat for either party.

15 Orme tells us of an engagement, rather a skirmish, on the 8th February (N.S.) in which the French did not venture to attack the troops with the convoy, being dispirited by the loss of 300 of their horse in the different previous skirmishes of the day. Dupleix, trying to protract the operations, asked the French to remain on the defensive and strengthen their entrenchments. The English, to make up for their deficiency in cavalry, solicited the Rajah of Tanjore for help in this direction. The latter promised compliance and actually sent some troops, but hastily recalled them on hearing that the Marathas had entered his kingdom.

Early in March, Murtazā Alī Khān was met at Valudāvur in state, on his way to Pondicherry, but he was not treated, as the Diarist remarked, with a tithe of the respect that was shown to Murari Rao. Further Dupleix is reported to have said that the Khān was "a mean fellow, quite unfit for his position." On his departure, he was given by Dupleix the title of Zulbasar Jang. But the latter demanded three lakhs of rupees that he had promised to pay and asked him to proceed to Tiruvannamalai, Tirukovilur, Kallakurichi, Sankarapuram and other places and to collect the revenues due from them and thus weaken the enemy. Murtazā Alī was not inclined to do so, and argued that if he occupied Arcot first, the rest of the fortresses could be easily taken. He departed, promising to pay at least a lakh of rupees and getting a mansab of 2,000 horse and a *naqqara* (kettle-drum).[16]

Throughout March the French operations round Tiruvati were dull; and this was due not only to the want of agreement between the French captain and Murari Rao, but also to other difficulties. The Diarist's entry for March 30, 1753, tells us of the seizure of Tiruvendipuram, three miles west of Tirupapuliyur, by Murari Rao and La Volonte, and that Muhammad Alī was in great difficulty for money and provisions, and therefore proceeded to Cuddalore, having put in a garrison at Tiruvati.

On the 1st of April, Murari Rao and his brother, Bhujanga Rao, advanced against Muhammad Alī and the English who were marching from Fort St. David, towards Tiruvati taking provisions with them. The Maratha horsemen made a dashing charge, threw the enemy into confusion and took their guns and provisions. Muhammad Alī and his *Bakshi*, Muhammad Abrar, were wounded; but Bhujanga Rao was killed; while Murari Rao had his horse shot under him. The Diarist remarks:—"Others of Murari Rao's people were killed; but the enemy lost more. Although our army retreated the Marathas fought gloriously. They showed two or three times as much courage as they usually do, and our people

16 Martineau, Vol. III, p. 292 and *Country Correspondence*, 1753—Letter No. 66.

disappointed them." This was the opinion of Dupleix who ordered a dress of honour and presents to be sent to Murari Rao.[17] It was hoped that the Marathas would cut off completely all communication with Fort St. David.[18] Murari Rao complained of the failure of the French soldiers in camp to assist him and of their refusal to fight the enemy. He required guns, shot and powder of which a small quantity was sent. News came of continuous skirmishing near Tiruvati to which Muhammad Alī Khān had retired. Dupleix was so anxious to hear the news of his death, that the Diarist remarks, in his entry for 8th April 1753, that he promised to give 1,000 pagodas and an elephant to him who would bring him the news of Muhammad Alī Khān's death. But Murari Rao's troops remained unpaid for two months; and no money was coming in, while Pondicherry had to pay three lakhs every month. The chief disease, more serious than that of military inefficiency, was that of financial ruin.

17 Orme testifies to the vigour of the charge of the Maratha cavalry on the English convoy which they followed from the vicinity of Fort St. David. He says that Bazin Row (Bhujanga Rao) was Murari Rao's nephew, the same who came to Clive's assistance after the seige of Arcot. The day ended with Lawrence assaulting the French near Tiruvati, but giving up the attempt owing to the strength of the French works.

18 The first three months of 1753 were ineffectually employed by Lawrence in bringing the enemy to a decisive engagement. His failure to do so *convinced him of the necessity of changing his plans.* Dupleix's plan was to approach Tiruvati and to expose it to two fires, from the west and the north, while communications should be interrupted from the side of Cuddalore; while other troops should operate on the south in the direction of Chidambaram and Bhuvanagiri. But Maissin, the new commander, though possessed of talent, would not listen to the suggestions of Dupleix. In the month of February, he did not accomplish anything to injure the enemy. In March the situation was not modified either. Dupleix asked in vain Murari Rao and Maissin to co-operate. The English situation also became desperate owing to difficulties of revictualling; and they were reduced to severe distress towards the end of March. In the action that took place on the 1st of April, Lawrence was assailed by the French army, three miles from Tiruvati and lost a part of his convoy. Murari Rao lost his brother. The English lost 53 soldiers. But Tiruvati continued to resist; and the English were holding the

At last it was learnt that Muhammad Alī Khān proceeded from Tiruvati to Fort St. David on the 21st April, that he was unable to pay his troops or to buy provisions and that Trichinopoly fort could no longer hold on unless he went there immediately, as the garrison was disaffected and inclined to the Mysoreans, having no money for their pay and provisions and that no more letters would be sent. After Muhammad Alī had advanced to Chidambaram, he was prevented for a time from going further by 2,000 of Murari Rao's horsemen. When he crossed the Coleroon, news came to him, according to the Diarist, that the Mysoreans had taken Trichinopoly (not true); and then he wanted to return to Cuddalore, but Murari Rao's horsemen attacked his troops and dispersed them on the bank of the Coleroon. The Diarist sententiously remarks that "Muhammad Alī Khān's misfortune began 15 days ago when he fled from Tiruvati. In another 15 days his business will be settled." To add to this, Hasan-ud-dīn Khān[19] who had fallen a prisoner into English hands in the first siege of Trichinopoly, made good his escape from Fort St. David; and this was expected to bring about an increase of misunderstanding between Governor Saunders and the Deputy Governor of Fort St. David, as well as between Muhammad Alī and the English

country with their mobile detachments. Maissin and Murari Rao were far from agreeing with each other; and there was even a talk of abandoning everything and retreating to Vaḷudāvur. Lawrence left Tiruvati for Trichinopoly on the 22nd. Astruc was instructed to follow Lawrence while Maissin should attack the English in their limits of Cuddalore and raze the town and destroy the garden at Manjakuppam. Dupleix thus hoped to compell Lawrence to retrace his march and leave Trichinopoly to Nañja Raja (Martineau, III, ch. 13).

19 Shaikh Hasan and Abdul Rahmān were first commissioned as captains of sepoys, in 1744; and both took a prominent part in the capture of Madras and in the expedition against Anvar-ud-dīn Khān. Shaikh Hasan took Tiruvati fort in July 1750. He had to suffer greatly from the mutinous spirit of his troops. According to Prof. Dodwell, Shaikh Hasan was reputed to be the man who slew Anvar-ud-dīn at Ambur. There is no hint of this in Burhan-ud-dīn's *Tuzuk-i-Wālājāh*. Shaikh Hasan, Abdur Rahmān, Bikhan Khān and Mīr Sāhib of Elavānāsur were the chief sepoy-leaders on the French side.

authorities. The story of Shaikh Hasan's escape is told at great length by the Diarist and resembles in some respects that of Shivaji's escape from Mughal custody at Agra. He contrived to escape in a box in which his food was usually conveyed to him. He narrated the story of his escape to the Diarist. His brother, Abdur Rahmān, who had risen high in the service of the Nizām and had later gone over to the Peishwa, got the latter to write to Muhammad Alī urging his release.[20]

The Diarist tells us of the correspondence that passed between the English and the French Governors regarding Muhammad Alī's grant of Tiruvati to the English and the consequent impropriety of the French attacking the place; and the latter retorted that the fort was first in his possession when Muhammad Alī seized it by force. Shaikh Hasan who had ambitions of his own, asked Dupleix why he had given the Arcot subah to Murtazā Alī Khān and declared that he would pay the revenues if it were given to him, adding that he had *parwanas* for the Vellore *killa* from Muzaffar Jang and Salābat Jang. The Governor told him that he could take possession of the Chetpattu fort and jaghir which had been assigned to him.

The beginning of May saw the approach of a crisis in the situation round Tiruvati. Murari Rao announced a victory that he secured over a body of English soldiers and sepoys that sallied out of Tiruvati, whom he beat severely. But he added that, though preparations were made to scale the fort, the attack had to be postponed. He was joined by Shaikh Hasan and renewed the attack; and he succeeded in capturing the fort on May 7th, in the evening. But, according to the Diarist, the English had sent off their property to Fort St. David on the previous night and departed with their weapons. In ignorance of this, the French went on firing cannon and mortars all the day; and when they finally entered the fort, they found only 29 French soldiers and 12 officers who had been formerly captured by the English. Papayya Pillai was appointed to the charge of the *Panchmahal* country,

20 *Country Correspondence, Military Department*, 1753, pp. 38-39.

comprising Tiruvati, Tirthanagari, Porto Novo, Bhuvanagiri and Venkatammalpettai; and orders were given for the demolition of the fort.[21]

It was only after the capture of Tiruvati, that the French control over the neighbourhood of the Gingee country became effective, at least partially. The capture of the Chidambaram pagoda from Mudamiah was followed by the seizure of the neighbouring *killas*. But the ravages of Maratha horsemen rendered cultivation impossible in the countries of Tirukovilur, Eravāsanallur, Gingee, etc.; and according to the Diarist, "not one cash has been received from the 150 and odd pargannahs of the Carnatic" (entry for July 19, 1753). Mutabar Khān of Ranjangudi seized, in July, Eravāsanallur and eleven other places; and he could not be dislodged without a large body of Maratha horse marching against him. Further, Murtazā Alī's troops, cowardly like their master, could not take the Tiruvannamalai fort, though they raised batteries round it and had to retreat, while the French troops who accompanied them, had to retrace their steps to Gingee. In October, the English, Muhammad Alī's people and those of Vettavalam made a night attack upon the French camp and forced Shaikh Hasan who had been sent to reinforce the ally to retire to Gingee. The enemy was in possession of the pargannahs of Uttaramerur, Tiruvattiyur and Salavakkam and extended his

21 For the capture of Tiruvati, see Orme, Vol. I, pp. 286-7. He says that the Marathas cut every man of the party who sallied from the fort. After this there was a mutiny among the remaining men of the garrison; and the captain, unable to prevent his men from getting drunk, was obliged to capitulate and was made captive along with them. Captain Chase who thus surrendered, died of a fever, soon afterwards, at Pondicherry. According to the *Diary and Consultation Book*, 1753 (Records of Fort St. George), Captain Chase, whom Major Lawrence had left in command, made a sally on the French attackers on the 26th April. On the 2nd May, an English party which sallied out was defeated by the Marathas who killed some and imprisoned the rest. The enemy took possession of the village, erected a battery and threw shells into the fort. Tiruvati surrendered on the 7th May, as the men refused to maintain the fort any longer and a breach was made and the defences destroyed. (Letter of Mr. Starke to Governor Saunders—dated 8th May).

power as far as Tindivanam and Merkanam. Muhammad Alī's troops captured Tirupati, slaying Muhammad Kamāl, its *amaldar*, who was maintaining French influence.

Operations round Trichinopoly—Negotiations with the Mysoreans (1753)

The Mysore army had borne no part in the operations when the surrender and subsequent murder of Chandā Sāhib occurred. His head was sent up as a trophy to Seringapatam and hung up over the Mysore gate.[22] Nañja Raja claimed Trichinopoly as we have seen; and Muhammad Alī was no longer able to conceal from the English his illegally formed agreement; but he coolly declared that he had never intended to observe the compact. At the same time he tried to deceive the Dalavāi with fresh promises that he would deliver up the town in two months and made over to him the revenues of the island of Srirangam and the adjacent region. The result was that the Mysorean intercepted supplies to the Nawab's garrison and the English troops, opened negotiations with Dupleix and contrived his best to gain the fort by treachery.[23] But all his attempts were frustrated by the cleverness of Major Lawrence.

In October, we saw Nañja Raja camping at Karur and recalling Innis Khān, the pay-master, from the camp of Muhammad

22 Wilks says that the head was taken by Muhammad Alī and delivered to Nañja Raja and sent by him to Seringapatam where it was suspended in a *cheenka* over the southern or Mysore gate to be gazed at by the multitude for three days, as a public trophy, "of the victories in which the troops of Mysore had as yet borne no very distinguished part." Mr. Orme was informed that the head was never carried out of the Carnatic.

23 The English victory at Bāhur checked the resolution of Nañja Raja of declaring openly for the French—See *Orme*, Vol. I, pp. 257-8. The Mysorean is alleged to have plotted to shoot Captain Dalton as he was about to march from Trichinopoly to join the Nawab at Tiruvati and it was discovered, from questioning one of the conspirators, that Khair-ud-din Khān, the Nawab's brother-in-law and commander of the fort, was also to be shot. The plots were discovered and frustrated.

Alī. In December the Madras Council thought it was now time to treat Nañja Raja as a declared enemy; and on the 23rd of that month (O.S.) Captain Dalton made an assault on the Mysorean camp under the north wall of Srirangam, but could not force his entry into the pagoda.[24] The Diarist received news from the Mysore vakil at Pondicherry that the Dalavāi had taken the fort. imprisoned some of the garrison, killed the rest and entertained 100 French soldiers formerly imprisoned there (entry for January 31, 1753). This seems to have been believed in even by Dupleix. This was possibly an echo of Dalton's set back in his attempt to capture the Srirangam pagoda. Nañja Raja (usually written as Nandi Raja by the Diarist) wrote in the middle of February to his *vakil* at Pondicherry, that as Balaji Rao's troops had advanced to Sirpi, Deva Raja, the chief Dalavāi, had written to him to leave a sufficient body of men at Srirangam and join him. He intended to march towards Mysore immediately and desired that the French and Murari Rao should combine to prevent the Peishwa's further advance into the Mysore country. He promised the French the subah of Arcot, retaining for himself Trichinopoly in case of success.[25] During the whole of March we do not hear anything

24 On the following night the English captured a choultry overlooking the southern gate of the Srirangam temple and bombarded the enemy; but they retreated, on account of an unconscionable feeling of panic, across the river, before a body of Maratha horse with a loss of 70 Europeans and 300 sepoys. After this Dalton lost all hope of driving the Mysoreans out of Srirangam. The affair took place on Dec. 25th (O.S.) *i.e.* 5th Jan. (N.S.). The charge against the English was led by Hari Singh, a Rajput *jamadar* of the Mysore cavalry, and the rival of Haidar Alī for military distinction. Captain Dalton had now to stand on the defensive and turned out, as a measure of precaution, the Mysore troops, to the number of 700, that were in the fort; while their captain, Gopal Raj, believed to be a brother of Nañja Raj, was kept in confinement.

25 For a summary of the negotiations between Dupleix and Nañja Raja see *Martineau,* III. *pp.* 310 *et seq.* The quasi-rupture between Nañja Raja and Murari Rao on one side and the English and Muhammad Alī on the other, which began on the day after the capitulation of Law, persisted. Lawrence had agreed, by a compromise, to allow Nañja Raja to remain under the walls of Trichinopoly, without participating in the

about Nañja Raja's movements from the Diarist. Nañja Raja's blockade of Trichinopoly was complete by March while there was no co-operation between Captain Dalton, the commander of the garrison, and Khair-ud-dīn Khān, the killedar of the fort; and provisions were getting thinner and thinner,[1] and could not come in. In April Muhammad Alī resolved to depart from Tiruvati for Trichinopoly; but his advance beyond Chidambaram and the Coleroon was prevented by a body of Murari Rao's horsemen. News was current then that Nañja Raja had actually taken Trichinopoly; a little later we are told by the Diarist that the Mysore troops had surrounded the fort and that Murari Rao's men were pursuing Muhammad Alī into the Tanjore country. On the 2nd of May the Diarist wrote that Muhammad Alī had set out from Kumbakonam with 1,000 English soldiers 5,000 infantry and 18 guns and had attacked the Mysore troops encamped against

military operations on this side. Perhaps the Mysoreans had been conciliatory only with the idea of entering the place with a force when the English should have gone away. Lawrence left Dalton with a force sufficiently strong to repel an attack. But Nañja Raja did not attack. A plan that he devised, to enter the town by a treason, opened the eyes of the English to the disposition of their former allies. Lawrence wanted to profit by the uncertainty that still prevailed among them; the Council of Madras was of another opinion. Having at last learnt for certain that he would have neither Trichinopoly nor "indemnite en tenant lieu," Nandi Raja declared himself at the same time against the English and Muhammad Alī and made a brisk attack on them in Srirangam (20th December). He could not maintain himself there, but two days afterwards, he attacked another English party commanded by Dalton himself, on the east of Trichinopoly, on the bank of the Kāveri. The English were forced, panic-stricken, and with appreciable loss, to the gates of Trichinopoly.

Nañja Raja however did not want to treat with Dupleix before knowing as to how he should act towards Muhammad Alī. On the 7th December Dupleix announced to the Mysore vakil that his master could have his friendship whenever he wanted it. At last, on the 24th February, 1753, Nañja Raja, acting in the name of his brother, the Regent, made to Dupleix, the following promises.

(1) I (Deva Raja) will recognise and be friendly with whomsoever you may nominate as the *naib* (lieutenant) in the province Arcot.

Trichinopoly; and the latter had retreated into Srirangam; also Murari Rao had sent 1,500 horse to the Mysore camp, while a body of French troops were attacking Chidambaram. The entry for the 23rd of May records a statement by Dupleix that Muhammad Alī had reached Trichinopoly by a stratagem, defeated Nañja Raja and his army and removed his treasure; and that the latter could not hold on, unless he was joined by the French troops from Tiruvati and by Murari Rao. On the 28th May, after the capture of the Chidambaram pagoda, Dupleix ordered Shaikh Hasan to collect men and join the Mysore camp, as Nañja Raja had repeatedly asked for his services. On the 4th June a bill of exchange for 3 lakhs was received from Nañja Raja, drawn payable in a month and a half, at which Dupleix greatly fretted. The French captured Vriddachalam and Kallakurichi a few days

(2) For the conquest of Trichinopoly, you will furnish bullets, cannon, powder, etc., and I shall pay 15 lakhs, 4 lakhs in advance and the balance after you should give me Trichinopoly and the *parwana* from Salābat Jang.

(3) For the grant of Trichinopoly and for getting me the *sanads* from Salābat Jang, I shall pay him whatever my vakil at his court should have agreed with him for *nazar* and durbar expenses, as soon as I should be in possession of the fortress.

(4) I shall pay the usual tribute that was paid from the time of Vijayaranga Chokkanatha Naicken, as soon as I get the sanad from Salābat Jang; besides I shall pay to the Company, through the Governor of Pondicherry, 3 lakhs annually.

(5) I shall give Karbbander to the French Company.

(6) (7) If Muhammad Alī should cede Trichinopoly, I shall take it, but not become his ally thereby. You in the possession of the fortress and country of Arcot and I, in the fort and country of Trichinopoly, should live in amity; if Mughals or Marathas should attack Trichinopoly or Seringapatam, you will help me; and if Arcot or Pondicherry is attacked, I shall send you help.

(8) After I get hold of Trichinopoly, I shall act according to your wishes with reference to Tanjore.

(9) I shall recall my vakils from our adversaries.

Martineau adds:—It is not to be doubted that Dupleix was thinking of seizing Trichinopoly on his own account, if chance should favour him.

later; and this, with their capture of Chidambaram from Mudamiah a few weeks before, enabled them to control the entire region to the north of the Coleroon.

Before the middle of June, Astruc and La Volonte had joined Nañja Raja, with 300 soldiers, guns, infantry, etc., at Srirangam; and they had entrenched themselves at Sandapettaimalai, beyond the Kāveri—the place being identified with what is known as the French Rock. On the 8th day after the French had encamped, La Volonte's troops were surprised in a night attack; and their camp was burnt, while their cannon and movables were carried off into the fort by the enemy. Nañja Raja was greatly irritated at this mishap which was not referred to by Orme and "must have been a very minor affair," according to Dodwell, somewhat exaggerated in the Diarist's record.

Some days later, the French troops under Astruc carried Kaḻudaimalai, about three miles from Trichinopoly, where they captured a gun and killed some infantry and ten Englishmen who were there. The French were then attacked by Lawrence and Muhammad Alī Khān's troops and had to retreat, abandoning their cannon, etc., and to flee to Nañja Raja's camp. "All the infantry, except the slain, flung away their arms and fled. Balaji Ghorpade, a sardar of Murari Rao's army, 5 or 6 jemadars and 20 or 30 troopers were killed. If the Marathas had not fought bravely, our whole army would have been destroyed. One of Nandi Raja's principal officers was also killed." (Diarist's entry for July 2, 1753).[26]

26 Lawrence's despatch to Madras, dated June 27, 1753, says that the previous day, "the enemy attacked one of our advanced posts, which being defended only by sepoys, they carried before we could get up to their assistance. Upon my marching out on the plain their whole army did the same; and a general action ensued in which the Nabob's troops were lucky enough to retake the post and repulsed the enemy which went off in such confusion that they left 2 pieces of cannon and a Haubitz behind them, likewise, their killed and wounded, among whom we found Bollapah, Moraree's nephew, who commanded all the Morattoes now with the Daloway. . . . Their loss was considerable both in men and horses; it must certainly give the Daloway a strange idea of his European Ally,

In July Muhammad Alī and Lawrence marched with their troops to Tanjore from whom they obtained 1,000 or 1,500 horse, 5,000 foot and a lakh of rupees; and then they made an alliance with the Tondaiman, the Marava (of Ramnad) and others.[72] As Nañja Raja could not stand before them, Astruc declared to Dupleix that he could not continue without assistance. Dupleix had to recall him. On the 25th of July the Diarist noted the contents of a letter received from Nañja Raja to the effect that Astruc had been quarrelling and had crossed the Coleroon with his army and reached Samayavaram, under pretence of Dupleix having recalled him. On an urgent entreaty from the Dalavāi, Astruc rejoined the camp. He was superseded by M. Brenier who

for though backed by so numerous an army, they behaved in a most dastardly manner." p. 121. *Diary and Consultation Book, Military Department*, 1753).

According to Orme, Trichinopoly was saved "by this success, which astonished even those who had gained it . . . . for, as the city would inevitably have fallen if the English had remained inactive, so the loss of it would have been hastened only a few days, if they had been defeated." (pp. 293-4 of Vol. I).

Burhan-ud-dīn, in his *Tuzuk-i-Wālājāhi*, describes Nañja Raja's erection of defences round about the Golden Rock and the French forces stationed on the hill opposite. He then tells of the Nawab's desperate resolution to attack the enemy. The hill came to be known from that day as *Fateh Pahadi* (hill of victory).

27 Both Dupleix and Nañja Raja intrigued with Pratap Singh of Tanjore and made him vacillate in his alliance with the English. They threatened that his country would be laid waste by Murari Rao's horse and bribed the Raja's chief minister, Sakkoji who succeeded in procuring the dismissal of Manoji who was of service to the English and the Nawab. Pratap Singh was on the point of signing a treaty of alliance with the French when a signal defeat of the latter induced him to return back to his old alliance (Venkasami Rao, *The Tanjore Manual*, p. 789; also *Wilks*, Vol. I, p. 197). In February 1753, Pratap Singh recalled his cavalry from joining the English at Tiruvati. In May–June he was dissuaded by the Mysoreans from supplying the English army at Trichinopoly with provisions. In July Mr. Palk, who was deputed to Tanjore, prevailed on him to declare openly and to order his troops to join the English under Lawrence who proceeded to Tanjore from Kunnandarkoil to which he had marched (Orme pp. 296).

had no better fortune than his predecessor.[28] The report was that Astruc had treated the Dalavāi very unfairly, by trying to swell the account against him and only desisting when he had obtained ready money and jewels amounting to five lakhs of rupees. Early in August there was a battle between the troops of Muhammad Alī Khān and those of Nañja Raja in which some horses and cannon of the former were captured by the latter. Nañja Raja wrote to Dupleix that Muhammad Alī, Manoji and others had retired into Trichinopoly, but meant to come out again and fight; but the French were ready to fly rather than encounter them, declaring that they could not stand with their small numbers against a superior enemy or attack them without being overthrown. Dupleix promised to send him reinforcements and the support of Murari Rao and Maissin. Lack of money seriously affected both Dupleix and the Dalavāi; and the former had to resort to the torture of one merchant in order to wring out money from him.

It was after the French defeat on September 21st, between the French Rock and the Sugar-Loaf Rock, that Dupleix became very depressed; he was so angry with Maissin who had returned from Trichinopoly that he ordered him not to appear in his presence, though Maissin was sick with dysentery on the day of the engagement and the command had devolved upon Astruc who had joined Brenier with reinforcement.[29]

28 Brenier sent de Cattano into Trichinopoly as a spy; Captain Dalton discovered his plans and compelled him to advise an escalade; the arrival of Major Lawrence prevented that attempt. Lawrence, with his force augmented by the Tanjoreans under Manoji, routed Brenier's force, 6 miles east of Trichinopoly (Aug. 7th). On the 23rd he pursued them to Uyyakondan which they abandoned. On the 21st September they were defeated and Uyyakondan was occupied.

29 For details of the engagement, see the General Letter of Lawrence to the Madras Council, dated 22nd Sept. 1753, in which he declared that an attack upon the French camp was absolutely necessary "though our prospects of success were not extraordinary, for besides their superiority in numbers, both of foot and horse, they were fortified with strong breastworks." Astruc and 100 soldiers were taken prisoners; and the Marathas saved the rest and prevented a pursuit. Lawrence himself was wounded in the arm. "The enemy are now gone to the Island, and I hear

In November a party of French soldiers and foot under Mainville who had superseded Maissin attempted to escalade the fort, as it was reported that the imprisoned Astruc had arranged with the sentries at the fort-gate, to pay them a large bribe, if, after making a show of resistance, they should open the gates to the assaulting party. The attempt was made without the knowledge of Nañja Raja or Murari Rao who were informed only after the assault was begun. When the French had entered the gate, they posted no troops there, but overturned the guns on the rampart into the ditch. La Volonte and Lambert who had been ordered to guard the gate with their men, did not appear; the English contrived to shut the gate, seized the powder and shot of the French party and fired against the men on the ramparts. About 400 men fell into English hands including 9 officers. It was believed that the English and Muhammad Alī must have laid a trap for the French; but the attempt proved to being very near to success.[30] When the news of the disaster reached Dupleix, he was "drowned in the ocean of sorrow"; and Pondicherry came to be "unlike itself and wrapped in darkness." Papayya Pillai, whom the Diarist heartily disliked, brought in false news of success which proved to be untrue. He was also guilty of torturing merchants and others into giving forced loans for raising money for Murari Rao. The year 1753 thus closed with the deepest gloom prevailing in Pondicherry and in the mind of Dupleix.

The Diarist shrewdly remarked that ever since the middle of September, Pondicherry was getting only news of the loss of

intend crossing the Coleroon. The Daloway must certainly give up the cause and the French without him are nothing." (pp. 157-8 *Diary and Consultation Books—Military Dept.* 1753). See also Malleson (pp. 399-404); but he makes mistakes with reference to dates, continuing to take into account the *O.S.* dates.

30 Orme Mss. India, III, 26, contain a copy of letter from Lt. J. Harrison, dated 13th December, 1753, and containing a short account of the attempted escalade of the 27th Nov., with the number of prisoners, killed, etc., *The Orme Collection of Mss.*, p. 285. Burhan-ud-dīn attributes the initial treachery to an officer of Muhammad Alī and the credit of the victory to Khair-ud-dīn Khān. He says that "the lamentations of 472 *Frangs* served as the musical instrument for their happy rejoicing."

armies, damage to ships, strength and success of enemies. The financial situation was so bad that the Governor had to write a *cowle* agreeing to take in troopers and foot-soldiers, but having no ready money to pay them, offered three lakhs of rupees in jewels in return for a loan (entry for October 22, 1753). European protests against Dupleix's high-handedness increased; and M. Duvelaer, the French Company's Director, is said to have remarked that Dupleix could neither rule nor manage and should not be continued as Governor; while the ladies and gentlemen of Pondicherry were all complaining of the high-handedness of Madame Dupleix in their letters to Europe.[31] Sententiously the Diarist remarks:—"How can the Governor expect success when all his actions are unjust? Victory will attend him only when his heart is right. I am certain of this" (entry for December 7, 1753).

31 The news of the French reverses from July 1752 was published by the English and transmitted by them to the French ministers to whom the French Company complained of Dupleix's policy and acts. This was brought by the Europe ships in August which also gave an account of the run on the French Company's funds, everyone wanting to sell his shares, even at 50 per cent. loss, in spite of the Minister's assurances to the contrary. (pp. 411-3 of *the Diary*, Vol. VIII).

CHAPTER XIV

PONDICHERRY UNDER GODEHEU

By the time that the Diarist's account is available to us in September 1754—there being an extensive gap from December 8, 1753 to September 8, 1754, due, presumably, to the entire disappearance of one volume of the original *Diary*—much had occurred. The French forces had failed in their last attempt to take Trichinopoly by assault; the conference of English and French deputies at Sadras had broken up; and M. Godeheu had landed at Pondicherry, with orders recalling Dupleix and with a mandate to bring the struggle with the English to a close and to free the French Company's trade from the encumbrances of war. The Diarist's account for September 1754 begins with "a new Governor, Godeheu, at that great *Gouvernement* which Dupleix had built for his own magnificence, but had scarcely occupied two years, and a Governor who was charged with the duty of reversing the policy of Dupleix, which for all its possibilities had obtained little beyond private fortunes, coupled with public disasters."

Ranga Pillai was sulky, because the new Governor kept him, at first, at a distance. He thought that the Diarist was afraid of Dupleix and unwilling to take part in business. The Diarist complained that Papayya Pillai, Dupleix's dubash, to whom the land-revenue had been rented and who was in arrears, had been imprisoned without his advice and that his own measures for recovering money from him had been disregarded, asserting that he would have managed to clear up the whole matter, but "what was done was like tying up air in a bag". Godeheu was persuaded, largely through M. Boyelleau, to take back Ranga Pillai into favour and entrust to him, as before, the affairs of the Tamils and the Muhammadans and the country business.[1] Dupleix who was

1 In the beginning of January, the Diarist was formally commissioned to take sole charge of all this business.

making hurried preparations for his departure to Europe, sent for Ranga Pillai, urging him to tender his advice to the Governor, even when not sent for and consulted, particularly in the grant of the leases of revenue, as to the persons to whom they should be given. From the entry for September 14, we learn that Godeheu took the Diarist into his confidence, asking him to " let bygones be bygones " and promising not to allow anyone else to have a hand in the management of the country affairs and those of the Tamils and Muhammadans, and adding that " I will see that none except our two selves manage matters."

The relations with the country powers displayed a very unsatisfactory aspect. Murari Rao wrote complaining that he had not received the promised contribution for 8 or 9 months and that Dupleix had made false charges against him, although he owed him more than 13 lakhs of rupees,[2] and forwarding to his vakils at Pondicherry, all the notes executed by the late Governor. Muhammad Alī sent a threatening letter through M. Maissin, warning the French to confine themselves to trade and not to exceed those limits and refusing to release the French soldiers that had been captured. Godeheu also complained that Bussy had not been writing to him at all; and the Diarist explained the matter by saying that Bussy had been hitherto managing all affairs without any interference and now he feared that some hindrance might arise. It was even suggested by the new Governor that the Diarist should send his men to get Salābat Jang's camp-news " without M. Bussy's knowing it." He was anxious about the visits paid by the vakils of Nañja Raja and Murari Rao to Dupleix and instructed Ranga Pillai to " watch who visits him and tell me." He had a letter written to Murari Rao that he should settle with the old Governor for the sums of money owing to him, or that he might set off his claims against the sum that Nañja Raja owed to the French, paying the latter whatever might remain after the adjustment. At the same time Murari Rao was to be exhorted not to abandon the French alliance. Nañja Raja

2 According to a despatch of Fort St. George, dated November 10, 1754, the French owed him 9 lakhs.

bitterly protested against the departure of Maissin, the French commandant, and charged the Pondicherry Government with having broken their promises to him, imploring that the French troops might be made to stay on at Trichinopoly. He agreed to give suitable hostages for the 15 lakhs of rupees, owing from him to the French, together with the cost of the *sibbandi*, if they should capture the Trichinopoly fort and give it to him; even otherwise, he would pay off the debt from out of the sum that the enemy had offered to give him.[3] Godeheu replied that he had arranged with the English for a truce of three months and that the Ḍalavāi would have to pay for the French troops from the time of their joining him; he also suggested, impliedly, that he might make his own terms with the enemy, adding, "if you get the 60 lakhs of rupees which were offered to you, what cannot be done with the help of so much money?" In the next letter to the Dalavāi, he wrote that Maissin had received orders to stay on

3 Orme remarks that "it is difficult to find an example of a prince conducting himself with more weakness than the Mysorean in the course of this war; the Nabob had procured his assistance by a promise which he never intended to perform . . . . The Nabob's breach of faith in refusing to deliver up the city to him, only served to exasperate his eagerness to get possession of it, which rendered him as great a dupe to the promises of M. Dupleix, as he had been to those of the Nabob; for it is certain that he at last discovered it himself, that the French never intended to give him Trichinopoly if they had succeeded in taking it; nor was he less deluded by his ally Morari-Row, who after persuading him to assist the French against the Nabob, deserted him as soon as his treasures began to fail. . . ." (Vol. I; Book V., p. 389).

Nañja Raja had to return to Mysore in the course of 1755, at the urgent summons of his brother, "having nearly exhausted the treasury in the expenses of this unprofitable war, added to a subsidy paid during most of the time to his Mahratta ally Morari Rao of Gooty and a loan of ten lakhs of pagodas to Muhammad Ali which was never repaid." According to Governor Saunders' despatch from Fort St. George, dated November 10, 1754, the Mysoreans trusted the French so little that they would have withdrawn long ago, "but that the Dalavāi's brother (Deva Rajah) fears for his life, should he acknowledge his defeat by withdrawal."

with his troops, "at which I was overjoyed, that you (Godeheu) thus escape the dishonour of reducing to despair him who has trusted the French these three years."

Dupleix's Departure for Europe—The Diarist's View

Dupleix departed for Europe by the *Duc d'Orleans,* on the morning of the 14th October, nearly 13 years after he landed from Bengal. He had hoped, according to the Diarist, to leave his bones in Pondicherry; yet now he had been "dismissed, accused and arrested." Sententiously the Diarist reflected—"Such is the fate of the man who seeks his own will without fear of God . . . Madame alone had caused all Dupleix's troubles; but he did not understand this till matters were irretrievable . . . He has eaten the fruit of his actions . . . I dwelt in truth and justice under his government; but from first to last, he regarded neither justice, nor truth. Without God's help no labours can serve to make one rich."

Dupleix had indeed continued to promise, even till the eve of his departure, to make good the losses that the Diarist had suffered through him, first on account of the lease of Tiruvati, Bhuvanagiri and other places which had been given to him for three years in 1749, but taken away later and transferred by Madame Dupleix to Rango Pandit; and, next, on account of the amount of half a lakh of rupees due on the balance of his private transactions with the late Governor.[4] The Diarist had prayed,

4 He thus wrote in the *Diary* for 15th October:—"From the day when the town became populous and flourishing till now, Europeans have made 40, 50, and 60 lakhs of rupees, have obtained the title of Nawab and ruled the country, using the Fish and other emblems of power. But I who was the root and support of this prosperity, have secured nothing but debt. I can blame nothing but my fortune." Dupleix to whom these words were addressed, was further told:—"others for their own benefit have given petitions complaining of the bribes they paid you; them you sent for and gave bonds to. You know well what sums I have paid; and God knows also. Your accounts, my heart and mind all bear witness. Scorning to be as unjust as others, I only ask for what you yourself promised me. Be pleased to stop the wound of my debts." Dupleix put

"with my head bowed towards my belly," that he might be paid the sums due to the Company and to others and waited even to the last moment of the ex-Governor's embarkation, thinking "it would be improper to speak of it in another's ear." He even showed Dupleix the petition that he had resolved to present to M. Godeheu, who had given an undertaking that the sum of 46,000 and odd rupees due on his private transactions, should be adjusted in the Company's accounts as well as the Covelong business. But Dupleix's ship sailed away in the early hours of that day (14th October); and the Diarist was left helpless.

Right and Left Hand Caste Disputes

Godeheu's administration was faced with the problems of caste disputes and factions between the Right and Left Hand caste groups.[5] We find the Diarist advising the Governor that when

the Diarist off with promises and told him to wait till the ship sailed. On the eve of his departure he said he was leaving at 7 or 8 o'clock the next morning and would then do what he wished. But the Diarist heard the guns announcing his departure at three in the morning. "So how could I see him? I can only continue my labour." Malleson gives a quite different picture of Dupleix's embarkation followed by the principal officers and employees and all the common people.

5 Similar disputes were frequent and significant in Madras and the country round Conjeeveram. The distinction between the two Hands is very old and was prevalent in all the Tamil and Canarese districts and also in some of the Telugu districts; it was absent in Malabar. A mythical account of the origin of the Left Hand castes is given in Inscription No. 489 of 1912 (South Indian Epigraphy) which is noticed on p. 109 of the Annual Report on South Indian Epigraphy for 1913. The earliest inscriptional reference to the Right Hand is a record of Rajendra Chóla Deva I (No. 341 of 1907). In the *Tondaimandala Śatakam*, we have got a reference to the unfriendly feelings between the Kammāḷars (Panchalars) and the Veḷḷaḷas, the respective principal elements of the Left and Right Hand groups. In Conjeeveram the differences between the two groups were more marked than in any other place. The Depressed Classes were also included in the divisions. Mr. Nelson, the author of the *Madura Country, a Manual*, (1868) thinks that religious differences had nothing to do with these distinctions. The Abbe Dubois and Dr. Francis Buchanan have remarked on the prominence of the

headmen were to be appointed in any caste, the caste-people assembled and chose two persons and reported their choice to the chief dubash who confirmed it. He also urged that the Governor should help in the rebuilding of the Vedapuri Isvaran Temple which belonged to the Right Hand castes and had been destroyed in 1748 and that the English at Madras and the Dutch at Negapatam had helped the construction of Hindu temples with money grants and monthly allowances and with the protection of sepoys and peons at festival times, to prevent disorder. He added that the town would not flourish unless the temple were rebuilt, and that, in the time of Governor Lenoir, when orders were received to destroy the Vedapuri Isvaran Temple, as a church had to be built on its site, there was a vigorous protest on the part of all the Hindu castes; and subsequently, orders were obtained from Europe that all should be allowed to follow their own respective religions

distinctions in the Mysore country about 1800. The Madras Consultations (for October, 30, 1707) have an entry regarding a paper, signed by President Baker, Agent Greenhill and Mr. Gurney in 1652 (only 12 years after the foundation of the settlement) for composing differences among the Right and Left Hand castes, which Governor Pitt got from the latter. (See *Fort St. George Records, Diary and Consultation Book for* 1707—pp. 75-76; J. T. Wheeler's *Madras in the Olden Time* (1882)—pp. 263-4; F. Buchanan's *A Journey from Madras, etc.*, Vol. I pp. 77-80; *The Madras Manual of Administration*, Vol. III. *Glossary*—pp. 1036–37; *South Indian Inscriptions*, Vol. II pp. 46-57; M. Srinivasa Iyengar's *Tamil Studies, First Series*—pp. 92 *et. seq*; and C. S. Srinivasachari on The Origin of Right and Left Hand Caste Divisions in *The Journal of the Andhra Historical Research Society*, Vol. IV, pp. 77–85; and V. R. R. Dikshitar, Around the City Pagodas in the *Madras Tercentenary Commemoration Volume*).

In the history of the city of Madras we find that the temples of Kachalesvarar was built about 1725 by the prominent merchants of the Left Hand group. The Ekambaresvarar Pagoda was built about the close of the 17th century by Alangatha Pillai, a *dubash* of the Right Hand group. The Kandaswami Temple is sacred to the Beri Chetty merchants of the Left Hand. The disputes between the groups had to be often put down with the help of troops; and separate parts in the town had to be assigned for them. The factions became sporadic in the second half of the 18th century and considerably diminished in the 19th.

and the Governor permitted a new temple to be built and allowed festivals to be conducted as men pleased.[6] M. Godeheu, while admitting that all this was true, said that he could give no orders without the Company's specific permission, "although it was the reason why the town had not thriven, because men could not follow the customs of their caste." When it was suggested that the Diarist should enlist the favour of Father Lavaur, the Superior of St. Paul's Church, for gaining his object, his only and proper answer was:—"Each should look to his own business; he who governs should treat all alike." The Diarist managed to persuade the Governor to permit the weavers who had gone away to return and live in peace under two heads of their own choice

[5] In Madras the Beri Chettis, artisans, oil-mongers, weavers and leather-workers were the chief elements in the Left-Hand faction; while the Veḷḷaḷas, the Arya Vysias, the Vanniars and the Adi-Dravidas belonged to the Right-Hand division. The grounds of quarrel were mostly with reference to the particular routes that the marriage and funeral processions of these castes should take, and the symbols and trappings that should adorn their processions and pandals, on occasions of festivity. The two factions were as ready to fall out with each other on the smallest provocation "as Orangemen and Ribbonmen were in Ireland or the Montagues and Capulets in Verona."

It was in the award given by the Council and President, in the earliest dispute between these castes in 1652-53, that the name of Chennapatnam, as applied to Madras, first occurs in an official document. The result of this award was that the eastern half of the Hindu town (known as Black Town, now George Town) came to be generally occupied by the Left Hand castes and the western half by the Right Hand ones.

6 The English seem to have pursued a quite different policy and adopted an attitude of friendliness and protection.

In Madras, the Chennakesava Perumal (the Town) Temple which was almost co-eval with the birth of the town, was for long under the special protection and patronage of the Company, whose Chief Merchant was usually its warden. It was commonly known as the Company's Pagoda; and the servants attached to the existing Town Temple, which has replaced the older one, wore, till lately, a badge bearing the words 'East India Company'—(See Davison Love's *Vestiges of Old Madras*, Vol. II p. 461 note 3). The Triplicane Temple was also managed for long by the Company's Chief Merchants. (cf. V. R. R. Dikshitar 'Some Madras Temples' in the *Handbook to the Indian Science Congress*, 1940).

and to release those who were in prison. He was also bold enough to tell Godeheu, when he inquired whether the people of Pondicherry desired war or peace with the English, that "the merchants, ryots and all people desire peace, and pray with all their hearts that God will be pleased to send some happy man to establish peace throughout the country and restore contentment to the people; and that only the smaller portion of the people, the sepoys, jemadars, officers, soldiers and troopers, who lived by plunder selfishly, desired that war should be continued."

Godeheu's Attitude towards the Country Powers

Meanwhile, Godeheu assured the Mysore vakil at Pondicherry that he had written to Maissin to remain with Nañja Raja, but to take care not to attack the English or Muhammad Alī Khān or their possessions. The vakil said that his master was concerned greatly about Madura as it belonged neither to Muhammad Alī Khān, nor to the English, but had been held by Ālam Khān for Chandā Sāhib and was now liable to be attacked from Trichinopoly and taken from Ālam Khān's people who were in occupation of it. Further, he added that Mahfuz Khān was about to attack Madura, and that, if it was so, permission should be given to attack him. To this Godeheu would only reply that all matters were to be settled with Maissin who was to remain with Nañja Raja.[7]

The Poligar of Udaiyārpālayam from whom no *peshkash* had been secured for the last three years was threatened with an attack by the French troops from Trichinopoly and Vriddachalam on his

7 Read below note 13. Orme says that "the Mysoreans could not be made to understand that they were no longer at liberty to commit hostilities against the English or the Nabob; and the regent, when advised by the French to return to his own country, said that he was under no obligation to regard any treaties that he had not made himself, that, therefore, he should never leave Seringham until he had got Trichinopoly, which he did not despair of effecting even without their assistance; finding however that the French thought themselves obliged to acquaint the English of any schemes that he might put in practice for this purpose, he offered the commanding officer, 3,00,000 rupees, if he would retire with the French troops to Pondicherry, and leave him

domains and with his own supersession. News came in that Murari Rao who was returning to his place, was plundering the country round Vellore, Arni and other forts and meant to do likewise all along his march. His vakil at Pondicherry was dismissed curtly, Godeheu refusing to pay the balance due to him under the agreement, on the plea put forward by M. Delarche that "the old Governor is gone; and so his business is closed." and that the matter could not be reopened.

The Peishwa, Balaji Rao, now sent a letter to Pondicherry, demanding the payment of *chauth* for the last two years and insisting that its collection should be in the hands of his own men under Narasinga Rao whom he now sent as his agent. The letter also solicited that the French should help the Marathas with troops, ships, cannon and powder for the capture of an island from the hands of the Habshis (Abyssinians). The Peishwa had sent a copy of his letter to Bussy demanding that the Arcot *chauth* should be paid to his agent. Bussy had then been sent to settle the Rajahmundry and Chicacole countries, to settle the *peshkash* of the zamindars and arrange for prompt payment and return speedily to the court of the Nizām.[8]

at liberty to carry on his projects without control: the English, however, were under no apprehensions of the effects of them; and at the request of the Nabob, a detachment of 500 Europeans and 2,000 sepoys were ordered to proceed into the countries of Madura and Tinnevelly to assist in reducing them to his obedience" (Vol. I, Bk. V, p. 380—4th edition).

8 Bussy marched in July 1754 with the bulk of his troops to see to the establishment of the French Government in the Circars as trouble was being given to Moracin, his deputy, by the Raja of Vizianagaram and other zamindars. He reported to Dupleix, in a letter of October 5, 1754, the settlement that he made of the revenues of the Circars which were expected to produce 31 lakhs for 1754-55. In his own *Memoirs*, Bussy estimated the sum total of the agreements with the various renters at 18½ lakhs for the year, a sum which, if fully realised, would have just met the expenses of the Deccan army. He returned to the Deccan at the close of 1754. Jāfar Alī Khān who had invited the Mahrattas from Nagpur, having no resource left flung himself on the clemency of Salābat Jang and went to Aurangabad to make his submission (See p. 253 above—Note 10 for Jāfar Alī Khān).

It was also noticed by the Diarist that Dupleix had imprisoned the agent of Abdul Nabī Khān of Cuddapah and released him only at the intercession of the vakils of Murari Rao and of Mysore, and since then nobody had been willing to go to Pondicherry and that "Dupleix has done so much like this that the whole country lost confidence in him." As a final stroke of the hand of misfortune that now seized Dupleix's reputation, the Diarist recorded that, on the 29th of October, the belfry of the Padre's Church that Dupleix had built and was able to complete only recently (opposite the house of the Diarist) collapsed, and the bell and the stone arch above fell near the church door and part broke into the church. The fall of the belfry was considered an ill-omen; and Dupleix had tried to make it loftier than the flag-staff itself. The Diarist concludes his observations with his usual sententious comment that "what is destined must happen, but only at the appointed time; and a man can neither escape, nor foresee destiny."

The Mysore negotiations dragged on through the month. The Dalavāi protested that Godeheu had agreed, without his knowledge, on a truce for three months,[9] with the English and Muhammad Alī and that he himself had no means or chance of getting the sum of 60 lakhs which they had offered him when Trichinopoly was being besieged and that, meanwhile, the English were gathering troops at that fort daily, while all the French troops had been recalled, "but 300 military and 1,000 foot with a commander." Godeheu had to reassure him that the English could do him no harm during the truce, that Europeans never broke their word and that Muhammad Alī was going to Cuddalore, The truce was deemed to commence from the 11th October, 1754; but it was very much doubted if a stable peace could be concluded. Major Lawrence wrote from his camp on October 6th, that Salābat Jang had written to Muhammad Alī, assuring him that he would be confirmed as the Nawab of the Carnatic and had also sent another letter to the Dalavāi with orders to return home and not continue

9 The true was to continue from the 11th of October 1754 to the 11th of January, 1755.

to disturb the Nawab.[10] Ranga Pillai lamented that when Chandā Sāhib's son came to offer congratulations to Godeheu on his name-day (November 4, 1754), he was received with a salute of 21 guns, as it implied that the Nawabs were still rulers, and that the French only servants. He wrote that ever since 1749-50, the French had been masters and the Arcot people had been under them; and now, by treating the Muhammadans as though they were still masters, the Governor had cast away half the glory that his nation had acquired; and he wailed, in his entry in the *Diary* for that day, that "the Governor had done this, because the time had come for all this glory to be lost, and Raja Lakshmi (the goddess of prosperity) was continued here by the influence of Jupiter only until M. Dupleix departed."[10a]

Meanwhile Murari Rao[11] who had agreed with Muhammad Alī, in return for a considerable sum, to leave the Carnatic, as he

10 Compare the fears expressed by the Mysore general with the letter of Major Heron, dated Tanjore, 22nd October, 1754 that ran as follows:—"My chief attention during the cessation of arms, will be to have a sufficiency of the above in store, that we may have nothing to do,. but take the field in the most advantageous situation when the cessation of arms expires." With regard to the French encamped in the Island of Srirangam, Colonel Killpatrick wrote on the 24th of October, 1754, that there were only about 150 Europeans and 500 sepoys with 2 guns, left on the Island, while the rest had marched back to Pondicherry; and the Mysore troops remained in the same situation as before. That officer also wrote to Madras that the French troops were very much inclined to desert and he was ordered to enlist all the Germans that came over to the British side and to send the French to Fort St. David (Records of Fort St. George, *Diary and Consultation Book, Military Department*, 1754; pp. 250 *et seq.*). The English kept one advantage in their hands, by not releasing 650 prisoners whom they had taken during the war, more than the French had taken from them (See Orme, Vol. I p. 377).

10a The Diarist wrote that this happened because neither the Councillors nor himself were consulted in the matter, which was done by M. Delarche—"as the proverb says: "Open your door, blind old woman"."

11 The Fort St. George Despatch of November 10, 1754, already quoted, says that the Nawab and the Raja of Tanjore had made an agreement with Murari Rao to leave the French and go home, for which

found his situation unprofitable, proceeded as noticed above, to the Arcot country where he extorted contributions from several *killedars* and harried the villages, carrying off the cattle. Abdul Wahāb Khān, a brother of Muhammad Alī, who had been left in charge of Arcot and the surrounding territory, was powerless to stop these depradations. Murari Rao complained to Godeheu that he had ordered his troops not to touch French territory and had trusted in Dupleix's word, but had not received the stipulated sum and that he would lay the burden on him and would abide by his decision.

The Reddi of Turaiyur[12] complained of Nañja Raja's aggressions against his country and urged that Godeheu should order the Dalavāi and Maissin not to interfere with him. Nañja Raja himself advised that the French Governor should have the Dutch and the Danes as mediators when discussing peace terms with the English; and that he should produce the *parwanas* given by Muzaffar Jang, Salābat Jang and Chandā Sāhib as against the grants to the English made by Nāsir Jang and Ghāzī-ud-dīn Khān, his elder brother. He concluded that "if you treat with the English without mediators, the matter will not be settled for centuries." In a further letter he complained that an agreement was made to give two lakhs of rupees to Maissin on account of his expenses for

Tanjore would pay him 3 lakhs and the Nawab would give him certain grants. The agreement was made some time back; and Murari Rao had been marching slowly, raising contributions on the way and had, by now, gone only as far as Polur; and it was doubtful whether he would continue his march. He had offered to join the English for 1¼ lakhs a month; but this was more than they could afford. The French were said to owe him 9 lakhs; and so there would be no reconciliation with them, unless the Mysoreans should find the money. Murari wished that the English would guarantee his treaty with Muhammad Alī; but "as Eastern princes make such terms in adversity as they never mean to observe in prosperity," the Presidency should try to avoid doing so.

12 In 1752 Ṭuraiyur was overrun by the Mysore and French troops who deposed the then poligar and appointed his cousin in his place. The Mysoreans continued to have a control over the poligar till they abandoned the Trichinopoly country in 1755 and left the French Government as the representatives of all their rights and pretensions in the Carnatic.

three months, for which one lakh worth of land was assigned on the banks of the Kāveri and the other lakh was assigned on Turaiyur. The French agents had received money from the poligar of Turaiyur for settling the affair at one lakh instead of two, as previously determined and were troubling the Dalavāi not to interfere in the affairs of that pālayam.

It was again lack of ready money that led the Governor to discharge most of the sepoys, guards and troopers posted in the several parganahs, immediately after the conclusion of the truce. But the differences that arose about the terms of the truce forced Godeheu, according to the Diarist, to order new enlistments and to desire the Pathan captains to send troops to their several camps; and on December 12, the Diarist was told by Godeheu that both Saunders, the Governor of Madras, and himself, would be returning to Europe in February as a definite peace could not be concluded.

The Situation at the End of 1754

The last two months of 1754 were very gloomy for the French cause; there was a marked decline in trade, while, Pondicherry itself passed through a time of severe depression. The heavy rains brought great losses; and the French and English factories at Porto Novo were washed away. As for building a factory at some other site, the Diarist remarked that, even according to the views of a French observer, the French were incapable of trade or government or administration and lost their temper easily; that the Dutch were best at trade and building purposes and the English might be half as good as the Dutch. The troops that returned from Trichinopoly served but to increase the insolence displayed by the soldiers towards peaceful citizens, " their cutting and stabbing men, their plundering the bazaars and the money-changers' shops and their stopping the work in the washing-place by stealing or burying the stamping-blocks." It was also resolved by the Council to segregate the Tamil population of Pondicherry in the western part of the town, separated from the European quarter by a wall with three gates, and to order that the Tamils should give up to those Europeans who wanted them, their houses east of the canal at cost price and those who required sites for building purposes would be given lands and gardens in Pavaḷapettai (coral merchants' quarter).

Godeheu himself confessed to the Diarist, according to the entry for December 7, 1754, that he also wanted to make money like former Governors, but in the manner of Lenoir and Dumas and by fair means, and not according to the methods of Dupleix whose "injustice was notorious." The Diarist told him that Lenoir sternly refused to take bribes offered by the Company's merchants and only made large profits in the Mocha trade; and that Dumas made money both by trade and by other means. Dupleix managed the country affairs by means of Delarche and Writer Ranga Pillai, and allowed all and sundry to make money in collecting rents and revenues from the country and to make deductions for various kinds of claims. It was possible to get, in the days of Dumas, large voluntary contributions as trade was very vigorous; but for the last ten years the town had been suffering from English hostility, bad trade and poor seasons, and the people had been living on what they had saved; and many would have nothing to live on "but for the country revenue and the sepoys." In this miserable situation, the Diarist still hoped to restore a measure of prosperity, if he should be entrusted with the management of the country business and that of the merchants and the mint-people, with the same powers as had been enjoyed in the time of Martin by the Company's Dubash: and, in that case, he would prevent the raising of complaints and settle everything within two months.

A statement of the Mysore vakil at Pondicherry that the Mysoreans had been in possession of the Tinnevelly country for nearly four years from the time of their occupation of it early in 1751 was supplemented by him with another that Madura was held before the truce neither by Muhammad Alī Khān, nor by the English, nor by the French, but by a Pathan soldier and that some Mysore troops were sent there before the conclusion of the truce;

and these seized a portion of the country and besieged the fort. The Mysore troops did not fight at all during the truce; but Muhammad Alī treacherously attacked them in the Tinnevelly fort, slew some of their captains and captured the place.[13] Godeheu was urged to inquire closely into the question whether Tinnevelly was captured now or before (*i.e.*, before the truce commenced). All that Godeheu could reply was that he would

13 From the time of the expulsion of the Marathas by the Nizām in 1744, the Madura country had been held by officers appointed by Anvar-ud-dīn and Muhammad Alī. A Record Office MS., quoted by Nelson (in p. 268 of Part III of *The Madras Country—A Manual*) says that Muhammad Alī and Mahfuz Khān ruled the country in subordination to their father and left it in charge of one, Mayana, in 1748, when they departed to assist their father against Chandā Sāhib. This Mayana was supplanted by one, Abdul Hakīmat Khān; and he, in his turn, was ousted by Ālam Khān, probably a relative of Mayana. Orme says that Ālam Khān, was a soldier of fortune who was in the service of Chandā Sāhib and of the Raja of Tanjore and who contrived to get recognised by his troops as the governor of Madura under Chandā Sāhib whom he acknowledged as his master. In the beginning of 1751, while Ālam Khān had been established in Madura, a detachment was sent by Muhammad Alī against that place, under Captain Cope, assisted by a body of Muhammadan cavalry under the Nawab's brother, Abdul Wahāb Khān. Cope had no battering cannon and was forced to withdraw after an attack of the walls, while the Nawab's troops went over to Ālam Khān. (Orme; Vol. I pp. 169–70).

While Orme does not notice any subsequent success of Captain Cope, Hindu accounts tell a different story. The Madura *Śrī-tāla* book tells us that Ālam Khān placed Mayana in charge of the Madura country, and the latter sold it to the Mysoreans; and Captain Cope called Kukku Sāhib in the chronicle, took possession of the place on behalf of the Raja of Mysore and was, soon afterwards, driven out by Veḷḷaiyan Sērvaikāran, the Dalavāi of the Ramnad Setupati and the minister of the Sivaganga ruler. These two besieged the fort for nearly 2 months, forced Cope to capitulate and crowned the adopted son of the late Nayak Queen, Minakshi, as the ruler of Madura. This person ruled for 16 months and was then deposed by three Muhammadan captains, who were, shortly afterwards, forced to give up the fort by Captain Cope and the Dalavāi of Ramnad who had allied themselves against him.

Nelson would plead for the substantial accuracy of this account of the *Śrī-tāla* book, in spite of its highly improbable features like

be writing to Maissin to ascertain and inform him what happened about the Tinnevelly country, the Madura fort etc., from beginning to end. He also accused the Mysoreans of carrying on discussions with Nawab Muhammad Alī and of giving the French nothing except empty words of friendship and co-operation in spite of repeated demands for the monthly expenses of the army. The

(1) Cope being described as the general of the Raja of Mysore; (2) his entering into an alliance with the Dalavāi of Ramnad; and (3) Orme not making any mention of these. He says that it is directly corroborated by the Record Office MS; and by a memoir supplied to him by a Muhammadan gentleman, and indirectly by other Mss. The Record Office Ms. says that Mayana sold the Madura country to the Mysoreans; that Kukku Sāhib, a Mysore general, took possession of Madura; and he surrendered the fort, after a siege, to the Ramnad Dalavāi and the Sivaganga minister, who crowned Vangaru Tirumala's son; and that these and their Nayak *protegē* were subsequently expelled by the Muhammadans; but it says nothing about Captain Cope's alliance with the Ramnad Dalavāi.

Ālam Khān went over in the beginning of 1752 to take part in the operations round Trichinopoly and was, soon afterwards, killed there. He appointed Mayana commander of Madura and Nabī Khān the captain of Tinnevelly. After the death of Ālam Khān and of Chandā Sāhib, Mayana intrigued with his son-in-law, Muhammad Barki, for the cession of Madura to some party or power. Thus Nelson gives his views of the whole series of transactions:—"Now it appears from Wilks; Vol. I Ch. VIII; that, early in 1752, a Mysore army marched to the assistance of Mohammad Alī, and it is quite possible, although neither Wilks nor Orme tells us anything about it, that a detachment of Mysoreans was commanded by Captain Cope, in his expedition against Madura, and if so, the fact of his being called a Mysorean general in the native Mss., would be very naturally accounted for. And on the supposition that he contrived to get possession of Madura, by paying to Mayana a sum of money advanced by the Mysoreans for the purpose, the account given in the *Śrī-tāla* book and in the Record Office Mss. becomes at once intelligible and credible. The Raja of Mysore was in possession of Dindigul at the time; and if he thought proper to buy the adjoining province of Madura, when professedly an ally of Mohammad Alī, who claimed to be its master, the transaction would of course be kept strictly secret. It is quite possible too that the terms of the transfer were unknown for some time to Captain Cope, ... and that he took possession of the fortress under the impression that it had been surrendered to Mohammad Alī."

vakil only replied that in the agreement between Dupleix and the Mysoreans, no definite payment was fixed and the soldiers and sepoys were to be counted and paid what was due; and since then they had not been counted, nor had a balance been struck; and the matter might be considered when the accounts should be settled. A letter was subsequently received from the Mysore Dalavāi that he would be paying not only the former dues according to the accounts, but also the cost of the army and supplies sent by the French, every month.

"However this may have been, whether Captain Cope was hoodwinked, or whether he was guilty of treacherous and unsoldierlike conduct, and whether or not he took possession of Madura, I think there can be no doubt that in the year 1752 the adopted son of Minakshi was declared king by Mayana and his colleagues assisted by the governments of Ramnad and Sivagangei . . . . . was then deposed . . . . . by his Mahometan patrons who seem to have been bought over by Mohammad Alī. Orme states that Mohammad Alī produced as evidence of his title to the sovereignty of Madura and Tinnevelly, a writing which purported to have been signed by Mayana, Mohammad Barki and Nabī Khān, and was dated 29th November, 1752; and it would seem not unlikely that this document, which acknowledged the justice of Mohammad Alī's claims, was executed shortly before Mayana found it convenient to relegate his client . . . . Mayana is said to have been in turn expelled by the Dalavay of Ramnad; but whether this is true or not, it is impossible to say. According to Orme Mohammad Barki was in possession of Madura in 1755. Perhaps, although he was attacked and defeated by the Ramnad Dalavay he was nevertheless permitted to retain Madura, as a tributary and vassal of Ramnad, and on condition that he disavowed Muhammad Alī's authority. Orme states that the *Poligar* of Maravar, by whom I suppose he means the Setupati, sided with Chandā Sāhib and the Mysoreans against Mohammad Alī; and it is therefore quite possible that he attacked Mayana when Mayana changed sides and sold himself to the Nabob."

This long extract from Nelson's work (pp. 271–73 of Part III) should naturally throw some light on the statements of the Mysore vakil that are summarised by our Diarist. Particularly, the profession of allegiance to Mysore by Mayana under the pressure of the Setupati, as stated by Nelson, may be said to be a support of the vakil's claim that the Mysore troops had seized a portion of the Madura country before the truce was concluded. Also, the Diarist records a sentence in his entry for March 19, 1755, that the Dalavāi claimed the Setupati for his ally. Mr. Dodwell, in

As for the Deccan, Godeheu only received a complaint from Muzaffar Khān[14] who had gone over to the service of Balaji Rao Peishwa, from that of Bussy, that he had been deprived, unjustly, of property worth 5 lakhs, by Bussy and his diwan, Rūmī Khān, who had made for themselves 30 or 40 lakhs in many ways and told many falsehoods about himself to Salābat Jang. The Peishwa wrote to Godeheu recommending that Muzaffar Khān and Hasan-ud-dīn Khān should retain their jaghirs and the insignia of the Fish Standard, the covered palankin and other honours. As Hirāsat Khān of Satghar, who had married Razā Sāhib's sister, had died without any legitimate son or brother, and as Murtazā Alī Khān of Vellore had designs of seizing Satghar, a letter was written to the English Governor to order Abdul Wahāb Khān, the subhadar of Arcot, not to attack Satghar nor do any harm.

The last entries of the Diarist for the year 1754 disclose, first, Godeheu's resentment that the second and other Councillors did whatever they pleased, that he did not hear of things that were going on and his insistance that, henceforth, nothing should be done without his orders; and next, that Clouet, brother of the Governor, was carrying a proposal to the Madras Government that there should be no war for 18 months from January, 1755, or until orders should be received from Europe about it.

Note I of p. 118 of Vol. IX of the *Diary*, states that "the Mysoreans might have taken the country before the truce, and also been dispossessed before that event"; and that, earlier in 1754, they were asking English help to obtain possession of these districts. Nelson's account also renders more intelligible the statements given by Dodwell; *viz.*, (1) In July 1752 the Mysore general sent a party to take possession of Madura, which was taken from him again, about the beginning of December, by the Maravans, "who, though in friendship with us, are like to keep it for themselves until we are in a better capacity to call them to account"; and (2) Heron, writing in October 1754, that he heard from the Nawab that Cope Sāhib endeavoured, with Mysore troops, to raise disturbances in the Madura country and plundered Tinnevelly.

14 For an account of him, see Ch. X: Employment of Sepoys by the French and Note 19 on p. 259 above.

THE END OF GODEHEU'S GOVERNORSHIP

On the second of January, 1755, Godeheu gave an order that all the people of Pondicherry, except Europeans, *viz.*, Tamils, Muhammadans and all Indians, should report news to the Diarist and do as he directed and presented him with a *sarpech* (ornament on the turban) *kalgi turra* and jewels, two pieces of broad cloth and two pieces of cloth of gold woven in silk, besides ordering a salute of 15 guns to be fired in his honour. This honour to the Diarist began his short-lived second spell of prosperity. It was followed by the announcement that, until news should arrive of a settlement between the English and the French in Europe, neither side should take up arms for 18 months.[15] In spite of the

15 The despatch from Governor Saunders to the English Company, dated January 12, 1755, says that at first Godeheu declined to conclude a provisional treaty, saying he had advice from France, of April 10, that Lord Holdernesse had told the Duke of Mirepoix that no treaty could be negotiated in India and that the Companies were issuing orders. Later, in order to bring matters to a crisis, Saunders proposed a truce (dependent on a provisional treaty) to continue till orders were received from Europe; and Palk and Vansittart were sent in a private capacity to furnish any necessary explanations and to require a positive answer in 3 days. The proposals were accepted, and when digested into regular form, were signed. The truce was proclaimed on the 1st of January. "The main considerations for making a truce are the infinite superiority of the French force, their great influence with the country powers, and the impossibility of a mere trading company to bear all expenses of war. If war had continued, the French, by means of their cavalry, could have protected their own territories and raided ours also; whereas we might have lost our own districts in attempting to seize theirs. Further the revenues remaining in the Nawab's power will probably enable him to reduce his debt." The conclusion of the truce was expected to revive the investments at Madras, Fort St. David and Salem and to increase the demand for imports from Europe. All troops except the necessary garrisons in the country forts could be called in and their batta stopped; and the sepoys could be quartered in the Nawab's territories at his expense. Dodwell—*Calendar of the Madras Despatches* 1744–1755: (pp. 252–3). See also the Consultation of the Madras Council, dated 6th December, 1754; the letters of Messrs. Palk and Vansittart to Saunders, dated 14th and 16th December, and the Consultation of the Council of the 22nd December (*Diary and Consultation Book* 1754, *Military Department*).

proclamation of the truce, the Diarist tells us of a body of English horse and sepoys seizing villages under Kiliyanagar and Koyappakkam and threatening to seize Acharapakkam, Chunampattu, Cheyyar and Kolattur and their occupation of the Karunguzhi country about the third week of January. Godeheu wrote to Saunders about the matter and to Pigot who succeeded him, about this and other acts of Muhammad Alī's troops; and he got from Pigot a reply that he had written to Abdul Wahāb Khān, the killedar and agent at Arcot, not to plunder the country in French occupation. A proclamation of the mutual release of prisoners was made at Pondicherry on January 28; and the next day, the English soldiers and officers, upwards of 500 in all, who were imprisoned at Pondicherry, were sent to Fort St. David, on the understanding that an equal number of French soldiers and officers should be sent to Pondicherry, and the rest to France, by way of England, on a Europe ship. The Diarist records that, in return for the release of the English soldiers in Pondicherry, 167 stout picked Frenchmen, with some Mestice and Topass servants arrived.[16]

When Godeheu prepared to sail for Europe, he promised Ranga Pillai that he would leave instructions with his successor, M. Leyrit, that all affairs concerning the Indian population of Pondicherry and the country people generally should be conducted through the Diarist himself and an order to this effect would be signed by himself and all the Councillors and sealed and handed over. According to the Diarist, the townspeople were fearful as to what might happen after Godeheu's departure. He had revived confidence to some extent and abolished the collection of tolls at Vaḷudāvur, which had been made part of the Company's *jaghir.* The Diarist rightly told him that trade would decay if both land and sea-customs were collected; and that former Governors desired to get rid of the tolls in order to promote the town's prosperity.[17]

16 According to a Fort St. George Despatch, the Nawab would still have about 700 Frenchmen after the exchange of prisoners.

17 In his entry for January 30, 1755, the Diarist had already advised the abolition of the toll for Vaḷudāvur and Villiyanallur, both in French limits.

Just prior to Godeheu's departure, the Diarist entrusted to him a *cahier* in French, recounting all his services to the Company since his accession to the office of the Company's Chief Dubash, early in 1746, in succession to Kanakaraya Mudali; even before this, Lenoir had sent him to Porto Novo and managed all trade through him; and his bales of blue cloth were stamped R and sent to Europe. Godeheu promised to show the document to the Company and the Ministers and secure for him a medal of recognition and rewards; and he said that he had written a note to Leyrit about the Diarist and to treat him well. The latter had no confidence in Barthelemy, Second in Council; and the Diarist tells us that Godeheu ordered him to do nothing without the consent of the Council, "for fear that he should shake all the fruit, ripe and unripe, from the tree."

Complaints reached Pondicherry of the disturbance created by the poligar of Vettavalam and the killedar of Eravāsanallur fort who seized the crops and revenues of the neighbouring tracts and even planned to plunder the neighbourhood of Villupuram and Tiruvati. As a number of mutual complaints had been made by the French and the English, of villages in the Karunguzhi country being seized after the suspension of arms, Saunders and Godeheu had agreed to appoint commissaries, two on each side, to investigate and report. They met in the beginning of February, but could hardly arrive at any agreement regarding even a single village. Du Rocher, one of the French commissaries, is described by the Diarist, as being very clever and capable, which was not to the liking of Barthelemy. The Diarist records that Mīr Sāhib (of Eravāsanallur) was seriously disturbing the Kallakurichi taluk yielding a revenue of two lakhs; and similar troubles affected the revenue of Wandiwash taluk which was about a lakh. He accused the English of throwing some obstacle in the way of a fair settlement and declared to Barthelemy that "they must be treated as they treat us."[18] He urged that troops should be sent against Mīr

18 Contrast the English Governor's letter of March 8, 1755, to the Company about this matter, in which he wrote that "the French seem disposed to protract matters, in order to keep possession, as long as

Sāhib who was suspected of being in the English interest and that, with the help of the pro-French poligars of the neighbourhood, he should be put down. The trouble about the killedar of Eravāsanallur was serious. And the strained relations with Nañja Raja grew only worse. Godeheu had always mistrusted the promises made by the Mysore vakil on behalf of his master who gave "nothing except words" and promised "anything". He had even threatened to withdraw the French troops from the siege of Trichinopoly. This he did on more than one occasion. On the other hand, the Mysore Dalavāi found his treasury empty and saw that war could not be conducted round Trichinopoly at a profit. He now complained that he had believed in Dupleix, given up his agreement with Muhammad Alī and for two years maintained his own *sibbandis*, at the same time bearing the cost of the French troops. Dupleix insisted on his continuing at Trichinopoly, though he had been summoned to Seringapatam and allured him with prospects of reinforcements from France. Godeheu recalled Mainville and sent Maissin who "spoiled everything". He concluded a truce with the enemy, but insisted that the Mysore troops and commander should not go back saying that, after the expiry of the truce, he would send large forces to capture Trichinopoly; and the truce was followed by another for 18 months. Now the English and Muhammad Alī had captured

possible, of villages they have no right to," and that the English should insist on "the revenues of the disputed villages being received by both parties jointly until the matter is settled."

According to Pigot, (*vide* his letter to the Company, dated 8th March, 1755), the poligars of the Arcot country were also indebted to the English Company and similar measures (like those taken by Heron against the poligars of Madura and Tinnevelly) were needed with them. Abdul Wahāb Khān, who was in charge of these parts, had applied for help; but since he was suspected of applying his collections to his private use, Pigot would send him no help from Madras till the Nawab should come up from the Madura expedition. The Commissaries were appointed after agreement with Godeheu, since many complaints were made by both the French and the Nawab of villages being seized after the suspension of arms.

the southern country (Madura-Tinnevelly) and the middle country (Dindigul ?) belonging to Mysore,[19] while Salābat Jang and Bussy advanced across the Krishna, threatening an invasion of the Mysore territory. Nañja Raja demanded that Trichinopoly should be given to him or Muhammad Alī should pay him his expenses and that the French should prevent Bussy and Salābat Jang from causing disturbances in Mysore. The Dalavāi was charged with having attacked the fort and town of Ariyalur and secured several lakhs of plunder; but he defended himself saying that Turaiyur was pledged to him for interest on the loans given by him to [Muhammad Alī] and that he had not exceeded his rights. The Diarist believed that Dusaussaye, the French commander with the Dalavāi, had been bribed to consent to and countenance his action in seizing Turaiyur.

The Interregnum till the Arrival of De Leyrit

The more stable did the position of Muhammad Alī become, the more marked were the honours that were paid by the Pondicherry authorities to Chandā Sāhib's son. Godeheu wanted to treat the French Nawab as if he were a real power; and we learn from the Diarist that the Commission of the three Councillors, with Barthelemy at their head, to whom the Governor's powers were entrusted in the five weeks of interregnum between

19 The English advised the Nawab to settle first the affairs of the Trichinopoly country. "This must be done by fair words and promises, because the terms of the agreement are that no one is to take possession of any district that is not at present in his hands. If you could get the people at Madura and Tinnevelly to take phirmaunds from you for the several districts and acknowledge you for their master, by promising them your favour and protection against all disturbers, you will then have a right to collect the revenues without any dispute. I have ordered Colonel Heron and Major Kilpatrick to assist you in this business." (Letter from Governor Pigot to Muhammad Alī, dated 17th January, 1755)—Heron marched for Madura on February 23rd and reached it on March 3. He advanced without opposition to Tinnevelly whence he sent out Captains Lee and Beaver with two parties against the poligars. He returned to Trichinopoly on June 6, leaving Mahfuz Khān in possession of the Madura and Tinnevelly countries.

Godeheu's departure and the arrival of Duval de Leyrit as Governor, continued to pay honours to Razā Sāhib which Ranga Pillai would not at all countenance. The Diarist was also not sparing in his condemnation of Barthelemy, stressing on his readiness to "do unheard-of things for whatever was offered him" and noting down how he was glad when Leyrit did not arrive by a certain ship by which he was believed to be coming. Leyrit, the *Directeur* of Bengal, arrived on the 25th of March and took up the office of Governor. The letters received in the previous week from the camp at Srirangam, reported the capture of Madura by Muhammad Alī and his intention to march against the Setupati with the aid of the Raja of Tanjore and the Tondaiman of Pudukottah; and of the flight of Mandumiyan (Mayana ?)[20] to the Setupati and the imprisonment of his wife and family in the Madura fort. Madura was plundered by Muhammad Alī Khān's people; and when Dusaussaye remonstrated with the English at the Trichinopoly fort that they should not help Muhammad Alī Khān to capture Madura and Tinnevelly or to attack the Setupati, they agreed to withdraw their troops within a week but, ordered the advance to Tinnevelly, as soon as they had sent the French commandant back to Srirangam. The Turaiyur affair was going on badly; Nañja Raja and Dusaussaye could not agree over the amounts of the presents that the new poligar should give the French Governor and officials; while the vakil of the old poligar continued to offer his own terms; and there was delay over the installation of the new poligar. Meanwhile, the truculent Mīr Sāhib of Eravāsanallur was secretly negotiating for a lease of his fort from Muhammad Alī for a period of 10 or 12 years.

20 Mr. Dodwell says that it might be Mudamiah.

The Setupati now offered to submit to the Nawab and apologised for his conduct during the war in siding with Chandā Sāhib and even offered to cede two settlements on the sea-coast of his country opposite to Ceylon, which would greatly facilitate the English communications with the Tinnevelly country; and Colonel Heron attacked the representative of Alam Khān in the fortress of Koilgudi, a strong pagoda situated about 8 miles to the east of Madura, to which he fled for protection.

The new Governor, de Leyrit, was told, the next day after he landed, that the Diarist had not been treated well since Godeheu's departure and had been hoping for some encouragement from him. Thereupon he urged the Diarist to attend to the Company's affairs as in Godeheu's time, at which Barthelemy was not pleased and went away to his house "with a downcast look". The Diarist was cautioned that the Governor was very close and only acted with deliberation, studying every plan in detail and that he should refrain from making hasty proposals to him.

CHAPTER XV

GOVERNOR DE LEYRIT AND HIS TROUBLES

The Diarist in the Favour of the New Governor

The Diarist noticed that the new Governor was obviously very close and would act only after much deliberation; and he was advised to refrain from making hasty proposals to him. On a suitable occasion, he told M. Leyrit :—"I was able to satisy M. Lenoir, M. Dumas and M. Dupleix, because they followed my advice. I never visit the Councillors, nor do I serve others. I deal direct with the Governor; nor do I visit others with gifts. . . . I have used my whole strength on behalf of him who governed, seeking only his gain, and satisfying myself with the glory. If now you also will listen to no advice but mine, and act accordingly, I will strive for your profit and win your favour." The Governor was obviously impressed with these words, and, in the language of the Diarist, vowed, calling on God to witness what he said, to do nothing without consulting him. Thereupon Ranga Pillai explained to the Governor "the character of all here and the profits they make, with proof of everything," as well as the affairs in the subordinate stations.

The Diarist subsequently wrote out in French an account of all that had taken place between Godeheu's departure and the new Governor's arrival, and this precious document was, according to Professor Dodwell, the one that was among the Gallois-Montbrun papers at Pondicherry and was shown to him.[1] Ranga Pillai's heart was now intent upon getting one personal honour to be

1 The document was dated March 29, 1755, and was published as an appendix to Vol. IX of the *Diary* (Translation). M. Dodwell is of the opinion that the letter was the Diarist's own and that it was only revised by M. Revne, with whose help, Ranga Pillai says, he wrote out the French account (*Note* 1—p. 228, Vol. IX of the *Diary*). The collection of papers was much damaged by the cyclone of 1916.

shown to him; *viz.*, that the *tambour*[1a] should be beaten at the Fort and the town-gates, as a mark of respect to him, since he was the leader (governor) of all the Tamils. To his great satisfaction, at the Governor's reception of the Company's merchants, the Diarist was personally invested by De Leyrit with a gold chain and pendant, the *turra* and *sarpech*, given 4 pieces of finest broad cloth and 18 yards of cloth of gold, and ordered a salute of 15 guns. Ranga Pillai also led the deputation of the Mahānāttārs to the Governor and cautiously hinted to the latter that he should not allow undue influence to others, and told him that "if you will listen to me alone, you and the Company will gain greatly, while you will earn the Company's gratitude." The Governor promised to give him the leases of Villiyaṇallur, Bāhur and Karaikal.[2]

The political situation of the French at Trichinopoly continued to be gravely jeopardised by financial difficulties. Nañja Raja, according to the Diarist, owed the French a balance of 22 lakhs and Murari Rao a sum of about 10 to 12 lakhs, while he continued to blame the French in every letter, ignoring his own obligations. M. Godeheu was blamed for having allowed the English, after the conclusion of the agreement, to seize the Madura and Tinnevelly countries, when the available French troops were all concentrated at Aurangabad, Masulipatam, and Trichinopoly. M. Godeheu could have then insisted on seizing half the country; but many districts continued in the English possession, with "only a few outlying places in ours."

1a The 'tambour' was formerly accorded only to the Deputy-Governor. The 'tambour-aux-champs' was reserved for the Governor. See for the significance of these honours *supra*, p. 32, note 15.

2 The Governor is characterised by Dodwell as a "cold, silent and haughty man, whose solemnity covered little but dullness, self-seeking and irresolution." "Those who wounded his feelings found him implacable in his resentment; but those who knew how to manage him found him plastic as clay." Ranga Pillai had been pointed out by Boyelleau and others as "the person who could, if he would, make De Leyrit's fortune." And we read that "so long as that impression lasted, the *courtier* on the whole enjoyed the Governor's favour, though not to the degree that he considered his due."

The Diarist told the Governor, on another occasion, that, as the successor of Dupleix, he was now a *mansabdar* of the Padshah; only he needed a jaghir in order to enable him to maintain his status and paraphernalia. Again, he advised the Governor not to be afraid of taking strong measures, and told him that it was not necessary to bring all to book, since "if we twist one or two, the others will be alarmed and will settle their affairs," and that former Governors had done so. After a few weeks had elapsed, the Diarist became bold enough to tell the Governor that the latter listened to what he said, but did not do accordingly; adding that this habit "brings discredit on those who transact business and belittles your service." The Governor was very fond of money and was advised to see that the commandants of troops did not prevent the amaldars from doing their work properly, and not to pay heed to their complaints and protestations, as otherwise rents could not at all be collected. So greatly did the Diarist rise in the favour of the Governor that he was told he was looked upon as nothing less than his minister, and that no one was so intelligent and broad-minded as himself; "for which reason both M. Dupleix and M. Godeheu had favoured you, though for a while under Madame Dupleix it was not so."

The Mysoreans in the Trichinopoly Country

Nañja Raja did not recognise that the Anglo-French truce of January 1755 prohibited his committing hostilities against the English and their allies; and he even requested the French to be pleased to retire with their troops to Pondicherry, if they, like Muhammad Alī and the English, thought proper to recede from their alliance. He continued his 'blundering' endeavours to obtain possession of Trichinopoly till the middle of April. The positive injunctions of his brother, Deva Raja, then induced him to depart, on account of a very serious domestic danger.[3]

3 Nañja Raja had stated that he had discovered the determination of the French to keep Trichinopoly for themselves, if they should succeed in its capture. When he departed, he left the French in possession

The Diarist who heard from the Governor of Nañja Raja's departure, told him that Dusaussaye, who had received about 50,000 to 60,000 (Rs.) from the Dalavāi and who could have forced him to stay on, should be held responsible; that it was not Dusaussaye that had been deceived or got nothing from the Mysorean; and that "careful inquiry will prove whether he (Dusaussaye) was deceived, or whether you (De Leyrit) were deceived by that letter." (Entry for the 11th April).

The day after that on which this entry was made, news was received at Pondicherry that Hari Singh and Manoji were going over to Trichinopoly from Tanjore in order to confer with Muhammad Alī; and that Nañja Raja, who had promised to leave Thana Singh and Hyder Alī Khān at Srirangam, had left for Mysore on the night of April 8, without doing so, since Dusaussaye disapproved of the terms he had offered.

An expedition had, in the meanwhile, been undertaken under Colonel Heron into the Madura and Tinnevelly countries, to collect the dues from the poligars. In the course of his operations, Heron experienced good treatment on the part of the Marava chief of Ramnad, who offered a free passage through his country for the English troops, promised to use his interest with the other poligars, sent his brother to their help with 3,000 men and several pieces of cannon, and pressed the English to build settlements in his dominions. This caused great jealousy in the minds of the rulers of Tanjore and Pudukottai; and they

of the island of Srirangam, the revenues of which had been formally given up by Muhammad Alī to the Mysorean (Wilks, Vol. I, p. 214).

Dusaussaye had refused to join Nañja Raja in a plan for a night escalade on the Fort, and had scornfully rejected a bribe of three lakhs of rupees offered by the latter, if he should feign a quarrel, march off, and thereby leave him at liberty to pursue his designs. It was even said that Nañja Raja's next project was to surprise the French and endeavour to cut them off; and Dusaussaye had written to Major Kilpatrick, assuring him that he would attack the rear of the Mysorean if the latter should make any attempt on Trichinopoly. (Cf. R.O. Cambridge—*An Account of the War in India from* 1750 to 1760 (1761), p. 87).

strongly protested against the English treating with the Marava. In their hatred of the Marava they had even raised forces to march into his country. The fact is, Manoji, the Tanjore general, had been personally affronted by the Marava, though the ostensible reason given for the hostility was the friendship that had subsisted between the Marava and the Mysorean. The English, under these circumstances, had perforce to pacify the Tanjore Raja and the Tondaiman, and ordered Colonel Heron to break off all negotiations with the Marava[4] till he should restore all the districts that he had taken from the King of Tanjore and the Nawab.

Heron himself at this stage, had to retire in disgrace from Madura. He was tried by a court martial for misconduct, for fraudulent collusion with Mahfuz Khān, the Nawab's brother, and for the neglect of the Nawab's instructions. He reached Trichinopoly early in June, after suffering a most disgraceful defeat in the Nattam Pass at the hands of the 'Colleries' (Kaḷḷars).

While this was the situation of the English, interesting events happened in Mysore. Nañja Raja hastened, by forced marches, to the help of his brother Deva Raja, who was besieged in Seringapatam by Salābat Jang, with the help of a strong force under M. Bussy. But before Nañja Raja could reach his destination, Deva Raja had been forced to agree to pay 56 lakhs of rupees which he could make up[5] only by requisitioning the plates and the jewels of the Raja's family and of the Hindu temples in the

4 Refer to the *Records of Fort St. George, Diary and Proceedings, 1755, Military Department*: Letters of Col. Heron to the President, dated Madura 4th March, and of A. Newton, dated Tanjore, 4th March, and the Government Consultation of 26th March. (pp. 47–53).

5 Only one-third of the amount could be made up; and the balance for which the acceptance of the *gomastahs* of the *sowcars* of Sriranga-patam was given by Deva Raja, was not at all realised. "Of the unhappy hostages, some died in prison, others escaped and after a period the remainder were released." The English treaty of 1768 says that Mysore was estimated to constitute half of the Carnatic Balaghat, of Bijapur and was asked to pay the Nizām a tribute of 3½ lakhs of rupees in 1755, including darbar charges.

town, and by prevailing on the *sowcars* of the town to give their *gomastahs* as hostages for the balance that remained. On learning this, Nañja Raja halted, and discharged one-third of his army, "not without great difficulty in paying their arrears." Nañja Raja then wrote to Pondicherry, suggesting that the Governor should write to Salābat Jang and M. Bussy to the effect that the whole amount of the *peshkash* money due from Mysore had been spent on the French army, and that they should collect only the usual *peshkash* and return what had been taken in excess. (Diarist's entry for April 24).

The Diarist gives, in his entry for April 25, the copy of a letter that he had received from Nañja Raja, dated April 14, in which he pleaded that he was an ally of the French, and that a suitable letter should be written by M. Leyrit to M. Bussy "who desires to break our friendship with the French instead of preserving it so long as the sun and the moon endure." Nañja Raja also requested Ranga Pillai to explain everything to Salābat Jang. He further warned the Diarist that the English should not be trusted, and that though they had concluded an agreement with the French, the Governor should write to his commandant at Srirangam warning him to stand on his guard against their attempts.[6]

The Pondicherry authorities could only assure Nañja Raja that Bussy and his European army were paid by Salābat Jang and were under his control, and should do as *he* desired. The French Governor could not interfere, but assured Nañja Raja thus:—"As you are my ally, we have protected your fort and

6 This was due to the fact that Dusaussaye had not only rejected Nañja Raja's plan of an escalade on Trichinopoly Fort and offer of a bribe, but also communicated the whole plan to the English Commander, Major Kilpatrick. A Madras Council Consultation of April 2|13, 1755, records a letter of De Leyrit communicating the news of Nañja Raja's proposed escalade and adding that "the representations made to him on that subject by the French Commanding Officer, far from diverting him from the enterprise, had served only to breed dissensions between them and him in so much that there was some reason to apprehend that he might turn his arms against their troops."

country hitherto. Otherwise you would have lost them. I have written to M. Bussy to help you as far as possible, and I will do so again; but you should pay our money speedily."[7] The Diarist suggested that the same might be written to the English and Muhammad Alī if they should protest against Bussy's activity on the ground that it was opposed to the treaty concluded with Godeheu. He wrote that "this device would meet all cases;" and the Governor agreed with him.

After thus satisfying the invaders before Seringapatam, the brothers, Deva Raja and Nañja Raja, continued to conduct the government as before, "whose usurpation, although complete in everything essential, left to the pageant Raja 'a considerable share of the exterior appendages of royalty'." The nominal ruler who had now attained the age of 27, became impatient of the restraint put upon him, and formed a crude plan to imprison the brothers and take the power into his own hands. The plan was duly reported by spies to the brothers; and Deva Raja advised the Raja to dismiss the evil counsellors and administered a mild remonstrance; but the latter burst into indignation, and replied with puerile threats. Deva Raja was for the adoption of only mild measures for restoring the ruler to a 'proper frame of mind';

7 A letter was written later, according to the Diarist, that Bussy and Salābat Jang had already given battle to Deva Raja and were on the point of capturing the fort (of Seringapatam); but immediately after the Governor's letter reached them, they ceased the attack, and demanded the usual *peshkash;* but the enemy made a reply that even that could not be paid; then the French decided to put a boy of the royal family on the throne, who was brought and installed with the usual ceremonies, in the name of the French. "But then a letter was written to M. Bussy who explained everything to Salābat Jang and settled the matter for 52 lakhs, for the payment of which a long period was allowed. Thereupon M. Bussy returned to Hyderabad with Salābat Jang's army." Neither Wilks nor *The Mysore Gazetteer* (new edition) makes any mention of the French invaders having set up a rival Raja to spite Deva Raja. The Diarist records in his entry for May 3, 1755, the details of the battle between Deva Raja and the Mysore troops. According to the Madras Despatch of October 27, 1755, Salābat Jang was reported to have collected 33 lakhs of rupees before he departed.

but Nañja Raja moved a column of troops against the palace, forced the Raja to take his seat on the throne; and cut off the noses and ears of his partisans in his very presence, in spite of the protests of his brother. Deva Raja was so deeply offended at this open contempt of his admonitions that he resolved to have nothing more to do with his brother. He actually departed from Seringapatam in February 1757, with all his adherents and with a large body of peons, and settled at Satyamangalam; and in order to get an income, he revoked the assignments of revenue made to Haidar Alī, and ordered them to be paid to himself; and the latter had to go over to Seringapatam from his faujdari of Dindigul.[8]

The Poligar Troubles

It was rumoured at Pondicherry that Deva Raja had died, and that that was the reason of Nañja Raja's departure from Srirangam. Nañja Raja's removal of Papu Reddi, the poligar of Turaiyur, who was under the protection of Dupleix and Godeheu, caused trouble. Papu Reddi sought French help in

8 Ranga Pillai has his version of the attempt of the Mysore Raja to free himself from the thraldom of the brothers. "The Raja, his mother and the Pradhān Pandit resolved to seize and imprison Nandi Raja and re-appoint the Pradhāni, Pandit Venkatapati Ayyan who was formerly Sarvādhikāri. But Nandi Raja and his elder brother Devaraja Udaiyar, learning this were on their guard and have seized Venkatapati Ayyan, the former Pradhāni and others of his party, and resolved to keep the Raja in the palace under close custody. Nandi Raja also suggested to his daughter who was the Rani that her husband should be put to death and her son placed on the throne. She would not consent, but told her husband about her father's intentions and warned him to be on his guard. The Raja collected 4,000 faithful men, and Nandi Raja also collected 200 European deserters; but Deva Raja went to his younger brother, his son-in-law and the Raja and pacified them. But Nandi Raja seized Venkatapati Ayyan, the Pradhāni, and his people who followed him, imprisoning them, plundering their houses and seizing 6 lakhs of pagodas. Nandi Raja set guards over the royal palace on the 12th day in the dark half of Asvija, (*i.e.*, November 1, 1755). Deva Raja tried to convince Venkatapati Ayyan, his son and several others of the folly of their plot

order to get back Turaiyur[9]; and the Governor tried to keep the poligars of Ariyalur and Udayārpālayam in check, so that they might not interfere in the Turaiyur affair. The French claimed control over Udayārpālayam as it was nominally under Gingee; but its poligar was playing off Muhammad Alī against the French and had been contriving, ever since the death of Chandā Sāhib, not to pay any *peshkash* to either. All that the Governor could do was to ask M. Maissin to threaten the poligars of Ariyalur and Udayārpālayam, so that they might not unduly interfere in the French affairs. A considerable amount of arrears was due from the neighbouring taluks. Chidambaram was demanded by Nawab

and said he should have communicated the plot. Venkatapati and his wife were chained and imprisoned in Manvallidrug and his son and son-in-law in another drug; and his brother and his wife were confined in Kapaldrug; while their houses and property were given to Nandi Raja. The whole town of Seringapatam was in a serious state of alarm; and the jemadars, officials, merchants and others feared of being falsely accused and punished." (Entry for December 1, 1755).

Several months later, in his entry for 19th August, 1756, Ranga Pillai reports what he had heard from the Mysore Dalavāi's Brahman *vakil* as to what had occurred about four weeks earlier. Deva Raja and Nandi Raja had resolved to kill the Raja and place on the throne a boy of five, the Pradhāni having been imprisoned in a hill-fortress four months earlier. The Raja however induced Shabaz Khān (Haidar Nāyak's elder brother) to quit service and secretly gave 50,000 gold pieces to Kande Rao, Haidar's *mutasaddi*, to be given to them (Haidar and his brother) in order to collect troops. Knowing this, the Dalavāi brothers closed all the gates of the fort, mounted guns against the palace. There was a battle the next day, in which the Raja and his followers sallied forth, and the Dalavāi's troops retreated. Nandi Raja then fired all the guns and entered the palace. The brothers first resolved to kill the Raja, but Krishna Raja Udayar's wife clung to him, and swore that they should kill her first. After much talk, they decided to imprison the Raja, his son and his wife, and the wife of Krishna Raja Udayar, in the palace under a guard. The *vakil* of the Peishwa is said to have protested to Nandi Raja against his action, and the Raja himself sent a letter to Poona by four camel-messengers recounting what had happened.

9 According to Orme, Turaiyur was ordered to be attacked by Maissin with a force of 500 Europeans and 1,000 sepoys. Captain Caillaud who wanted to oppose him was asked by the Madras Government to desist.

Abdul Nabī Khān of Cuddapah; but his vakil was told that nothing could be definitely decided owing to the 18 months' truce between the English and the French. The fort of Chetpattu which had been taken from Mīr Āsad by Chandā Sāhib and made over to Shaikh Hasan, was given, after the capture of the latter by the English in the battle of Srirangam, into the possession of Papayya Pillai and Nizar Muhammad Khān. As there was no agreement between the two, Nāzir Muhammad, who was in charge of the *killa,* joined Muhammad Alī and the English.

Abdul Wahāb Khān, the younger brother of Muhammad Alī, had created considerable disorder in the Arcot country, of which he was in charge, and squandered away the revenues. The Madras Governor advised Muhammad Alī to settle with his family at Arcot. Accordingly, after Heron's expedition had returned to Trichinopoly, and the troops had rested for some time, the Nawab began his march north on the 9th July (20th N. S.), being escorted by 300 Europeans and 1,000 sepoys under Captain Polier. The march was made through the country of Tanjore, as the rivers were swollen with floods, and as some risk was apprehended from Maissin's troops then lying before Ariyalur. In the Tanjore country the Nawab received Manakji (Manoji) who assured him of his master being ready to serve him with 5,000 horse in the Carnatic, in spite of the Mysore general having offered him 50 lakhs of rupees for forsaking the Nawab. These protestations of friendship on the part of the Tanjoreans were declared by the Nawab to Captain Polier to be "all a lie." After halting at Fort St. David,[10] the Nawab arrived near Arcot on

Maissin had his own way at Turaiyur, deposed its poligar and reinstated his cousin and predecessor. He then proceeded against the Poligars of Ariyalur and Udaiyārpālayam, who, according to the English, had never made any submissions of fealty either to the French or to the Mysoreans. Caillaud was now ordered to march from Trichinopoly; and the English Governor threatened to send another force from Madras, if Maissin should persist. After this, De Leyrit ordered Maissin to desist.

10 The Diarist and the Governor De Leyrit both suspected that Muhammad Alī would not be going over to Arcot without some new object. (p. 356 *Diary,* Vol. IX).

August 19 (O. S.), and was, before he made his state entry into the capital, invited to pay a visit to Madras by a deputation headed by Major Lawrence. The deputation was requested by the Nawab, to announce in full darbar, that the poligars and other tributaries should submit their accounts without delay, lest they should be forced to it.

At Madras, which he visited on the 28th August (O. S.), the Nawab urgently requested military assistance in order to force the Arcot poligars to pay up their heavy arrears. It was resolved to take half the monies that might be collected and to send a force of 300 Europeans and 1,500 sepoys under Major Kilpatrick to help the Nawab. The latter objected, on the score of loss of dignity, to the transfer of the management of certain taluks to the Company, and finally agreed to give Ponneri and Pudupet which were worth about 30,000 pagodas a year.

One remarkable feature about Muhammad Alī's march to Arcot is noticed by Ranga Pillai. The troops never resorted to plunder on their way. Wherever they halted, they sent word of assurance to the amaldars that they would not plunder, nor tread down the crops, so that no complaint might afterwards be made; and "the people thereabouts are saying that they have never before seen troops march so quietly and they are astonished at it. These troops are under complete discipline." (Entry for Aug. 11, 1755). Ranga Pillai also notes the respect shown to Muhammad Alī at Madras, his stay in Louis Madeiros' garden (the present Government House garden in Mount Road), and a display of fireworks and other entertainments in his honour. Ranga Pillai also says that Muhammad Alī was to be given an allowance and desired to remain at Madras, and that he was much dejected as his amaldars had been directed not to do any act of authority without orders from the English who had sent their own people to Arcot and other places.[11] The Diarist heard at Pondicherry

11 The Fort St. George Despatch to the Secret Committee, dated October 27, 1755, says that, in order to secure for the Company a proportionate share of the rents at which the Arcot countries might be let out, the Nawab had promised to report when any countries were about to be

that Muhammad Alī had agreed to accept Rs. 240,000 from Yachama Nayak of Venkatagiri, two lakhs from the Damarla Poligar of Kalahasti, inclusive of darbar expenses, and a lakh and a half from the Raja of Karveti or Bommarajapalaiyam—all these sums having to be paid at Madras by the sowcars. Also, Murtazā Alī Khān of Vellore had agreed to pay a lakh of rupees, and supply 500 troopers and 200 horse. The killedar of Satghar had settled for Rs. 50,000. Muhammad Alī was able to collect or settle these sums, without any complaint; nobody could question his title; and on December 7, the English flag at Arcot was replaced by that of the Nawab. The Fort was named Muhammad Nur (Muhammadpur); and the Nawab himself was to be henceforth called Umdat-ul-Mulk, Siraj-ud-Daula Bahādur Dilāwar Jang (Entries for December 6th and 19th).[12] Ranga Pillai expressed a doubt whether the countries of the poligars were worth the amounts stipulated; but he admired the Nawab as "one who behaves calmly and discreetly, without precipitation," and he attributed this assurance on the part of Muhammad Alī to the fact that the

leased, so that the Company's share might be settled before the *cowle* should be given. Much of the Arcot country was leased out to the principal inhabitants of Madras who agreed to pay the greater part of the sum of 8 lakhs of rupees granted to the Company, with orders on the renters, payable half in May, and half in September (1756). The Nawab had also promised half the revenues of Madura and Tinnevelly, though he expected nothing for the time being, owing to the cost of the troops sent to punish the rebels, over and above half the tribute paid by all the poligars under him. W. Percival was to accompany the Nawab and to be present at all the transactions with the poligars or their vakils, to receive the Company's half of the tribute and to control the expenditure involved in the expedition.

12 By reason of De Leyrit's threats, Kilpatrick, who was sent to help the Nawab was ordered 'to repulse force by force'; should the French support the Arcot poligars. Before December, Kilpatrick had marched towards Bangāru Yāchama Nāyak's pālaiyam, and encamped for nearly a month outside its limits at Killenore. After the Nawab finished his business with Yāchama Nāyak, the army marched into Bommarāja-pālaiyam where it stayed for a whole month. The reduction of the minor poligars was left to the Nawab's country forces. The army returned to Arcot in January 1756.

Marathas were strong enough to establish or overthrow the Padshāh, while Salābat Jang's dominions were being overrun by the Peishwa, and Murari Rao had seized the country belonging to Coja Nāmat-ullah Khān, the subahdar of Adoni, with its dependencies and *killas.* Only part of the Hyderabad country remained in the possession of Salābat Jang; "but even there he could not keep order, for he had no money to pay the army and had to wink at much." The year 1755 ended with Muhammad Alī triumphantly and securely settled at Arcot, and his flag flying, in the place of the English flag, even over the forts of Kāveripākkam and Timiri, though he himself was prostrated by a severe illness.

One sad comment on the state of the political morality of the Europeans at Pondicherry is noted by the Diarist in his entry for December 6th, 1755. It is as follows:—"When the Europeans formerly had the renters under them, they said that they had lost 1½ lakhs of rupees . . . . . Mm. Vēry and Solominiac wrote that they had borrowed Rs. 10,000 in excess. . . . . The same is the case with other European sureties. As you are dealing with this carefully, falsehood cannot succeed, but truth will appear."[13]

The affair of the Vellore killedar was seriously taken up in the beginning of the new year. Murtazā Alī had always been perfidious in his behaviour. He had sworn on the holy *Quran,* acknowledging the right of Muhammad Alī, and offering to pay up the tribute due from him. His insincerity became obvious, when Muhammad Alī claimed the fulfilment of his promises. Indeed,

13 Dodwell remarks on this state of affairs thus:—"Ranga Pillai mentions many details in which he had no personal interest. The Second, as Sepoy Paymaster, draws for twice as many as were actually with the colours; one officer appropriates part of the Turaiyur *peshkash*; another levies a rupee on every traveller passing by Gingee; The Company's servants oblige the merchants to supply them with cloth, while the Company's Investment has still to be provided. In short, as the Diarist observes, Dupleix might have taken money for himself, but he had at least kept a sharp lookout for the misconduct of others, whereas De Leyrit suffered all to do very much as they pleased. (*Diary*: Vol. X, Introduction p. VIII).

in one place, Ranga Pillai records that Muhammad Alī fell sick after eating betel sent him by the wife of Safdar Alī Khān of Vellore, and resolved to capture that fort, " as the Vellore man had attempted to poison him." (Entry for January 24, 1756).

Kilpatrick marched on Vellore towards the end of January; but as the place was found to be very strong, it was decided not to attack it but only to intimidate the faujdar. De Leyrit at this stage, disputed the Nawab's right to Vellore, and threatened to oppose any English intervention. Letters were also written from Pondicherry to Murtazā Alī Khān that he need not pay *peshkash* to Muhammad Alī, and that, if it was demanded from him, he might reply that he was " our (French) ally," and that " we (De Leyrit) had forbidden him to pay *peshkash;*" and he was assured that troops would be sent if he were attacked. Murtazā Alī's bending the knee to Muhammad Alī was taken by the French as an indication of his general worthlessness, and the opinion was held that, " if he had only done as we told him, he might have ruled the subah of Arcot ". 300 Frenchmen and 300 sepoys were thereupon sent from Pondicherry for Vellore. It was sanguinely hoped by the Diarist that the despatch of French troops would save Murtazā Alī in Vellore, Nāzir Muhammad at Chetpattu (where he was opposed by Mīr Āsad Khān at the head of Muhammad Alī's troops), and Abdul Rahmān at Elavānāsur which was intended to be attacked by Khair-ud-dīn Khān. The English Council at Madras feared that a party of French troops might be easily admitted into the Vellore Fort, "in which case it would have been difficult ever to expel them." Fortunately for the English, discipline was none too evident among the French troops. M. Saubinet, who used to be merciless in his punishments, was stabbed to death at Gingee by his officers who resented his sternness and, even more, his jobbery. Indeed, as already remarked, peculation was rife at Pondicherry, especially among those officials who had the sepoy and cavalry management.

The English, in the meanwhile, surrounded the Vellore fort and raised batteries. Khair-ud-dīn Khān abandoned his attack on Elavānāsur, and joined his master at Arcot; and even by the middle of February, Murtazā Alī could not get any reinforcements from the French. Their troops were only encamped near Tiruvati and "plundering our own country."

Robert Orme was at this stage deputed by the Madras Government to negotiate with Murtazā Alī, and he set out on February 19 to Vellore. Already, ten days before this, the faujdar, finding that the English army remained under the walls of Vellore, in spite of De Leyrit's protest, had agreed with Kilpatrick to pay 100,000 pagodas and Rs. 25,000 for the removal of the troops, and indeed paid Rs. 20,000 as earnest money. But now, finding that he could hope to get better terms from the new English envoy, he refused, on the 22nd February, to fulfil his engagement with Kilpatrick. Orme would not interfere, and promptly left for Arcot. Murtazā Alī, however, would not treat with anyone but Orme. The latter had perforce to come back to Vellore, and hold a conference with its faujdar. Early in March, Orme returned to Madras; while Kilpatrick, after some time spent before Vellore, marched to Arcot, as the Presidency considered it better to await another opportunity, rather than relax their demands on Murtazā Alī. During all this parley, a body of 700 French soldiers and 1,500 sepoys lay between Chetpattu and Gingee, some forty miles from Vellore.

The Marathas and Murari Rao on the Scene

The Diarist reports that Kilpatrick, who was before the Vellore Fort, was subsequently reinforced by troops under Sayyid Yūsuf and Muhammad Abrār Khān; and he demanded four lakhs of rupees from Murtazā Alī. Thereupon Murtazā sent word to Madras; and Mr. Orme was sent as envoy. He first conferred with Muhammad Alī at Arcot, and then with Murtazā Alī in the Vellore fort, and returned with presents to Madras; and Governor Saunders was in a position to write to Kilpatrick asking him to withdraw his troops and proceed to Arcot, as the Vellore affair had been settled for two lakhs or a lakh and a half (entry for March 2, 1756).

Muhammad Alī thereupon arranged to occupy the Tuttippattu and Agaram pargannahs, dependent on Vellore and sent some troops to Padaivīdu and Mūlakkādu. He even planned to send the newly entertained horse and foot to Madura and Tinnevelly. News of the English capture of Gheriah reached Arcot at this time; and 60 guns were fired by the fort and the army as a token of joy. De Leyrit suspected the Diarist, on the report of his enemies, of helping Muhammad Alī with news from Pondicherry.[14] The troops despatched to the help of Murtazā Alī Khān, returned at the end of March from Chetpattu, beyond which they had not proceeded. Meanwhile, things did not improve for Murtazā Alī; and he wrote to the Peishwa for the contingent of 10,000 horse which he had promised in return for their daily pay. Balaji Rao was now reported to have made peace with Salābat Jang and despatched his cousin, Sadasiva Rao, with 30,000 horse and artillery towards Savanur and Bankapur (February, 1756). Balaji Rao had also started on an expedition into Mysore in 1754-55, in the course of which he extorted one-fourth of the revenue either in cash or in bills from every village through which his army passed, and further stormed the fortress of Hole Honnur on the Bhadra river. Joining Salābat Jang's army beneath the walls of Seringapatam, Balaji demanded a vast sum from Mysore as arrears of tribute due to him. It was now that M. Bussy obtained an audience of the Peishwa, on behalf of both the Nizam and the Dalavāi, and won his good opinion. The Maratha ruler was deeply impressed by "de Bussy's bearing, his studied courtesy, his unruffled temper, and above all, by his vast capacity for military and civil affairs[15]"; and he was persuaded that it was useless to make further demands on Mysore. The Peishwa thereupon withdrew his army from Seringapatam, but he overran Jamkhandi, and fought a series of actions at Harihar, Bagalkot,

14 The Diarist openly complained to the Governor that Mm. Du-Basset, Delarche and Moraein had joined together to bring heavy and unfounded charges against him.

15 Kincaid and Parasnis—*A History of the Maratha People;* Vol. III p. 34.

and other places (1755). At the same time, Mahadji Purandare plundered Bednur; but he quarrelled with Muzaffar Khān, the commandant of the Maratha artillery, who had been trained under the French; and the latter left the Peishwa's service, and entered that of the Pathan Nawab of Savanur. The refusal by the Nawab to comply with the Peishwa's demand for the surrender of Muzaffar Khān led to the formation of a league between Murari Rao Ghorepade (who would not acknowledge the Peishwa) and the Pathan Nawabs of Savanur, Cuddapah and Kurnool, and of a counter-league between the Peishwa and the Nizām. A powerful expedition was despatched by the latter against Savanur. The Peishwa himself met the Pathan Nawabs and Murari Rao near Savanur, and drove them, after inflicting a severe defeat, to take shelter in its fort. Salābat Jang and Bussy soon arrived at the place, and a regular siege began: Bussy's artillery poured, it was said, more than 250,000 shells into the fort; and the tremendous effect of the cannon has "passed into legend." Murari Rao now deserted to the Peishwa; and the Nawab of Savanur submitted. He surrendered Muzaffar Khān to the Peishwa, and further gave an indemnity of 11 lakhs and the districts of Belgaum, Sholapur and Hubli (May, 1756).

In the course of the siege Murari Rao had given to Bussy a bond which had been executed in his favour by the Pondicherry Government and which had not been redeemed; and Bussy had spoken of it to both the Peishwa and the Nizām on behalf of Murari Rao. The matter was reported to the Peishwa, and he communicated it to Shāh Nawāz Khān. The latter had been thirsting for an opportunity to alienate the Nizām from Bussy; and he now painted his action in the blackest colours, asserting in fact that Bussy had received a rich bribe from Murari Rao. This was the beginning of the great rupture between Bussy and Salābat Jang.[16]

16 See Letters No. 115, dated 3-7-1756 containing a report of Muzaffar Khān's movements, No. 116 indicating negotiations with Murari Rao Ghorepade to whom Amrit Rao was specially deputed as conciliator; No. 121, dated 8-2-1756 giving the news of the investment of Savanur;

The Diarist reported on January 25, 1756, that a battle had been fought between Murari Rao and the Peishwa's younger brother on the banks of the Krishna. Later, he gives us the news that the crafty and jealous Tāra Bai, whose inveterate hatred of the Peishwa had not abated a jot, had written to Murari Rao that she would send 30,000 horse and a sum of 30 or 40 lakhs, if he would seize the Nana (the Peishwa) by treachery in battle, and that he had replied asking for the despatch of the troops (entry for February 20th, 1756). Murari, the Diarist continues, was subsequently encamped near Savanur with 12,000 horse, 8,000 foot and 10,000 followers (*stomam*), and fought a hard battle with the Peishwa who had crossed the Tungabhadra. He then refers to Balaji Rao's besieging Savanur which was garrisoned by Murari Rao's forces. Murari Rao, we are told, was in great straits from a scarcity of provisions; and the Peishwa sent word at the same time to the Nawab of Savanur that, unless he delivered up Murari Rao and his sardars, he would destroy the fort, (entry for 2nd March, 1756). By the end of March, the Diarist had heard that Balaji Rao and Salābat Jang had combined, that the Savanur affair had been settled, and that both had marched their armies in two stages towards Mysore, which greatly troubled the Pathans of Cuddapah and other places, and also disconcerted the mind of Muhammad Alī, who thereupon resolved to send two envoys to discuss matters with them. The Diarist had heard echoes of the severity of the French shelling of Savanur fort, and he also noted the gossip, of course false, to the effect that Murari Rao, Muzaffar Khān and others had been killed, that Bussy had been wounded, and that the Rao and the Khān had been chained together by the Peishwa.

and *No.* 129, detailing that the Peishwa had besieged Bagalkot and Murari Rao, Muzaffar Khān and the Nawab of Savanur were preparing to oppose him. (G. S. Sardesai—'*Selections from the Peshwa Daftar*, No. 28.—*Peshwa Balaji Rao, Karnatak Affairs* 1740–1761).

Affairs in the Madura Country

Colonel Heron's troops, accompanying the Nawab's forces, set out from Trichinopoly about the middle of February. At Manapar, where the Nawab desired to stay till the tributes of the four principal poligars of the neighbourhood should be paid, it was resolved to attack the Poligar 'Lachenaig'; and in the attempt to overcome the barriers raised by him to cover the advance to his principal town, some serious loss of troops occurred. After this, the Nawab returned to Trichinopoly; and the troops proceeded to Madura[17] together with Mahfuz Khān. The gates of Madura were thrown open to them without any resistance and apparently without any treachery. A deputation from the Setupati awaited them; and Colonel Heron entered into an alliance with the Marava chief upon his own responsibility. Mayana, who had been appointed by Ālam Khān as the governor of Madura, had fled to Koilkudi, a few miles off to the west, and entrenched himself in the strongly built pagoda of Tirumbur. The temple was therefore stormed, notwithstanding the inefficiency of the sepoys; and what was worse, Heron and Muhammad Yusuf, the captain of the sepoys, burnt down the gates with fire, and allowed the troops to plunder the pagoda and carry off a large number of idols which were very sacred to the Kallars of the neighbourhood.[18]

Leaving a garrison of Europeans and sepoys in Madura, Col. Heron moved off to Tinnevelly in the end of March 1756. From the latter place, he sent two parties under Captains Lee and Beaver to compel the poligars to settle their accounts; and they did it with very little loss. Kattabomma Nayak, the most considerable of these, however, was attacked by one of the

17 For an account of the situation at Madurá see the writer's note No. 13 in Ch. XIV on pp. 285–8, above.

18 According to Orme, the people of the country held the troops in utter detestation for this exploit; Nelson writes of it thus:—"It is observable that, contemptible as was the value of the plundered articles, this circumstance is the only one recorded in the Record Office Ms. in connection with Mak'hphuz Khān's stay in Madura." (*The Madura Country, A Manual;* Part III, p. 274).

detachments; and the fort of Nellikota was stormed by another. Meanwhile, the Marava chief of Ramnad, who had offered and even despatched 5,000 men under the command of his brother, to assist Heron in the reduction of the poligars of the Tinnevelly country, was thrown away by Heron who had received strict orders from the Presidency to break off all connection with him, as the King of Tanjore and the Tondaiman of Pudukottai strongly declared that they could place no reliance on the friendship of the English if the latter should ally themselves with their mortal enemies, the Maravas. The revenues of the expedition were not equal to the expenditure on the army. Mahfuz Khān embezzled a portion of the tributes realised; and Colonel Heron received with avidity presents from those who had accounts to settle. Mahfuz Khān and Heron's interpreter colluded together to make the condition of the country appear less advantageous than it really was, and as the result of it Heron persuaded himself into giving Mahfuz Khān the charge of the Madura and Tinnevelly countries for a yearly rental of Rs. 1,500,000.[19]

After returning to Madura, Heron moved off towards the Nattam Pass, where he suffered a disgraceful defeat at the hands of the Kallars and lost a considerable part of his baggage. At the town of Nattam he was joined by a detachment from Trichinopoly; and Mahfuz Khān returned to Madura. Heron eventually reached Trichinopoly on the 16th of June.

An inquiry was held into Heron's conduct; and he was suspended from his seat in the Council; but he applied for a court martial. Mahfuz Khān placed Barkat-ullah in charge of Madura, where a fakir planted a small mosque on the top of the unfinished Rāyagopura, and would not remove it in spite of the entreaties and remonstrances of the people.

Ranga Pillai records in his *Diary* an agreement said to have been arranged by the English with Muhammad Alī, on the latter's visit to Madras, to the effect that the Nawab was to bear the cost

19 For a clear and full account of Heron's doings see Orme (4th Edn.) Vol. I, pp. 380-395; and R. O. Cambridge, *An Account of the War in India*, pp. 83–86.

of the establishment at Trichinopoly, that the Poligars' *peshkash* was to be given to the English, and that Mahfuz Khān was to be recalled by 'proper persons.' In the meanwhile, Mahfuz Khān could not make full headway against the rebels. According to the Nawab's understanding with the English, the latter were to get half the revenues of Madura and Tinnevelly. Mahfuz delayed payment of the balance of Rs. 121,000 due from him under the pretext of his heavy expenses in defending the country against the poligars, and later on contended that he required the Nawab's authority for the payment. Titarappa Mudali, a Tinnevelly merchant, was prepared, at this stage, to rent the country for 12 lakhs of rupees; but the Nawab doubted his capacity to collect the revenues in so turbulent a region; and the Madras Council invited that person to go to Madras to explain his plan.

De Leyrit had remonstrated that the southern expedition of Heron was in itself a breach of the truce with M. Godeheu, and that the southern districts belonged to themselves in virtue of various rights derived from Chandā Sāhib and the Mysore Dalavāi. The English answered these remonstrances with "arguments equally specious;" and De Leyrit did not think it worth while to interrupt the expedition at the risk of renewing the war.

CHAPTER XVI

BUSSY AT HYDERABAD AND OTHER MATTERS

PROPOSAL TO HELP THE DANES AT TRANQUEBAR

ABOUT the end of June 1756, there was a change of Governors at Fort St. David, Mr. Clive taking charge from Mr. Starke who visited Pondicherry on his way to Madras. He was received with considerable, but punctilious, ceremony. The Pondicherry Council resolved to send help to Tranquebar as the Danes had quarrelled with the Raja of Tanjore, and to despatch a ship with 400 sepoys and 250 soldiers. When the English came to know of this, they remonstrated that no such help should be given, that the Tanjoreans and the Tranquebar people should be left to themselves and that if reinforcements should be sent, they would intercept the ship conveying the soldiers and prevent her from proceeding; and the French Governor felt that, in view of the prevalence of the 18 months' truce, he should not ignore the remonstrance. The ship did not proceed, but letters were sent by land to Karikal and Chidambaram with orders for the despatch of soldiers and sepoys to Tranquebar; and even these letters were later on countermanded.[1] Ranga Pillai writes of a letter to the Raja of Tanjore, saying that, according to the terms sent home,

1 Governor Pigot and the Madras Council wrote on the 4th July 1756, to President Krog and the gentlemen of the Council of Fort Dansborg at Tranquebar, offering to settle the difference between them and the Raja of Tanjore and advising avoidance of the commencement of hostilities, "considering the tranquillity which at present subsists in this country, we think it would have been more eligible to have tried first the way of accommodation, and as there are the strongest ties of friendship between our two Nations, and we are also in strict alliance with the King of Tanjore, you might have availed yourselves of our good offices which you might have been persuaded we should most readily have employed." *Records of Fort St. George.' Diary and Consultation Book, Military Department*, 1756—p. 214. See also letter of the same date to the King of Tanjore (175 of *Country Correspondence*) and a letter to M. De Leyrit as entered in the *French Correspondence*, No. 39.

help might be afforded to the Tranquebar people if attacked, and therefore troops were being sent and that if the Raja desired peace with them and wrote to that effect, peace would be concluded. Already, early in June, news was received of the British Government's orders to seize French vessels and of the probability of war breaking out; and the Madras Council desired Admiral Watson to prevent troopships from reaching Pondicherry; while it was reported that the French Company had despatched 11 ships with 3,000 men to India. Clive, writing from Fort St. David, on the 2nd July, gave out his opinion on the matter in the following words:—"I cannot take upon me to give any advice upon so nice a subject, on the one side our acquiescence (in French help to the Danes being permitted) may sink us in the opinion of the people of the country; on the other, it may serve to strengthen our alliance with the King of Tanjore on which much will depend in case of a rupture between the two Nations; . . . It seems to me odd, that the Governor of Tranquebar should not apply to the English for their mediation."[2]

De Leyrit's first attitude towards the situation was that the alliance subsisting between the French and the Danes did not permit him to refuse the succour which they demanded and that he

The Tranquebar Council wrote to Madras, even on the 4th of July, that they had asked for assistance and succour from the Frenchmen "as the most nearest European nation seated unto us here, for so much the better to defend us against the said King (of Tanjore)" and that they announced this to the English as friends and allies in Europe "to the end that you not at all in the least manner will assist these Heathens against us being a Christian nation, but rather adjuvate us to forward our righteous weapons against this inhuman people."

Clive wrote from Fort St. David on the 6th July that the French design of sending a reinforcement to Tranquebar was entirely dropped, but that Law and five other officers had embarked with 150 soldiers for Masulipatam.

2 Letter addressed to Governor Pigot and members of the Select Committee at Madras—See Forrest: *Madras and Bengal Papers 1688—1758*—Vol. II—Chronological List of Clive's autograph letters, May 1756 to March 1757—No. 3.

would not lose "a moment of time" in despatching a ship with soldiers and sepoys. He concluded that he only thought it proper to give this advice to Mr. Watson.

The Committee at Fort St. George feared that they could not have any pretence for desiring the Admiral to stop the French ship as De Leyrit had given public notice to Watson; but they suspected that the French would seize the opportunity to form for themselves some new establishments at the expense of the ruler of Tanjore; and they saw "no method of endeavouring to prevent this so eligible as the using our interposition to put a stop, if possible, to hostilities, by recommending to both parties to enter upon an amicable accommodation of their dispute and to render the assistance of the French to Tranquebar unnecessary." (Military Consultation of 4th July, 1756.)

Dismissal of Bussy by Salabat Jang

On July 14, the Diarist heard that three men-of-war had arrived in Madras and that orders had been given to prohibit the despatch of goods and letters to Pondicherry. Also, Mr. Wynch was to be sent to Fort St. David as the Second in Council, while Captain Clive was to march to Trichinopoly and other places as commissary for war and was only waiting for formal orders from Europe. Twelve French ships, including four of the King's, were believed to be on their way to India, while it was rumoured that twenty men-of-war which had been sent out, were lying, ten in one place and ten in another. It was feared that Salābat Jang would be on the English side on account of his dispute with Bussy; and the English anticipated grants of country "like the man who had a vessel of flour." Salābat Jang's letter to the English asking for assistance was received at Madras on June 14th; then Bussy had been dismissed. As his alliance would bring the English all the desired advantages, the Madras Committee accepted the offer at once and began to make preparations for the despatch of troops to him. But on July 13, news came of the loss of Kasimbazar and of the threatened danger to Calcutta from Nawab Sirāju'd daulā. Nevertheless, on a fresh application from Salābat Jang, the

Madras Council resolved to persist in sending the Deccan expedition; but when the preparations had been completed, alarming news was received on the 3rd of August about the imminence of the fall of Calcutta and the desperate plight of the English in Bengal, on which it was resolved to send to Bengal the reinforcements and to suspend the Golconda expedition.

The Diarist wrote in his entry for July 15, 1756, that when Bussy and Salābat Jang disagreed, the former went in May to Hyderabad in great anger, and there he fell out with its killedar, slew him, plundered the whole city and even despoiled the houses of the merchants and seized the fort. Thereupon Balaji Rao's horse, Janoji Nimbalakar, Raja Chandrasen's son and Malhar Rao Holkar's troops, consisting of 20,000 horse, surrounded M. Bussy and his army and gave battle; and Salābat Jang himself who was four days' journey on the way, also surrounded him. This news was reported in a letter written in Persian and dated at Golconda, 4th of Shawwal, *i.e.* 3rd July (N.S.)[3] Bussy was encamped at Kolemahal, near Hyderabad with his 2,000 soldiers and 8,000 infantry; Rummī Khān, vakil, was sent to Ibrāhīm Alī Khān, *gomastah* of Zāfar Alī Khān of Hyderabad; after some discussion, on June 28, they quarrelled and Rummī Khān was killed by Ibrāhīm Alī Khān. Some of the inhabitants fled with their property; but others were seized and plundered. When Salābat Jang heard of this, he marched to Hyderabad with his army and 20,000 Maratha horse; and Bussy's people were being killed as they came out of the city.

On July 16, the Diarist wrote[4] that the Governor's face fell as he read the letters received from Bussy at Golconda and

3. The Peishwa was informed, by letter, by Nilo Narsinha, of the removal of Muzaffar Khān from the service of the Nizām and of the differences that had arisen between the Nizām and Ramachandra Rao Jadhav. This letter was dated 24-3-1756 (?). And the next letter (No. 166—*Selections from the Peshwa Daftar; No. 25—Balaji Baji Rao Peishwa and the Nizam*, 1740-1761), dated 4-4-1756, tells us that the Peishwa's agent wrote from Bijapur of the differences that had arisen between Salābat Jang and his French supporters.

4 Salābat Jang took the field against Savanur—Bankapur (lying about 30 miles to the north-west of Hampe—Vijayanagara) in February

suspected that they brought news of disturbances, while information had come already that Ellore, Rajahmundry, Chicacole, Mustaphanagar and other places had been seized. The next day a Mughal mansabdar from Salābat Jang reached Pondicherry, bringing letters ordering De Leyrit that Nawab Muhammad Alī should be put in possession of the Carnatic subah and that all moneys due should be paid to him. The envoy was not received with the courtesy due to his position. It was only on the following day that the Diarist heard the news of the expulsion of the English from Calcutta and the occupation of that place by the Nawab of Bengal, the Diarist writing down the name of Alī Vardi Khān as the Nawab, being probably ignorant of the succession of Sirāj-ud-Daula.

1756; it had been arranged by the Diwan, Shāh Nawāz Khān, that Balaji Rao Peishwa should march from Poona, about the same time, to punish Murari Rao whose territory adjoined the country of Savanur—Bankapur on the east. Both the armies met and agreed to assist each other in the reduction of their disobedient vassals, beginning with Savanur which was now reinforced by Murari Rao with a large body of Marathas headed by himself. Murari Rao now offered to Bussy to relinquish his claim upon the French Company for which the Government of Pondicherry had given him a bond, if the French general would effect his reconciliation with Balaji Rao upon moderate terms. Negotiations were conducted by Bussy; and Shāh Nawāz Khān secretly rejoiced at this new turn. Both the Nawab of Savanur and Murari Rao submitted to their respective superiors; and Murari Rao gave up to Bussy the bond of the French Company. Now, Shāh Nawāz Khān represented to Salābat Jang that Bussy preferred the interests of the French Company with Murari Rao to those of the Nizām with his vassals; and the French had never supplied any money to him from the province of Arcot although it was now five years since they had been entrusted with its administration; while Muhammad Alī was soliciting the same patents for himself, proferring an annual tribute of 32 lakhs of rupees and an immediate present of 12 lakhs, as soon as he should receive the patents. There was probably no truth in the alleged offers of Muhammad Alī; but Bussy believed them. Jāfar Alī Khān who had been deprived of the rule of Rajahmundry, because it was ceded to the French Company, was very hostile to Bussy and the French party. He had accompanied the army of Salābat Jang and now persuaded him that if he would remove the French troops from

On the 20th July, 640 soldiers and 200 sepoys were sent under Saubinet aboard a ship to Masulipatam on their way to join Bussy who was said to be surrounded in Hyderabad fort by Maratha horse and by the army of Salābat Jang. The Diarist also recorded in his entry for that day that the English had sent 4 ships with 900 soldiers and some sepoys against the Nawab of Bengal, though it was also rumoured that those troops had been destined for Hyderabad to help Salābat Jang. The history of the plan for an alliance with the Marathas and of the abandonment of the scheme to send an English expedition to the Deccan is given as an appendix to this chapter.

Bussy's Stand at Hyderabad

The Diarist plaintively wrote that the times were out of joint, that the Maratha troubles and the last ten years' plunder had ruined the country, the land lay uncultivated and the people had

his service, their place would be immediately supplied by an equal body of the English with whom he had been keeping up a correspondence.

Shāh Nawāz Khān communicated the designs of his party to Balaji Rao and even suggested to him that Bussy could be removed, in the easiest manner, by assassination. Balaji Rao rejected this proposal with disdain and also refused to open hostilities against the French troops. He had an idea of attaching Bussy to his own service, if the quarrel between him and Salābat Jang should become irreconcilable. Shāh Nawāz Khān ordered Bussy to retire, with his troops, out of the Nizām's territories without delay, promising not to molest them in their retreat if they should avoid all hostilities. Bussy moved out some distance from Salābat Jang's camp, giving out that he intended to proceed to Masulipatam and despatched letters to Pondicherry asking them to send all available troops to that place, while Salābat Jang despatched letters and an agent to the English Presidency requesting a body of troops to assist in expelling the French out of his dominions; and his letter was received at Madras on the 14th of June. Balaji Rao had proposed to Bussy, immediately after his separation from Salābat Jang, that the French troops should act as auxiliaries to the Marathas on the same terms as had been granted by the Nizām. Bussy declined the offer, stating that he depended on orders from Pondicherry. Nevertheless, Balaji detached a body of 6,000 horse under the command of Malhar Rao Holkar with orders to accompany Bussy till the latter should be free from pursuit or

been scattered. Labour was very scarce and what little cultivation there was, was hindered by the interference of the commandants so that the amaldars, in spite of their troops, could not manage the country nor collect anything either by kind words or threats or force or fine or any other punishment. The amaldars took leases on the security of substantial Europeans; and these latter took the money and very often did not pay the amounts they had guaranteed, but "also mismanaged affairs, misappropriated the collections and allowed their people to do the same." The injustice done by the commandants and Europeans had become marked since De Leyrit became the Governor; and so, neither town nor country prospered. With his usual mind, the Diarist explained that it was no use blaming the Governor for all the misfortunes which were caused by the bad stars; but from the middle of August, prosperity would revive and the Governor and himself would acquire glory and understanding.

molestation by the Nizām. After 8 days Bussy dismissed the Maratha troops; then Jāfar Alī Khān came in hot pursuit of the French, with 25,000 men, horse and foot; and the French were troubled by a poligar near the bank of the Krishna which they were able to ford; while Jāfar Alī Khān was prevented from pursuit by floods in the river. Bussy now turned to Hyderabad outside whose walls he encamped, hoping to get provisions and money therein. The city-bankers were quieted by his assurances that no violence was intended and lent him money on his own credit, with which he paid off his sepoys. They clamoured for more and began to desert in large numbers. Some of Bussy's bullocks were attacked and taken by the troops of the district, whereupon he sent Rummī Khān to the governor of the city for demanding their restoration on compensation. Hot words passed between them; and the governor, Ibrāhīm Alī who was nephew and son-in-law to Jāfar Alī Khān, was fatally stabbed by Rummī Khān who was also killed. This incident did not seem to have created a panic in the city. Just then, 12,000 Maratha horsemen who were in Salābat Jang's service, appeared on the scene and ordered Bussy to surrender all his artillery, except 6 guns that he had brought from Pondicherry and to give up all his Mughal dignities. Bussy refused and held that he had these dignities from the Mughal Emperor and not from Salābat Jang. These events took place between the 14th and 27th of June 1756.

On August 16 (N.S.) news was received at Pondicherry that war had been declared between England and France on February 23 and that even before the declaration the captain of the King's squadron had left France with 12 men-of-war. There was also conveyed at the same time news of the rumoured return of Dupleix with a few ships, which the Europeans at Pondicherry could not believe.

Law and Saubinet had to halt at Bezwada as their route to Golconda to relieve Bussy was obstructed, due to heavy rains. Murari Rao's vakil brought a letter to Pondicherry from his master which said that Balaji Rao had been seeking to trouble Bussy and obliging him to depart, in order that he might join the English and make Salābat Jang do as he desired. When Salābat Jang attacked Savanur, he communicated to Bussy the whole matter which, however, the latter did not believe. The Carnatic subah had been confirmed in the name of Muhammad Ali, besides the promise of the Ellore, Rajahmundry and Chicacole countries on condition of English help being rendered to Salābat Jang. Murari offered to help the French, though Salābat Jang had requested him to send help against Bussy and he had, in response, sent Muzaffar Khān and a small army.

On September 3, news of what happened at Hyderabad 15 days back, reached Pondicherry. This was to the effect that Law was asked by Bussy to march towards Bhongir and drive away Salābat Jang's forces sent thither to seize the treasures of Bussy and Haidar Jang lodged there; Law put the enemy troops to flight and also inflicted severe losses on Muzaffar Khān, Munawar Khān and others who attacked him. He then joined Bussy with 300 Europeans, 2 guns and the few sepoys that remained. After this Salābat Jang opened negotiations with Bussy; and Muhammad Alī who had been joyfully collecting forces to send to Salābat Jang became downcast and depressed.[5]

5 Law had set out from Masulipatam, at the head of 160 Europeans, 700 sepoys and 5 guns on July 16. When he was detained at Bezwada by heavy rains, he was joined by another body of troops despatched from Pondicherry. At the head of the combined forces, Law reached

News had reached Pondicherry by September 5, of the reconciliation of Salābat Jang with Bussy and Law. Bussy was received by Salābat Jang with all honours; and it was decided that both parties should be at peace and that Chicacole, Rajahmundry, and other districts and the Carnatic *subah* given in jaghir for the expenses of the establishment, should be continued as before. Each party should continue in possession of the countries they actually held; and Bussy was not to interfere in the management or *peshkash* and he must confine himself to his cavalry and military and his countries. This reconciliation took

Megnapara, about 50 miles from Hyderabad on the 10th of August. Salābat Jang who had reached Hyderabad on August 1st, preferred to attack Law's relieving column to the more showy plan of making an assault on Bussy's entrenched position in Char Mahal on which Muzaffar Khān proposed an assault. Muzaffar Khān induced a number of sepoys in Bussy's camp to desert him. Bussy had kept up a secret understanding with Janoji Nimbalakar and Ramachandra Jadhav, two Maratha chieftains in the service of Salābat Jang, and arranged with them, that, in the projected attack on Law, they should only feign to take a part and hang out distinctive banners to indicate to the French captain that he had nothing to fear from them. Intimation of this understanding was duly sent to Law. Law's running fight with the enemy's troops from the 11th to the 15th August, through the hilly country up to Hayatnagar and Bussy's beating up Salābat Jang's camp with one part of his forces and sending the other to help Law to join him; and the victorious entry of Law into Hyderabad on the next morning—these were followed by Salābat Jang's offer of peace and by the formal reinstatement of Bussy on August 20, in all his previous dignities, titles and honours. The skill and gallantry of D'Arambure in this fight are greatly praised by Colonel Malleson. This exploit of Bussy, and Law "rather resembles Clive's successes at Plassey than any more stubbornly contested victory." There was little hard fighting. The English vakil, Vasudeva Pandit, writing from Salābat Jang's camp, August 17, 1756, says that the Maratha sardars, Janoji, Lakshman Cadagula and Bala Rao, attacked Law all along the road, till they arrived at the village of Singavarem within 10 cosses of Golconda. At that place there was fought a smart engagement. At length Law finding himself in great distress, bribed Janoji's son with 10,000 pagodas and by that means entered safe into the city. (p. 151—*Records of Fort St. George, Country Correspondence, Military Department*, 1756).

place on August 22nd and presents were given on August 23rd.[6] There were held at Pondicherry a thanksgiving service and a grand banquet in honour of Bussy's triumph.

The Diarist describes, under his entry for September 22, 1756, the contents of a letter written by Salābat Jang before the reconciliation was effected, with a complaint against Bussy. The letter was actually handed to the Governor on the above date when it had become superfluous and useless. It runs as follows:— "Long ago, when Muzaffar Jang left Pondicherry, Dupleix sent Bussy with him with an army on condition of his paying 1½ lakhs of rupees a month. I continued to pay this sum accordingly. When news came that Ghāzī-ud-dīn Khān was marching to attack me, I ordered Bussy to collect forces and promised to pay him two lakhs of rupees per month. Bussy had conducted himself to my entire satisfaction; therefore I managed all affairs by his advice as the chief man. While at Masulipatam, he wanted that country to be assigned for his pay. As the treasury was low, I assigned to him the five mahals of Chicacole, Rajahmundry, Ellore, Murtazanagar, etc., yielding a revenue of 32 lakhs of rupees a year. Thereafter he asked me to give him Mustaphanagar on condition of his paying its value. I gave him this place, accordingly, yielding a revenue of 7½ lakhs. When four years elapsed, he wanted it to be granted to him for thirty years. Although this large sum was due from M. Bussy, yet I took no notice of it considering his good conduct and services. But after Coja Qalandar Khān's son had joined him, he no longer treated me with his former respect, but assumed state and spoke as though I was his inferior. Even then I passed over his language and showed him due respect. When I was halting at Golconda,

6 Orme says that the reconciliation took place on the 20th. Bussy could not get the surrender to him of Muzaffar Khān and of the late deserter Mahmud Khān, nor the removal from office of Shāh Nawāz Khān. Jāfar Alī Khān came to Bussy and made his submission, and Janoji Nimbalakar delivered back the Arabs and the Abyssinians whom he had shut up in Golkonda. Bussy contrived to capture Mahmud Khān. Muzaffar Khān subsequently entered the service of the Peishwa and was put to death for a conspiracy.

he posted guards to seize me, and coming to me said, "you are too poor-spirited to be fit to be my master". I replied to him calmly in spite of this insult, but as I learnt that he intended to seize me by treachery, I strengthened myself, and having passed Savanur and Bankapuram without violence, I induced him to depart and gave him his dismissal. I have also ordered the country assigned to him for his pay to be resumed. In future I shall write to you when I stand in need of your help. Please write recalling your people in my country."

The Nawab of Cuddapah, in a letter that was received at Madras on the 1st of October, said that he had designed to go to Salābat Jang's relief, but he heard when he reached his headquarters that Bussy, "with submission and obedience and with his hands tied, waited upon His Excellency (Salābat Jang), and obtained his gracious pardon," for which reason he deferred the march—a very curious, but effective way, as diplomacy then stood, for gaining the English good will.

Account of the Palace Revolution in Mysore (1756)

Krishnappan, the Mysore Dalavāi's Brahman *vakil*, told the Diarist of the occurrences in *Adi*, in the beginning of August, 1756, between the Raja of Mysore and Nañja Raja, the *Sarvādhikāri* of the *Dalavāi*, Devaraja. Both these rose against Chikka Krishnaraja Udayar II (1734–66 A.D.) as he whom they got married and installed on the throne, hearkened to evil advisers and sought to imprison or destroy them and appoint others in their place. They resolved to kill him and place on the throne, a boy of five, born of Nañja Raja's daughter. Venkatapathi Ayyan, the *pradhani*, who had ill-advised the Raja, had been seized four months' back and imprisoned in a hill fortress; now they had the royal palace surrounded by their own troops. But the Raja induced Shabaz Khān, the elder brother of Haidar Nayak, and secretly gave 50,000 gold pieces to Kande Rao, Haidar's *mutasaddi*, to be given to the Muslim brothers, in order to collect troops and men with whom to attack the fort next day. Knowing this the rebel brothers had the gates closed, the fort surrounded with their own troops, Europeans and *topasses* who had been hired at Trichinopoly and guns mounted on the walls facing the palace. Then, on the next morning, the Raja and his men, a thousand in all, sallied forth with drawn swords and a battle ensued in which 500 fell on either side. Nañja Raja's own troops retreated and the Raja withdrew to his palace. Nañja Raja then fired all the guns mounted on the walls, slaying men, women and female servants and others, a hundred in all; and then he and his brother entered the palace and ordered all the Raja's people who survived to be imprisoned. They resolved also to kill the Raja, but the wife of (Dodda) Krishna Raja Udayar clung to him and vowed that they should kill her first. After much talk they decided to imprison the Raja, his wife and child and this woman under a close guard. The Peishwa's vakil remonstrated to Nañja Raja against this action. Thereupon Nañja Raja sent his men to bring the Raja out of the fort; and immediately afterwards the Raja sent a letter to the Peishwa by four camel messengers reporting what had happened. The fort[7] was afterwards very closely guarded.

MISCELLANEOUS MATTERS TO THE END OF FEBRUARY, 1757

Madame Barthelemy, in the course of a conversation with the Diarist, describing the contents of a letter of M. Rich, late Governor of Karikal, said that Dupleix had not yet visited the King or his Ministers, his goods and property had been removed to the Company's godown and that he had been confined to his

7 Wilks mentions of a conspiracy whose aim was to persuade the wife of the Raja, who was then *enceinte*, to remove her husband by poison. But both the lady and Deva Raja would have nothing to do with such a plan. Deva Raja and Nañja Raja were entirely disagreed with regard to the measures to be pursued towards the Raja. Nañja Raja was instigated by Viranna, his second in command, who had "the reputation of instigating upon all occasions the violent proceedings of his principal" Nañja Raja barricaded all the avenues to the palace and lined the walls with troops. A parley was rejected; and a heavy fire

house and he was worse off in Paris than an Indian coolie. She also said that affairs in Pondicherry were being ruined, because De Leyrit could not control the Europeans. Dupleix, however, according to another account, seems to have written to his attorney, Du Bausset, and to De Larche directing them to pay his creditors out of the revenue of his Vaḷudāvur jaghir which was estimated by Godeheu to be about Rs. 125,000 a year. Three copies of the accounts were to be prepared by Du Bausset who was planning to send them to Europe by three different ships.

An important but casually noticed fact has some interest. One day in October, when the Diarist went into the sorting godown, he found that only cloth for the Europeans was being baled; while one remarked that if Europeans made the merchants under them get them cloth, the Company could not expect to make a profit or get good cloth. M. Barthelemy who was of the Company present, added that things had begun to go wrong under Dupleix, and now, under De Leyrit, they had been completely spoilt.

The French at Pondicherry, began to press Nañja Raja for the moneys due from him, so that the Raja of Mysore might think that "as we are pressing Nandi Raja, we may help to bring him into subjection on condition of securing what is due to us or such sum as he had offered to the Nana." The Diarist told the Governor that the Raja desired French assistance to overthrow his rebellious *Sarvādhikāri* and that if letters and men be sent now, he thought that French affairs would prosper.

was opened from the palace which did considerable execution. Soon the gates were blown open with guns and the defenders abandoned the walls and fled for concealment to the courts of the women's apartments. Leaving Virạnna in charge of the gate, Nañja Raja proceeded to the interior of the palace, forced the Raja to sent himself in the hall of audience and, in his presence, put many of his adherents in irons and had the noses and ears of the others cut off and themselves turned out into the street.

Deva Raja had protested against this outrageous proceeding and now resolved to renounce all future intercourse with his brother. He wanted to avoid a direct contest and departed for Satyamangalam with a large body of followers, in February 1757. (pp. 220–221 of Vol. I of *History of Mysoor*, (1869 *ed.*)—also Note 8 on pp. 303–4 above.

In yet another place, the Diarist reports Du Bausset as remarking that the Governor knew nothing and no answer could be had from him under three months, whereas in an hour Dupleix would decide a thousand matters. Further, he heard that the French King and Ministry were well disposed towards Dupleix and had proposed to send him out as Governor; but it was put off because of the proposed marriage of his elder brother's son and Madame Dupleix's daughter; and also he wanted to wait till his health should be better. "Should there be trouble here, M. Dupleix will come; otherwise he will not." The Diarist was silent, thinking it wise not to make any remarks.

M. Boyelleau recommended ironically that the Villupuram *ryots* who had demanded 50 per cent as their share of the produce, whereas under the Muhammadans they were said to have been allowed only 30 or 35 and the previous renter had allowed them 40 and 45, should not be given even 40 per cent. that the Governor allowed them, but they might be beaten with rods. It was pleaded that if the country were mountainous or forest, 40 and 45 per cent would be reasonable, but 30 per cent should be enough in the case of river-fed lands. The *tafrik* (additional assessment) of 25 per cent imposed by the previous renter, had to be remitted owing to troubles in the country. The ryots now demanded that they should be allowed 2 per cent of *paṇṇaikkattu,* (bundle of corn in the straw given to the labourers at harvest time) besides their share of 40 per cent. Boyelleau was of the opinion that they might be allowed a half-share.

Ranga Pillai frequently and bitterly complained that, though he had been given charge of the country by Godeheu, the sureties enjoyed the revenues for nearly a year and a half without paying anything and the Governor did not check them, but only desired him to pay. Thus the money due to the Company had been scattered among many. "Some country was lost owing to the English troubles; and there were losses owing to the commandants and sureties." And Ranga Pillai bewailed this miserable state of affairs."[8]

8 The *beriz* from Villupuram was reduced from 1,85,000 to 75,000 rupees; and the lessees paid handsome bribes for this.

Thus the year 1756 came to an end with the *Courtier's* accounts getting into a very bad state, wherein the Governor himself remitted a considerable portion of the balances due from the amaldars, saying that they need not make good what was paid for presents and contingencies, but only the balance still due; and this was because the amaldars had paid large sums as presents to the Governor so that he might get something for himself and the rest might manage their business as they pleased. All this came on the top of the commandants and sureties not paying back what they had taken. All these factors contributed to the rapid decay of cultivation; and to make matters still worse, the Governor sent the Councillors into the country in the sowing season itself. The Diarist could only exclaim, "I have had nothing to do with all this."[9]

Further, he heard that the Governor had directed Lambert to march to Srirangam with a body of 100 sepoys and accompanied by his own *dubash,* Kandappa Mudali who was given his own signet-ring and guarded by an escort; and he surmised that both these were going with the Governor's orders to seize the property said tc be lying in great store in the Ranganathaswami temple at Srirangam and bring it to Pondicherry. He believed that he had passed through a period of misfortune in the last two months and the evil influence of Jupiter would weaken with the end of December. He thus wrote:—"As it was time of misfortune for me, everyone pilfered the money in the country, instead of sending it to me; moreover, the harvest was bad; and I fell into arrears to the Company; the Governor did not enquire into this, but entrusted the country management to M. Desvaux . . . All this ended in loss and there was not enough money for this year (*Dhatu*) 1756–7." He also escaped attack from an elephant in rut which rushed at him and broke a verandah pillar of his house. (Entry for December, 23, 1756).

9. For some account of the Diarist's financial transactions see *Un Livre de Compte de Ananda Ranga Poulle*—tr. by R. P. O. Bernadotte, with introduction by E. Gaudart (1930) pp. 34–37.

Plague and pestilence ranged fearfully at Arcot, Vellore, Wandiwash and other places; and 15,000 people, Europeans, Hindustanis, Muhammadans, and Pariahs died in Arcot alone; and even these came to believe in the efficacy of sacrifies and offerings to the fearsome deities that presided over these diseases, which indeed, were believed to have traversed from Mysore to Tiruvannamalai; and even Europeans and Muhammadans wore margosa leaves in their head-dress to propitiate the diety. In his own house, Annaswami had small-pox.

The new year, 1757, began with renewed complaints on the part of the Diarist about the mischief of the amaldars being asked to give *nazars* to the Governor at the rate of 25 pagodas a lakh, in the house of M. Desvaux and, as a consequence, being given the option to remit the arrears for the cyclic years of *Bhava* (1754–55) and *Yuva* (1755–56) as they pleased, "on their agreeing to give *nazars* to the Governor, Desvaux" and others. Ranga Pillai openly expressed that he had only incurred De Leyrit's displeasure owing to his evil stars, he had never deceived him nor given false accounts and the renters were responsible for any mistakes, finally adding that the Governor replied angrily that "his favour was of no use to me as I had every one except him on my side." M. Boyelleau told him that ships from France were expected to arrive within the inside of a month with letters giving him as much authority as Godeheu had given him and that favourable orders would be received about the Diarist's affair. Boyelleau was enjoying the favour of Godeheu who was greatly displeased with De Leyrit for not having carried out the instructions left behind at his departure.

A curious order is noted by the Diarist to the effect that as the amaldars had been delaying the despatch of money on the plea of the disturbances raised by the Goddess Māriyamman, 50 guards with 30 Christian peons and catechists were sent in the beginning of February to Villupuram, in the region round which the Goddess was said to have been seen by several persons and to have demanded sacrifices and offerings, to seize men and give 50 stripes to those who said that they were possessed and to convert them into Christians. Still the Goddess continued to dominate the minds of the people and when the amaldar of Wandewash wanted to send money, he was told by her in a vision that she would rule the country for nine years and therefore the money should be given to her, instead of to the ruler. The peon who was about to take the money, bled at the nose and the mouth; and even the Christian Savariraya Pillai had to give Rs. 1,000 for her propitation, if his younger brother should be cured of the dysentery that had seized him on his merely declaring that he would defy the Goddess. Strange things happened in Mailam.

The *Courtier* who had no pleasant time of it at all, recorded little of interest of the stirring political revolution that was taking place in Bengal. Only, towards the end of February, he wrote that the Javanese had made an attack on the Dutch trading in the Java country; and that the English who sent away their ships when they had recovered Calcutta, had been surrounded and slain by the Nawab of Bengal and the city had been recaptured. What a perversion of truth?

APPENDIX

HISTORY OF THE PLAN FOR AN ALLIANCE WITH THE MARATHAS

The driving of the French out of the Deccan was always deemed essential for the Company's success in the Carnatic; and the Bombay Council had projected an alliance with the Marathas who were easily a match for Salābat Jang; and they had written of the feasibility of an alliance with the Peishwa at any time. This was the view of the Madras Council (*vide* their letter of March 1, 1756, to the Secret Committee) when they were not aware of the exact destination of the Company's troops sent out to Bombay. The Madras Council recommended to the Bombay Committee, even then, to immediately undertake the projected expedition to remove the French influence over Salābat Jang. The Madras Council believed that there was great probability of success as Bourchier of the Select Committee at Bombay reported that he could at any time enter into a firm alliance with the Marathas. The Bombay Presidency had been ordered by the Company to cultivate friendship with the Marathas. The expedition from Madras which had been organised was to be despatched either to Bombay or to the northern part of the Coromandel Coast, as might seem most advantageous. The Secret Committee from London had written to Bourchier at Bombay on March 26, 1755, that a secret treaty should be made with the Marathas, under the cloak of an expedition against Angria, to attack Salābat Jang and his allies; and the treaty should be arranged by the Governor of Bombay himself in order to keep the matter as secret as possible; while the Select Committee at Madras was ordered to co-operate with Bombay and a cypher was sent for secret correspondence between the Governors of Madras, Bombay and Bengal. A diversion on the Masulipatam side was expected to facilitate the projected operations. The Marathas must solemnly engage not to come to any compromise either with Salābat Jang, his friends or allies, for money or portions only of the territories unjustly seized by the latter; and they might be induced to proceed to the Carnatic, especially if the kings of Tanjore or Mysore should desire their assistance and provided the Select Committee of Fort St. George raised no objection. The Marathas might be consulted about drawing some of the princes near Vizagapatam into the alliance and about the recovery of the Divi Island and the English factories near Masulipatam; and if the Marathas were not to join in this plan, the artillery, stores and men were to be sent round to the Coromandel Coast.

Difficulties seemed to have risen. The Company's Secret Committee wrote to the Select Committee at Madras, on February 13, 1756, that many weighty objections had been raised against the plan of a joint campaign by the English and the Marathas in the Deccan, "as the Marathas would be more likely to pursue their interests than ours and all their inroads show their principal object to have been plunder and if the English had joined in attacking the Moghal's Government it would be an insult to the authority from which English privileges are derived." Therefore the Bombay Committee was directed not to proceed with the plan; but, if circumstances compelled joint operations with the Marathas, there should be an explicit stipulation that "the English expenses be defrayed, they have a due share of the contributions levied, and that they be not obliged to act against the Mughal."

On March 15, 1756, proposals were received from Balaji Baji Rao for an English contingent; and the Madras Government resolved to send him 200 European soldiers and 1,000 sepoys and also a train of artillery; and according to the Madras Private Committees of March 15, and May 18, 1756, it was believed that the cession of Gheriah might induce the Peishwa to enter into a firm alliance with them. Bussy's dismissal by the Nizām happened while this was the subject of negotiation between the Select Committees of Madras and Bombay. Salābat Jang's letter desiring an English detachment, reached Madras on June 14; and it was at once resolved to send a body of men, including 400 Europeans and a park of artillery; the expedition took some time to organise; but before it could start, there came on July 13, news of the capture of Kasimbazaar by the Nawab of Bengal and on August 13, of the latter's capture of Calcutta. "This, in spite of opposition, which Orme says, in his private correspondence, was due to private interests, determined the abandonment of the English schemes in the Deccan."—pp. 98-99—Dodwell's *Dupleix and Clive.*

CHAPTER XVII

SOME EVENTS OF 1757

THE DIARIST'S ACCOUNT OF THE DOINGS OF THE SUCCESSIVE GOVERNORS OF PONDICHERRY

THE Diarist continued his complaints about the non-settlement of his affair by the Council. He was not in a mind to supply the Governor with the usual paraphernalia when the latter proposed to proceed to Gingee. In the entry for Thursday, March 24, the Diarist informs us that Salābat Jang had reached Adoni with 30,000 horse and that the Peishwa himself had crossed the Krishna with double that number of cavalry and halted near Savanur, Bankapur and Gadwal and that both of them were said to be coming to Arcot and to the south. Curiously enough, after this we come across the following piece of information under the caption—"Particulars of the Governors of Pondicherry"—wherein he gives the following interesting account of the various Governors from the time of Martin.

Flacourt, who was the Second in Council under Martin, (1701–06), acted as Governor when Martin became too ill to attend to business and continued to be in charge till the arrival of Dulivier from Bengal, who was Governor on two occasions, first from February 1707 to July 1708 and for the second time, from about September 1713 to about August 1715. Hebert and Dulivier were General and Governor respectively up to the middle of 1718. Nainiya Pillai, the Chief Dubash, was imprisoned by Dulivier without consulting the Councillors. Nainiya Pillai appealed to the Duke of Orleans, the Regent of France, for reinstatement. The Diarist states that Hebert and Dulivier were both of them punished for this act of injustice (1718–19), the former being removed from office and deprived of his property and sent to Europe in custody and the latter degraded. La Prévostiére who now became Governor (1718-1721), had Kanakaraya Mudali removed from the office of Chief Dubash to which he had been appointed by Hebert. The Diarist says here that the Company and the Ministers were persuaded to order that no member of Kanakaraya Mudali's family should hereafter be appointed *Courtier*. This was in 1718, July. It may be remembered that Nainiya Pillai was an uncle of the Diarist and had invited the latter's father, Tiruvengadam Pillai, who was previously trading at Madras, to settle at Pondicherry in 1716. Hebert had disgraced Nainiya Pillai and ill-treated his son, Guruva Pillai. Guruva Pillai had gone to France and personally represented the injustice done to him and his family before the Regent, the Duke of Orleans. Both he and Tiruvengadam Pillai were restored to their previous positions by La Prévostiére who had become the *ad interim* successor to Hebert. The Telugu work entitled "Ānanda Rangarātchandamu" which is a treatise on prosody and is dedicated to Ananda Ranga Pillai, by its author Kasturi Rangayya Kavi, contains, in its introduction, an account of the genealogy and family of Ranga Pillai. It also tells us how Tiruvengadam Pillai grew to be powerful at Pondicherry and helped in securing justice and honour for his relative, Guruva Pillai, from the French King himself. Ananda Ranga Pillai perhaps utilised the family traditions and the journal maintained by Nainiya Pillai for his information. His account as given here is not wholly correct, particularly with reference to the dates of the accession and departure of the Governors and of Nainiya Pillai's disgrace and restoration.

We have read above that Lenoir, who was Governor for the first time in the years 1721–23, had always a high regard for Tiruvengadam Pillai and encouraged the Diarist, who was then an young man, to continue the work on which his father had been engaged. Thus Lenoir is praised as the fittest and cleverest governor and as "a very capable, just and intelligent man". During the first Governorship of Lenoir, French credit was built up with native merchants in spite of a lack of steady and continuous supply of goods and bullion from France. During his second Governorship which began in 1726, Ranga Pillai's rise to influence at Pondicherry really began. His cousin, Guruva Pillai, had died in 1724; and his father Tiruvengadam Pillai followed him to the grave two years later. Ranga Pillai himself had already become the chief native merchant of the French trading-house at Porto Novo. Now we read that, during the nine years' governorship of Lenoir, the prosperity and power of Pondicherry grew by leaps and bounds. So also did the influence and wealth of the Diarist.

Thus Lenoir is praised by our Diarist:—" Lenoir was very able and clever, and established a name as bright as the sun by enquiring justly into all matters. Pondicherry which was but a jungle became a town; huts became storeyed houses; and walls were built round the town. He sent ships with merchandise to Manilla, Mocha, Achin, Malacca, Quedah, Perak and other distant places whither ships had never before been sent, and carried on trade to the extent of five or six lakhs, thus bringing in large profits for the town and for the Company, so that, during his ten years' rule, people declared that, of all places, Pondicherry was the most just and truthful, that its merchants and inhabitants were the wealthiest, that it could supply all kinds of goods to other parts of the country, and that it could procure the goods from all other places; and the townspeople, the out-villagers, the Company's Directors and others in Europe all prayed that he would continue for ever as Governor. Moreover, by great efforts, he obtained from the Nizām a *parwana* for the coinage of rupees in Pondicherry and 3-swami pagodas for the Yanam factory equal in fineness to the Madras *karukku* pagodas,[1] and thus made the town prosperous. He ruled in such a way that the Nizām and other Muhammadan rulers and the European and Carnatic governments and others, pronounced that God had been pleased to make truth, justice, ability, broadness of mind and all other good qualities dwell in the person of M. Lenoir and that he was fit to occupy the throne of Delhi itself. This great man sailed for Europe by the Lys (captain, M. Dordelin) at one o'clock on the night of the 27th

1 Kuruki pagodas had three standing figures strongly marked and a plain granulated reverse. They were coined at Tiruvāmur, for Madras which began to mint pagodas as early as 1661. These were coined for the Nawabs of the Carnatic. The Kuruki and star pagodas were very popular.

Puraṭṭāśi, Rākshasa, corresponding with October 8, 1735, thus causing more grief than the loss of parents or treasure".

Governor Dumas got permission from Nawab Dōst Alī Khān to coin rupees and pagodas at the Pondicherry mint which would be current in the country and gave the means of livelihood to many, as well as profits to the Company. For protecting the families of Dōst Alī Khān and the Muhammadan nobles of Arcot in the troublous times of the invasion of Fateh Singh and Raghuji Bhonsle, he got from the Emperor of Delhi, a mansab of 4,500 horse with a standard and *naubat.* The Company and the Ministers sent him the Cross of St. Michael for having obtained the Nawab's permission to coin rupees at Pondicherry.

Dupleix assumed charge of the Governorship on January, 14, 1742, with all the Mughal dignities that were enjoyed by his predecessor. "He was destined to hear the beating of *naubat* in Pondicherry which no other European in India had been fortunate enough to enjoy, and to have the Padshah's standards borne before him." The Diarist claimed special credit for himself and responsibility for the successes of Dupleix in the operations against the English in the years 1746–48. For the subsequent political triumphs of Dupleix right down to the installation of Salābat Jang as the Nizām, he got the Order of St. Michael for his victories and also the title of Marquis.

With this, our Diarist's account of the Governors of Pondicherry ends. We do not know the particular reason why he was at so much pains to embody all the details about the French Governors at this point of his narrative.*

He took up this narrative, perhaps as a fond memory of his, in this time of political and financial depression, of the former days of his own prosperity and great influence which were certainly on the wane under Godeheu and De Leyrit.

Bussy and Vijayaramaraju of Vizianagaram

The Diarist at first wrote that Vijayarāmarāju was killed in a fight at Chicacole, along with a number of his followers and that

* See appendix at the end of the book entitled 'Nainiya Pillai and Guruva Pillai'.

Bussy marched to Viziyanagaram and captured and plundered the town. This highly inaccurate account was later rectified in the entry for March 26, in which the Diarist purports to relate the news of Vijayarāmarāju's death, as reported by Pīr Muhammad Sāhib of Bimlipatam. When Bussy quarrelled with Salābat Jang, Shaikh Ibrāhīm was suspected of treachery against his master. He sought shelter with a Telugu zamindar, Ranga Rao of Bobbili, and also made friends with Vijayarāmarāju. Bussy therefore marched against Ibrāhīm Khān and was joined by Haidar Jang, son of Jāfar Alī Khān, and some other sirdars from Ellore and Rajahmundry. They camped first at Kasimkota. Vijayarāmarāju sent word secretly to Ibrāhīm Alī Khān at Bobbili advising him to depart before troubles should begin. Similar advice was given by Ranga Rao of Bobbili himself to Ibrāhīm Alī Khān. Thereupon Shaikh Ibrāhīm left Bobbili and hid himself in a distant place. Vijayarāmarāju had a grudge against Ranga Rao as for a long time the latter had not shown him due respect. With this object he persuaded Bussy, after joining him, to seize the Bobbili fort and country and also kill Ranga Rao. Thereupon the combined armies of Bussy and Vijayarāmarāju marched by way of Chicacole and encamped at Bobbili which was about 100 miles off. Negotiations were then begun with Ranga Rao; but as he would not come to an agreement, Bussy advanced with a small body of troops to attack the fort. About 5,000 of Ranga Rao's men came out and fought so boldly that Bussy's men had to retreat. Vijayarāmarāju was indignant at this, mounted his elephant and advanced against the fort of Bobbili. He beat off Ranga Rao's people, approached the fort, crossed the ditch by filling it with bundles of straw and scaled the walls, while Bussy's men successfully scaled the walls on the other side, after a very severe fight in which 18 officers, 200 soldiers, 2,000 foot and 1,000 artillery people on Bussy's side and sepoys, guards, Carnatic infantry sirdars, making 5,000 in all on the side of the Raja, had perished and the ditch had become red with blood. When the fort had been captured, Bussy warned Vijayarāmarāju that he should not leave even a single child alive in the fort. All the people were slain including even pregnant women and Ranga Rao himself; but his younger brother survived and was recommended by Vijayarāmarāju to Bussy to be spared and to be treated for his wounds.

Sometime afterwards, one of Ranga Rao's people who had escaped, went to Vijayarāmarāju's tent and asked permission to see him on the plea that the Rao's younger brother had refused to have his wounds dressed. Vijayarāmarāju admitted the man into his tent; but the guards who searched him did not find out a folding knife that he had secreted in his dress. Being allowed to approach, he ripped up the Raja's belly with the knife, so tearing the intestines that he immediately died.[2] Bussy in great grief communicated this sad event to Jagapathi Raja, the son of Vijayarāmarāju's elder brother, who was his heir and in charge of Vizianagaram, and promised to give him the Bobbili fort and also territories yielding two lakhs of rupees. For generations the rulers of Vizianagaram had been *mansabdars* of 7,000 horse and possessed the privilege of the fish standard.

Bussy arrived at Rajahmundry towards the end of 1756 with a large force, for stabilising the French dominion and for recovering arrears of tribute. Vijayarāmarāju had persuaded Bussy to remove his own powerful rival, the Raja of Bobbili; consequently Bussy proposed to Bobbili that he should give up his fort, but receive other lands of great extent and value in another part of the Circars; but this proposal was received by Ranga Rao as an insult. Unfortunately, one of Bussy's detachments was cut up in the woods in the neighbourhood of Bobbili; and in his anger, Bussy determined to expel that chief and all his family. The result was " one of the most ghastly stories which even Indian

2 A book entitled 'Account of the Bobbili Zamindary,' written by the then Maharajah of Bobbili and published in 1900, tells us that the founder of the house was Peddarayadu. In 1652, he entered the district in the train of Sher Muhammad Khān, the then faujdar of Chicacole. For services to the faujdar, Peddarayadu was eventually granted the Razam Hunda (or estate). His son, Lingappa, built the fort and town of Bobbili and called it Peddapuli, (*i.e.*, large tiger), out of compliment to the name, Sher (tiger), of the patron of the founder. The word was

History has got to record." The historian, Robert Orme, has given a very graphic description of the defences of Bobbili and of the attack of the French on it. The attack commenced on the 24th January, 1757 (O. S.). The garrison fought with the heroism of despair; and at last, when Ranga Rao saw that there was no hope of continuing the resistance, he asked his followers to put their wives and children to death, in order to preserve them from violation by Europeans and the more ignominious ill-treatment at the hands of the retainers of Vijayarāmarāju. They set fire to all the habitations in the fort and stabbed without remorse all the women and children who attempted to escape from the flames. Then they resolved to die on the walls; and none of these defenders quitted with life the rampart where they gathered round their chief, who was shot down by a musket ball. None of them would accept quarter, but each fell only in the last agony of resistance or suffering. When the victors entered the fort, they found everywhere desolation and fire; but an old man led a boy from a distant recess and told M. Law, the French Commandant, that the child was the son of Ranga Rao, whom he had preserved against his father's will. Bussy was horrified at what he saw before him and would not go into the shambles in the fort,[3] but received very

corrupted into Pubbuli and Bobbuli and at length became Bobbili. A son of Sher Muhammad was rescued from the hands of rebels at Rangavaka near Palasa in Ganjam by Lingappa; and for this service he was granted twelve villages and the hereditary title of Ranga Rao. After three lives, Gopalakrishna succeeded to the estate. In his time, at the end of 1753, the Northern Circars were taken possession of by the French; and the Chicacole and Rajahmundry Circars were leased out to Pedda Vijayarāmarāju of Vizianagaram.

Another retainer of Sher Muhammad Khān, was Pusapati Madhavavarma, the ancestor of the Vizianagaram family; and the rivalry between the houses of Bobbili and Vizianagaram is said to be as old as the time of their settlement in the district.

3 The historic fort which was the site of this slaughter is on the west side of the present town, and is marked by an obelisk bearing inscriptions on stone, commemorating the tragedy. In these inscriptions and also in the popular ballad on the subject of the fight, which is entitled "Rangaraya Charitamu," Vijayarāmarāju is said to have been slain by a single individual, named Tandrapapiah, a sirdar of the fort

kindly the boy and his guardian and straightway appointed the boy lord of the territories which he had previously offered the father (Ranga Rao) in exchange for the domains of Bobbili. On the third night after the massacre, the camp was alarmed by a sudden tumult in the quarters of Vijayarāmarāju. Two of the soldiers of Ranga Rao had escaped from the carnage and somehow gained admission into Vijayarāmarāju's tent at night when they found him alone and asleep. Vijayarāmarāju was extremely corpulent, in so much that he could scarcely raise himself from his seat without assistance; the two men, restraining their very breath, struck in the same instant with their poniards at his heart; the first groan brought in a sentinel, who fired, but missed; more immediately thronged in; but the murderers, heedless of themselves, cried out, pointing to the body, 'Look here! We are satisfied.' They were instantly shot by the crowd, and mangled after they had fallen; but had stabbed Vijayarāmarāju in thirty-two places. Had they failed, the other two remaining in the forest were bound by the same oath to perform the deed or perish in the attempt."

This tragedy of Bobbili was a momentous historical event in the annals of the Northern Circars. Vijayarāmarāju had been easily induced by Jāfar Alī Khān, the Nazim of Chicacole to join him in opposing the entry of the French. From the alliance, he was, shortly afterwards, seduced by the offer of Bussy to give him a lease of the two circars of Chicacole and Rajahmundry at a very favourable rate. Jāfar Alī then called in the Marathas to his aid. They devastated these two circars from end to end and

at Razam. Two members of the Bobbili family escaped from the massacre; namely Ranga Rao's brother, Vengal Ranga Rao, and his infant son, Venkataranga Rao, who was usually known as Chinna Ranga Rao. They fled to Bhadrāchalam and returned after the French occupation was superseded by the British and got possession of the fort at Razam. According to our Diarist, Vijayarāmarāju was born in the year, *Sarvadhāri*, and died in *Dhātu* in his 49th year. His estate extended over 40 killas and many temples; and his full title was Sri Pūsappātti Mastamandala Raya Manne Sultan; and he had the right of pearl umbrellas and the fish-standard.

returned with an enormous booty. Jāfar Alī had courted the alliance of the English at that date; and he did not allow his allies to molest the English factory at Vizagapatam, while they were permitted to plunder the Dutch factory at Bimlipatam. Moracin, the French administrator of Masulipatam, not having sufficient troops with him to reduce the united forces of Vijayarāmarāju and Jāfar Alī had to seduce the Raja by the very favourable leases offered for two circars. Orme says that this temptation was most effective. When Jāfar Alī allowed the Dutch factory of Bimlipatam to be plundered and burnt by the Marathas, Moracin detached all the forces he had, about 150 Europeans and 2,500 sepoys, to join Vijayarāmarāju. There was a big battle at Tummapalam, near Anakapalle, between the Marathas and Vijayarāmarāju. The fight was maintained irregularly for several hours; but at last the Marathas had to give way before the fire of the French artillery. They tarried some days longer in the neighbourhood and then crossed the Godavari at a ford which they had discovered and retreated through the circars of Ellore and Kondavidu. In July 1754, Bussy came from Hyderabad to Masulipatam and thence went over to Rajahmundry where he settled the details of administration of all the new French acquisitions. Jāfar Alī Khān could not expect any further help from the Marathas and, having no other resource left, threw himself upon the mercy of Salābat Jang. During the months of Bussy's troubles caused by the crisis of his rupture with Salābat Jang in the summer of 1756, his orders on the revenues of the Circars were generally dishonoured by the renters and the poligars, to whom it had been publicly notified by the Nizām's *durbar* that the grant of the Circars to the French had been resumed. Even Bussy's own governor of Chicacole, Ibrāhīm Khān, disavowed his authority. The only leading chief who continued to be faithful to Bussy and assured him of his regular payment of tribute was Vijayarāmarāju. "One night, when little expected, and most wanted, a man came to Charmaul, and, being permitted to speak in private with Mr. Bussy, delivered, with the message of Vijayarāmarāju, a sum of gold, as much as he could carry concealed under his garments.

It was sufficient for the present want, and the same man afterwards furnished more as necessary." (Orme, Vol. II, p. 103).

Bussy arrived at Rajahmundry in the third week of December 1756, with the object of collecting the balances due in the Circars and providing for the future regularity of the payment of dues. On the approach of the French and dreading punishment for his ingratitude, Ibrāhīm Khān, the Faujdar of Chicacole, fled away to Aurangabad. Vijayarāmarāju, confident in the proofs that he had given of his attachment to Bussy, met him with a large army and with several other loyal chiefs.

After the tragedy of Bobbili, Bussy proceeded through the northernmost part of the Chicacole circar; and at one time he even talked of marching to the aid of Sirāj-ud-Daula in Bengal through Cuttack; but he heard of the continuous successes of the English in Bengal and of their capture of Chandranagore and therefore abandoned that plan and resolved upon an immediate retaliation by attacks on the English factories in the Circars.

The Marathas in the Carnatic

The Diarist noted that the Peishwa encamped in the beginning of April, about 4 or 5 leagues from Seringapatam, as the Raja of Mysore had invited him to seize and imprison the Dalavāi and the Sarvādhikāri, with the promise of giving him half the kingdom and a daily allowance of Rs. 15,000. The Peishwa seized the fort of Sira, whose Nawab, Dilāwar Khān, was given a *jaghir*. Dilāwar Khān was the last of the Mughal governors of Sira[4] who played a prominent part in many of the contests between the rivals for the *masnad* of the Deccan.

4 Sira attained to its highest prosperity under Dilāwar Khān and is said to have contained 50,000 houses. An elegant palace erected by him, now all in ruins was the model on which those of Bangalore and Seringapatam came to be built. A fine garden was also made, called the Khān Bagh, which was kept up by Haidar and may have suggested the Lal Bagh at Bangalore. The ruins of a large quarter, to which tradition assigns the name of Latapura, may yet be seen to the north-west of the fort.

Sira itself was founded by one, Rangappa Nayak, early in the 16th century, "the selection of the site being due, as is commonly related of

Subsequently, the Diarist heard that the Raja of Mysore who had adopted Nañja Raja's son, had marched with him to Satyamangalam with 2,000 horse. Nañja Raja had removed the Brahman minister whom he had previously imprisoned, to the fort of Seringapatam and declared that if the Peishwa should approach, he would kill the Dorai and even the Brahman ministers and others and then kill himself. The news was that about 40,000 of the Peishwa's horse had taken possession of the country as far as Kolar, and that the Peishwa would encamp at Arcot in the course of the year, after conquering Mysore.

The Peishwa was later on reported to have concluded a treaty with Mysore and departed northwards and that the fort of Seringapatam was closed for ten days and nobody was allowed to go, by the orders of Nañja Raja. The Marathas had already conquered Sira. They now demanded *chauth* from the Nawab of Cuddapah; and when he resisted them, they attacked his fort, slew him and occupied his country. Balwant Rao Mehendale is reported by the Diarist, in the last days of August, as halting in the Kadappanattam[5] forest near Vellore, with 10 or 15 thousand horse and as having sent the major portion of his troops to seize Madanapalle, Gurramkonda, etc., under the Cuddapah man (?). Hearing this, Nawab Abdul Nabī Khān of Cuddapah marched against Balwant Rao with five or six thousand horse; and the latter had decided to rejoin with his followers the main body of his army, where it lay encamped, after worshipping the God in Tirupati. Balwant Rao was in general charge of the Maratha operations in the

other forts in the country, to the turning of a hare upon the hounds in pursuit". It was captured by Randullah Khān, the Bijapuri general, whose lieutenant, Mālik Husain, was appointed its governor (*cir.* 1638). Mālik Husain completed the fort that had been already begun by Rangappa Nayak. Mughal rule was established over it after the conquest of Bijapur in 1687; and Sira became the capital of the new province, composed of the districts south of the Tungabhadra. Kāsim Khān, its first Mughal governor, introduced the Mughal revenue system; and his successor, Khaiflyat Khān, was an equally good ruler.

5 Kadapanattam is about 35 miles, W.S.W. of Chittore and at the head of Talapolla Ghat. It had 2 forts and was formerly the head-quarters of a taluk.

country from Cuddapah to Bednur. According to the *Selections from Peshwa Daftar, No. 28—Peshwa Balajirao: Karnatak Affairs, 1740–1761,* Mehendale gave a sum of money to Murari Rao Ghorepade for expenditure on his troops, enforced payments from the dowager Rani of Bednore and tried hard to speed up the work of realizing the tributes due from the Raja of Mysore, giving him no quarter. Letter No. 198 in that book conveys the congratulations of the Peishwa to Balwant Rao Mehendale at Cuddapah, heartily congratulating him on his victory over Nawab Abdul Majīd Khān, who was killed in action with the Marathas on the 24th September 1757, and also congratulating all those who made special exertions in the fight.[6] This victory of Balwant Rao was gained over the Pathan chiefs.

The Diarist notes how Arcot was struck with consternation by the arrival of the Marathas at Cuddapah; and Nawab Muhammad Alī, apprehending the incursions of some of the parties into its neighbourhood, sent the women and children of his family to Madras for safety. According to Orme, Cuddapah surrendered

6 A great difficulty is experienced in arriving at an accurate list of the Nawabs of Cuddapah. Mr. J. D. B. Gribble has the following note. (*Manual of Cuddapah District,* 1875).

"At the commencement of the eighteenth century, the then Cuddapah Nabob was a man of considerable influence. This was Abdool Nabbee Khān, who consolidated under his exclusive rule the districts of Sidhout, Gandikota, Cumbum, Gurramkonda, and Punganoor, and even extended his conquests as far as the Baramahal, from which he only retired after levying heavy requisitions from the Seringapatam treasury. The rule of the Cuddapah Nabob appears to have lasted for some time over Baramahal, for when in 1759 Hyder overran that district, we find him, for the first time, coming into collision with the Cuddapah Nabob. This rise of power in Cuddapah was, however, temporary, and though we find the Cuddapah Nabob playing an important part in the Carnatic affairs in 1750, the superior strength of Hyder soon effectually destroyed his influence. I would wish before leaving this era to give a list of the Cuddapah Nabobs, but the absence of any trustworthy data renders this very difficult. The first Nabob is said to have been Abdool Nabbee Khān, the grand-father of the man of the same name whom I mentioned as conquering Punganoor in 1714. This would probably

after a struggle, on the 15th of July; while a strong detachment of the Marathas invested Ambur from which they levied contributions and their parties scoured the valley of Vaniyambadi quite up to the gates of Vellore. His agent, Amrit Rao, negotiated with the Nawab, soon reached Arcot, demanded four lakhs as arrears due from the subah, and consented to take two lakhs in ready money and the Nawab's rescripts (or orders) on the killedars of the forts and the poligars for 2½ lakhs more.

Murari Rao had accompanied Balaji Rao in his expedition to Seringapatam. Balwant Rao was opposed, when he attacked and took Hoskote, by all the Pathan Nawabs, who now proposed that all of them should combine in an alliance with the English, the Nawab of Arcot and the Mysoreans, not only to oppose the Marathas at this crisis, but to prevent all Maratha incursions to the south of the Krishna in the future. In this Murari Rao had taken the lead; and both Murari Rao and the Nawab of Cuddapah had offered to march against Balwant Rao at Kadappanattam if the English troops would join them there. The Madras Government could spare no troops and was in reality as much afraid of them, as they were of the Marathas entering the province.

bring the origin of the family to about 1640 or 1650, but it is clear that there must have been several chiefs previous to that time for the Mahomedan rule was established soon after the battle of Tellicottah in 1564. Abdool Nabbee Khān may, however, have been the first of a new family. If this was the case, the second is unknown. The third was Abdool Nabbee Khān before mentioned, who had ceased to rule, at all events, before 1732, when we find an inscription speaking of his son Mahazid Khān as the Nabob. When this man died, he left an infant son, and the Nabobship appears to have been assumed by his brother Mahasim Khān. Elsewhere this Nabob appears to be called Moochee Meer and was killed in 1751, when he was succeeded by his nephew Abdool Alim Khān, the son of the former Nabob. This prince was the last of his race, and was conquered by Hyder Alī in 1780." C.P.

See also Brown—*An Ephemeris etc. from A.D.* 1751 *to* 1851—p. VII—under 1747—Abdul Nabī Khān Mayana, who according to him ruled Cuddapah from Saka 1658 to Saka 1669 (1736–7 to 1747–8). Was this Mayana related to the Mayana connected with Madura? (see above pp. 285–8, footnote).

They therefore resolved to procrastinate the negotiations with Amrit Rao who was invited to come to Madras along with the Nawab. Amrit Rao soon saw that the English merely wanted to gain time till news of information from Europe should reach them as to the outbreak of war with France and strongly protested against the evasion; and finally it was agreed that 3,000 Maratha horse should immediately join the troops at Conjeevaram and proceed with them to attack the French army. Meanwhile, Balwant Rao despatched a contingent to capture the villages in the neighbourhood of Gooty and to collect their revenue. Balwant Rao was later on very much agitated about the arrival of French ships at Pondicherry in September. Even in December we find that Balwant Rao had not yet finished his task at Cuddapah, The Nawab of Cuddapah had taken a very prominent part not only in the events leading to the assassination of Nāsir Jang but also in the subsequent tragedy of the murder of Muzaffar Jang.

The Diarist tells us at some length of the reception given to Mīr Nāmatullah Khān, the trooper who brought the presents from Balaji Rao Peishwa to Pondicherry. The accompanying message said that, although the Carnatic *chauth* had not yet been paid as promised, no demands had been made out of regard for M. Bussy; but there should be no delay any longer. The Mīr Sāhib is said to have said that everyone knew that the Muhammadans kept no promise at all, but the Europeans always did and therefore they should see by their conduct that the belief was justified.

Amrit Rao set out in the end of June with about 1,000 horse, left 400 horse in Vellore and thereabouts and approached Arcot with 600 horse; and upon learning this, Muhammad Alī went out to receive him (Entry for July 22nd). A little later we read that Murtazā Alī Khān received Amrit Rao, gave him a feast and was arranging about *chauth* and that the Maratha would go later to Muhammad Alī (at Arcot) who was expecting him and had prepared lodgings. Amrit Rao's horse plundered the country as far as Vaniyambadi, Ambur, Tiruppattur and Virinchipuram. At last, when Amrit Rao actually reached Arcot, he entered into an agreement with Muhammad Alī for 8 lakhs of rupees, 5 lakhs on the mortgage of the countries and 3 lakhs on mortgages with the killedars. Muhammad Alī promised to send him some money as soon as he should reach Madras by way of Conjeevaram. The Diarist thus remarks on the situation of Muhammad Alī: "I conclude from this agreement of Muhammad Alī Khān and his departure, that he is like betel-nut in a nut-cutter, for about 15,000 of the Nana's horse are at Satghar, Amrit Rao is near at hand with 1,000 more, and the French army is close by, engaging the English. He therefore, thinking that there would be danger in resistance, sent his wife to Madras and Mylapore, and himself entered into this agreement in order to escape. I do not think that he is sincere."

Amrit Rao proceeded, along with Muhammad Alī, to Madras, where he was lodged at Tiruvottiyur; and the Nawab agreed to pay him some money so that he might help him instead of withdrawing his 1,000 horse. The Diarist also heard that the merchants and rich men at Madras were sending their property away to Pulicat and other places for safety and they greatly feared that the disaster of 1746 would befall them again.

In this connection, the Diarist gives us a realistic account of the demolition of the Old Town in Madras. The French who were in occupation of that city for three years down to August 1749, planned to retain it permanently; and they demolished the Indian houses of Black Town which adjoined the north wall of the fort and formed a glacis with the debris; thus the southern half of the Black Town, along with its walls and the Company's garden-house in Peddanaickenpetta, were demolished by them for the better protection of the fort from the fire of an enemy. The old pagoda in Black Town which now stood by itself and the remaining portion of Old Black Town were pulled down in 1757 and the debris was utilised for the rebuilding of the fort. Thus Old Black Town ceased to exist; and the name was now given to the two suburbs of Muthialpetta and Peddanaickenpetta that had grown up respectively to the north and west of it. The Diarist naturally makes much of the reported destruction of the existing houses in Old Black Town. The Perumal Pagoda must have come down forthwith. The Diarist's note on this is as follows: "When the French formerly captured Madras and hoisted their flag, the Perumal temple, the Iswaran temple and all the houses up to Sunguvar's house were allowed to stand. Their destruction has now been ordered and the fact was published by beat of tom-tom. So the merchants went to Mr. Pigot (the Governor) and asked him how he could destroy such ancient temples. He replied, 'The town is in danger and it is therefore necessary to demolish them. If you agree quietly, well and good; if not, I shall send men to destroy them.' Thinking that it was no use seeking to bargain with him, they requested him to give them a month within which to remove the idols from the temples before their destruction and to find houses elsewhere. He refused this, but gave only 15 days. When the French captured the town before and hoisted their flag, half the town was destroyed and now the whole will go to ruin, and the name of Madras will be forgotten. At first the town was very prosperous; then it lost half its greatness; and now the very name of the town will disappear; therefore the time has come to destroy the remaining houses".[7]

The French Capture of Vizagapatam (1757)

Bussy was said to have been checked by a strong poligar on his way north to Bengal and to have returned to Chicacole with great loss. This was the news that the Diarist heard about the middle of May. Early in June the news reported by the Diarist was that Bussy had appointed Law to the governorship of Ellore and Rajahmundry and directed him to take possession of all the English ports, Vizagapatam, Melapalle, Kapulapalayam, Kopagiri and Bandarmalanka at the mouth of the Godavari and ordered the white flag to be hoisted in these places.

"M. Law therefore obtained the assistance of Reddi Polavaram Raja, Mangapati Devu, Nuvugidu Appa Rao, Mugalturru

7 (Refer also to H. D. Love—*Vestiges of Old Madras;* Vol. II, Chapter xxxviii. pp. 526-527); and C. S. Srinivasachari's *History of the City of Madras* (1939)—pp. 165 *et seq.*

Venkata Raja, Peddavaram Jagapati Raja, etc., zamindars, with their large armies, including Europeans, artillery and munitions of war and commanders, and having halted near Yanam, he sent out detachments which captured Melapalle, Kapulapalaiyam, etc., factories belonging to the English situated east of Yanam and mentioned above, and ordered the French flag to be hoisted there. He then despatched an army to attack Mr. Andrews, captain of the English troops holding the fortress in the port of Bandamurlanka, situated four leagues south of Yanam.[8] The English captain fled after fighting for one day, so our troops removed the English flag and hoisted the white flag. As M. Bussy has ordered M. Law to march with his army towards the English port of Vizagapatam, which was to be attacked jointly, M. Law would proceed thither. This is the news which Pīr Muhammad has heard from the messengers. By the Hindu science of astrology, it was foretold that, in the year Iswara, all the English ports would pass into the hands of the French who would hoist the white flag in them. Accordingly the English forts and ports are falling into French hands, and all may rest assured that all places, from England in Europe to Madras and Fort St. David in India, will pass into French hands. I am sure that this will happen." (Entry for Monday, June 5th).

The French captured the English factory at Vizagapatam on June 26th; and Mr. Smith, its governor, two councillors, 200 soldiers and some officers were also captured. One Frenchman was killed; and all the councillors, soldiers and others were imprisoned by the French captain. The reduction of Vizagapatam was reserved for himself by Bussy; but being sure of his

8 The English had attempted (very vainly) to secure concessions on the northern coast in order to protect their trade from the consequences of the French occupation of the Circars, and their expulsion from Masulipatam. But they had neither troops nor fortifications worth the name, even at Vizagapatam. Andrews was the covenanted servant in charge of these temporary factories, not a soldier as Ranga Pillai seems to suppose. (Dodwell).

prize he remained at Chicacole until he had settled the affairs of that circar. On the 24th of June, the van of Bussy's army appeared before Vizagapatam.

According to our Diarist, it was Law that marched with an army from Bussy's camp to attack the fort. He said that Law had hoisted the French flag and captured Smith, the English commander (entry for July 17 and 18, 1757). Orme says that on the same day when the van of Bussy's army appeared in sight, the English Company's ship *Marlborough,* anchored in the road; and the Chief Engineer of Madras who was then on board the ship, on his way to Bengal, landed, inspected the fortifications and gave it as his opinion that the extent of the fort could not be defended even with a much greater force; he advised therefore that all the Europeans should be immediately embarked and the sepoys, with two or three officers, should be left to make the best capitulation they could; but all the boats and fishermen had deserted in the night and it was very difficult for people to go out into the sea, the wind being so strong. The next day at noon, the main body of Bussy's army asked the English to surrender and the capitulation of the place was signed in the night. All the Europeans, whether troops or inhabitants, were to be prisoners of war. The sepoys and natives were free to go where they liked. All the Company's property became the spoils of the victors, but Bussy gave back every property that anyone claimed as his own. He permitted Mr. Perceval, the chief of the factory, and several other officers to proceed by the *Marlborough* that was then anchored off Bimlipatam, to Bengal. Evidently the Diarist confused Smith, a factor at the place, with Perceval, the chief.

The despatch of the Select Committee at Madras to the Secret Committee of the Court of Directors, dated July 30, 1757 says that a peon from Vizagapatam reported that Bussy appeared before it on June 24, that the *Marlborough* anchored there on the 25th and that it surrendered on the 26th of June. The *Marlborough* sailed immediately for Bengal with Perceval, the Chief of Vizagapatam and others on board and the French were now able to control all the coast from Bandar to Vizagapatam. There was a great deal of rejoicing at Pondicherry over the capture of Vizagapatam. The Diarist heard on August 3, 1757, that Bussy was at Vizagapatam with a very large body of men and Mr. Perceval had agreed in writing that the custom about the bearing of arms by those taken in war should be observed and that they should be ready to appear when required and then the officers were allowed to depart.

The other English factories in the circars had been seized by this time. Early in May the factory at Madapollam was captured; but its chief, Andrews, contrived to send away all the Company's goods by sea before its capture. He himself retired to the Dutch factory at Palakollu but was obliged to surrender himself to the French. Nellipalli and Bandarmalanka were seized shortly afterwards. The Diarist reporting in one place that "Our people seized Bandamurlanka and another port and sent to Masulipatam those whom they had seized." The capture of Vizagapatam formed the crowning act of the French for the year. From Vizagapatam the French army proceeded to Rajahmundry where it stayed for some time. Then it moved northwards to keep under control the refractory poligars who showed a tendency to resist.[9]

9 (Orme. Vol. II, p. 261). "In consequence of his orders the Europeans he had left in garrison at Rajahmundrum, when joined by more from Masulipatam, marched against the factories of Madapollam, Bandermalanka, and Ingeram, which stand near the sea on three different arms of the Godavari. The natives here weave excellent cloths at cheap rate, and the three factories annually furnished 700 bales for the Company's market in England. Ingeram only had soldiers, and only 20, and all the three factories surrendered on the first requisition. The reduction of Vizagapatam, as being nearer, Mr. Bussy reserved to himself; but being sure of his prize, remained in the city of Chicacole until he had settled the affairs of this government."

(*The Madras Despatches* 1754-1765, p. 102). "The superiority the French in the North has proved fatal to the English settlements. On hearing from Calland of the French approach, Andrews removed most of the Company's effects from Madapollam on his private sloop which proceeded first to Vizagapatam and thence to Bengal. He sent all the military to protect Nallapalle, but they were intercepted. He himself took

MILITARY AFFAIRS IN THE CARNATIC COUNTRY— A RESUME OF EVENTS FROM 1755 TO 1757

We saw that Colonel Heron's expedition to the south was questioned by De Leyrit as a breach of the truce with Godeheu, because the southern districts belonged to the French in virtue of various rights derived from Chandā Sāhib and the Dalavāi of Mysore. Heron marched for Madura in February-March 1755. A few days later came the news that the Mysoreans had left Srirangam, perhaps with the aim of assisting the rebellious poligars against the English; and so, early in April, Heron was ordered to return to Trichinopoly without delay from which he sent out two detachments to compel the poligars of that district to settle their accounts. Even when Heron had received the orders to return to Trichinopoly, he turned aside at the request of Mahfuz Khān to attack Pulitevar in his fort, as that poligar was the only one who had not submitted. But finding that he could not take that place even with the help of heavy guns, Heron returned to Madura, and subsequently to Trichinopoly, in June 1755, having lost a part of his baggage in a surprise attack by the Kallars in the Nattam Pass. An official inquiry was held on Heron's conduct. He was suspended from his seat on the Council and tried by court martial.

The Nawab, Muhammad Alī, entered Arcot in triumph with English troops as his escort, about the end of August; but as the Arcot poligars were in heavy arrears of tribute to him, he requested the English Government for military assistance and was urged, in return, to transfer the management of certain countries to the Company. The Nawab objected to this course on the ground of the loss of dignity that he would incur. The Madras Select

refuge in the Dutch factory at Palicol, but had to surrender. The fortifications and buildings at Nallapalle were completely destroyed. Madapollam, Ingeram, Bandarmalanka, and Sankarapalaiyam are now in French possession, and it is rumoured that Vizagapatam also surrendered to Bussy on June 26. The *Marlborough* is reported to have touched at Vizagapatam the day before its surrender."

See also D. F. Carmichael—*A Manual of the District of Vizagapatam* (1869)—p. 182 *et seq.;* H. Morris: The Godavery District (1878) chh. IX & X.

Committee finally agreed to accept Ponneri and Pedipattu, where the Company's fine cloths were woven and which were worth about 30,000 pagodas a year, on the same terms as Chingleput, in addition to orders for eight lakhs of rupees on the renters of the Arcot countries payable in two instalments. The Nawab also promised to settle the Company's share of the rent before he gave any *cowle* to the renters, many of whom were expected to be selected from the principal inhabitants of Madras. The Nawab also promised to give the English half the revenues of Madura and Tinnevelly, though nothing could be expected from them immediately on account of the cost of the troops still in the field against the poligars of those regions as well as half the amount of the tributes paid by all the poligars under him. An English agent, a member of the Secret Committee, William Percival, was to accompany the Nawab and be present at all his transactions with the poligars or their vakils and to receive the Company's half of the tribute. The Nawab's government was in an unsettled condition. Half the province was in French hands and several prominent killedars claimed independence of the Nawab on one ground or another, the most notable among them being Murtazā Alī Khān of Vellore.

Salābat Jang entered the Mysore country with Bussy in March, and collected 33 lakhs of rupees before he departed from that kingdom. The Mysoreans withdrew from Srirangam in the latter part of March, probably on account of Salābat Jang's incursion into their own dominions.

The English had to interfere in order to restore some lands seized from the Raja of Tanjore by the Marava of Ramnad; and there was some likelihood of a war breaking out between the former and the Tondaiman of Pudukottai on account of two forts made over to the latter by Manoji Appa, the general of Tanjore.

The army that was sent to accompany the Nawab for the collection of arrears of tribute, finished its business with reference to the demands made on Bangaru Yachama Naick and on the zamindar of Bommarajapalayam.

By reason of the threats of De Leyrit, the English captain of the troops with the Nawab was asked to repulse force by force, should the French support the Arcot poligars. Fortunately, they did not do so. The English forces were strengthened with additional troops sent from Madras, in order to support the Nawab's demands on Murtazā Alī Khān of Vellore and marched on that place towards the end of January. Governor Pigot of Madras now got a letter of remonstrance from De Leyrit, disputing the Nawab's claim of suzerainty over Vellore and threatening to oppose the English Company's intervention. The English captain was even informed by the Select Committee that, if the French should march to the help of Murtazā Alī—information having been received that 300 French and 300 sepoys had left Pondicherry in the course of January 1757—he might summon them to retire and if they refused, might attack them. Murtazā Alī's vakil made overtures with the English at Madras for an accommodation; and Orme was sent to negotiate with him by reason of his knowledge of the Muhammadan language. The faujdar had agreed to pay one lakh of pagodas if the English troops should retire; and the Secret Committee at once ratified and returned the agreement to him. Meanwhile, Orme's arrival induced the faujdar to hope that better terms could be had and he thereupon refused to fulfil his agreement and refused to treat with anyone but Orme. The faujdar would not listen at all to Orme's remonstrances; and the latter had to return to Madras; and all the while, a body of 700 Frenchmen and 1,500 sepoys lay threateningly between Gingee and Chetpattu, some 35 miles from Vellore.

In the southern Carnatic, Mahfuz Khān who was the Nawab's deputy, delayed the payment of his balance of over a lakh and a quarter on the pretext of very heavy expenses incurred by him in defending the country against his poligars.

Murtazā Alī of Vellore, Nāzir Muhammad Khān of Chetpattu and Mīr Sāhib of Elavānāsur were the only chiefs who remained practically independent of Nawab Muhammad Alī. Mīr Sāhib threatened to call in the French, if any troops should be sent against him. The English felt that it was not safe to attempt to reduce these chiefs so long as a French army was in their neighbourhood. They advised the Nawab to make a general defensive alliance offered by the Nawab of Cuddapah. The English claimed that, under the provisional treaty of 1754, they were entitled to assist Muhammad Alī to collect the tributes due from the poligars dependent on the Nizāmat of Arcot. The French contended that only the Nizām, Salābat Jang, could say properly who was the Nawab of Arcot. The French correspondence on the subject is contained in the *Military Sundry Books* of the Madras Records. De Leyrit contended further that the truce of Godeheu was confined only to the Carnatic and that, while the French were at liberty to help Salābat Jang in the Deccan, the English might not, in their turn, help Muhammad Alī in the south. The English naturally said that this argument would justify their immediate interference in the Deccan as against Bussy. On this point hung the plans projected by the Madras Council in consultation with the Bombay Committee for an expedition into the Deccan to destroy French influence at Salābat Jang's court.

With regard to the long-disputed rights over certain villages in the Karunguzhi taluk, a personal conference between De Leyrit and Pigot was actually proposed. We get occasional glimpses from the Diarist about these transactions and about the French commissaries purposely dragging on the negotiations regarding the contested places. The French fortified Villiyanallur and Porto Novo, upon which De Leyrit was asked to reduce them to their former state.

Muhammad Alī had made over to the English the revenues of Madura and Tinnevelly, the collection of which was leased out to Titarappa Mudali for three years on an average of twelve lakhs per year, half of which was to be paid over to the Company, as agreed to by the Nawab. The Madras Government was anxious, as we saw above, in the year 1756, to send an expedition into the Deccan to counteract French influence. They received, in the middle of June, Salābat Jang's request for help after he had dismissed Bussy. But a few weeks later, came the news of the loss of Kasimbazaar and of the imminent danger to Calcutta from

Sirāj-ud-Daula; and Major Kilpatrick was immediately sent to Bengal with about 250 troops. But when Salābat Jang made a fresh request for help, the Madras Committee again resolved to persist in the Deccan expedition. However, when in the course of August, news came of the loss of Calcutta and all the Company's settlements in Bengal, the Deccan plan had to be completely abandoned. July and August of that year saw also the crisis in Bussy's relations with Nizām and his ultimate triumph over and reconciliation with the latter.

Two Europe ships arrived at Pondicherry in April and a third in June; and it was feared that more help might come from Europe to Pondicherry after the monsoon. The Madras Government hoped to finish the Bengal affair before news was received of the expected declaration of war with France and to recall Clive and his troops for the defence of Madras when once war should be declared.

The second Madras expedition to Bengal was despatched, consisting of the Company's troops under Clive. The army which was despatched to Vellore continued to remain at Arcot. On complaints from the Nawab that the Tinnevelly poligars were still resisting Mahfuz Khān, it was decided to send the sepoy commandant, Yūsuf Khān, with 1,000 troops from Trichinopoly to Mahfuz Khān's help. On Yūsuf Khān's arrival the rebels dispersed; but he could not be recalled owing to the suspicious conduct of Mahfuz Khān, who would not deliver the country to the renter Titarappa Mudali, but stayed on at Madura and turned out the Company's sepoys from the fort there. Mahfuz Khān declared, in justification of his attitude, that his discharged troops would not allow them to leave Madura till their arrears had been paid and that it was they and not himself that had turned out the Company's sepoys and he could not control their action. Caillaud, the English commandant at Trichinopoly, was asked to settle this affair.

In the course of 1756, the Nawab did not stir out of Arcot. Murtazā Alī was in ostensible friendship with the English and demanded from them permanent exemption from the tributes to the Nawab. The English also remained nominally friendly with the killedars of Chetpattu and Elavānāsūr. They established an alliance with Balaji Rao Peishwa who was then engaged in his Karnatak expedition and promised to send a detachment to his camp to be maintained at his expense.

No reply was received from Balaji Rao till September. Then he wrote that as he had settled the affair of Savanur, he did not need the British troops at once, but he would visit the Carnatic after the monsoon, when he desired that the body of troops should be ready to join him. At the same time, the Madras Council attempted to negotiate a treaty with the King of Mysore for the recovery of the Company's debt. But Mysore had been bled twice by the Marathas and once by Salābat Jang and was moreover torn by civil war. A correspondence was however kept up with it through Orme. A friendly correspondence was also kept up with the Nawab of Cuddapah.

The disputes between the English and the French over the taluk of Karunguzhi and the neighbourhood continued. De Leyrit, however, suspended the fortifying of Porto Novo and Villiyanallur on receiving the English complaint, but would not demolish what had already been built.

On November 12, 1756, news was received of the declaration of war with France and it was immediately communicated to all the garrisons in Bengal. The Madras Government when it sent Clive to Bengal, had reserved the power to recall him in the event of war with France. This was necessary in view of the danger of the English situation in the Presidency. At the end of the year 1756, it was felt that the northern settlements were under the grave risk of being lost and the possessions in Arcot were barely defensible. Madura was actually possessed and Tinnevelly was threatened by the rebels. Towards the end of October, Bussy and Law went to the Northern Circars, but Vizagapatam was then protected by a warship in the roads and it was thought that the French might not attack the northern settlements, lest the English should attempt reprisals and prevent them from collecting their revenues as usual. The Nawab again wanted that the English should attack the killedars of Chetpattu, Elavānāsur etc. But nothing was done lest the French might come into the field with equal forces. Mahfuz Khān was again troublesome and Caillaud was ordered to march to Madura to undertake the Sisyphian task of bringing him round; while Orme's secret negotiations with Mysore did not produce any results. Meanwhile, the strengthening of the walls and bastions of Fort St. George went on. Colonel Forde, with about 100 Europeans and 300 sepoys, went to assist the Nawab's army to expel Najībullah Khān, a brother of the Nawab and the renter of Nellore who had refused to pay his rents. News came that d'Auteuil, with 200 Frenchmen, was advancing to attack Mīr Sāhib, (an ex-commandant of French sepoys, known by the name of Shaikh Abdur Rahmān) the killedar of Elavānāsur, on account of his devastation of the French districts. The party was repulsed near the fort, on April 2, by Mīr Sāhib; but as the latter died, a few days after this attack, of a wound which he had received, and as d'Auteuil had received reinforcements from Pondicherry, the late killedar's brother abandoned the fort and left the French to occupy it on April 13. Having been warned that the French disputes over Elavānāsūr, Udayārpālayam, etc., were only to be utilised as a justification to cover a sudden attack on Trichinopoly, the Madras Committee, on April 11, ordered a party of 50 men thither from Fort St. David, and warned Caillaud to remain near Madura, so that he might return immediately to Trichinopoly if necessary. M. d'Auteuil moved from Elavānāsur to Vriddhachalam where he was joined by men despatched from all the French garrisons. He marched on May 4, and on May 7 was repulsed in an attack on Udayārpālayam. Having agreed with the poligar for the payment of a sum of money, on May 11, he moved so rapidly on Trichinopoly that on the next day his advance guard was enabled to pitch camp at Srirangam.

The Diarist's note on the capture of Elavānāsur is as follows:—" As for Elavānāsur, the fort was said to have been captured by Aumont who advanced against it from Tirukkovilur. Mīr Abdul Rahmān, *i.e.,* the Mīr Sāhib, fled from the place. It was even reported that in the first day's fight, a shot struck Mīr Sāhib and he was expected to die. M. d'Auteuil was said to have written to the Governor that Mīr Sāhib had died of his wounds and his younger brother and others had departed with their horse and families and goods, while 10 men from the fort of Tyagar (Tyagadrug) in the vicinity hoisted the English flag at Elavānāsur, saying that they were for the English. M. d'Auteuil, Aumont and others marched to the fort, removed the English flag and hoisted the French flag. On hearing of the fall of Elavānāsur, the killedar of Chetpattu wrote to Nawab Muhammad Alī and hoisted the white flag, thus making it appear that it had passed into their possession. Mīr Sāhib's women and others were seized and imprisoned."

To return to the narrative:—d'Auteuil who marched from Elavānāsur to Srirangam, took his post at Woriur, but the English thought that the reinforcements from Fort St. David were quite enough for the defence of the fort of Trichinopoly. M. d'Auteuil had about 800 Frenchmen and 2,000 sepoys with him. It was rumoured that about 300 of the French troops were planning to join the rebels of Madura. The English determined that they would send as much available reinforcement to Trichinopoly as was possible in the circumstances, especially since the French had drained all their garrisons to supply d'Auteuil with men. Colonel Forde's men from Nellore, Polier's company of Swiss troops and the sepoys and troops from Karunguzhi were to make up the reinforcements. The French abandoned Uttiramerur to Polier, though it was shortly afterwards retaken by them. It was suggested that Forde should, on his way south, retake and demolish Uttiramerur and, if possible, capture the garrison. It was even planned that if Caillaud could get into Trichinopoly and engage the French, Adlercorn who was sent with the Madras troops, was to reduce the French strongholds to the south. If the French should return from Trichinopoly to Pondicherry by land, Adlercorn was to engage them if he should feel confident of success.

Caillaud failed to secure Madura by the attempt at escalade that he made on it, while Forde, having attacked and taken Nellore. joined Adlercorn. Adlercorn was asked subsequently to reduce

Wandiwash. It was expected that he would be joined by the Nawab's troops and by those of the killedar of Chetpattu. The principal object of Adlercorn's movements was the removal of d'Auteuil; and it was effected by the arrival of the news of the English capture of Chandernagore, on receipt of which d'Auteuil was straightaway withdrawn to Pondicherry and Adlercorn was directed to return to Madras in order to avoid the expense of keeping up troops in the field.

The Chevalier de Soupire and the Chevalier de Dure, his second, arrived at Pondicherry with the Regiment of Lorraine and a company of artillery on September 9, 1757; and they were received with all honours by De Leyrit and the Council. The Diarist tells us that he heard from Mahē that eight Europe ships were sighted off that place and that they were probably those of Count de Lally's squadron that was expected soon. In reality, they were the squadron of Bouvet that brought the troops of Soupire. Bouvet returned from the Bay almost immediately after he landed the troops, on the ground that he was short of shot and that two of his ships were too high in the water even as it was, the shot being used as ballast in them. Mr. Dodwell says that his return was really due to his fear of being caught up by the approaching monsoon. Soupire was definitely instructed not to interfere with the administration and trade of Pondicherry and the country. Ranga Pillai continued to entertain hopes, based on the calculations of his Brahman astrologers, that King Louis XV was bound, according to his stars, to conquer the Muhammadan kingdoms in India and that he himself would share the King's prosperity.

The Diarist tells us that Diwan Sampati Rai who was hated by Muhammad Alī, was seized and imprisoned by the English at Madras and sent to Arcot on the ground of his intrigues with Mahfuz Khān and Najībullah Khān. Orme informs us that the Nawab left the government of Arcot when the French troops approached it in September, in the hands of his brother Abdul Wahāb, assisted by Sampati Rai and Abrār Khān, the Bakshi. The confusion in Arcot was then so great that almost everybody was suspected of treason and even Abdul Wahāb was not immune from the Nawab's fears of disloyalty; and a party of sepoys seized Sampati Rai and put him in confinement. It was not until a few days had passed that the English could at all restore to Muhammad Alī his peace of mind; but Abdul Wahāb Khān, who had retired, in like fear of injury to himself from disloyal chiefs, to Chittore, refused to return, began to enlist troops and corresponded with the Marathas.

In September, Pondicherry became stronger by about a thousand men owing to Soupire's arrival. This superiority of the French compelled the English to recall troops from the neighbouring country to Madras and also Caillaud who had taken possession of Madura, to return to Trichinopoly. Soupire began to prepare on October 2nd, for his campaign, along with d'Auteuil. The Diarist gives us the news that Barkatullah, the deputy of Mahfuz Khān delivered the fort of Madura to the English for a sum of Rs. 40,000, on the same day when Soupire arrived at Pondicherry. Caillaud evacuated the fort and marched to Trichinopoly, leaving the sepoy commandant, Yūsuf Khān, at Madura; and the Diarist tells us that Mahfuz Khān, the Mysore army and Haidar Alī would soon capture the Madura fort. News was also recorded by him that the French captured Chetpattu on the 13th October, seizing its killedar, Nāzir Muhammad. A large number of French soldiers must have fallen in the escalade. The French lost many soldiers before Chetpattu where the killedar continued to fight even in the streets after he had lost the fort; and his family then destroyed themselves. Then they occupied Tiruvannamalai which was abandoned on the French approach. Then the French army had to return to Pondicherry for the monsoon. Soupire had encamped part of his troops at Vaḻudāvur from the beginning of October, with a view to intercept any body of English troops that might be sent from Fort St. David or to prevent any succour from Madras for the killedar, Nāzir Muhammad. The main body of his troops remained at Pondicherry, awaiting the arrival of Lally's armament; and thus the year 1757 drew towards its close, with the Diarist hoping that Lally would make the French glory shine once more.

CHAPTER XVIII

GROWING TROUBLES—ARRIVAL OF LALLY

TROUBLES IN THE INDIAN TOWN OF PONDICHERRY

WE saw that from the time of the reinforcements including the famous Regiment of Lorraine and consisting of about a thousand soldiers from France, landing at Pondicherry in September under the Chevalier Soupire, the French position on the coast had become somewhat strengthened. The English were at that time too weak to offer any open opposition to them. Soupire immediately took the field after landing and encamped at Vaḻudāvur near Pondicherry. The first important event was the capture of the fortress of Chetpattu from Isārat Muhammad Khān who was killed in the course of the attack, followed by the plunder of the place including the cannon, guns and other weapons in the fort.

A very important matter about which our Diarist dwells at some length is with reference to the recrudescence of troubles between the right and left hand castes regarding their respective temple rights in the town of Pondicherry. The immediate occasion for this was the complaint of some blacksmiths and carpenters regarding the proposed taking out in procession of their Goddess Kali for the *Pārvēttai Vijayadasami* festival, along with the idols of Varadaraja Perumal and Kālahastīsvaran. They presented a petition to the Governor and got from him the necessary permission. Ranga Pillai, when he heard the news, felt greatly pleased, but remarked that, in this matter, it was only the consent of the right hand castes people that was required and not the permission of the Governor; but he carefully added that they had done wisely in getting the Governor's consent and advised them further to go and seek permission from the *Nāttārs* of the important right hand castes like the Kavarais, the Idaiyars, the Agamudaiyārs, the Veḷḷāḷars, the Kaikkōḷars[1] etc., and to " ask them softly to be

1 The Kaikkōḷars were a left-hand caste and not of the right-hand as was wrongly entered by the Diarist. According to some authorities on South Indian ethnography, Kaikkōḷan Dasis except those who are specially

pleased to allow your idols to be carried in procession along with Dharmaraja, Māriyāthāḷ, etc., idols, so that the procession may be more magnificent, and you, their servants, will be pleased." They replied that they would not approach anybody or beg other people with soft words when they had secured the Governor's permission; and the latter would certainly see to the proper performance of what he had promised, through Vinayakam Pillai. Ranga Pillai however narrated to them the past history of such disputes in Pondicherry and said that the right hand castes people would, in all probability, not agree easily in the present case.[2]

This present dispute assumed some importance. The Governor's agent interviewed some leaders of the right-hand castes who stubbornly maintained that they would not suffer a new thing to be done; and when they were threatened with the stopping of the procession of their own deity, they replied that they would

engaged by the Beri Chettis and Kammālans, were placed in the right hand faction. (Refer to note on Right and Left Hand Castes, by the author, *J.I.H.* Vol. XIII, Part II, Sec. XIII of the Historical Material, etc. 3; and also to the authorities quoted by him in foot-note 5 therein), and also to the paper by the author entitled 'Right and Left Hand Castes Disputes in Madras in the early part of the 18th Century'—published in the *Proceedings of the Twelfth Public Meeting of the Indian Historical Records Commission*, held at Gwalior, in December 1929, (Calcutta, 1930). —Refer *supra pp.* 275-77. Refer also to the Madras Council Consultation of 15th January, 1708, that "both (Right and Left hand) castes complain against the Kaicullawarrs and the oilmen that they were very fickle in their castes, that they were sometimes of one caste, and sometimes of another, which give trouble to both castes . . . . when the weavers declared for the Left Hand and the oilmen for the Right Hand which they were ordered to keep to, or be severely punished."

2 "When in M. de la Prévostiére's time the left-hand caste people tried to take Kalahasti Iswaran (the left-hand caste God) in procession, although Tiruvengada Pillai Avargal and Narasappa Nayakkan Avargal pleaded on their behalf, the right-hand people refused to yield. Again, although M. Lenoir searched the records 40 or 45 days and explained the whole matter to the right-hand caste people, the latter did not agree. But when M. Lenoir requested them to consider the case specially, they yielded."—Ranga Pillai's *Diary*, Vol. XI—Entry for Oct. 22, 1757, pp. 72–73.

rather see that happen than consent to this request. Though the Diarist advised them to do as the Governor directed, they persisted in maintaining their ground that they would agree to everything that might be suggested, but would not give way in an affair concerning their caste customs. Of course, the Diarist was deemed by his enemies to have been instrumental in having incited the right-hand castes people to refuse to accede to the Governor's wishes. The Governor naturally forbade the procession of Varadaraja Perumal, unless that of Goddess Kali also should be allowed to be taken out; and the net result was that the *pārvēttai* procession was not held on the proper day. Since the Governor allowed the Kālahastīsvaran procession, the Diarist communicated the order to the authorities of that temple; but they did not care to conduct their procession without Varadaraja Perumal accompanying it. The latter procession was thus not held for the first time since the town was founded. It was only several days later that the Governor finally agreed to the celebration of the *pārvēttai* festival for Varadaraja Swami and for Kālahastīsvaran. The attitude adopted in Pondicherry by the French towards the conduct of Hindu religious festivals and worship was certainly generally marked by a spirit of non-interference. The Hindus and Muhammadans of the settlement were allowed to have their own temples and mosques and to worship therein freely, though, on one occasion, we read that the Pondicherry Council imprisoned some natives who had repaired their temples without permission; but when it was explained that the Hindu residents believed that they had always the right to do this by virtue of the religious freedom impliedly accorded to them and long enjoyed by them, they were released, though the men who actually carried out the repairs were publicly reprimanded.

Miscellaneous Matters Recorded by the Diarist

After the landing of Soupire's reinforcements, active preparations were begun for the renewal of military operations, particularly against the English at Fort St. David. Soupire ordered the French troops from Vaḷudāvur to march to Arcot and capture it. The Governor De Leyrit keenly felt the lack of money; and both he and Soupire demanded the immediate payment of an alleged arrear of four lakhs of rupees due from the Diarist, according to the accounts kept of the country leases. The Diarist contended that his lease ran on for a term of five years, on the expiry of which the country management was taken away from him without his being informed; and that, according to the inquiries made of the renters by the Governor's commissaries, thirteen lakhs of rupees were still due on account of the lease to the lease-holder and therefore the Council still owed him nine lakhs. The Governor persisted in demanding from him payment within a week, of two lakhs out of the alleged four lakhs of his dues, on pain of his being put in prison. Then followed the conversation given below which shows how deeply and markedly the once powerful *courtier* had fallen out of favour and how much the frowns or favours of a Governor could alter the fortunes of even the most influential and wealthy Indian in an European settlement.[3]

3 The matter is given *in extenso* on account of its value in reflecting one important phase of life at Pondicherry.

"I (Diarist) replied, 'The Gods return no answer to men, but Kings are the voice of Gods. Should a God depart from truth, who can hinder Him? All power here is yours; and if your will is to act unjustly or untruly, none has authority to resist. Instead, therefore, of waiting a week to imprison me, imprison me now or punish me or do what you will with me. I stand before you. I cannot pay you two cash, so do not think that I shall be able to pay you two lakhs for fear that you will imprison me a week hence. Now, therefore, do what you will.'—'Why,' he (Leyrit) said, 'that is just how you have cheated me all along.' I answered: 'When you are in authority you are my father and God and all. The moment I understood that I had lost your favour, I concluded that my bad time had begun and confined myself to my house, and had nothing further to do with money transactions. I have come to the Fort once in four or five days to visit you, and then returned home, waiting for my bad time to end and my good time to begin. However much I lost and whatever people did to my hurt, I have kept quiet lest my words should bring on trouble. But since you think thus, my bad time still continues. You may therefore do what you will and I shall suffer it.'—'You have cheated me thus,' he replied, 'go.' I answered, 'I do not

An incident reported by the Diarist was about the attempted handing over to M. Moracin the Chief of Masulipatam, of the English ship, *Restitution*, by means of a plot hatched by the French prisoners who were on board. The ship was alleged by the Diarist to carry two lakhs of gold mohurs despatched by Clive from Calcutta to Madras. Mr. Dodwell considers that it is unlikely that the ship carried the large sum of money mentioned by the Diarist.[4]

The Diarist reported that Moracin landed the two lakhs of gold mohurs, rice, cloth etc., together with the English soldiers and sepoys, put Frenchmen on board in their stead and wrote to Pondicherry to that effect. Immediately the Diarist, greatly battered by fickle fortune, felt that a change in French fortunes was about to begin and congratulated himself that, just as French prospects began to decline from November 1756, when a French ship despatched to Mahē with five lakhs of rupees and goods was captured by an English ship from Tellicherry off the Mahē roads, so English fortunes would begin to decline from this capture of an English ship (Entry for November 14, 1757). Such was the keen optimism that marked the Diarist even at this stage.

mind whether you believe me or not. My father came here fifty years ago, and died 33 years ago. (The Diarist's father first settled in Pondicherry in 1716 and died in 1726) and always I have secured the Governors' kindness and not their anger, and they, in turn, have earned glory, not infamy. But in your time, I have received not kindness but anger, and this may bring dishonour to you, although God has placed you in a position of authority. I am but your servant and the country will extol or blame you for the good or evil that appears. God has been pleased to bless you with fortune, so you know everything, and your pleasure and my fortune are one."

4 The following is the account given in the despatch from the Select Committee at Madras to the Secret Committee, dated March 13, 1758. "The Chandernagore prisoners have been sent down by a cartel ship, the *Restitution*, for which Leyrit promised a safe conduct; but she was seized by the French prisoners and carried into Masulipatam. She has since arrived at Pondicherry. Leyrit refuses to return her at present on the pretext that the English broke the capitulation of Chandernagore. This at present prevents an exchange of prisoners."

In December, negotiations were begun again with the Peishwa; and presents were sent to him as well as to his younger brother (Raghunatha Rao), his vakil Balwant Rao and others. A strange rumour based upon a prophecy was recorded by the Diarist that the horoscope of the Peishwa naturally meant that he would be so fortunate as soon to displace the Mughal Emperor from the throne of Delhi and occupy it himself; and now, on the birth of a son to the Peishwa, the astrologers who cast his horoscope, said that the child would ascend the Padshah's throne at Delhi in the month of *Āvaṇi, Bahudānya,* corresponding to August-September 1758; and so the Peishwa was making preparations to realise that great contingency.[5]

5 The events that took place in the rotten heart of the Mughal Empire and that enabled the distant Diarist to hope for the fulfilment of his prophecy may be summarised here briefly in order to give the reader an idea of the extreme probability of the realisation of this aim. In April 1757 Ahmad Shāh Abdālī resolved to avenge the seizure at Lahore of Mīr Mannu's son by the insolent Ghāzī-ud-dīn Imad-ul-Mulk, advanced to Hindustan, took Delhi, where his soldiers committed a massacre and despatched a detachment which surprised the people of Muttra at a religious festival and killed many. And in June of that year, the Afghan returned to his kingdom, leaving Najīb-ud-Daula, as Amir-ul-Omara to protect the Emperor Ālamgīr II, from Ghāzī-ud-dīn. Raghunath Rao, the Peishwa's younger brother, marched from Rajputana to Delhi about the end of July after the dreaded Afghan had retired, and called upon Najīb-ud-Daula, to pay the customary chauth as in the reigns of Muhammad Shāh and his son, on the ground that the lands assigned to the Marathas in lieu of chauth had been occupied by Najīb and he was therefore personally responsible for the amount in cash. This demand was backed up by two contingents of Maratha soldiers, of Naro Sankar from Jhansi and of Sakaram Bapu from Jaipur. The subahdari of Agra was given by the Peishwa to Malhar Rao Holkar who nominated his own deputy to rule there. Proceeding from Agra as their base, the Marathas crossed the Jumna and sent a net-work of detachments to occupy the Doab up to the bank of Ganges, in June and July. Though they avoided Delhi at first, their approach caused *great trembling and scarcity of grain* in the capital. Najīb-ud-Daula advised the weak Emperor to prepare for boldly opposing the Marathas, if they should offer any attack.

In the last days of December the Diarist heard rumours that came from Madras that peace had been made in the previous September between the French and the English in Europe, while the Europeans at Pondicherry said that the English had given out only such news, because they were awaiting reinforcements and that it was too soon to expect news and that if really it had come, the French would have also received it. Bussy's army was said to have been then encamped outside Masulipatam. Again,

About the middle of July, Sakaram Bapu, the diwan of Raghunath Rao, and Tatya Gangadhar, the diwan of Malhar Rao, established their headquarters at Patparganj and plundered the grain-dealers engaged in bringing supplies to the capital. Najīb-ud-Daula ran a line of trenches outside the city, but soon withdrew most of his men from this line to the new city. The rest of the month of July and the first week of August were spent in mutual expectations of further developments. Then the Marathas from the east bank of the Jumna began to cross over to the Delhi side by boat in small parties and took their first stand about 20 miles south of the city. Their most advanced foragers were at first driven back, but they returned in greater strength, plundered the neighbourhood of Safdar Jang's tomb and a quarter of the old city, even looting several houses. Najib-ud-Daula tried to negotiate with the Maratha generals at Patparganj; but the latter demanded the removal of all his troops from the fort and his own evacuation of the city. Raghunath Rao attacked Delhi on the 11th of August 1757. One division of the Marathas entered the old fort and plundered old Delhi. A second division attacked the river bank, south-east of the city, while Ghāzī-ud-dīn visited Raghunath Rao and Malhar Rao for cementing his alliance with the invaders. Next day, the attack continued; and for a few days afterwards, bands of Maratha horsemen were sent round the city walls, while Najīb closed all the city gates and posted artillery and troops at each of them. The Marathas and Ghāzī-ud-dīn covered a semi-circle round the western side of Delhi and were entrenched opposite the Kashmir gate in the north-east. Fighting was renewed about the end of August. Thus, the learned Sir J. N. Sarkar described the situation at Delhi in the face of a Maratha attack. "Najib declined to resign his post or leave the capital unless Imad did the same on his part, and he offered only five lakhs. He preferred death in fight to the dishonour of accepting his enemies' exorbitant demands; he abused the Emperor for his cowardice and treachery and intercepted his letters to Imad. The Emperor was helpless, neither side would listen to him." Imad continued to fume over the Ruhela outrage on his harem (done by Najīb's orders

it was said that the French and English ships were reported to be sailing towards Mahē and Tellicherry for an engagement, and that when this became known at Cuddalore, the Governor ordered all the inhabitants to quit the place and so men were departing. Again, the Diarist tells us that Ghāzī-ud-dīn, who was then playing a most unenviable part in the politics of Delhi and had become, after the death of his father, Ghāzī-ud-dīn II, in 1752, the Amīr-ul-Omara with the title of Imad-ul-Mulk, was written to, asking for the grant of a *mansab* and *jaghir* to De Leyrit, the same as had been formerly granted to Dupleix and that a letter had been received on the 26th of December from Ghāzī-ud-dīn, granting to De Leyrit a mansab for 7,000 and to Mr. M. De Larche, one for 5,000 horse, and stating that jaghirs would be granted for the same honours in the Carnatic or in Hindustan. The mansab letter is also said to have conveyed a request to the Governor and to De Larche, asking for the supply of 1,000 soldiers and 200

in the course of repelling the Marathas) and Raghunath grumbled at his august personality being ignored and Najib negotiating with Malhar, whom Raghunath hated." (Page 150—*Fall of the Mughal Empire;* Vol. II, 1754–1771).

The most interesting feature was that Malhar Rao tried to soften Raghunath Rao and Ghāzī-ud-dīn; and at last Najīb consented to visit Malhar and accept any terms that the latter might dictate. The triumph of Maratha arms is best read in the words of Professor Sarkar who says that, "from the entry in the official history of the reign, the Emperor, as requested, sent robes of honour to Malhar to make new appointments at his own discretion; the persons inducted to office, after putting their *khilats* on, made their bows to Raghunath Rao in his tent." Thus the Marathas became supreme and Antaji Manakeshwar was appointed Imperial Faujdar of the environs of the capital. Raghunath Rao, however, was always apprehensive of a return of the Afghan invader. The Marathas however plundered Thaneswar on the way, took Sarhind in March 1758 and finally Lahore in April and thus completed the nominal conquest of even the Punjab. Thus Raghunath Rao is regarded as having carried Hindu paramountcy, i.e., *Hindu-pad-padshahi*, up to Attock; but this was really a hollow show and financially barren. It was possible for the Peishwa to have amicably marked out the Maratha and Afghan spheres of influence in Northern India.

artillery men, together with guns, powder, shot and other munitions of war. The Diarist believed that this was the reason why Ghāzī-ud-dīn sent the mansab letter.[6]

Bitterness Between De Leyrit and Soupire

The new year (1758) began with an open manifestation of the jealousy entertained by De Leyrit of Soupire on the ground that Ananda Ranga Pillai with his meticulous knowledge of the details of the previous administrations held that it was the Governor that was in charge of the administration of the country and that it was himself alone that should be visited by the amaldars, the ryots and the *mahānāttārs* on all ceremonial and official occasions. In ignorance of this, De Leyrit had told the amaldars and the ryots to pay their respects to Soupire, who shrank from accepting responsibility and was only in charge of the army.[7]

On the 14th of January, the Diarist heard that Soupire and De Leyrit had quarrelled so much that the latter was in fear of

6 Imad-ul-Mulk's policy, during the period of about six years when he was the Chancellor of the Mughal Empire (1752–58), was always one of open and vindictive opposition to the other powerful elements in the Mughal state, like Surajmal, Shūja-ud-Daula and Najīb Khān, the last of whom became the most powerful potentate in Northern India after Ahmad Shāh Abdālī's return to Afghanistan in April 1757. Najīb Khān greatly humiliated Imad, as was pointed out in a previous foot-note, on the occasion of the Maratha attack on Delhi in the autumn of 1757. Imad-ul-Mulk had always relied upon Maratha aid, but he knew that Maratha friendship and alliance depended upon the cash nexus and his own administrative incapacity prevented his regular payment of the sums due for the Maratha soldiers being maintained at Delhi. It was now that he thought of getting help from the French in the Carnatic. For a fuller account of Imad's policy and movements till 1758, see Chapter I, Sec. 2 and 3 of Sir Jadunath Sarkar's *Fall of the Mughal Empire*, Vol. II, (1754–1771).

Thus Ranga Pillai would maintain the superiority of the Governor who was also the Commandant-General. He wrote as follows in his *Diary*:—"The French recovered (Pondicherry?) from the Dutch on February 1, 1701 and hoisted the white flag; and the *mahānāttārs* did not visit the King's people in charge of the Fort when M. Martin was

being run through by the other, had left the *Gouvernement* and had taken up his residence in the old house of Dupleix, situated to the north of the Fort. The fault seems to have been that De Leyrit sent all the papers and communications to Soupire who took advantage of it to interfere in everything, instead of leaving the army alone in the Fort to act under Soupire's orders and himself attending to all other affairs of the administration. The situation was so bad that De Leyrit was afraid of even the *mahānāttārs* visiting him without Soupire's knowledge, while the merchants were cautioned to do so only secretly.

Soupire complained very bitterly of the very unsatisfactory condition of the administration and, particularly, of the bad state of the finances. He sent his own men to inquire how matters were going on in the country parts and got a report that affairs were very bad.[8]

Governor. When M. Hébert came as Governor in 1708, he brought a letter from the King which he gave to the King's people, and, after sending them back to Europe, remained himself in the Fort. During the Governorship of M. Lenoir, M. Lebo, the King's man, arrived in 1728 as the chief in command of the Fort and troops. M. Lenoir thought that he would be powerless if this man commanded the Fort without regard to him, and, writing to Europe, obtained a letter from the King for his removal. So M. (La Farelle) was the only Major-General, and, ever since M. Lenoir's time, the Governor has been called Commandant-General. Now M. Soupire is the Brigadier who has come to conduct the war. The first in military rank is called Marechal de France; next to this is the Lieutenant-General; below this is the Marechal-de-camp; below him is Brigadier; then Colonel; then Commandant; then Capitaine; then Major, and lastly the officers. These are the ranks of men in the army; their duty is to fight and they have nothing to do with administration. The Minister, then the General, then the Governor, and lastly the Councillors, are the people in charge of the administration of the country, and these should be visited by the amaldars, the ryots and *mahānāttārs*. In ignorance of this, M. Leyrit told the amaldars and ryots to visit M. Soupire, the Brigadier, and so the Governor has spoiled everything." (pp. 93–94 of the *Diary*, Vol. XI).

8 The Diarist's entry for Feb. 11, contains an account of what was supposed to have passed between Soupire and De Leyrit on the basis of this report and in the presence of the Councillors. Soupire said "What

Even otherwise, the King's soldiers were said to have created great trouble among the inhabitants. The King's officers were said to have been in arrears of their pay for three months and when they asked De Leyrit for payment, he retorted that they could take service elsewhere if they pleased, that the Company had no money and he could pay them only when money should be obtained.

Ranga Pillai found his own fortunes very perverse in every respect. He heard from two of the King's officers that Lally spent several months with Dupleix, writing down everything about the condition of affairs in India and what establishments would be required and what forces should be sent from Europe for conquering the whole country right up to Delhi. This was evidently a reference to the memoir that Lally prepared on the state of India, advocating the reversal of Dupleix's policy. The Diarist exclaimed: "I have not written a quarter of what they said in praise of M. Lally's talents, but enough to show what kind of man he is."

De Leyrit even gave away Ranga Pillai to Soupire, telling him that he deceived everyone and was worth nothing and it was only Barthelemy that championed his cause and declared that he was upright, while the Company was greatly indebted to him. From all these, the Diarist could only hope that, with the arrival of Lally, his fortunes might possibly change, particularly as the evil influence of the asterism, *Rahu,* had expired in his horoscope and the three years of misfortune predicted thereby had come to an end just about a month before.

In February 1758, an attempt was made by the French administration to make a demonstration against Fort St. David. De Leyrit and Soupire marched on the 25th with 300 soldiers, 200 foot and one gun to Marikrishnapuram almost within the sight

a government is yours! Instead of urging the people to attend to the cultivation, the men you send into the country beat the ryots and harass them by unlawful means to obtain money from them. How can money be expected from the country like that? and how will you be able to pay the Company?"

of Tēvanāmpatnam, where they fired with the gun two or three times, poured out several volleys of shot with their small arms and plundered the surrounding villages. Upon this, the people of Manjakuppam, Tiruppadirippuliyur and Cuddalore fled in panic towards Fort St. David; but the commander of the latter place fired on them with four guns, whereon they returned; also it was said that in four or five days, troops would be marching on Fort St. David. The general situation was that the French were believed to have got a superiority on the coast on account of the expected arrival of Lally's squadron.

Shortly before this incident happened, the Diarist had heard of the set-back to the fortunes of the Marathas that took place in February. We saw that Amrit Rao, the Maratha agent, had reached Arcot and from thence proceeded, along with Muhammad Alī, to Madras and compelled the Nawab to pay him a large sum. Now the Pathan Nawabs made an attempt at the vindication of their strength against the Marathas. Abdul Nabī Khān, the cousin-german and the nearest relation of the late Nawab of Cuddapah who had been killed in battle in the previous year, entrenched himself at Siddhout, a very strong fortress near his head-quarters. The other Nawabs stood on their defence in their respective fortresses. Balwant Rao, the chief agent of the Peishwa, sent vakils to negotiate with Abdul Nabī and at the same time despatched troops to harry the estates of the chiefs of Kālahasti and Venkatagiri, namely, Dāmarla Venkatappa and Bangaru Yachama Nayak. He himself appeared before Nellore and attacked Najībullah Khān, the brother of Muhammad Alī, who was in charge of that place, in order to prevent the latter from marching against the Nawabs with a large body of French troops which he heard were advancing to join him from Bussy's army. Najībullah paid immediately a sum of money satisfying the expectations of Balwant Rao, who had, however, meanwhile plundered the fair towns of Venkatagiri and Kālahasti and frightened their poligars, who immediately gave him bonds and securities for the payment of their tributes to the Nawab. Balwant Rao and his troops then returned to Cuddapah where he made a treaty with Abdul Nabī

Khān agreeing to divide the subah of Cuddapah equally with him. Then he took possession of Gurramkonda and later marched back to Sirpi with orders that Amrit Rao should join him there.

Abdul Wahāb Khān, another brother of Nawab Muhammad Alī, moved about the same time to Chittoor from Chandragiri near Tirupati; and Murtazā Alī of Vellore, with the help of the troops of Abdul Wahāb and also those of the Marathas under Amrit Rao, now marched against Tiruppattur and in the beginning of February, began an assault on that fort. The day after the assault was begun, a cannon ball killed Amrit Rao on which the garrison sallied out, routed the besiegers and took their cannon; and the Marathas immediately retired to join the main body of their troops under Balwant Rao, while the others returned home. Below is given the version of the death of Amrit Rao as the Diarist heard it.[9]

In February 1758, we have details given by the Diarist regarding the accounts of the country management during the years of *Bhava* and *Yuva* (1754-56) and also of the subsequent year of *Dhāthu*. Reference has already been made to the commandants of troops receiving money from the renters illegally and the European sureties appropriating large sums for themselves from the country revenues. Ranga Pillai gives a statement of account of the payments he had made in ready money and in grain, besides what he had paid to the sepoys and the commandants.

9 "When Amirta Rao, the Nana's man, marched against Vaniyambadi and Tiruppattur forts, the Navait Pathans who were in possession of those forts sent word to Amirta Rao that they were ready for war. Amirta Rao replied, inviting them to battle, divided his army into three detachments, posting them in three places, himself waiting with ten horse in a place of safety. The Navaits, learning this, secretly marched with 200 horsemen by the foot of the mountain and appeared before Amirta Rao's troops. Immediately Amirta Rao mounted his horse, advanced with ten horsemen, and fell upon the enemy who lost ten horses, but who managed to kill Amirta Rao's ten horsemen and wound him severely. Amirta Rao was carried to Tiruppattur fort, and his wounds dressed, but at the time of the removal of the third dressing, he died, whereon his troops retreated." (p. 105 of the *Diary*, Vol. XI).

He claimed also certain sums that should have been properly credited to his account, like the amounts of commission due to him, the amounts paid to the European sureties, the sums violently seized by the commandants, the losses sustained on account of troubles caused by them and the sums spent on the repairs of tanks and canals. He objected to the addition of 10% for *rusum* (*i.e.*, customary perquisites) and for *sādalwār* (*i.e.*, contingencies etc.), as being improperly included and therefore as causing him a loss of five lakhs and odd in all. Since July 1756, *i.e.*, the beginning of the second quarter of *Dhāthu*, commissaries inspected the country and took possession of it; and hence the Diarist was not able to demand the arrears which were due for his part of the lease. The *amaldars* were not allowed to speak to him either about the country or about general affairs; and he was put to great trouble. He represented that he had sustained, on the whole, a loss of eight lakhs of rupees during the two years of his management and maintained that he was given at first a lease for five years and was made to pay the whole stipulated amount when the yield was only five-eighths. He also pleaded that Godeheu had told him to take up the management of the country with a lease for five years for the present and that if he should find it difficult to collect the lease amount in one year, he might pay it in the course of the succeeding year and assured him that, in the matter of collection of rents, he would enjoy the same powers of punishment as the *subahdars* of old and that the Governor would have nothing to do with the business save to help him when necessary. Ranga Pillai had early complained that the country was in a miserable condition and money had to be advanced to the cultivators who had run away and who had to be promised liberal *vāram* rates in order to be brought back and that it would take two years for the land to recover. Now the Governor would not listen to all his pleadings and statements and the only course left to him was to be patient and bide a return of luck. On the 27th February, a proclamation was issued by the Governor limiting the rate of interest for Europeans to 8% per annum as in Godeheu's time. Now the new Governor reiterated the rates though these had not been observed, and money-lenders usually charged from 10 to 12% per month.

The Diarist's entry for the 1st of March shows that English reinforcements to the extent of twelve ships, including five ships from Bengal and laden with goods and rice had reached Madras. Soupire bitterly blamed De Leyrit that he had, on plea of lack of money, unwisely refrained from attacking Madras when it was weak and so had lost chances of success; and now, Madras had been greatly strengthened. Their mutual recriminations are interesting as reported by the Diarist.[10]

Evidently these ideas of De Leyrit's unpatriotic avarice were current in France itself and reports of his alleged embezzlement of public funds had been brought by Soupire from France.

This was not the worst. An incident is reported by the Diarist, under entry for March 8, of a serious altercation between one of the King's officers and Desvaux, the latter being charged by the former of having robbed the Company in conjunction with De Leyrit and therefore speaking so hotly that the former in anger gave him severe blows with his cane. Desvaux and De Leyrit went to Soupire and asked him angrily if such uncivil behaviour could be tolerated. Soupire replied equally angrily that this, or even worse, would be done if money could not be had and that M. Lally should learn the whole matter on his arrival.

10 To Soupire's charge, "M. Leyrit replied, 'Did I refuse money when the Company had not?' M. Soupire replied, 'You are right; how could the Company have any money when all that had been collected had been shared among you? Do I not know that you have 1,20,000 pagodas in M. Desvaux's house to be sent to Europe by the Portuguese ship? You say that you have not a single cash for pay, but you have money to send to Europe. You have ruined the country and so prevented the Company from receiving money. You seem to think I do not know that M. Desvaux has been the agent of many of you in embezzling money, but I know everything.' M. Leyrit replied, 'You say that I have 1,20,000 pagodas ready to send by the Portuguese ship. If you will prove this, I will give you twice as much at once.' M. Soupire replied, 'I will prove not only this, but other things too.'"

De Leyrit then went to his own room, his anger and wrath having somewhat abated. The Diarist says: "Nobody knows what will happen; English sloops and ships are cruising about, sometimes in, sometimes out of sight." After this incident, De Leyrit and Soupire took meals in separate rooms, apart from each other and without speaking with one another. De Leyrit, fearing what Soupire might do, sent for the Company's Commandant and sought his protection; and the latter assured him that he would call on the Company's officers and soldiers to do their utmost, should Soupire contemplate any act of violence. Further scenes like this occurred. On one occasion, Soupire roundly charged De Leyrit, Delarche, Barthélemy, Desvaux and Du Bausset with having stolen the Company's moneys and threatened that, if they should not render a complete account, he would confiscate their properties and get them punished.[11]

The strain went so far that Soupire had to forbid the Tamils to go upstairs in the *Gouvernement* and the sentry on duty should first carry De Leyrit's letters to the officers in waiting who should give them first to him in order that they might be read both by him and by De Leyrit in the presence of both of them and no letter should be taken away until the Governor should have read it out to him.

Abdul Wahāb Khān wanted the help of 500 Europeans and 20 cannon, powder and shot, saying that he had 2,000 horsemen and as many foot and that he had received a grant of the Arcot subah and with French help, he would be able to march to and capture Arcot and that he desired to receive the same treatment as was given to Chandā Sāhib formerly.

The Peishwa's vakil wrote that Razā Sāhib had not delivered the goods promised and therefore he had sent an angry remonstrance to the latter. Great efforts were made for securing support for Razā Sāhib as it was expected that Lally was bringing

11 "You and M. Barthelemy shall be chained, beaten and hanged; and the others shall be hanged outside the South Gate; and your *dubashes* shall be hanged outside the Fort for all to see. When M. Lally arrives, I will place the accounts before him and cause him do all this,

out the King's orders that the Muhammadans should be given the management of the country and that Razā Sāhib should be appointed to the subah of Arcot. The Diarist also describes, in the course of his narrative, the plot formed at Trichinopoly about December 1757, by a Frenchman, named La Forge, for the release of the French prisoners imprisoned in that fort by attempting to seduce certain Frenchmen who had taken service with the English. The plot was, however, betrayed to the English Commander Caillaud who ordered the physician concerned (i.e. La Forge) to be hanged. The Diarist says that De Leyrit had been informed of this attempt by the conspirators and had directed all the French troops in Srirangam to be alert on the particular day fixed for the *coup* and to march out at a moment's notice. He also says that the physician and the fifteen Frenchmen whom he had conspired with, were all of them hanged. The English Military Consultations for January 12, 1758, tell us, however, that the betrayer did not believe in the promise held out to him and said that "the French would be paying the arrears with blows."

The end of March also saw disorder continuing on account of the soldiers and an officer going about threateningly with drawn swords in their hands in the streets and the Nayinar, as the head peon of Pondicherry was called, pleading that he could not seize them as he was unarmed. The English ships which had arrived on the coast were cruising about threateningly against the approach of Lally's fleet.

Lally's Landing

Early in April, Pondicherry was all agog expecting the daily arrival of Lally whose ships had been sighted this side of Mahē; and cattle, fowls and other things were being got ready against the approach of his fleet. De Leyrit himself removed to Dupleix's old house outside the citadel. The rumour began to prevail that Lally and his squadron would not be coming in that month, as it

and, should he not come, I will do it myself." (Soupire's words as written by the Diarist, entry for March 12, 1758, pp. 123–4 of *Diary*, Vol. XI).

usually blew violently in the Bay and that he wanted first to take Tellicherry and another English port and would come to the Coromandel only afterwards. De Leyrit was so much disliked by Soupire that his good ally, Desvaux, would not be allowed into the fort; and the general once refused to sit at table along with De Leyrit, as Desvaux was also seated by his side.

The Diarist got the alarming information from Bishop Noronha that De Leyrit had been telling Soupire that he himself was the worst of the Tamils, the Bishop himself was the worst of the Portuguese and M. Boyelleau was the worst among the French. Bishop Noronha further told him that the *dubashes* of De Leyrit and Desvaux and two other persons, who had been most guilty of peculation, would be duly hanged on Lally's arrival, outside the fort, while a number of guilty Europeans would be sent back to Europe, as Soupire had made a full enquiry and reported all that he had heard to Lally. There was no end to Soupire's complaints against De Leyrit for his not giving him any money at all, though he had been believed to have made about 20 to 30 lakhs of rupees.

On April 28, an English ship was sighted off the coast, while news was received of Lally's arrival in the Pondicherry roads. Lally had been named Syndic of the Company, Commissary for the King and Commandant General of all the French establishments in India. The English ships fired shots, one of which fell close to Lally's ship and another even struck it. Lally immediately ordered a gun to be fired, struck the flag he was flying and hoisted a red one. He was received by Soupire who rowed up to his ship; while, half-way to the shore, De Leyrit welcomed him. Lally was received with a salute of 21 guns. Immediately after landing, he ordered[12] that Soupire should proceed to help him in the attack on Fort St. David which he had planned, while the ships following him were to make off at once to the place.

12 "M. Lally having left Europe in May last, reached Mascareigne in December and stayed there forty days; he sailed again on January 26, reached Karikal on the afternoon of April 27, (corresponding with *Chittirai* 18), where a captain went ashore to get news as D'Ache was unwell, and then, setting sail, reached Pondicherry at noon on the 28th.

He ordered also the European officers and soldiers, the German troops and foot to march at once by land to Fort St. David that very night. He further demanded that 4,000 earth-diggers and bullocks should be got ready as well as powder, shot and guns, munitions of war and provisions which should be sent on at once. Lastly, he posted some of the King's soldiers at the Fort gates with orders to allow no one to go out and wrote letters describing what should be done as soon as the ships should reach the Fort St. David roads.

De Leyrit set about vigorously to collect horses, cattle, coolies etc., without delay and also attended to the unloading of Lally's goods from the ships. On the next day, *i.e.*, April 29th, the Diarist heard news that Tiruppadiripuliyur had been plundered the previous night, and Cuddalore was seized that morning and plundered and set on fire; but he believed that this news could not be true. It was also said that Manjakuppam, to the west of Fort St. David, was seized, while entrenchments were dug round the fort and shots were fired into it. When nine English ships from Madras arrived in the afternoon to reinforce the Cuddalore troops, the nine French ships already engaged in attacking the fort opened fire on them. The two ships which came with Lally to Pondicherry now hoisted sail and stood to the east to intercept the English ships, which they attacked. The ships of both sides then put out and the sound of firing from them ceased towards the evening. "Each man tells a different story and each minute brings different news " was the remark of the Diarist on this.

Lally (*Memoire*, p. 39) says that on his arrival in the roads his vessel, the *Comte de Provence*, was saluted by five-shotted guns, three of which passed through her and two damaged the rigging. D'Ache (*Third Memoire*, p. 8) says that as soon as Lally went on board the *Comte de Provence*, he hoisted the square flag at the main-mast as the sign of his rank. A comparison of these statements with the narrative in the text suggests that Lally's flag was the reason why his vessel was not recognized as being French. The firing evidently was not part of the formal salute of welcome as Malleson (*The French in India*, p.–515) supposed."

The Siege and Surrender of Fort St. David

Soupire marched to Fort St. David on the 29th; but when he and Lally reached that place, the troops demanded why they should be left to die of starvation instead of falling in the field by the hand of the enemy. Lally at once returned in a great rage to Pondicherry and angrily roused De Leyrit from his sleep several times in the course of the night; and the Diarist tells us that it was this continuous nocturnal teasing that made Lally violently hateful to De Leyrit in a single day. Orders were given by Lally to the Marquis de Conflans who had set out for the north, to return. Likewise, strict instructions were given to De Leyrit that he should consult Lally in everything and carry out all his orders correctly.

Two of the vessels of the English had run ashore in the engagement referred to above and had to be burnt. The Diarist says that the remaining ships were damaged and put to flight; but according to English records, the latter obtained a slight, though not a decisive, advantage over the French fleet.[13]

13 "Report the arrival of 11 French ships under the command of D'Ache, with Lally as Commander-in-Chief of all the French forces. They appeared off Fort St. David April 27–8 dropping anchor, 2 lying out to sea, and 2 proceeding to Pondicherry. Pococke and Steevens sailed southward from Madras April 17, with His Majesty's ships, the *Yarmouth, Elizabeth, Tyger, Cumberland, Weymouth, Salisbury, Newcastle* and *Queenborough*. Pococke put into Negapatam, and having sailed by Karikal and other southern ports, reached Fort St. David—April 29. The French on his appearance, put out to sea. Pococke chased them. The two fleets formed a line of battle about noon; but it was not till 3 o'clock in the afternoon that the engagement began 10 leagues northward of Pondicherry. After 2 hours, the French Admiral broke the line and bore away, followed by the other 8 ships, and on being joined by the other two which had been away to leeward, 'hauled their wind' to the south-west. The masts and rigging of our squadron were so much damaged that they could not sail so well to windward. The French reached the coast at Alambarai where one of them, the *Bien-Aime*, 74 guns, was obliged to run ashore. The rest reached Pondicherry while ours were repairing their damages between Sadras and Covelong. Lally reached Pondicherry the 28th." The same letter

A great obstacle confronting the French was the difficulty of sending sufficient provisions for the troops at Fort St. David. An order was given that all the liquor and arrack stored in Pondicherry were not to be sold, but were to be given over to the Government for the use of the troops in the field.

On May 4, the Diarist heard the news that, in the third watch of the previous day, French troops marched to Cuddalore and hoisted the white flag; while a proclamation was made that any English sepoy would be killed at sight. Lally himself had arrived at the Cuddalore Garden House on the 1st of May and had detatched the Comte d'Estaigne across the Gadilam river to reconnoitre and take a post near Cuddalore. The place remained in the same condition of fortification as when attacked twelve years before by Dupleix. It was surrounded on the three land sides with a rampart and small bastions, but had no ditch or other advance defences. It was open on the sea side, but the approach to this side was flanked by two bastions at the extremities; and the French attackers, according to Orme, thought that the sea face was also defended.

Lally proposed, even on the 2nd of May, a conference with the English Commandant at Fort St. David, on the subject of the feeding of the French prisoners[14] and also on that of the surrender

(Despatch from the Select Committee at Madras to the Secret Committee of the Company, dated May 20, 1758) tells us that though the English squadron prevented the French from landing more men, they had been collecting all their forces at Fort St. David, being posted at the Garden-House (present residence of the Collector of South Arcot) and at Cuddalore which being of great extent, was surrendered by the two companies of sepoys left there. The opinion was that everything possible had been done for the defence of Fort St. David, the provisions had been plentiful and the garrison was as large as could be spared from Madras. The crew of two ships threw themselves into the fort when their ships were surrounded by the French squadron.

14 The practice was that even when soldiers of one side fell into the hands of the enemy, they were still a burden on their former masters, Thus the French had to feed their own men in the hands of the English. Muhammad Alī deemed this 'the European style of treating prisoners. Dupleix laid the blame for this practice on Lawrence and the English

of Cuddalore. Major Polier, the commander at Fort St. David, went to Lally and after much discussion, it was agreed on the 3rd that Cuddalore should be delivered up at sunrise on the 4th, provided a battery of heavy cannon had at that time been made ready to open fire, and then the English garrison at Cuddalore would be permitted to retire to Fort St. David with their arms and field ammunition and the French prisoners therein should be released and sent over to proceed to any of the neutral ports of the south like Tranquebar or Porto Novo where they were to remain until the fate of Fort St. David should be decided.

The Diarist has given us plenty of information about the discontent that became manifest in Pondicherry even immediately after the arrival of Lally. The hurry which marked Lally's advance on Fort St. David, had prevented him from collecting the necessary number of coolies and other labourers for the seige operations required for the reduction of that place. A number of the Indians of the settlement were pressed into service and employed in carrying earth and burdens and doing other services. Orme remarks: "The violence created terror; the disgrace indignation." The head peon was very busy collecting provisions and men. The Diarist's own *agraharam* was practically denuded of supplies of rice, ghee, fowls, sheep and other provisions in order to provide for the soldiers and sailors landed from the French ships, which also disembarked 32 chests of silver. He was forced to give up all his horses except two lame ones, even they being demanded at one time.

The Diarist tells us that Boyelleau was appointed to make an inventory of the goods found in Cuddalore on its surrender, and Lally declared before the Councillors—so we read in the *Diary*—that he would not talk with them until Fort St. David and Madras should have been captured.

who were deemed to have begun it. But "whoever may have been responsible for it, the burden falling on the French in 1752 (and later) after a series of set-backs must have been grievous." (W. H. Dalgleish: *The Company of the Indies in the Days of Dupleix* (1933), p. 176.)

Lally rejoined the troops before Fort St. David on the night of May 10th; there had been no fighting, but English ships were cruising to and fro near the coast. On May 12th, there was some sharp fighting in Fort St. David, where they raised a battery south of the Pennar river. Lally set out again to Fort St. David on the evening of the 14th. The situation in Pondicherry was very bad. All the pack-bullocks had been seized, rice and paddy were very scarce; while ten months' pay, amounting to 17 lakhs, was owing to the soldiers and officers who had accompanied Lally. On the 15th, the Diarist heard that the French had occupied the ground to the north of Fort St. David, comprising the Dutch factory and the sand-hills, as well as the entrenchments on the south. Great efforts were made by De Leyrit to get men to transfer the three mortars required most urgently by Lally. On the 16th, Lally's troops attacked the Uppalavadi Battery[15], and the Company's

15 Fort St. David stood in the angle where the canal running from the Gadilam river near its mouth to the Pennar, joins the former. The bed of the Pennar was 1,800 yards to its north. Its garrison consisted of 1,600 sepoys, lascars and topasses, about 620 Europeans including 80 invalid pensioners and 250 seamen landed from the two ships which had run ashore.

'By many additions and improvements Fort St. David was now become a fortification armed at all points; but the original defect of want of space in the body of the place still remained; being only 140 feet from W. to E. and 390 from N. to S. The four bastions at the angles mounted each 12 guns. The curtains, as well as the bastions, were surrounded by a faussebray with a brick parapet. The outworks were a horn-work to the north, mounting 34 guns; two large ravelins, one on the east, the other on the west; a ditch round all, which had a cuvette cut along the middle, and was supplied with water from the river of Tripapolore; scarp and counter-scarp of the ditch faced with brick; a broad covered way excellently pallisaded, with arrows at the salient angles commanding the glacis, and the glacis itself was provided with well-constructed mines. All these works, excepting the horn-work, were planned by Mr. Robins, but the horn-work was raised before his arrival in India with much ignorance and expense, the whole being of solid masonry, and the rampart too narrow to admit the free recoil of the guns. The ground to the north of the fort, included by the sea, the rivers of Panar and Tripapolore, and the canal which joins them, is a

troops, the Chukklers' Battery, which was soon captured. Lally cut off the reinforcements that were sent from the Fort to strengthen the fighters in the Uppalavadi Battery which he captured, killing 40 soldiers and 300 sepoys. Two batteries had thus been taken and there were only two more. The sound of guns was heard at Pondicherry all through the 17th evening. The next day, a lakh of rupees was collected somehow by De Leyrit and sent to Lally for the army expenses. The latter also contrived to lade a ship with cannon, bombs, shot, powder chests, bundles of leaves and other things; and labourers had to be impressed for the task with extraordinary difficulty; and the Diarist noted that the Governor would not spare even Chettis, merchants and Brahmans for the purpose. He had to protest, when he was asked to provide 1,000 labourers at a very short notice, that he could secure only 300 and that all the available men in the town had gone to the camp and no more coolies were forthcoming.

The Diarist reported on the 19th May that two men came out from Fort St. David to treat for peace with Lally, offering to surrender the fort and the Company's goods therein, on condition of being allowed to depart with their arms and goods and money. Lally is said to have declared that only the women in the fort could go away without interference, but the men must lay down their arms and march out under guard and not like victors with

plot of sand, rising in several parts into large hillocks, which afford good shelter against the fort. On the edge of the canal, 1,300 yards to the north of the fort, stood on obsolete redoubt, called Chuckly-point. It was of masonry, square, mounted eight guns, and in the area were lodgments for the guard; the entrance was a pallisaded gate under an arch, but the redoubt was not enclosed by a ditch. About 200 yards to the right of this stood another such redoubt, on a sandhill called Patcharee. Four hundred yards in the rear of these redoubts was another sandhill, much larger than that of Patcharee, on which the Dutch had a factory-house called Thevenapatam; but the house had lately been demolished; and a fascine battery of five guns was raised on the hill. In a line on the left of this hill, and on the brink of the canal, was a gateway, with a narrow rampart and battlement." (Orme's *History of Indostan*, Vol. II, p. 307—See also Orme's Plan of Fort St. David with the French Attack, May, 1758 in Vol. III (of the 4th ed.)

their goods and weapons. By now 50 or 60 Europeans seemed to have died and there were left only about 150 Europeans and 100 topasses. This attempted negotiation is not mentioned by Orme or in the English records.

There was no active firing heard on the 20th; and only slight firing marked the operations of the next day. The French had been provisioned on a plentiful scale and Lally was held to be conducting the attack very carefully; and an English ship that appeared opposite Fort St. David soon put out to sea, being warned of the danger.[16]

Aumont marched against Devikottai with some troopers, soldiers and foot and plundered Achalpuram in the neighbourhood; and a body of Europeans and sepoys, 500 strong, was encamped before Devikottai, reinforced by 400 or 500 of Gadai Rao's horsemen who hoped to secure their favour and prevent them from plundering the country. De Leyrit withdrew all troops from Srirangam on Lally's orders, whereon the English at Trichinopoly marched out, seized the place and carried away 125 guns and a lakh of pagodas worth of powder and shot. Parts of the forts of Chettupattu, Tiruvarangam and Kallakurichi were demolished and deserted.

By May 28, Lally was said to have completed four batteries at the camp and intended to carry the Fort by assault on the third day. A meeting of D'Ache and the Pondicherry administration was held that day to decide about attacking the English ships and Madras. D'Ache, the admiral, put out to sea for action, while the English ships were drawing near and had fired on the Alambarai fort. On the 1st of June, the Diarist heard that shells broke the flag-staff at Fort St. David and damaged the first storey which had

16 The English admiral, Pococke, after his encounter of April 29th, began repairing the damages of his ships between Sadras and Covelong. He was off Alambarai (a French possession) on May 13th; he was not inclined to attack the French ships if he could not encounter them outside the Pondicherry roads. If the French avoided a second action with him, Pococke intended to proceed to Fort St. David to assist it if possible. Pococke could not get south of Alambarai (May 26th).

to be pulled down, while the guns from Cuddalore destroyed the southern wall. The powder-magazine also exploded, killing many. At 9, on the morning of the 2nd June, there being no drinking water available at all, the white flag was hoisted on the fort and the keys were brought out under another. The commandant was imprisoned and the rest were made to sign *parole.* Though it was rumoured that about 60 lakhs worth of property had been got in the fort, besides a *jhul* (horse-cloth) set with precious stones, the treasure that was actually brought to Pondicherry could not have been worth more than a lakh and a half of rupees. Wynch, the Governor of Fort St. David, Sloper, the Chief of Cuddalore and other English Councillors and officers were brought to Pondicherry and lodged in the old Gouvernement.[17]

Lally himself, immediately after the surrender of Fort St. David, set out for Devikottai, even on the 3rd June. He accompanied the troops as far as Chidambaram and sent a party against Palayamkottai which surrendered. Devikottai likewise capitulated to D'Estaing who appeared before it on the 4th and its garrison retreated through the Tanjore country to Trichinopoly. Lally made a triumphant entry into Pondicherry on the evening of the 9th and proceeded to a magnificent *Te Deum* and a very sumptuous entertainment.[18] (** Orme says that he made his triumphal entry on the 7th).

17 The articles of capitulation are recorded in the Madras Military Consultations of June 12; and the resolution of the council of war held on the 1st, in the Military Consultations of June 27th. These explain the condition of the garrison and the reasons for surrender. The charge was made that Lally did not keep even one of the articles.

18 "As M. Lally was returning victorious, preparations were going forward from early morning to three o'clock to-day; the officials, vakils, merchants, *mahānāttārs* and various people from the bound villages and Villiyanallur were told of his coming; those who could not give nazars were supplied with rolls of silk, dresses of honour, pieces of cloth, pagodas and rupees; the *naubat,* standards, music and dancing-girls, elephants and camels, flags and the other marks of honour were ordered to be brought; I set out with all marks of honour.................In front of us went people with music and dancing-girls, flags, standards and other marks of honour. Behind us came troopers with drawn swords; next to these

Ranga Pillai was held up in honour by Montmorency to Lally as the Company's *Courtier* and presented him with gifts. He arranged for the visit of the *mahānāttārs,*[19] *monegārs* and others to Lally on the next day, the 10th, and presented them one by one, to the great man. The *Diary* gives an exhaustive list of the *nazars* given by them and proudly recorded that he procured an order for the release of almost all that were in prison.

came the General on horseback; then came officers and gentlemen, and lastly the *naubat* was carried. *Tōraṇams* had been tied in every street; plantain trees and cocoanut branches had been erected; water sprinkled; *kōrai* spread and other decorations made from the Bound-hedge to the town. M. Lally, as he came, observed all these decorations. When he entered the gate, a salute of 21 guns was fired, and then four Councillors received him. As he passed by the mint, M. Leyrit, the Governor, M. Barthelemy and the other Councillors escorted him to the Capuchin's Church, where mass was heard, a salute of 21 guns fired, followed by another when he entered the Fort."

(Ananda Ranga Pillai's *Diary,* Entry for June 9. Vol. XI, pp. 194-6).

19 Among the *mahānāttārs* were the Veḷḷāḷas, the Chettis, the Kōmuttis, the painters (of cloth), the Kaikkōḷars, washermen, carpenters and blacksmiths, the Vāṇiyans (oil mongers), gold-smiths, brass-smiths, betel-leaf sellers, the Shaṇiyans, the coral-merchants, the Agamudaiyāns, the indigo-merchants, the pressing people, the potters, the cloth merchants, the arrack-renters, the shroffs, the grocers, the people of the country management besides the renters of the different districts, the Company's merchants and the vakils of the Indian potentates. The list given on pp. 201–203 of the *Diary*: Vol. XI, is very instructive as to the organisation of the Indian society of Pondicherry in its relation to the administration.

CHAPTER XIX

THE BEGINNING OF THE END—LALLY'S CAMPAIGNS

LALLY'S DOINGS IN THE TANJORE COUNTRY

AFTER the capitulation of Fort St. David, the French troops had plenty of trouble; and the authorities were impatiently hustled by Lally about the provision of money, food etc., for the projected attack on Madras. An English sloop was captured near Negapatam and brought to Pondicherry, laden with sugar and rice. The Diarist's office in the flower-garden was broken into and guards were posted there; and naturally he felt worried very much over this act of official aggression. The European troops were sent to Tindivanam on the way to Madras. Vessels were laden with provisions for the purpose. On the last day of June news was received by Ranga Pillai that Bussy had left Golconda with all his troops, not even leaving a single European behind; and the countries in the coast had been seized by Vijayarāmarāju's men. Lally who went to Karikal with a view to getting money from the Tanjore ruler, could not meet even his own expenses. He proceeded, after experiencing difficulties on the way, to Tiruvalur on the road to Tanjore, without settling anything with the Raja whose general Manoji, intercepted his path with 2,000 horse and 5,000 foot. When Lally's troops reached Ammāpēttai about twelve miles east of Tanjore, a battle was fought in which the Tanjore troops advanced boldly, but finally retreated in panic; and the French marched on and encamped near Māriamman Kovil, four miles east of Tanjore. The Diarist was not, however, sure whether this item of news was true. Lally had broken his word to protect the houses of the merchants and others at Nagore and sold that town's plunder to a German for two lakhs of rupees and diamonds worth 12,000 francs. The Hindu images in the temples of Kīvaḷur and Tiruvalur had been carried away by the people in fear of the French. The Dutch at Negapatam were approached for the loan of a lakh of rupees and for provisions. Their governor, Vermont, promised to supply the provisions, but declined the loan. The Danes at Tranquebar were also said to have supplied some provisions.

The Diarist heard that Koyaji Ghangte, the Tanjore adventurer[1] had offered, through the priests of St. Paul's Church, to pay forty lakhs besides the expenditure incurred by the army, if Tanjore should be captured and given to him, while Muthayyar from Udaiyārpālayam had offered to become a Christian, to pay two lakhs and to defray the expenses of the campaign, if Udaiyārpālayam should be captured and given to him. Also, another offer of a lakh and a half was said to have been made on condition that Papu Reddy and his people were given Ariyalur and Turaiyur. Father Lavaur attempted to persuade Lally to come to a decision. Writing on July 18, the Diarist gave a brief account of the engagement at Kōvilveṇṇi, in which the Raja's troops retreated and fled, leaving two cannon and thirty match-locks in the enemy's hands. The Tanjore horse attacked and plundered Tirumalarāyanpattanam and the neighbouring māhāṇams. Haidar Nayak from Mysore had passed Karur with 2,000 horse on his way to join Lally. When Lally encamped at Māriamman Kovil, the Raja opened negotiations and first consented to settle the affair for thirty lakhs, offering to pay ten lakhs in ready money; but Lally

1 *Vide* above—footnote 18 on pp. 93–95 on the sons of Tukoji Raja: Kōyaji was the champion of the Kāṭṭu Raja.

Father Lavaur, it seems, had suggested to Lally that the real means of his getting money was to undertake an expedition against Tanjore as Sahuji who had twice been expelled from the country in 1739 and who, taken up by the English for their own purposes in 1749 and thrown aside when no longer of any use to them, had continued to live ever since a pensioner on their bounty and now came to Pondicherry. Father Lavaur, the Jesuit, thought that this pretender might be made use of to frighten the ruler of Tanjore, his nephew, upon whom the French had a claim for 55 lakhs of rupees in consequence of a bond given to Chandā Sāhib and made over by his son. Razā Sāhib, to Dupleix. Lally however, marched unwillingly upon Tanjore. This Sahuji was very likely one and the same person with Saiyaji, the second son of Tukoji and the Kāṭṭuraja. Father Lavaur is held by Dodwell to have been sincere in his advice to Lally. According to Hamont, Lally had this expedition in view even before he landed at Pondicherry.

demanded, in addition, the fort of Tirukāttuppaḷḷi with a view to using it as a base for his intended attack on Trichinopoly.

Lally's troops were very deficiently provided with draught cattle, ammunition and provisions. He had plundered Nagore from which, however, the merchants had had time to remove all their valuable effects. At Kīvaḷur, eight miles inland from Negapatam, he was told by deceptive informers to expect an immense amount of gold. Here, Lally, "ransacked and dug the houses, dragged the tanks, and took the idols out of the chapels, but no treasures were found; and the idols proved to be only of brass". Further, mistaking for spies six unhappy Brahmans who lingered about his camp to try to recover their images, he had them shot away from the muzzles of the guns.

On July 25, the Raja of Tanjore and his general, Manoji Appa, directly opened negotiations with Lally for peace terms. These were naturally protracted; and in their course, the Tanjore horse effectively prevented provisions from reaching the French camp, which had to be entrenched on account of the virtual blockade maintained by the enemy. Rumours regarding the negotiations reached the Diarist daily. He, however, did not judge that the affair could be settled very satisfactorily so soon and would not place any reliance on the news that filtered. Thus, on the 1st of August, he heard that Manoji had given Lally's envoy 20,000 gold pieces and also promised to send 500 horse and 1,000 foot, with rice and provisions for the attack of Trichinopoly. Again, the next day, he heard that 7½ lakhs of rupees had been promised. Later, we learn from him that no letters had been received from Lally's camp and that rumours were prevalent of a pitched battle having been fought. We hear also that the Raja of Tanjore was hurt by the treatment of Lally and, being supported by the promises of the English, bade defiance to the enemy. Early in August batteries were erected against the Tanjore fort; a breach was effected on the 7th and the decisive attack itself was to take place on the 8th. But just on the morning of that day, news was received by Lally that the French Admiral, D'Ache, had been attacked and beaten by English ships and the latter were threatening Karikal which formed the base of his Tanjore operations. Then Lally had, with him, supplies only for two days. Anyhow, a breach having been effected, the French captains were eager that the assault should follow; but Lally suddenly made up his mind to retreat in the direction of Karikal. On the 9th of August, the Tanjoreans, having got to know the intention of Lally, made a sudden sally on his camp. They were repulsed, but not before 100 Europeans had been killed and a great quantity of ammunition blown up. There was, indeed, even an attack upon Lally personally, which might have succeeded, had it not been for the assailant being shot dead at the nick of time by one of his personal followers. The same night, Lally spiked his heavy guns and retreated towards Tiruvalur. But the next morning, the Tanjoreans pursued his troops, cut off a number and took two guns and some mortars. The Diarist describes, in his entry for August 6, an attack of Manoji Appa with 2,000 horse on Lally's troops which, failing, enabled the French to open a fierce cannonade on the fort. The Diarist's account of the final repulse of Lally from Tanjore is as follows:—" This is the news of to-day—When at about three o'clock on the morning of August 9, M. Lally's troops were about to attempt to scale the walls of the Tanjore fort with the aid of heaps of straw, the Tanjore Raja's troops opened the north gate and attacked M. Lally's provision camp, half an hour before our troops were to move; a severe battle followed, in which five or six Europeans were killed on the Tanjore side and 500 or 600 Europeans besides three high officers on M. Lally's. In consequence M. Lally and our troops retreated to Tiruvalur leaving everything behind. Razā Sāhib who had marched from Karikal to Tiruvalur and visited M. Lally at the latter place means to attack the fort again with the help of the Setupati and the Tondaiman. It is not known whether the English ships have left Karikal. Savarirāyan is going about, prostrating himself before the ships' captains in order to make his peace with them ". (Entry for Wednesday, August 16).[2]

2 The figures of casualties of Lally's side are greatly exaggerated.

The Diarist tells us that the Dutch ship, *Haarlem,* which was intercepted and brought into the roads, was deprived of its store of gold and silver bullion worth two lakhs of rupees, and the captain was given a bill payable in Europe for the amount, including a profit of about 15%. The pretence was made that as the French had no money in India, the French King had made an agreement in Europe that any ship containing gold and silver might be detained and the money taken, in return for bills payable in Europe. The real motive was that the ship was seized in revenge for the Dutch inaction when a French ship (the *Rubis*) was taken in the roads of Negapatam.

Lally had to spike his cannon and burn his tents and guns on his retreat. He was in great anger with the Pondicherry Council at not having been supplied with money for his camp expenses or with provisions, powder and shot. The confusion at Pondicherry was great; and the Diarist remarks that Lally's complaints against the councillors were not justified. "M. Lally is wrong to blame all the councillors wholesale like this, for, before his departure, when he asked me whether Tanjore could be attacked, I advised him not to go, as the rivers and canals would be full, the fields in cultivation, and the ground so deep that the troops could only march with great difficulty. In spite of this, he blames us all. He should blame only those who advised him to go". (Entry for Monday, August 21). D'Ache was preparing to return to Mascareigne as he had already suffered severely from the attack of the English fleet and as he now heard that six fully equipped English men-of-war were approaching Bombay.[3] Lally returned to Pondicherry on August 28; and on the last day of the month news was received of the return of Bussy from the north. According to English records we learn that the earlier accounts of the Diarist had greatly exaggerated the French losses. Caillaud had been ordered to join the king of Tanjore with all the troops that could be spared, in case it should be possible to cut off the enemy's retreat to Pondicherry; and Pocock had been desired to co-operate

3 This is deemed to be the reason for his departure; but he did not seem to have urged it.

with Caillaud, while Lawrence marched south to prevent assistance being sent to Lally from Pondicherry. But when the last (Lawrence) reached Chingleput, he learnt that the enemy had recrossed the Coleroon, and therefore returned to Madras. Pocock was cruising off Karikal and Negapatam to protect the English ships coming from England and intercept hostile reinforcements. "Caillaud's former orders in the event of an appearance of attack on Madras, to march to the coast with all the Europeans and Coffrees of Trichinopoly and come here with the Squadron, have been renewed, although Palk and Lawrence consider the measure is now unnecessary."[4]

In September Lally left for Wandiwash and the English abandoned Chingleput as soon as Soupire crossed the Pālār; and the French were soon strengthening the forts of Chingleput, Karunguzhi and Chetpattu, which forts they had taken, as well as Tiruvannamalai, Chengamma etc. Taqī Sāhib of Wandiwash submitted to Lally and made friends with him. Lally seems to have said to the renters and others that they need not render accounts of the rents paid or the balance due from them to any one but himself and that they should even give him the accounts which they had already given to others and that they might raise horse and seize all the country they could. There is a large gap in the Diary from September 17, 1758 to January 23, 1759 and this period was occupied chiefly with Lally's siege of Madras and its failure.[5] Ranga Pillai merely noted that Lally took up all power

4 (Despatch from the Select Committee at Madras to the Secret Committee, Fort St. George, October 5-10-1758.) *Military Despatches to England*, Vol. 2, pp. 21-45.

5 (The detailed events of the siege were recorded in Public Department Sundry Book, Vol. XIII, 1758-59, entitled 'Journal of Transactions during the Siege of Fort St. George.' The volume was compiled by the Secretary to Government, Josiah du Pre. It contains 461 folios, of which 161 constitute the journal proper, the remainder consisting of tabular statements and returns, and copies of letters despatched and received during the siege. A journal maintained by Mr. John Call, the Engineer, was published in 1761 in Cambridge's 'Account of the War in India'. In the following pages the official account is followed, but the plan

on himself and signed all orders himself, thus putting De Leyrit completely into the background. The coin and plate obtained from the Dutch ship proved to be two lakhs and thirty-three thousand nine hundred pagodas weight of gold, mostly in coins struck with human figures, $9\frac{3}{4}$ fine and the total value of the whole quantity was $3\frac{1}{2}$ lakhs of rupees. Bussy was said to have sent a *hundi* for a lakh and a half, though the Diarist put it down at three lakhs. News was also received early in September that Soupire had camped to the next of Tiruvannamalai and Chetpattu, while Bussy and Moracin had reached Nellore on their way to Madras. The situation in Pondicherry was so bad that Lally went to the length of threatening to assault and kick De Leyrit in open council; but De Leyrit put up with all these in a cowardly manner. The Diarist reports a remark of a Frenchman on the situation:—' The Company is gone, and Pondicherry is like a bird that has lost a wing, and, being unable to fly with the other, must perish in spite of every effort. M. Lally respects nobody, but beats, abuses or otherwise disgraces them; so that sixteen officers have gone home by the ship which sailed for Europe, and others say that they will do the same '. The conduct of Father Lavaur had alienated even De Leyrit, Desvaux and others.

Events During and After the Siege of Madras

When the Diary begins again on January 23, 1759, the first entry is that Muhammad Alī Khān's son who was in Fort St. George, was killed by French fire and that all the Tamils and several European settlers with their women had quitted the place.

which accompanies the narrative is reproduced from Cambridge. 'The Indian Records Series: D. Love: *Vestiges of Old Madras*', Vol. II, Page 539). There is, a plan of Fort St. George and the Black Town, as it was when besieged by the French: 12th December, 1758; in Cambridge's book, reproduced in a reduced form by Love. A similar plan is furnished by Orme who also gives an enlarged plan of the north front. The Pondicherry archives contain three coloured drawings of the Fort executed in 1758-59. The French force was estimated at 3,000 Europeans, horse and foot, 500 native cavalry and 3,000 sepoys. The British garrison consisted of about 1,750 Europeans and 2,200 sepoys. The French had

By January 14, the siege had practically begun to prove to be a lost cause; and news arrived from Bombay that Admiral Pocock was sending two men-of-war and four Company's ships for the relief of the besieged at Madras. On January 21, we hear that a sally of the English made at the foot of the glacis, drove out the enemy and destroyed some of their works. On the 23rd the French worked up the basis by sap and opened a battery against the north ravelin; the next day they formed a lodgement on the crest of the glacis. A week later they opened a breaching battery which was however badly constructed and from which the shot flew high.[6]

reached Vandalur on the 6th of December; Lawrence fell back from St. Thomas' Mount to the Choultry Plain on the 10th December; on the 12th Lally cannonaded the Choultry Plain and drove in the detachments; Lawrence retreated to the Island and then to the Fort, leaving small bodies to guard the approaches to the Black Town. Captain Preston had a body of troops at Chingleput and Major Caillaud was ordered to join it from Tanjore and to operate against the enemy's line of communications.

The French troops occupied the Black Town on the 14th December. Early in the morning on the 17th February, 1759, they abandoned their trenches and batteries and retreated.

The siege lasted 67 days; and for 46 days the defenders sustained a vigorous bombardment. The French left behind 52 guns. The chief actions during the siege were: (1) Draper's action in Peddanaickenpetta, in the Black Town, on the 14th December; and (2) Caillaud's action near St. Thomas' Mount on the 9th February. (See Orme: Vol. II, pp. 384 *et seq.*, Book X—Love's *Vestiges of Old Madras*, Vol. II, Ch. XL; and Cambridge: *The War in India* (1761).

6 "The enemy opened 3 batteries January 6; their maximum fire was from 26 guns and 9 mortars. Their attack was on the north, as the Black Town afforded them cover from which to open the Royal Battery at 450 yards. A few days later, they opened other batteries enfilading all the northern side. They advanced by sap to 30 yards from the crest of the glacis, where they raised a battery against the right face of the north ravelin; but this was ill-constructed and their cannon was destroyed by our fire as often as they opened their embrasures. Their next battery on the crest of the glacis proved no better. None of our defences have been destroyed. Every disabled gun has been replaced and the damaged works repaired. Our fire therefore was so superior

Ranga Pillai mentions the death of Saubinet and also that Caillaud from Madura and Muhammad Yūsuf Khān had visited Abdul Wahāb Khān at Chandragiri, captured Tiruvaḷḷūr and other places and then marched to Poonamallee. Lally sent a body of soldiers and *Kallars* to oppose their advance; and, as usual, he raged against the commandant of this body for failing to scale the walls and capture Chingleput when it was but slightly defended. The Diarist also tells us that the English Governor Pigot, General Lawrence and others met in council and resolved to resist to the last and not to surrender even though the walls should be destroyed or scaled. He heard that the northern works of Fort St. George had been brought down, fetching the curtain along with them and that the French had occupied the covered way and were in a fair way to success. He also mentions a reference to the intrigues carried on against Lally in the French camp itself which led to the arrest of several officers, their deportation to and their imprisonment in Pondicherry. The names of two of these officers are given by him. Lally found proofs of their sending letters to the English, according to his *Memoires*.

On the 1st of February the Diarist heard that an English squadron of nine ships had reached Galle and Colombo, that contrary winds and currents would prevent it from coming to the rescue of besieged Madras before the middle of March and he felt

that they were forced to retire to the Royal Battery after springing a mine which opened the counterscarp of the ditch before the salient angle of demi-bastion, which by that time was actually breached; but palisades had been erected before the enemy could interrupt its repair by musketry fire."

"An army of observation, consisting of 50 Europeans from Chingleput, a large body of sepoys from Trichinopoly, and some country horse, commanded first by Preston and then by Caillaud jointly with Yusuf Khān, the Commandant of the Sepoys, proved of great service by distracting the enemy, who four times sent large detachments against them unsuccesfully."

[Despatch from the Secret Committee, Madras to the Company, Military Despatches to England, dated February 21, 1759.]

Refer also to the diurnal chronicle of the siege operations given by Colonel Love—*Vestiges*: Vol. II, pp. 540 *et seq.*

that by that time, Madras would have been captured. In spite of these hopes, the wealthy inhabitants of Pondicherry, including Christians, were secretly sending their goods to Negapatam and Tranquebar; and for the past one month, people had been going away from the town on the pretext of visiting Rameswaram.

The next important item of news reported by Ranga Pillai is that on the 9th February.[7] Abdul Wahāb Khān, Muhammad Yūsuf Khān and Caillaud marched against the French besiegers who were suffering from want of provisions and took up a position at St. Thomas' Mount. Thereupon Lally—the Diarist mistook the General's relative Col. Michel Lally, who was sent—attacked the English troops at St. Thomas' Mount, inflicted heavy losses on them and scattered them in all directions. The Diarist reports the deaths of both Caillaud and Yūsuf Khān in the action. Of course, the story of the death of these two was purely fictitious; and according to Orme, the action was a drawn one, both sides falling back with a number of losses. The Diarist next reported that Abdul Wahāb Khān and his Bakshi were also made prisoners. A detailed account of this action is given by Orme who says that the cavalry of the French inflicted more loss than they suffered. Towards the evening, the French retreated towards the east, crossed the river and took up their quarters in the village of Marmalong (Mambalam). Caillaud had practically no ammunition left with him; and he could not have retreated, if pressed by the enemy in the open plain. By next morning he arrived at Vandalur and soon afterwards reached Chingleput in safety.

7 Caillaud's engagement with the French at St. Thomas' Mount is the second of the notable operations of the siege, as already pointed above. Throughout the siege Lally had been harassed by the detachment at the Mount under Captain Preston and Muhammad Yūsuf Khān which constantly threatened his communications. Lally resolved, early in February, to attack the Mount in force and sent a detachment of 800 cavalry and 1,800 infantry, one-third of the number being Europeans, under his relative Colonel Lally, with orders to annihilate Preston. But two days before this, Caillaud who had returned from a mission to Tanjore in search of mercenaries, reached the Mount and took over the command as the senior officer. The native contingents were commanded

Bussy had meanwhile come to Pondicherry owing to ill-health while six or seven English vessels reached Madras on the 16th. The Diarist does not give us any details regarding Lally's retreat[8] from Madras except that he heard he had reached Poonamallee with his troops on his way to Arcot (Entry for the 19th February), and then marched by way of Tiruvaḷḷūr and Tiruppachur to Kāveripauk. He says, reflecting on the fortunes of the French, that Madras was plundered, the fort was blown to pieces, the houses within it were demolished by shells, the walls destroyed and beaten into the ditch. Yet the fort was not taken and the glory redounded to Mr. Pigot the English Governor; but Lally was not to blame—this is repeated several times. Also Madras escaped because Fort St. David was destroyed. Then, in a sad vein, he continues that only his own prosperity would bring prosperity to the French cause and that it was but just that their misfortunes should coincide with his own.

by Muhammad Yūsuf and Abdul Wahāb, the Nawab's younger brother, on whom, however, little reliance could be placed. Abdul Wahāb's horsemen were repulsed easily by the French cavalry and fled to Chingleput. The French put up a hot fire and their infantry repeatedly attacked the English advanced post and captured it. They, however, did not assault the main position and drew off to the Adyar river in the evening. Caillaud remained on his ground till 8 p.m. (Caillaud's replies to queries regarding the details of this action are found in the Orme Mss. in the India Office—Vol. LXII. (S. C. Hill's *Catalogue of the Orme Collection*: (1916)—Orme Mss. O.V. 62 (14)). In a letter, dated 28th June, 1778, Caillaud wrote to Orme that "the European cavalry had no chance with the black cavalry, *à l'arme blanche*".—which accounts for the French cavalry halting and firing with their carbines, instead of charging with the sword." (*Ibid.*, p. 126).

8 Generally it has been held that Lally's retreat from Madras was caused by the arrival of the English squadron on the coast. Six English ships were descried to the northward on February 16th; and early on the 17th, Lally abandoned his trenches and batteries and retreated. A letter from Lally to De Leyrit, dated 14th February and intercepted by Caillaud, shows that the resolution to raise the siege had been taken two days at least before the appearance of the English ships. Even in January he had received news of the approach of the English fleet and had written to Leyrit that he had no more than a month at the farthest

Events after the Retreat from Madras

One of the usual accompaniments of the warfare of those days was that the Marathas who were invited by the English, plundered Conjeevaram and other places unchecked. Pondicherry itself was threatened by the English vessels. Moracin was sent, instead of Bussy, to proceed to Masulipatam in consequence of the news that the English and Ananda Raja, the son of Vijayarāmarāja, of Vizianagram had advanced against that place, plundered its suburbs and were about to launch an attack on the fort. Soon afterwards, Brereton, the commander of the English troops which advanced from Madura, scaled the walls of the Conjeevaram fort, (*i.e.* the big temple of the place) and slew some of the Muhammadans inside. They also occupied the town itself. Lally had left for Wandiwash and there was much privation for want of money for his expenses. Soupire had reached Tiruvati. On April 22, news was received that Masulipatam had been captured. The English scaled the walls of the fort and captured it at dead of night. They flew Salābat Jang's flag on the fort, and it was said that the Nizām himself had come to Bezwada. The French at Pondicherry merely said that they could not explain the capture of Masulipatam with its 600 soldiers and 3,000 or 4,000 foot except by ill-luck. The loss of the place was a serious blow to the French; and De Leyrit wrote to Lally at Wandiwash that his recall of Bussy and Moracin had lost for the French Salābat Jang's support and entirely ruined French influence in the Deccan and the Northern Circars.[9]

to complete his enterprise (Leyrit's *Memoire*. p. 281). "Their opportune arrival, however, hastened the enemy's retreat and doubtless saved Black Town from destruction." Lally's letter showed that he despaired of success and had resolved to burn the Black Town. In his hasty retreat he destroyed the powder-mills in Egmore, but left the Black Town intact. English fire had destroyed no less than 33 of the enemy's cannon and left them few serviceable guns.

9 [Pigot's letter of June 28, 1759.] The following is an account of the English successes in the Circars:—"Forde's expedition succeeded beyond expectation. After defeating the French near Rajahmundry, December 7, 1758, he was prevented from investing Masulipatam, by

Lally's conduct at Wandiwash at this time was equally outrageous. He hanged in the public street the dubash of the Commandant for an act of alleged embezzlement. He took to task Razā Sāhib, who ran away from Wandiwash to Pondicherry without telling anybody and gave the Arcot subah to be managed by one, Ramalinga Pillai, a petty clerk. Lally then advanced on Conjeevaram and attacked the English on the banks of the Sarvathīrtham tank. There were losses on both sides; but a number of French troopers including a few soldiers and officers deserted to the English side; the troops then quitted Conjeevaram and marched to Tiruvattur (Cheyyar) and Wandiwash. Lally himself was expected to return to Pondicherry. Thus ended the glorious scheme of destroying the English power at Madras. "Thus from misunderstanding the course of events and the state of affairs in different places, M. Lally is mismanaging business, showing himself to be indiscreet and unaccustomed to positions of responsibility. People say that our period of misfortune has turned men's minds. I have written it accordingly". So wailed the Diarist with his glomy forebodings of the impending ruin of Pondicherry and the French cause.

In Pondicherry itself, towards the end of the siege operations at Madras, an attempt was made to issue token parchment rupees which were to pass current at their face value and the parchment money were to be paid to the Company's officials, sepoys and peons and to be accepted by the Company. Immediately after the issue of a proclamation to this effect, the shroffs and cloth-merchants closed their shops in protest. Two days later, *i.e.*, on the 21st of February, the governor had to summon the choultry writers and tell them that the bazaar people need not be compelled to accept

differences with the Raja, until March 7. On the night of April 7–8, he took it by assault, making the Marquis de Conflans and the whole garrison prisoners—no less than 500 Europeans including 100 officers and officials, a number exceeding that of the attacking army. Two ships from Pondicherry with reinforcements anchored there 8 days later under Moracin, the former Governor. He afterwards proceeded to Ganjam hoping to raise fresh opposition by means of a disaffected Raja there. But we hear he has failed and re-embarked."

the parchment money; on this assurance being given, the bazaars were reopened. Confusion also began to prevail in the settlement owing to the misbehaviour of the European troops, who molested the towns-people and said, in their defence, that they had not received any pay from the Company and had nothing to live upon and so were reduced to demanding money with threats. Well-dressed people were asked to pay Rs. 4 or Rs. 5; and the others were allowed to go free for six *fanams* or a rupee. The Governor did nothing; and things became so bad towards the end of April, that a few European officers and writers went breaking into the houses in the streets of the native town. The Diarist tells us that if the Europeans had not gone to camp, the situation would have been easily worse. In May, the Governor had to post the European residents, officials, councillors etc., at the fort, the sea-gate, the ramparts and the gates surrounding the town. Each one had his place assigned and all were ordered to assemble at the firing of two guns and the hoisting of their red flag; so afraid were they of an English attack.

The Diarist felt a premonition, on the occasion of his father's annual ceremony which fell on the 17th of May, that he would not perform that ceremony next year at Pondicherry though he hoped even yet that his fortunes would turn round the corner. He felt that after Lally's arrival he would bring fresh troubles to those under the influence of Venus and Mercury; and he told a friend that when Lally entered Pondicherry, on the night of the 18th, Saturn had entered the fort.

Lally would not admit even De Leyrit into the citadel and had resolved, so we read, to imprison the Governor and his friends and also the Tamils under them, seize their houses and property, look into their accounts and confiscate their wealth to the Company. The object of Lally was to get money urgently needed for the pay of his army before Wandiwash. There was a rumour that Conflans had been bribed to deliver Masulipatam to the English. In June the situation became worse. The Diarist's entry for the 8th tells its own tale. "The misconduct of the Europeans in the town, their plundering, ravishing women, and other misdeeds have gone beyond all limits. Men say that injustice daily increases. I cannot describe their sufferings but only mention them briefly here and there. The parchment money has already been sold at a discount of 15 to 50 per cent; but to-day I myself saw one or two persons selling it at a discount of 60 or 65 per cent.; so I write it, and I have heard that ten or twenty persons have sold it at that rate. Those who have to pay the Company and the lessees gain much, and the Europeans also. The *Arumpatai's* people have made lakhs by cheating the Company. Others have suffered much loss and are broken-hearted ".

Ranga Pillai promises to give us details about the capture of Masulipatam, as communicated to him by Mattal Reddi Naicken, dubash at that place, written on Krishnapaksha 10th S.S. 1681. But he apparently forgot to enter the letter in the *Diary* when his autograph rough draft was written fair. Lally was foolish enough to order the imprisonment of Nagoji Naicken, the diwan of Bussy, in the Vaḷudāvur fort; and Bussy himself was put under arrest at his house on the suspicion that he was concealing his correspondent with Salābat Jang. This reported arrest probably meant that Bussy was no longer permitted to visit Lally. Bussy himself was much annoyed and alarmed at this; and the rumour prevailed that his words would no longer be regarded with any weight by Salābat Jang or the Peishwa. De Leyrit and the Councillors were much alarmed at this action of Lally in alienating and humiliating Bussy.

Lally tried to enlist the help of Murari Rao and hoped to secure his alliance through Father Noronha, Bishop of Mylapore. The English ships were cruising on the Tanjore coast and the alliance of the Raja of Tanjore was eagerly sought after. It was thought that Lally intended that De Leyrit should be removed from his office. Even at this moment Lally claimed to make Razā Sāhib, the subah of Arcot and resolved to recognise him as the Nawab. To this arrangement, De Leyrit and Desvaux would not give their consent; and Lally said that he did not care. The Diarist was surprised that the French, to whom the *subah* was given by Muzaffar Jang and Salābat Jang, should themselves appoint another master to lord it over the country. Neither Dupleix nor his successors could enjoy the management of the country as disorder prevailed intensively.

The Muhammadan management had also failed. Razā Sāhib was to enjoy a jaghir and also all the revenue from the country except Trichinopoly and Tanjore as well as the *peshkash* due from the poligars and the killedars. The Diarist also heard that Basālat Jang, the younger brother of Nizām Salābat Jang, had claimed the Arcot subah and the country south of the Krishna as they had been given to him and that he was coming down with a body of 10,000 horse and 6,000 foot by way of Cuddapah and Nellore.

In the entry for July 29, the Diarist records the news of the first step of the revolution that replaced Salābat Jang by Nizām Alī Khān and that the two brothers had quarrelled even to the point of death.[10]

Early in August, news came from Salābat Jang that Bussy was experienced in the affairs of the Deccan and that he alone could keep the poligars, Marathas, and killedars in order and therefore either Lally was requested to come or to send Bussy to his court; and then there was a threat given at the end; "if you will do neither of those, your troops and jemadars, who enjoy countries etc., here will be dismissed, and I shall seek English help and manage

10 "Nizām Alī Khān who has been living in Shāh Nawāz Khān's house, went to his elder brother Salābat Jang's and said that he would not depart unless he was given the twenty lakhs of rupees' worth of property belonging to his wife, and then set guards on his house, attempting to imprison Salābat Jang, seize all the property, and rule the country. But the *amir-ul-umaras* (chief nobles) under Nizām Alī Khān, the jemadars, etc., disapproved of such treatment of Salābat Jang and told Nizām Alī Khān that they could not countenance such unjust behaviour as they had vowed not to raise a finger against Salābat Jang. The latter will either kill Nizām Alī Khān or be killed by him. The two brothers have thus quarrelled even to the point of murder. Owing to the atrocities committed at Golconda, the merchants and inhabitants are leaving it, and people say that the town will be destroyed, anarchy will prevail, and the destruction of the Muslim power is at hand."—Entry for July 29.

affairs as I think best ". To this letter of Salābat Jang it was agreed that no reply should be given until a letter should be received from Nizām Alī Khān. Evidently the French had some knowledge of the course of events at the Nizam's court, which was to end in the deposition of Salābat Jang.

Lally proceeded with his recognition of Razā Sāhib as the Nawab, gave the *parwana* for Tyagadrug to the son of Imām Sāhib and held the function of the installation of Razā Sāhib with a ceremony at which De Leyrit was also present. Unfortunately the rope of the flag-staff broke in the middle in the process of the flag-hoisting; and Ranga Pillai immediately prognosticated evil, saying that, in the people's opinion, the breaking of the flag-staff rope signified his (the Nawab's) death within a few days.

Murari Rao who had been written to by Father Noronha, agreed to send a body of 1,000 horse and musket people, besides some *coffres* and *topasses* in return for two lakhs of rupees and the payment of each horseman at ¾ of a rupee daily. Four sardars of Murari were also said to be coming. On August 4, the English vessels which had been cruising off Negapatam, appeared in the Pondicherry roads and caused great consternation. All the Europeans assembled at the fort with their guns; and shot and powder were made ready at the beach. News was received, a few days later, of the English capture of Louisbourg in Canada and of the declaration of war by Denmark against France. The English marched against Kāvēripākkam, intending to proceed from thence to Arcot and camped their troops at Lalapet, Ranipet and Uttaramallur. The French commander who was encamped at Wandiwash complained of want of provisions, while it was feared that Razā Sāhib and his people would be running back to Pondicherry out of fear within the current month. The English were beaten twice in their attempt to advance to Arcot. They were driven from Tirupati by the Marathas and retired towards Arcot, intending first to take Kāvēripākkam and Timiri. Being fore-warned of this, the French had made preparations and managed to repulse them twice and to make them retreat to Conjeevaram. The English were themselves in some want of money and depended upon Bengal and Bombay, for the usual supplies had not been got by importation from Europe. The net result was that, after months of manœuvring, the French cantoned their troops at Wandiwash and Chetpattu and withdrew the rest to Pondicherry, while the English troops were cantoned at Conjeevaram and Chingleput; and the only fruit of the campaign for the English seems to have been the recovery of the Conjeevaram and Tiruppāchur countries. Thus there was a temporary stalemate in the situation in the Carnatic for the time being.

Growing Confusion in Pondicherry

The lack of money at Pondicherry resulted in a forced money-levy on the citizens from De Leyrit downwards. The houses of those who refused to contribute were liable to plunder by the troops, according to a resolution of the Council. De Leyrit was to be shortly removed from the Governorship; but until a successor should come, he was to continue nominally in office, but in reality without power. In his entry for August 17, the Diarist tells us that the *Mahānāttārs*, two from each caste, were brought in to give a list of the properties of the towns-people; and when they professed ignorance, they were shut up in a room for a length of time. The next day they assembled in the choultry and Ranga Pillai was persuaded to pacify them into a good state of mind. They said they had never agreed to make out a list of properties of the towns-people. Soon afterwards the head-peon and two other prominent Hindus were imprisoned in the west gate of the fort, while their houses were searched. Lally met the *Mahānāttārs* and the Company's merchants and assured them that he would act impartially, that he proposed to build ramparts round the fort and make other preparations for the defence of the settlement and they should join together and lend him 8 or 10 lakhs of rupees which would be returned with interest at 12%, and for the security of which, the Villiyanur or Vaḻudāvur country would be mortgaged to them and allowed to be managed by them. Lally promised to give an agreement to this effect and requested the

Mahānāttārs to send four of their number, along with Ranga Pillai, and settle the business. The four representatives met Lally on August 24th, in the presence of the Diarist and a few others and were told that two lakhs of rupees were required for the repair of the town-walls and a larger sum for paying the soldiers and *sibbandhis* and that they should pay an initial portion of this sum in four days. An idea of the corruption that persisted even now can be had from the entry of the Diarist that the choultry-writer and his assistants had been told to write an account for twice the sums as shown in the lists prepared according to the means of the different castes. Lally urged the Diarist to accompany the collectors of the contribution in their rounds. He even offered to mortgage the Gingee or the Tiruvati country, with 12% interest and to include the amount borrowed by De Leyrit in the bond. The proclamation of the Council assuring the payment of interest was translated into Tamil; but the usual delay took place in the preparation of the quota-list of contributions by the respective communities. The levy of a tax of five in twenty was ordered; but those who had property worth only ten pagodas were exempt. There was disagreement between the Diarist and La Selle who was commissioned to collect the contributions. On September 1st, the *Mahānāttārs* were compelled to sign for an extra sum making in all a lakh of pagodas. In spite of this, they would agree to pay only 70,000 pagodas and nothing more. The Diarist advised Lally that he could collect ten or fifteen thousand pagodas every week. Some of the *Mahānāttārs* were treated badly by La Selle; and they were imprisoned in the dungeon, or kept in custody. The Madras merchants closed their shops in alarm at the imprisonment of the *Mahānāttārs.* La Selle complained to Lally that the Tamils were threatening him; and the latter thereupon ordered their houses to be searched and all guns, swords and other weapons found in them to be seized and brought into the fort. At last, after repeated pressure, they signed for 81,000 and odd pagodas, after having been kept under duress from sunrise to 2 o'clock in the night. The treatment accorded to Kandappa Mudali and others was horrible; and the Diarist declared that he had never seen such a thing in all his life. A petition presented to Lally with the recommendation of Father Lavaur made him agree to the reduction of the stipulated payment to 70,000 pagodas. But Lally did not change his mind as was thought he might. The Diarist himself was asked to pay 5,000 pagodas and protested that it was only in the previous December he paid 10,000 rupees; and the *dubash* of La Selle assured him that he would be excused from paying the amount if only he would make the *Mahānāttārs* pay speedily.[11]

La Selle was suspected by the Diarist of secretly arranging to receive bribes and to trouble the *Mahānāttārs* with the hope that, in their alarm, they would give him something. Meanwhile, news was received of the naval action off Negapatam between D'Ache and the English Admiral Pocock. Throughout September the work of collecting the contribution continued; and towards the last week of that month the English ships reached the Pondicherry roads and D'Ache arrived at the settlement. There was an action at Wandiwash on the 22nd between the English and the French; and Ranga Pillai says that the English captain had to retreat to Tiruvattur leaving a large number of wounded. This was only Colonel Brereton's rash attempt to seize Wandiwash; but it was to have for its sequel the decisive French defeat at the hands of General Coote.

11 It is interesting to know from the list prepared by La Selle, the material condition of the respective communities. "56 Veḷḷālas have agreed in writing to pay 7,550 rupees; 113 Agamudaiyāns 7,800 rupees; 45 Idaiyans 900 rupees; 91 Kōmuttis 6,000 rupees; 28 Kavarais 600 rupees; 33 Shāṇārs 600 rupees; 13 Eḷavāṇiyans 800 rupees; 9 Mucchiyars 400 rupees; 169 Chettis 12,000 rupees; 5 Kammāḷas 500 rupees; 32 Paḷḷis 1,600 rupees; 26 Brahmans 8,000 rupees; 12 individuals 2,215 rupees; 71 Christians 7,500 rupees; Venkatachala Mudali 750 rupees; Ayyamperumal 600 rupees; Mīr Alī Nayakkan (?) 150 rupees; and Mīr A'azam 750 rupees. Let the amounts be collected according to the list." La Selle wanted that, in addition, small sums should be collected from others, including dancing-women, washermen, barbers and Paraiyas. The Tamils had their contributions fixed very high. The Brahmans' share of the tax was fixed at 12,000 pagodas, finally, of which more than half was to be paid by two individuals and the balance by the rest of the community.

CHAPTER XX

THE END—THE DEATH OF THE DIARIST AND THE FALL OF PONDICHERRY

INTENSIFIED DEPRESSION AT PONDICHERRY

THE contributions levied from the Tamil castes of Pondicherry did not amount, after all, to much. On September 16th, 1759, the fleet of Admiral D'Ache was sighted off the Pondicherry roads, along with a Dutch ship he had taken. It had encountered the English fleet off Nagore and Karikal; and in the engagement the masts and hulls of two of the English ships were damaged; but just when they were about to surrender, a frigate came to their help and a hard north wind also set in. The smoke from the English cannon enveloped the French ships, of which two or three were damaged and had their masts injured. The Diarist wrote that two of the disabled English ships were burnt and that the people from Karikal, Tranquebar and other places said they saw the light of the burning ships. This was, however, a mere rumour and not true.

The French fleet landed 1,000 soldiers and 1,000 coffres and silver which, when minted, was expected to yield about 160,000 rupees. D'Ache and Lally quarrelled quickly enough; and De Leyrit and Bussy were summoned to patch up the difference. But D'Ache would not even see them at first and merely replied, in an inexplicable fit of petulance; "What is it to you whether I go to Mauritius or some other place? I shall do as I think best and will neither inform you, nor listen to your words." Then when he was asked whether he would go and attack the English ships remaining at Negapatam, he said: "Whether I attack or not, what has that to do with you? I will do as I please and shall sail to-night."

D'Ache did not allow his men to land, but even recalled those who had come ashore. On the September 18th, the Diarist wrote that D'Ache had set sail the previous night with his fleet. He was really unwilling to reveal his designs to Lally, though he averred later on that he had not intended to quit the coast, but only planned to sail northward and seize Masulipatam and that he had merely kept the project secret from every one for fear of the enemy's spies. D'Ache returned to Pondicherry on the 23rd in consequence of the protest sent to him after his departure, in time to drive from the neighbourhood the English fleet, which appeared in the Pondicherry roads on the 26th night. He disembarked on the 29th, only to sail away two days later.

The Dasara festival which fell at this time, was not at all marked by any signs of festivity and rejoicing. All that the Diarist would say was that the town was in a state of affliction, there was mourning in every house and many householders had gone away to Tirupati on pilgrimage; while others, including a large number of Brahmans, had gone to Mayavaram to bathe in Kāveri. He wished that the ships of D'Ache had remained for at least a fortnight so that trade could be stimulated. Lally and D'Ache, he remarked, quarrelled like " cat and rat."

Towards the end of September the Diarist wrote of a rash attempt of the English to seize Wandiwash in which their losses were, in reality, twelve officers and 195 rank and file. D'Ache had finally landed about 800 European sailors and 400 coffres; but he retired from the coast on October 1st. Bussy was appointed second in command and ordered to proceed to Wandiwash with the European and coffre troops. The middle of October witnessed an open threat at desertion to the enemy by the soldiers of the Lally and Lorraine regiments,[1] a number of whom marched out of the camp at Wandiwash towards the site where the English had been previously encamped. On receipt of this news Lally sent over a lakh of rupees, which had then been got ready with considerable difficulty. The next day, the Diarist heard that the mutinous soldiers who had deserted at Wandiwash, attacked the place, plundered the camp and the country, ravishing women and inflicting other losses, on which Taqī Sāhib, the killedar of the

1 Orme (II, p. 528) tells us that the mutineers elected their own commanders and spread the discontent to Bussy's men at Arcot. A general amnesty quelled the movement in time.

fort, closed the gates and remained within the walls together with some French officers and sardars.

In November, there was an exchange of prisoners between the English and the French sides. By the middle of that month the Diarist exclaimed that if Lally should continue to govern the town like this for another two months, not a single Tamil family would remain and perhaps he himself would also be forced to leave; and then Lally would be left alone with the soldiers and even they would be probably deserting him. Orders were given towards the end of the month to collect as much as possible of the property of the rich families and the Europeans living in the town, because the Company was on the point of sinking and had no money to pay even the *sibbandhi*. News also reached the Diarist of an attack by the French troops sent to reoccupy Srirangam, on the English near Samayavaram and their assault on the Srirangam temple and their merciless plundering of two streets therein. The Diarist heard that just as the French had attacked Srirangam, the English threatened and surrounded Wandiwash, plundering a street and setting fire to a few houses, with the hope that the French troops would be thereby recalled from Srirangam.

The beginning of December saw that rice could not be had in the town even at 1½ measures a *fanam* and many were starving. Lally thereupon issued desperate instructions, asking the merchants to bring paddy and other grain from outside somehow, without any hindrance or any duty to pay. It being the time of the Karthigai festival, many pilgrims who set out for Tiruvannamalai, had to return as a battle was threatening in the neighbourhood. On the 1st of December Lally received the news of the English capture of Wandiwash. Thereupon some soldiers and coffres were dispatched with powder and shot from Pondicherry to strengthen Gingee and other places. In Madras the prevailing famine in rice had been averted by the importation of two or three ship-loads from Bengal. Famine conditions prevailed also in Cuddapah and the country to its northward. The inevitable march of English arms resulted in their occupation of Cheyyur, Chūnāmpattu and Alambarai and their tying *toranams* in these places in token of their occupation. In the Council meeting that was held on the 6th, there was an open quarrel between Lally and De Leyrit following an exchange of violent words. De Leyrit who had been quiet and restraining himself so far, now began to say that Lally had not the power to restrain or punish him.

Disasters Leading to the Battle of Wandiwash

A lone ray of hope was entertained by the Diarist, who heard that the French had beaten and driven off the English troops who attacked Karunguzhi. With regard to the capture of the fort of Wandiwash, the Diarist heard that the English took away Taqī Sāhib, the killedar, along with his property in the fort worth 400,000 rupees, including numerous small chests containing jewels and other valuables. The truth was, that when the English entered the fort, owing to the surrender of the French party there, Coote was waiting to see whether the killedar would carry out all his promises; and when the troops claimed all the contents of the fort, as their prize, the English commander had to issue a special order. Taqī Sāhib seems to have sent off all his valuables before ever the siege was begun.[2]

2 "Colonel Coote, who had been appointed to the command of the army in the Carnatic, arrived at Madras on the 27th October 1759, and joined the troops, who were in cantonments for the rains at Conjeevaram, on the 21st November. His arrival at once put a better complexion on the state of affairs. On the 25th November, he marched towards Arcot, with a view to deceiving the French as to his intentions, while on the same day he detached Major Brereton towards Wandiwash. Brereton captured the petta at Wandiwash by assault on the 27th November, and Coote, who had seen nothing of the enemy in the neighbourhood of Arcot, made a forced march and joined Brereton on the 28th. On the 30th, the fort was delivered up without the necessity of assaulting it, the casualities of the British during the short siege only amounting to five men wounded."

"As the French, who were at Chettupattu had made no attempt to interfere with his movements, Coote next resolved to attack Karunguli, another fort, which was commanded by Colonel O'Kenelly, an Irishman in Lally's regiment. On the 4th December, the petta was occupied, and Coote opened fire on the fort on the 6th. On the 10th, the

Moracin, who had been sent to Ganjam and had quarrelled with Kalingattu Narayana Das of Mohirry, his principal ally in the Circars, had to return to Pulicat from whence he arrived at Pondicherry on the 12th December.[3]

The whole expedition of Moracin was unlucky from start to finish. The Madras trading house of Tawker which till very

garrison surrendered, the French marching out with their arms, whilst the sepoys were disarmed and set free. The British loss was only one officer and three men killed." (Page 8, Murland's '*Baillie-Ki-Paltan*', *being a History of the 2nd Battalion, Madras Pioneers, formerly the IV Madras Pioneers*, 1759–1930).

The Madras Council's despatch of February 16, 1760 says that 2 batteries were opened on the 29th November; and the next day, a breach being made, the old killedar, Taqī Sāhib, offered to pay a sum of money and deliver up the French garrison on condition of being continued in his government. But before the offer was accepted the French troops surrendered at discretion, including 6 officers and 53 privates. "The place though so often threatened was never before captured." Taqi Sāhib was confined at Madras and Nawab Muhammad Alī insisted that he should be made to pay up ten lakhs of rupees, being the arrears of tribute due to himself and should not be released.

3 The circumstances that led to his failure may be briefly summarised. Moracin went over to Ganjam at the northern extremity of the Chicacole Circar, where the French had a trading station and persuaded a neighbouring chief, by name, Narayan Deo of Mohirry who was the enemy of Raja Vijayaram Raz to help him in attacking Vizagapatam and Vizianagaram. The preparations of Moracin were not satisfactory, while his ally was not seriously inclined to help him. Scarcely had Moracin's miserable expedition begun its march and reached Berhampur when Narayan Deo openly deserted it and forced it to return to Ganjam. Soon there was open hostility between the French and their ally who actually besieged Moracin in the factory at Ganjam and even wrote to Clive in Bengal that he would help him in the destruction of the French force, if a detachment should be sent from Calcutta. Actually Clive sent a body of 60 Europeans by sea, who reached Ganjam and persuaded Moracin to go away with his European troops. But he landed at Cocanada where Jagapati Raz of Samalkotta, another enemy of Ananda Raz, joined him with promises of support which however came to nothing. Moracin had therefore to sail away to Pondicherry, and his troops at Ganjam who could not do anything further had to follow in his wake. Only 150 returned, out of the 500 that went.

recently had been a very prosperous firm, is mentioned by the Diarist as having sent a merchant from that place, who bought the diamonds taken from the English ship, *Grantham*, for 54,000 pagodas, payable in forty days.[4]

Even now hopes were entertained that the French Company would soon be sending large sums of money and a number of ships. Murari Rao's horse, numbering 1,500, reached Arcot, nominally for the help of the French; and as usual, they plundered Conjeevaram. The French troops also left Srirangam, posting there a small body of Europeans and coffres. The unhappy year 1759 ended with the compulsory exaction of 1,000 pagodas from the *mahānāttārs* of Pondicherry, this claim being urged as the last balance due on account of the previous demand on them, with the assurance that they would not be made to pay any more contribution. Thus the Diarist felt comforted for the moment and wrote that "the evil from which the town has been suffering is declining and will disappear this month."

The fateful year 1760 begins with the Diarist's complaint that not even 100 looms were at work in Pondicherry where there were previously as many as 1,500 looms. The body of troops left by

4 Prof. Dodwell has this very interesting piece of information regarding the past history of that house. The Tawkers, to whom Nilakanta belonged, are a sub-division of the Paj Khedaval sub-caste of Gujarati Brahmans [Enthoven, *Castes and Tribes of Bombay*, i, 322]. From documents and information communicated by the courtesy of Mr. Nanabhoy Davay and Mr. Mallikarjuna Dugget, the second of whom is himself descended from a brother of the Nilakanta Tawker in question, it appears that Nilakanta and two brothers traded jointly in precious stones at Madras, Poona and Munimadugu. They opened a joint house at Madras in 1761, though from the reference above they must have traded in Madras earlier; Nilakanta survived both the other brothers and died in 1779. In the following generation, the family died out in the male line; and the widows of two of Nilakanta's nephews founded in 1807 a temple and charity at the village of Ayanavaram, *alias* Viswanathapuram, near Madras. This charity still exists, and is under the management of Mr. Mallikarjuna Dugget. Besides maintaining temple-worship and feeding Brahmans, the charity is also intended to feed and lodge Gujarati travellers." (P. 454, *Ananda Ranga Pillai's Diary*. Vol. XI).

Moracin in Ganjam returned to Pondicherry in a condition of complete starvation. The Maratha horse plundered the Poonamallee, Tiruppachur and Mylapore countries and created further unrest.

There is a gap in the diary from January 11 till the end of February—a period marked by the great victory of Coote at Wandiwash over the French.[5]

5 The loss of Karunguzhi and of Wandiwash fort taught Lally the necessity of concentrating his forces; and he consequently assembled his army at Arcot by calling in all detachments. Early in January 1760, Coote also arrived in the neighbourhood of Arcot and both sides were busy for some days out-bidding each other for the services of Murari Rao and the body of horsemen that he commanded. These latter were ravaging the whole country as noted by the Diarist; and they did it with such success that cattle were sold at the time at the rate of 7 or 8 per rupee. At last, the Marathas to the number of 3,000, joined the French; and thereupon Lally moved about the 10th of January from Arcot to Tiruvattur; and halting at the latter place, he returned north made a dash for Conjeevaram, hoping to seize large supplies thein. Meanwhile, Coote sent his baggage to Kāvēripākkam and when he heard of Lally's dash on Conjeevaram, hastened to that place soon after the French had withdrawn from it to Tiruvattur. Lally's plan was now to divert the attention of Coote with a part of his army while he attempted to capture Wandiwash with the remainder. Consequently, he left Bussy with the main body of his army at Tiruvattur and himself marched towards Wandiwash where he began to prepare batteries to reduce the Fort. Coote moved from Conjeevaram to Uttiramerur and in his turn planned to wait until Lally should become fully engaged in the siege operation, when he could either attack the besieging or give battle to the covering force of Bussy. Bussy saw through Coote's design and urged Lally vainly to desist from the siege and to keep together all the French forces. Lally however gave Bussy a free hand and the latter at once joined him before Wandiwash. Batteries were opened against the French on the 20th January. On the 21st, Coote marched from Uttiramerur with his cavalry for reconnaissance. Soon, finding that the main rampart was breached, he ordered his infantry to join him at once; on the morning of the 22nd, Coote assembled his troops for battle in three lines, the last being all the cavalry and the first time being composed entirely of two European battalions with sepoys equally divided on either flank.

Orme tells us that when the cannonade once commenced, the brunt of the fighting fell entirely on the Europeans in both the armies; and the

THE SITUATION AFTER THE BATTLE OF WANDIWASH

The Diarist, writing again from March 1st, tells us that six ships with powder and shot were on their way from Madras to attack Pondicherry and that the English troops had occupied places about Gingee and were marching towards Pondicherry by way of the Perumukkal killa.

Next day he heard that Perumukkal was being actually attacked. Perumukkal was almost halfway between Chettupattu and Pondicherry; and the French troops stationed at Mortandi Choultry, an outpost of Pondicherry, retreated towards the town.

There now began an exodus of the citizens from Pondicherry including Christians, Labbais and Tamils who were given ready money in exchange for their goods, silver etc. De Leyrit and the Councillors were put in charge of the inner fort, while the other Europeans were to guard the battery at the corner of the sea-wall and Lally himself was to guard the outer defences. The panic-stricken people were allowed to go out freely, to the extent of nearly half the town, as the Diarist says; but he records, with pride, that " my own relatives and family remain here."

A party of the English force before Perumukkal attacked the French troops and drove them to the Perumbai Hill and even to the Valudāvur Gate. And even the Europeans stationed at the several outposts who were unwilling to face the enemy, retired to the bounds.

sardars of the sepoys of the English side complimented Coote on his victory, and "thanked him for the sight of such a battle as they had never seen." The English took 24 pieces of cannon, besides large quantities of ammunition and stores. The French lost 200 Europeans besides 160 taken prisoners, among whom was Bussy, who was permitted by Coote to proceed to Pondicherry on *parole*. In Madras, the victory caused "joy almost equal to that of Calcutta on the victory of Plassey." The French troops fled to Chettupattu and thence to Gingee and shortly afterwards retreated to Pondicherry. Coote secured the surrender of Chettupattu on the 29th of January and a week later, began the siege of Arcot which fell after a resistance of five days. On the last day of February Tiruvannamalai surrendered to a detachment of English troops under Captain Smith; and Coote marched to Perumukkal which finally submitted on the 4th of March, though the first assault made on it was unsuccessful.

Lally, for fear that if people departed in further numbers, provisions would not be brought in, tried to prevent a further exodus and to induce the bazaar people to open their shops. The English troops alarmed Perumbai and the neighbouring places on the 8th March. Bussy,[6] who had given the *parole* after Wandiwash, was now asked by Coote to surrender himself. Lally offered to ransom him in accordance with a cartel arranged in Europe; but Coote declined the ransom and insisted on the surrender of Bussy and of two other officers, who had likewise given the *parole*. Bussy departed from Pondicherry for Madras on the 9th. The European households sent away their women and children from the place.

Chandā Sāhib's son was put in charge of the corner battery of the west wall of the town and the adjacent ditch and was asked to guard it with 500 sepoys who were to be maintained at his own cost, till French ships should arrive with supplies. The Diarist himself was asked to guard a rampart on the walls of the fort with a body of 50 sepoys at his own expense and to entertain further sepoys for the protection of the Tamils. He querulously complained, reiterating all his old grievances that he had been unduly deprived of his jaghirs and made to suffer other losses. But he agreed to do his duty at the critical time, saying that he should not fail "when the Company is on the verge of ruin, for I have lived here 50 years under the French flag, serving the Company and eating its food so that the very blood in my veins

6 Coote had allowed Bussy and two other French officers to return to Pondicherry on *parole*. Lally had, even in the previous September, forwarded to Pigot the cartel for the exchange of prisoners concluded between the French and the English at Sluys (in February). In November 1759, there was a general exchange of prisoners. The English would not deliver up the prisoners subsequently taken, to the number of 400, unless the French should discharge the accounts of expenditure for the maintenance of those prisoners. Pigot said that Lally obliged all his officers at Pondicherry on *parole* to carry arms in the late action and regretted that Bussy should have been allowed to return to Pondicherry as his arrival as a prisoner in Madras should have had a great effect on Indian opinion.

is the Company's." But he insisted that he could not control the sepoys who might be employed and offered to pay the money for their maintenance, though it might reduce him to the necessity of selling his houses and property. The Diarist tells us further that the European troops committed all sorts of atrocities and the English horse advanced in two's and three's, plundering up to the bound-hedge of the town. He compared the condition of Pondicherry to the times of the deluge and wrote that "it is beyond the power of the *dorais* (Europeans) to save us, God alone can." News was recorded by him that the Alambarai fort, 20 miles north of Pondicherry, was captured and the Europeans in it were sent prisoners to Madras, while the English troops were marching from that place against Vaḻudāvur. (Entry for March. 13.) Alambarai surrendered on the 12th March.

The Nāttārs of the different castes like the Veḷḷālas, the Kōmuttis, the Chettis and the Elavāṉians and the Agamudayāns were asked to bear the pay of bodies of sepoys proportioned to their interest; but they expressed their difficulties.

When the European residents were asked by Lally to prepare for marching to battle, two of them said it would not be decent for them to go and they would not leave the fort, whereupon Lally got infuriated, ran at them with a horse-whip and ordered their imprisonment. A few others were also fettered. The soldiers of the regiments of Lorraine and Lally, 300 or 400 in all, were set to guard the houses in the Fort; and the Diarist says that while the inhabitants of the Tamil streets were not particularly alarmed, the Europeans were more afraid of their houses being plundered and therefore they intended leaving the town with their children. Lally is said even to have threatened De Leyrit and the Councillors with summary punishment, and told them that he could deal (by virtue of the King's commission) with the Governor and the Councillors as he pleased, remarking: "Be careful in future; or I will apply the adze to you. Till now you were all ignorant of my authority. Now at least know it." Lally marched on the 22nd of March as far as Kunimedu in order to attack the English at Alambarai. He made a desperate attempt to invite those who went away from the town to return and live quietly.

LOSS OF KARIKAL AND VALUDAVUR

The English army proceeded from Alambarai on their way to attack Gingee which the French still continued to hold. The Madras Council proposed to attack Karikal next, by landing marines and joining them to a detachment from Pondicherry. Karikal was first raided by a small party of Englishmen that landed from some English ships in the roads; and soon batteries were raised in order to be ready for attack, and by the end of the month the English had occupied the villages round the settlement with a view to make a final assault on the fort.

To pass on to a personal reflection of the Diarist:—The Diarist completed 51 years of his life on the last day of March. Of course, as usual, he indulges in a lot of interesting speculation about his future based on astrological calculations of his horoscope. He still believed that his fortunes would improve and that from that day and from the year, *Vikrama*, i.e., 1760–61, prosperity would daily increase for 54 years in the place of the adversity that had been seen till now. According to his horoscope and according to the *Simsumara Chakra*, an astrological chart drawn in the shape of a crocodile, showing the god's planets and stars, with the sun controlling the affairs of kings, the moon controlling the affairs of the nobles, the planets influencing the fortunes of the officers of state and the stars controlling the destinies of private individuals. The Diarist lost a tooth on the right side of his lower jaw and, with that, was freed from his ailments. He expected that, perhaps, good things would emanate from the influence of the *Savya Chakra*, literally the right hand side, meaning the Sun's passage from Aries to Virago in the dexter direction, comprising 54 years, 9 years being allowed for each of the six signs.[7]

7 The Sun's passage, which had just been completed, from Libra to Pisces, also comprising 54 years allowing nine years for each of these six signs, forms the night or *Apasavya Chakra*. In the first three signs of the *Apasavya Chakra*, prosperity decreased, but was not severely felt; but in the three signs following, ending with Pisces, there was a progressively evil influence which exhibited itself in famine throughout the

At Karikal the English seized the old fort on the bank of the river and the people in the town were asked either to depart quietly or to have their houses sealed up, if they could not remove their goods and they were further assured that the houses so sealed would be carefully guarded by sepoys, both when the French continued to be in occupation of the place and when the English should come to occupy it. After some indifferent fighting, the French troops became unable to endure the shells of the English besiegers, made terms and delivered the place to the enemy on the 5th of April. The capture of Karikal by the English was well worth the trouble, because it afforded a constant and certain inlet into the territories of Tanjore and its revenue including the farming of the numerous villages dependent on it, while the customs of the port was more than sufficient for the expenses of the garrison.[8]

Early in April, Coote appeared near Valudāvur, a good country fort, 9 miles to the west of Pondicherry, with a large

land and a decrease in riches and revenues owing to the troubles among the Rajas. So all the prosperity which was seen here on each during the *Savya Chakra* gradually declined by Pisces, the last of the signs in *Apasavya Chakra.* From to-day and from the year Vikrama, prosperity will daily increase for 54 years in place of the adversity that has been seen till now, according to my horoscope and according to the *Simsumāra Chakra.* From Tuesday the 23rd Panguni, commences the (dark half of the lunar) month of Chittirai of the year Vikrama. According to the mundane figure and according to the solar year calculations of those who prepared almanacs, good and bad, are to be seen from Wednesday, the first of Chittirai, when the Sun enters Aries. (*Ananda Ranga Pillai's Diary*, pp. 28–29, Vol. XII).

8 According to the Engineer John Call, writing to Col. Draper, the place should have defended itself for a month at least. For an account of the operations at Karikal, see Orme, Vol. II, Book XII, pp. 617–624; and also appendix to Vol. XII of *Ranga Pillai's Diary*, pp. 409–11, containing the letter from Call to Draper, taken out from the Newcastle Mss. by Prof. Dodwell. Major Monson commanded this expedition. Men from Alambarai and troops from Trichinopoly co-operated. The garrison consisted of 7 officers, 91 soldiers and 250 sepoys. On his way back the English commander took Chidambaram on the 19th and Vriddhachalam on the 27th, securing the surrender of the garrison at both places.

body of horse and foot, for reconnoitering purposes and began to raise batteries against the fort, while the French army, though encamped on the neighbouring Perumbai Hill, only looked on and even allow themselves to be attacked and to retreat to Olukarai, Reddipalayam and the Bound-hedge.[9]

The *mahānāttārs* in Pondicherry were again pressed for contributions and additional tax-levies, and even imprisoned, on their demurring, in the dungeons of the walls. On April 16, the Diarist reported that Coote captured the Vaḷudāvur fort by escalade, taking the French soldiers and sepoys therein as prisoners and hoisting the English flag, though on that day the garrison was only summoned to surrender by Major Robert Gordon who conducted the siege and agreed to do so the next morning.

The English seized also the Villiyanallur country, hoisted the flag on the Villiyanallur Gōpuram and tied *tōranams* (as a token of their occupation) right up to the bound-hedge. On April 17, there was a battle between the English and the French troops at the Perumbai Hill, from which the latter retreated, allowing the victors to tie *tōranams* of occupation in Ariyānkuppam. Ranga Pillai mourned that all the villages in the vicinity of Pondicherry should have thus come to be occupied by the enemy; the only exception was Kaḷāpattu to the north. In Pondicherry itself, the people, being continuously pressed to pay taxes, became further alarmed. De Leyrit told the *mahānāttārs* that the Company most urgently needed two lakhs of rupees for immediate expenses and even asked them to sell their ear-rings and rings. After a great deal of protestation, the *mahānāttārs* and the Company's merchants were duly imprisoned in the dungeons of the west gate of the fort. The Diarist, in his capacity as the *Courtier* of the Company, was asked to testify to the property of the towns-people, but categorically replied that he could not do so, as all the previous demands for assessment had not been successful; but he promised

9 A thick-set hedge of palmyra, prickly pear and thorny bushes preventing the passage of men and horse. Such bound-hedges encircled Madras and Cuddalore also. The bound-hedge usually linked blockhouses defending the fort on the land side.

to see whether a smaller sum could not be collected. Even De Leyrit was convinced that further compulsion would merely result in a further exodus.

At last, the *Mahānāttārs* were persuaded to agree to pay Rs. 50,000 on the condition that only gentle measures should be adopted towards them. Lally was even now not satisfied and presented to the Council a list containing demands of contributions from the principal persons of the several castes classified in three categories. The Diarist was asked to examine the list and make out impartially an assessment for two lakhs of rupees, having due regard for each man's present means and difficulties. After a great deal of haggling and bargaining, the men contrived to mount up the assessment to two lakhs, after having been kept in custody for nearly 24 hours, not having been supplied with even drinking water and having been threatened to be put in the dungeons and to be shipped off to Mascareigne. Thus the month of April ended, when 10 or 12 English ships were in the Cuddalore roads and the Maratha sardar, Balwant Rao, had approached Cuddapah with 20,000 or 30,000 horse, while the English themselves indulged in frequent and almost daily assaults from Vaḷudāvur and the Council was desperately anxious to secure the help of Hyder.[10]

10 At that time, Hyder Alī realised his danger from the minister, Khande Rao, who was plotting against him, and cast about to get some place of refuge immediately for his own treasures, and consequently for his own person. He preferred Tyagadurg, a strong fort in the Carnatic about 8 miles east of Kallakurichi, by reason of the difficulty of access to it from Mysore, and the impregnable nature of its fortifications.

About this time a French emissary, styling himself as the Bishop of Halicarnassus, arrived at Trichinopoly with proposals to Hyder to join the French in expelling the English from Arcot. He further told Hyder that the convention agreed upon between the English and the French in 1755 was a mere truce; and both proposed to themselves separate advantages from acceding to it. This emissary was Antonio de Noronha (1720–76) who was appointed by Chandā Sāhib as governor of San Thomé in 1749 and subsequently arrested by Admiral Boscawen. He later went to Europe and got the titular Bishopric of Halicarnassus. He was a pseudo-nephew of Madame Dupleix. For an account of his

THE ALLIANCE WITH HYDER ALI

To anticipate the narrative and trace the operations of the English against the Mysore troops, the following account is given:—

Lally, finding no other means of procuring relief, immediately sent two more officers to Hyder begging his help early in 1760. It was agreed that Hyder should immediately send a body of 2,000 horse and 3,000 sepoys with artillery; and on their arrival at Tyagadurg, they were to be given both the forts of Tyagadurg and Elavānāsur, with the dependencies of both, which were to remain in the possession of Hyder in perpetuity as long as the flag of France existed in India. This army was to be paid at the rate of 100,000 rupees a month, from the day of their arrival at Tyagadurg. Ten eighteen-pounders were to be given as a present to Hyder, exclusive of the artillery in the two forts. His troops were to be furnished with ammunition, while serving for the French, who, after the Carnatic should be cleared of the English, were to assist him in conquering the southern countries of Madura and Tinnevelly. Besides the number already stipulated, Hyder Alī engaged to supply 1,000 horse and 2,000 sepoys more, in consideration of which half the countries which should be recovered in the Carnatic were to be given over to his government, excepting the French Company's dominions of Villiyanallur, Vaḻudāvur. Bāhur and Alaṃbarai; "the territory of Vellore, as belonging to Mortizally, their ally, and the districts dependant on Trinomalee, having been granted in appanage to Rajasaheb, the son of Chundasaheb were likewise exempted and whatever portion of the Carnatic should fall into the hands of the Mysorean was to be delivered back to the French in proportion to the progress of the acquisition in the southern countries".[11]

activity in South India, *see* J. A. Ismael Gracias: *Dom Antonio Josē de Noronha Evēque D'Halicarnasse—Les Aventures D'un Pseudo Neveu de Madame Dupleix*—trans. into French from the Portuguese by H. De Closets D' Errey (1933).

11 *Orme,* British Military transaction in Hindustan, Vol. II. pp. 637–638.

The whole negotiation was kept strictly secret; but on the 24th May, 1760, Colonel Coote received intelligence of this alliance by a letter from one of his correspondents in Pondicherry telling that M. Lally was preparing a considerable detachment to march and join Hyder Alī at Tyagadurg.

Sir Eyre Coote was of the firm opinion that Hyder Alī was at Seringapatam busy with his own affairs at the Mysore court; anyhow, to console himself, he sent out his men to reconnoitre the whole field of that rumoured activity. But nothing happened for several days to confirm the news; and Coote began to think that it was a mere rumour thrown out by M. Lally himself to frighten him. But all of a sudden, he was dislodged from this pleasant fancy, when he received a confirmation of it, from Krishna Rao, whom he had despatched to Volconda (Vālikandapuram) to find out the truth of the rumour.

On the 4th June 1760, the first division of the Mysore troops under Makhdūm Alī, the brother-in-law of Hyder, consisting of 1,000 horse and 2,000 sepoys arrived at Tyagadurg and began roaming over the country in their attempt to collect cattle, when they were met by Krishna Rao and his men near Vālikandapuram. Some sharp skirmishes ensued between the two armies; Krishna Rao was utterly routed; and he now applied to Coote for help. At this time he was further informed that a large force of the Mysoreans was in Tyagadurg. This new fear, added to the defeat which he had already suffered, made poor Krishna Rao hurry back to protect the district of Vriddhachalam, which had been entrusted to him and to safeguard which he urgently wrote to Colonel Coote for fresh reinforcements.

Early in June 1760, the Mysore troops stationed at Dindigul, had commenced hostilities against the poligars dependent on Trichinopoly; and it was reported that they intended to get possession of the pass of Nattam which would preclude any immediate communication between Trichinopoly and Madura. The Nawab, getting scent of Hyder's activity in his own country, immediately sent a detachment to Madura with instructions to attack his troops at Dindigul and thus divert his attention. Another detachment was sent to the help of Krishna Rao who was seriously hampered by Hyder at Vālikandapuram. This corps immediately marched on the 10th June 1760, accompanied by 25 coffres, two companies of sepoys, 1,600 black horse, and an iron gun with five European gunners.[12]

Colonel Coote had by this time captured every French fort of importance in this province, Tyagadurg and Gingee excepted, and had completely surrounded Pondicherry with his forces.[13] The Mysorean army, now augmented by the French troops from Tyagadurg, appeared before Tirukoyilur on the 10th June and threatened it. The few sepoys who were kept as its garrison refused to submit, whereupon the enemy opened a sharp fire and obliged them to surrender. After capturing this place, the victorious troops marched against another fort, a few miles to the east, whose garrison of sepoys took to flight on their approach.[14]

The Mysoreans now left for Trichinopoly. In the meantime, Col. Coote had detached a corps under Major Moore to encounter this new danger. As Moore's ill luck would have it, the renters and heads of villages in the land, not knowing how soon they might have new masters, gave no assistance to his detachment which now suffered for want of provisions; misled by false intelligence, they advanced from Villupuram towards Tirukoyilur and arrived at Tiruvati on the 23rd June, where they halted for the day. Apprised of the English approach, M. Lally at once detached 50 of his European cavalry to join the Mysorean troops who were on their way to Pondicherry. Col. Coote was equally sharp, and immediately getting intelligence of the French, sent the whole of his remaining cavalry under Vasserot.[15] The Mysorean immediately got the news of the arrival of Col. Coote's troops and skulking away from his place of encampment, set off along the Vanar, and towards the evening reached Ariyankuppam, three miles in the rear of the French camp at Perumbai.

12 Orme, II, p. 641.

13 Wilks, History of Mysore (2nd ed.), I, 414.

14 Orme, II, p. 641.

15 Orme, II, p. 642.

The terms of the agreement between the French and the Mysorean having not been finally settled, the latter now sent an officer appointed by Hyder to the French Council. At this juncture they heard that M. Lally was called back to France. Hence they insisted that M. De Leyrit and all the members of the Council should sign the treaty and, if they did not do so, they would not help them in future. The French Council was in such a desperate plight and so much in utter need of help at this critical moment when their very existence in Pondicherry was threatened by Col. Coote, that they signed the treaty somehow on the 27th June, whereupon the Mysorean officer returned to the camp promising to give all the help that could be given.

On the 30th June, Col. Coote detached another small body of soldiers to Major Moore, who had by this time joined Krishna Rao, with the explicit order that he might strengthen himself in his encounter with the whole body of the Mysoreans on their march to Pondicherry. Poor Moore was once again misled in his calculations by the village people who, as we have already seen, had learnt to hate all the Europeans as tyrants; and he came to know of the exact location of the Mysorean troops only after they had passed out of his reach.

M. Lally who was reported to be leaving India, anxiously awaited the arrival of the Mysore army. Col. Coote also remained inactive for a period of 20 days, at the end of which he went to Madras on the 6th July and returned immediately on the 14th. On the very next day after his arrival he received intelligence from Major Moore that the Mysoreans had started from Tyagadurg with a very large convoy of provisions. This intelligence was confirmed the next day; and Coote immediately despatched Colonel Monson, who took possession of Perumbai directly opposite Villiyanallur. The English were now safely stationed. Their army possessed the whole space in front of the river of Ariyānkuppam; and nothing was feared from the rear except the danger that the Mysoreans were coming. But before the Mysorean troops could join the French, they had to pass the English camp.

Unfortunately for the English, both the detachment of the Mysoreans and that of Major Moore arrived at the same moment in front of Tiruvati.[16] The Mysoreans had 4,000 horse well mounted, 1,000 sepoys and 2,000 Europeans; while Moore had 180 European infantry, 30 coffres, and 50 horses and a small body of Krishna Rao's sepoys. Unmindful of his decided inferiority and being elated with the idea that the English were victorious wherever they went, he engaged the Mysore troops in a pitched battle at Tiruvati on July 19, the result of which was an utter rout for the English. Orme gives the casualities as 15 killed and 40 wounded.[17] But Ananda Ranga Pillai says, in his report of the battle, that "the English have lost 100 or 200 killed, 100 or 200 wounded and 50 taken prisoners and that 200 or 300 of the English have retreated to a nearby fort.[18] The loss on the side of Mysore, he says, was only about 100 men; Hyder was much elated with the intelligence of this success, and sent reinforcements, considerably exceeding the stipulated number.

The sad news reached Coote, the next day, when he immediately determined to wipe out this failure by wresting Villiyanallur from Lally. On the 20th July at 10 o'clock, the English luckily captured Villiyanallur fort and hoisted their flag and fired 21 guns as a demonstration of victory.[19] Orme remarks that had the French commander at Villiyanallur fort delayed a bit or held out the siege for a bit longer, the disaster would have been averted, for Lally was advancing to its relief with his own troops and a body of the Mysoreans.[20]

A Worsening of the Situation

In the month of May, the situation became worse. Even Appavu, the nephew of the Diarist, was imprisoned in the dungeon on the 27th of April and threatened with transportation to Mascareigne, in spite of very earnest pleadings. The Diarist was shown a list of 60 persons peremptorily assessed for a total of

16 Orme, II, p. 645.
17 Orme, II, p. 645.
18 *Ananda Ranga Pillai's Diary*, XII, p. 235.
19 *Ananda Ranga Pillai's Diary*, XII, p. 236.
20 Orme, History of Mysore (2nd ed.), III, p. 649.

nearly 6 lakhs. On the 4th May, an English ship ventured near and was met by the guns of the three French vessels inshore and by a brisk fire from the ramparts. A body of English horse also appeared near the bound-hedge on the west. The Diarist was, in his own turn, threatened with punishment and obliged to agree to pay Rs. 10,000 in a month's time. Other merchants were treated even worse. Every day prominent citizens were either compelled to pay large sums or put in the dungeon for default or even delay.

When Tanappa Mudali, the younger brother of the famous *courtier,* Kanakaraya Mudali, was threatened with imprisonment in the dungeon, the Diarist, forgetting all his old jealousies and dislike of that family, said:—'His family has been great and respectable for three generations, for his grandfather, father, and elder brother have been the Company's *courtiers,* so he should not be treated disrespectfully, to say nothing of his state of health. Moreover, although with Europeans it is no rare thing for a man, however high in office, to be imprisoned, you should not ignore our Tamil feelings, for we regard it as a disgrace. Besides he does not refuse to pay anything at all, but offers Rs. 10,000, so that he is not guilty of any serious misdeed and should not be put in the dungeon.' (Entry for May 10th.)

On May 11th, the Diarist heard that when Lally's soldiers and sepoys attacked Cuddalore on the previous day, many of the Indian merchants who had taken refuge there, perished by drowning in the river, and the town itself was plundered[21] while the European soldiers and sepoys who were lying wounded in its hospital, were carried off.

21 The French had abandoned Cuddalore on its capture and demolished the parapets of the bastions, torn down the gates and made several breaches in the ramparts. Lally perhaps intended to retake the place, and the English officer in charge was asked to keep a special guard. This French attack, mentioned by the Diarist, took place on the night of the 10th of May. The next day, the English were reinforced by two companies of sepoys and a few European horsemen. On the 12th, a French force, stronger than the preceding one, again attacked Cuddalore but had to retreat to Fort St. David and thence across the Pennar.

The Diarist mentions that, on the 20th, the English who lay in ambush at Cuddalore in expectation of a further French attack, opened fire, when the French advanced with a much larger body of men arranged in five divisions. They were forced to retreat; and among their slain was the commandant of the European Regiment of Lorraine.

In the meanwhile, the imprisonment of citizens in the dungeons of Pondicherry went on merrily. In the third week of May, news was received that Hyder Nayak accompanied by Birki Venkata Rao, had reached Anandagiri with 3,000 horse, 5,000 foot and 11 pieces of cannon.

A very curious rumour regarding Bussy's alleged treacherous offer to the English to help in the seizure of Pondicherry is recorded by our Diarist in his entry for the 24th of May (Saturday); thereupon Sama Rao, Bussy's vakil at Pondicherry, was imprisoned and his papers seized. Thus the Diarist wrote on the matter:— 'Ten days ago M. Lally was saying (so Europeans relate) that he had heard letters had been written to the English offering them help to capture Pondicherry and that the writers of these letters would be arrested. Everyone was therefore wondering what would happen. What gave colour to this rumour was that M. Bussy had been visiting the English. Nagoji Nayakkan, his diwan, is staying at Vellore; and, as Sama Rao is M. Bussy's vakil, secret letters must have passed. On learning this, M. Lally put Sama Rao in prison, returning his pagodas but keeping his papers, and, should anything be revealed by them, it will go hard both with M. Bussy and Sama Rao; otherwise the matter may end quietly.''[22]

Bussy had surrendered to the English at Madras; but on April 7, he had been allowed with others to return to Pondicherry. Paddy now began to be carried away forcibly from private houses; but in no house was any large quantity of it to be found. The choultry writers removed half the quantity of stored paddy from certain houses and the entire quantity from others. Instances of

22 On March 11, he had surrendered his *parole;* but on April 7, he had been allowed with others to return to Pondicherry, where he remained for some time (Military Consultations, 13th March and 7th April 1760).

Europeans themselves quarrelling over trifling matters were common; and even Lally was implicated in some of these. The Diarist melted articles of gold and silver from his house and managed to pay over Rs. 6,000 out of the demand for Rs. 10,000 made of him. Skirmishes near the Perumbai Hill with the English were fairly frequent. In a few days, however, the guns at Perumbai had to be removed and mounted on the mud walls at the bound-hedge and the two guns at the Cuddalore point were ordered to be brought in.

Early in June, Hyder's horse reached Tyagadurg; and his vakil, Venkaji Pandit, came to Pondicherry to discuss the preliminaries of the terms of agreement. Padre Noronha of Mylapore, called elsewhere the Bishop of Halicarnassus, went to meet Hyder Nayak at Tyagadurg, along with 200 German troops; and the latter joined the commandant of Gingee and defeated the English troops encamped at Tirukoyilur. This was the Diarist's version. Towards the end of June, 2,000 Mysore cavalry under Hyder's brother-in-law Makhdūm Alī, who was always styled only as Nayakkan by the Diarist, reached Villiyanallur. The next day Lally visited the Mysore troops, which had been plundering, on their way, at Tiruvati, Panruti etc. The Mysore horse marched in the afternoon of June 25 to Kasupalayam, where they had a skirmish with the English troops. Negotiations regarding the final terms of the alliance between Makhdūm Alī, Hyder's brother-in-law, and Lally were arranged. The terms discussed by the Council on the 28th and finally accepted were, according to the Diarist, as follows:— 'The Mysore troops are to assist the French in all affairs, obtain Arcot for them and defeat the English; in return, they are to receive Tyagadurg, Tiruvannamalai, the Elavānāsur and Sankarapuram countries and Vālikandapuram, as jaghir, with two lakhs of rupees a month for pay after two months, and half the country that may be conquered hereafter, exclusive of the Valudāvur, Villiyanallur and Bahur countries; the French are to help the Mysoreans in the capture of the Madura and Tinnevelly countries, after which the latter are to restore half the country which they shall have received in these parts, and help the French to capture Trichinopoly fort and, besides, are to supply 4,000 oxen immediately. When the Mysoreans desired that Tyagadurg should first be given, M. Lally replied that he would do so as soon as he had received the 4,000 cattle.'

The Diarist tells us that the Mysore representatives left at midnight, thinking that no affair could prosper where so much distrust was shown. Consequent upon this withdrawal of the Mysore men, the English horse advanced from Vaḻudāvur to Villiyanallur and the bound-hedge and the French troops retired from the Perumbai Hill to within the bounds. The tension between Lally and the Council became so bad that De Leyrit was actually forbidden his door by the General in the presence of some 100 officers and Europeans gathered; and the Diarist rejoiced that God was returning on De Leyrit a thousand times the humiliation that he had imposed on others. The negotiations with the Mysoreans were resumed about the condition of the supply of 4,000 cattle, as the latter would naturally feel much chagrined over this point, being Hindus and therefore being naturally averse to the supply of oxen for consumption. This point was finally settled, as also that of giving Tyagadurg to the Mysoreans.

In July, commodities and food supplies became scarce; and in his entry for the 8th of that month, the Diarist gives the following rates as being the prices at which the provisions were sold that day.

Rice	$1\frac{1}{4}$ or $1\frac{3}{8}$ measures a fanam;
Dholl	$1\frac{1}{8}$ measures a fanam;
Pulse	$1\frac{3}{4}$ do.
Green gram	$1\frac{1}{8}$ do.
Ragi	$1\frac{3}{4}$ do.
Black gram	$1\frac{1}{4}$ do.
Gingelly oil	3 fanams a seer;
Castor oil	$2\frac{3}{4}$ fanams a seer;
Ghee	2 rupees and 4 fanams a tūkku (*i.e.*, $6\frac{1}{4}$ seers);
Tamarind	2 fanams a tūkku;
Pepper	1 rupee and $2\frac{1}{2}$ fanams a tūkku;
Chillies	3 fanams a tūkku;
Turmeric	$1\frac{1}{4}$ do.
Mustard	$2\frac{1}{2}$ do.
Cumin	1 rupee and 6 fanams a tūkku;
Fenugreek	$2\frac{1}{2}$ fanams a tūkku.

The prices rose still higher in the succeeding weeks. Thus, according to the Diarist, the prices prevailing on September 6, were as follows:—

Lamp oil	5 seers a pagoda.
Gingelly oil	6 seers a pagoda.
Ghee	1 seer for five fanams.
10 areca nuts	1 fanam.
Dried nuts	1 palam for 1 fanam.
Chillies	3 palams for 1 fanam.
Paddy	1 big measure for 1 fanam.

He added also that ghee, vegetables, grain and oil could not be had at all and the others only in small quantities. If, in the next eight days, things were not brought in, nothing would be left for sale in the town. Small quantities at least could still be got, as goods were being brought in by stealth both at night and by day.

Bishop Noronha went to meet the Mysore troops at Tiruvati and Tyagadurg, and to escort them. Imām Sāhib's son who was at Tyagadurg, had been urging that Hyder could not be trusted as he had betrayed his former master and was now secretly helping the English and that the fort should not be entrusted to him. He was, however, suspected of sowing discord, because he wanted to enjoy Tyagadurg as his jaghir. The Bishop was sent with a body of troops to see that Tyagadurg was duly delivered over to Mysore and to make terms with the Mysore captain. All the while, there were frequent skirmishes by the English troops at Vaḻudāvur and attacks on the Villiyanallur fort, wherein provisions were diminishing. So great was the danger of an imminent English attack that all the town-gates round the fort were closed except the Villiyanallur gate alone. The only consoling fact was that the Mysore troops which were advancing towards Pondicherry, had made a sudden attack on the English encamped at Tiruvati and put them to flight. An advance body of 1,500 Mysore horse arrived at Ariyānkuppam. Nevertheless, the English captured the Villiyanallur fort on July 20th, though the whole body of the Mysore troops had by that time reached Ariyānkuppam. The English capture of Villiyanallur was a very cruel surprise. It destroyed all hopes of final relief in the minds of the Europeans of

Pondicherry. Orme tells us that, just on the eve of the capture of Villiyanallur, Lally was preparing for a general action with the English army and had in fact begun to advance for its relief with his own troops and with the Mysoreans.

Makhdūm Alī, the brother-in-law of Hyder, who was at the head of the Mysore troops, was received, along with Bishop Noronha, by Lally with presents and a salute (July 21). The next day the Diarist reported continuous fighting between the English and the French troops at Olukkarai. The presence of Mysore troops only increased the severity of the prevailing famine conditions; and rice was available only at eight small measures per rupee. Sick horses were killed and cut out for meat by Pariahs and topasses as rice could not be had at all. A wild attempt was made by a body of the German hussars accompanied by 600 or 700 of the Mysore horse to march northwards, in order to bring back the French prisoners guarded in St. Thomas' Mount. The Diarist heard and recorded a rumour that they had captured Governor Pigot of Madras and fifty others when they were at play in a garden near St. Thomas' Mount; and even Lally believed this rumour and was elated for the moment. At last, the Diarist heard, on July 30th, of Pigot's actual arrival at the English camp, in the vicinity of Pondicherry, in order to press for a more vigorous and quicker offensive.

In the beginning of August, the situation had become so bad that there were only about 10 or 15 bazaars still open in the whole town; and everyone had sold whatever paddy he had and only one-eighth of a *marakkāl* could be had for a fanam. The Mysoreans seized the choultry in the Diarist's Tiruvengadapuram Agraharam which was founded by his father nearly fifty years ago and carried away therefrom the red-wood pillars, rafters, reapers, beams etc. Ranga Pillai grieved over this loss most bitterly and remarked that they would only plunder and ruin the town still further and not at all win any success. He wrote that "the Mysoreans and even the Pariahs among them, treat French officers and people of the Government more like dogs than men; this is the result of M. Lally's seeking the assistance of the Mysoreans, who value the French as naught."

Makhdūm Alī complained of a lack of a sufficiency of provisions for his troops; he even threatened to depart to Gingee and Villupuram and demanded that enough rice should be given to him at the rate of one *pakka* measure per head and horse-gram for the horses. Consequently rice was allowed to be carried out of the town to the Mysore army without any hindrance. Then Makhdūm had an ugly interview with Lally, in which he demanded the payment of two lakhs of rupees and said that the two months' limit mentioned in the agreement had expired and he would be departing the next day. Lally contrived to pacify Makhdūm by saying that the Europeans had been assessed for a tax of several lakhs of rupees which they would be paying in a week. The assessment on the Tamils was attempted to be exacted with more than the usual amount of oppression. Meanwhile, the English were raising batteries on every side for the final operations against Pondicherry. The Mysore troops plundered Karukudikuppam, Pākkumudaiyāmpattu and other places, destroying and plundering the houses on the plea that they had nothing else to subsist on. The Diarist grieved over the hanging of a Brahman by Lally on the complaint of some sepoys of the Mysore army, after his nose and ears had been cut off. The Diarist wrote that all these years since the town was founded, no Brahman had been hanged. The Mysore army was at last allowed to go to Gingee whence they should send provisions here and prevent supplies from reaching the English. De Leyrit told the Diarist on August 14th that so little was left in the town that the provisions would not suffice for the people for more than a few days. On the same day, the Mysoreans marched away to Gingee as they had been threatening to do and many of the townspeople went along with them. The English raised batteries by the Chunnāmbāru in order to capture the Ariyānkuppam fort. An Assembly Nationale consisting of all Europeans high and low was convened for the 18th of August to consider the desperate financial situation, at which Lally blamed De Leyrit for not having laid in provisions enough to last a year as he was asked to do from Wandiwash; and it was feared that the sepoys would desert to the enemy and means must be found to give the officers and men their pay. He asked the Great Council to concert measures to find the money. It was decided to tax the Europeans; and Moracin and Courtin were to visit their houses, demand the tax and receive whatever their means permitted them to pay.

THE DEATH OF THE DIARIST AND THE END OF THE FRENCH DOMINION

Pigot, the Madras Governor, arrived at Vaḻudāvur with a body of 1000 sepoys and 200 horse, as the Diarist wrote, " in order to blacken the faces of the Frenchmen, who had formerly announced that they had captured him." Pigot went over to Cuddalore and then to Perumukkal, where a Council of the English was held to decide whether, after so much expenditure, Pondicherry should be attacked or not. On August 26th, 30 sepoys threatened to desert to the enemy because they had received no pay and one of them selected by lot was blown from the cannon's mouth. The English were everywhere raising fortifications close to Pondicherry. Pariahs and Europeans entered the houses of the Tamils on the pretext of orders given to them to drive off all the cattle available. Another Great Council of Europeans, which met on the last day of August, is said to have been told that Lally was not desirous of continuing in command and had decided to resign. De Leyrit was very much put out; and the Diarist tells us that he sent his goods to the house of a friend in order to move away from the fort at the last moment; and everything now depended upon the arrival of the expected squadron. The fort itself appeared deserted. Soon news came that four English ships had arrived at Cuddalore with 500 soldiers and some sepoys and it was feared that the town would fall within the next fortnight.

In September, there was an attempted attack on the English batteries at Mortāndi Chāvadi; but it resulted only in a retreat. On the 9th, Lally himself sent word to De Leyrit saying that four English ships, 500 soldiers and some sepoys had landed at Cuddalore and Pondicherry would have to be surrendered to them in about 15 days. On the 9th, there was heavy firing from the English batteries at Mortāndi Chāvadi. The English had occupied all the ground up to the bound-hedge. Gingee was believed to have been captured on September 12th. The scarcity of paddy was so great that Lally threatened to drive out every Tamil and asked the soldiers to break open the houses; and a proclamation was issued that everyone should certify to the amount of paddy in his house. At last the Diarist planned to send to Sadras some of his moneys and jewels under the protection and in the name of an English prisoner who had obtained a passport and was sailing for Madras.

The *Diary* breaks off on September 24th when Ranga Pillai sent off his goods. It is begun again from Saturday, January 10, 1761, shortly before the end, not by Ranga Pillai himself, but probably by his nephew who continued to keep the diary after Pillai's death. The entry for that date tells us that Ranga Pillai was too ill to sail by the chelinga arranged for him and he could only travel by road. The next morning, Pillai complained of difficulty in breathing. At 1 o'clock in the afternoon he took a little food. In the evening he felt greatly fatigued and very thirsty. Throughout the night, he suffered and perhaps felt that death was at last coming upon him. The next day Ranga Pillai signed his last letter in which he wrote to the addressee: "You may not see me hereafter"; and when signing it, he added " this must be considered my last letter." At last, four days after Ranga Pillai had been carried to the burning place, Coote's English grenadiers replaced the French guard at the Valudāvur Gate and the English flag was hoisted over Fort Louis. Pillai was only 52 when he died; but the misery of the times and his own decline hastened his end. Thus disappeared an acute Indian observer who was better informed on political matters than any other Indian of the times and whose diary contains more authentic detail of a political nature than that which any other Indian at Pondicherry could have kept. He knew most intimately all that went on in the Indian quarter and was very accurate and discerning in watching the course of the trade and feeling the pulse of the popular sentiment. " His mind was a storehouse of diplomatic precedents; and he could tell with unfailing accuracy whose *vakil* should receive *pān* from the Governor's own hand, and whose from that of an inferior, how far the Governor should go to meet an embassy from the Nawab and with what salutes presents from Poona and Hyderabad should be greeted. He was the standing authority on the customs and privileges of the castes at Pondicherry, a matter of no small moment when an inadvertent permission . . . might provoke a riot that would set the whole Indian quarter by the ear." He possessed great experience and displayed a striking degree of authenticity in his narrative, recording accurately enough even rumours and " more authentic detail of a political nature than that which any other Indian at Pondicherry could have kept." He was fully conscious of his own worth and dignity; but his vanity was " less personal than ancestral." His grief was at its greatest when he chronicled the destruction of his father's choultry by the Mysoreans and when he recorded the final disasters that swept away all Dupleix's dreams of greatness. He displayed the beginning of the end of the French power through Indian eyes. He wrote in September 1760 that things were so bad that " either a new Governor with reinforcements must come to save the town or I must leave it." He entertained the idea of leaving the town only when it was too late for him to do so; even at the last moment he hesitated to leave by the boat that was arranged to take him to Madras; and Providence ordained, with more than justice to his life, that his bones should be reduced to ashes in the soil of Pondicherry which he so much loved.

APPENDIX A

NAINIYA PILLAI AND GURUVA PILLAI

THE family of Ananda Ranga Pillai was "one of the first to yield to the call of France." Its head, Nainiyappa Pillai, enjoyed a sound trade at Madras; he later settled at Pondicherry and obtained from its Superior Council the lease of tobacco and betel for two years at the rate of 2,400 pagodas per year (September 1704). When in 1708 the merchants of the French Company at Pondicherry demanded an increase of 20% on the price of cloth supplied by them for export to Europe, Nainiyappa Pillai offered to supply the goods at a cheaper price and thus released the Council from the difficulty caused by the collusion of the contracting merchants. When the Company was obliged to realise a part of its agent's (Lazare de Motta's) coral and could not find suitable purchasers for it, Nainiyappa contrived to have it sold at a good price. As a reward for his faithful service, Chevalier Hébert appointed him *Courtier* in the place of Lazare de Motta who was the first of the Dubashes of the French Company, having been appointed to that office in 1676 and who continued to function till December 1708. In the words of Hébert, Nainiyappa was "a man of parts and much esteemed." He exercised considerable influence with the Hindu population of the settlement; but his appointment as *Courtier* met with a vigorous opposition from the Jesuits who had been authorised by a Royal Edict of 1695 to settle in all the French factories in India and had closely followed the Capuchins to Pondicherry. The Jesuits had been in general charge of the Indian Christians; and they now levelled various accusations against Nainiyappa who was, however, supported, at that time, by Hébert with all his authority. Dulivier arrived at Pondicherry in October 1713 with orders to arrest Hébert and send him back to France. He now found himself face to face with an order from Louis XIV endorsed on the petition of the Jesuits who had requested (1) that the post of Mudaliar (chief of the Indians) or *Courtier* should always go to a Christian, (2) that all the great temples of

Pondicherry should be closed down except that of Isvaran in the Madras Street and that of Perumal in the Weavers Street; and (3) that Nainiyappa should be immediately dismissed. Louis XIV had admitted these demands, but made a marginal note on the petition that the closure of the temples should be done with great tact and moderation and that the Governor and the missionaries should act in concert in this respect; and Nainiyappa should be given six months' time to become a Christian in good faith; and if he did not comply within the period, he was to be replaced by a Christian.

Louis XIV's order which was dated 14th February, 1711, but was not transmitted by the Directors of the Company to India till about three years later, on account of their fear of its possible consequences, ran thus :—" This item (closure of temples) is granted; but this kind of innovation should be made with great tact and moderation on the part of the Governor and the missionaries and they should act in concert."

The Pondicherry Council feared an exodus of all their Hindu subjects if they were denied the free exercise of their temple worship. They felt that it would be possible for them to make use of Nainiyappa's influence with the Hindu castes and thereby to carry out the decision of King Louis regarding the closure of temples, especially that of the Linga (Vēdapurīsvara, which was actually destroyed by command of Dupleix in September 1748 during the siege of Pondicherry by Admiral Boscawen), situated to the north of the Church of the Jesuits; and in order to satisfy them, they associated with Nainiyappa, a Christian named Savari, with the title of co-Mudaliar, empowering them both to " act together with the same powers, honours, prerogatives and eminences in all affairs, attached to the office (of Mudaliar) without any difference or distinction of first and second." They also declared that Nainiyappa was " the most qualified in all the coast as regards commercial matters " and had " great influence in the court of the Carnatic " and that they had " no native, be he Christian or heathen, to replace him in his post whom we can trust in the present circumstances when the Moors are actually in league to retake the *aldées* (villages) which have been given to the European nations by the Nawab."

The co-Mudaliar, Savari, had influence only with the small community of the Indian Christians; and thus Nainiyappa continued to be the real chief of the Malabars (Hindus). But there was continued agitation at Pondicherry over the attempt to close the temples; and the Jesuits accused Nainiyappa of instigating them. They pressed the Governor to enforce completely the royal orders; and the latter prohibited all ceremonies in the temples and all religious processions accompanied by music, as well as funeral processions, on Sundays and Catholic holidays. On the 3rd February 1715, the Governor refused permission to the heads of the castes to perform, on the following day which happened to be a Sunday as well as the New Moon day, the essential *Amāvāsya* ceremonies; and this led to the desertion of the entire Hindu population of the town which remained empty for four days till the Governor and Council gave a solemn guarantee to them as to the free exercise of their religion and thus persuaded the Hindus to return to their homes.

Meanwhile, the Chevalier Hébert had gone to France and made his peace with the Jesuits who were very influential at the court of Versailles and had won the favour of the Minister of Marine and the Directors of the Company. He was acquitted of the charges brought against him and restored to his position in India with plenary powers and with the title " Envoy of the King and General of the Nation ". Dulivier was stripped of all authority and forced to retire from the service of the Company (July 1715).

Hébert had since resolved to dismiss Nainiyappa; the latter was, however, strongly supported by the merchants of the Company of St. Malo who now monopolised all the trade with India, since the failure of the *Compagnie des Indes* and knew well that without the help of the Hindu *Courtier* they could not find cargoes for their ships. This only delayed Hébert in the execution of his resolve; and soon after the ships of the Malouins had sailed away from the roads of Pondicherry, he had Nainiyappa arrested on a charge of complicity in the riots of the 4th February, along with some other Indians. The *Courtier* was subjected to a sham inquiry and sentenced by Hébert, with the forced consent of the Council, to whipping at a public place, to a fine of 8,000 pagodas, to rigorous imprisonment for three years and to subsequent banishment.

This piece of cruel injustice roused the indignation of the Europeans of the settlement and particularly that of M. Jacques Vincent, Accountant of the Company of St. Malo, who took up warmly the cause of the disgraced *Courtier* and advised him to petition the King for a revision of his trial and sentence. On the intervention of the merchants of the St. Malo Company, the Minister of Marine ordered Hébert to re-establish Nainiyappa in his office and to appoint a Christian as his assistant. But Nainiyappa, broken in heart and health, had died in prison, a few days before the order of restitution arrived in August 1717, while his goods had been already seized on the pretext of recovering the fine imposed on him. On subsequent enquiry it was found that Hébert and his son had misappropriated for themselves a good portion of Nainiyappa's properties, jewels and bills. Hébert had also revenged himself on Tiruvengadam Pillai who had settled in Pondicherry on the invitation of his brother-in-law, Nainiyappa and had refused to give a loan solicited by him. Tiruvengadam Pillai had also been subjected to a mock trial by Hébert and sentenced by his authority alone, without the concurrence of the Superior Council of Pondicherry being secured, to 50 strokes by the whip at the hands of the executioner; he was charged, in addition, with having offered a bribe to Hébert for the commutation of this sentence, though at the time of the trial, the Pillai, having been driven out of Pondicherry, was actually living at Madras. M. Jacques Vincent (who was the first husband of Madame Dupleix) easily proved the falsehood of the charge of attempted bribery and secured the cancellation of the sentence imposed on Hébert by the Supreme Council.

A Royal Decree of February 1718 cancelled the sentence against Nainiyappa and ordered an inquiry by a special commission into the complaints preferred against Hébert and his son.

Hébert was dismissed; and since Boyvin d'Hardancourt (who was one of the colleagues of Martin and then the Chief of Chandernagore), who was appointed to succeed him, had died some time prior to the communication of the order, La Prévostière, First Councillor at Pondicherry, became the *ad interim* Governor and had to enforce the orders against Hébert who had, meanwhile, transported his properties to Madras for safety and also destroyed the incriminating records against him. After a time, Hébert and his son were arrested and an inquiry soon showed that they had defrauded the Company to the tune of more than 100,000 *livres* and also exacted huge sums from private parties. The commission appointed to revise the trial of Nainiyappa annulled the sentence against him, and also those against the other Hindu leaders who had been condemned along with him (January 1719). Though the honour of Nainiyappa was thus fully rehabilitated, his family was completely ruined in fortune.

An appeal was preferred to the King of France by Guruvappa, the eldest son of Nainiyappa, who was advised by Jacques Vincent and several other Frenchmen interested in his family, to go to France and seek justice directly from the King. He embarked on board an English ship from Madras in February 1719, with the full permission of his guardian, Tiruvengadam Pillai, his paternal uncle, Nallatambi, and his two brothers, Muthiappa and Venkatachalam who supported his claim demanding from Hébert and his son, all the expenses of his voyage to Europe, the claim being attested by, and deposited with, the Pondicherry Council.

Guruvappa was well received at the French court, through the recommendations of Dulivier and the merchants of St. Malo; and the Regent, the Duke of Orleans, took a personal interest in his cause. On September 10, 1720, the Council of the King ordered the *Compagnie des Indes* to pay to the heirs of Nainiyappa, 10,060 pagodas (deposited by Hébert in its chest, as being the proceeds of the sale of the goods of Nainiyappa) which, with interest calculated from the date of deposit, at 10%, came to upwards of 13,953 pagodas. This sum was paid partly to Guruvappa in Paris under the surety of Dulivier, and partly in Pondicherry to him and his brothers in August 1723. But this compensation made good only a fraction of the fortune lost for the family.

Guruva Pillai was, however, appointed *Courtier* and *Mudaliar* of Pondicherry by the reformed *Compagnie des Indes.* He had been converted to Catholicism during his stay in France and baptised in the Royal Chapel at Versailles with the Christian names of Charles Philippe and with the Dauphin, (King Louis XV) acting as his god-father. He was raised to be a noble and received the title of Chevalier of the Order of St. Michel. He returned to Pondicherry on the 16th August 1722. On the 18th, 2 days after his arrival, he was sworn in as *Dubash, Courtier* and Chief of the Malabars; and his uncle, Tiruvengadam Pillai, became his deputy. Chevalier Guruva Pillai died prematurely in August 1724 and was interred in the Cemetery of St. Lazare. He was a good Christian; and his wife had also been baptised in January 1723, in the Capuchin Church. He was succeeded in his office by Pedro Kanakaraya Mudali whom Hébert had appointed in the place of Nainiyappa and who had been dismissed by La Prévostiérc. Ananda Ranga Pillai was 14 years old at the time of the death of his cousin, Guruva Pillai. His father, Tiruvengadam Pillai breathed his last in 1726.

(Abstracted from the French of M. Edmond Gaudart's Introduction to *Un Livre de Compte de Ananda Ranga Poulle*— traduit du Tamil par le R. P. Oubagarasamy Bernadotte (1930— Paris and Pondicherry, Societe'de l'Histoire de L'Inde Française) pp. XV—XXV and translated kindly by Mr. R. Bhaskaran).

APPENDIX B

NOTICES OF SOME FRENCHMEN MENTIONED BY THE DIARIST.

(BY COURTESY OF MON. EDMOND GAUDART)
KINDLY TRANSLATED FROM THE FRENCH
BY MR. R. BHASKARAN

(1) *Dubois* was a merchant and ship-owner who was in mercantile connection with Ananda Ranga Pillai; he is often mentioned in the *Diary*. On the 25th July 1748, a search was ordered in the House of Dubois and the letters and accounts of Mahe de la Villebague and his brother, Mahe de Labourdonnais whose agent Dubois was, were seized. (Cf. Ananda Ranga Pillai's *Diary*, Vol. V, p. 71). Dubois had a brother named Dubois de la Rousseliere (Jacques), (born at Nantes and died at Pondicherry on the 15th August 1750.)

(2) *Andre Boyelleau*, born at Paris on the 12th July 1712; had had a long career in the service of the Company. Arriving at Pondicherry about 1736, he died there on the 15th July 1788. His tomb is in the old cemetery of the Church of Notre Dame des Anges. Married on the 27th July 1740 to Jeanne Julienne Arthur widow of Nicolas Olivier le Faucheur. At the date of his loan (advance) to Ananda Ranga Pillai, Boyelleau occupied the office of Secretary to the Council Superieur and of Greffier Notaire (probably some kind of Public Recorder or Register of Documents).

(3) *The Younger Duplan* or *Duplan de Laval*, born at Versailles in 1712. He married at Pondicherry on the 1st April 1742, Marie Martin, widow of Nicolas Leride. He arrived at Pondicherry as a first grade clerk in 1738. (Cf. Correspondence of C. S. T. II, p. 217). On the 17th November he was Secretary of the Council and was appointed Councillor. The advance to Ananda Ranga Pillai to which he agreed was for the delivery of bleached cloth.

(4) *Desfrenes* was a servant of the Company. We do not find this name, spelt in this way in any public register. It is often cited in the *Diary* of Ananda Ranga Pillai. On the 6th June 1739 he accompanied Dumas on a visit to P. Loyere to congratulate him on his nomination to the Bishopric of Siam. On the 28th July of the same year he embarked as supercargo on a ship bound for Moccha. In 1743 he made another voyage to Moccha on board the "Neptune" and was captured by the Angria pirates. In 1746 he was among the employees taken to Madras to administer that town. (Cf. Ananda Ranga Pillai's *Diary*, Vol. I, 96, 99, 210, 218; Vol. II, 160, 360; and Vol. III, 5, 6).

(5) *Jacques Baleine Dulaurens,* born in Paris. In 1722 he was Secretary of the Conseil Superieur; and he married on the 3rd February 1723, Marie Gallyot de la Touche. He had six children:—

1. Madeleine, Barbe, 7th November 1723.
2. Jacques, Joseph, 21st October 1725.
3. Louis, Charles, 11th February 1727.
4. Marie, Generieve, 1st December 1728.
5. Marie, Francoise, 19th October 1730.
6. Antoine, Francois, 20th December 1732.

He had been made Councillor on the 8th December 1738 and died on the 25th October 1749, aged 50. Two of his sons had been in the service of the Company at Pondicherry. One of them, Jacques Joseph, in the record of his marriage with Agnes, Brigitte Decasse (18th June 1753), is described as employed under the Company, from which we can infer that, recruited locally, he had continued in subordinate posts. The other, Antoine, Francois, studied in France and obtained the title (degree) of an Advocate of Parlement. At the time of his marriage to Jeanne Desjardin (25th July 1758) he was a clerk of the first grade. After the destruction of Pondicherry in 1761, he was Notary at Tranquebar and was appointed Registrar of the Conseil Superieur in 1785.

(6) *Pierre, Benoit, Gallyot de la Touche,* born at Pondicherry on the 5th October 1718, son of Louis Gallyot de la Touche,

Captain of the port and Barbe Audibert de Boutteville and godson of Governor Benoit Dumas; he was employed in the service of the Company and married on the 11th October 1746 Adrienne Osterhaen, daughter of the manager of the Loge Hollandaise (Dutch Lodge) at Porto Novo. (Cf. Resume des actes de l'Etat Civil Vol. I, p. 182, Vol. II, p. 82. Ananda Ranga Pillai's *Diary,* Vol. II, p. 381).

(7) *Louis Barthélémy,* born at Montpellier, arrived in India in 1729 appointed by the Company to the post of clerk (Cf. Cor. C. S. Vol. I, p. 334); he was put in charge of the administration of Madras on the capture of the town by Labourdonnais and occupied at Pondicherry the office of Second (which means Assistant) to the Conseil Superieur. He retired from service in 1759 and died on the 29th July 1761.

(8) *Alexandre Legou,* born at Tours and died at Pondicherry on the 12th January 1754 at the age of 70. Made member of the Conseil Superieur; in the capacity of Councillor since 1718 was its oldest member (doyen) down to about 1748. He had married Marie Audibert de Boutteville by whom he had a son, François Xavier, who was employed in the service of the Company and married on the 30th January 1750, Colombo Desplat de Flaix.

One of the daughters of Alexandre Legou, Catherine, married, on 30th July 1750, Nicolas Champion d'Ancy, Captain of Infantry; and she died on 30th June 1752. Another daughter, Petronille, had married on the 10th August 1747, Jean Baptiste le Riche, under-merchant and assistant at Karikal.

(9) *Noel, Michel Guillard,* born at Rouen, was appointed Councillor on the 15th June 1741 (Cf. Cor. C. S. Vol. III, (p. 349). Commanded (governed) at Masulipatam and Yanoan and filled at Pondicherry the office of Attorney-General (Procureur General) and that of Treasurer. Frequently mentioned in the *Diary* of Ananda Ranga Pillai. He had married one of the daughters of Alexandre Legou, named Marie, who died at Pondicherry on the 21st October 1756.

(10) *The Chevalier Pierre du Bausset* born at Marseilles in 1711, son of Joseph du Bausset, Seigneur de (Lord of)

Roquefort and Margeuritte Thommassin. He obtained, on the 15th November 1738, an Ensign's commission in one of the infantry companies maintained by the Company at Mahe. He was made Sub-Lieutenant on the 10th January 1741. (Cf. R. 28. Archives de Pondicherry, Brevets and Commissions). He abandoned the military career and was appointed sub-merchant in 1742 and councillor on the 17th November 1752. Dupleix reproached him for lack of enthusiasm and expedition, but esteemed him so much that, on his return to France, he nominated him jointly with Delarche as his (representative) agent in India. Du Bausset fulfilled his charge with great probity and remained true to Dupleix. He thus displeased the Directors of the Company and, in the same manner as Delarche, had to resign his office of Councillor in 1759.

Pierre du Bausset had married at Pondicherry on the 9th January 1741, Marie Leridé, born at San Thomé (Madras). He had eight children, of whom one, Louis François, born on the 14th December 1748, was the author of the Life of Bossuet and of the Life of Fenelon and became Cardinal, Peer of France and Academicien. Madame du Bausset died at Pondicherry on the 14th April 1757.

(11) *Henri Alexandre Delarche*, born at Pondicherry (4th January 1720) of Jean Henri Delarche (native of Paris), Infantry Captain, and Marie Rolland, native of Pondicherry. He entered the service of the Company and obtained on the 17th November 1752 a Councillor's commission (charge or office). His knowledge of Oriental languages, especially Persian, made him the interpreter of Dupleix in all his negotiations with the princes of India. He was one of the very few employees recruited in the country (*i.e.* locally) who had attained the highest rung of their career. He was also one of the few assistants of Dupleix who had been observed with leniency by their chief. Dupleix reproached him only for his great vanity, but excused it in him, considering it a "common defect in a child of India."

Henri Alexandre Delarche had married at his first wedding on the 27th May 1743, Jeanne, Madeleine Elias. He had by this union, two children:—Louis, Jacques Henri baptised on the 25th January 1752 and died on the 26th March 1756—and Jeanne Baptiste Josephine, baptised on the 21st September 1752. He married for the second time, on the 16th October 1757, Barbe Cornet, daughter of Mathurin Etienne Cornet. Charged by Dupleix with the administration of his goods and the settlement of his debts, jointly with Bausset, he had, like the latter, to resign in 1759 his office of Councillor.

(12) *Léon de Moracin,* born at Bayonne in 1708, son of Jean de Moracin, Esquire, and Marie Plaisance Béhic. The India Company had in him one of its better agents. Arrived in 1730 at Pondicherry, he was sent to Masulipatam where his brilliant qualities soon won for him the title of Governor of the town and Administrator of the four provinces of the Northern *Circars* which had been ceded to us to meet the expense of keeping up our Deccan forces. Léon de Moracin was a prudent colleague of Bussy and at the same time his faithful friend. By his wise and far-sighted administration of these provinces, he spared him all financial difficulties, and made it possible for him to pursue advantageously his mission at the court of the *Souba* (Subha). Recalled by Lally almost at the same time as Bussy, Moracin had not much trouble in justifying himself, so that Lally sent him with a detachment of 400 Europeans to the relief of the Marquis de Conflans besieged in Masulipatam. He arrived there too late, the town having already fallen into the power of the English. After the loss of our Establishments in 1761, Moracin returned to France and took an active part in the campaign of accusations against Lally.

De Moracin had married, at Pondicherry on the 19th October 1751, Marie, François Desnos de Kerjean, widow of Choisy. He had thus become the nephew of Dupleix. He was appointed Councillor on the 17th November 1752.

(13) *Jean Baptiste Vincent.* One of the sons of Madame Dupleix who had five by her first marriage with Jacques Vincent. The one in question here, is probably Jean Baptiste who was an officer in the Company's troops and served in the Deccan army.

What makes this supposition probable is the circumstance of the payment made by Vincent to the account of the Abbé de Fage At this date, the 18th March 1752, Jean Baptiste Vincent was still at Hyderabad. He came a little later to and died at Pondicherry on the 16th August 1752.

(14) *Faye (Abbé de)*—Secular clergyman—found himself at Pondicherry during the siege of 1748. He wrote a very detailed account of it. Dupleix charged him to carry himself this account to the court and adjoined him to his nephew, De Kerjean, whom he sent to France to carry there the lucky news of the raising of the siege. They went to take passage at Madras on the Company's ship which was to proceed to the Isle of France, but had to disembark at Pondicherry on the 11th November 1748, the vessel being in too bad a state to continue its voyage. (Cf. Ananda Ranga Pillai's *Diary*, Vol. VI, pp. 28 and 56).

(15) *Antoine de Bury*: The omission of Christian names renders identification difficult.

Arrived in India about 1714 with the commission of the Sub-Lieutenant, Antoine de Bury had there a long military career and retired from the service with the rank of Lieutenant Colonel. He had married on 25th February 1716 at Pondicherry, Elisabeth Cosson de Lalande. He died there on the 20th October 1750 at the age of 74 years. He had three sons, Jean Baptiste (baptised 16 June 1718); Jacques (born 26th November 1719), Pierre, Benoit (born 30th December 1720).

APPENDIX C

ENTRY OF ANANDA RANGA PILLAI FOR *PRAMŌDHŪTA*, MĀRGAḶI 8TH SATURDAY—1750 DECEMBER *16TH*

(DISCOVERED BY M. G. JOUVEAU DUBREUIL FROM A TRANSCRIPT OF THE DIARY IN FRANCE—RELATING TO A PORTION MISSING FROM THE TRANSCRIPT FROM WHICH THE ENGLISH TRANSLATION WAS MADE)

" The Diarist went to the *Gouvernement* and paid his respects to Mon. Dupleix; he heard the news that Himmat Bahadur Khān disclosed (to French spies) all the dispositions of Nāsir Jang's camp at the time when the latter was assassinated. Mon. Dupleix desired to be informed as to when and where Muzaffar Jang was (at the time of the assassination). He was told that when Nāsir Jang was about to mount on his elephant on this last occasion, Muzaffar Jang was taken from his prison in camp, mounted an elephant with two men on either side of him with drawn swords pointed at his neck and with definite instructions to cut off his head, on order from Nāsir Jang; his elephant was stationed at a distance of ten spaces from that of the Nizam. As soon as Nāsir Jang found himself insulted by Himmat Bahadur Khān and gave the order that Muzaffar Jang's head might be cut off, he himself was killed and his head cut off; while Himmat Bahadur approached Muzaffar Jang, saluted him, while the guards set over him, lowered their swords, saluted him also and descended. Himmat Bahadur Khān immediately mounted Muzaffar Jang on the elephant of Nāsir Jang and proclaimed him to all the assembled people. A standard of white silk showing in gold the sun's rays and face was raised on another elephant. The head of Nāsir Jang was raised aloft on a javelin. Further firing of cannon etc. was stopped. The camp of Nāsir Jang was surrounded and the tents where his treasure was kept were closely guarded. The French officers on the spot went and saluted Muzaffar Jang who embraced them and expressed his gratitude.

[This short account shows some instructive details regarding the exact course of events that happened at the death of Näsir Jang and the elevation of Muzaffar Jang.]

(The author is indebted to Professor G. J. Dubreuil for permitting him to give this summary of an extract, hitherto unpublished, from the *Diary* of Ananda Ranga Pillai. He is informed that there are available with him several similar entries of the Diarist in places which have been hitherto marked by lacunae and for which no entries have been available. Mon. Dubreuil has, from an examination of a transcript preserved in France, alighted on these extracts. Their full text, when available to the student, will fill up many gaps in our knowledge of the matter furnished by the Diarist.)

BIBLIOGRAPHY

List of books and documents quoted or referred to:—

A Catalogue Raisonnée of Oriental Manuscripts in the Library of the College of Fort St. George: 3 vols. W. Taylor. 1857.

A Descriptive Catalogue of the Oriental, Mss., collected by C. Mackenzie, edited by H. H. Wilson, Vols. I & II; 1828.

A Comprehensive History of India: Vol. I. H. Beveridge, 1865.

A Revised and Enlarged Account of the Bobbili Zamindari: 1907.

A General History of the Pudukkottai State: S. Radhakrishna Aiyar, (1916).

A Glossary of Judicial and Revenue Terms of British India, etc.: H. H. Wilson, 1855.

An Account of the War in India from 1750 to 1760: R. O. Cambridge, 1761.

A History of the Mahrattas: Vol. I, 4th Edition. James Grant Duff, 1912.

A History of the Maratha People: Vols. II and III. *Kincaid, C. A.*, and *Parasnis, D. B.*; 1918.

Ānandarangarātchandamu: Kasturi Ranga Kavi, Vavilla Edition, 1922.

Anandaranga Vijaya: Srinivasa (*ms.*)

Asiatic Annual Register, 1802.

J. Scott: *Ferishta's History of Dekkan*, etc. (comprised in six parts)—2 Vols.—1794.

Bengal and Madras Papers: ed. by G. W. Forrest—3 Vols.

Press List of Bengal and Madras Papers: 1746–85; (1902).

Baillie-ki-Paltan, being a History of the 2nd Battalion; Madras Pioneers, formerly the IV Madras Pioneers, 1759–1930: H. F. Murland, 1932.

Calendar of the Madras Records 1740–44: H. H. Dodwell, 1917.

Catalogue of the Mss. in European Languages of the India Office Library: Vol. II, Part I. S. C. Hill. 1916.

Catalogue of the Home Miscellaneous Series of the India Office Records: S. C. Hill, 1927.

European Manuscripts in the India Office Library: Vol. II, Pt. II; *Minor Collections and Miscellaneous Mss.*: Kaye and Johnston, Section I: 1937.

Castes and Tribes of South India: Vols. VII and VIII. E. Thurston and K. Rangachari. 1909

Castes and Tribes of Bombay: R. E. E oven.

Census of India Report: 1891.

Chronological List of Clive's Autograph Letters, 1756–1757.

Coins of South India: Sir Walter Elliot (1886).

Country Correspondence: Military Department, 1753.

Dupleix and Clive: H. H. Dodwell, 1920.

Dupleix et l' Inde Française 1749–54. A. Martineau. Vol. III, (1927).

Dupleix: *Ses Plans Politiques; Sa Disgrace*; P. Cultru. 1901.

Dupleix d'apres sa Correspondance inedite. T. Hamont. 1910.

Du Livre de Compte de Ananda Ranga Poulle by R. P. O. Bernadatto; *Introduction* by Edmond Gaudart, 1930.

Factory Records; Fort St. George: Vol. V.

Fall of the Mughal Empire: Vol. II. 1754–1771. Sir J. N. Sarkar, (1936).

Fort St. David Despatches.

Fort St. George Records: *Diary and Consultation Book*, 1707.

History of Hyder Naik: By Mir Husein Ali Khan Kirmani, and translated by Col. Miles, 1842.

History of the Military Transactions of the British Nation in Indostan: Robert Orme, 3 Vols. Madras Reprint, 1861.

Historical Sketch of the Kingdom of Pandya: H. H. Wilson, 1838.

History of Tinnevelly: R. Caldwell, 1881.

Histoire des Inde Orientals: Abbe Guyon, 1744.

History of the Decisive Battles of India: G. B. Malleson. 1883.

History of India, J. Mill, Vol. III: 1848.

History of the Carnatic up to 1749: Paupia Brahman

History of the City of Madras: C. S. Srinivasachari, 1939.

History of India as told by its own Historians, Vol. VIII: Elliot and Dowson. 1877.

History of the French in India: Malleson, 1893.

Hobson-Jobson: *A Glossary of Anglo-Indian Colloquial Words and Phrases*: Col. Yule and A. C. Burnell. Edited by William Crooke, New Edition, 1903.

Indian Ethnography: *Encyclopaedia of Indo-Aryan Research*: Sir A. Baines. 1912.

India Office: *Miscellaneous Letters 1749–50*: H. H. Dodwell.

Journal of Indian History: [*The Historical Material in the Private Diary of Ananda Ranga Pillai*, 1736–61.]: Vols. VI to XVII: C. S. Srinivasachari.

Journey from Madras through the Countries of Mysore, Canara and Malabar—3 Vols.—1807. F. Buchanan.

Later Mughals: W. Irvine. 2 Vols. Edited by J. N. Sarkar. 1921–22.

Les Cyclones a lo Cote Coromandel; Alfred Martineau, 1917. Pondicherry.

Les Française des l'Inde la Relation du Siege de Pondicherry: M. Vinson, 1894.

Life of Lord Clive: G. W. Forrest, 2 Vols. 1918.

Life of Robert, Lord Clive: Sir John Malcolm, 3 Vols. 1836.

Life of Maharaja Tukoji Rao Holkar, II: M. W. Burway. 1925.

Lights' Report (Military Consultations), 1871.

Manual of the Cuddapah District: J. D. B. Gribble, 1875.

Madras in Olden Times: J. Talboys Wheeler, 1882.

A Manual of the Pudukottai State: (1st & 2nd Ed.). S. Radhakrishna Iyer and K. R. Venkatarama Iyer, 1921 and 1938.

Manual of the Vizagapatam District: D. F. Carmichael, 1869.

Memoirs of Captain Dalton: C. Dalton. 1886.

Memoir pour Bussy expositif de ses creances sur la Campaigne de Indes. 1764.

Memoir pour la Sieur de La Bourdonnais, 1894.

Mir Shahabuddin—R. D. Banerjee, in the *Muslim Review*, Vol. II.

Military Despatches to England, Vol. II.

Nawab Muhammad Ali and the Siege of Arcot: C. S. Srinivasachari. *Indian Historical Quarterly*, Vol. XIV.

Notice sur la Chronique en Langue Tamile et sur la Vie D' Ananda Ranga Pillai: A Gallois Montbrun, 1849.

Oriental Historical Mss. Vol. II. Ward's Survey.

Oriental Biographical Dictionary: T. W. Beale. Revised by H. G. Keene, 1894.

Public Despatches from England, Vol. 51.

Records of Fort St. George: *Diary and Consultation Book* of 1752.

Records of Fort St. George: *Country Correspondence of* 1753: *Military Department*, No. 2.

Report on the Old Records of the India Office with Supplementary Note and Appendices. Birdwood, (Second Reprint), 1891.

Report on the Dutch Settlements: Hodgson, 1818.

Report on South Indian Epigraphy, Madras, 1913.

Selections from the Peshwa Daftar: ed. by G. S. Sardesai—

No. 6. Ramaraya's struggle for power: letters, 167, 168, 180 and 201.

No. 28. Peishwa Balaji Rao, Karnatak Affairs, 1740–61.

No. 20. The Bhonsles of Nagpur, 1717 to 1774.

No. 25. Balaji Rao and the Nizam, 1740–61.

Some Madras Temples by V. R. Ramachandra Dikshitar in the *Handbook to the Indian Science Congress, Madras*, 1940.

South Indian Inscriptions, Vol. II. E. Hultzsch & V. Venkayya, Madras. 1916.

Tamil Studies. I Series. M. Srinivasa Iyengar. 1914.

Tuzaki-Wālājāhī of Burhan-ud-dīn Ibn Hasan: Vols. I & II. Translated by Dr. S. M. H. Nainar, Madras University, (1934—1939).

The Armies of India: G. McMunn.

Ananda Ranga Pillai, the 'Pepys' of French India

The Chronology of Delhi History: J. N. Sarkar, in the *J.B.O.R.S.* Vol. XVIII, Pt. I.

The Chronology of Modern India, 1494–1894. James Burgess, 1913.

The Company of the Indies in the Days of Dupleix: W. H. Dalgleish, 1933.

The East Indian Chronologist: Anonymous.

The Godavari District: H. Morris, 1878.

The History of the Punjab: Sayyad Muhomed Latif. 1891.

The Historical Sketches of the South of India in an attempt to trace the History of Mysoor: Col. Mark Wilks. 2nd Edn. 2 Vols. 1869.

The Indian Historical Records Commission; Proceedings and Transactions of Meetings, Vol. I to XV.

The Journal of John Hallyburton: *Orme Mss. in the India Offices; Coast and Bay Extracts.*

The Madras Despatches, 1744–55. H. H. Dodwell, 1920.

The Madras Despatches, 1754–65. H. H. Dodwell, 1930.

A Calendar of the Madras Records (1740–44): H. H. Dodwell, 1917.

Manual of the Administration of the Madras Presidency. 3 Vols: Edited by C. D. Macleane, 1885.

The Madras Tercentenary Commemoration Volume, 1939.

The Madura Country: *A Manual*: J. H. Nelson, 1868.

A Collection of Treaties, Engagements and other Papers of importance relating to British Affairs in Malabar: W. Logan, 1891.

The Maratha Rajahs of Tanjore: K. R. Subrahmaniam. 1927.

Military Despatches to England. Vol. II.

The Muslim Review, Vols. I—IV. Calcutta.

The Mysore Gazetteer, Vol. II—Parts I—IV. New Edition. 1930.

The Nizam, Vol. I. H. G. Briggs.

The Pirates of Malabar, J. Biddulph, 1907.

The Private Diary of Ananda Ranga Pillai: 12 Vols. Translated from Tamil. F. Price and H. H. Dodwell, (1904–1928).

The Rise of the British Power in the East: M. Elphinstone. Edited by E. Colebrook. 1887.

The Journal of the Andhra Historical Research Society, Vol. IV.

The Siege of Madras in 1746 and the Action of La Bourdonnais: G. W. Forrest, 1908.

The Seir Mutaqherin or Review of Modern Times; being A History of India. A. H. 1118 to 1914. Calcutta Reprint.

The South Arcot Manual: J. Garstin, 1878.

The South Arcot Gazetteer: Vol. I. Francis, 1906.

The Tanjore District Manual: T. Venkasami Rao, 1884.

The Tanjore District Gazetteer: F. R. Hemingway.

The Trichinopoly District Gazetteer: F. R. Hemingway, 1907.

The Tellicherry Records.

The Universal Traveller: Thomas Salmon.

The Vizagapatam District Gazetteer: W. Francis, 1907.

Vestige of Old Madras, 1640–1800. H. Davison Love. 3 Vols. 1913.

Vieux Pondichéry 1673–1815. Histoire D'une ville coloniale française: par M. V. Labernadie. 1936.

Dom Antonio José De Noronha Évêque D' Halicarnasse: J. A. I. Gracias; tr. par H. De Closets D'Errey. 1933.

Histoire de Gingi: Rao Saheb C. S. Srinivasachari, tr., par Edmond Gaudart, 1940.

Un Livre De Compte De Ananda Rangapoule par le R. P. O. Bernadotte, 1930.

Créole Et Grande Dame (Johanne Bégum, Marquise Dupleix) par Mme. Yvonne Robert Gaebele.

Histoire Détaillée Des Rois Du Carnatic par Narayampoulle: tr. par Gnanou Diagou, 1939.

Sources for the History of British India in the XVIIth Century: S. A. Khan. 1926.

INDEX.

INDEX

References are to Pages and Notes given.

A

D

G

L

M

N

O

T

W